Tasting the Dish
Rabbinic Rhetorics of Sexuality

by

Michael L. Satlow

Scholars Press
Atlanta, Georgia

Tasting the Dish
Rabbinic Rhetorics of Sexuality

© 1995
Brown University

Library of Congress Cataloging-in-Publication Data
Satlow, Michael L.
    Tasting the dish : rabbinic rhetorics of sexuality / by Michael L. Satlow.
      p.   cm. — (Brown Judaic studies ; no. 303)
    Includes bibliographical references.
    ISBN 0-7885-0159-3 (cloth : alk. paper)
    1. Sex in rabbinical literature. 2. Sex—Religious aspects—
Judaism. 3. Rabbinical literature—History and criticism.
4. Incest—Religious aspects—Judaism. I. Title. II. Series.
BM496.9.S48S26   1995
296.3'8566—dc20   95-38540
                                                                   CIP

ISBN 978-1-93065-83-4 (paper : alk. paper)

Printed in the United States of America
on acid-free paper

Table of Contents

Preface xiii
Abbreviations xvii
I. Introduction 1
   A. Rhetoric: The Art of Persuasion 7
   B. Using Rabbinic Documents 10
   C. Assumptions about Sexuality 11
   D. Sources and Conventions 13
      1. Terms 13
         (1) Tannaitic Documents 13
         (2) Talmudim 14
II. Incest
   A. Rhetoric of Definition 19
      1. Forbidden Liaisons 19
         (1) Incest and Marriage 19
            (a) Example 1: The Raped and Seduced Woman 20
            (b) Example 2: "A Woman and Her Daughter" 23
            (c) Conclusions 24
         (2) Prohibited Sexual Partners 26
            (a) Who is Forbidden 26
            (b) Reasons for the Prohibitions 27
               i. Arguments from Scripture 27
               ii. Logical Argumentation 30
               iii. Arguments from Appearances 33
               iv. Arguments based on Sociological Factors 35
               v. Conclusions 37
         (3) Proselytes and Gentiles 28
      2. Defining Act 41
      3. Non-Rabbinic Parallels 42
      4. Conclusions 44
   B. Rhetoric of Categorization 44
      1. Origin 44
      2. Punishments 47
         (1) Tannaitic Sources 47

			(2) Talmudim 50
		3.	Non-Rabbinic Parallels 51
		4.	Conclusions 52
	C.	Rhetoric of Liability 52
		1.	Determination of the Transgression 53
			(1) Tannaitic Sources 53
			(2) Talmudim 54
		2.	Mitigating Circumstances 55
		3.	Non-Rabbinic Parallels 55
	D.	Rhetoric of Progeny of Forbidden Liaisons 56
		1.	*Mamzer:* Legal Status 56
			(1) Tannaitic Sources 56
			(2) Talmudim 58
		2.	*Mamzer:* Social Stigma 59
		3.	Non-Rabbinic Parallels 60
		4.	Conclusions 62
	E.	Rhetoric of Association 62
		1.	Non-Rabbinic Parallels 63
	F.	Rhetoric of Defining the Other 64
		1.	Defining Gentiles 64
		2.	Defining the Evil Jew 65
		3.	Non-Rabbinic Parallels 66
	G.	Rhetoric of Apologetics 68
		1.	Cain 68
		2.	Yo'abed and Amram; Sarah and Abraham 69
		3.	Reuben 70
		4.	Non-Rabbinic Parallels 72
		5.	Conclusions 72
	H.	Rhetoric of Temptation 72
		1.	*Yi'ud:* The Prohibition on Seclusion 73
		2.	"Nature" and Sinai 76
		3.	Non-Rabbinic Parallels 77
		4.	Conclusions 77
	I.	Divine Punishment 77
		1.	Non-Rabbinic Parallels 78
	J.	Conclusions 79
III.	Sex Between Jews and Gentiles
	A.	Rhetoric of Definition 84
	B.	Rhetoric of Progeny 84

Table of Contents vii

    1. Jewish Woman and Gentile Man.................................84
        (1) Tannaitic Sources.......................................84
        (2) Yerushalmi...85
        (3) Bavli...88
    2. Jewish Man and Gentile Woman.................................92
        (1) Legal Status..92
        (2) Affronts to God...93
    3. Non-Rabbinic Parallels...95
    4. Conclusions...95
  C. Rhetoric of Defilement and Prohibition............................96
    1. Men...96
        (1) Tannaitic Sources.......................................96
        (2) Yerushalmi...97
        (3) Bavli...98
    2. Women..98
    3. Non-Rabbinic Parallels...101
  D. Rhetoric of Divine Retribution...102
    1. Personal Retribution...102
    2. Communal Retribution..103
  E. Rhetoric of Association...104
  F. Rhetoric of Apologetics...105
    1. Moses..105
    2. Solomon..106
    3. Samson...107
    4. Esther...108
    5. Conclusions..108
  G. Rhetoric of Temptation...108
  H. Rhetoric of Threat..109
    1. Non-Rabbinic Parallels...116
  I. Conclusions..117

IV. Non-Marital Sex
  A. Rhetoric of Definition...120
    1. Bî3ilat znut..121
        (1) Non-Marital Intercourse............................121
        (2) Non-Procreative Intercourse......................123
        (3) Non-Rabbinic Parallels..............................125
        (4) Conclusions..125
    2. Defining Act..126
        (1) Non-Rabbinic Parallels..............................128

- B. Rhetoric of Categorization..129
  1. Intercourse with a Married or Betrothed Woman...........129
  2. Woman, Maiden, Minor...130
  3. Authority..131
  4. Priest's Daughter...131
  5. Seduction and Rape..132
     (1) Non-Rabbinic Parallels..134
  6. Summary..135
- C. Rhetoric of Liability..135
- D. Rhetoric of Impurity...136
- E. Rhetoric of Progeny..137
- F. Rhetoric of Association..139
  1. Adultery...140
     (1) Association with Theft...140
     (2) Shame...141
  2. Other Forms of Non-Marital Sex......................................144
     (1) Witchcraft..146
- G. Rhetoric of the Other..146
  1. Licentiousness...148
  2. Non-Rabbinic Parallels...152
- H. Rhetoric of Divine Retribution...153
- I. Rhetoric of Temptation..155
  1. Women as Daughters...155
  2. Women as Wives...156
  3. Rhetoric of Women as Temptresses and Seductresses..158
     (1) Female Sexual Desire..158
     (2) Male Sexual Desire...159
     (3) The Temptress...160
     (4) Controlling Desire..163
  4. Non-Rabbinic Parallels...167
  5. Conclusions..169
- J. Rhetoric of Threat...169
  1. Legal Penalties..170
     (1) Prohibition of an Adultress.......................................170
     (2) Economic Penalties...171
     (3) Non-Rabbinic Parallels...172
  2. Rhetoric of Threat...173
     (1) Public Display..173

Table of Contents ix

		(2)	Humiliation	175
		(3)	"Measure for Measure"	177
			(a) Adulteresses	177
			(b) Adulterers	179
			i. Tannaitic Sources	179
			ii. Yerushalmi	180
			iii. Bavli	181
			iv. Non-Rabbinic Parallels	181
	K.	Summary and Conclusions		182

V. Homoeroticism
   A. Rhetoric of Definition 186
      1. Prohibited Partners 186
         (1) Hermaphrodites 186
            (a) Non-Rabbinic Parallels 187
         (2) Female Homoeroticism 188
            (a) Non-Rabbinic Parallels 191
      2. The Defining Act 192
   B. Rhetoric of Categorization 193
   C. Rhetoric of Liability 194
      1. Active and Passive Male Lovers 194
      2. Age 197
      3. Non-Rabbinic Parallels 198
   D. Rhetoric of Association 198
      1. Vice-Catalogues 198
         (1) Non-Rabbinic Parallels 200
      2. Bestiality 201
   E. Rhetoric of the Other 203
      1. Non-Rabbinic Parallels 205
   F. Rhetoric of Divine Retribution 206
      1. Non-Rabbinic Parallels 207
   G. Rhetoric of Temptation 208
      1. Non-Rabbinic Parallels 211
   H. Passivity/Activity, Female/Male 212
      1. Passivity 212
         (1) Non-Rabbinic Parallels 214
      2. Activity and Power 217
         (1) Non-Rabbinic Parallels 219
   I. Conclusions 220

VI. Non-Procreative Sex

A. Non-Procreative Liaisons 224
　　　　1. Sex with an Infertile Woman 224
　　　　　(1) Levirate Marriage 224
　　　　　(2) Soṭah Ordeal 225
　　　　　(3) Mistaken Marriage 227
　　　　　(4) Licentiousness 227
　　　　2. Sex with an Infertile Man 230
　　　　3. Conclusions 231
　　　B. Family Planning 232
　　　　1. Contraceptive Sponge (Mok) 232
　　　　2. Oral Contraception 235
　　　　3. Coitus Interruptus and Anal Intercourse 236
　　　　　(1) Bi2ah Shel2o kedarkah 238
　　　　　(2) "Overturning the Table" 239
　　　　4. Other Non-Procreative Sexual Activities 242
　　　　5. Abstinence and Child Abandonment 243
　　　　6. Non-Rabbinic Parallels 244
　　　C. Wasted Seed 246
　　　　　(1) Tannaitic Sources 250
　　　　　(2) Amoraic Dicta 254
　　　　　(3) Redactorial 256
　　　　　(4) Summary 259
　　　　1. Non-Rabbinic Parallels 260
　　　D. Conclusions 262
VII. Marital Sexuality
　　　A. Sexual Obligations Between Husband and Wife 265
　　　　1. Female Sexual Rights 265
　　　　　(1) The 3Onah 265
　　　　　　(a) Tannaitic Traditions 266
　　　　　　(b) Yerushalmi 269
　　　　　　(c) Bavli 272
　　　　　(2) Sex on Friday Night 278
　　　　　(3) Other Discussions of Female Conjugal Rights 280
　　　　2. A Husband's Right to Sex 282
　　　　　(1) Economic Penalties for Refusal of Sex 282
　　　　　(2) Marital Rape 286
　　　　4. Reasons for Sexual Rights and Obligations 290
　　　　　(1) "Happiness" 290
　　　　　(2) Procreation 293

Table of Contents   xi

                      (3) Non-Rabbinic Parallels 294
        B. Marital Sexual Behavior 296
            1. *Niddah* 296
            2. Modesty 298
                (1) Sex in the Light 298
                      (a) Non-Rabbinic Parallels 302
            3. Rhetorics of Eugenics 303
                (1) Palestinians and Babylonians 310
        C. Conclusions 313
VIII. CONCLUSIONS
        A. Assumptions: Toward a History of Rabbinic Sexuality 315
            1. The Nature of Sex and Gender Expectations 316
            2. Marital and Non-Marital Sexuality 317
            3. Sexual Desire 320
        B. Rabbinic Rhetorics of Sexuality 320
            1. Legal Rhetorics 321
            2. Non-Legal Rhetorics 323
        C. Implications for Future Research 327
            1. Implications for the Study of Rabbinic Literature 328
            2. Hellenism and the Rabbis 330
            3. Rhetoric and Reality 331
            4. Gender Relations 332

Preface

This book is about the intersection of two topics, rabbinic constructions of sexuality and the rhetoric that the rabbis of late antiquity used to promote their sexual mores. In the first goal I follow the recent works of David Biale, Daniel Boyarin, and Howard Eilberg-Schwartz, who have begun to ask not just what the rabbis *legislated* about sexuality, but how they *understood* it: what assumptions about sexuality inform rabbinic dicta and law? How are rabbinic sexual assumptions manifested within the rabbinic literature, and how are the statements produced within one set of sexual assumptions understood when transmitted to a culture that has a very different understanding of sexuality?

Despite their own occasional claims to the contrary, the rabbis of late antiquity had little coercive power. Their power depended upon their ability to persuade. Rabbinic "texts," be they originally written or oral, represent attempts not only to convey tradition but to win adherents to that tradition. Any (successful) speaker or writer attempts to make arguments only to a particular audience. This study asks what kinds of arguments the rabbis thought would be effective within their own cultures. How did these rabbis attempt to persuade each other, and perhaps even a larger community, to practice only "sanctioned" sexual behavior?

Although the extant rabbinic documents from late antiquity – which contain virtually all that we know about the rabbis – are relatively uniform, within these documents one can discern deep fissures between rabbinic circles. *Rabbinic "culture" was not a monolithic entity.* One of the primary conclusions of this study is that one cannot talk of "a" rabbinic view of sexuality or set of rhetorics. Palestinian and Babylonian rabbis held often extremely different assumptions about sexuality. This should come as no surprise: although linked by texts, traditions, and some travel between the communities, Palestinian and Babylonian rabbis functioned in radically different cultural milieus.

Any comprehensive study of rabbinic sexuality intersects with many broader issues: the nature of rabbinic documents; rabbinic modes of argumentation; rabbinic self-perception and power; the influence of non-rabbinic thought on the rabbis; gender expectations; and the relationship between rhetoric and reality. As this study progressed, I became increasingly aware of the vast and complex web within which I had entangled myself. I hope that simply through my collection, organization, and analysis of rabbinic texts on sexuality this study will contribute to, and continue to stimulate, the developing dialogue on rabbinic sexuality. I will be happy if this study also makes some modest contributions to those areas with which it intersects.

This study is a revised version of my dissertation, completed at the Jewish Theological Seminary of America in 1993. Many people contributed to this work, and it is a privilege for me to be able to thank them.

My adviser, Shaye J. D. Cohen, was unstinting with his time and advice. he saved me from numerous errors; helped me to clarify issues of importance; improved my prose; and encouraged me to publish this book with *Brown Judaic Studies*. My debt to him is enormous.

Bernadette J. Brooten, Richard Kalmin, Sarah Pomeroy, and Burton Visotzky all read and commented upon this entire manuscript. Jacob Neusner read the Introduction and Conclusion and offered many trenchant comments. Judith Hauptman read Chapter 5. Daniel Boyarin read Chapter 6, and was kind enough to share the proofs of his book *Carnal Israel* with me. All shortcomings in this book would only have been magnified without their comments.

Teachers too numerous to name have contributed to my intellectual development, allowing me to reach this point. Particularly influential, however, have been: Baruch Bokser *(z"l)*, Gerson Cohen *(z"l)*, Steven Fraade, Isaiah Gafni, and Yosef Yahalom.

I have been fortunate to enjoy financial support while writing this book. An Interuniversity Fellowship (1989-91) and Lady Davis Fellowship (1990-91) for study at Hebrew University, Jerusalem, supported me as I was beginning this project. A Stroock Fellowship in Ancient Judaism from the Jewish Theological Seminary (1991-92) and a Charlotte W. Newcombe Dissertation Fellowship (1992-93) allowed me the freedom to complete the dissertation. As I have prepared the dissertation for publication in its present form I have benefited from the resources of the Judaic Studies Program at the University of Cincinnati. I thank all of these organizations.

Only my wife, Jacqueline Romm Satlow, fully understands how difficult completing these revisions has been for me, and I thank her for her understanding and support. Finally, my parents, Frank and Felsa

Satlow, instilled in me the love for ideas and intellectual discourse that drove me daily. Their emotional support has been unceasing, and it is to them that I, with pleasure, dedicate this work.

Abbreviations

ADRN	Abot d'Rabbi Nathan
Aḥare	Aḥare Mot
Albeck	Albeck, ed., *The Mishnah*
ANRW	Aufstieg und Niedergang der Römischen Welt
ʿArak.	ʿArakin
Arukh	Kohut, ed., *Arukh*
ʿAbod. Zar.	ʿAboda Zara
b.	Babylonian Talmud (Bavli)
BA	Babylonian Amora
Bab. Tal.	*The Babylonian Talmud with Variant Readings*
B. Bat	Baba Batra
BDB	Brown, Driver, Briggs, *Lexicon*
Bek.	Bekorot
Ber.	Berakot
Beṣ.	Beṣah
Bik.	Bikkurim
B. Meṣ.	Baba Meṣiʿa
B. Qam.	Baba Qama
CD	Damascus Document
Coll.	De Collatio Legum Mosaicarum et Romanarum
CTh.	Codex Theodosius
D.	Digest
Deut. Rab.	Deuteronomy Rabbah
D.S.	Diqduqe Soferim
ʿEd.	ʿEduyyot
ʿErub.	ʿErubin
FIRA	S. Riccobono, *Fontes Iuris Romani Antejustiniani*
GCS	Die grieschischen christlichen Schriftsteller
Gen. Rab.	Genesis Rabbah

Ginzberg, *Leg.*	L. Ginzberg, *Legends of the Jews*
Git.	*Giṭṭin*
Ḥag.	*Ḥagiga*
Hor.	*Horayot*
Ḥul.	*Ḥullin*
Jastrow	M. Jastrow, *Dictionary of the Targumim*
Jub.	*Jubilees*
Ker.	*Keritut*
Ketub.	*Ketubot*
Let. Aris	*Letter of Aristeas*
Lieberman, *Tos.*	S. Lieberman, ed., *The Tosefta*
Lieberman, *Tos. Kip.*	S. Lieberman, *Tosefta Ki-fshuta*
m.	*Mishnah*
Maʿas. S.	*Maʿaser Sheni*
Mak.	*Makkot*
Meg.	*Megilla*
Meʿil.	*Meʿila*
Mekh.	*Mekhilta d'Rabbi Ishmael*
Mekh. d'RASHBI	*Mekhilta d'Rabbi Shimon ben Yohai*
MGWJ	*Monatsschrift für Geschichte und Wissenschaft des Judentums*
Mik.	*Miqwaʾot*
Moʿed Qat.	*Moʿed Qaṭan*
Naz.	*Nazir*
Ned.	*Nedarim*
Nid.	*Niddah*
NJPS	*Tanakh*, Jewish Publication Society
OED	Oxford English Dictionary
PA	*Palestinian Amora*
par.	Parallel
Pes.	*Pesaḥim*
Ps. Sol.	*Psalms of Solomon*
P.W.	Pauly and Wissowa, ed., *Realencyclopädia*
Qidd.	*Qiddushin*
Qod.	*Qodshim*
San.	*Sanhedrin*
Shab.	*Shabbat*
Shebu.	*Shebuot*
Sib. Or.	*Sibylline Oracles*
Sifre Deut.	*Sifre Deuteronomy*
Sifre Num.	*Sifre Numbers*
Sokoloff	M. Sokoloff, *Dictionary of Jewish Palestinian Aramaic*

Abbreviations

Soṭ.	*Soṭah*
Sukk.	*Sukkah*
t.	*Tosefta*
Taʿan.	*Taʿanit*
Tem.	*Temurah*
T. Iss.	*Testament of Issachar*
T. Jud.	*Testament of Judah*
Wörterbuch	J. Levy, *Wörterbuch*
y.	Palestinian Talmud (Yerushalmi)
Yebam.	*Yebamot*
Zav.	*Zabim*
Zeb.	*Zebaḥim*

1

Introduction

Sexuality is a cultural and societal construct. Although the sexual act is physiological, the ways in which cultures of different times and places discuss sex acts, the assumptions that underlie these understandings, the categories into which they group them, and the use to which this extensive web of discourse is put, varies widely. Only recently has the study of sexuality gained academic credibility.[1] Following Foucault's suggestions, these histories of sexuality do not evaluate and judge evidence of sexuality within the context of our own assumptions, but rather, they attempt to describe "sexuality" as it existed and worked in its context, as well as the assumptions that underlie it.[2] Recently,

---

[1] See Arnold I. Davidson, "Sex and the Emergence of Sexuality," *Critical Inquiry* 14 (1987): 16-48.
[2] See, for example, Michel Foucault, *An Introduction*, vol. 1 of *The History of Sexuality*, trans. Robert Hurley (New York: Random House, 1980), and, *The Use of Pleasure*, vol. 2 of *The History of Sexuality*, trans. Robert Hurley (New York: Viking, 1985), and, *The Care of the Self*, vol. 3 of *The History of Sexuality*, trans. Robert Hurley (New York: Random House, 1984).
  Foucault was preceded by Kenneth James Dover, *Greek Homosexuality* (London: Gerald Duckworth, 1978), which perceptively examined the role of homosexuality in ancient Greece. Prior to Dover's work, studies of sexuality in antiquity were limited to medical and philological studies, as well as prurient surveys. Both of these approaches continue to be pursued. On medicine, see Aline Rousselle, *Porneia: On Desire and the Body in Antiquity*, trans. Felicia Pheasant (New York: Basil Blackwell, 1988) and, "Observation féminine et idéologie masculine: Le corps de la femme d'après les médecins grecs," *Annales: Économies, sociétés, civilisations* 35 (1980): 1089-115; G. E. R. Lloyd, *Science, Folklore and Ideology: Studies in the Life Sciences in Ancient Greece* (Cambridge: Cambridge University Press, 1983); Ann Ellis Hanson, "The Medical Writers' Woman," in *Before Sexuality: The Construction of Erotic Experience in the Ancient Greek World*, ed. David M. Halperin, John J. Winkler, and Froma I. Zeitlin (Princeton: Princeton University Press, 1990) 308-37.

scholars have paid increased attention to constructions of sexuality in the pagan and Christian societies from antiquity.[3] These studies have been informed by methodologies drawn from anthropology, sociology, literature, and feminist scholarship.[4]

Application of these new methodologies to rabbinic sexuality (c. 200 C.E. to 600 C.E.), on the other hand, has increased only in the last few years. The reasons for this delay are not difficult to discern: both technical and methodological hurdles confront the student of rabbinic sexuality. Rabbinic documents are written in languages not accessible to most classicists and these texts constitute unique genres that are often difficult to decipher without extensive training. Further, the texts, especially the Talmudim, are extensively edited compilations of many earlier sources. Source-critical approaches to these texts are still being developed (see below).

On sexual language, see P.-E. Pierrugues, *Glossarium eroticum linguae latinae sive theologiae* (1826; rpt. Berlin, 1908); G. Vorberg, *Glossarium Eroticum* (Stutgart, 1932); J. N. Adams, *The Latin Sexual Vocabulary* (London: Duckworth, 1982); Amy Richlin, *Garden of Priapus: Sexuality and Aggression in Roman Humor*, rev. ed. (New York: Oxford University Press, 1992); Jeffrey Henderson, *The Maculate Muse: Obscene Language in Attic Comedy*, 2d ed. (New York: Oxford University Press, 1991).

[3]Most recent work on sexuality in antiquity are based on Foucault's work. See David M. Halperin, John J. Winkler, and Froma I. Zeitlin, ed., *Before Sexuality*; David M. Halperin, ed., *One Hundred Years of Homosexuality* (New York: Routledge, 1990); John J. Winkler, *The Constraints of Desire* (New York: Routledge, 1990). The appearance of these books prompted several reconsiderations of Foucault's method. See Amy Richlin, "Zeus and Metis: Foucault, Feminism, Classics," *Helios* 18 (1991): 160-80; Bruce Thornton, "Constructionism and Ancient Greek Sex," *Helios* 18 (1991): 181-93; Camille Paglia, "Junk Bonds and Corporate Raiders: Academe in the Hour of the Wolf," *Arion*, 3d ser., 1 (1991): 139-212.

For recent discussions of sexuality in early Christianity see Peter Brown, "Late Antiquity," in *From Pagan Rome in Byzantium*, ed. Paul Veyne, vol. 1 of *A History of Private Life* (Cambridge: Harvard University Press, 1987) 235-311, and, *The Body and Society: Men, Women and Sexual Renunciation in Early Christianity* (New York: Columbia University Press, 1988), and, "Bodies and Minds: Sexuality and Renunciation in Early Christianity," in *Before Sexuality* 479-93; Elaine Pagels, *Adam, Eve, and the Serpent* (New York: Random House, 1988); Elizabeth A. Clark, "Sex, Shame, and Rhetoric: Engendering Early Christian Ethics," *Journal of the American Academy of Religion* 59 (1991): 221-45; Joyce E. Salisbury, *Church Fathers, Independent Virgins* (New York: Verso, 1991).

[4]For examples, see David Cohen, "Sex, Gender, and Sexuality in Ancient Greece," *Classical Philology* 87 (1992): 145-60, esp. 160; Amy Richlin, ed., *Pornography and Representation in Greece and Rome* (New York: Oxford University Press, 1992).

Introduction

Methodologically, the difficulties are even more prominent. Can one even talk of a rabbinic "sexuality"?[5] That is, did the rabbis consider sex acts as part of the same domain, or did they see different sexual liaisons or acts as part of different discursive domains? Second, compared to the evidence considered by classicists, evidence on sexuality among Jews in antiquity appears monochromatic. Whereas the Roman historian can consider visual arts, graffiti, laws, philosophical tracts, medical writings, satires, love poetry, epigrams, and works of history, the evidence for Jewish views of sexuality in the rabbinic period consists only of scattered written statements found throughout a comparatively homogeneous literature.[6] Finally, the links between rabbinic literature and its audience, not to mention the actions of the daily lives of Jews in Palestine and Babylonia, are largely unknown.[7]

Previous studies of rabbinic sexuality have focused almost exclusively on legal material. The first post-rabbinic writings on Jewish sexuality, primarily commentaries on talmudic legal dicta or legal compilations, date from as early as the eleventh century.[8] Not "dispassionate" at all, these legal codes were meant to guide the daily life

---

[5]Dover, for example, has shown that Greek homosexuality did not exist merely as a component of the domain of "sexuality"; rather, it was integrally bound up in social relations, both those that we would term "sexual" and those that we would not (*Greek Homosexuality* 60-68, 201-2).

[6]Very little extant Jewish art from this period can contribute to the study of Jewish sexuality in antiquity, and the relationship between the relevant extant art and the rabbinic sources is far from certain. While, for example, the frescoes from Dura Europas might reveal the attitudes toward nudity of a Jewish community on the edges of the Roman Empire, they make little contribution to the study of sexuality in Palestinian and Babylonian rabbinic communities.

More important are the erotic motifs on lamps recently found in archaeological explorations in Israel. These, however, have yet to be fully published. See Lawrence E. Stager, "Eroticism and Infanticide at Ashkelon," *Biblical Archaeology Review* 17:4 (1991): 34-53, 72. For treatments of comparable Roman sources, see Michael Grant, *Eros in Pompeii: The Secret Rooms of the National Museum of Naples* (New York: William Mowwor, 1975); Otto J. Brendel, "The Scope and Temperament of Erotic art in the Greco-Roman World," in *Studies in Erotic Art*, ed. Theodore Bowie and Cornelia V. Christenson (New York: Basic, 1970) 3-108.

[7]For some preliminary comments on the Bavli's intended audience, see David Kraemer, "The Intended Reader and the Bavli," *Prooftexts* 13 (1993): 125-40.

[8]A compilation of material was made in early Gaonic times in the treatises *Derekh Eretz*. See Michael Higger, *The Treatises Derek Erez* (New York: Manchester, 1935). The first code of Jewish law, Maimonides's *Mishnah Torah*, compiles these laws under the title, *Hilkhot 'isurei bi'a*, the laws of forbidden intercourse. This was followed by the *Tur*, which titled its compilation of laws dealing with sexuality *Hilkhot pîriyah vîribiyah*, the laws of procreation, and then Joseph Karo's *Shulkhan 'Arukh*, which included compilations on both procreation and "wifehood" (*'ishut*).

of their contemporary audiences. They created a single "law" that governed sexuality. For every action, there is a single, unambiguous law. Opinions from earlier sources that were not ultimately accepted as "law" were either passed over or relegated to the margins as "minority" opinions. This attitude has informed the later scholarly works whose goal was to describe and analyze Jewish sexuality rather than to lead people in daily life.[9] Even Preuss, writing a history of rabbinic medicine,

---

[9] The first "modern" book on Jewish sexuality (excluding the works of the Christian Hebraists, who addressed Jewish sexuality only in passing) is, to my knowledge, Benedetto Frizzi, *Dissertazione di polizia medica sul Pentateuco in riguardo alle leggi, e stato del matrimonio* (Pavia: P. Galeazzi, 1788). On Frizzi, see B. Dinaburg, "B. Frizzi and His Book 'Petah Enayim,' on the Character of the Italian Haskalah," *Tarbiz* 20 (1949): 241-64 (Hebrew). Frizzi, and the many German writers in the century that followed him, composed legal surveys with an apologetic flavor. See Z. Frankel, "Gründlinien des mösaisch-talmudischen Eherechts," *Jahrserbericht des jüdisch-theologischen Seminars* (Leipzig: H. Hunger, 1860); P. Buchholz, *Die Familie in rechtlicher und moralischer Beziehung nach mösaich-talmudischer Lehr* (Breslau: Schetter, 1867); Ludwig Lichtschein, *Die Ehe nach mösaisch-talmudische Auffassung und das mösaische-talmudische Eherecht* (Leipzig: Otto Wigand, 1879); Leopold Löw, "Eherechtliche Studien," reprinted in *Gesammelte Schiften*, 3 vols. (Hildesheim: Georg Olms, 1979) 3:13-334; Jacob Neubauer, *Beiträge zur Geschichte des biblisch-talmudischen Eheschließungsrechts, Eine rechtsvergleichend-historische Studie* (Leipzig: J. C. Hinrichs'sche, 1920). On Neubauer's book, see the review of Max Eschelbacher, "Zur Geschichte des biblisch-talmudischen Eherechts," *MGWJ* 65 (1921): 299-322.

The American writers on Jewish sexuality too were focused on the legal material, and were aimed at portraying the moral "health" of Jewish sexuality. For examples, see M. Mielziner, *The Jewish Law of Marriage and Divorce in Ancient and Modern Times and Its Relation to the Law of the State* (Cincinnati: Bloch, 1884); Louis M. Epstein, *Marriage Laws in the Bible and the Talmud* (Cambridge: Harvard University Press, 1942), and, *Sex Laws and Customs in Judaism* (New York: Bloch, 1948). On the latter, see the review by Michael Higger, "Sex Laws and Customs in Judaism," *Jewish Quarterly Review* 39 (1948-49): 425.

Recent writers on Judaism have paid only passing reference to sexuality, and what they did write are also strictly legal surveys. See, for example, George Foot Moore, *Judaism in the First Centuries of the Christian Era*, 3 vols. (Cambridge: Harvard University Press, 1927-1930) 2:268-70; Immanuel Jakobovits, "Sex," *Encyclopedia Judaica*, 16 vols. (Jerusalem: MacMillan, 1971) 14:1206-7; Haim Cohn, "Sexual Offenses," *Encyclopedia Judaica* 14:1207-8; S. Safrai, "Home and Family," in *The Jewish People in the First Century: History, Geography, Political History, Social, Cultural and Religious Life and Institutions*, ed. M. Stern et al., 2 vols. (Philadelphia: Fortress, 1976); Ephraim Urbach, *The Sages: Their Concepts and Beliefs*, trans. Israel Abrahams (Cambridge: Harvard University Press, 1975) 471-83; Thomas Gergely, "Vous ne suivrez pas les desirs de votre coeur et de vos yeux ...," *Judaisme et comportement sexuel, Religion et tabou sexuel*, ed. Jacques Marx (Bruxelles: Editions de l'Université de Bruxells, 1990) 117-27.

includes most of his discussion of sexuality in a chapter labelled "Gerichtliche Medizin" ("Legal Medicine").[10]

Daniel Boyarin and David Biale have recently attempted to move beyond this legal approach to the study of rabbinic sexuality.[11] Both authors apply modern methodologies developed in fields such as anthropology and gender studies to the rabbinic material, and both are sensitive to the "tensions," the ambiguities and dialectics, found within the rabbinic discourse on sexuality.[12] In his brief chapter on rabbinic sexuality, Biale attempts to show that in this material there are three distinct dialectics: asceticism/gratification; procreation/pleasure; and collective imperatives/individual needs.[13] Boyarin's goal is to unmask the "cultural tensions" inherent in rabbinic texts on sexuality. "[T]he equivocations in the texts will be taken as evidence for tensions in the

---

[10]Julius Preuss, *Biblisch-talmudische Medizin: Beiträge zur Geschichte der Heilkunde und der Kultur überhaupt* (Berlin: S. Karger, 1921). The English translation is *Biblical and Talmudic Medicine*, trans. Fred Rosner (New York: Sanhedrin, 1978).

[11]David Biale, *Eros and the Jews* (New York: Basic Books, 1992); Daniel Boyarin, *Carnal Israel: Reading Sex in Talmudic Culture* (Berkeley and Los Angeles: University of California Press, 1993). Much of this book has appeared previously. See Daniel Boyarin, "Literary Fat Rabbis: On the Historical Origins of the Grotesque Body," *Journal of the History of Sexuality* 1 (1991): 551-84 (= "The Great Fat Massacre: Sex, Death, and the Grotesque Body in the Talmud," in *People of the Body*, ed. Howard Eilberg-Schwartz [Albany: State University of New York Press, 1992] 69-100), and, "Internal Opposition in Tamludic Literature: The Case of the Married Monk," *Representations* 36 (1991): 87-113, and, "Reading Androcentrism Against the Grain: Women, Sex, and Torah-Study," *Poetics Today* 12 (1991): 29-53, and, "'Behold Israel According to the Flesh': On Anthropology and Sexuality in Late Antique Judaisms," *Yale Journal of Criticism* 5 (1992): 27-57, and, "'This We Know to be Carnal Israel': Circumcision and the Erotic Life of God and Israel," *Critical Inquiry* 18 (1992): 474-505.

[12]Previous works have attempted to apply gender studies to rabbinic sources, but these have paid only passing notice to sexuality *per se*. For example, see Judith Hauptman, "Images of Women in the Talmud," in *Religion and Sexism: Images of Woman in the Jewish and Christian Traditions*, ed. Rosemary Ruether (New York: Simon and Schuster, 1974) 184-212; Judith Baskin, "The Separation of Women in Rabbinic Judaism," in *Women, Religion, and Social Change*, ed. Yvonne Yazbeck Haddad (Albany: State University of New York Press, 1985) 3-18; Judith Romney Wegner, *Chattel or Person? The Status of Women in the Mishnah* (New York: Oxford University Press, 1988); Léonie J. Archer, *Her Price is Beyond Rubies: The Jewish Woman in Graeco-Roman Palestine* (Sheffield: Sheffield Academic Press, 1990). See also Howard Eilberg-Schwartz, *The Savage in Judaism: An Anthropology of Israelite Religion and Ancient Judaism* (Bloomington: Indiana University Press, 1990).

[13]Biale, *Eros* 33-59, 229. Although these dialectics might be present in rabbinic literature, these dualisms are so broadly conceived that one would be hard pressed to find a society, Jewish or not, ancient or modern, that does not reflect them. See my review of this work in *Shofar* 12 (1994): 114-16.

society."[14] This is a mode of reading he terms "cultural dialectics," the discovery of rabbinic "solutions" to particular cultural "problems." Rabbinic discussion of sexuality cannot be reduced to monolithic law. Rather, Boyarin claims, a careful reading of selected rabbinic texts reveals that their authors were frequently ambivalent about issues of sexuality. not only do these texts not promote a monolithic law, but the very tensions and their solutions reflected within these texts are diverse. That is, Boyarin demonstrates that different groups of rabbis had different sexual ambivalences and solutions.[15]

The strengths of both of these works are their sensitivity to both the complexity of the rabbinic sources and the nuances and contradictions of these texts. Both are correct to reject monolithic models, especially legal, of rabbinic sexuality, and to refuse to harmonize the rabbinic sources. Following feminist scholarship that has extensively discussed the relationship of language to power, both Biale and Boyarin discuss the institutional control of sexuality and sexual desire (e.g., marriage and the study of Torah).[16]

Neither of these works, however, is in any sense comprehensive. Both use a very limited number of sources, which they (for the most part) do not subject to source-critical or philological analysis. Moreover, neither author attempts to "describe" rabbinic sexuality except on the grossest level. That is, although both Biale and Boyarin find "tensions" within the literature, they do not directly address the dual problems of sexual *assumptions* and the discourse of *persuasion* employed by the rabbis to promote their own sexual mores. Our understanding of how sex "functioned" in a given rabbinic or Jewish community in antiquity, how people thought about sex and how they (or at least the elite) attempted to regulate sexuality, remains meager.

This study has three goals: (1) to identify the rhetorical strategies by which the rabbis of late antiquity sought to promote their sexual mores; (2) to isolate and identify the different voices on sexuality within this

---

[14]Boyarin, *Carnal Israel* 15.
[15]See also my review of *Carnal Israel* in *Journal of the History of Sexuality* 5 (1994): 297-300.
[16]For examples of feminist discussions on this issue see Sheila Rowbatham, *Woman's Consciousness, Man's World* (Baltimore: Penguin, 1973) 32-33; Mary Daly, *Gyn/Ecology: The Metaethics of Radical Feminism* (Boston: Beacon, 1979); Jean Bethke Elshtain, "Feminist Discourse and its Discontents: Language, Power, and Meaning," *Signs* 7 (1982): 603-21; Sherry B. Ortner and Harriet Whitehead, ed., *Sexual Meanings, the Cultural Construction of Gender and Sexuality* (Cambridge: Cambridge University Press, 1981); Christine Brooke-Rose, "Woman as a Semiotic Object," *Poetics Today* 6 (1985): 9-20; Catherine MacKinnon, *Feminism Unmodified: Discourses on Life and Law* (Cambridge: Harvard University Press, 1987).

literature; and (3) to uncover some of the assumptions and constructions of sexuality and their development (or misreading) throughout the rabbinic literature of late antiquity. Each of these goals warrants a brief discussion.

Rhetoric: The Art of Persuasion

Aristotle succinctly defines "rhetoric" as "the faculty of discovering the possible means of persuasion in reference to any subject whatever."[17] Whereas in ancient Greece and Rome the study and practice of rhetoric most frequently concerned itself with strategies of oral persuasion, any linguistic attempt to persuade a listener/reader can be termed "rhetorical."[18] Scholars have recently emphasized the importance of persuasion in fields in which an objective "logic" was formerly thought to the sole adjudicator of conflicting paradigms and opinions, especially in science and law.[19]

The importance of persuasion in the "enforcement" of norms and mores becomes paramount both in private zones and in societies that lack the power of coercion. The regulation of sexuality, an essentially

---

[17] Aristotle, *The Art of Rhetoric* 1.2.1 (trans. J. H. Freese, *Aristotle* 12.22 [LCL; Cambridge: Harvard University Press] 15). See also Plato, *Republic* 2, 359a-61c.

[18] For traditional surveys of classical rhetoric, see George Kennedy, *Classical Rhetoric and Its Christian and Secular Tradition From Ancient to Modern Times* (Chapel Hill: University of North Carolina Press, 1980), and, *Greek Rhetoric Under Christian Emperors* (Princeton: Princeton University Press, 1983). Recently, some scholars have begun to examine rhetoric in its broader sense in late antiquity, especially in early Christianity. See Averil Cameron, *Christianity and the Rhetoric of Empire: The Development of Christian Discourse* (Berkeley and Los Angeles: University of California Press, 1991); Peter Brown, *Power and Persuasion in Late Antiquity: Towards a Christian Empire* (Madison: University of Wisconsin Press, 1992).

[19] The two early most influential expositors of the role of "persuasion" within hermeneutical systems are Thomas S. Kuhn, *The Structure of Scientific Revolutions*, 2d ed. enl. (Chicago: University of Chicago Press, 1970); Jürgen Habermas, *Communication and the Evolution of Society*, trans. Thomas McCarthy (Boston: Beacon, 1979). For a review of the extensive philosophical discussion that these books have engendered, see Richard J. Bernstein, *Beyond Objectivism and Relativism: Science, Hermeneutics, and Praxis* (Philadelphia: University of Pennsylvania Press, 1983).

The ideas that emerged from this discussion have recently been applied to law: how does one arrive at (or critique) a "good" or "correct" judicial decision? See especially Owen M. Fiss, "Objectivity and Interpretation," rpt. in *Interpreting Law and Literature: A Hermeneutic Reader*, ed. Sanford Levinson and Steven Mailloux (Evanston, IL: Northwestern University Press, 1988) 229-49; Stanley Fish, "*Fish v. Fiss*," rpt. in *Interpreting Law* 251-68; Steven Mailloux, "Rhetorical Hermeneutics," rpt. in *Interpreting Law* 345-62; Richard Weisberg, *Poethics and Other Strategies of Law and Literature* (New York: Columbia University Press, 1992) 3-47.

private activity which like other private activities (e.g., eating and drinking) is essentially resistant to legal coercion, has always been (and continues to be) "enforced" extra-legally. That is, because societies cannot successfully legislate sexual mores, they develop controlling discourses in such diverse areas as medicine, religion, and social relations. Successful societal rhetorics, those that persuade people to follow "sanctioned" sexual norms, are far more effective than coercion ever could be. If, for example, a society wished to regulate a given sexual practice (e.g., masturbation), medical discourse that is, ideally, internalized by its members (e.g., "you will go blind") will be more effective than simple legal prohibition.

It has long been recognized both that the rabbinic communities in late antiquity lacked coercive powers and that persuasion is a primary goal of the documents of these communities.[20] Rabbinic rhetoric, its power to persuade Israel that the Judaisms that they articulated are the correct ones, gave the rabbis their power; it was not rabbinic power that justified their rhetoric. Yet the strategies of rabbinic rhetoric, an examination of the arguments that different rabbinic circles thought persuasive, has not been undertaken.

The primary goal of this study is to examine the rhetoric used by the rabbis to discuss sexual norms. These rhetorical strategies are of two distinct types, which I will refer to as legal and persuasive. By "legal rhetorics" I refer to rabbinic discussions of the law, their attempts to define transgressions, categorize them, and establish issues of liability. Rabbinic rhetoric, for example, defines the transgression called "adultery" (what must occur with whom); puts this transgression into a category based on prescribed punishments; and elaborates both circumstances that mitigate this transgression (e.g., one of the partners was a minor) and the liability occurred when an act of adultery also involves other transgressions (e.g., sex with one's mother).

"Persuasive rhetorics" are those arguments that seek to promote sexual norms by other than strictly legal means. Into this category I place such rhetorics as the threats of human and divine retribution; association with other transgressions; and the activities of the "other": all of these rhetorics are intended to dissuade people from engaging in certain sexual activities. The identification of the lack of sexual self-control with the

---

[20]See Jacob Neusner, *A History of the Jews in Babylonia*, 5 vols. (Leiden: E. J. Brill, 1969-1970) 2:282-87; 3:220-29, and, *Talmudic Thinking: Language, Logic, Law* (Columbia, S.C.: University of South Carolina Press, 1992) 175-87; Lee I. Levine, *The Rabbinic Class of Roman Palestine in Late Antiquity* (New York: Jewish Theological Seminary of America, 1989) 127-33, esp. 131: "A number of sources indicate that the extent of rabbinic influence was directly dependent upon the majority of the people's acceptance of their authority."

"other," for example, seeks to dissuade such behavior by Jews by making that behavior "definitional." Within each rhetoric as applied to a particular sexual liaison or activity, I attempt to identify (1) themes or consistencies and (2) provenance of the discussion (Palestinian or Babylonian, early or late). Certain themes or even types of rhetoric, we will see, are limited to certain rabbinic groups.

This study is organized topically. The first chapters, on incest, sex between Gentiles and Jews, non-marital sex, and homoeroticism, all deal with forbidden sexual partners. The next chapters, on non-procreative and marital sex, deal with discussion of sexual acts. This division into the "who" and the "how," sexual liaisons and sexual acts, derives from modern sociological discussion.[21] This organization also highlights the differences between the rhetorical strategies employed by the rabbis in their discussions of "who" one should or should not have sex with, and "how" one should sexually conduct oneself.

Rabbinic texts are often very complex, blending different formal characteristics, rhetorics, and discursive strategies. Throughout this study I break apart these complex texts in order to recover and analyze the rhetorics of which they are comprised. The danger of such an approach is that it obscures the relationships between and interaction among these rhetorics. In some cases I attempt to analyze extended passages in order to show how these texts might have functioned as a whole. More frequently, however, I analyze only the component rhetorics. My goal has been to isolate the "building blocks" of these texts; how the redactor(s) combined and utilized these rhetorical strategies requires further study.

When applicable, I explore how a text might have *functioned* in its cultural formation.[22] Unlike Boyarin, who is more interested in how texts express "solutions" to cultural "problems," I am interested in how these texts might have been read, what message the reader would take from the text, and how that message might have influenced social, especially gender, relations. These texts, for example, might have in and of themselves functioned as controlling devices. Because so little is known of the society in which these texts functioned, such explorations are ultimately speculative, but I believe that they will have value in providing further study of the cultural formation of different types of rabbinic Judaism.

---

[21]See Jeffrey Weeks, *Sexuality* (Sussex: Ellis Horwood, 1986).
[22]For an example of how texts "work" in societies, see Clifford Geertz, *The Interpretation of Cultures: Selected Essays* (New York: Basic, 1973) 3-30.

Using Rabbinic Documents

It is commonly accepted that rabbinic documents are highly stylized compositions constructed from earlier sources. Over the past several years Jacob Neusner has challenged the validity of constructing rabbinic thought from the fragments of "sources" found in the redacted rabbinic documents. Because, Neusner asserts, each rabbinic document has been redacted according to an often polemical purpose, one can only recover the thought of the authorship of the documents, not of the documents' sources.[23] Others, without directly refuting Neusner, have developed source-critical programs for stratifying these rabbinic documents, especially the Babylonian Talmud.[24] Ultimately, these scholars maintain, many of the component sources are recoverable. The ramifications for the study of rabbinic thought and history are obvious: Neusner would ask, what is the thought of a particular document (e.g., what does the *Mishnah* say about Torah?) but deny the validity of asking, what is the thought of rabbinic circles of a various time or place, whose ideas are scattered through different documents.

This debate is far from settled. This study attempts to steer a middle course. Discussion of each rhetoric is organized *by rabbinic document*, yet at the same time I apply source-critical methodologies to the talmudic sources. Hence, I have organized this study "openly," explicating and comparing the rhetorical strategies utilized by, as well as the assumptions embedded in, rabbinic documents with those that emerge from the dicta of different rabbinic circles (as attributed in the documents). This organization occasionally results in stylistic

---

[23]For recent statements, see Jacob Neusner, *How the Talmud Shaped Rabbinic Discourse* (Atlanta: Scholars Press, 1991) 105-53, and, *Sources and Traditions: Types of Compositions in the Talmud of Babylonia* (Atlanta: Scholars Press, 1992) 1-9. Neusner does recognize the occasional possibility of isolating sources in the Bavli. See Jacob Neusner, *The Bavli's Massive Miscellanies: The Problem of Agglutinative Discourse in the Talmud of Babylonia* (Atlanta: Scholars Press, 1992) 255-68.

[24]See especially David Halivni, *Sources and Traditions: A Source Critical Commentary on the Talmud, Tractate Shabbath* (Jerusalem: Jewish Theological Seminary of America, 1982) 5-27 (Hebrew), and, "Contemporary Methods of the Study of Talmud," *Journal of Jewish Studies* 30 (1979): 192-201; Shamma Friedman, "A Critical Study of Yevamot X with a Methodological Introduction," in *Texts and Studies: Analecta Judaica*, ed. H. Z. Dimitrovsky (New York: Jewish Theological Seminary of America, 1977) 275-441 (Hebrew). For critiques of these writers, see Jacob Neusner, ed., *The Formation of the Babylonian Talmud* (Leiden: E. J. Brill, 1970).

Some scholars have recently directly addressed the issues posed by Neusner. See especially Richard Kalmin, "Quotation Forms in the Babylonian Talmud: Authentically Amoraic, or a Later Editorial Construct?" *Hebrew Union College Annual* 59 (1988): 167-87.

awkwardness. Nevertheless, my goal is as much to present the evidence as it is to advance my own interpretation of it, and because these conclusions have ramifications far beyond the area of sexuality, it is important for the reader to see all the evidence on which these conclusions are based.

My own conclusion, as will hopefully become clear throughout this study, is that sources attributed to Babylonians and sources attributed to Palestinians, regardless of document, show a *coherency in thought and assumptions*. These coherencies are far stronger than those displayed by individual rabbinic documents. I return to this issue in the Conclusion.

Assumptions about Sexuality

A history of rabbinic sexuality would answer the question, how did different rabbinic circles "construct," or understand, sexuality? What "deep" assumptions underlie their dicta? What happened to dicta composed upon one set of assumptions when they were transmitted and interpreted in a culture with an entirely different set of sexual assumptions?

Although this is not a history of rabbinic sexuality in that sense, it does, I believe, point toward such a history. The issues of the assumptions that inform the rabbinic dicta and their subsequent interpretation arise frequently in examination of these sources; indeed, one frequently-discussed rhetoric, "Temptation," is a construction of sexual desire. My use of non-rabbinic (e.g., Greek, Roman, Christian, and Jewish-Hellenistic) data is toward this end. Whereas the rabbinic material on sexuality is often fragmentary and has not been extensively studied, contemporaneous non-rabbinic material provide relevant areas of comparison. This data can frequently help in the interpretation of the rabbinic sources. Moreover, *many Greek and Roman sexual assumptions find strong parallels to those displayed in rabbinic sources attributed to Palestine.* While my goal is not to compare rabbinic and non-rabbinic sexual discourse, these parallels suggest that interaction between Roman, Hellenistic, and Palestinian rabbinic culture occurred on a "deep" level that up to now has not been noticed.[25] I return to this in the Conclusion.

The methodology that I use here owes much to anthropology. We know only too well the difficulty of trying to understand the workings of one culture while standing in another. Previous studies of rabbinic writings on sexuality have adopted, more or less, a diachronic approach,

---

[25]Although much more work has been done on non-Jewish than on rabbinic sexual discourse, there is much left to do. The methodology that I am attempting here has not been applied to the non-rabbinic material. It is my hope that my brief comparisons will spark further study of non-rabbinic material along these same lines.

interpreting texts in line with the interpretive traditions (usually legal) that have crystallized around them over the course of centuries. This study aims to be synchronic, evaluating the rabbinic material against other contemporaneous evidence while, to the extent that it is possible, ignoring how this evidence was read by later interpreters. I make no claim to objectivity: this method is inherently subjective, involving a constant shuttling between perspectives. Theoretically, this approach is close to Gadamer's "fusion of horizons." As Richard Bernstein explains:

> What are we doing (or rather what is happening to us) when we try to understand a horizon other than our own? We already know [that] ... the idea that we can escape our own standpoint and leap into the horizon of the past – is not the right answer. For this is impossible ... Rather, what we seek to achieve is a "fusion of horizons," a fusion whereby our own horizon is enlarged and enriched.[26]

Any attempt to explain the sexual assumptions of the rabbis in late antiquity must fuse the standpoint of the modern interpreter (which in itself represents a range of methodological horizons) with the fragmentary pictures that emerge from both rabbinic and contemporaneous non-rabbinic data. This study attempts to fuse these horizons.

This study does not seek to explain the sexual life of the "average" Jew or rabbi in antiquity. Societal conditions are noted where they are relevant to the discussion of the place and function of the text in society, but I have attempted to avoid the specious assumption that these texts necessarily reflect actual sexual practice. Stories of rabbis exhibiting extreme modesty in intercourse does not lead to the conclusion that "Jews were modest in sexual behavior," any more than the rabbinic assertion that Jews are not to be suspected of homoeroticism leads to the conclusion that there was little or no Jewish homoeroticism in antiquity. It is possible that Jews really were modest in intercourse and that there really was little Jewish homoeroticism in antiquity. But these texts are anything but accurate descriptions of societal practice and cannot serve as evidence for what people were actually doing.

It must be kept in mind throughout that for all that is not known about the culture that produced and read these texts, we do know that at least in their redacted form they were written by men for a male audience. Whether or not the texts are misogynistic is not our concern,

---

[26]Bernstein, *Beyond Objectivism and Relativism* 143. See Hans-Georg Gadamer, *Truth and Method*, trans. Garrett Barden and John Cumming (New York: Seabury, 1975) 269-71.

but without a doubt they are androcentric.[27] Any reconstruction of rabbinic sexuality thus must be exactly that, sexuality as discussed and recorded by a small elite group of male religious leaders. The inaccessibility of women in these texts is frustrating, for discussions of women's sexuality is primarily confined to strategies of control of women's sexuality. This issue too is explored.

Sources and Conventions

This study is, I hope, more or less comprehensive for the tannaitic documents and the Talmudim. Occasionally I use sources from the Midrash Aggadah, especially *Genesis Rabbah* and *Leviticus Rabbah*. My own preliminary studies show that the conclusions and distinctions made in this study persist in other contemporaneous rabbinic documents.

Terms

Throughout this study I use the following terms:
- **Tannaitic** – referring to the work of rabbis who lived between approximately 70 C.E. and 250 C.E. in Palestine.
- **Baraitha** – a source that is identified as tannaitic, but is found outside the *Mishnah*.
- **Amoraic** – referring to the work of rabbis living in both Palestine and Babylonia, after the end of the tannaitic period until the close of the Talmudim, about 425 C.E. in Palestine and 500 C.E. in Babylonia. Amoraim are noted by provenance (Palestine or Babylonia) and generation.[28]

    The "redactor" refers to the anonymous editors who compiled the Yerushalmi and the Bavli.

Tannaitic Documents[29]
1. *Mishnah* – A collection consisting mainly of laws promulgated by rabbis between 70 C.E. and 220 C.E., organized topically.[30]

---

[27]See Boyarin, *Carnal Israel* 240.
[28]Unless noted, all references to the provenance and generation of amoraim follow H. Albeck, *Mavo' l'Talmudim* (rpt. Tel Aviv: Dvir, 1987).
[29]Note that I have not included the *'Abot d'Rabbi Natan*. While this document without doubt contains earlier material, I have not considered it here due to its late recension date. It would be worthwhile to compare the sexual attitudes and assumptions expressed there with the conclusions of this study.
[30]See Abraham Goldberg, "The Mishnah – A Study Book of Halakhah," in *The Literature of the Sages*, ed. S. Safrai, 2 vols. (Philadelphia: Fortress, 1987) 1:211-51; H. L. Strack and G. Stemberger, *Introduction to the Talmud and Midrash* (Minneapolis: Fortress, 1992) 119-66. The *Mishnah* probably contains material from before 70 C.E., but these sources are very difficult to recover and verify. See Jacob Neusner, *Rabbinic Traditions About the Pharisees Before 70*, 3 vols. (Leiden: E.

2. *Tosefta* – Another collection of tannaitic dicta.[31]
3. *Mekhilta d'Rabbi Yishmael* – a commentary on the book of Exodus, consisting mainly of halakhic material, but containing some exegetical commentary.[32]
4. *Mekhilta d'Rabbi Shimon b. Yoḥai* – a fragmentary commentary on the book of Exodus, roughly parallel to the *Mekhilta d'Rabbi Yishmael*.[33]
5. *Sifra* – a commentary on the book of Leviticus, consisting mainly of short halakhic statements.[34]
6. *Sifre Numbers* – a commentary on the book of Numbers, consisting mainly of halakhic statements but also containing exegetical material.[35]
7. *Sifre Deuteronomy* – a commentary on the book of Deuteronomy, similar in character to *Sifre Numbers*.[36]

Talmudim

1. Yerushalmi – also called the Palestinian Talmud. A mixture of tannaitic, amoraic, and redactorial material commentary on the *Mishnah*. Redacted in its final form in Palestine in the early fifth century, C.E.[37]

J. Brill, 1971). Unless noted, citations of the *Mishnah* follow the text of H. Albeck, ed., *The Mishnah*, 6 vols. (rpt. Tel Aviv and Jerusalem: Dvir and The Bialik Institute, 1988).

[31]There is great uncertainty about the redaction date and purpose of the *Tosefta*. See Abraham Goldberg, "The Tosefta – Companion to the Mishnah," in *The Literature of the Sages* 1:283-301; H. Albeck, *Mavo' l'Talmudim* 51-78; Strack, *Introduction* 167-81.

Citations follow Saul Lieberman, ed., *The Tosefta*, 4 vols. (New York: Jewish Theological Seminary of America, 1955-88) for Orders Zera^cim, Mo^ced, Nashim, and tractates Baba Qamma, Baba Meṡi^ca, and Baba Batra. All other citations are from M. S. Zuckermandel, ed., *The Tosefta* (rpt. Jerusalem: Wehrman, 1970).

[32]For comments on these and the following tannaitic documents, see Strack *Introduction* 269-99. Unless noted, all citations follow H. S. Horovitz and I. Z. Rabin, ed., *Mekhilta d'Rabbi Ishmael* (rpt. Jerusalem: Wehrman, 1970).

[33]All citations follow J. N. Epstein and E. Z. Melamed, ed., *Mekhilta d'Rabbi Shimon b. Yoḥai* (rpt. Jerusalem: Hillel, n.d.).

[34]All citations follow J. H. Weiss, ed., *Sifra* (Wien: Jacob Schlossberg, 1862).

[35]All citations follow H. S. Horovitz, ed., *Sifre Numbers* (rpt. Jerusalem: Shalem, 1992).

[36]See Steven D. Fraade, *From Tradition to Commentary: Torah and Its Interpretation in the Midrash* Sifre to Deuteronomy (Albany: State University of New York Press, 1991) 17-21 185-86, n. 56. All citations follow Louis Finkelstein, ed., *Sifre on Deuteronomy* (rpt. New York: Jewish Theological Seminary of America, 1969).

[37]See Abraham Goldberg, "The Palestinian Talmud," in *The Literature of the Sages* 1:303-19; Z. Frankel, *Mavo' HaYerushalmi* (1870; rpt. Berlin: Louis Lamm, 1923) (Hebrew); Baruch M. Bokser, "An Annotated Bibliographical Guide to the Study of the Palestinian Talmud," *ANRW* 2.19.2 (1979): 139-256; Strack *Introduction* 182-207. All citations follow the Venice edition.

2. Bavli – also called the Babylonian Talmud. Like the Yerushalmi, but much larger and redacted in its final form in Babylonia in the late fifth or early sixth (or perhaps even seventh) century C.E.[38]

All translations, unless noted, are my own.[39] My division of rabbinic texts into lettered paragraphs is primarily based on source-critical criteria; this division also facilitates subsequent discussion. I have opted to leave several terms throughout this study in their transliterated form. Sometimes I do this for precision, at other times because I do not feel that a single English word can capture the semantic field of the original. The Hebrew word *carayot*, for example, can cover a range of sexual activities, and it is precisely the ambiguity of the term that contributes to its rhetorical force. When I leave a term transliterated I indicate at its first appearance its approximate meaning, and the reason that I do not translate the term.

Most of the non-rabbinic sources, especially the classical and Christian writings, are widely available. Thus, I note editions for these sources only when unusual or when I feel it necessary.

Names of rabbinic documents are capitalized when referring to the actual document, but left in lower case when used as adjectives (e.g., *mishnaic*). They are also left in lower case when referring to a particular pericope. Hence, "the *Mishnah*" is a document, but "the *mishnah*" is the passage of the *Mishnah* under discussion.

---

[38]See Abraham Goldberg, "The Babylonian Talmud," in *The Literature of the Sages* 1:323-45; David Goodblatt, "The Babylonian Talmud," *ANRW* 2.19.2 (1979): 257-336; Strack *Introduction* 208-44. For discussion of the dating of the Bavli, see Richard Kalmin, *The Redaction of the Babylonian Talmud: Amoraic or Saboraic?* (Cincinnati: Hebrew Union College Press, 1989).
[39]Biblical translations generally follow the *Tanakh: A New Translation of the Holy Scriptures According to the Traditional Hebrew Text* (Philadelphia: Jewish Publication Society, 1985).

2

Incest Restrictions[1]

All societies restrict sexual contact between members of the same kinship group. In some societies, these restrictions are limited to contact between mothers and sons, in others between those able to find a common male descendant four generations back.[2] The taboo, though not the form that it takes in each society, is universal.

As with the variegated forms of the restrictions on sexual contact within a group, the discourse that surrounds such restrictions varies from culture to culture. Hence, for example, the very term "incest," derived from the Latin *incestus*, meaning impure or unchaste, implies a rhetoric of purity and pollution.[3] Embedded in the very word is the concept that commission of the act is impure and liable to moral censure.[4] Anthropologists have shown that this is but one of many rhetorics that are used to control these sexual relationships.[5]

---

[1]For summaries of Jewish laws of incest, see L. Löw, "Eherechtliche Studien" 86-97; Lichstschein, *Die Ehe* 35-41; Mace, *Hebrew Marriage: A Sociological Study* (London: Epworth, 1953) 142-64; Mielziner, *Jewish Law* 33-41; L. Epstein, *Marriage Laws* 220-63; J. D. Eisenstein, "Incest," *Jewish Encyclopedia* 6:572-74; Haim Cohn, "Incest," *Encyclopedia Judaica* 8:1316-18; "גילוי עריות" *Encyclopedia Talmudica* 6:105-15 (Hebrew); Stephen D. Ricks, "Kinship Bars to Marriage in Jewish and Islamic Law," in *Studies in Islamic and Judaic Traditions*, ed. William M. Brinner and Stephen D. Ricks, 2 vols. (Atlanta: Scholars Press, 1986) 1:123-28.

[2]In Roman Egypt, for example, it appears that sibling marriage and intercourse were permitted. See Keith Hopkins, "Brother-Sister Marriage in Roman Egypt," *Comparative Studies in Society and History: An International Quarterly* 22 (1980): 303-54. The Nuer are at the other extreme. See E. E. Evans-Pritchard, *Kinship and Marriage among the Nuer* (1951; rpt. Oxford: Clarendon Press, 1990) 29-48. See also Robin Fox, *Kinship and Marriage* (1967; rpt. Cambridge: Cambridge University Press, 1989) 54-76.

[3]*OED* 5:149.

[4]See for example, *P.W.*, sv. *Incestus*, (p. 1246): "...ist ein aus dem Gebiete des fas herstammender Begriff und bedeutet dort ein den religiösen Satzungen

In this chapter, I explore the rhetorics used by the rabbis in their discussions of restrictions on sexual contact between kin.[6] Leviticus 18, 20, and assorted shorter passages in the Bible contain lists of women with whom sexual contact is prohibited to the Israelite male.[7] Rabbinic literature also speaks from this point of view: in rabbinic law, it is always the woman (defined by her relationship to the male kin) who is prohibited to her male kin. Kinship for purposes of these laws are reckoned by both "blood" (consanguinity) and marriage (affinity).[8] That these forbidden women are perceived in rabbinic literature as a distinct group is seen in the inclusion of all of these women in the rabbinic term ʿarayot (see below). While for convenience I will use the term "incest" throughout this chapter, I will return at the end to the question of whether this term, and the discourse it implies, is fitting for discussion of the rabbinic material.

Before categorizing and analyzing the rabbinic rhetorics of the incest restrictions, a word on kinship terminology is in order. The Bible contains nine kinship terms: son (בן); daughter (בת); father (אב); mother (אם); brother (אח); sister (אחות); uncle (דוד) (probably paternal); father-in-law (חתן); and daughter-in-law (כלה). Terms for all other relationships are constructed from these words (rabbinic terminology adds a few more, which will be noted when relevant). Hence, what in English might be

---

zuwiderlaufendes unzüchtiges Verhalten." See also Luc de Heusch, "Les vicissitudes de la notion d'interidit," in *Religion et tabou sexuel*, ed. Jacques Marx 9-16.
[5]The Nuer, for example, create a discourse of threat around incest. See Evans-Pritchard, *Kinship* 39.
[6]I avoid the use of the word "family" because the rabbinic concept(s) of what constituted the "family" has yet to be sufficiently explored. For some preliminary remarks, see Miriam Peskowitz, "'Family/ies' in Antiquity: Evidence from Tannaitic Literature and Roman Galilean Architecture," in *The Jewish Family in Antiquity*, ed. Shaye J. D. Cohen (Atlanta: Scholars Press, 1993) 9-36.
[7]Biblical laws on sexual contact between kin: Lev. 18:6-18; 20:11-14, 17, 19-21; Deut. 23:1; 27:20, 22-23. I do not here deal with the biblical laws in and of themselves. See Karl Elliger, "Das Gesetz Leviticus 18," *Zeitschrift für die alttestamentliche Wissenschaft* 67 (1955): 1-25; Stephen F. Bigger, "The Family Laws of Leviticus 18 in Their Setting," *Journal of Biblical Literature* 98 (1979): 187-203; S. Loewenstamm, "'Arayot," Encyclopedia Biblica 6:388-90 (Hebrew); Baruch A. Levine, "Excursus 5: Family Structures in Biblical Israel," in *The JPS Torah Commentary: Leviticus* (Philadelphia: Jewish Publication Society, 1989) 253-55; Jonathan Ziskind, "Legal Rules on Incest in the Ancient Near East," *RIDA*, 3d ser., 35 (1988): 79-109.
[8]Epstein acknowledged the inappropriateness of the term "incest" when dealing with these rabbinic restrictions, and substituted the term "consanguineous" (*Marriage Laws* 257). Although morally neutral, this term too is imprecise, as many of the prohibited relationships are based on affinity rather than consanguinity.

termed a "first-cousin" must be expressed in Hebrew in one of six ways: a mother's/father's sister's/brother's son/daughter. The point is that the Hebrew requires a specificity lacking in the English phrase "first-cousin." In my translations I will preserve this specificity.

Rhetoric of Definition

Rabbinic literature attempts to define the incest restrictions in two ways: *who* is prohibited (the dominant rhetoric) and the commission of *what* act defines the transgression. Each of these rhetorics will be considered separately.

FORBIDDEN LIAISONS

In discussions of *who* is prohibited, I consider two distinct issues. The first is that of differentiating sexual contact with kin from marriage with kin. In many cultures, including rabbinic, these issues become confused.[9] The second issue considered is the criteria, implicit and explicit, by which kin are included in these lists of sexually forbidden women.

Incest and Marriage

For the most part, the biblical restrictions on sexual contact between relatives is aimed at relatives whose nakedness a man may not reveal (including, a fortiori, marriage).[10] This emphasis is shifted in Palestinian rabbinic sources to marriage. Discussion of the incestual restrictions within tannaitic sources nearly always focuses on marital restrictions; a tendency echoed in the Yerushalmi.[11] Babylonian sources, by contrast,

---

[9]See Robin Fox, *The Red Lamp of Incest* (New York: E. P. Dutton, 1980) 2-6.

[10]Relatives whom a man is prohibited from "revealing their nakedness" (לא תגלה ערותן): your mother (Lev. 18:7); wife of your father (Lev. 18:8; see also Lev. 20:11); your sister, maternal or paternal (Lev. 18:9); daughter of your son or daughter of your daughter (Lev. 18:10); half-sister on father's side (Lev. 18:11); sister of your father (Lev. 18:12); sister of your mother (Lev. 18:13); wife of the brother of your father (Lev. 18:14); daughter-in-law (Lev. 18:15; see also Lev. 20:12); wife of your brother (Lev. 18:16); woman and her daughter (Lev. 18:17). On the word *'ervah* in its biblical context, see Levine, *Leviticus* 119.

Relatives a man is prohibited from "taking" (לא תקח): daughter of wife's son or daughter (Lev. 18:17); a sister of one's wife in her lifetime (Lev. 18:18); woman and her mother (Lev. 20:14).

[11]The vast majority of this discussion is centered on the levirate marriage: "When brothers dwell together and one of them dies and leaves no son, the wife of the deceased shall not be married to a stranger, outside the family. Her husband's brother shall unite with her: take her as his wife and perform the levir's duty. The first son that she bears shall be accounted to the dead brother, that his name may not be blotted out in Israel," (Deut. 25:5-6). Several biblical narratives revolve around the levirate marriage (e.g., Gen. 38; Ruth). On these, see Biale, *Eros* 11-20. This is discussed at *m. Yebam.* 1:1, 3; 3:4-8; *m. Qidd.* 2:7; 3:10. See also

mirror the biblical concern of sexual contact between kin. Two examples, tracing the Yerushalmi's and Bavli's treatment of the same *mishnah*, can highlight this dichotomy.

Example 1: The Raped and Seduced Women

A vivid illustration of the divergent views and concerns of Palestinian and Babylonian rabbis regarding incest can be seen in their treatments of *m. Yebam.* 11:1:

> A. One can marry [the normally prohibited relatives of] a woman whom one raped (נשאין על האנוסה) or seduced...
>
> B. A man can marry a woman raped by his father, or seduced by his father; or a woman raped by his son, or seduced by his son.
>
> C. Rabbi Yehudah prohibits a woman raped by his father or seduced by his father.

The logic of (A) is that rape and seduction do not cause affinity, hence they do not restrict a man's capability of contracting valid marriages with the woman's relatives. (B) follows from this position that intercourse alone does not cause affinity: because a woman who is raped or seduced by a man never gains the status of "wife" of that man, the man's son or father can marry her. Rabbi Yehudah (C) dissents from this view. Note that throughout this *mishnah*, the only concern is that of marriage, not intercourse with any of these women.

The *Tosefta* attempts to explain Rabbi Yehudah's dissent:

> Rabbi Yehudah forbids the woman raped or violated by his father, as it is said "Do not uncover the nakedness of your father's wife; it is the nakedness of your father," [Lev. 18:8]. Later it says, "No man shall marry his father's wife, and he will not reveal the skirt of his father," [Deut. 23:1] and it says, "[If a man comes upon a virgin...and he seizes her and lies with her...] she shall be his wife..." [Deut. 22:28-29].[12]

The *tosefta's* explanation is economical. A man is not allowed to have intercourse with the wife of his father. The *tosefta* here employs the exegetical technique of *smikut:* since in Deuteronomy the restriction against having sex with one's father's wife directly follows the verses that command that a man must marry the woman he rapes or seduces, it is possible to equate a raped or seduced woman with the wife of the father. Because, then, a woman raped by one's father is counted as the wife of his father, marriage to her is governed by the prohibition against

---

m. Sanh. 7:4, which adds the motif of the effect of widowhood from engagement and marriage and its effect on the consanguinity regulations.
[12] *t. Yebam.* 12:1.

intercourse with one's father's wife.[13] According to the *Tosefta*, Rabbi Yehudah holds that intercourse renders a woman a "wife," at least for purposes of reckoning incest restrictions.

While the *Tosefta* focuses on Rabbi Yehudah's dissent, the Yerushalmi focuses on the first clause in the *mishnah*:

> A. One can marry [the relatives of] a woman one raped, etc. [*m. Yebam.* 11:1]. Read the *mishnah* thus: Marry *after* the rape and *after* the seduction. [E.g.,] If he raped a woman, he can then marry her mother. If he seduced a woman, he can then marry her daughter. One who rapes or seduces a married woman is liable.
>
> B. R. Yoḥanan [PA 2] said, they taught [this *mishnah*] concerning marriage. If he marries a woman and afterwards he raped her mother, then he is liable. If he married a woman and afterwards raped her daughter he is liable.[14]

(A) recognizes that the *mishnah* potentially subverts Lev. 18:17, which prohibits sexual contact between a man and a woman and her daughter. Whether a man married a woman before he had intercourse with her daughter or after is a distinction not known to the Bible. Intercourse with a woman, according to the Bible, should preclude the possibility of intercourse with her mother. The Yerushalmi, apparently, ignores, avoids, reinterprets, or rejects this biblical assumption.[15]

In the Bavli there is a more complex view.

> A. Here we learn, as the Rabbis taught, if one raped a woman it is permitted to marry her daughter; if he married a women he is forbidden to marry her daughter.
>
> B. An objection was raised: One who is suspected [of intercourse] with a woman is forbidden to her mother and her daughter! [The answer:] This is a rabbinical prohibition.
>
> C. And every place there is a rabbinical prohibition, [can it be taught] "they marry" [i.e., this *mishnah*] from the outset? [No,] our *mishnah* refers to after her [i.e., the raped woman's] death.
>
> D. Whence this ruling? As the Rabbis taught, in all [the biblical verses on prohibited liaisons] it says "lies" and here it says "takes" [or, marries] to teach you that the Torah prohibits "taking" [i.e., marriage].

---

[13]See also *t. Sanh.* 10:2 (par. *Sifre Deut.* 246 [p. 275]) which states that a man can marry the "wife" of his father if in fact the "wife" is forbidden to his father.

[14]*y. Yebam.* 11:1, 11c (par. *y. Sanh.* 9:1, 26d).

[15]*y. Yebam.* 11:1, 11d, and similarly at *y. Sanh.* 9:1, 26d-27a. See also *y. Yebam.* 1:1, 2c. Curiously, the *sugya* continues with *m. Ḥul.* 5:3, which refers to liability incurred in the slaughtering of an animal and its mother on the same day. This *sugya* completely subverts the original meaning of *m. Ḥul.* 5:3.

E. Rav Papa [BA 5] said to Abaye [BA 4], but this would apply to his sister! As it is written, "if a man takes his sister, the daughter of either his father or his mother." [Lev. 20:17]. Here "taking" is prohibited; [are we to say] intercourse is permitted?

F. He [Abaye] replied, when "marriage" alone is stated in the Torah, if she is suitable to marry [it means] marriage; [but] if she is suitable [only] for intercourse then intercourse [is meant].[16]

G. Raba [BA 4] said, if he raped a woman, he is permitted to marry her daughter. From here [it is proven] — it is written "The nakedness of *your* son's daughter, or of *your* daughter's daughter — do not uncover their nakedness..." [Lev. 18:10]. Thus, the daughter of *her* son and the daughter of *her* daughter can be revealed [i.e., one can have intercourse with them].

H. But it is written, "Do not uncover the nakedness of a woman and her daughter; nor shall you marry her son's daughter or her daughter's daughter..." [Lev. 18:17]. How [are these texts to be reconciled]?

I. Here [Lev. 18:10] [we refer to a case] of rape, here [Lev. 18:17] to marriage.

J. Can I reverse it? [No,] in respect to forbidden relatives "his own flesh" is written, and this applies to marriage. With rape, "his own flesh" does not apply. [i.e., in Lev. 18:17, but not Lev. 18:10, the word "flesh" (שארה) is written. Lev. 18:10 cannot be applied to rape because the term designates kinship].

K. "Rabbi Yehudah forbids a woman raped by his father, etc.": Rav Gidal [BA 2] said in Rav's name, what is Rabbi Yehudah's reason? It is written, "No man shall marry his father's former wife, so as to remove his father's garment," [Deut. 23:1]. "His father's garment" – the garment that his father saw he shall not reveal.

L. And how do we know that Scripture refers to rape? From that which is above: "[If a man comes upon a virgin who is not engaged and he seizes her and lies with her...] the man who lay with her shall pay the girl's father fifty [shekels of] silver..." [Deut. 22:28-23:1]. And the Rabbis? If the texts were adjacent it would be as you say. But here they are not adjacent, and it is required for the statement of Rav Anan [BA 2] as Rav Anan said in the name of Shmuel [BA 1], the text speaks of the woman awaiting the levirate decision of his father. And what does "his father's garment" mean? The garment that is fitting for his father [i.e., a woman his father is permitted to marry] he shall not uncover.[17]

This *sugya* is a discourse on the difference between intercourse and marriage with a woman, with results quite different from those of its parallel in the Yerushalmi. In (A) through (D) the difference between sex

---

[16]These clauses are reversed in MS Oxford Opp. 248.
[17]*b. Yebam.* 97a.

and marriage is explored. (D) posits that the mishnaic permission given to a man to marry the daughter or mother of a woman he raped or seduced derives from the phrasing of the relevant scriptural verse. In (E) and (F) the ramifications of this stance, namely that a man would be permitted to have sex with his sister, are explored. (F) rather lamely resolves the problem: although Lev. 20:17 uses the word "taking," we should not think that intercourse with one's sister is permitted because here "marriage" does not really mean marriage – because marriage with one's sister is a priori forbidden – so it must mean intercourse. Instead of following-up the circularity of this argument, the *sugya* moves on to (G) and (H), which discuss the relationship of a man to the daughter of a woman he raped. Raba (G), citing Scripture, affirms that a man can marry such a woman. (H) cites Scripture in objection, and (I) and (J) address the objection. (J) rejects the tannaitic notion that rape might cause a marital relationship with its attendant consequences.

In the continuation of the *sugya*, the divergence between the Bavli, which recognizes that the biblical incest restrictions extend to non-marital sex, and the Palestinian sources, which interpret the restrictions as marriage restrictions, is even clearer. The reason for Rabbi Yehudah's dissent, that a woman raped by a man's father is forbidden to that man, is reconsidered. Although the same scriptural verses are cited as employed in the *Tosefta*, their use is unique. In the tannaitic sources, Rabbi Yehudah's decision is justified by saying that a woman whom his father raped is considered, for purposes of these restrictions, "his father's wife." (K) records a true intercourse prohibition. That is, Deut. 23:1 is read to be referring to a father and son sexually sharing a woman rather than as a prohibition against sexual contact with one's father's wife.[18] (L), seeking to justify the position of the rabbis, cites another Babylonian amora who argues that the verse used by Rabbi Yehudah, according to Rav Gidal's explanation (K), has a much more limited application than had previously appeared.

While the legal differences between the Palestinian and Babylonian sources and documents are negligible, they have different foci. The concern of the Palestinian sources, even those cited in the Bavli, is mainly on marriage: how might sex influence future marriage possibilities? Babylonian sources are far more sensitive to the biblical incest restrictions *qua* incest restrictions, not necessarily connected to issues of marriage.

---

[18]See the parallels at *b. Yebam.* 4a and the theoretical statement on *b. Ber.* 21b. On the difference in interpretation between the Bavli and Yerushalmi see also Halivni, *Sources* 3:7-8.

Example 2: "A Woman and Her Daughter"

The *Mishnah* attempts to define the meaning of Lev. 18:17: "Do not uncover the nakedness of a woman and her daughter...":

> These are burned: One who has intercourse with a woman and her daughter... Included in "a woman and her daughter" are: his daughter, daughter of his daughter, daughter of his son, daughter of his wife, daughter of her daughter, daughter of her son, his mother-in-law, mother of his mother-in-law, mother of his father-in-law...[19]

This *mishnah* is apparently based upon Lev. 18:17 and 20:14. According to Lev. 20:14, a man who has sexual contact with a woman and her mother is liable for death by burning, specifies burning in the case of a liaison between a man and a woman and her mother. The first three restrictions prohibit intercourse (or marriage) with a man's own female descendants. The rest of the prohibitions concern a man's wife's female ascendants and descendants. By the end of the *mishnah*, one's father-in-law's mother is being counted as part of "a woman and her daughter." The *mishnah* has expanded the biblical emphasis to include relationships caused by affinity. While preserving the biblical language concerning incest restrictions, the *mishnah* shifts the emphasis to marital relationships.

As its commentary on the passage, the Yerushalmi imports the *sugya* on *m. Yebam.* 11:1 (cited above). The *mishnah*, according to the Yerushalmi, is to be interpreted as referring to marriage, not intercourse. The Bavli, by contrast, states at the beginning of a long *sugya* on this *mishnah*, "'One who has intercourse with a woman whose daughter he married' is not taught [in the *mishnah*], rather, 'One who has intercourse with woman and her daughter' showing that both are forbidden."[20] Intercourse and marriage are clearly distinguished, and this *mishnah* is interpreted as applying to both of them.

Conclusions

The Bible records a number of prohibitions against a man having sexual intercourse with his kin. Tannaitic sources and the Yerushalmi consistently reinterpret these prohibitions as referring to marriage: a Jew is prohibited from marrying these women.[21] The Bavli returns to the

---

[19]*m. Sanh.*, 9:1.
[20]*b. Sanh.* 75a.
[21]See also, for example, *y. Yebam.* 2:4, 3d (par. *y. Yebam.* 11:1, 11c), which cites with some variations a tannaitic tradition reported in the *Sifra Qod.* 9:17 (92c). This tradition, attributed to Rabbi Huna [PA 3] here (but Rav Huna [BA 2] in *y. Sanh.* 9:1, 26d), emphasizes that it is through marriage (not sexual contact) that the incest restrictions are transgressed.

notion that these restrictions refer to intercourse. It should be noted that in the *sugyot* from the Bavli surveyed here, no Palestinian amoraim appear. Similarly, the relevant *sugyot* in the Yerushalmi contain very few statements of Babylonian amoraim. The significance of this fact that become clearer later in this chapter. For the moment, it is the difference between the Palestinian and Babylonian conceptions of the biblical incest restrictions that is important. *Palestinians display a heightened interest in the effect that incest restrictions have on marriage.*[22] The coherence between the assumptions expressed in different documents is less compelling than the coherence between all the Palestinian and Babylonian documents.

Lévi-Strauss was the first anthropologist to note that incest prohibitions translate into a "rule of exogamy:" if men are prohibited from marrying women from their own group, they are forced to marry women from other groups, thus forging bonds with these other groups.[23] Concern with incest and with exogamy are not necessarily connected.[24] The Palestinian rabbis interpret incest restrictions as restrictions on endogamy: the primary application of the incest restrictions is in determining marriage restrictions.[25] Babylonians interpret the incest restrictions more widely.

---

[22]Similarly, they might also be more concerned with the children of these liaisons (see below). There might also be a hint of this in *Sifra Qod.* 9:13 (92b). Trying to explain the use of the word (חבל) in Lev. 20:12, which prohibits a man from having sexual contact with is daughter-in-law, the *Sifra* writes: על שם שתיבל את החום, "because he mixed the line." This obscure line might refer to a concern in lineage (see Rashi on Lev. 20:12). The text, however, might be corrupt.

[23]See Claude Lévi-Strauss, *The Elementary Structures of Kinship*, trans. James Harle Bell and Richard von Stumer (Boston: Beacon Pres, 1969) 19, 51, 481. See also Bronislaw Malinowski, *The Sexual Life of Savages* (1927; rpt. Boston: Beacon Press, 1987) 425, 433; Evans-Pritchard *Kinship* 29-48, esp. 44. Lévi-Strauss's extreme structuralist approach is not universally accepted. Se Pierre Bourdieu, *Outline of a Theory of Practice*, trans. Richard Nice (1972; rpt. Cambridge: Cambridge University Press, 1991) 1-71.

[24]See Fox, *Red Lamp* 146-51.

[25]I do not argue that Palestinians were exogamous rather than endogamous. It appears, in fact, that Jewish Roman Palestine was an endogamous community. See, for example, S. Belkin, "Levirate and Agnate Marriage in Rabbinic and Cognate Literature," *Jewish Quarterly Review* 60 (1969-70): 275-329. Although the Romans were exogamous, endogamous influences might have derived from Hellenistic or other Middle Eastern sources. See Robert F. Murphy and Leonard Kasdan, "The Structure of Parallel Cousin Marriages," *American Anthropologist* 61 (1959): 17-29, and, "Agnation and Endogamy: some Further Considerations," *Southwestern Journal of Anthropology* 23 (1967): 1-14. An examination of Jewish marriage in late-antiquity is a desideratum.

Prohibited Sexual Partners

Rabbinic literature attempts both to define more exactly those sexual partners prohibited by the Bible and to expand the prohibitions to include other "related" women not specified in the Bible. In this section, I examine the ways in which scriptural prohibitions are made more exact; additions to the lists of prohibited sexual partners; and the rhetoric used to justify these prohibitions.

Who is Forbidden

Despite the many studies of the rabbinic incest restrictions, there has been little discussion of the underlying logic which has informed rabbinic additions to the biblical incest laws.[26] All of the rabbinic additions to these regulations for which no reasons are given are of one of three types: they add maternal/paternal specificity; they add generational specificity; or they "fill in" relationships that were not prohibited by or directly derived from Scripture.

In several places tannaitic sources attempt to clarify ambiguous biblical incest regulations. For example, Scripture states that a man should not have sexual contact with the wife of his brother (Lev. 18:16, 20:20). Without citing Scripture, the *Mishnah* clarifies this prohibition: it includes the wives of both one's maternal and paternal half-brother.[27] This same concern can also be found in a list of prohibitions in the *Tosefta* that enumerates the "secondary restrictions from the words of the Scribes," a category alluded to in the *Mishnah*.[28] A simple reading of the list shows this desire for exact specificity. The sexually prohibited women are: the mother of one's mother; the mother of one's father; the wife of the father of one's father; the wife of the father of one's mother; the wife of the brother of one's mother, related paternally; the wife of the brother of one's father, related maternally; the wife of the son of one's son; and the wife of the son of one's daughter. The prohibited women are specified exactly.

Within this same list there are examples of the other two types of unjustified additions to the incest restrictions. The *Tosefta*, for example, prohibits the wife of one's paternal grandfather, an extension of the prohibition against sexual contact with the "wife of one's father." Of the third type are, for example, prohibitions against the wives of one's mother's brother from a shared father and of one's father's brother from

---

[26]See n. 1.
[27]*m. Yebam.* 1:1.
[28]*t. Yebam.* 3. See *m. Yebam.* 2:3, 4; 3:2-4. This categorization, and the difference in terminology, will be discussed below.

a shared mother.[29] The "equivalent" relatives from the other maternal or paternal side (e.g., the wife of one's father's brother related paternally), are thought to be already included in the scriptural prohibitions.

In the Talmudim too unjustified additions to the incest restrictions – which occur almost solely in Palestinian sources – are based upon the three reasons stated above.[30]

Reasons for the Prohibitions

When the rabbis attempt to justify additions to the biblical incest prohibitions, they base themselves on arguments from Scripture; logic; appearances; or sociological concerns.

Arguments from Scripture.

The most common form of Scriptural argument is that based upon analogy, as illustrated by the following passage:

A. "[If a man marries] a woman and her mother, [it is depravity...]" [Lev. 20:14]. I only know about a woman and her mother, whence the scriptural prohibition on her daughter, the daughter of her daughter, and the daughter of her son? Behold, it says here [in Lev. 20:14] "depravity" and it says there [Lev. 18:17][31] "depravity." Just as "depravity" which is stated there [Lev. 18:17] [means] her daughter and the daughter of her daughter and the daughter of her son, so too "depravity" which is stated here [includes] her daughter and the daughter of her daughter and the daughter of her son.

B. What is the scriptural source to make males as females [i.e., kinship reckoned through the male line as kinship reckoned through the female line]? Behold, you [can] argue: it is said here "depravity" and it is said there "depravity." Just as "depravity" which is stated there [Lev. 18:17] makes males as females so too depravity which is stated here [Lev. 20:14] makes males as females.

---

[29]This appears to create an old kinship system. One is forbidden from sexual contact with the wife of one's paternal uncle, whether related to one's father maternally or paternally, but is, on one's mother's side, prohibited from sexual contact only with the wife of an uncle who shares a father with one's mother. This is either an oversight or an indication (or vestige?) of a kinship system in which paternity is a more important determinant of kinship than maternity. It is possible that the parallel found in the Yerushalmi (*y. Yebam.* 2:4, 3d), deliberately substitutes for this relationship "the wife of the brother of his mother," thus instead of referring to the maternal half-uncle with a common father indicates the simpler case of the maternal uncle.

[30]On adding generational specificity, see *b. Yebam.* 21a-22a. On "filling in," see *y. Yebam.* 2:4, 3d (Bar Kapra [PA 1] is credited with adding to the list of prohibited sexual partners one's mother's father's mother and one's father's father's mother).

[31]"Do not uncover the nakedness of a woman and her daughter; nor shall you marry her son's daughter or her daughter's daughter and uncover her nakedness; they are kindred; it is depravity."

C. And what is the scriptural source to make the bottom [i.e., descendants] like the top [i.e., ascendants]? Behold, you [can] argue: it is stated there "depravity" and it is stated here "depravity." Just as "depravity" which is stated there [Lev. 18:17] makes the bottom like the top so too "depravity" which is stated here [Lev. 20:14] makes the bottom like the top.[32]

Sifra uses the occurrence of the word "depravity," זמה, in two related Scriptural verses in order to elucidate the Lev. 20:14. Since Lev. 18:17 explicitly extends the prohibition against sex with a woman and her daughter to include granddaughters, the rabbis read Lev. 20:14 to also be referring to multiple generations. (B) and (C) function similarly: both use the relationships explicitly stated in Lev. 18:17 to help interpret Lev. 20:14. The result is scriptural justification for prohibitions not explicitly stated in Scripture, such as the daughters of one's sons and daughters.

Neusner has noted the *Sifra's* polemical preference for scriptural over logical proof.[33] Indeed, the *Sifra* uniformly tries to anchor the *Mishnah's* incest restrictions in Scripture.[34] The *Sifra* complements this effort with a strong polemic against the use of logic to deduce the incest restriction. The prohibited liaisons can be deduced only from Scripture (as interpreted in "approved" ways); any attempt to logically derive them will be bound to fail. In several places the *Sifra* goes out of its way to show that a fortiori reasoning, or "logic," דין, cannot be used to determine the prohibited liaisons.[35] Renunciation of the use of logic to derive incest prohibitions can also be found *Sifre Numbers*.[36]

The Yerushalmi too attempts to stay close to Scripture in discussions of definition.

A. R. Yosi [PA 5] said, "his aunt (דודתו), [the shame of his uncle he revealed]" [Lev. 20:20] is necessary to exclude the wife of his maternal brother.

B. What is the reason? It is said here [Lev. 20:20] "his aunt" and it is said there "...or his uncle or his uncle's son shall redeem him..." [Lev. 25:49]. Just as when Scripture says "uncle" there [Lev. 25:49] it is the paternal brother of his father, so too "his aunt" which is written here [Lev. 20:20] means the wife of the paternal brother of his father.

C. Also the wife of his brother one learns from "his aunt." Just as when Scripture says "his aunt" it is the wife of the paternal brother

---

[32]*Sifra Qod.* 9:16, 17 (92c) (par. *y. Yebam.* 2:4, 3d; *b. Sanh.* 75a).
[33]See Jacob Neusner, *Sifra: An Analytical Translation*, 2 vols. (Atlanta: Scholars Press, 1988) 1:1-53, esp. 30-31.
[34]See *Sifra Qod.* 10:10 (92d); 10:12 (92d); 11:6 (93a); 11:8 (93a).
[35]See Sifra *Aḥare* 13:14 (86b) *Qod.* 10:10 (92d); 10:12 (92d); 11:8 (93b).
[36]*Sifre Num.* 7 (p. 11).

of his father, so too when Scripture says "wife of his brother" [Lev. 18:16] Scripture means the wife of his paternal brother.

D. Up to this point [this is according to] R. Akiba. How does R. Ishmael respond?

E. R. Ishmael taught: It is said here [Lev. 18:16] "wife of his brother" and it is said there "If a man marries the wife of his brother, it is indecency *(niddah),*" [Lev. 20:21]. Just as in the case of *niddah* there is permissibility after a prohibition [i.e., one is first forbidden to a menstruant and then after her menses permitted] so too the wife of his brother from his father is permissible. This excludes the wife of his maternal brother for whom there is no permissibility after the prohibition.[37]

Rabbi Akiba is attributed with a complex syllogism (B-C) of scriptural analogies to arrive at the proposition presented in (A): that Scripture does not prohibit a man sexual contact with his maternal half-brother's wife. (B) demonstrates that the words "his aunt" can refer only to the wife of one's paternal uncle. (C) applies this logic to the prohibition against the "wife of one's brother," concluding that only the paternal half-brother could be meant.

A second exegesis is then offered in R. Ishmael's name. (E) appears to be responding to the exegesis of (C): one learns that "wife of one's brother" refers only to the wife of a paternal brother not from the syllogism of (C), but from a combination of scriptural analogy and deduction from laws of the menstruant. This definition depends upon, but moves further from, Scripture than that of (B) and (C).[38]

Given these two exegeses, it is interesting to note that (A) appears to accept without reservation the logic of (B) and (C), attributed to R. Akiba. R. Ishmael's alternative explanation, which depends upon logical argumentation, if known to R. Yosi (A) was ignored by him. Whether or not (B) through (E), which appears to form a coherent unit, is authentically tannaitic (it is not paralleled in tannaitic documents), the late Palestinian amora accepts only the scriptural argument ascribed here to R. Akiba.

The reluctance of the Yerushalmi to stray far from Scripture in derivations of incest prohibitions can also be seen in the following short tradition:

---

[37]*y. Sanh.* 7:5, 24c.
[38]Note that R. Ishmael focuses on the question of which relatives a man is allowed to marry after the affine connection has been broken, an issue which appears elsewhere in the Yerushalmi *(y. Sanh.* 7:8, 24d). These traditions emphasize the strength of maternity, at least among tannaitic rabbis, for incest reckoning – uterine brothers may never share a wife.

A. Up to now [we have been discussing] the daughter of the daughter. Whence do we learn the daughter?

B. Rav [BA 1] said, if he is cautioned about the daughter of the daughter, is it not all the more so in regard to his daughter?

C. If he suffers extirpation [for violating] his daughter's daughter, is it not all the more so for his daughter?

D. According to whom? Hezakiah taught, "When the daughter of a priest ('ish kohen) defiles herself through harlotry," [Lev. 21:9].

E. Scripture says "'ish" [which is extraneous] in order to indicate that one who has intercourse with his daughter from a woman he raped is punished by burning.[39]

Even Rav's a fortiori argument (B and C), implicitly based on Scripture, cannot stand alone. Ultimately it is the strained scriptural exegesis in (D) and (E) that justifies the prohibition of sexual contact with one's daughter from a woman that one raped. Like the *Sifra*, the Palestinian sources in the Yerushalmi appear to rely more on Scripture as sources for incest prohibitions.

In the Bavli, Scripture is rarely used alone to justify the prohibitions against intercourse with female kin. In fact, the Bavli often rejects the use of Scripture alone for this purpose. More or less parallel *sugyot* in the Yerushalmi and Bavli on this topic show a striking difference in this regard. An example of this occurs in the citation in the Yerushalmi and the Bavli of the tannaitic tradition from the *Sifra* that reckons male kin as female kin and ascendants as descendants (cited above). The Yerushalmi's treatment of it is brief and unremarkable, but in the Bavli it triggers a long redactorial passage that applies logic and counter-examples to every clause and relationship enumerated in the tradition.[40] In a parallel *sugya*, on the derivation of the prohibition against the maternal and paternal aunt, the Yerushalmi uses Scripture (citing a *baraitha*) while the Bavli again prefers logical argumentation.[41]

Logical Argumentation.

There are, of course, many types of "logic." The logical, or argumentative, hermeneutic of rabbinic circles is vast but has yet to be rigorously analyzed.[42] Nevertheless, at least in the case of incest restrictions, it is clear that self-conscious argumentation is used far more frequently in Babylonian than in Palestinian rabbinic sources.

---

[39] *y. Sanh.*, 9:1, 26d.
[40] *y. Yebam.* 2:4, 3d; *Sifra Qod.* 9:16, 17 (92a); *b. Sanh.* 75a-b.
[41] *y. Sanh.* 7:4, 24c; *b. Yebam.* 54b.
[42] For some preliminary comments, see David Kraemer, *The Mind of the Talmud* (New York: Oxford University Press, 1990) 36-37, 79-98.

Tannaitic sources, to my knowledge, never justify the imposition of incest restrictions with logical argumentation.[43] Within the Yerushalmi, logical argumentation is used only to justify pre-existent, or scripturally determined, prohibitions:

A. Rav [BA 1] said, all whom the Torah prohibits to a man from the female side, similarly the wife of the male relative [of the same degree] is prohibited. [For example,] the sister of one's father, a female, is forbidden, [hence in the case of] the brother of one's father, a male, his wife is forbidden. The sister of one's mother, a female, is forbidden, [hence in the case of] the brother of one's mother, a male, his wife is forbidden. The daughter of one's son, a female, is forbidden, [hence in the case of] the son of one's son, a male, his wife is forbidden. The daughter of one's daughter, a female, is forbidden, [hence in the case of] the son of one's daughter, a male, his wife is forbidden.

B. Rabbi Ya'akov the Southerner [PA 5] said before Rabbi Yosi [PA 4], you have another two. One's mother [is prohibited from the] Torah. The mother of one's mother is a secondary [restriction] to it. They prohibited the mother of one's father because of the mother of one's mother. The wife of one's son [is prohibited from the] Torah. The wife of the son of one's son is a secondary [restriction] to it. They prohibited the wife of the son of one's daughter because of the wife of the son of one's son.

C. Rabbi Mattenaiah [PA 5-6] said, you have another two. The wife of one's father [is prohibited from the] Torah. The wife of the father of one's father is a secondary [restriction] to it. They prohibited the wife of the father of one's mother because of the wife of the father of one's father.[44] The wife of the brother of one's paternal brother [is prohibited from] the Torah. The wife of the maternal brother of one's father is a secondary [restriction] to it. They prohibited the wife of the maternal[45] brother of one's mother because of the wife of the maternal brother of one's father.[46]

(A), attributed to an early Babylonian amora, advances an argument of logical symmetry. The wives of men who stand in the same degree of relationship as biblically prohibited women can thus be prohibited. Hence each biblical prohibition (all of which have women as their objects) implies a prohibition on the wife of a kinsman. Sometimes, as in the case of the wife of the brother of one's father, this woman is already prohibited biblically (Lev. 18:14); in the other examples cited in (A), there is no overlap with the biblical prohibitions. (B) and (C) employ this logic

---

[43]This excludes a fortiori reasoning, which is always based on scriptural analogy and is used in the tannaitic material.
[44]In MS Leiden, from the beginning of (C) to here is found only in the margin.
[45]In MS Leiden, "maternal" is found only in the margin.
[46]y. Yebam. 2:4, 3d.

in a somewhat different form. According to these late Palestinian amoraim, one can prohibit women based on a chain of logical symmetry. Prohibitions from Scripture imply secondary prohibitions: logical symmetry is then used to prohibit an equivalent maternal or paternal kinswoman. Together, the prohibitions enumerated in (B) and (C) account for all the relationships included in a list of incest restrictions cited at the beginning of this *sugya*. This logic, then, is used only to justify pre-existent restrictions rather than to add new ones.

Qualitatively and quantitatively, the Bavli's use of logic far exceeds the Yerushalmi's. Occasionally, the Bavli itself demonstrates this difference between Palestinian and Babylonian use of logical argumentation:

A. Come and hear: When R. Yehudah bar Shila [PA 4] came he said, they say in the West that every scriptural prohibition that applies to a female, they forbid as a secondary restriction the equivalent male's wife.[47]

B. Raba [BA 4] said, this is a general rule? His mother-in-law is prohibited from Scripture (*'ervah*), the wife of his father-in-law is permitted; the daughter of his mother-in-law is prohibited from Scripture, the wife of the son of his mother-in-law is permitted; the daughter of his father-in-law is forbidden from Scripture, the wife of the son of his father-in-law is permitted; his step-daughter is prohibited from Scripture, the wife of his step-son is permitted; the daughter of his step-son[48] is prohibited from Scripture, the wife of the son of his step-son is permitted.

C. What did Rav Yehudah bar Sila include? Did he not include the wife of the maternal brother of one's mother, because every scriptural prohibition that applies to a female, they forbid as a secondary restriction the equivalent male's wife.

D. What is the difference between these [relations in B] and this [in C]? In this case [C] she becomes kin in a single act of betrothal; in those [relations in B] two acts of betrothal are necessary.[49]

The logical principle attributed to Palestine (A) is cited and then ridiculed by Raba (B). The redactor (C) offers an alternative application of the principle. (D) separates the cases by saying that the women referred to in (B) are related through two acts of marriage, while those in

---

[47]כל שבנקבה ערוה בזכר מרו על אשתו משום שניה. It is interesting to note that this is similar to Rav's statement, cited above, in *y. Yebam.* 2:4, 3d. Rav, however, does not refer to secondary restrictions, which enter the *sugya* attributed to later Palestinian amoraim.

[48]Following most manuscripts. The printed edition reads חורגתו.

[49]*b. Yebam.* 21b.

(C) are related only through a single act of marriage.[50] In this example, both sets of logical argumentation, (A) and (B), are harmonized. Argumentation and categorization are used by both the Babylonian amora and the redactor.

Arguments from Appearances.

Only the Yerushalmi explicitly prohibits certain relatives on the basis of appearances, that is, although a union might be perfectly legal, it is prohibited because others might misunderstand the true circumstances and thus be led to transgression.

- A. R. Zerikan [PA 3] in the name of R. Ḥaninah [PA 3] said, the wife of one's father-in-law is forbidden because of appearances (מראית העין).
- B. Do not say that this is a scriptural [prohibition]. Behold, David married Rispah, the daughter of Ayyah, as it is said, "I gave you your master's house and possession of your master's wives..." [2 Sam. 12:8. This proves that marriage to the wife of one's father-in-law is permitted].
- C. R. Yermiah [PA 4] in the name of R. Leazar [=R. Eleazar, PA 3] said, two step-children raised in one house are forbidden to marry because of appearances.
- D. A case came before R. Ḥaninah b. Abbahu [PA 4]. He said, let them marry in a place where no one knows them...[51]

The prohibition in (A) appears to be based on the fear that sexual contact (or perhaps only marriage, as in [D]) with one's father-in-law's wife would *look like* and might be confused with sexual contact with one's true mother-in-law, which is prohibited. Similarly, sexual relationships between step-children (C) are prohibited because outsiders might mistakenly assume them to be relationships between true siblings. (C) especially is somewhat strained. This argument from appearances assumes that a person who sees the liaison and mistakenly assumes that the two step-children are true siblings, will think that a union between siblings is not a transgression, and might thereby be led to marrying her or his sibling. The taboo against a liaison between siblings, however, would have been too well-known to conceive of a situation in which a person is misled to having sex with one's sibling. Alternatively, this text might be based on an assumption that a man harbors a strong sexual

---

[50]Harmonization through categorization is very common in the Bavli. Here, however, the specific axis along which these groups are separated might indicate an elementary kinship theory, by which kinship might "weaken" across marriage bonds.

[51]*y. Yebam.* 2:4, 3d.

desire for his sister.⁵² If so, then the real fear reflected in this text would be that a man who believes that he sees two siblings having sex will himself be tempted to initiating sexual contact with his sister. In any case, the relationship is prohibited out of fear for how others will interpret and respond to it.⁵³

There is, to my knowledge, only a single argument from appearances used in the Bavli to justify the incest prohibitions. It is employed in a discussion on proselytes:

- A. Rabah [BA 3] said to Rav Naḥman [BA 3], has the master seen this one [rabbi] of the rabbis who came from the West and said, they ask in the West whether they apply the secondary restrictions to converts or do not apply the secondary restrictions to converts. He said to him, now if even scripturally prohibited liaisons are imposed [on converts rabbinically] so that they will not say that they came from a [religion of] strict holiness to one of lesser holiness and the Rabbis did not impose other restrictions; is it a question that the Rabbis would have imposed secondary restrictions?

- B. Rav Naḥman [BA 3] said, converts – since they came up, let us say something about them. Maternal brothers cannot serve as witnesses [for each other] but if they did, their testimony is valid. Paternal brothers can testify [for each other] from the start.

- C. Amimar [BA 5-6] said, maternal⁵⁴ brothers can also testify [for each other] from the start.

- D. And how is this different from the scripturally prohibited relations (מש מעריות)? The laws of prohibited relations are transmitted to all, but [the laws relating to] testimony are transmitted to the Court, and [the members of the Court would know] that a convert is like a new-born [i.e., considered to be without relatives].⁵⁵

In this discussion of the application of the secondary restrictions to Gentiles, there is an implied argument from appearances. According to rabbinic law, a convert to Judaism is like a "new-born," all former kinship ties are broken. Yet, according to Rav Naḥman (A), those female

---

⁵²See below. The assumption that a man sexually desires his sister is not an unusual one. Anthropological data has shown cultures in which sibling desire is very carefully guarded against. See especially Malinowski, *Sexual Life* 437-440. In nearby Egypt, not long before the composition of this text, brothers and sisters of all classes were marrying. See Hopkins, "Brother-Sister Marriage."

⁵³There are two alternative readings of this text: (1) as mentioned in the last note, Egyptian siblings used to marry. Hence, perhaps it was feared that the appearance of sibling intercourse would seem to mimic non-Jewish practice; (2) the motivating factor was shame. Such behavior would appear shameful and impudent, thus worthy of societal censure.

⁵⁴MS Munich reads "paternal," but this appears to be a scribal error. See *Bab. Tal.* 3.1:245.

⁵⁵*b. Yebam.* 22a.

kin that Scripture prohibits to Jewish men are also imposed by the rabbis on proselytes, so that they will not say that their new religion is easier, or less holy, than their old. The meaning of this is not totally clear: who precisely are the "they" (Gentiles, proselytes, or Jews?) and why do the rabbis not want them to think this? The second reason given is a little clearer. (D), stated anonymously, says that the reason for imposing these restrictions on proselytes is that "the laws of prohibited relations are transmitted to all." Apparently this redactorial statement reflects a fear similar to that of "appearances" in the Yerushalmi. The fear is that Jews might see converts marrying normally forbidden relatives and not knowing why they are legally entitled to marry who they are (a difference known to the Courts, who administer testimony), will imitate them.

Arguments based on Sociological Factors.

Only in the Bavli are incest restrictions justified on what appear to be the basis of contemporary societal conditions or at least assumptions about them.

- A. Rav [BA 1] said, four women have a limitation [i.e., they, but not their ascendants or descendants, are forbidden]. Rav knew of three: the wife of the paternal brother of the mother; the wife of the maternal brother of the father; and his daughter-in-law.
- B. Zeiri [BA 1] adds also the wife of the father of his mother.
- C. R. Naḥman b. Isaac [BA 4] said, your [= Zeiri's] mnemonic is, that above Rav's.
- D. Why does Rav not include [Zeiri's addition]? [Because] she [the wife of the father of one's mother] might be confused (מיחלפא) with the wife of the father of one's father.
- E. And Zeiri [can he answer this]? It is common for him to go there [his father's family], but it is not common for him to go there [his mother's family]. [Hence, there is no fear of confusion].[56]

According to the redactor (E), sociological factors can explain an opinion that the wife of the father of one's mother is not prohibited. Apparently, the assumption in (E) is that one has closer contact with one's father's family than with one's mother's family (perhaps indicating patrilocal marriage among Babylonian Jews at the time of the redactor). Regardless of the (if any) underlying reality, there is a willingness demonstrated here that is not seen in tannaitic sources or the Yerushalmi to advance sociological arguments in determining prohibited relationships.

---

[56]*b. Yebam.* 21a.

A second example of this argumentation occurs later in the same *sugya*. Here, Rav's reference to "his daughter-in-law" ([A], above) is explained:

> Abaye [BA 4] said to Raba [BA 4], I will explain it to you: it is like the daughter-in-law of the house of Bar Tzitai. Rav Papah [BA 5] said, like the daughter-in-law of the house of Papa bar Abba.[57] Rav Ashi [BA 6] said, like the daughter-in-law of the house of Mari bar Isaac.[58]

That both Rashi and Tosafot struggle to integrate this comment into the *sugya* highlights the obscure nature of the argument. One cannot understand the passage without knowing the family situations to which it alludes. Ye this does not stop these late Babylonian amoraim from making the argument and the redactor from including it.

The immediate continuation of this *sugya*, discussing restrictions on aunts, evinces two additional sociological arguments:

A. They asked them, what is the law concerning the wife of the maternal[59] brother of one's mother? Did the Rabbis forbid the wife of the maternal brother of the father and the wife of the paternal brother of the mother because there is a [common] paternal side, but not forbid this because there is no [common] paternal side or perhaps it is not different?

B. Rav Safra [BA 3] said, she [the wife of the paternal brother of the mother] herself is forbidden [as a preventive measure], shall we establish a preventive measure for a preventive measure?

C. Raba [BA 4] said, are not all of them forbidden as preventive measures for preventive measures? One's mother is prohibited from Scripture, the mother of one's mother is a secondary restriction,[60] and they prohibited the mother of one's father because of the mother of one's mother. What is the reason? Everybody calls them "of the house of the grandmother" (כולהו דבי אימא רבתי קרו.)

D. The wife of one's father is prohibited from Scripture, the wife of the father of one's father is a secondary restriction, and they prohibited the wife of the father of one's mother because of the wife of the father of one's father. What is the reason? Everybody calls them "of the house of the grandfather" (דבי אבא רבה).

E. The wife of the paternal brother of one's father is prohibited from Scripture; the wife of the maternal brother of one's father is a

---

[57]Following most manuscripts.
[58]*b. Yebam.* 21b.
[59]MS Munich 95 reads "paternal."
[60]Contrast the sources surveyed above (especially *m. Sanh.* 9:1 and the commentary on it), which derive authority for prohibition of one's grandmother from Lev. 18:17 or 20:14.

secondary restriction; they prohibited the wife of the paternal brother of one's mother because of the wife of the maternal brother of one's father. What is the reason? Because everybody calls them, "of the house of the uncle" (רבי דודי).[61]

Who is an "uncle"? (A) entertains the idea that the wives of some "uncles" and not others are prohibited because the uncles are related through the father. That would assume that kinship travels more "efficiently" through the paternal line than the maternal. The two prohibited wives of uncles are enumerated in Rav's list of the three relatives that have a limitation. (A) attempts to do what Rav never did, to tell us why in fact these relationships are prohibited. The redactor might here be basing the question on assumptions about the relative strength of paternal kinship, examples of which we have also seen above.

(B) does not answer the question posed by (A). Instead, it cites a well-worn objection, usually left unattributed, that is used throughout the Bavli for a variety of subjects.[62] According to this objection, once an object (or in this case wife or sexual partner) is declared rabbinically prohibited, one does not legislate a second restriction to protect the first. In (C) through (E), Raba shows that this principle does not apply. Each paragraph ends with a statement, probably from the redactor, that indicates that maternal and paternal grandmothers, step-grandmothers, and aunts (through marriage) are colloquially considered the "same." Whereas all of our other sources go through great pains in order to precisely identify relatives, the redactor here conflates these distinctions by saying that usually the word "grandmother," for example, indicates both the maternal and paternal grandmother, and that this is reason enough to forbid this relative even though she is at least three logical degrees removed from any scriptural prohibition. Again, we find an allusion to contemporaneous kinship attitudes at the heart of the argument.[63]

---

[61] *b. Yebam.* 21b.
[62] See, *b. Beṣ* 3a (redactor); *b. Shab.* 11b (Raba); *b. ʿErub.* 4b (redactor), 99a (Raba); *b. Yoma* 11a (redactor); *b. Sukk.* 6b (redactor); *b. Yebam.* 109a (Rav Naḥman); *b. ʿAbod. Zar.* 21a (redactor); *b. Ḥul.* 85b (redactor), 104a (redactor); *b. Nid.* 67b (redactor).
[63] Another example of sociological argumentation can be found in *b. Yebam.* 97a-b. A tannaitic tradition (*t. Yebam.* 4:5), cited in this *sugya*, forbids a man who is suspected of having had intercourse with a woman from marrying her relatives. An unattributed statement in the *sugya* limits its application to during the life of that woman. It is possible that the redactor interpreted the tannaitic statement as being based in the fear that a man will marry a woman in order to gain easier access to one of her relatives. It is unlikely that this is the original reasoning behind the tannaitic statement. See below.

Conclusions

Palestinian sources much more frequently employ scriptural proofs and shun logical proofs in extending the incest restrictions than do Babylonian sources. Palestinian, and perhaps Babylonian, sources do employ arguments from "appearances" in extending these prohibitions. Only Babylonian sources utilize sociological arguments as justification or illustration of these prohibitions.

Proselytes and Gentiles

Both the Yerushalmi and the Bavli discuss the application of incest restrictions to proselytes and Gentiles. The differences between the discussions within these two documents appear to reflect different assumptions about kinship.

The Yerushalmi clearly regards kin related through the mother as "more" related than those related through the father.

- A. A Gentile who converts and who was married to a woman and her daughter or a woman and her sister, he weds (כונס) one of them and sends the other away. When does this apply?[64] When he did not have intercourse (הכיר) with one of them from the time of his conversion. But if he had intercourse with one of them after his conversion, he takes her as his wife. If he had intercourse with both of them, because he had intercourse, he had intercourse [i.e., he retains both as wives].

- B. A convert – [if married to] his sister [before he converts], whether paternal or maternal, he sends her away [after he converts], according to R. Meir. R. Yehudah says, his maternal sister he sends away, his paternal [sister] he retains.

- C. The sister of his mother [if he is married to her] he sends away, the sister of his father he retains, according to R. Meir. R. Yehudah says, the maternal sister of his mother he sends away, the paternal sister of his mother he retains. The remainder of all the forbidden relatives he weds (כונס) and does not send away. It only says here "weds" – but it is forbidden at the beginning [i.e., a convert cannot begin a relationship with one of his relatives after her converted, but if he began one and then converted, he is allowed to continue the relationship].

- D. A Gentile – [if married to] his sister, whether paternal or maternal, he sends her away, according to R. Meir. R. Yehudah says, his maternal sister he sends away, his paternal sister he retains.

- E. The sister of his mother he sends away, the sister of his father he retains, according to R. Meir. R. Yehudah says, the maternal sister of his mother he sends away, the paternal sister of his mother he retains.

---

[64]From the beginning of (A) to here is in the margin of MS Leiden.

Incest Restrictions

F. R. Ḥanin [BA 2?][65] said, the opinion of R. Meir is understandable to us: "Hence a man leaves his father and his mother [and clings to his wife]..." [Gen. 2:24]. This encompasses related women from both his father and his mother.

G. R. Bibi [PA 3] [said] from this it follows that the sister of one's father is forbidden because she is from the line of his father (שהיא סמוכה לאביו). The sister of one's mother would be forbidden to him because she is from the line of his mother.

H. R. Shimon son of R. Aibo objected, is it not written, "Amram took to wife his father's sister Joḥabed," [Ex. 6:20]. From this, Israel did not even behave as the sons of Noah [i.e., Gentiles, who are commanded not to marry their fathers' sisters]!

I. R. Hila [PA 3] said, it is both from his father and from his mother.

J. They objected to R. Meir. Is it not written "And besides, she is in truth my sister, my father's daughter though not my mother's..." [Gen. 20:12, referring to Sarah]. R. Meir said to them, is this proof? [Does not the verse continue,] "and she became my wife"?

K. What is the result? R. Yoseh [PA 3 or 4] said, every incest restriction [transgression of which] the court of the Jews requires the death penalty also applies to Gentiles, and every incest restriction [transgression of which] the court of the Jews does not require the death penalty does not apply to the Gentiles.

L. They objected: Behold, intercourse with one's sister requires the death penalty, and this is not forbidden to Gentiles!

M. R. Hila in the name of R. Shimeon ben Lakish [PA 3] [said], "[For anyone who does such things is abhorrent to the Lord,] and it is because of these abhorrent things that the Lord your God is dispossessing them before you," [Deut. 18:12]. This teaches that God punishes only [on account of transgressions about which] God [first] admonished.[66]

Although the tannaitic opinions expressed in (A) through (E) are not paralleled in any tannaitic source, they exhibit characteristics familiar to the tannaitic and Palestinian sources previously surveyed, namely a concern with marriage and precise identification of forbidden relatives. Because the convert is considered "new born" and without kin, her or his obligation to adhere to many of the incest rules is nominal and academic. That is, a new convert cannot transgress an incest restriction because she or he legally has no relatives. This clearly did not sit very well with the rabbis in this *sugya*. The opinions in (A) through (C) attempt to restrict a proselyte's right to marry his kin. The last line of (C), a gloss by the redactor, acknowledges the problem: if previous incestuous relations

---

[65]Following MS Leiden.
[66]*y. Yebam.* 11:2, 12a (partial par. *Gen. Rab.* 18:5 [pp. 165-66]).

were confirmed after conversion through intercourse, they remain intact. Otherwise, they are to be dissolved. A parallel discussion occurs for Gentiles in (D) and (E), although without the redactorial gloss.

The prohibition of some relatives to proselytes extends only to women related maternally. Not only do neither R. Meir nor R. Yehudah suggest that a kinswoman related only through the father be sent away, but Rabbis Meir and Yehudah (C) even explicitly permit a male proselyte to remain married to his paternal aunt. The importance placed on incest prohibitions that derive from uterine descent might be based in one of two assumptions. First, it is possible that this is an argument from appearances: Jews are assumed to be more likely to confuse relatives of the mother with "real" relatives, thus making them more likely to be led astray. That is, if a Jew saw a proselyte married to his maternal aunt there would be more likelihood that the Jew would recognize this marriage as a violation of an incest restriction than if the Jew saw the proselyte married to a paternal aunt. The second, and more likely, possibility is that kinship through the mother was considered stronger than kinship through the father. This would be in line with the recently formulated (or still developing) matrilineal principle.[67] Proselyte and Gentile men were permitted to their paternally related kinswomen while forbidden from their maternal counterparts precisely due to either popular belief or rabbinic polemic that identified kinship more strongly with the mother. As we have seen, this appears not to have been the case in Babylonia.[68]

The rest of the *sugya* concentrates on application of the law to Gentiles. The tannaim in (D) and (E) attempt to define precisely incest restrictions for Gentiles. From (F) on, the argument becomes less one of definition and concentrates more on the general applicability of incest restrictions to Gentiles.

The parallel *sugya* in the Bavli demonstrates different assumptions about kinship.[69] The *sugya* itself is sparse, basically a streamlined version of the tannaitic traditions recorded in the Yerushalmi. Informative, though, is the redactorial discussion that directly precedes this *sugya*.[70]

---

[67]On the matrilineal principle and its history, see, Shaye J.D. Cohen, "The Origins of the Matrilineal Principle in Rabbinic Law," *AJS Review* 10 (1985): 19-53.

[68]I do not mean to suggest that these different kinship attitudes had necessary legal ramifications. Babylonians could focus on kinship structures that gave primary importance to paternity without negating the tannaitic rule that the status of the mother of a child determines that child's status. On the other hand, kinship structures that gave primary importance to maternity might have given rise to the matrilineal principle.

[69]*b. Yebam.* 98a-b (par. *b. Sanh.* 58a).

[70]*b. Yebam.* 97b.

In this discussion, the redactor entertains the notion that some Babylonian amoraim "call" a person after his or her father, and others after his or her mother. This sociological fact has important legal ramifications. In a society, for example, that "calls" people after the father, a proselyte who marries a paternal relative will be known to be marrying a relative, thus potentially leading Jews astray. This relativistic attitude among Babylonian amoraim (according to the redactor) might account for the relative neglect of these tannaitic traditions cited in the Bavli, which are more rigid. Such rigidity would have appeared confusing to the redactor. That is, the different kinship structures in which the tannaitic traditions (and Yerushalmi) were framed and in which the Bavli's redactor worked might have influenced the latter's understanding of these received traditions.

DEFINING ACT

What sexual act defines incest? That is, how much sexual contact can take place between men and the women sexually prohibited to them before they have committed a "transgression?"

All rabbinic sources are virtually unanimous in labeling intercourse – whether vaginal or anal, whether it resulted in ejaculation or not – as the "defining" sexual act. While the *Mishnah* does not give any reason for its ruling, *Sifra* derives its ruling from the biblical laws concerning the menstruant.[71] According to Lev. 20:18, "[If a man lies with a woman in her infirmity] and uncovers her nakedness, he has laid bare her flow (*he'erah*) [and she has exposed her blood flow; both of them will be cut off from among their people]." The word *he'erah* (הערה), which appears to be superfluous, is interpreted as indicating the first stage of intercourse, *me'erah* (מערה). The first stage of intercourse with a menstruant, insertion of the penis into the vagina (and probably anus), renders a couple liable for violation of the biblical stricture against sex during menstruation. The passage then offers a number of scriptural analogies that extend this position to the other forbidden liaisons of Lev. 20. In both the Yerushalmi and the Bavli insertion is assumed to make the incestuous couple liable.[72]

According to a single tradition found only in the *Sifra*, any physical contact between a man and a woman forbidden to him is prohibited. This too is argued from scriptural analogy to the menstruant, to whom it

---

[71] *m. Yebam.* 6:1-2; *m. Ker.* 2:4; *Sifra Qod.* 11:2 (93a).
[72] See *y. Yebam.* 6:1, 7b; 6:2, 7b; 11:1, 11c. These discussions are paralleled in the Bavli: *b. Yebam.* 55b-56a, 22b; *b. Soṭ* 26b.

is forbidden to "draw near." This rule is then extended to the other kin in Lev. 18.[73] The Bavli, citing a Palestinian amora, rejects this position.[74]

NON-RABBINIC PARALLELS

This rabbinic legal rhetoric of definition has many parallels within both Greek and Roman legal literature. The most pronounced of these is that of the exogamous rule. Even in ancient Greece, which was an endogamous society, the discourse on "incest" was centered on (accidental) marriage rather than sexual contact; note, for example, the famous case of Oedipus, which was based upon his accidental marriage with his mother.[75]

Since Roman society was exogamous, it is no surprise that incest restrictions in Roman law also center on restrictions on marriage with kin.[76] Nearly every surviving Roman law mentioning or referring to incest includes a reference to marriage.[77] It is in fact part of the legal definition of incest: *"Si quis ex his, quas moribus prohibemur uxores ducere, duxerit, incestum dicitur committere."*[78] Questioning the reason behind the Roman incest regulations, Plutarch too frames the problem and its potential answers in reference to marriage.[79]

This same tendency is found in the Jewish-Hellenistic and Christian writers. Philo interprets incest as referring to marriage,[80] and a case of incest reported in the New Testament, 1 Cor. 5:1, refers to a man actually

---

[73]*Sifra Aḥare* 13:1 (85d).
[74]*b. Shab.* 13a (par. *b. 'Abod. Zar.* 17a).
[75]See also A.R.W. Harrison, *The Law of Athens* (Oxford: Oxford University Press, 1968) 22–23, esp. n. 3.
[76]On Roman exogamy, see Egon Weiss, "Endogamie und Exogamie im römischen Kaiserreich," *Zeitschrift der Savigny-Stiftung für Rechtgeschichte* 29 (1908): 353-69; Brent D. Shaw and Richard P. Saller, "Close-Kin Marriage in Roman Society," *Man*, n.s., 19 (1984): 432-44.
[77]See *D*.23.2.53 (Gaius); *D*.23.2.17 (Gaius); *D*.23.2.12.3-4 (Ulpian); *D*.23.2.15 (Papian); *D*.23.2.14.2, 4 (Paulus); *D*.23.2.39.1 (Paulus); *D*.12.7.5.1 (Papinian); *D*.23.2.68 (Paulus); Gaius *Inst.* 1:59-63; *Gnomon of the Idios Logos* sec. 23 (*BGU* 5.1210, in Riccobono, *FIRA* 2:473-74); *CTh* 3.12; *CIC* 5.5.5-6.

Only *D*.23.2.56 (Ulpian) refers to the crime of *incestus* regarding a non-marital liaison: keeping one's sister's daughter as a concubine. Mommsen also comments on this Roman conflation of incest and marriage (Theodore Mommsen, *Römisches Strafrecht* [1899; rpt. Barmstadt: Wissenschaftliche Buchgesellschaft, 1961[687). Non-legal sources use the term more loosely. See Tacitus *Ann.* 12.8 and Dio 58.22.3, and on this issue Jane F. Gardner, *Women in Roman Law & Society* (London: Croom Helm 1986) 126.
[78]*D*.23.2.39.1 (Paulus).
[79]Plutarch *Moralia (The Roman Questions)*, 289D-E: Διὰ τί δὲ τὰς ἐγγὺς γένους οὐ γαμοῦσι; Among the proposed answers Plutarch includes one that is frankly anthropological. See also *Moralia (The Roman Questions)* 265D.
[80]Philo *Spec. Laws* 3.25

living with his father's (former) wife.⁸¹ Of all the early Jewish and Christian writers, only Josephus reads Lev. 18 as referring to intercourse rather than marriage.⁸² Even the few incest laws found in the Dead Sea Scrolls, although stricter than rabbinic laws, focus their attention on marriage rather than intercourse.⁸³

A scholarly appraisal of the similarities of the actual kinship prohibitions in roman and rabbinic law has not yet been done, but there are clearly many parallels.⁸⁴ Like the rabbinic law, Roman law was concerned with precisely defining the prohibited relationships.⁸⁵ Moreover, the rabbinic issues with proselytes find some parallels with the Roman laws on marriage restrictions applied to adopted and manumitted Romans.⁸⁶

Passages from the Dead Sea Scrolls too employ this rhetoric of definition. The *Temple Scroll* records in language very similar to the scriptural wording a number of incest restrictions, modified to emphasize the prohibition on marriage.⁸⁷ One change in the scriptural restrictions is the prohibition for a man to marry his maternal or paternal niece, a stricture found also in the *Damascus Document*.⁸⁸

If the legal definitions are in some cases parallel, the rhetoric of justification more often is not. Scripture is the determinant for the rabbis, *mores*, "ways, customs," for the Romans.⁸⁹ Diocletian, if the attribution is to be trusted, invokes the concepts of the gods' desire and legitimacy of

---

⁸¹See Gordon D. Fee, ed., *The First Epistle to the Corinthians: The New International Commentary on the New Testament* (Grand Rapids: William B. Eerdmans, 1987) 200-1; 1 Cor. 7:36-38.
⁸²Josephus *Ant*. 3.274. He uses the phrase τὸ μίσγεσθαι.
⁸³See *11QTemple* 66.12, 16-17 (ed. Yadin, 2:298-300); *CD* 5.7-11, and on this Chaim Rabin, *Qumran Studies* (London: Oxford University Pres, 1957) 91-93.
⁸⁴See the comments by Aline Rousselle, "Vivre sous deux droits: La pratique familiale polyjuridique des citoyens romains juifs," *Annales: Économies, sociétés, civilisations* 45 (1990): 845.
⁸⁵See, for examples, *D*.23.2.17.2 (Gaius); *D*.23.2.12.1, 3 (Ulpian); *D*.23.2.15 (Papinian); *D*.23.2.68 (Paulus). Specificity in these restrictions appears to increase in later laws, perhaps under the influence of Christianity. See *CTh*. 3.12.1, 3, 4; *CIC* 5.4.17 (attributed to time of Diocletian and Maximiam), 19 (dated 405 C.E.).
⁸⁶See *D*.23.2.17 (Gaius); *D*.23.2.12.4 (Ulpian); *D*.23.2.14.2 (Paulus).
⁸⁷*11QTemple* 66:11-17 (ed. Yadin, 1:299-300).
⁸⁸*11QTemple* 66:17 (ed. Yadin, 1:300); *CD* 5.8-11. On the latter, see Joseph A. Fitzmyer, "Divorce among First-Century Palestinian Jews," *Eretz-Israel: Archaeological, Historical and Geographical Studies* 14 (1978): 103*-10*. The prohibition is derived (?) from Lev. 18:13.
⁸⁹See above and Augustine *City of God* 15.16, who acknowledges that incest violations were rare *per mores*.

the offspring in outlawing mother-son incest among the Persians.[90] One Roman law is justified with reference to *naturale ius* and *pudor;* a marriage of a man to his daughter is called *contra pudorem*.[91] The employment of shame as justification for incest laws is paralleled in Philo, though it is not found in the rabbinic corpus.[92] Josephus, the only other Jewish-Hellenistic writer who defines incestuous relationships, calls these liaisons "the greatest evil."[93]

CONCLUSIONS

The Palestinian rabbinic legal rhetoric mirrors Greek and Roman legal rhetoric in its concern with incestuous marriages. Babylonian legal rhetoric, truer to the biblical rhetoric, considers cases of incestuous intercourse. Palestinian lists of incestuous liaisons, to which Babylonians appear to have made few additions, with their emphasis on specifics also mirror Roman legal writings. Where rabbinic and non-rabbinic sources part is their justifications for the imposition of these laws. Non-rabbinic sources mainly use language of shame, and perhaps natural law, to condemn these liaisons. Palestinian rabbis rely mainly on Scripture; Babylonian rabbis on a combination of Scripture and logic. Both Palestinian and Babylonian rabbis use arguments from appearances, and Babylonian rabbis alone use sociological argumentation.

Rhetoric of Categorization

Rabbinic laws on incest are categorized within rabbinic literature based on origin and punishment.

ORIGIN

Incestual prohibitions, according to the *Mishnah*, fall into one of two categories: those that derive from Scripture, *'isur 'ervah* (אסור ערוה) or a second type, called *'isur miṣvah* (אסור מצוה).[94] The *Mishnah* itself clarifies this term: "*'isur miṣvah:* secondary [restrictions[from the rulings of the

---

[90]*Coll.* 6.4 (dated to 294). On this See H. Chadwick, "The Relativity of Moral Codes: Rome and Persia in Late Antiquity," in *Early Christian Literature and the Classical Intellectual Tradition in Honorem Robert M. Grant,* ed. William R. Schoedel (Paris: Éditions Beauchesne, 1979) 144-51; and more generally Alfredo Mordechai Rabello, "De Collatio Legum Mosaicarum et Romanarum," *Shenaton ha-Mishpat ha-Ivri, Annual of the Institute for Research in Jewish Law* 1 (1974): 231-62 (Hebrew). See also A.D. Lee, "Close-Kin Marriage in Late-Antique Mesopotamia," *Greek, Roman, and Byzantine Studies* 29 (1988): 403-13.
[91]D.23.2.14.2 (Paulus). See also Cicero *Pro Cluent.* 12-13.
[92]Philo *Spec. Laws* 3.25. On this passage see Isaak Heinemann, *Philons griechische und jüdische Bildung* (Breslauy: M. & H. Marcus, 1932) 280-81.
[93]Josephus *Ant.* 3.274.
[94]*m. Yebam.* 2:3-4.

Scribes."[95] The category is defined according to the origin of the restrictions included in it. Curiously, these restrictions are never detailed in the *Mishnah*.[96]

The *Tosefta* by and large replaces the *mishnaic* category of *'isur miṣvah* with the term "secondary restrictions" (שניות).[97] The *Tosefta* both lists these prohibitions and attempts to sort restrictions left undifferentiated in the *Mishnah* into these categories. This is most clearly seen in the example of the restrictions placed on intercourse with the woman who has gone through the procedure of release (*ḥaliṣah*) from the levirate marriage. After the release, she is forbidden to several of the relatives of the man (the levir) who released her. According to *m. Yebam.* 4:7, she is forbidden to the levir's father; father's father, son; son of his son; brother; and son of his brother. On this the *Tosefta* elaborates:

> Four [relatives of the man who released her] are liable from the Torah and four are secondary to them. His father, his son, his brother, and the son of his brother, these are liable on account of her. The father of his father, the father of his mother, the son of his son, and the son of his daughter, these are secondary to them...[98]

Where the *Mishnah* offers an undifferentiated list, the *Tosefta* divides the *Mishnah's* list into two categories, one of relations restricted by scriptural authority (*'isur 'ervah*) and one of relations "secondary" to them.

The origin of these restrictions had, according to the *Tosefta*, concrete legal ramifications. According to the *Mishnah*, a woman married to a man forbidden to her as a secondary restriction forfeits rights to her marriage settlement (*ketubah*).[99] The *Tosefta* explains,

- A. Because he is fit and she is fit, [so] they fined her her *ketubah* so that it will be easy for him to divorce her.

- B. Rabbi said, in this case [marriage of a High Priest to a widow] it is words of Torah [i.e., Scripture commands it], which need no strengthening, but in this case [incestuous marriage] it is words of Scribes, which need strengthening.

- C. Another opinion: In that case [marriage of a High Priest to a widow] he persuades her to marry him. In this case [incestuous

---

[95] *m. Yebam.* 2:4. On this passage, see Jacob Neusner, *The Mishnaic System of women: A History of the Mishnaic Law of Women* (Leiden: E.J. Brill, 1980) 54-55.
[96] It is interesting to note that this term always appears in conjunction with the term *'isur qedushah*, in which are included the restrictions placed on the marriage of priests. See *m. Yebam.* 3:3, 3:4, 9:3.
[97] The *Tosefta* also has discussions that involve only the two categories found in the *Mishnah*. See *t. Yebam.* 6:5.
[98] *t. Yebam.* 6:4.
[99] *m. Yebam.* 9:3.

marriage] she is persuaded to marry him (חו הרגילה את עצמה שתנשא לו).¹⁰⁰

Three explanations are offered for the fine. Two are sociological: (A) is meant to influence his behavior, and (C) punishes her for her behavior. (B) asserts that the punishment is based on the origin of the restrictions. Because the couple are forbidden to each other only on authority of the Scribes, a more severe punishment is imposed on them so that the restrictions will not be taken lightly.

In the Yerushalmi, categories of *'isur miṣvah* and *'isur qedushah* are hardly used. They appear in a single short *sugya* and even here are not developed as categories.¹⁰¹ The Yerushalmi does, however, discuss the secondary restrictions. The justification for a category of secondary restrictions is derived from Scripture: "From where do we learn about the secondary restrictions? R. Huna [PA 3 or 4-5] said, from the word *'ha'el'* [Lev. 18:24], which means hard, thus we learn [from its appearance in this verse, which refers to the incest restrictions] that there are those [restrictions] lesser than these."¹⁰² In contrast to the *Mishnah*, this statement asserts that the secondary restrictions have scriptural authority.¹⁰³

Like the other sources, the Bavli prefers the designation of "secondary restrictions" to *'isur miṣvah*. Most of the occurrences of the term *'isur miṣvah* in the Bavli are found in one of three contexts: (1) in a citation of a *Mishnah* that contains the term;¹⁰⁴ (2) in discussion of a *Mishnah* that contains the term (with no discussion of the term itself);¹⁰⁵ or (3) in definitions of the term (derived from tannaitic sources).¹⁰⁶ All other references to these restrictions are subsumed under the rubric "secondary restrictions."

---

¹⁰⁰*t. Yebam.* 2:4.
¹⁰¹*y. Yebam.* 2:3, 3d.
¹⁰²*y. Yebam.* 2:4, 3d. My translation follows the interpretation of *b. Yebam.* 21a (discussed below) as understood by the *Pnei Moshe*. According to him, this interpretation of *ha'el* derives from the use of a similar word in a clearly negative context in Ezek. 17:13.
¹⁰³In this same *sugya*, cited above, two late Palestinian amoriam distinguish between incestual restrictions from Scripture and those "secondary to them." They then comment that the rabbis forbade other relatives based on these secondary restrictions. There is no sign in these statements that the Palestinian amoraim saw the secondary restrictions themselves as the product of the "Scribes." That is, unlike the restrictions that the rabbis imposed, the secondary restrictions are simply assumed.
¹⁰⁴*b. Sanh.* 53a.
¹⁰⁵*b. Yebam.* 20a-b; 28b.
¹⁰⁶*b. Yebam.* 20a; *b. Sanh.* 53b. Only in a single *sugya* does the redactor use the term as part of a dialectical discussion. See *b. Yebam.* 9a.

Incest Restrictions

A lengthy discussion, entirely among Babylonian amoriam, clearly supports the notion that secondary restrictions carry the authority of the Scribes.[107] Although these amoraim attempt to find a "hint" to the secondary restrictions in the Torah, they never appear to actually attribute the secondary restrictions with scriptural authority.[108]

PUNISHMENTS

The punishments for violation of incest restrictions referred to in the Bible are: the death penalty (Lev. 20:11, 12); the death penalty by burning (Lev. 20:14); extirpation from God *(karet:* Lev. 18:29; 20:17); and dying childless (Lev. 20:20, 21). These punishments are, in the biblical verses, applied sporadically and unsystematically. Rabbinic, especially tannaitic, literature on the other hand uses these punishments as an organizing principle, dividing and categorizing the incest restrictions according to the punishments decreed for their violation.

Tannaitic Sources

Although the Bible never suggests that some violations of the incest restrictions can make one liable for lashing and pecuniary penalties, the *Mishnah* assumes it, and separates those transgressions from the ones that are punished with death:

1. These are the women who have a fine [i.e., who collect a fine for the following outrages]:...a man who has sexual contact with his sister, the sister of his father, the sister of his mother, the sister of his wife, the wife of his brother, the wife of the brother of his father, and the menstruant – they have a fine; even though they are punished with extirpation, there is no death penalty imposed by a court.

2. These are the ones [= women] who do not collect a fine: if one has sexual contact with his daughter, the daughter of his daughter, the daughter of his so, the daughter of his wife, the daughter of her son, the daughter of her daughter – they do not collect a fine, because he [i.e., the male violator] is obligated with his life, which is given at the hands of the court; and anyone who is obligated with his life does not pay money, as it is said: "[When men fight, and one of them pushes a pregnant woman and a miscarriage results], but no other damage ensues, the one responsible shall be fined [according as the woman's husband may exact from him, the payment to be based on reckoning]," [Ex. 21:22].[109]

---

[107]*b. Yebam.* 21a.
[108]Instructive is the parallel found in this sugya to R. Huna's statement in the Yerushalmi. Attributed to Raba [BA 4] (but in the manuscripts, Rav Huna [BA 2]), the exegesis is prefaced with the question, "where might there be a *hint* in the Torah of the secondary restriction?" From the start, this exercise excludes the possibility that these restrictions have actual scriptural authority.
[109]*m. Ketub.* 3:1-2. On this passage, see Lawrence H. Schiffman, "The Samaritans in Tannaitic Halakhah," *Jewish Quarterly Review,* n.s., 75 (1985): 332-33. Lashing

According to this passage, the incest restrictions are of two types: those that are punished by extirpation (and are not said in the Bible to incur the death penalty) and those that are punished by the death penalty. The separation between monetary penalties and the death penalty is then derived from Ex. 21:22.[110]

Under closer scrutiny, however, the division enumerated in these passages is not as neat as it appears. Intercourse with one's mother is not on the first list, although no death penalty is specified for it in Scripture. Similarly, intercourse with one's father's wife or one's daughter-in-law, both singled out by the Bible as being punishable by death (Lev. 20:11 and Lev. 20:12 respectively) is not on the second list.[111] It is possible that one's mother was excluded from the first list for apologetic reasons: it does not look particularly good that intercourse with one's mother is seen as a lesser transgression than intercourse with one's step-grandchild. It may be possible to explain the exclusion of the other relationships by reference to the apparent biblical basis of *m. Ketub.* 3:2. The relationships enumerated in *m. Ketub.* 3:2 all derive from a conflation of Lev. 18:17, which proscribes having sex with a woman and her daughter, and Lev. 20:14, which decrees the death penalty on the man having sex with a woman and her mother. *m. Ketub.* 3:2 uses the paradigm of Lev. 18:17 (only descendants are discussed), but implicitly derives the death penalty from Lev. 20:14. One's father's wife and daughter-in-law may have been excluded from this list because they do not fit into this paradigm of Lev. 18:17. In any case, it is interesting to note that all three missing relationships appear in *m. Sanh.* 7:4, and transgression of each makes one liable for stoning.

According to *m. Sanh.* 9:1 (cited above), nine incestuous sexual liaisons are punished by death by burning. These relationships derive from Lev. 18:17 and 20:14.[112] The death penalty by stoning serves as another punishment around which the *Mishnah* organizes the incest

---

for those designated in *m. Ketub.* 3:1 is imposed in *m. Mak.* 3:1. Note the lack of specificity (e.g., maternal or paternal relatives) in these passages when compared to *m. Yebam.* 1:1-3. *m. Yebam.* 1:1-3 seeks to define the relationships, *m. Ketub.* 3:1-2 to categorize them. No effort is made to harmonize them. Note that this passage seems to assume, contra Lev. 20, that only the male faces capital punishment.

[110]When, according to this text, "other damage" does ensue, the punishment is "eye for eye...life for life." Monetary punishments and corporeal punishment are separated.

[111]According to the Tosafot Yom Tov, *ad loc.*, the reason for this is simply that הוא הושייר.

[112]Although Lev. 20:14 prescribes burning only for the man who has intercourse with a woman and her mother, the *Mishnah* expands this penalty to include intercourse with a woman and an ascendant or descendant of two generations.

Incest Restrictions

restrictions.[113] The *Mishnah* does not clarify whence the penalty of stoning for the relationships enumerated here are derived.

The *Tosefta* accepts the *mishnaic* groupings, without contributing to it. In its references to those *mishnayot* that do categorize incest restrictions according to punishment, the *Tosefta* tends to discuss issues of liability.[114]

Tannaitic midrashim justify the punishments imposed by the *Mishnah* on certain incest violations. In the *Sifra*, stoning and burning are derived by scriptural analogy. Stoning is derived from the occurrence of the phrase "their blood guilt is upon them" (דמיהם בם) in the relevant verse (Lev. 20:11, 12) and in Lev. 20:27, which mandates stoning for a witch.[115] Burning is applied to the relationships enumerated in Lev. 18:17 through scriptural analogy with Lev. 20:14.[116]

The categorization based on punishment is more fully conceptualized in *Sifre Deut*. In two passages in *Sifre Deut*. the incest restrictions are divided into three groups based on the punishment incurred for their transgression: those that require extirpation, those that require death administered by a human court, and those that violate a negative precept (thus incurring lashing).[117] In neither of these passages, though, is Scripture used to justify the categorizations. Instead, the categorizations are used to explain the verse under consideration. According to Deut. 25:7, "But if the man does not want to marry his brother's widow, his brother's widow shall appear before the elders in the gate and declare, 'My husband's brother refuse to establish a name in Israel for his brother; he will not perform the duty of the levir'." *Sifre Deut*. atomizes this verse:

- A. 'And if the man does not want [to marry his brother's widow]...' not that God does not want it.

- B. I have excluded the incest restrictions whose violation incurs the death penalty administered by the court, but still I have not excluded the incest restrictions whose transgressions incur extirpation in heaven's hands. Thus Scripture says, '[...his brother's widow shall appear...and declare,] My husband's brother refuses [to establish a name in Israel for his brother],' – not that God refused.

- C. I have [now] excluded those incest restrictions that incur extirpation in heaven's hands, but still I have not excluded those incest restrictions that violate [just] a negative precept. Thus Scripture

---

[113] *m. Sanh.* 7:4.
[114] See below. For the passages dealing with the punishments, see *t. Sanh.* 10:2; *t. Mak.* 4:9.
[115] *Sifra Qod.* 9:12, 13 (92a-b); 11:24 (93d).
[116] *Sifra Qod.* 9:16 (92c).
[117] *Sifre Deut.* 215 (pp. 248-49), 289 (p. 308).

says, '...he will not perform the duty of the levir,' – and not that God will not perform it.[118]

Deut. 25:7 is read as referring to three groups of incest restrictions, each based on a different punishment. The goal of the passage is to prove that the ceremony of release of the levirate widow is not necessary if intercourse with the levir would violate any of the incest restrictions. This atomization was hardly necessary to met that goal. Rather, the division of these restrictions into three categories based on punishment was simply taken for granted.

According to Scripture, the punishment for intercourse with one's uncle's wife or brother's wife is childlessness (Lev. 20:20, 21). Neither the *Mishnah* nor the *Tosefta* mention this. Only the *Sifra* discuses it:

> If they [i.e., the partners of the incestuous liaison] have children, they will bury their children [or sons]. If they do not have children they will die without children. And although there is no proof [for this interpretation] there is a hint: 'Thus said the Lord: Record this man as without succession, one who shall never be found acceptable; for no man of his offspring shall be accepted...' [Jer. 22:30].[119]

Using the verse from Jeremiah as a (self-consciously) nominal proof text, the *Sifra* concretizes the ambiguous threats of Lev. 20:20 and 21. The common formula that follows these midrashim, "here we hear about the punishment, but we do not hear about the formal prohibition" (עונש שמענו אזהרה לא שמענו), emphasizes that *Sifra* does not see this punishment as supplementing another form of punishment administered by a human court. Rather, dying childless *is* the punishment for sexual contact with one's aunt or sister-in-law. This grouping, indicated by Scripture but developed by *Sifra*, is totally ignored in *Mishnah* and *Tosefta*.

Talmudim

The Yerushalmi adds little to the mishnaic categorization of punishment. In the Yerushalmi all of the traditions that attempt to derive the mishnaic penalties for violations of incest restrictions are tannaitic.[120]

In many respects, the Bavli follows the tannaitic categorization of incest restrictions based on their punishment.[121] Where either early

---

[118]*Sifre Deut.* 289 (p. 308).
[119]*Sifra Qod.* 11:7 (93a); 11:9 (93b).
[120]In *y. Sanh.* 9:1, 26d, the derivation of the penalty of burning is cited in passing. Derivation for stoning is not even hinted. See *y. Sanh.* 7:4, 24c-d, which concentrates on liability and definition.
[121]See, for examples, *b. Sanh.* 53b, 54a, 75a-76a.

Incest Restrictions   51

Babylonian amoraim or the redactor diverge from the tannaim is their understanding of punishment as representing a hierarchy. Once one cracks the code of which punishment (or rather, death by which method) is more severe, the Bavli assumes, then one can derive a hierarchy of transgressions. In a discussion of whether a man's father's mother is prohibited to him, the Bavli argues:

A. ...According to the one who says that burning is more severe, it is possible to object [to the previous analogy]. Why is she forbidden? Because [intercourse with] her mother [is punished] by burning. Can you say that about his mother, [intercourse with whom is punished] with stoning?

B. Furthermore, [intercourse with] his mother [is punished] by stoning, can [intercourse with] the mother of his mother [be punished] by burning [i.e., can it be a more serious transgression]?

C. Furthermore, just as in her case you do not make a division between her mother and the mother of her mother, so too in his case you do not make a division between his mother and the mother of his mother.

D. And according to the one who says that stoning is more severe, the analogy cannot be deduced from this difficulty...[122]

A hierarchy is not actually in place, but the language and assumptions of these punishments as reflecting a hierarchy in severity is. This language is pervasive in the Bavli.

NON-RABBINIC PARALLELS

In only a single passage does Roman law approach the rabbinic categorization of incest restrictions based on importance or primacy. The rubric *ius gentium*, the law of the nations, is applied to a group of incest restrictions, defined by Paulus as marriage with an ascendant or descendant.[123] Whether we see in this an idea of the laws that all (known) nations hold in common,[124] or whether we accept Gaius's assertion that this is equivalent with "natural law,"[125] we see here an entirely different rhetoric of justification of incest restrictions than the rabbinic categories of "primary" and "secondary" restrictions.[126] Never in rabbinic sources is the distinction between primary and secondary

---

[122]*b. Sanh.* 75b.
[123]D.23.2.68. See also D.48.5.39(38).2.
[124]Suggested by Susan Treggiari, *Roman Marriage: Iusti Coniuges From the Time of Cicero to the Time of Ulpian* (Oxford: Clarendon Press, 1991) 39.
[125]Gaius *Inst.* 1.1.
[126]One that might, incidentally, be post-Classical. See Gardner, *Women in Roman Law* 135, n. 35. She follows Antonio Guarino, "Studi sull' "incestum," "*Zeitschrift der Savigny-Stiftung für Rechtsgeschichte (Röm. Abt.)* 63 (1943): 247-48.

incest restrictions based on either of these possible interpretations of the *ius gentium*, even if legally this concept might parallel the rabbinic application of the scriptural prohibitions to the Gentiles.[127]

There is no true equivalent in roman law to the rabbinic categorization of transgressions by punishment. There is an isolated statement by Gaius that marriage with collateral kin is forbidden but the penalty is "not as much" *(non tanta)* as that mandated by marriage with an ascendant or descendant.[128] The rabbinic enterprise of categorizing these liaisons by punishment, especially in the absence of any implied hierarchy, would have been wholly incomprehensible to the Romans. Mommsen's certainty notwithstanding, it is not even clear in most of the sources what punishment other than nullification of the marriage an incestuous marriage could warrant.[129]

CONCLUSIONS

Tannaitic sources categorize incest restrictions by origin and punishment. Later rabbinic sources, while redactorially dependent on these earlier sources, do not develop these categories. The division of incest restrictions into biblical and secondary restrictions is commonly accepted in all rabbinic sources. While there was broad agreement that these sources were from the authority of the Scribes, one view in the Yerushalmi connects them to Scripture.

Neither of the Talmudim creates its own categories in dealing with these restrictions. Neither type of categorization is paralleled in Roman legal documents.

Rhetoric of Liability

Several legal discussions of incest within rabbinic literature contains rhetoric that (1) seeks to establish the precise "count" for which one is

---

[127] Boaz Cohen suggests that the two are equivalent, and that natural law is evident in rabbinic writing (Boaz Cohen, "Peculium in Jewish and Roman law," reprinted in *Jewish and Roman Law*, 2 vols. [New York: Jewish Theological Seminary of America, 1966] 1:339-41). I find his case unconvincing – although the application of certain laws to those outside the group is indeed held in common by both Jews and Romans, there is no real evidence that both rabbis and Roman jurists justify and/or conceive of this application in a similar way.
[128] Gaius *Inst.* 1.60.
[129] According to Theodor Mommsen, *Römisches Strafrecht*: "Dass nach der ursprünglichen Ordnung die Blutschande mit dem Tode bestraft ward, kann trotz des Fehlens ausdrücklicher Zeugnisse nicht bezweifelt werden," (688). Toward the sixth century Roman law imposed a financial penalty for the commission of incest. See *CIC* 5.5.5-6 and Justinian, *Nov.* 12. It is possible that Mommsen refers here to *CTh* 3.12.3, which hints that incestuous marriages were punished with burning. The actual law, however, is not extant.

Incest Restrictions 53

considered guilty; and (2) discusses those factors that mitigate the assignment of guilt.

DETERMINATION OF THE TRANSGRESSION

Most of the rhetoric of liability on incest concentrates on how many and which transgressions are incurred when a single incestual act falls under more than one rubric.

Tannaitic Sources

The *Mishnah* presents a simple example of this sort of rhetoric:

A. ...If one [i.e., a man] has intercourse with his mother he is liable on her account both for sexual contact with one's mother and for intercourse with the wife of one's father. Rabbi Yehudah says: he is only liable for [the transgression of] intercourse with one's mother.

B. If one has intercourse with the wife of one's father, he is liable on her account for intercourse with the wife of one's father and for adultery, whether it is during the life of his father or after the death of his father, whether [he died while they were] betrothed, or while they were married.

C. If one has intercourse with his daughter-in-law he is liable on her account for sexual contact with his daughter-in-law and for adultery, whether it is during the life of his son or after the death of his son, whether [the son died while they were] betrothed or while they were married...[130]

Intercourse with one's mother (A), a wife of one's father (B), or one's daughter-in-law (C) violates more than one sexual restriction. This *mishnah* attempts to clarify exactly which transgressions are committed. In another passage, the *Mishnah* demonstrates how a single act of intercourse can violate up to six sexual restrictions, most of which are violations of incest restrictions.[131]

The *Tosefta* develops this rhetoric far beyond the *Mishnah*. Several times the *Tosefta* refocuses mishnaic passages that show little interest in issues of liability to this area. According, for example, to *m. Yebam.* 3:10:

If two men betrothed two women and when they entered the wedding canopy exchanged brides, they are liable for adultery. If they were brothers, they are liable for [violating the restriction against intercourse with] the brother's wife. And if they were sisters, they are liable for [violating the restriction against marriage to] a woman and her sister. And if they were menstruants, [they are liable for violating the restriction against intercourse with] a menstruant...

---

[130]*m. Sanh.* 7:4.
[131]*m. Ker.* 3:5-6.

The *mishnah* presents a hypothetical case where two men accidentally (?) exchange women to whom they were betrothed. On this, *t. Yebam.* 5:9 elaborates:

> If two men betrothed two women and when they entered the wedding canopy exchanged brides, they are liable for sixteen transgressions, due to the fact that they are brothers, [their wives] sisters, [the women are] menstruants, and for adultery. If they are not brothers they are liable for twelve. If [the wives] are not sisters they are liable for eight. If [the wives] are not menstruants they are liable for four. If the men are adults and the women minors they are liable for two. If the women are adults and they are minors they are liable for four. If their fathers married them they are liable for eight.

In contrast to the *mishnah*, this passage begins with the situation that would yield the most transgressions. It concludes with another issue of liability, not mentioned in the *mishnah*: the effects of age on guilt. In other passages, the *Tosefta* adds discussions of issues of liability to *mishnaic* passages that are not concerned with this issue.[132]

Among the tannaitic midrashim, there is a single attempt to establish precisely the transgression incurred by sexual contact with a woman to whom more than one prohibition applies.[133]

Talmudim

If the tannaitic sources explore how many transgressions a given incestuous liaison can produce, the Yerushalmi attempts to reduce and universalize them. Thus, in a *sugya* commenting on *m. Sanh.* 7:4 (cited above), the redactor writes, "fleeing from the serious prohibition [one of the incest restrictions] and adhering to the easier prohibition [intercourse with another man's wife] is not possible..."[134] The cases under discussion, in the *Mishnah*, the *Tosefta*, and even in the preceding part of the *sugya* in the Yerushalmi, are specific, centering on whether a man who has had intercourse with a forbidden relative who is also married can be held liable for adultery. The Yerushalmi's redactorial statement, on the other hand, asserts that when it is possible to hold someone responsible for more than one transgression, only the more serious should apply. The assertion is unnecessary, as it does not even address the original problem, which was whether the transgressor should be held liable for two transgressions, not whether he should be held liable only for the lesser one. This kind of universalization seems limited to the

---

[132]See, for example, *t. Sanh.* 10:1-2, which comments upon *m. Sanh.* 7:4. For another example, see *t. Mak.* 4:9.
[133]*Sifra Qod.* 9:12 (92b).
[134]*y. Sanh.* 7:8, 24d.

redactor. Other discussions of this topic, when confined to statements of amoraim, are more localized.[135]

Like the Yerushalmi's rhetoric of liability, the Bavli's too tends to reduce complicated "transgression counts" into a single transgression. For example, *b. Sanh.* 53b-54a cites a series of tannaitic sources that interpret biblical verses in a fashion that usually assigns two transgressions to a single sexual act. These are followed by amoraic and redactorial discussion limiting the transgression to a single count. They then reinterpret the biblical verses in order to solve the exegetical problem.[136]

MITIGATING CIRCUMSTANCES

Intention is considered necessary in order to assign liability for incest violations. According to the *Mishnah*, guilt can only be assessed within an incestuous liaison if the person was a willing participant. Hence, age (minor/adult) and wakefulness (asleep/awake) impact the assignation of guilt.[137] The *Tosefta* more directly states that intention and willingness are key factors in the determination of guilt of the participants of an incestuous liaison.[138] The *Sifra's* discussion of this issue is limited to exculpation of a minor.[139] Neither the Yerushalmi nor the Bavli develop any rhetoric on this topic beyond that of the tannaitic sources. The contributions of both documents is the use of the tannaitic traditions to formulate broader principles that govern liability over a range of topics.[140]

NON-RABBINIC PARALLELS

In Roman legal sources too the age and intention of the participants of an incestuous liaison are taken into account in determination of liability.[141] Unlike rabbinic law, in Roman law a woman was assumed to

---

[135]See *y. Sanh.* 7:8, 24d (before the tradition just referred to); *y. Yebam.* 11:1, 11c.
[136]The superfluity in the verse that generated the original interpretation is usually re-explained by the redactor to refer to the continuation of the prohibition after the death either of the wife or, in the case of an in-law, of the man to whom she is married. See also *b. Yebam.* 20a and *b. Sanh.* 75b. *b. Yebam.* 22b is structurally very similar to this one.
[137]*m. Yebam.* 6:1; *m. Ker.* 2:6, 3:7.
[138]*t. Yebam.* 5:1; *t. Ker.* 1:16, 18.
[139]These comments focus on the superfluous appearance of the word "man" (איש) in Lev. 20:11, 12, 14, 17, 20, 21. See *Sifra Qod.* 9:12 (92a); 9:15 (92c); 10:10 (92d); 11:6 (93a).
[140]See, for example, *y. Yebam.* 6:1, 7b; *y. Sanh.* 7:5, 24c (par. *y. Shab.* 7:2, 9d); *b. Yebam.* 55a-56b; *b. Ker.* 2b-3a, 11a-b.
[141]See *D.* 48.5.39(38).1 (Papinian). See also Treggiari, *Roman Marriage* 38-39. For a comparison of some aspects of the use of age as a legal determinant in Roman and Jewish legal sources, see B. Cohen, *Jewish and Roman Law* Heb. sec. 1-9.

be ignorant of the degrees of kinship, and was thus only held liable to the incest restrictions *iure gentium*, which she was expected to know.[142] Neither Roman nor Jewish-Hellenistic writers discuss the case where more than one transgression applies to a single act of sexual contact.[143]

Rhetoric of Progeny of Forbidden Liaisons

Most of the rabbinic rhetoric on the children conceived by incestuous liaisons centers on their legal status. The term most frequently applied to these children is that of the status of *mamzer (mamzeret* [f.]; *mamzerim*]m. pl.]). The number of sources on and complexity of the issue of the *mamzer* is staggering, and a comprehensive study is a desideratum. Here I only sketch a picture of how the different sources link the *mamzer* to children conceived by incestuous liaisons. Palestinian and Babylonian sources, I show, us this rhetoric differently.

MAMZER: LEGAL STATUS

Tannaitic Sources

The term *mamzer* (ממזר) occurs only twice in the Bible (Deut. 23:3; Zech. 9:6) and its meaning in these texts cannot be determined philologically or contextually. Clearly in Hellenistic times its meaning was still in dispute, as the Septuagint translates each of these two occurrences differently.[144] Two passages in the *Mishnah* attempt to define the term:

>   A. Who is a *mamzer*? [Any child conceived from intercourse with] any relative [who is forbidden in the Torah with the phrase] "one shall not come upon" [i.e., have intercourse with]. These are the words of Rabbi Akiba.
>
>   B. Shimon the Yeminite says: [Any child conceived from intercourse with] any [woman, intercourse with whom is punished by] extirpation in the hands of heaven. And the *halakah* is according to him.[145]
>
>   C. Rabbi Yehoshua says: [Any child conceived from intercourse with] any [woman, intercourse with whom is punished by] the death penalty at the hands of the court.

---

[142]See D.48.5.39(38).7, and on this Treggiari, *Roman Marriage* 281, n. 105.
[143]Although Roman legal material does discuss the overlap of adultery and incest. See Treggiari, *Roman Marriage* 281.
[144]Deut. 23:3 (2): ἐκ πόρνης; Zech. 9:6 ἀλλογενεῖς.
[145]On this phrase see J.N. Epstein, *Introduction to the Text of the Mishnah* (Jerusalem: Magnes Press, 1964) 687 (Hebrew).

Incest Restrictions 57

> D. Rabbi Simeon ben Azzai said: I found a scroll of genealogy in Jerusalem and written in it [was]: So and so is a *mamzer* as a result of adultery. This supports the opinion of Rabbi Yehoshua...[146]
>
> ...Anyone who does not have the ability to contract a betrothal with him, but she can contract a betrothal to others – the child is a *mamzer*. And who is this? One who has intercourse with one of the incestuous relationships that are enumerated in the Torah...[147]

These passages offer competing definitions of the *mamzer*. The first passage bases definition of the *mamzer* on the wording of the biblical verses on incestuous prohibitions and on the punishments that they specify. Categorization by punishment is not only utilized, but given concrete legal application.

The second passage operates according to a broader theoretical framework. This passage is located in the middle of a unit that seeks to define the status of children resulting from liaisons of partners of varying legal statuses. Children of incestuous liaisons are *mamzerim* because their parents lack the ability to contract a valid marriage with each other, although the child's mother is fit to contract a valid marriage with another man.

These two passages employ two different, though not mutually exclusive, rhetorical strategies. The first attempts to link the *mamzer* specifically to liaisons which the Bible forbids, whereas the second is based on the ability to contract a valid betrothal.[148]

The *Tosefta* attempts to harmonize the mishnaic opinions about definition of the *mamzer*. According to *t. Yebam.* 1:10, even the Schools of Hillel and Shammai agreed on the definition of a *mamzer*: only one born from a liaison that both violated a scriptural incest restriction (*'isur 'ervah*) and that is punishable by extirpation.[149] Of the three opinions expressed in *m. Yebam.* 4:13, this rule is most in accordance with that of Shimon the Yeminite, which the *Mishnah* accepts as normative.[150]

---

[146]*m. Yebam.* 4:13.

[147]*m. Qidd.* 3:12.

[148]These rhetorical differences also apparently underlie other, less explicit references to the *mamzer* in the *Mishnah*. *m. Yebam.* 4:12, for example, is clearly based on the disagreement in *m. Yebam.* 4:13. Other passages, though, regard the *mamzer* as generated from (usually) adulterous liaisons. See *m. Yebam.* 10:1 (and *m. Git.* 8:5) and 10:3.

[149]Hebrew:

...אמ' ר' אלעזר אע'פ שנחלקו בית שמיי כנגד בית הלל בצרות, מודים שאין הולד ממזר, שאין ממזר אלא מן האשה שאיסורה איסור ערוה וחייבין עליה כרת.

[150]There is a curious redundancy in the phrasing of this passage from the *Tosefta*. Because the rabbis never on their own call any transgression punishable by extirpation – recognized by Simeon the Yeminite in his formulation of this rule –

Another passage in the *Tosefta* also seeks to find consensus among the differing opinions of the definition of the *mamzer*.

> A. Rabbi Akiba agrees that in the case of [marriage of] a widow to a high priest; or a divorcee or woman released from the levirate marriage to a common priest, that even though [these relationships are designated in the Torah by the term] "Do not have intercourse with," the child is not a *mamzer*, because a *mamzer* is only made via an incestuous union.
>
> B. Rabbi [!] Shimon the Yeminite agrees that in the case of one who has sexual contact with his wife while she is menstruating that even though [this liaison is designated in Scripture as punishable by] extirpation, the child can only be a *mamzer* if born from an incestuous union.[151]

Neither the definition of R. Akiba nor that of R. Shimon the Yeminite is perfect, because their application results in the labeling of certain persons as *mamzerim*, whom, a priori, we know are not. The *Tosefta* resolves these problems by limiting their definitions only to intercourse with kin (שאר בשר). Despite their disagreements, the two tannaim, according to the *Tosefta*, agree that an incestuous liaison is necessary for conception of a *mamzer*.

Talmudim

The primary interest of the Yerushalmi's discussions of the definition of the *mamzer* is the determination of the scriptural bases upon which the definitions expressed in the *Mishnah* rest.[152]

The Bavli too contributes little to the discussion of the legal status of children of incestuous liaisons. One passage, however, seeks to expand R. Akiba's already inclusive definition of the *mamzer*:

> A. What is the scriptural support for Rabbi Akiba's position [that a *mamzer* results from any forbidden liaison]? As it is written, "No man shall marry his father's former wife, so as to remove his father's garment," [Deut. 23:1]. "His father's garment" – the garment that his father saw he shall not reveal. And he holds as R. Yehudah who said that the verse refers to a woman raped by his father, that is those violating negative commandments, and near to it [is the verse] "A *mamzer* shall not be admitted into the congregation of the Lord..." [Deut. 23:3].
>
> B. Thus from these are a *mamzer*, and according to Rabbi Simai [PA 1] who increased [Rabbi Akiba's category to include children] of liaisons that violate negative commandments and which are not

---

there was no need to include the phrase איסור ערוה. That is, any liaison punishable by extirpation is necessarily an *'isur 'ervah*.

[151]*t. Yebam.* 6:9.
[152]*y. Yebam.* 4:15, 6b-c; 11:2, 11d; *y. Sanh.* 9:1, 27a.

Incest Restrictions

[labeled in the Torah as] "kin," and to Rabbi Yishabab [a late tanna] who from the word "and not" [in Deut. 23:3] derives that [Rabbi Akiba's position] even includes those liaisons that violate a positive commandment.[153]

(A), composed mainly of tannaitic material, hermeneutically links the case of intercourse with the wife of one's father to the *mamzer*: this linkage reappears often in rabbinic discussions that seek to derive the application of the *mamzer* by analogy to liaisons similar to that with the wife of one's father. (B) expands on this, reporting two traditions which, if applied, would swell the ranks of *mamzerim*. These extreme Palestinian positions are, to my knowledge, repeated nowhere else.

The Bavli's discussion of the definition of the *mamzer* presented in *m. Qidd.* 3:12 is much richer.[154] Even here, though, the focus is on hermeneutics and derivation rather than on definition and application.

MAMZER: SOCIAL STIGMA

What did it mean to be a *mamzer/et* in Jewish antiquity? According to the bible, the *mamzer* was not "to be admitted into the congregation of the Lord," (Deut. 23:3). The rabbis interpreted this to mean that a *mamzer/et* was not allowed to marry another Jew who did not also have a defective legal status.[155] Otherwise, the *mamzer/et* had legal rights equal to all other Jews. In the Yerushalmi there are hints, though, that the disability of the *mamzer/et* went beyond the strictly legal:

A. ...[A]s Rabbi Ḥaninah [PA 1] said, once in sixty or seventy years the Holy One, blessed be He, brings a plague into the world and wipes out the *mamzerim* and takes with them legitimate people so as not to publicize their sins...[there follows a number of traditions on theodicy].

B. Rav Huna [BA 2] said, a *mamzer* does not live for more than thirty days.

C. Rabbi Zeira [PA 3] once came up to here and he heard voices calling, *mamzer, mamzeret*. He said to them, what is this? Note what Rav Huna said, for Rav Huna said, a *mamzer* does not live more than thirty days.

D. R. Ya'akov bar Aha [PA 3-4] said to him, I was with you when Rabbi Ba [=Abba, PA 2 or 3] said, Rav Huna said in the name of Rav [BA 1], a *mamzer* does not live more than thirty days. When? When he is not known [as a *mamzer*]. But if he was known, he lives.[156]

---

[153] *b. Yebam.* 49a.
[154] *b. Qidd.* 67b-68a.
[155] See, for example, *m. Qidd.* 4:1. In Qumran, this verse was apparently interpreted as referring to entrance into the priesthood rather than marriage.
[156] *y. Yebam.* 8:3, 9c-d. See also *y. Qidd.* 3:12, 64c.

This passage reflects the stigma borne by the *mamzer/et*. On the one hand, because of the potential societal repercussions of marriage of a secret *mamzer/et* to a "fit" Jew, it was important that the *mamzer/et* not hide his or her legal status. On the other hand, a public stigma is borne by those that do reveal their status. According to Rabbi Ḥaninah (A), even if the child *mamzer/et* survives the first thirty days, the adult will not live past sixty or seventy years, and at that time he will cause suffering for the whole community. The Palestinian interpretation of Rav Huna's statement (D) seeks to promote the public disclosure of the status of the child by threat, most likely reflecting a stigmatized view of the *mamzer/et*. The depth of this stigma is also shown in a parallel to this sugya in the Yerushalmi, in which a man who is uncovered in public as a *mamzer* cries out that his life is ruined.[157]

Finally, a tradition found only in the Bavli should be considered:

A. R. Yehudah ben Naḥami, the translator of Reish Lakish [PA 2], said, the entire portion [dealing with the blessings and the curses] refers only to the adulterer and the adulteress, as it is said, "Cursed is the man who makes a graven or molten image...," [Deut. 27:15].

B. Is "cursed" enough for him?

C. Rather, the verse speaks of one who has intercourse with an *'ervah* and [thereby] bears a son and he [the son] goes among the Gentile and worships idols. Cursed are his mother and father, who are the cause of this![158]

In (A), the adulterer and adulteress are condemned with the entire force of the curses enumerated in Deut. 27:15-26.[159] In (C), a remarkable transformation occurs. Now the verse is interpreted s referring to a violation of incest restrictions. Apparently, the shame that the child would bear would compel him to leave the Jewish community. Thus, his parents bear the guilt – and should feel the shame – of giving birth to an idolater. (B) and (C) are almost certainly not of the same source as (A), and are most likely redactorial. If so, then this is the single piece of evidence in the Bavli of the application of a rhetoric of stigma to the child of an incestuous union (as well as a rhetoric of shame applied to the parents). Unlike the discussions in the Yerushalmi, however, there is no necessary assumption here that the child is a *mamzer*.

---

[157] *y. Qidd.* 3:12, 64c.
[158] *b. Soṭ.* 37b.
[159] It is unclear to me how this exegesis works. It might turn on the continuation of the verse, which talks of setting the idol up in a secret place. The midrash might equate the secrecy of idol worship with the secrecy of adultery.

NON-RABBINIC PARALLELS

The notion that children of incestuous marriages were legally disadvantaged is found also in both Greek and Roman sources. Athenian citizenship in the fifth century B.C.E., for example, was given only to the children of two legally married Athenian citizens.[160] This requirement apparently continued in Hellenistic cites.[161] Children of incestuous liaisons would not, most likely, be considered *nothoi*.[162]

Romans too required that both parents of a child be citizens for the child to be a citizen. According to Gaius, a child of two partners who do not possess *connubium*, i.e., the legal ability to contract a valid marriage, follows the status of the mother.[163] In the same passage, he equates the status of children of incestuous marriages with those of "promiscuous" (*vulgus*) liaisons, all of whom would be *spurii*.[164] Boaz Cohen has argued that *spurii* were functionally equivalent to *mamzerim*, an assertion that has recently been dismissed.[165] A *spurious*, like a *nothos*, could not register in the citizenship roles and had a subordinate right of inheritance.[166] One can presume from the great importance placed by the

---

[160]See Aristotle *Pol.* 3.19 (1275b 21-22; 3.3.4-6 (1278a 27-40); 6.2.9-10 (1319b 2-10). On these passages, see Jean-Marie Hannick, "Droit de cité et mariages mixtes dans la Grèce classique," *L'Antiquité Classique* 45 (1976): 133-48. Most relevant to this discussion is the Periclean law on *nothoi* of 451/0 B.C.E. See *Ath. Pol.* 26.4; Plutarch *Per.* 33. Although no Greek source known to me explicitly discusses the legal status of children of incestuous relationships, they without doubt would not have been legitimate (*gnesios*).

[161]See P.M. Fraser, *Ptolemaic Alexandria*, 3 vols. (1972; rpt. Oxford: Oxford University Press, 1986): 76-77.

[162]Following the suggestion of Patterson that the *nothos* and *nothē* were children of a special status, who were both "illegitimate" and specially recognized by their father. See Cynthia B. Patterson, "Those Athenian Bastards," *Classical Antiquity* 9 (1990): 40-73. Cf. D.M. MacDowell, "Bastards as Athenian Citizens," *Classical Quarterly*, n.s., 26 (1976): 88-91; P.J. Rhodes, "Bastards as Athenian Citizens," *Classical Quarterly*, n.s., 28 (1978): 89-92; R. Sealey, "On Lawful Concubinage in Athens," *Classical Antiquity* 3 (1984): 111-33.

[163]Gaius *Inst.* 1.64; Ulpian 5.7.

[164]See also *Coll.* 6.2.4 (Ulpian): "*Si quis eam quam non licet uxorem duxerit, incestum matrimonium contrahit: ideaque liberi in potestate eius non fiunt, sed quasi vulgo concepti spurii sunt.*"

[165]B. Cohen, "Laws of Persons," *Proceedings of the American Academy of Jewish Research* 16 (1947): 1-37. According to S. Cohen, "The rabbis do not have a category corresponding to the *spurious*, and the Romans do not have a category corresponding to the *mamzer*," (S. Cohen, "Matrilineal Principle" 43). While this appears to be true, a more detailed investigation is needed of the relationship between the *nothos, ou gnëios, spurious,* and *mamzer,* and more broadly the nature and understanding of illegitimacy in antiquity.

[166]According to the *lex Aelia Sentia* and *Papia Poppaea* (4 C.E.). See J.A. Crook, *Law and Life of Tome, 90 B.C.-A.D. 212* (1967; rpt. Ithaca: Cornell University Press, 1984) 47, 107; W.W. Buckland, *A Text-book of Roman Law from Augustus to Justinian,* 3d

Romans on family, although there is no evidence on the topic, a social stigma attached to these children.

As in the Greek sources, the Romans do not develop a rhetoric that explicitly discusses the legal status of children of incestuous liaisons.[167]

CONCLUSIONS

A rhetoric that focused on children of forbidden liaisons had potentially serious legal and social ramifications for the lives of these children. Thus, this rhetoric also served as a control of sexuality: forbidden partners could never hope for "fit" (*kasher*) children. The more inclusive the application of the legal status of *mamzer*, the tighter the control that this rhetoric sought to exert.

Tannaitic sources struggle over the inclusivity of the status. The *Tosefta* suggests that it applies only to incestual relations. The survival of opinions of Palestinian "extremists," as well as the lack of evidence that the *mamzer/et* was stigmatized in Babylonia, suggest that Palestinians were more comfortable with (or found more effective) the use of this rhetoric as a social control than were the Babylonians. Although there might be a relationship between the categories of *mamzer, spurious*, and *nothos*, the rabbinic sources differ from Roman and Greek sources in that they actively link incest to the legally disadvantaged child.

Rhetoric of Association

Violation of incestuous restrictions is often referred to in rabbinic literature by the term *giluy 'arayot* (גילוי עריות) or a cognate. This term originates in the wording of Lev. 18, which prohibits men from revealing the *'ervah* (singular of *'arayot*), "shame," of kinswomen. In the *Tosefta*, the tannaitic midrashim, the Yerushalmi and the Bavli alike this transgression is frequently grouped with murder and idolatry to form a trope.[168] Hence, when it appears in this list, *giluy 'arayot* often lacks a distinctive meaning. This list of three is itself used to designate

---

ed. (Cambridge: Cambridge University Press, 1963) 105 n. 2; Raphael Taubenschlag, *The Law of Greco-Roman Egypt in the Light of the Papyri 332 B.C.-640 A.D.* (New York: Herald Square, 1944) 107 n. 17. The *spurious*, however, should not be considered merely a Roman equivalent of the *nothos*. The Romans themselves commented that the *nothos* was a unique Greek institution. See Quintilian 3.6.96-97.

[167]The most explicit attempt to develop such a rhetoric is made by Plato, *Rep.* 461C, and his discussion is far from clear.

[168]See *t. Ned.* 2:4; *t. B. Meṣ.* 6:17; *t. Sanh.* 8:6; *t. 'Abod. Zar.* 8:4; *Sifra Aḥare* 13:8 (85a); *Mekh. Yitro Baḥodesh* 2 (p. 207); *Mekh. B'shelaḥ* petiḥta (p. 82); *Sifre Deut.* 254 (p. 280), 343 (p. 396); *y. Sheb.* 4:2, 35a; *y. Sanh.* 3:6, 21b; *Gen. Rab.* 31:6 (p. 280); *b. Yoma* 9b, 82a; *b. Ketub.* 19a; *b. Soṭ.* 5b; *b. 'Arak.* 15b and the sources listed below. For discussion of this trope, see Burton L. Visotzky, "Mortal Sins," *Union Seminary Quarterly Review* 44 (1990): 31-53.

exceptional evil, the worst thing that a person or group can do. At some period, perhaps pre-rabbinic, the specific acts themselves become subordinate to the meaning of the trope. When rabbis wanted to denounce or condemn other transgressions they would add them to this list. This occurs at almost every layer of the rabbinic sources.[169]

The term *giluy ʿarayot* is ambiguous: although primarily used to refer to incest restrictions, it can also refer to any of the sexual transgressions noted in Leviticus 18. Moreover, it appears to undergo no shifts of meaning in different rabbinic documents.[170]

Outside of this vice-catalogue, violation of incest restrictions is not associated with other transgressions.

NON-RABBINIC PARALLELS

In the Jewish-Hellenistic literature, only the *Psalms of Solomon* uses this rhetoric, associating incest with adultery and perhaps sexual contact with a menstruant.[171]

Vice-catalogues are common in Christian literature. Acts 15:20 enumerates four regulations that Gentiles should continue to observe, abstention from things polluted with contact with idols; from fornication *(porneia)*; from eating animals that were strangled; and from drinking blood.[172] Haenchen suggests that *porneia* here refers to the incestuous relations of Lev. 18.[173] The list is different than in the rabbinic sources

---

[169]See *Sifra Aḥare* 13:10 (86a); *y. Yoma* 1:1, 38c; *y. Taʿan.* 3:3, 66c (this source adds public charity collectors who steal to this list, an addition missing from a parallel at *y. Sanh.* 6:9, 23d); *y. Peʾa* 1:1, 15d; *b. Git.* 6b; *b. B. Bat.* 88b.

[170]In addition to the sources cited above, see *b. Pes.* 25a; *b. Sanh.* 57b. In pre-rabbinic Hebrew documents, עריות nearly always means "nakedness" or something tainted. From Qumran, see *1QH* 12.25; *11QTemple* 58.17 (ed. Yadin, p. 264); *1QS* 7.14. The Zadokite documents (5.9-10) contain the only use of the term with the meaning of incest restrictions. On this, see *The Zadokite Documents*, ed. Chaim Rabin (rpt. Oxford: Clarendon Press, 1958) 18-19.

[171]*Ps. of Sol.* 8:9-12 (ed. Charlesworth, 2:659).

[172]The textual tradition is not entirely certain. Different witnesses leave out (or add) a regulation, including the one referring to fornication. See F.F. Bruce, ed., *The Acts of the Apostles: The Greek Text with Introduction and Commentary* (Grand Rapids: William Eerdmans. 1990) 342 for a discussion of the manuscript evidence.

According to Jack T. Sanders, "...that Luke presents these four restrictions on Gentile Christian behavior as the concluding decision of the Apostolic Council is not in doubt," *(The Jews in Luke-Acts* [Philadelphia: Fortress Press, 1987] 376, n. 98).

[173]Ernst Haenchen, ed., *The Acts of the Apostles: A Commentary* (1965; rpt. Philadelphia: Westminster, 1971) 449, n. 4.

(food restrictions are submitted for murder), but the same ambiguity over the term of sexual conduct, *porneia*, remains.[174]

Early Christian literature after the New Testament, following Hellenistic models, continues to employ the form of the vice-catalogue.[175] They are common in the *Didache*, which associates sexual sins (though not particularly incest) with other transgressions.[176] This form develops into a list of mortal sins, employed most violently and articulately by Tertullian.[177] Here, as in the rabbinic sources and in Acts 15:20, there is an air of ambiguity about "fornication": sometimes it refers to incest, but more often its meaning is broader.

To my knowledge, early Christian literature, like rabbinic literature, does not associate incest with other transgressions outside of this trope.

Rhetoric of Defining the Other

Incest is, according to rabbinic literature, characteristic of two "other" groups, Gentiles and particularly evil Jews. Tannaitic rhetoric favors the first identification, amoraic and later rhetoric the latter.

DEFINING GENTILES

Apart from a single passage in the *Tosefta* that identifies the rabbinic trope of the three transgressions as part of the Noahide laws, only the tannaitic midrashim seek to identify violation of the incest restrictions with non-Jews.[178] The *Sifra* explains Lev. 18:3, "You shall not copy the practices of the land of Egypt where you dwelt, or of the land of Canaan to which I am taking you; nor shall you follow their laws," to mean that Egyptians and Canaanites – and by extension all Gentiles – participate in the sexual practices excoriated throughout Lev. 18.[179] This tradition might not merely be making an obvious exegetical observation, that due to the placement of Lev. 18:3 the sexual transgressions (which immediately follow) are "obviously" associated with the Egyptians and Canaanites. Elsewhere, it states: "...[J]ust as the deeds of the Canaanites

---

[174]See Matt. 5:32; 19:9. For a discussion of the ambiguity of the word *porneia* in the New Testament, see Bruce Malina, "Does *porneia* Mean Fornication?" *Novum Testamentum* 14 (1972): 10-17.

[175]See Anton Vögtle, *Die Tugend- und Lasterkataloge im Neuen Testament* (Münster: Verlag der Aschendorffschen Verlagsbuchhandlung, 1936) 223-24; Ehrhard Kamlah, *Die Form der katalogischen Paränese im Neuen Testament* (Tübingern: J.C.B. Mohr, 1964) esp. 103-48. For a short summary of the scholarship on this form see Peter Zaas, "Catalogues and Context: 1 Corinthians 5 and 6," *New Testament Studies* 34 (1988): 622-24.

[176]See especially *Didache* 2; 5.1.

[177]See Tertullian, *De pud.* 19; Visotzky, "Mortal Sins," 37-43.

[178]See *t. 'Abod. Zar.* 8:4.

[179]*Sifra Aḥare* 9:8 (85c-d); 13:8, 10 (85a).

are steeped in idolatry, in violation of the ʿarayot, in murder, in male homoerotic intercourse, and in bestiality, so too are the deeds of the Egyptians like them..."[180] Leviticus 18 contains prohibitions against all the sexual prohibitions listed, but idolatry is only hinted at and murder is nowhere specified. Later, in fact, theft and blasphemy, neither appearing in Lev. 18, are added to this list.[181] The attribution of these and other transgressions to Gentiles appears also in other tannaitic midrashim.[182]

Separation is the goal of this rhetoric.

> "And I have set you apart from other peoples to be Mine," [Lev. 20:26]. If you are separated from the nations then you are Mine and if not then you are [of the sort of] King Nebuchednezzar and his comrades. Rabbi Eleazar ben Azariah says, [regarding the tradition] that a man should not say, it is impossible to wear *shatnez*, it is impossible to eat swine, it is impossible to have intercourse with a forbidden relative. Rather, [he should say] whatever I do is possible, but my Father in heaven decreed [that I do not do it]. [Regarding this tradition,] what is the scriptural basis? Scripture says, "And I have set you apart from other peoples to be Mine," this is one who separates from sin and accepts the kingdom of heaven.[183]

Obeying the incest restrictions willingly, with the knowledge that one is free not to, helps to separate Israel from the rest of the nations. The incest restrictions, like eating pork or wearing clothing mixed of wool and linen (!), are made a definitional issue, separating Israel from "Nebuchednezzar" – the paradigm of the evil Gentile.[184] In other traditions, named Gentiles are portrayed as involved in incestuous liaisons.[185]

DEFINING THE EVIL JEW

If the tannaitic midrashim use the rhetoric of violation of incest relations to separate Jew from non-Jew, the later sources use it to

---

[180]*Sifra Aḥare* 13:8 (85a).
[181]*Sifra Aḥare* 13:10 (86a).
[182]See *Mekh. Yitro Baḥodesh* 2 (p. 207) and *Mekh. B'shelaḥ* petiḥta (p. 82); *Sifre Deut.* 254 (p. 280); *Sifre Deut.* 343 (p. 396).
[183]*Sifra Qod.* 11:24 (93d).
[184]Although abstinence from port was a well-known Jewish trait in late antiquity, Jewish observance of the laws of *shatnez* went unnoticed by non-Jewish authors in antiquity. See Shaye J.D. Cohen, "'Those Who Say They Are Jews and Are Not': How Do You Know a Jew in Antiquity When You See One?" in *Diasporas in Antiquity*, ed. Shaye J.D. Cohen and Ernest S. Frerichs (Atlanta: Scholars Press, 1993) 4-8. The inclusion of *shatnez* in this list may have been a rabbinic attempt to encourage adherence.
[185]According to *b. Pes.* 54a, Zibeon, one of the descendants of Esau (Gen. 36:24), committed incest with his mother.

separate bad Jew from good Jew. Both the Yerushalmi and the Bavli identify the three transgressions of idolatry, murder, and violation of the *giluy 'arayot* as those that one should die rather than commit: they mark the bounds of acceptable Jewish behavior.[186] In the Yerushalmi the term *giluy 'arayot*, almost always found as part of the trope that includes murder and idolatry, represents the paradigmatic state of sinfulness (or the sinner *par excellence*).[187]

Whereas the Yerushalmi appears to use violation of incest restrictions as a code for general heinousness, the Bavli adds to this an association with Jewish "sectarians." Although Gentiles, even particularly and pardigmatically evil ones such as Pharoh and Nebuchednezzar, are not accused in the Bavli of violating incest restrictions, the evil Jewish kings are. According to one tendentious source in the Bavli, Aḥaz annulled the incest restrictions; Manaseh had intercourse with his sister; and Amon had intercourse with his mother.[188] Another text tells of a Jewish sectarian whose dream is interpreted by a sage to mean that he had had intercourse with his mother and sister.[189] In this story, the sectarian's dream is interpreted without moral judgment. In a parallel in the Yerushalmi, however, the sage prefaces his interpretation to the *man* (בר נש, which does not denote a sectarian) by saying, "may that man's breath expire."[190] You did something so horrible, said the rabbi, that you deserve to die. For the Bavli the activity (among others included in this *sugya*) is to be identified with a sectarian, but for the Yerushalmi it is emphasized as an heinous act that anyone, Jew or Gentile, can commit.

NON-RABBINIC PARALLELS

Alone among the Roman historians, Tacitus accuses the Jews of illicit intercourse; it is possible that this refers to the rabbinic sanction for a man marrying his sister's daughter, a union singled out as illegal in Roman sources.[191] Later Roman laws accuse the inhabitants of

---

[186]*y. Sheb.* 4:2, 35a; *y. Sanh.* 3:6, 21b; *b. Sanh.* 74a-b.
[187]See *y. Git.* 5:9, 47b; *y. B. Meṣ.* 5:13, 10d; *y. Ḥag.* 1:7, 76a; *y. Sheb.* 1:2, 33a.
[188]*b. Sanh.* 103b. On this See David Novak, *The Image of the Non-Jew in Judaism* (New York: Edwin Mellen, 1983) 204.
[189]*b. Ber.* 56b. The printed edition reads צדוקי, but many of the other printed editions and manuscripts read מינא. See *D.S. ad loc.* For discussion of passages like this, see Burton L. Visotzky, "Prolegomenon to the Study of Jewish-Christianities in Rabbinic Literature," *AJS Review* 14 (1989): 47-70. For a source critical discussion of this entire passage see Abraham Weiss, *Studies in the Literature of the Amoraim* (New York: Horeb, 1961/62) 264-70 (Hebrew).
[190]*y. Ma'as. S.* 4:9, 55b.
[191]Tacitus, *Histories* 5:2: "*inter se nihil inlicitum.*" It is also possible that this is a much more general reference to Jewish lustfulness. For this interpretation, see

Mesopotamia, under the influence of the Persians, of violating incest restrictions.[192] Some scholars have accepted this charge as reflecting reality.[193]

Separation and identification with the other is the primary Jewish-Hellenistic rhetoric used in discussion of the incest restrictions. According to the *Letter of Aristeas*, the majority of "other" people engage in homoerotic intercourse and "defile" (μολύνουσιν) their mothers and daughters, in contrast to the chaste behavior of Israel.[194] In *Jubilees* the sexual conduct of Lot and his daughters (the fruit of which were Ammon and Moab, outsiders) was stridently condemned, in contrast to the apologetic treatment of Reuben's sexual misconduct with his father's wife.[195] The *Sibylline Oracles* describe life under a foreign kingdom in which all kinds of incestuous liaisons will take place.[196] Philo identifies the Persians, Greeks, and Egyptians as violators of incest restrictions.[197] Josephus reports a rumor that Berenice cohabited with her brother.[198]

Early Christians use incest for both internal and external arguments. Violation of the incest restrictions becomes a stock charge against heretical groups in the early Church literature.[199] On the other hand, Origen notes (and not with approval) the Persian custom of a woman marrying her son.[200] Minucius Felix reports a charge leveled by pagans that Christians engage in incest – a charge that he quickly turns back on his accusers.[201] Lactantius opens his accusation that pagan priests

---

Menahem Stern, ed., *Greek and Latin Authors on Jews and Judaism*, 3 vols. (Jerusalem: The Israel Academy of Sciences and Humanities, 1980) 2:40-41. But see Tacitus *Annals* 12:5 ff. for use of this expression in regard to the liaison of Claudius and Agrippina. The Romans apparently saw marriage with a niece, the daughter of a brother or sister, as defiling. See Pliny, *Ep.* 4.4-10; Juvenal 2.29-33. The rabbis, however, did not see a distinction between their own and Roman behavior in this matter. See *Gen Rab.* 17:7 (p. 158); *ADRN*, ver. B, 8 (p. 24). A parallel at *b. Sanh.* 39a lacks reference to the incestual relationship.
[192]*CIC* Nov. 154. See also the sources noted by Chadwick, "Relativity of Moral Codes" 146-51.
[193]See A.D. Lee, "Close-Kin Marriage" 403-13.
[194]*Let. Aris.* 152.
[195]*Jub.* 16:7-9. For Reuben's sin, see below.
[196]Sib. Or. 7:43-45.
[197]Philo *Spec. Laws* 3.13 (Persians); 3.15 ff (Greeks); 3.23 (Egyptians).
[198]Josephus *Ant.* 20.145. Manuscripts render this clause differently, though the meaning remains clear in all the versions. See also Juvenal 6.156-60.
[199]See, for example, Clement of Alexandria *Strom.* 2.3. See also Burton Visotzky, "Overturning the Lamp," *Journal of Jewish Studies* 38 (1987): 72-77.
[200]Origen *Contra Celsum* 5.27. This charge, also made by Philo (see above), is a stock one against the Persians.
[201]Minucius Felix *Octavius* 9.2, 6-7; 31.1. On this charge, see also, Athenogoras *Leg.* 3; Origen *Contra Celsum* 6.27; and the discussion in G.W. Clarke, *The Octavius of Marcus Minucius Felix* (New York: Newman, 1974) 215-16, n. 116.

commit incest with the words *"non enim de nostro, sed ex illorum numero"*; they do it, not us.[202] Tertullian too argues that the nations of the world are steeped in the mortal sins (of which fornication/incest was one).[203]

Rhetoric of Apologetics

Several biblical characters are said, according to the definitions of Lev. 18, to have committed incest. Lot had intercourse with his two daughters (Gen. 19:30-38); Abraham's wife, Sarah, was his paternal half-sister (Gen. 20:12); Reuben had intercourse with Bilhah, his father's concubine (Gen. 35:22); Judah had intercourse with Tamar, the widow of two of his sons (Gen. 38:18); Moses was the child of Amram and his paternal aunt (Ex. 6:20); Ammon had intercourse with his paternal half-sister Tamar (2 Sam. 13:14); and Absalom had intercourse with the concubines of his father, David (2 Sam. 16:22).[204] Incestuous relations can also be inferred among the first generation of humankind, all of whom according to the Bible were descended from Adam and Eve.[205] Rabbinic literature tries in several places to wrestle with the problem of associating Israel's founders and heroes with commission of what was seen as one of the worst of transgressions.

CAIN

The *Sifra* uses Lev. 20:17 as a starting point for an apologetic for Cain. According to Lev. 20:17, "If a man marries his sister, the daughter of either his father or his mother, so that he sees her nakedness and she sees his nakedness, it is a disgrace *(ḥesed hu')*...*"* The Hebrew word used here for "disgrace" (חסד) much more commonly means "compassion, grace:"

> "It is a disgrace" – perhaps you will say that Cain married his sister. Hence Scriptures says *ḥesed hu'*. From its beginning the world was created only with much *ḥesed*, as it is written, "I declare, your steadfast love is confirmed forever...," (כי-אמרתי עולם חסד יבנה) [Ps. 89:3].[206]

The midrash is a brilliant word-play. The rabbis read Ps. 89:3 as, "I declare, *ḥesed* will build the world." This hyperliteral reading of Ps. 89:3 allows for a scriptural analogy. What is this *ḥesed* that built the world?

---

[202]Lactantius *Div. Inst.* 5.9.15-16 (ed. Brandt, 427).
[203]See Visotzky, "Mortal Sins" 38.
[204]The rabbis also assume that David married two sisters, Michal and Merav. They solve this problem by saying that he married one after the death of the other. See *t. Soṭ.* 11:18; *b. Sanh.* 19b.
[205]I omit from discussion here the incident between Lot and his daughters (Gen. 19:30-35) because Lot, and his children by his daughters, are in rabbinic literature associated with dangerous outsiders. Thus, a rhetoric of apologetic is never employed in discussion of this incident.
[206]*Sifra Qod.* 10:11 (92d).

Incest Restrictions

From the word's appearance in Lev. 20:17, we learn that it is intercourse between a man and his sister. Cain's implied act of incest is deflected into an activity sanctioned by God for the purpose of the multiplication of people on earth. The tradition is clearly apologetic: it hardly helps to elucidate the phrase from Lev. 20:17, *ḥesed hu'*, that triggered it. This tradition also recorded in both the Yerushalmi and the Bavli.[207]

YOḤABED AND AMRAM; SARAH AND ABRAHAM

In the middle of a discussion on the obligation of Gentiles to observe the incest restrictions, the Bavli cites three apologetic traditions.

A. Come and hear: "Amram took to wife his father's sister Yoḥabed," [Ex. 6:20]. Is this not his maternal aunt? No, it is his paternal aunt.

B. Come and hear: "She is in truth my sister my father's daughter though not my mother's..." [Gen. 20:12], implies that the sister of one's mother is forbidden. This is logical. Was she his sister? She was the daughter of his brother and because of this there is no difference whether she was [was related] paternally or maternally, [for] she is permitted [to him]. But he [Abraham] said to him [Abimelekh], she is kin of a sister to me paternally, not maternally.

C. Come and here: Why did Adam not marry his daughter? so that Cain would marry his sister...[208]

(A), a tradition found in modified form also in the Yerushalmi, disposes of Amram's apparently incestuous union by clarifying the relationship between him and Joḥabed. As we saw above, several tannaim argued that a Gentile man (that is, all men before the giving of the Torah) is allowed to keep his paternal, but not maternal aunt as a wife.[209]

(B) offers a more subversive explanation for the apparent contradiction. In the verse, Abraham is trying to explain to Abimelekh why he told him that Sarah was his sister. Backpedaling, Abraham admits that she's only his half-sister from his father's side. But we know from Lev. 18:9 that this relative too is forbidden! As in (A), this unstated objection might be answered that the Torah, and the incest restrictions, had not yet been revealed. Instead, the Bavli argues that Abraham really meant to say that Sarah was his niece, the daughter of his brother, a relation not only permitted but even condoned. If in fact Sarah is Abraham's niece, why does he tell Abimelekh that she is his sister? The next clause responds to this problem. The peculiar phrase "kin of a sister" is explained by Rashi to mean "...'she is my sister, daughter of my

---

[207] *y. Sanh.* 9:1, 26d; *y. Yebam.* 11:1, 11c. See below for the tradition in the Bavli.
[208] *b. Sanh.* 58b (partial par. *Gen. Rab.* 18:5 [p. 166]).
[209] See the parallels to this tradition at *y. Yebam.* 11:1, 12a; *Gen. Rab.* 18 (pp. 165-66).

father,' because she is the daughter of my brother the son of my father and is [thus] called his sister..." The Bavli here goes to far greater lengths to clear Abraham of suspicion of incest than it did to clear Amram.

(C) reframes the apologetic for Cain. Perhaps uncomfortable with terming God's relaxation of the incest restrictions *ḥesed*, the Bavli instead implies that the "compassion" was actually exercised by Adam, by not marrying his daughter, allowing her to Cain.

REUBEN

An apologetic most likely likes behind the mishnaic comment that "the incident of Reuben is read but not translated."[210] The verse about Reuben's affair with Bilhah, his father's concubine (Gen. 35:22), is not skipped during the public recitation of the Torah but the translator, whose job was to translate the Hebrew recitation to Aramaic, is to leave it untranslated. This tradition is not commented upon in the Yerushalmi. The Bavli records a story *(ma'aseh)* that a certain Rabbi Ḥaninah ben Gamliel went to Kabul (a district in Northern Palestine) and instructed the translator not to translate Gen. 35:22, an action that was praised by the "Sages."[211]

The Bavli contains a more extended apologetic for Reuben:

A. R. Shmuel bar Naḥmani [PA 3] said in the name of R. Yoḥanan [PA 2], anyone who says that Reuben sinned is mistaken, as it is written, "Now the sons of Jacob were twelve in number," [Gen. 35:22] which teaches that all were accounted as one [i.e., were equal to each other].

B. But how do I explain "[Reuben went] and lay with Bilhah, his father's concubine...," [Gen. 35:22]? It teaches that he disturbed the bed of his father, and Scripture blames him *as if* he lay with her.

C. R. Shimon ben Eleazar said, that righteous man [Reuben] was saved from that very sin [i.e., sleeping with Bilhah], and the [opportunity for] the incident never came. Is it possible that his descendants should stand on Mt. Ebel and say, "Cursed be he who lies with his father's wife...," [Deut. 27:20], and yet he committed this sin?

D. But how do I explain "[Reuben went] and lay with Bilhah, his father's concubine...," [Gen. 35:22]? He demanded [the requite of] his mother's insult.[212] He said, if the sister of my mother was co-wife to my mother, should the slave woman of the sister of my

---

[210]*m. Meg.* 4:10; *t. Meg.* 3:35. On this expression, see P.S. Alexander, "The Rabbinic Lists of Forbidden Targumin," *Journal of Jewish Studies* 27 (1976): 177-91; Michael L. Klein, "Not to Be Translated in Public – לא מתרגם בציבורא," *Journal of Jewish Studies* 39 (1988): 80-91.

[211]*b. Meg.* 25b.

[212]According to the text, עלבון אמו תבע. I have been unable to find a similar usage of תבע outside of Palestinian texts. See Sokoloff 574, s.v. תבע.

mother [also] be a co-wife to my mother? He rose and disturbed her bed.

E. Others say, he disturbed two beds. One of the Shekhinah and one of his father, that is as it is written, "[Unstable as water, you shall excel no longer; For when you mounted your father's bed, you brought disgrace –] my couch he mounted!" [Gen. 49:4].

F. This is like [a discussion among tannaim]. "Unstable *(paḥaz)* as water..." R. Eliezer said, you were hasty *(paztah)*, you were guilty *(ḥavtah)*, you degraded *(zaltah)*...[there follow a series of such exegeses, all attributed to tannaim].

G. Rabban Gamliel said, still we need [the explanation of] the Modiite. R. Eleazar the Modiite said, reverse the letters and interpret! You trembled *(zaza'tah)*, you withdrew *(ḥarta'tah)*, sin fled *(parḥah)* from you.

H. Raba [BA 4], and some say R. Yermiah bar Aba [BA 2], you remembered *(zakarta)* the punishment of the matter, you became sick *(ḥalita)* with a serious illness, and you separated *(parashta)* yourself from sin.[213]

Units (A) and (B) are structurally similar to units (C) and (D). Both (A) and (C) purport to record Palestinian traditions that dismiss the possibility that Reuben had intercourse with his father's concubine. (B) and (D) are unattributed objections to these traditions: the verse explicitly states that Reuben sinned! They answer that Reuben's act was actually not very serious, perhaps even excusable, but that Scripture credited him with a serious transgression (perhaps because more was expected of him). (E) is an alternative rendering of Reuben's sin. The conclusion of the tradition is that Reuben's transgression was more serious than that reported in (A) and (C), but less than that recorded in Scripture.

In (F) a number of tannaitic traditions attribute to Reuben three actions, the words for each of which begin with a different letter of the פחז *(paḥaz)*, "unstable." Two of the traditions in this passage attempt to find in this word, part of Jacob's blessing to Reuben, a hint of Reuben's sin. The third, along with the one in (G) (which uses the same hermeneutic but with the letters of *paḥaz* reversed), seek to find a hint of Reuben's innocence. (H), the only passage attributed to a Babylonian amora in this section, also seeks to exculpate Reuben.

The Palestinian attributions are, I think, to be trusted. (B) through (G) are to varying degrees of precision paralleled in *Genesis Rabbah*, and as noted, there is at least one linguistic phenomenon particular to

---

[213] *b. Shab.* 55b.

Palestine.²¹⁴ These traditions alone reflect a tension between reading Scripture literally and reinterpreting this problematic verse (Gen. 35:22). The single Babylonian addition, (H), favors an apologetic approach. The *sugya* itself is constructed to emphasize the opinion that Reuben did not transgress.²¹⁵

NON-RABBINIC PARALLELS

There are a few cases of apologetic rhetoric regarding the incest in the Jewish-Hellenistic literature. Pseudo-Philo excuses Judah and Tamar (his daughter-in-law), and the incident is in fact wholly missing from Josepus's *Antiquities*, "presumably for apologetic reasons."²¹⁶ *Jubilees* excuses Reuben's sin with Bilhah on the grounds that the law (i.e., the incest restrictions) had not yet been revealed to the people.²¹⁷ And whereas *Jubilees*, as mentioned above, condemns Lot's intercourse with his daughters, Josephus excuses it.²¹⁸

Origen too offers an apologetic for Lot's daughters, but for entirely different reasons. Lot's daughters initiated intercourse for the purpose of procreation, something infinitely better, in Origen's opinion, than the activities of the fornicators who have sex for pleasure.²¹⁹ The "apology" is used to make a homiletical point, rather than defend the characters of the Hebrew Bible, an enterprise that would little interest Origen.

Conclusions

Palestinian sources, especially early ones, do engage in apologetic rhetoric.²²⁰ The content of these rabbinic apologetics do not conform to that of any known pre-rabbinic apologetics. The Bavli preserves several of these sources, perhaps to further its own interest in excusing those biblical "heroes" said by Scripture to have committed incest. None of these apologetics appear directed at countering Christian attacks.

---

²¹⁴*Gen. Rab.* 97 (p. 1205-6), 98 (pp. 1253-54).
²¹⁵The passages from *Genesis Rabah*, although they ultimately also favor such an opinion, give the other side a fairer hearing.
²¹⁶Ps. Philo *LAB*, 9.5. On this and Josephus, see Louis H. Feldman, "Josephus *Jewish Antiquities* and Pseudo-Philo's *Biblical Antiquities*," in *Josephus, the Bible, and History*, ed. Louis Feldman (Detroit: Wayne State University Press, 1989) 64.
²¹⁷*Jub.* 33:1-17.
²¹⁸Josephus *Ant.* 1.205.
²¹⁹On this, see Uta Ranke-Heinemann, *Eunuchs for the Kingdom of Heaven* (1988; rpt. New York: Doubleday, 1990) 51-52. There might be a rabbinic echo here. Although Lot's action is unequivocally condemned in rabbinic literature, this condemnation in the Bavli (*b. Naz.* 23b) immediately precedes the strange rabbinic dictum גדולה עבירה לשמה ממצוה שלא לשמה.
²²⁰It is interesting to note that some less-sympathetic biblical characters are not excused for their incestual actions. Amnon, for example, is said to have lost his penis in a hair of Tamar's (*b. Sanh.* 21a, attributed to R. Yitzḥak).

Rhetoric of Temptation

In my interpretation above of *y. Yebam.* 2:4, 3d, I suggested behind this tradition is the assumption that a man harbors sexual desire for his sister. The issue of lust, or the *yeṣer hara'*, "evil desire," is considered more fully in Chapter 4. Here I will note those few places that support this idea that the danger, or threat, of lust extends to kin.

YIḤUD: THE PROHIBITION ON SECLUSION

At the end of a *mishnah* describing the laws that forbid a man to remain alone with a woman (*yiḥud*), it states, "A man remains together with his mother and with his daughter, and sleeps together with them, [even] with flesh touching. If they are grown, she sleeps in her garment and he sleeps in his garment."[221] Mother and daughter are the only women explicitly excluded from the rules against seclusion. When one of the partners is still pre-pubescent, they can sleep together naked with no fear of temptation. When both have passed puberty (that is, either the man's daughter or the woman's son) then although still permitted to sleep together, they take the precaution of wearing clothes. While regarding the danger as slight, the *Mishnah* obviously still sees the danger of temptation between a man and his mother or daughter.[222]

If the mother and daughter are "privileged," one's sister and mother-in-law, according to the *Tosefta*, are not. "[In the case of] one's sister and one's mother-in-law, and the remainder of all the [female] relatives mentioned as forbidden in the Torah, a man should not be alone with [them] unless there are two others also present."[223] This passage continues with restrictions against (male) seclusion with other females, including Gentiles, and other males. Lust does not differentiate between these objects of desire. Note that the *Tosefta* singles out one's sister and mother-in-law as particularly tempting.

These exceptionally tempting relationships do not remain constant in later sources. According to a tradition in the Yerushalmi cited as tannaitic, a man is forbidden to remain alone with his mother-in-law and the sister *of his wife*.[224] A tradition attributed to R. Yoḥanan [PA 2], permits a man to remain alone with his mother, daughter, or sister, and

---

[221]*m. Qidd.* 4:12.
[222]One's sister might also be seen as presenting a particular temptation. See *m. Ker.* 4:1-2.
[223]*t. Qidd.* 5:10. There is an apparent parallel in *ADRN*, ver. A, 2 (p. 5a), but according to Lieberman this tradition deals with another matter. See *Tos. Kip.* 8:979.
[224]*y. 'Abod. Zar.* 2:1, 40c.

even to live with the first two.²²⁵ Although apparently rejecting the stringent rule in the *Tosefta*, he still regards the brother-sister relationship with some suspicion.²²⁶

The Bavli explicitly connects the rules of *yiḥud* to incest. According to a statement attributed to Rav Yehudah in the name of Rav *yiḥud* was legislated after the incident between Amnon and Tamar.²²⁷

Like the Yerushalmi, the Bavli appears to maintain a distinction between the temptation posed by one's mother and daughter and that posed by the remainder of his relatives. In places, the redactor of the Bavli appears to follow the *Mishnah* in regarding a man's mother as posing less of a danger than other women:

A. Rav Yehudah [BA 2] said in the name of Rav Asi [BA 1], a man is permitted to remain secluded with his sister, and to live with his mother and with his daughter.

B. When he said this before Shmuel [BA 1] he said, it is forbidden to remain secluded with any of those women forbidden to him, and even with an animal.

C. But we learned: A man remains together with his mother and with his daughter, and sleeps together with them, [even] with flesh touching. This is a refutation of Shmuel.

D. But Shmuel can respond, according to your reasoning, as it was taught, one's sister and one's mother-in-law, and the remainder of all the relatives mentioned as forbidden in the Torah, a man should not be alone with unless there are witnesses. With witnesses, yes, but without witnesses, no [it is forbidden].

E. Rather, this is a tannaitic disagreement, as it was taught: Rabbi Meir said, they cautioned me because of my daughter. Rabbi Tarfon said, they cautioned me because of my daughter-in-law.

F. A certain student mocked him [Rabbi Tarfon]. Rabbi Abbahu [PA 3] said in the name of Rabbi Ḥaninah ben Gamliel, it was only a few days before that student "stumbled" with his mother-in-law.²²⁸

The *sugya* begins with a debate between Babylonian amoraim. Surprisingly, Shmuel (B) is advocating a position stricter than the *Mishnah's* (C).²²⁹ The redactor uses the tradition from the *Tosefta* (D) to

---

²²⁵*y. Soṭ.* 1:1, 16b; *y. Qidd.* 4:11, 66c (here the attribution is R. Yoḥanan in the name of R. Shimon b. Yoḥai).

²²⁶But see *ADRN*, ver B., 8 (p. 24), which assumes that a man would not want to marry his sister because familiarity breeds contempt.

²²⁷*b. Sanh.* 21a-b (see *D.S.* 9:49 and par. *b. ʿAbod. Zar.* 36b).

²²⁸*b. Qidd.* 81b.

²²⁹I argue in Chapter 4 that Babylonian rabbis are generally more concerned than Palestinian rabbis with male desire. Shmuel's statement here appears to accord with this suggestion.

Incest Restrictions 75

derive an answer for Shmuel. (E) is an unparalleled tannaitic tradition in which we can see that the redactor distinguished between the sexual "danger" posed by one's daughter and that posed by one's daughter-in-law.[230] (F) emphasizes the danger of a female in-law. Sisters and female in-laws represent a much greater sexual temptation than do mothers and daughters.[231]

The logical consequence of this attitude is that a man must also beware lest one's wife has intercourse with her son-in-law:

> R. Yehoshua ben Levi [PA 1] said three things in the name of the Men of Jerusalem...and be cautious with your wife and her first son-in-law. Why? Rav Ḥisda [BA 3] said, because of sexual transgression. Rav Kahana [BA 3?] said, because of money.[232]

As the Jewish man must be particularly careful about seclusion with his mother-in-law, so too should he guard his wife against the threat of her son-in-law. It is possible that Rav Kahana's explanation refers to the fear that a woman will squander her husband's money on her son-in-law, perhaps trying to win his affection (or, on the other hand, having been manipulated by him).

It is not clear from this short passage why R. Yehoshua ben Levi warns for particular caution with one's *first* son-in-law.[233] One of two assumptions may be at work. First, it is possible that the first son-in-law posed a particular threat because the woman has not yet grown accustomed to the occasional presence in her house of men other than her immediate family. As long as she has not internalized the son-in-law as forbidden to her, he represents a danger. By the time she has additional sons-in-law she would have made this mental transition. This focus of female desire (that of the mother-in-law for her son-in-law) is, as we shall see in Chapter 4, much in line with the Palestinian construction of sexual desire.[234]

Alternatively, there might be a fear that when one dies, if there are no surviving sons the first son-in-law will gain possession of the leadership of the family, claiming the estate, and in a particular act of hubris, one's widow also. The true possibility of this happening is

---

[230]Even if the tradition is authentically tannaitic, the first line, "this is a tannaitic disagreement," is redactorial. The statements themselves are not necessarily in conflict.
[231]See also *b. Sanh.* 21b (par. *b. ʿAbod. Zar.* 36b; *b. Qidd.* 80b).
[232]*b. Pes.* 113a.
[233]This troubled the Rashbam, who writes, ‎‏ומיהו הוא הדין לכל חתנים? אלא שמן הראשון‏‎ ‎‏צריך ליזהר חמיו יותר.‏‎ (*b. B. Batra* 98b, s.v., ‎‏בי תמרה‏‎).
[234]See also *t. Yebam.* 2:4, which attributes desire for incestuous marriage to women. My argument that this explanation might lie behind the statement of R. Yehoshua ben Levi is tentative. See below.

irrelevant; there might still have existed an almost primal fear of this new man in the family. This explanation, I think, would fit better with the comments of the Babylonian amoraim.[235]

"NATURE" AND SINAI

A tannaitic tradition hints that before the giving of the Torah at Sinai, the Israelites were "naturally" prone to incestuous unions.

> "Moses heard the people weeping, every clan apart..." [Num. 11:10]. Rabbi Nehurai used to say, this teaches that Israel was grieving when Moses told them to restrain from intercourse with relative, and it teaches that a man used to marry his sister and the sister of his father and the sister of his mother and when Moses told them to restrain from the forbidden kin they grieved.[236]

Without the law, administered by Moses, Israel would still commit incest. Behind the midrash is an assumption that the law is a necessary defense against the "natural" desire presented by a man's sisters and aunts. A glance at the context of Num. 11:10 shows that the Rabbis were in no way responding to an urgent exegetical need. The midrash is informed by the underlying assumption that this incestual desire is primal and natural.

The Bavli contains a variant form of this midrash:

> R. Shimon ben Gamliel taught...Every commandment that Israel accepted with discord, such as the sexual restrictions (as it is written, "And Moses heard the people weeping, every clan apart..." [Num. 11:10] about affairs of its family) they still do with discord...[237]

This text implies a certain determinism. Because Israel "wept" over reception of these sexual restrictions (something not at all clear in the actual biblical verse), the community is fated to always have problems with these restrictions. The Bavli's version differs from the tannaitic one in two ways. First, there is no mention of *specific* female relatives who pose a sexual danger. Secondly, the Bavli added to the problem of

---

[235]Otherwise, it is difficult to place the comment about money. If, as was likely, marriage was patrilocal in Babylonia, then a day-to-day fear of the son-in-law would make little sense. There would have been a greater chance of the couple living matrilocally if the son-in-law was the intended heir. This explanation is admittedly speculative. It is also possible that the first explanation applies to Babylonian assumptions, and the second to Palestinian, or both or neither to either.

[236]*Sifre Num.* 90 (p. 91). See the parallel in *Sifra Aḥare* 13:4 (85d-86a). Another expression of the same idea can be found in *Sifre Num.* 115 (pp. 127-28). See below for a parallel in the Bavli.

[237]*b. Shab.* 130a. See also *b. Yoma* 75a.

individual lust for kin a communal "problem." The incest restrictions are seen as imposed over unruly sexual desire, and that that desire was not fully conquered with the giving of the law.[238]

NON-RABBINIC PARALLELS

Greek and Roman literature contain, to my knowledge, no parallels to this rhetoric about the natural sexual temptation of kin. If anything, there is an opposite attitude. According to Plato, "unwritten custom" and natural sentiments keep men from having intercourse with their kin.[239] In his retelling of the Oedipus story, Seneca, for example, emphasizes that incest is "against nature."[240] Josephus however might assume that one is especially attracted to his mother when he separates intercourse with one's mother from other acts of incest.[241] Christians, of course, are very concerned with the danger of sexual temptation, although it does not appear that they regarded incest as a particular temptation.[242]

Conclusions

Unlike Greek sources, tannaitic sources appear to view the sexual desire of one's kin as "natural." These sources perceive the sexual temptation presented by one's sister and mother-in-law to be greater than that presented by one's mother and daughter(s), a distinction much in line with anthropological observations made in many societies.[243] It is possible that later amoraim, and especially the redactor of the Bavli, refocused on the danger presented by female in-laws.

Divine Punishment

The end of the Lev. 18 states that because the previous occupants of Canaan transgressed the sexual restrictions, the land "spewed" them forth (Lev. 18:28). This biblical threat of divine punishment for violation of the incest restrictions is only briefly mentioned in rabbinic sources. The connection of incest transgressions, pollution of the land, and

---

[238] See also b. Mak. 23b (par. b. Ḥag. 11b) which if referring to incest, also reflects the danger of temptation.
[239] Plato *Laws* 838A-B.
[240] See Elaine Fantham, "Nihil Iam Ivra Natvrae Valent: Incest and Fratricide in Seneca's *Phoenissae*," in *Seneca Tragicus: Ramus Essays on Senecan Drama*, ed. A.J. Boyle (Victoria: Aureal, 1983), 61-76. I discuss the meaning of the term "against nature" in Chapter 5.
[241] Josephus *Ant.* 3.274, where he terms intercourse with one's mother "the greatest sin," κακὸν μέγιστον.
[242] On the Christian view of the danger of sexuality, see James A. Brundage, *Law, Sex, and Christian Society in Medieval Europe* (Chicago: Chicago University Press, 1987) 64-65.
[243] See Fox, *The Red Lamp* 22.

communal punishment (usually exile), is made in Palestinian sources.[244] A tradition in the Yerushalmi attributes the destruction of Sodom to commission of the three major rabbinic sins, murder, idolary, and fornication.[245]

In a variation on this theme, a tannaitic tradition proposes that not only is Israel exiled as a result of these transgressions, but God is also exiled.

> "When you go out as a troop against your enemies, [be on your guard against anything untoward,]" [Deut. 23:10]. "Be on your guard against anything untoward" – I hear about purities and impurities and tithes Scripture says, "[...let Him not find anything] unseemly [among you and turn away from you]," [Deut. 23:15]. I only know about "unseemly" [things], what is the scriptural basis to include [in the meaning of this verse] idolatry, bloodshed, and blasphemy? Scripture says, "unseemly" – just as [sexual sins] are special because on their account the Canaanites were exiled and they caused God's presence to depart, so too any act on whose account the Canaanites were exiled and that causes God's presence to depart...[246]

This midrash combines the rhetorics of separation and threat of divine communal punishment. Israel is commanded, according to this midrash, to avoid those transgressions most commonly associated with Gentiles, including incest. Violation will lead to communal as well as divine exile. During a time when there is no Temple, when Palestine is under Roman occupation and in some sense the Rabbis perceived themselves as already living in exile, this midrash "updates" the threat of Lev. 18:28. Incest leads both to identification with Gentile and to causing the Divine presence to depart. The physical act of exile has already been realized, but the banishment of God's presence can still be avoided.

There is no rhetoric of personal, divine punishment for violations of incest restrictions.

NON-RABBINIC PARALLELS

Curiously, the need for a communal purificatory ceremony after an incident of incest, not discussed in rabbinic sources, is common to the

---

[244]*Sifra Aḥare* 13:8 (85a); 13:10 (86a); *y. Yoma* 1:1, 38c (led to the destruction of the First, and in one opinion also the Second Temple); *b. Shab.* 33a; *b. Sheb.* 7b.

[245]*y. Sanh.* 10:3, 29c. This tradition is derived from the atomization and exegesis of Gen. 18:20 – it has no basis in any part of the actual biblical narrative of the story.

As with the other uses of the term *giluy 'arayot*, it is impossible to identify with certainty the referent of this term. Here it might refer to fornication generally or to incest. If it refers, though, to homoeroticism, it would be one of the very few places that attribute this sin to Sodom. See Chapter 5.

[246]*Sifre Deut.* 254 (p. 280). See also *Sifre Deut.* 343 (p. 396).

Incest Restrictions 79

ancient Greeks and the Romans.[247] Among Jewish-Hellenistic writers, a trope of the evil communal consequences of incestuous unions is more common. *Psalms of Solomon* suggest that incest led to the destruction of Jerusalem.[248] Philo uses a fabricated history of the Persians and Greeks to demonstrate that violation of the Jewish incest restrictions lead to communal strife and destruction.[249]

Generally the Christian literature employs a rhetoric of divine punishment more frequently than found in either the rabbinic or pagan literature. There are a number of different interpretations of 1 Cor. 5:1-5 but all of them emphasize the disastrous end – be it personal or communal – resulting from the incest.[250] The seriousness of incest, and its concomitant punishment, is emphasized by Tertullian.[251]

Conclusions

In their discussions of the incest restrictions, Palestinian and Babylonian rabbis hold different assumptions. Palestinian sources cited by the Bavli frequently have more in common with Palestinian sources from other Palestinian documents than they do with the views expressed by the Babylonian sources, even within those very *sugyot* in which they are cited. That is, it appears that the Bavli reports these Palestinian traditions more or less faithfully, but incorporates them according to its own understanding of them and the editorial agenda of each *sugya*. This is a point to which I will frequently return.

To the extent that the evidence allows, then, it is possible to relate the sexual assumptions and rhetoric of Palestinian and Babylonian rabbis. Palestinians feared endogamy more than sexual relations between relatives. This fear helps to explain Palestinian emphasis on a rhetoric about the children of such liaisons. By threatening the legal status of the children, they apparently hoped to discourage such marriages. This also helps to explain the Palestinian leniency about seclusion with kin when compared to the Babylonians. Palestinians also deploy rhetorics that

---

[247]The most notorious example in ancient Greece being Oedipus, but see also Harrison, *The Law of Athens* 22-23, n. 3. Tacitus *Ann.* 12.8 tells of the purifications offered on the day of Claudius's marriage to his niece, Agrippina.
[248]*Ps. Sol.* 8:9-10.
[249]See Philo *Spec. Laws* 3.16 (Greeks); 3.17-19 (Persians).
[250]Compare the following two interpretations: J. Duncan and M. Derrett, "'Handing Over to Satan': An Explanation of 1 Cor. 5-7," *RIDA*, 3d ser., 26 (1979): 11-30; Adela Yarbro Collins, "The Function of 'Excommunication' in Paul," *Harvard Theological Review* 73 (1980): 251-63.
[251]Tertullian, *De pud.* 13 (ed. Reifferscheid and Wissowa, 243-44). About the man referred to in 1 Cor. 5:1, he says: "*...quem scilicet auferri iussisset de medio ipsorum, multo magis utique de animo.*"

identify incest as a behavior that goes beyond the pale of acceptable Jewish behavior and that threatens communal punishment for violation of these restrictions. This latter rhetoric might be related to the nearly exclusive use by Palestinian rhetoric of "appearances" as an argument for the imposition of certain incest restrictions. Because incest threatens the whole community, everybody is expected to watch the behavior of their neighbor.

Babylonian rabbis based some of their incest rhetoric on sociological factors. Kinship among the Jews of Babylonia has yet to be adequately studied, but preliminary observations here indicate great emphasis on the paternal line. This might help to explain certain Babylonian treatments of Palestinian sources that emphasize matrilineal descent. Babylonians also put more stress than Palestinians on the possibility of non-marital sexual relationships between kin, particularly emphasizing the sexual danger posed by a man's female in-laws. The idea that the avoidance of incest depends upon one conquering his other "natural" desire might also inform the Babylonian identification of incest with sectarian Jews: incest is a symbol of the ultimate manifestation of the heretic's general hubris and lack of sexual self-control, the opposite qualities of those found in pious Jews (see Chapter 4).

One rhetoric found only fleetingly in these sources is that of purity. The stain or pollution associated in non-Jewish ancient writings with incest, and indicated by the (English) word itself, is lacking from rabbinic sources. The rabbinic attempt at incest control is unique in other ways as well. Many societies construct a rhetoric of threat of natural or medical disaster around the incest taboo; a strategy not dissimilar from our own modern biological rhetoric about the potential ills of inbreeding [252] In Rome, among the Stoics and in at least one law, incest is termed "unnatural," one of very few sexual offenses that receive this label.[253] Philo, Roman law codes, and Cicero employ rhetorics of shame for incest.[254] And as we have seen, Philo shares with the non-Jewish sources a rhetoric that identifies incest with the (external) other.

Within these broad observations of Palestinian and Babylonian rabbinic cultures, chronological change should not be ignored. From a rhetorical point of view, these are most obvious in the legal rhetorics of

---

[252] See Françoise Hértier, "The Symbolics of Incest and Its Prohibitions," in *Between Belief and Transgression: Structuralist Essays in Religion, History, and Myth*, ed. Michel Izard (1979; rpt. Chicago: Chicago University Press, 1982) 152-79.
[253] See Elaine Fantham, "*Stuprum*: Public Attitudes and Penalties for Sexual Offenses in Republican Rome," *Echos du Monde classique/Classical Views* 35, n.s., 10 (1991): 289, n. 60 and the references cited there.
[254] In addition to the laws cited above, see Philo *Spec. Laws* 3.25; Cicero *Pro Cluent.* 12-13.

category and liability. Tannaitic sources actively employ forms of both rhetorics that are foreign to Scripture and in some cases to Roman legal thought. Later sources are uninterested in developing such rhetoric. A second difference between tannaitic and later sources is the use of rhetoric of the "Other." More than any other source, the tannaitic midrashim actively link incest to Gentiles, a rhetoric that is virtually absent in later sources.

All of these observations, and proposed differences, can properly be evaluated only in the context of a broader examination of the rabbinic rhetorics on sexuality. Do the differences posited here apply as well to rabbinic rhetoric on other areas of sexuality? The issues and questions raised here will guide examination of these areas.

If the incest restrictions define a rule of exogamy, restrictions on marriage between Jews and Gentiles define a rule of endogamy. In the next chapter, I examine rabbinic rhetoric on sex and marriage between Jews and Gentiles.

3

Sex Between Jews and Gentiles[1]

Commenting on the Jewish "hate and enmity" for all Gentiles, Tacitus writes that Jewish men "abstain from intercourse with foreign women."[2] Although the verity of his claim might be questioned, Tacitus's comment does echo a strong rhetorical tradition found in Jewish writings of both the Second Temple and Talmudic periods.[3] S.J.D. Cohen has noted the post-biblical origins of this rhetoric as it applies to intermarriage.[4] Rabbinic laws on intermarriage have, in fact, been frequently discussed. In this chapter I will focus on intercourse, not intermarriage, between Jews and Gentiles, women and men. While much of the material that I will discuss has been previously considered, it has yet to be synthesized into a coherent account of the rabbinic rhetoric on sexual relations between Jews and Gentiles.

---

[1] On this topic, see L. Löw, "Eherechtliche Studien," 3:108-200; Lichtschein *Die Ehe* 66-71; Mielziner *Jewish Law* 45-54; Gerhard Kittel, "Das Konnubium mit Nicht-Juden im antiken Judentum," *Forschungen zur Judenfrage* 2 (1937): 30-62; L. Epstein, *Marriage Laws* 145-219; J. David Bleich, "The Prohibition Against Intermarriage," *Journal of Halacha and Contemporary Society* 1:1 (1981): 5-27; Shaye J.D. Cohen, "From the Bible to the Talmud: The Prohibition of Intermarriage," *Hebrew Annual Review* 7 (1983): 27-39, and, "Solomon and the Daughter of Pharaoh: Intermarriage, Conversion, and the Impurity of Women," *Journal of the Ancient Near East Society* 16-17 (1984-85): 23-37.
[2] Tacitus *Hist.* 5.5.2: *"alienarum concubitu abstinent."*
[3] On the verity of his claim, see Martial, a contemporary of Tacitus, who accuses his female lover of intercourse with a Jew *(Ep.* 7.30). Note that all pagan rhetoric on intercourse between Jews and Gentiles is directed as the case of Jewish men with Gentile women. See also Meleager *Anth. Graec.* 5.160; Martial *Ep.* 11.94 (a Jewish poet steals Martial's boy!). Marriages between Jewish women and Gentile men, however, are recorded. See Jean Juster, *Les Juifs dans l'Empire Romain: Leur condition juridique, économique et sociale*, 2 vols. (Paris: Paul Geuthner, 1914) 2:45 n. 5.
[4] S. Cohen "From the Bible to the Talmud" 28.

Rhetoric of Definition

One cannot discuss intercourse between Jews and Gentiles without a clear sense of the boundary lines that separate Jews from Gentiles. As recently noted, for Jews in antiquity these boundary lines were sometimes maddeningly fuzzy.[5] Yet only a single rabbinic passage on sex between Jews and Gentiles directly addresses the problem of definition: "R. Ḥiyya bar Abba [PA 3] came to Gabla and saw Jewish women pregnant by proselytes who were circumcised but had not immersed...He came before R. Yoḥanan and he said to him, announce that their children are *mamzerim.*"[6] According to this passage, in which R. Ḥiyya bar Abba assumes that the child of a Gentile man and a Jewish woman is a *mamzer* (see below), male proselytes who had not ritually immersed after their circumcision are not considered Jewish.

Rhetoric of Progeny

The rhetoric on the children of Jews and Gentiles forms the bulk of the rabbinic discussion on mixed liaisons. Most of this rhetoric centers on determining the legal status of a child of such a liaison, although there are a few scattered dicta that raise other issues.

JEWISH WOMAN AND GENTILE MAN

Tannaitic Sources

As mentioned in Chapter 2, *m. Qidd.* 3:12 contains four clauses on the status of children of different liaisons. Most determinations of the status of children are made on the basis of which of the parents have the ability to contract a valid marriage with a Jew. Among several omissions in this passage is explicit reference to the status of the child of a Gentile man and a Jewish woman. Also, according to none of the opinions expressed in another passage which attempts to define the *mamzer/et, m. Yebam.* 4:13, would the child of a Jewish woman and Gentile man be considered a *mamzer/et.*

Several other tannaitic dicta, however, including one from the *Mishnah* itself, do label such a child a *mamzer/et.*[7] Many other tannaitic sources simply assume that the child of such a union is a *mamzer/et.* For example, one exegesis of Lev. 24:10, which refers to the son of an Egyptian man and Israelite woman, mentions in passing that this man is

---

[5]See, for example, Shaye J.D. Cohen, "Conversion to Judaism in Historical Perspective: From Biblical Israel to Post-Biblical Judaism," *Conservative Judaism* 36:4 (1983): 31-45, and, "Crossing the Boundary and Becoming a Jew," *Harvard Theological Review* 82 (1989): 13-33; and "'They Who Say They are Jews'."
[6]*b. Yebam.* 46a (par. *b. 'Abod. Zar.* 59a).
[7]*m. Yebam.* 7:5; *t. Qidd.* 4:16; *t. 'Ed.* 3:4; *Sifra Emor* 5:4 (97c); 14 (104c).

a *mamzer*.⁸ The *Tosefta* acknowledges the logical contradiction between the assignment of the status of *mamzer* to children of these unions and the mishnaic definition of status of children:

> A. If a Gentile or slave has intercourse with a Jewish woman and bears from her a child, the child is a *mamzer*.
>
> B. R. Shimon ben Yehudah says in the name of R. Shimon that a *mamzer* comes only from a woman [intercourse with whom] is a violation of the incest restrictions (*'isur 'ervah*) and subjects her to the penalty of extirpation.⁹

R. Shimon ben Yehudah (B) disagrees with (A), opting instead for a conflation of two definitions of the *mamzer/et* expressed in *m. Yebam.* 4:13. This leaves a somewhat confused state in the tannaitic sources: several traditions assume that a child of a Gentile man and Jewish woman is a *mamzer/et*; there are two competing sets of legal principles (*m. Qid.* 3:12; *m. Yebam.* 4:13) on the status of children, neither of which includes the child of a Gentile man and Jewish woman;¹⁰ and a passage from the *Tosefta* recognizes, but does not resolve, the conflict. No clear legal answer emerges from the tannaitic sources.

Yerushalmi

The debate over the children of these liaisons continued among the rabbis throughout late antiquity. The longest discussion of the Yerushalmi on this issue is a well-crafted composition that argues for the

---

⁸*m. Yebam.* 7:5; *t. Qidd.* 4:16; *t. 'Ed.* 3:4; *Sifra Emor* 14 (104c). The former source is attributed to Hananiah ben Adai. Although the text for *t. 'Ed.* 3:4 might be corrupt, these sources might be evidence for a relatively late dating of *m. Qidd.* 3:12 and *m. Yebam.* 4:13. That is, the prevalence of the opinion that the child of a Gentile man and Jewish woman is a *mamzer* may have preceded the attempts both to define status based on ability to contract valid marriages (*m. Qidd.* 3:12) and to define the *mamzer* based on categories of punishment (*m. Yebam.* 4:13). Such a dating would help to account for the contradictory views expressed in the literature, and the persistence of these opinions throughout the talmudic period. But see S. Cohen, "Matrilineal Principle" 28, 34-36.

The *Sifra's* tradition, after calling the man a *mamzer*, says that he "converted," implying that he was regarded as a Gentile rather than a *mamzer*. These two opinions on the status of a child of a Gentile man and Jewish woman appear to have been conflated. See V. Aptowitzer, "Spuren des Matriarchats im Jüdischen Schriftum (Schluss)," *Hebrew Union College annual* 5 (1928): 274-77; Israel Francus, "The Halakhic Status of Children Born From Mixed Marriages in Talmudic Literature," *Sidra: A Journal for the Study of Rabbinic Literature* 4 (1988): 101 (Hebrew).

⁹*t. Qidd.* 4:16.

¹⁰S. Cohen has shown how *m. Qidd.* 3:12 might logically include the case of the child of the Jewish woman and Gentile man, but this is speculative and appears unlikely ("Matrilineal Principle" 32-33).

"defectiveness" of these children. After reporting several stories about *mamzerim* that indicate that it was not easy to be a *mamzer* in the rabbinic culture of antiquity, the *sugya* addresses the liaison of a Jewish woman and Gentile man:

A. It is taught: If a Gentile man or slave has intercourse with a Jewish woman, the child is a *mamzer*. R. Shimon ben Yehudah says in the name of R. Shimon, a *mamzer* comes only from a woman [intercourse with whom] is a violation of the incest restrictions *('isur 'ervah)* and makes her liable to the penalty of extirpation.

B. Both [positions] derive from a single biblical verse: "No man shall marry his father's former wife..." [Deut. 23:1].

C. R. Meir explained that just as the former wife of his father is special because he [i.e., the son] cannot contract a valid marriage with her, so too any woman with whom one cannot contract a valid marriage, any child [thereof] is a *mamzer*.

D. Rabbi Shimon ben Yehudah explained that just as the former wife of his father is special because she cannot contract a valid marriage with him, but if she has the ability to contract a valid marriage with others, the child [of a man and his father's former wife] is a *mamzer*, this excludes a Gentile and a slave, who cannot contract a valid marriage with this woman and any other [woman].

E. Rabbi Shmuel bar Abba [PA 3] objected to the first teaching: a levirate widow who has sexual intercourse [not with her levirate husband], does not have the ability to contract a valid marriage either with him or with others, yet the child is fit [i.e., not a *mamzer*].

F. Rabbi Yannai [PA 1] said in the name of Rabbi, if a Gentile or slave have intercourse with a Jewish woman the child is a *mamzer*.

G. Rabbi Yoḥanan [PA 2] and R. Shimon ben Lakish [PA 2] both say that the child is a *mamzer*.

H. Rabbi Ya'akov bar Aḥa [PA 3-4], R. Shimon bar Abba, Rabbi Yehoshua ben Levi [PA 1] said in the name of Rabbi Yannai as Rabbi,[11] the child is not [totally] fit, nor [totally] disqualified, but is disqualified [if female] from marrying a priest.

I. R. Yonathan [PA 3] went with R. Yehudah HaNasi to Ḥamatha d'Geder and taught there that the child is fit.

J. Rabbi Zeria [PA 3] said [of] that child, he goes and ascends.

K. Rabbi made him disqualified *(mêzuham)*; his [i.e., Rabbi's] son [made the son of a Jewish woman and Gentile man] disqualified from the priesthood; his [i.e., Rabbi's] son's son made him fit.[12]

L. R. Ba bar Zivda [PA 3] said in front of all the rabbis that the child is fit.

---

[11]"as Rabbi" is missing in MS Leiden.
[12]This follows the emendation of Francus, "The Halachis Status of Children" 100.

M. R. Bibi [PA 3] said in front of R. Zeira in the name of R. Ḥanina [PA 1] that the child is fit.

N. R. Zeira said, not from this [do we learn]. We do not learn a report from an oral report (הברה).

O. Rabbi Ḥezkiah [PA 4-5] said, I know the beginning and end. Rabbi Ḥama bar Ḥanina [PA 3] was going up to Ḥamatha d'Geder. He came to his father. He said to him, be careful – there are blemished people there – do not disqualify them (דלא תפגע בהון).[13]

(A) cites *t. Qidd.* 4:16. (B) to (D), from the redactor's hand, attempts to show how the two parties in (A) arrive at their positions. (E), a refutation of (D), is left unanswered, implying that in contrast to the first opinion in the *Tosefta*, R. Shimon ben Yehudah's position that the child of a Jewish woman and Gentile man is fit, does not rest on biblical authority. (F) and (G) are opinions of three Palestinian rabbis that the child of such a liaison is a *mamzer/et*.[14]

At this point, the *sugya* appears to reverse itself. (H) reports that some of the very rabbis cited above declaring the child a *mamzer/et* actually hold a different opinion, that the child is permitted to marry any Jews, except, if a female, she cannot marry a priest. (I) goes a step further, asserting that the child is fully fit. (J) and (K), in a somewhat amused and detached tone, comment that the position of the child of such a liaison improves as the generations progress. That is, according to (J) the legal status of children of Gentile men and Jewish women have been improving because (K) the rabbis are holding increasingly lenient positions. In (L) and (M) the position that the child is fully fit is reiterated.

Instead of progressing toward the expected conclusion, that the child of such a liaison is fully fit, (N) and (O) suddenly revert to the stricter opinions, reversing the *sugya* yet again. The force of (N) is to void (L) and (M) of legal authority. (O) purports to relate an alternative tradition to (M). Whereas in (M) R. Ḥanina is credited with declaring children of Jewish women and Gentile men fully fit, (O) suggests that the person was R. Ḥama bar Ḥanina, implying that (M) is defective. (O) never states that R. Ḥama bar Ḥanina thought that such children were fit (or even not *mamzerim*); only that his father advised him *not to state* that they are unfit.[15] The advice of his father was for diplomatic rather than legal reasons. Thus, his father's advice not to trumpet an opinion that these children are unfit suggests that R. Ḥama bar Ḥanina in fact did think that these "blemished" folk were disqualified. My suggestion is not that an

---

[13]*y. Qidd.* 3:14, 64c-d.
[14]See also *y. Yebam.* 7:6, 8b-c for parallels.
[15]My translation follows Sokoloff, s.v., פנע.

actual opinion should be attributed to an actual R. Ḥama bar Ḥanina. Rather, it is that the wording and placement of (O) cause a reversal in the *sugya*, leading the reader to believe that R. Ḥama bar Ḥanina held such an opinion, thus supporting the halakic opinion that these children are not entirely fit.

(O) also contains a second reversal. By using the same place name, Ḥamatha d'Geder, as indicated in (I), (O) also implicitly advances itself as an alternative tradition to (I). In (I), as in (M), rabbis declare the child of a Jewish woman and a Gentile man fit. This is not to say that (O) really does have any connection to (I). Again, like its reversal of (M), the wording and replacement of (O) cast doubt for the reader on the authenticity of the lenient traditions. As a whole, then, the *sugya* preserves a powerful halakic opinion (the child of a Jewish woman and Gentile man is fit) with which the redactor evidently disagrees. The editing of the *sugya* conveys the redactor's disapproval of this stance, and leaves the reader, if looking for a legal solution to this problem, with the impression (if not legal support) that the child of a Gentile man and Jewish woman is not fully (if at all) fit.

Other brief discussions in the Yerushalmi and other Palestinian documents too preserve the opinion that child of a Jewish woman and Gentile man is a *mamzer/et*.[16] Moreover, even the assertions in the Yerushalmi that the child of such a liaison is a legitimate Jew are qualified. A *sugya* that cites only Babylonian amoraim, all of whom agree that the child is not a *mamzer*, focuses on disqualifying the child, if female, from marrying a priest.[17]

Bavli

The Bavli consistently attributes the position that the child of a Jewish woman and Gentile man is a *mamzer/et* to Palestinian rabbis. Babylonians, and the redactor, are on the other hand found most often supporting the position that these children are fit. This can most easily be seen in a long *sugya*, from which I will cite excerpts, that seeks to determine the status of these children:

A. Rabah bar bar Ḥanah [BA 3] said in the name of R. Yoḥanan [PA 2], all agree that if a slave or Gentile has intercourse with a Jewish woman the child is a *mamzer*.

B. According to whom does "all agree" [refer]?

C. It is Shimon the Yemenite because although Shimon the Yemenite said that violations of [simple] prohibitions (חייבי לאוין) do not

---

[16]*y. Ketub.* 3:1, 27a-b (redactor); *y. Yebam.* 7:7, 8c (redactor); *y. Git.* 1:5, 43c (R. Yoḥanan); *Lev. Rab.* 32:4 (pp. 742-43).
[17]*y. Yebam.* 4:5, 6c.

produce a *mamzer*, because they [i.e., the simple prohibitions] apply when there is potential for valid marriage, but here, in the case of a [male] Gentile and slave, because there is no potential for a valid marriage it is similar to those unions punishable by extirpation.

D. There is an objection: If a Gentile or slave has intercourse with a Jewish woman the child is a *mamzer*. Rabbi Shimon ben Yehudah says that a *mamzer* results only from a violation of the incest restrictions, punished by extirpation.

E. Rav Yosef [BA 3] said, according to whom does "all agree" [refer]?

F. It is Rabbi. Although Rabbi said that these words apply only according to Akiba...in the case of a Gentile or slave [who has intercourse with a Jewish woman] he agrees [that the child is a *mamzer*].

G. As when Rav Dimi [BA 3-4] came [from Palestine], Rav Yitzḥak bar Abudimi [PA 1] said in the name of our Rabbis, if a Gentile or a slave has intercourse with a Jewish woman, the child is a *mamzer*.

H. Rabbi Aḥa [PA 4], prince of the fort (שר הבירה), and R. Tanḥum the son of Rabbi Ḥiyya of Kfar Akko [PA 3] redeemed a captive who came from Armon to Tiberia. [She] was pregnant from a Gentile. They came from R. Ami [PA 3]. He said to them, it was R. Yoḥanan, R. Eleazar, and R. Ḥanina who said that if a Gentile or slave has intercourse with a Jewish woman, the child is a *mamzer*.

I. Rav Yosef said, is it an advantage to list names [or authorities]? Rav and Shmuel in Babylonian and R. Yehoshua ben Levi [PA 1] and Bar Kapara in Palestine – and some say to switch "Bar Kapara" with "Elders of the South" – who say, if a Gentile or slave has intercourse with a Jewish woman the child is fit.

J. Rather, Rav Yosef said, it is Rabbi [whose authority it was. Then (G) is cited again as proof]...

K. Rabbi Yehoshua ben Levi said, the child is tainted *(mêqulqal)*.

L. To whom [is the child tainted]? I could say [to marry into] the congregation [i.e., Jews]. But Rabbi Yehoshua said that the child is fit except for the priesthood, for [even] all the amoraim who call the child fit agree that it is unfit *(pagum)* for the priesthood...[here is a discussion about deriving this rule from the case of the High Priest married to a widow].[18]

M. Abaye [BA 4] said, why do you rely on Rav Dimi? Rely on Rabin [BA 3-4], for when Rabin came he said, Rabbi Nathan and Rabbi Yehudah HaNasi agree to permit [the child]. Who is Rabbi Yehudah HaNasi? Rabbi.

N. And even Rav agreed and permitted [the child]. Once a man came before Rav and asked him, what is the law if a Gentile or slave has

---

[18]Francus asserts that this section was a late addition to the *sugya* ("The Halakhic Status" 106).

intercourse with a Jewish woman? He said to him, the child is fit. He said, then give me your daughter [i.e., he was the child of a Jewish woman and Gentile man]. He [Rav] said to him, I will not give her to you. Shimi bar Ḥiyya [BA 2] said to Rav, people say that a camel in Medea dances on [the measure of] a *qav*. Here is the *qav*, here is the camel, here is Medea, and there is no dancing [Rashi: you permit something new, now prove your words and give him your daughter]. He said to him, if he was like Yehoshua ben Nun I would not give my daughter to him. He said to him, if he was like Yehoshua ben Nun [then] if Master [i.e., you] does not give him [his daughter] others would give [their daughters] to him. When he [the son of the Jewish woman and Gentile man] would not leave from before him [Rav], he fixed his eye on him and he died.

O. Rav Mathneh [BA 2 or 4] agreed to permit [the child].

P. Rav Yehudah [BA 2] agreed to permit the child, as when [one] came before Rav Yehudah he said to him, go conceal your identity or marry one like you; and when [one] came before Raba he said to him, either go abroad or marry one like you.[19]

(A) and (H) directly attribute to Palestinians the position that a child of a Gentile man and a Jewish woman is a *mamzer*, and (G) reports this as a common position in Palestine. In (I) a Babylonian amora tacitly recognizes a difference between Babylonians and Palestinians on this issue by showing that there are authorities in *both* places who permit such a child. Given the clear statements in the Yerushalmi that do permit such a child, the choice of examples chosen by the Bavli is odd: the statement attributed to R. Yehoshua ben Levi (K) does not say that he believes the children of such liaisons fully fit.[20] Only the redactor's explanation in (L), apparently a late addition, somewhat salvages the tradition. Abaye, in (M) next attempts to contest (G), but his tradition is confused. Not only is the version in (G) rather than (M) attested in another parallel in the Bavli,[21] but the chronology of (M) does not work: a BA 3 or 4 reports a position of a man who lived about a century

---

[19]*b. Yebam.* 44b-45a.
[20]What exactly R. Yehoshua ben Levi does mean is not clear. His comment, that the child is מקולקל has generally been taken to mean that if a woman, she cannot marry a priest (a synonym of מזוהם). This is the only such use of the term in rabbinic literature known to me. Apparently, this term was also puzzling to the redactor or later reader, who added (L) attempting to clarify it.

It is also possible that the force of מקולקל was moral rather than legal. Generally, the root קלקל denotes disgrace through immorality. The child of such a union would be a palpable disgrace of an "immoral" liaison.
[21]*b. Yebam.* 70a.

earlier.²² The Bavli does not relate a single unambiguous tradition of the Palestinian tradition that the child of a Jewish woman and Gentile man is fully fit.

The next attempt to promote the more lenient view (N) is transitional. Rav lived between the age of the tannaim and the amoraim, and is reported to have spent part of his life in Palestine and part in Babylonia. Perhaps this helps to explain his acceptance of the lenient Babylonian position on the child of a Jewish woman and Gentile man, but only with ambivalence about his decision. "Even if he was like Yehoshua ben Nun," Rav declares, he would not give his daughter to this man. According to the medieval commentator the Maharasha, Rav's reason is that although the son of a Jewish woman and Gentile man might be fit and virtuous, marriage with him would (following L) disqualify his daughter from (re)marrying a priest. Because there is no sign in this text that Rav either followed the law of (L), or in fact that (L) would apply to the man's wife rather than daughter, the Maharasha's explanation is hard to accept. Rather, I suggest, the reason is simpler: Rav shared with many in his community an unease with such a possibility. This communal attitude is reflected in (P), in which the rabbis appear to be more certain in their decisions but acknowledge the societal prejudices. Rav rules like a Babylonian rabbi, but behaves according to his time.²³

Babylonian amoraim after Rav are not portrayed as hesitant to declare the child of a Jewish woman and Gentile man fully fit. After a similar discussion about the repercussions of a liaison between a slave (or partial-slave) and a Jewish woman, the *sugya* concludes, "And the law is: if a Gentile or slave has intercourse with a Jewish woman, the child is fit, whether she is unmarried or married."²⁴ Other statements scattered throughout the Bavli, some parallel to the *sugya* cited above, also show the differences between Palestinian and Babylonian rhetoric on this issue.²⁵

---

²²Francus, "The Halakhic Status" 99-100 asserts that Abaye confuses the statements of Rabbi and his grandson. This assertion is supported by the Yerushalmi passage cited above (K).
²³I argued in Chapter 2 that there is no sign in the Bavli of attaching a societal stigma to the *mamzer/et*. Here note that there is a stigma in Babylonian society attached to children of Jewish women and Gentile men that clearly runs independently of any relation to the *mamzer/et*.
²⁴*b. Yebam.* 45b.
²⁵*b. Yebam.* 16b-17a (attributed to a BA 6 and which even attempts to ease the prohibition of a *mamzer* from marrying a Jewish woman), 46a, 70a, 99a; *b. Qidd.* 68b, 70a; *b. 'Abod. Zar.* 59a.

Jewish Man and Gentile Woman

Legal Status

There is less legal controversy surrounding the offspring of Jewish men and Gentile women. According to several tannaitic sources, the child of a Gentile woman, by any father at all (except a *mamzer*), is considered a Gentile.[26] The child born of a Jewish man and a Gentile woman is, according to the *Mishnah*, a Gentile: "Any [woman] who does not have the potential to contract a marriage either with him or with any other man. Who is this? The child of a female slave or [female] Gentile."[27] This law, dated by S. Cohen to the early rabbinic period, is modeled on Roman accounting of citizen status.[28]

Both Talmudim contain similar traditions that justify this status with a biblical proof-text.

> A. From where in Scripture do we know about a Gentile woman? Scripture says, "You shall not intermarry with them," [Deut. 7:3].
>
> B. We find that they do not have the potential to contract marriage.
>
> C. From where in Scripture do we know that the child [of a Jewish man and Gentile woman] is of her status?
>
> D. R. Yoḥanan [PA 2] said in the name of R. Shimon ben Yoḥai, Scripture says, "For they will turn your child away from Me [to worship other gods...]," [Deut. 7:4]. "Your child" – one who comes from a Jewish woman is called "your child." "Not your child" – one who comes from a Gentile woman is not called "your child" but "her child."
>
> E. Ravina [BA 5] said, from this we learn that the child of your daughter, who comes from [i.e., has as a father] a Gentile man, is called your child.[29]

In this passage, Deut. 7:4, which interdicts all marriages between Jews and those of the seven nations in Canaan, is interpreted as referring to the union (not necessarily marital) between Jewish men and all Gentile women.[30] This, in turn, justifies the status of such children according to *m. Qidd.* 3:12. The association of intercourse between Gentiles and Jews

---

[26] See *Mekh. Mishpatim* 2 (pp. 250-51); *Sifre Deut.* 215 (p. 249); *Sifra Emor* 6:3 (109d). These sources all say that the child of a Gentile slave-women from a Jewish father is a slave. Note that in these sources there is no condemnation of this liaison.
[27] *m. Qidd.* 3:12. See also *m. Yebam.* 2:5.
[28] See S. Cohen, "Matrilineal Principle" 30-32, 34-35, esp. 42-46. See also Taubenschlag, *The Law of Greco-Roman Egypt* 104-8. See especially D.1.5; Gaius *Inst.* 1.48-96.
[29] *b. Qidd.* 68b. (D) and (E) are paralleled at *b. Yebam.* 17a, 23a.
[30] See Francus, "The Halakhic Principle" 94.

with idolatry will be considered below. The Yerushalmi contains a very similar version of this tradition, but lacking Ravina's comment (E).[31]

A single tradition dissents from this decision. Yaakov of Kfar Niburaia (PA 4) is said to have issued a ruling in Tyre that the child of a Jewish man and Gentile woman is considered a Jew.[32] Although he was forced by a rabbi to retract his view, we may presume that he was not the only person in late rabbinic Palestine to ignore rabbinic authority on this matter.[33]

Affronts to God

A single tradition evinces a different kind of rhetoric on children of liaisons between Jewish men and Gentile women. According to the *Mishnah*, "If one says, '"Do not allow any of your offspring to be offered up to Molech," [Lev. 18:21], and do not give from your seed to impregnate an Aramaean woman' – forcefully silence him."[34] The *mishnah* condemns those who, while publicly reading Lev. 18:21, interpret, rather than literally translate, this verse. This interpretation may have been a common one; it is attested in Targum Jonathan on this verse (see below).

The Talmudim offer slightly different versions of the same tradition as their only commentary to this *mishnah*. In the Yerushalmi, we read, "R. Yishmael taught, this is one who marries an Aramaean woman and

---

[31]*y. Yebam.* 2:6, 4a; *y. Qidd.* 3:14, 64d. S. Cohen seems to consider it likely that no comment such as Ravina's is found in the Yerushalmi because the Yerushalmi assumes that R. Shimon ben Yohai's exegesis (D) extends also to the case of the child of a Jewish man and Gentile woman ("The Matrilineal Principle" 35). It is also possible that the Yerushalmi never does logically connect the two halves of the "marilineal principle." If so, then the marilineal principle, as known today in Jewish law, is essentially a Babylonian product.
[32]*y. Qidd.* 3:14, 64d (par. *y. Yebam.* 2:6, 4a).
[33]On the "heresy" of Yaakov of Kfar Niburaia, see O. Irsai, "Ya'akov of Kefar Niburaia – A Sage Turned Apostate," *Jerusalem Studies in Jewish Thought* 2:2 (1982/3): 153-68, esp. 157-63 (Hebrew). There is no contemporary evidence on whether the society at large accepted the opinion of the rabbi or that of Yaakov of Kfar Niburaia. See also, Ze'ev Falk, "On the Historical Background of the Talmudic Laws Regarding Gentiles," *Immanuel* 14 (Fall, 1982): 102-13.
[34]*m. Meg.* 4:9. In Albeck's text, the clause reads, ומזרעך לא תתן לאעברא בארמיותא. MSS Kaufman, Codex Paris, and Codex de Rossi 138 all have למעברא in place of לאעברא. In his notes to this *mishnah*, Albeck (2:368) interprets this clause to refer to teaching one's child the laws and ways of Gentiles. My translation follows Jastrow, p. 131, s.v., אעברא. Both understandings depend on how one takes the double pun on the biblical verse: (1) does זרע mean semen or one's child; (2) and does עבר mean "transfer," which is closer to the biblical meaning, or "impregnate?" Targ. Onkelos translates Lev. 18:21 ומבנך לא תתן לאעברא למולך, using the same word for "transfer" that the *Mishnah* employs, if I am correct, for "impregnate."

bears[35] from her children, [who] establishes enemies of God."[36] In the Bavli, the version appears as, "The School of R. Yishmael taught, the verse [Lev. 18:21] refers to a Jewish man who has intercourse with a Samaritan (כותית) woman and bears from her a son (for idolatry)."[37]

Two differences between the Yerushalmi's and Bavli's versions of this short tradition should be noted. First, the Yerushalmi specifically mentions marriage where the Bavli refers only to intercourse. The Yerushalmi's focus on marital relations when compared to the Bavli's was noted in the last chapter, and recurs in other discussions in the Yerushalmi on sex between Jewish men and Gentile women.[38]

Second, the Yerushalmi's version labels these children as "enemies of God." The Bavli's version follows the tamer interpretation referred to in the *Mishnah*, that these children will turn to idolatry. Whereas the Bavli uses this tradition to explicate an unclear clause in the *Mishnah*, the Yerushalmi uses that same tradition to advance the argument that children of such liaisons are affronts to God.[39] This goes beyond the rhetoric of Deut. 7:3-4, which the Talmudim use to dissuade intermarriage due to a possibility of a "leading astray" of the Jewish spouse.[40]

---

[35]This reading is from the parallel at *y. Sanh.* 9:11, 27b. Our text has the apparently corrupt מעמיד.
[36]*y. Meg.* 4:10, 75c (par. *y. Sanh.* 9:11, 27b). Finklestein records this tradition in the *Sifre Deut.* 171 (p. 218) but it is not found in any extant manuscript. The addition was based on citation in manuscripts of the *Yalkut Shimoni*.
[37]*b. Meg.* 25a. The last two words, "for idolatry," are not found in MS Munich 95 nor, it appears, in Rashi's version. A parallel version can be found in *Sifre Deut.* 171 (p. 218), although this might be a later addition. See also *Midrash Tannaim* (pp. 109-10), which Hoffman corrects from *Sifre Deut.* On this see Gary G. Porton, *The Traditions of Rabi Ishmael*, 3 vols. (Leiden: E.J. Brill, 1977) 2:200-1. On intermarriage between Jews and Samaritans, see L.H. Schiffman, "The Samaritans in Tannaitic Halakhah" 328-34.
[38]See *y. Sanh.* 2:6, 20c; *b. Yebam.* 76b. On the Yerushalmi passage, see S. Cohen, "Pharaoh's Daughter" 32. The Yerushalmi, in contrast to the Bavli, seems to suggest that Solomon did not actually marry his wives, but only used them for sexual purposes. Sex with Gentile women might be bad, but marriage with them is worse. See below for a fuller treatment of these passages. See also *y. Sanh.* 2:3, 20b, in which a marriage between a Jewish man and Gentile woman produces a line of descendants that ultimately causes disaster for Israel.
[39]See also *b. Soṭ.* 37b, discussed in Chapter 2.
[40]I do not think that there is any import to the use of the term "Samaritan" in the Bavli's version. This might have been a substitution made by the censor, and is to be read as referring more generally to Gentile woman. If, however, "Samaritan" really was intended, then this would lend further support to my argument that the Bavli uses this tradition in an exclusionary way, rather than the Yerushalmi's inclusionary version.

Non-Rabbinic Parallels

As discussed in Chapter 2, among both Greeks and Romans, citizenship generally was granted only to those who had two citizen parents. In "mixed" marriages, those between citizens and non-citizens, the children generally followed the status of the parent with inferior status.[41] Children that resulted from non-marital mixed liaisons generated less commentary. Because men, in both Greek and Roman cultures, had free and sanctioned sexual access to a variety of non-citizen women (e.g., *hetairai*, slaves, prostitutes) children of such relationships were not given a stigmatized status within their communities: they were simply not given a status. Such children would either be the sole responsibility of the women who bore them or would be slaves, depending on the mother's status.

Conclusions

When a Jewish woman in Late Antiquity had intercourse with a non-Jewish man, and returned to her family's home carrying a child by him, there was bound to be some anxiety. Palestinian rabbis are identified with the legal position that labels the children of such liaisons *mamzerim*. The relevant *sugyot* in the Yerushalmi, while citing contrary opinions, are edited so as to support this position. Like the Greeks and Romans, the child was accepted into the community, but with a stigmatized status. Despite Babylonian leniency on the legal status of these children, they too appeared to attach a stigma to them.

By comparison, intercourse between a Jewish man and Gentile woman was relatively unproblematic. The woman was assumed to take the child back to her family: it is removed from the community. Although Babylonian and Palestinian rabbis agree that the status of a

---

[41]This was almost always the mother. In Rome, for example, stable sexual relationships between citizen men and non-citizen women, marriage to whom was not possible, occurred in the context of concubinage. The children, as mentioned in Chapter 2, would have followed the status of the mother. See Susan Treggiari, "Concubinae," *Papers of the British School at Rome* 49 (1981): 59-81; P.R.C. Weaver, "The Status of Children in Mixed Marriages," in *The Family in Ancient Rome: New Perspectives*, ed. Beryl Rawson (Ithaca: Cornell University Press, 1986) 145-69, and, "Children of Freedmen (and Freedwomen)," in *Marriage, Divorce, and Children in Ancient Rome*, ed. Beryl Rawson (Oxford: Oxford University Press, 1991) 166-90; W.W. Buckland, *A Manual of Roman Private Law* (Cambridge: Cambridge University Press, 1939) 63-64. Stable sexual relationships between citizen women and non-citizen men was almost inconceivable, but surely the children of any such unions would not have been considered citizens.

See also Joseph Mélèze-Modrzejewski, "Un aspect du 'couple interdit' dans l'antiquité: Les mariages mixtes dans l'Égypte hellénistique," in *Le couple interdit: Entretiens sur le racisme*, ed. Léon Poliakov (Paris: Mouton, 1977) 53-73.

child of a Jewish man and Gentile woman is a Gentile, in a single tradition the Yerushalmi seeks to label these children as enemies of God. This tradition, however, indicates particular concern on the part of Palestinians with intermarriage, as opposed to non-marital intercourse between Jewish men and Gentile women. In the conclusion I will address the issue of how this rhetoric might have functioned within the society in which it was framed.

Rhetoric of Defilement and Prohibition

Tannaitic and amoraic, Palestinian and Babylonian sources all employ a rhetoric of defilement in discussing sexual contact between Gentiles and Jews. Sexual contact with Gentiles, according to this rhetoric, conveys ritual pollution to Jews. Because the rhetoric of defilement was applied unevenly to male and female Gentiles, I consider them separately.[42]

MEN

Tannaitic Sources

"Gentiles and the convert and the resident alien do not convey ritual impurity by flux, and although they do not convey ritual impurity by flux, they convey ritual impurity as those in flux in all respects," the *Tosefta* states.[43] According to rabbinic purity laws, a male Jew who experiences a seminal emission, especially an abnormal one, becomes impure and conveys ritual impurity. Although Gentiles are not subject to ritual defilement, they are nevertheless considered to be in a permanent state of impurity, capable of defilement of the same type as a Jew who has had a seminal emission. Obviously intended to keep a social distance between Jews and Gentiles, this rule is not explicitly connected in tannaitic sources to sexual contact. That is, it is likely that the intent of this rule was to keep social distance between *males*, as men too would have been able to contract impurity from those considered to impart impurity like those in a state of flux (see below). Gentile semen, in fact, when mentioned in the *Mishnah* is considered "pure." Hence, the

---

[42]On the issue of Gentile defilement generally, see G. Alon, "The Levitical Uncleanness of Gentiles," reprinted in *Jews, Judaism and the Classical World* (Jerusalem: Magnes Press, 1977) 146-89; A Büchler, "The Levitical Impurity of the Gentile in Palestine Before the Year 70," *Jewish Quarterly Review*, n.s., 17 (1926-1927): 1-81. Büchler dates the imposition of levitical impurity on Gentiles as a strategy to prevent intercourse between Jews and Gentiles to the first century C.E. for women and after 70 C.E. for men (15, 20-21). I disagree with this dating, but do agree with him, *contra* Alon, that these laws were of rabbinic origin.

[43]*t. Zav.* 2:1. See also *Sifra Metzora, Zavin*, 1 (74d): בני ישראל מטמאין בזיבה ואין הגוים מיטמאים בזיבה. ואף על פי שאינן מטמאים בזיבה מטמאין כזבים. Note that *m. Zav.* 2:1, which declares that "all" convey impurity by flux, does not include a Gentile in its list.

Sex Between Jews and Gentiles 97

Mishnah informs us that if a Jewish woman secretes semen from a Gentile lover after three days, she is not defiled.⁴⁴ The tannaitic rhetoric of purity and defilement of Gentile men is not linked to sex.

Yerushalmi

A tradition in the Yerushalmi explicitly links Gentile purity and sexual contact. According to the "Eighteen Decrees," a list of enactments allegedly made by the School of Shammai on the eve of the destruction of the Temple, among those things prohibited were "their [i.e., Gentile] daughters, their semen and their urine."⁴⁵ Gentile women are forbidden to Jewish men (presumably marriage is meant) but it is Gentile *semen*, rather than the expected "their sons," that is found in the continuation. In an alternative version attributed to R. Shimon b. Yoḥai, cited shortly after this tradition, the expected "their sons and their daughters" replaces the reference to semen. The inclusion of Gentile semen in this tradition confuses the redactor: Gentile semen, as we know, is "pure!" "Semen is always accompanied by urine," is the answer.⁴⁶ Perhaps because the excepted ruling that Gentile semen does not defile is ultimately irreconcilable with the statement of the "Eighteen Decrees," a rhetoric of defilement of Gentile semen is not used anywhere else in the Yerushalmi.

If the Yerushalmi does not pursue the rhetoric of the defiling quality of Gentile semen, it might shift this rhetoric to one of prohibition. The *Tosefta* records a tradition that begins by enumerating the various men intercourse with whom disqualifies a woman from marrying a priest, that is, renders her a *zōnah*. This is followed by a statement attributed to R. Yoseh: "Anyone whose child (*zarʿo*) is fit, she [who had intercourse with him] is fit. Anyone whose child (*zarʿo*) is disqualified, she [who has intercourse with him] is disqualified."⁴⁷ Lieberman interprets the word *zarʿo* here to refer to children.⁴⁸

The Yerushalmi cites a slightly different version of this tradition:

A. If they [i.e., the men] are not fitting to come in to [the congregation of] Israel, they [i.e., the women they have intercourse with] are disqualified, and they are: a boy aged nine years and a day; an Ammonite, Moabite or Egyptian convert; a *mamzer*; a *ḥallal*; a *natin*; if [any of these men] have intercourse with a Jew, the daughter of a Levite, or the daughter of a Kohen [i.e., priest], they disqualify her from [marrying] a priest.

---

⁴⁴*m. Mik.* 8:4. See also *t. Mik.* 6:7; *m. Shab.* 9:3.
⁴⁵*y. Shab.* 1:4, 3c. Alon contends that these laws were in effect well before the period of their alleged enactment ("Levitical Uncleanness" 156-68).
⁴⁶*y. Shab.* 1:4, 3d.
⁴⁷*t. Yebam.* 8:1.
⁴⁸Lieberman, *Tos.* 5.1:24, note to line 3.

B. R. Yosi [PA 3] says, all whose semen disqualifies, his intercourse disqualifies. Anyone whose semen does not disqualify, his intercourse does not disqualify.[49]

(A) lists the men who disqualify a woman from marrying a priest. (B) creates a syllogism: it is the *semen* that disqualifies, hence intercourse with one with disqualifying semen is disqualified. It appears the R. Yosi reads the *Tosefta's* use of the root zr^c to refer to semen rather than children. Another tradition in the Yerushalmi is even clearer, mentioning a "disqualified drop" of semen.[50] Instead of a rhetoric based on the power of Gentile semen to cause impurity, a rhetoric is developed that gives the power of disqualification to semen. This idea is then read into the *Tosefta's* tradition, which is based on the status of the children. A rhetoric of purity is transformed into a rhetoric of prohibition.

Bavli

A similar rhetoric occurs in the Bavli. The redactor – curiously, except for one case, only the redactor – commonly uses the phrase "disqualified/fit drop of semen," usually applied to the *mamzer* or the convert.[51] Although, then, the redactor is familiar with the concept that the semen itself can disqualify or be "unfit," this rhetoric is not applied specifically to liaisons between Jews and Gentiles. The inapplicability of the purity of Gentile semen to sexual intercourse between Jews and Gentiles is highlighted in a *sugya* that discusses the "Eighteen Decrees." According to Rav Naḥman bar Yitzḥak [BA 4], Gentiles are considered as if they were in a permanent state of flux, the result being an avoidance of homoerotic intercourse with Jewish *boys*.[52] There is no attempt to link the tradition of regarding Gentiles in a state of permanent flux to sexual contact with Jewish women. The Bavli maintains, like the Yerushalmi, that if a Gentile man had intercourse with a Jewish woman, then the woman is disqualified from marrying a priest.[53] Never is this rhetoric applied to the semen itself or to the statutory impurity of the Gentile.[54]

WOMEN

Three successive *mishnayot* discuss the purity of non-Jewish women:

---

[49] *y. Yebam.* 7:5, 8b (par. *y. Soṭ.* 4:6, 19d).
[50] *y. Yebam.* 8:3, 9c, attributed to R. Ḥagai [PA 4] in the same of R. Pedat [PA 3-4].
[51] *b. Yebam.* 78a; *b. Soṭ.* 27a (Shmuel); *b. Qidd.* 78a; *b. Sanh.* 36b (par. *b. Nid.* 49b); *b. Hor.* 13a; *b. 'Abod. Zar.* 20a.
[52] *b. Shab.* 17b (par. *b. 'Abod. Zar.* 36b). For a discussion of this passage, see Chapter 5.
[53] *b. Soṭ.* 26b; *b. Yebam.* 45a, 68b-69a; *b. Qidd.* 75b. These are all attributed to R. Yoḥanan [PA 2].
[54] In fact, *b. Nid.* 34a-b explicitly discusses the fact that Gentile semen is not impure.

1. Samaritan women are considered menstruants from their cradles. And Samaritan men cause impurity...because they have intercourse with menstruants...

2. Sadducean women, when they follow the customs of their ancestors, are like Samaritan women. But if they separate [from them] and follow the customs of Israel, they are like Israel. Rabbi Yosi says, they are always considered like Israel until they separate and follow the customs of their ancestors.

3. The blood of a Gentile woman and the "pure" [i.e., non-menstrual[]] blood of a female leper – the School of Shammai declares it pure, and the School of Hillel says, [it is] like spittle and like urine...[55]

These passages appear to be organized by the decreasing power of the menstrual blood to convey impurity. Samaritan women and their husbands are irredeemably impure. Sadducees are impure only if they follow their traditional purity laws; but if they follow rabbinic purity laws, they are considered like all other Jewish women for purposes of the menstrual regulations. A menstruating Gentile women might or might not convey impurity, but even if she does, as the School of Hillel holds, then it is a different, less severe, kind of impurity.[56]

The Yerushalmi too suggests a certain leniency regarding the purity of Gentile women. In the discussion of the "Eighteen Decrees," the (im)purity of Gentile semen is discussed, but the Yerushalmi does not offer any discussion of impurity regarding the prohibition of Gentile women.[57] More telling is a story:

A. Once a man came to have intercourse with the slave-women of Rabbi.

B. She said to him, if my mistress does not immerse, I will not immerse.

C. He said to her, but are you not like an animal?

D. She said to him, and did you not hear [i.e., do you not know] that one who has intercourse with an animal is stoned, as it is written...[58]

This passage is not entirely clear: most puzzling is the meaning of (B).[59] What seems to be clear is that the slave-woman is using her non-

---

[55]m. Nid. 4:1-3. See also t. Nid. 5:1, 2, 5.
[56]Later sources, as shown below, interpret the School of Shammai's statement to mean that it is the urine that mixes in with the blood that makes it impure. This is not necessarily the stance of the Mishnah.
[57]y. Shab. 1:4, 3d. See the emendation proposed by Saul Lieberman, *Ha Yerushalmi Kiphshuto* (Jerusalem: "Darom", 1934) 50-51.
[58]y. Ber. 3:4, 6c.
[59]According to Louis Ginzberg, the slave-woman threatens that if her mistress begins to immerse after intercourse, which at present she does not do, then she too will begin to immerse, and because everyone would know that she had had

immersion as a reason not to have intercourse. Her potential lover says that it does not matter if she immerses, for, the logic seems to be, that because she is a Gentile immersion has no effect. Her menstrual blood is like that of an animal, not human and therefore not conveying impurity to her lover.[60] Her retort, although clever, does not exactly deny this assertion: if I am like an animal, she says, you still cannot have intercourse with me, for then you would be guilty of bestiality. (C) is left unrefuted.[61]

A tradition in the Bavli, however, does state that Gentile women were considered as statutory menstruants. This tradition, whose context I examine in more detail below, is aimed directly at those Jewish men who might consider intercourse with a Gentile woman:

- A. When Rav Dimi [BA 3-4] came [from Palestine] he said, the Court of the Hasmoneans decreed that one who has intercourse with a Gentile[62] woman is liable for intercourse with NSGA [the mnemonic for a menstruant, a slave-woman, a Gentile woman, and a married woman].

- B. When Ravin [BA 3-4] came [from Palestine], he said [he is liable] because of NSGZ [which is the mnemonic for intercourse with] a menstruant, slave-woman, a Gentile woman, and a *zōnah*.[63]

To my knowledge, aside from the brief discussion in *m. Nid.* 4:3, this is the first application of the laws of the menstruant to Gentile women. Two historical claims are made in this passage. (A) claims that these statements of liability originated during the Hasmonean period. There is no other evidence that supports this attribution, and the appearance of this tradition so long after its alleged origin, when unattested in earlier sources, mitigates against the verity of this claim.[64] The attribution of

---

intercourse, both she and her lover would be shamed (*A Commentary on the Palestinian Talmud*, 3 vols. [New York: Jewish Theological Seminary of America, 1941] 3:244 [Hebrew]). This strikes me as strained.

[60]This appears to be a play on the legal principle that a convert has no relatives, which is based on the idea (exegetically derived from Gen. 22:5) that Gentiles are a people "like the ass." See *b. Yebam.* 62a; *b. Ketub.* 111a; *b. Qidd.* 68a; *b. B. Kama* 59a; *b. Nid.* 17a; *Gen. Rab.* 56:2 (pp. 595-96).

[61]This tradition raises other, more elusive issues. How is this tradition meant to be read? Although apparently meant to be witty, it also seems to rest on the assumption that its audience would not find the scenario – namely, that female slaves are made available sexually by their masters – implausible.

[62]The printed version in *b. Sanh.* 82a reads "Samaritan woman," but it is clear from the parallel at *b. 'Abod. Zar.* 36b and the manuscripts that "Gentile" is meant.

[63]*b. Sanh.* 82a (par. *b. 'Abod. Zar.* 36b).

[64]Josephus, however, suggests that for a Jewish woman to marry a Gentile man was a "transgression of the ancestral laws," παραβῆναί τε τὰ πάτρια νόμιμα πείθεται (*Ant.* 20.143, referring to Drusilla). Josephus probably refers here to "custom" rather than any kind of enacted law.

this tradition, in (A) and (B), to Palestine is more problematic. The ruling reflected here is nowhere found to my knowledge, in Palestinian documents, nor are they attributed here to Palestinian amoraim. It is likely that this rhetoric is Babylonian.[65] In any case, this passage reflects a unique rhetoric.

NON-RABBINIC PARALLELS

A parallel to this rhetoric of defilement can be found in the book of *Jubilees*:

> And there is no remission of forgiveness except that the man who caused defilement of his daughter will be rooted out from the midst of all Israel because he has given some of his seed to Molech and sinned as to defile it. And you, Moses, command the children of Israel and exhort them not to give any of their daughters to the Gentiles and not to take for their sons any of the daughters of the gentiles because that is contemptible before the Lord.[66]

S. Cohen points out that this passage is an exegesis of Lev. 18:21.[67] Although the prohibition applies to liaisons between Jewish men and Gentile women and vice versa, the first part of this citation applies only to the Jewish man who gives his daughter as a wife to a Gentile man: he has "given some of his seed to Molech." Whereas Lev. 18:21 makes no reference to defilement, the passage from Jubilees cannot seem to say it enough. Philo too views intercourse with a Gentile woman as conveying some type of impurity.[68] If this reflects a stronger use of the rhetoric of defilement from this period, it is possible that the rhetoric faded in time,

---

[65]A tradition recorded in *b. Shab.* 16b might also reflect this rhetoric. R. Naḥman bar Yitzḥak [BA 4] cites *m. Nid.* 4:1, in his own name, with the comment that this law too was enacted along with the "Eighteen Decrees." It is possible, although there are no manuscript variants known to me, that his use of the term "Samaritan woman" was broad, and meant to include all Gentile women. Although this use of the term כותית would be irregular, it could explain why he did not cite this source as tannaitic.

The concept that a Gentile woman is considered a menstruant appears to continue in Babylonian circles, as it is attested in *Derekh Eretz Rabah* (ed. Higger, pp. 273-74). Higger considers this a work of post-talmudic Babylonia (pp. 19-20). See also the commentary of Marcus van Loopik, *The Ways of the Sages and the Way of the World* (Tübingen: J.C.B. Mohr, 1991) 50-52.

[66]*Jub.* 30:10-11 (ed. Charlesworth, 2:113).

[67]S. Cohen, "From Bible to Talmud" 34-35. On the connection of this passage to the traditions of R. Ishmael, cited above, see also Ch. Albeck, *Das Buch der Jubiläen und die Halakha* (Berlin: Hochschule für die Wissenschaft des Judentums 47, 1930) 27-29.

[68]See Philo *Moses* 1.285-304, the story of Zimri and Pinḥas. By slaying those who had had intercourse with the Midianite women, the "zealots" purged the "defilement of the nation": τὸ μὲν μίασμα τοῦ ἔθνους ἐκκαθαίρουσι. It is unclear if this defilement resulted from the intercourse or from the idolatry.

surviving in the rabbinic period as the power to disqualify a woman to marry a priest.[69]

Rhetoric of Divine Retribution

According to the rabbis, two types of divine retribution result from intercourse between Jews and Gentiles, personal and communal. Sources that posit personal punishment are all of Babylonian provenance, while Palestinian sources posit only communal punishment for this liaison.

PERSONAL RETRIBUTION

The Bavli contains two passages that suggest that God will punish the Jewish man who has intercourse with Gentile women.

A. "They pass through the Valley of Baca [or, weeping]..." [Ps. 84:7].

B. At that hour they [wicked Jews] warrant Gehenna, and Abraham our father comes and brings them up and receives them, except for a Jew who has had intercourse with a Gentile woman, because his foreskin is drawn up and he [Abraham[does not recognize him [as a Jew].[70]

The exegesis apparently by the redactor, is playful. The verse from Psalms (A) is said to describe the Jews going through Gehenna, but then emerging from this "Valley of Weeping." (B) cleverly links intercourse with a Gentile woman with "drawing up" the foreskin, that is, denial of the covenant and idolatry. Because Abraham no longer recognizes them as Jews, they are doomed to suffer damnation. A second tradition, cited

---

[69]Admittedly, this is speculative. It is also possible that the motif of intercourse with a Gentile man disqualifying a Jewish woman from marriage with a priest is directly generated from Lev. 18:21. According to the continuation of the verse, ולא תחלל את–שם אלהיך. The verb חלל is frequently used in rabbinic literature to indicate either a priest who is not fit to serve or a woman who is forbidden to marry a priest. The acceptance of the identification of Lev. 18:21 with liaisons between Jews and Gentiles leads naturally to the exegesis that such liaisons would cause a Jewish woman to be disqualified from marrying a priest. On the acceptance of this exegesis of Lev. 18:21, (apparently) polemicized against in the *Mishnah*, see G. Vermes, "Leviticus 18:21 in Ancient Jewish Bible Exegesis," in *Studies in Aggadah, Targum and Jewish Liturgy in Memory of Joseph Heinemann*, ed. Jakob J. Petuchowski and Ezra Fleisher (Jerusalem: Magnes Press and Hebrew Union College Press, 1981) 108-24. See also Abraham Geiger, *Urschrift und Uebersetzungen der Bibel in ihrer Abhängigkeit* (Breslau: Julius Hainauer, 1857) 299-305.

[70]b. 'Erub. 19a. Note a parallel Palestinian tradition, *Gen. Rab.* 48 (p. 483), in which Abraham sends to Hell those who kill infants in order to take their foreskins to disguise their own circumcisions. In this tradition, though, there is no connection to sex.

below in the name of Rav, threatens scholars with loss of disciples and priests with loss of sons if they have intercourse with Gentile women.[71]

COMMUNAL RETRIBUTION

Two traditions assert that intercourse between Jews and Gentiles results in collective punishment of the Jewish community. As with the examples of personal retribution, these sources address only the case of intercourse between a Jewish male and a Gentile female.

One tradition links the creation of Rome, the subjugator of the Jewish state and destroyer of the Tempe, to Solomon's marriage to the daughter of Pharaoh.[72] Solomon's marriage to the daughter of Pharaoh is mentioned several times in the Hebrew Bible.[73] Although most of these passages register no disapproval, as S. Cohen has noted, a few of the biblical passages and several sources from the Second Temple period to condemn Solomon's intermarriage on grounds that the foreign wives led Solomon into idolatry.[74] Only rabbinic writings, however, proffer the idea that this marriage led to the creation of Israel's arch-enemy. According to the account of the Yerushalmi,

> R. Levi [PA 3] said, on the day that Solomon was made a son-in-law to Pharaoh Necho, king of Egypt, [the arch-angel] Michael descended and stuck a reed in the sea and it caused alluvium to collect and a great thicket was made and this is the great city that is in Rome.[75]

A slightly different version is found in the Bavli, also attributed to a PA 3.[76]

---

[71] b. Sanh. 82b. Cited below, p. 113, as (D).
[72] See Paul Rieger, "The Foundation of Rome in the Talmud: A Contribution to the Folklore of Antiquity," *Jewish Quarterly Review*, n.s., 16 (1926): 229, who appears to view these traditions as referring not to the creation of the city of Rome in its role as destroyer of the Temple, but instead to "the foundation of a city, of the type that was current in Asia Minor." This interpretation robs the tradition of the moral overtones clearly indicated by their contexts. See also Samuel Krauss, *Persia and Rome in the Talmud and Midrashim* (Jerusalem: Mosad Ha-Rav Kook, 1948) 14-19 (Hebrew).
[73] 1 Kings 3:1, 7:8, 9:16, 24 all report the marriage without moral judgment. 1 Kings 11:1-2; 2 Chron. 8:11; Neh. 13:26 are all condemnatory. On these passages and their post-biblical history, see Jacob Lassner, *Demonizing the Queen of Sheba* (Chicago: University of Chicago Press, 1993) 9-35.
[74] See S. Cohen, "Solomon and the Daughter of Pharaoh" 23-30. The connection of mixed intercourse to idolatry will be considered below.
[75] y. 'Abod. Zar. 1:2, 39c.
[76] b. Sanh. 21b (R. Yitzḥak) (par. b. Shab. 56b). The same attributions are found in MS Munich 95. These *sugyot* are alluded to by the redactor at b. Nid. 70b. The tradition is also found in MS London Margoliouth 341, Add. 16, 406 of *Sifre Deut.* 52 (p. 119).

The *marriage* (in all of these sources marriage is explicit) of a Jewish man to Gentile women, according to these primarily Palestinian sources,[77] leads to punishment of the entire community.

Rhetoric of Association

The Hebrew Bible clearly connects the threat of idolatry for a Jew intermarrying a man or woman to intermarriage with the seven nations of Canaan: "for they will turn your children away from Me to worship other gods," (Deut. 7:4).[78] Ezra (9:1-2) expands the scope of this prohibition even to Gentiles not of the seven nations, but applies it only to Jewish men marrying Gentile women. Philo and Josephus for the most part follow Ezra's exegesis, although in Philo's paraphrase of Deut. 7:3-4 he acknowledges the power of a Gentile male to lead his Jewish wife astray.[79] These sources all focus on marriage between Jewish men and Gentile women.

This association of idolatry with intermarriage, and even simple sexual liaisons between Gentiles and Jews, continues in the rabbinic period. According to a *mishnah*, "if one steals the libation vessel, or curses the divining tool, or has intercourse with an Aramaean [i.e., Gentile] woman, zealots harm him."[80] Alon has argued that a connection to idolatry links these three clauses.[81] Less subtle is a tradition found in *Sifre Deut.* discussing Solomon's marriage to Pharaoh's daughter:

> "King Solomon loved many foreign women in addition to Pharaoh's daughter...," [1 Kings 11:1]. [Since] "Pharaoh's daughter" is included [in "many foreign women"], why is she singled out? It

---

[77]Shmuel, like Rav, lived between the time of the tannaim and amoraim, even to the point were sources that are in other places attributed as tannaitic are attributed to him. See the sources cited in Baruch Bokser, *Post-mishnaic Judaism in Transition* (Chico: Scholars Press, 1980) 458, nn. 84-85. Hence, his views might reflect Palestinian or Babylonian assumptions.

[78]The Hebrew Bible is fairly consistent in portraying the danger of Gentile women leading Jewish men to commit idolatry. See Atalia Brener, "נשים זרות במקרא" *Beit Mikrah* 30 (1984-5): 179-85.

[79]See Philo *Spec. Laws.* 3.29 (a paraphrase of Deut. 7:3-4); *Moses* 1.295-304 (the story of Pinḥas); Josephus *Ant.* 4.125-55 (story of Pinḥas); 8.190-96 (Solomon's intermarriages); 11.139-41 (paraphrase of Ezra story). On these passages, see S. Cohen, "From Bible to Talmud" 26-27; and, "Solomon and the Daughter of Pharaoh" 28-29.

[80]*m. Sanh.* 9:6.

[81]See G. Alon, "Studies in Philonic Halakhah (C)," *Tarbiz* 6 (1934): 33-34 (Hebrew). Although Alon's attempt to link this *mishnah* to Philo's "halakhah" is questionable, his interpretation of the *mishnah* is more plausible than that offered by Martin Hengel, *The Zealots: Investigations into the Jewish Freedom Movement From the Period of Herod I Until 70 A.D.*, trans. David Smith (Edinburgh: T.&T. Clark, 1989) 186-90, who interprets the *mishnah* as referring to magical practices.

is to teach that he loved her more than all the others and she caused him to sin more than all the others.[82]

The sin, of course, is idolatry. Solomon's great love for a foreign woman led him into sin. The causative, "she caused him to sin," clearly is dependent on Deut. 7:3-4. The Talmudim too accept the association of Solomon's liaisons with Gentile women and his (or their) idolatry.[83]

The only other set of traditions, to my knowledge, that explicitly links intercourse with Gentiles to idolatry are those that are connected with the work of the prophet Balaam. In these traditions, after failing to curse Israel Balaam conceives a plan to lure Jewish men, by inflaming their passions with Gentile women, to practice idolatry.[84] This tradition too is found in the tannaitic and amoraic, Palestinian and Babylonian sources.

Rhetoric of Apologetics

Several biblical characters are said to have had sexual liaisons with Gentiles: Moses (Ex. 2:21; Num. 12:1); Solomon (esp. Neh. 13:26); Samson (esp. Judges 14:2-3); and Esther (Est. 2:17). I will briefly examine the rabbinic rhetoric of apologetics associated with each of these figures.

MOSES

Moses married the daughter of the Midianite priest Yitro. This match was criticized in the Bible for unknown reasons: "Miriam and Aaron spoke against Moses because of the Cushite woman he had married: 'He married a Cushite woman!'," (Num. 12:1). In its commentary on this verse, *Sifre Num.* identifies this Cushite woman as Zipporah, Yitro's daughter, and posits that the complaint against Moses was that he stopped having sex with his wife.[85] There is no hint of disapproval or apology for the "intermarriage." Other tannaitic documents as well do not express disapproval of this marriage.

Later sources do recognize this marriage as potentially problematic. both the Yerushalmi's and Bavli's version of the story of Pinḥas, cited below, contain a tradition that Zimri criticized Moses for his marriage to a non-Israelite, a detail missing from the parallel tannaitic account.[86] A second tradition in the Bavli also reflects a criticism of Moses's marriage:

---

[82]*Sifre Deut.* 52 (p. 119).
[83]*y. Sanh.* 2:6, 70c; *b. Yebam.* 76a-b.
[84]For Balaam's mission, see Num. 22:2-24:25. These traditions are cited and examined in depth in Chapter 4. This tradition is from the first century C.E., if not earlier. See Geza Vermes, *Scripture and Tradition in Judaism* (Leiden: E.J. Brill, 1961) 162-64.
[85]*Sifre Num.* 99 (pp. 98-99).
[86]*y. Sanh.* 10:2, 28d; *b. Sanh.* 82a-b, (J) cited below. Compare to *Sifre Num.* 131 (p. 172).

"Rabbi Eleazar said, always a man should cleave to good men. Behold Moses, who married Zipporah, begat Jonathan; Aaron, who married Aminadav, begat Pinḥas."[87] Moses's marriage produced Jonathan, identified earlier in this *sugya* as a sinner, and Aaron's produced Pinḥas, the consummate zealot. R. Eleazar seems to be arguing that Moses produced bad children because his father-in-law was not a "good" man, but an idolator.[88] The intermarriage is condemned due to the father-in-law rather than to any of Zipporah's actions.

To my knowledge, no rabbinic source attempts to reply to these attacks. Post-talmudic sources will feel constrained to justify this union on the grounds that Zipporah was a pious convert to Judaism.[89]

SOLOMON

In his study of the exegetical traditions of Solomon's marriage to foreign wives, S. Cohen points out that by and large, "Solomon was left to wallow in his sin."[90] Rabbinic sources excoriate Solomon for his violations of prohibitions against the multiplication of wives (Deut. 17:17), intermarriage, and the idolatry that resulted from his intermarriages.

There are, however, two rabbinic attempts to justify Solomon's actions. According to one *sugya* in the Yerushalmi, (1) Solomon did not actually marry foreign women, but only had intercourse with them; and (2) he married them only in order to convert them.[91] The former is intriguing precisely because of its improbability; the *sugya* itself indicates that this possibility is contradicted within the Bible itself (Neh. 13:26). Nevertheless, the possibility of Solomon only having intercourse with Gentile women was apparently seen as less problematic than his actually marrying them. Idolatry here, as in Deut. 7:3-4, is connected to marriage rather than sex.[92] In a parallel *sugya* in the Bavli, Babylonian amoraim are attributed with identical arguments.[93]

---

[87]*b. B. Batra* 109b.
[88]Note that "cleaving," ידבק, to good men would here be read as marrying their daughters.
[89]See Louis Ginzberg, *Legends of the Jews*, 6 vols. (1925; rpt. Philadelphia: The Jewish Publication Society of America, 1947) 6:136, n. 791.
[90]S. Cohen, "Solomon and the Daughter of Pharaoh" 32.
[91]*y. Sanh.* 2:6, 20c. On this, see S. Cohen, "Solomon and the Daughter of Pharaoh" 32.
[92]Ginzberg *Legends* 6:282 n. 16 says that this and other traditions reflect "differences in the attitude toward intermarriage." S. Cohen dismisses this statement without argument ("From Bible to Talmud" 28, n. 16). The main purpose of these traditions is to excuse Solomon's behavior. This assumes that there were differences of attitude toward intercourse and marriage with Gentile women. Similarly, ascribing a proper motive to Solomon (that is, to convert his wives) assumes that this could to some degree exculpate him. This latter

SAMSON

Samson marries a Philistine woman (Judges 14:1-3) and consorts with a Gentile prostitute (Judges 16:1, 4). As in their treatment of Solomon, the tannaitic sources make no effort to exonerate Samson. In fact, these sources emphasize his sinfulness, mainly in respect to general licentiousness rather than intermarriage *per se*.[94]

In the Yerushalmi, Samson is condemned specifically for intermarriage:

A. It is written, "When he [Samson] came to the vineyards of Timnah...," [Judges 13:5].

B. Rav Shmuel b. Rav Yitzhak [PA 3] said, it [the verse] teaches that his father and his mother were showing him the vineyards of Timnah sown with diverse species. They said to him, my son, just as their vineyards are sown with diverse species, so too their daughters are sown with different species.[95]

Samson is warned off Philistine women because, it appears, they are promiscuous.[96] No attempt is made to excuse Samson for his intermarriage, and to my knowledge there is no discussion in the Yerushalmi of his relationship with Delilah.

An extended passage in the Bavli faults both Samson and Delilah.[97] Palestinian and Babylonian amoraim are attributed with statements that emphasize Samson's lustfulness.[98] A long, mainly tannaitic passage plays off Delilah's name *(dldl* is the Hebrew root for "weaken") to suggest that she weakened him in a variety of ways. In this same

---

assumption does in a sense represent a difference in attitude toward intermarriage. If, on the other hand, Ginzberg does mean that this would fully exculpate Solomon – that there was an attitude that with the proper motive intermarriage could be justified – then Cohen is correct to dismiss this assertion.

[93]*b. Yebam.* 76a-b. Rav Yosef (BA 3) is ascribed with the position that Solomon married these women to convert them, and Rav Pappa (BA 5) with the position that he did not actually marry them. See also *b. Shab.* 56b, which states that Solomon never actually practiced idolatry: either his wives inclined his heart that way and he resisted, or he is held liable for the sins of his wives, whom he did not prevent from worshipping idols.

[94]See *m. Soṭ.* 1:8, 17d.

[95]*y. Soṭ.* 1:8, 17d.

[96]Their daughters, like their fields, are "sown" with different kinds of "seed." The implication is that Samson would not be marrying a virgin.

[97]*b. Soṭ.* 9b-10a.

[98]One is in the name of R. Ami [PA 3]. The other is a tradition in the name of Rabbi Yoḥanan [PA 2] which states that while Samson was in prison, all used to bring their wives to him for impregnation. Tacked on is a statement attributed to R. Papa [BA 5], "Thus they say, [leave] before a wine drinker wine, and before a ploughman figs." Samson has a "taste" for women, so all left before him he will seek to "consume."

passage Samson is also praised for his work as a judge, but no attempt is made to exonerate his behavior.

ESTHER

According to the Bible Esther became the queen of the Persian king Artaxerxes. This intermarriage is crucial to the story, in which her intervention with the king saves the Jewish community. Jewish literature of the Second Temple period sought to justify Esther's liaison. In the Greek additions to the Book of Esther, for example, Esther prays that God knows that she "abhors the bed of the uncircumcised and any alien."[99] Her relationship with the king is conducted purely for the good of the community.

Rabbinic sources do not attempt to justify this liaison. Nor, however, is Esther's liaison condemned. According to one tradition, Mordecai is portrayed giving advice to the king on how to win Esther's favor.[100] Another *sugya* asks how Esther could have committed such a transgression, publicly no less. Abaye [BA 4] answers that "she was really soil," that is, she was passively "tilled" and so deserved no opprobrium. Raba [BA 4] responds that because the king had intercourse with her for his own pleasure rather than in order to persecute the Jews, her cooperation was not forbidden.[101]

CONCLUSIONS

The conclusions to this section are negative. Not once do the rabbis engage in apologetic rhetoric for sex between Jews and Gentiles. In discussions of Jewish men, they in fact tend to exaggerate the sin. They treat Esther's liaison as inconsequential.

Rhetoric of Temptation

As we saw in the last chapter, prohibitions against seclusion with members of the opposite sex were imposed because it was assumed that the men and women, even if related, sexually desire each other. The *Mishnah* and *Tosefta* also apply rules against seclusion to Gentile men and Jewish women. According to the *Mishnah*, a woman is allowed to remain in a room alone with two (Jewish) men, the assumption being that each

---

[99]*Additions to Esther* 14:15.
[100]*b. Meg.* 13a. See also *b. Meg.* 15b, in which angels are credited with inciting the king to lust for Esther. On this passage, see Samuel Tobias Lachs, "Sexual Imagery in Three Rabbinic Passages," *Journal for the Study of Judaism* 23 (1992): 245-56.
[101]*b. Sanh.* 74b. This *sugya* develops from a question of whether one should submit to death rather than commit a sexual transgression. Although, then, this tradition is not intended to address the topic of sex between Jews and Gentiles, it is notable that nevertheless Esther is not condemned for the liaison.

Sex Between Jews and Gentiles

man will be embarrassed to approach her sexually in the presence of the other.[102] Another *mishnah* prohibits a Jewish woman from remaining alone with Gentiles because "they are suspected of sexual transgressions (*'arayot*)."[103] According to the *Tosefta*, a woman should not remain alone "even with a hundred Gentile men."[104] Both women and Gentiles were thought to lack sexual control (see Chapter 4). These passages assume that because Gentile men have no shame, they will not prevent each other from approaching the woman. Neither the Yerushalmi nor the Bavli add to this rhetoric.

There is very little rhetoric that suggests that Gentile women were considered particularly attractive, or sexually tempting, to men, or the reverse.[105] Gentile men were to be avoided because they were lascivious, not because they were thought desirable.

Rhetoric of Threat

Traditions that record actual punishments being meted out to those who have intercourse with Gentiles are relatively rare. An apocryphal tradition attempts to explain an enigmatic statement in the *Mishnah* that the priestly course of Bilgah "always divided [the showbread] in the South, because their ring was fixed and their window sealed."[106] According to the *Tosefta*, one possible reason is that this priestly course was punished was because the daughter of Bilgah, the progenitor of the course, "apostasied and married an officer, one of the Greek princes."[107] Aside from the historical unreliability of the tradition, it is questionable whether the *Tosefta* means to connect the punishment of the Course of Bilgah solely to intermarriage.[108]

Two traditions in the Bavli record Babylonian rabbis, acting against the Persian authorities, flogging men caught having intercourse with

---

[102]*m. Qidd.* 4:12.
[103]*m. 'Abod. Zar.* 2:1.
[104]*t. Qidd.* 5:10.
[105]The single tradition of this kind known to me states, in reference to the case of Dinah, that a woman who has had intercourse with a non-Jew cannot separate from him: אמר ר' חוניה, הנבעלת מן ערל קשה לפרוש (*Gen. Rab.* 80:11 [pp. 966-67]).
[106]*m. Sukk.* 5:8.
[107]*t. Sukk.* 4:28. The tradition is repeated without comment in *y. Sukk.*5:8, 55d; *b. Sukk.* 56b.
[108]Before marrying she did apostasy. Moreover, in the continuation of this tradition she mocks the altar of the Temple after the "Greeks" succeed in capturing it. According to Lieberman this is the disgrace that led to the punishment (*Tos. Kip.* 4:909).

Gentile women.[109] A Palestinian source might refer to a rabbi castigating the Jewish men of Sepphoris for sexual liaisons with Gentile women.[110]

Of a more theoretical nature is a passage in the *Mishnah* that gives permission to the "zealots" *(qan'aim)* to injure, among others, one who has intercourse with a Gentile woman.[111] Although this statement receives no tannaitic amplification, Palestinian and Babylonian amoraim who commented upon it related it to the biblical story of the act of Zimri and the figure of Pinḥas. These commentaries are the longest and most coherent rabbinic compositions on intercourse between Jews and Gentiles.

According to the biblical account, immediately after the prophecies of Balaam the Israelites began "whoring with the Moabite women," (Num. 25:1) and turning to other gods. As God orders Moses to kill the leaders of this idolatry:

> Just then one of the Israelites came and brought a Midianite woman over to his companions, in the sight of Moses and of the whole Israelite community who were weeping at the entrance of the Tent of Meeting. When Phinehas, son of Eleazar son of Aaron the priest, saw this, he left the assembly and, taking a spear in his hand, he followed the Israelite into the chamber and stabbed both of them, the Israelite and the woman, through the belly. Then the plague against the Israelites was checked.[112]

The earliest rabbinic commentary on this passage is from *Sifre Numbers*. After Pinḥas saw that no one was prepared to do anything after seeing the man, Zimri, and his Midianite lover,

A. [H]e stood in his Court and detached the point [of his spear] and placed it in his belt and was leaning on his staff [i.e., the lance] and he set out.

B. They said to him, Pinḥas, where are you going?

---

[109] *b. Ber.* 58a (attributed to R. Shila. The printed edition reads that he was caught with an Egyptian woman, but manuscripts replace this with the more general "Gentile woman." See *D.S.*1:326); *b. Ta'an.* 24b (attributed to Court of Raba). On these passages, see Jacob Neusner, *A History of the Jews in Babylonia* 2:32-35; 4:36-37.

[110] *y. Ta'an.* 3:4, 66c. The reference is to the vague "acts of Zimri." The act of Zimri as recorded in the Bible and discussed in talmudic literature was, as shown below, intercourse with a Gentile woman. But the talmudic use of this phrase is not necessarily consistent. See, for example, *b. Soṭ.* 22b, which appears to use the phrase "acts of Zimri" to refer to general transgressions. The reference in this tradition to the "plague," however, echoes that of the biblical story of Zimri, cited below.

[111] *m. Sanh.* 9:6.

[112] Num. 25:6-8.

C. He said to them, [the tribe of] Levi is not greater than [the tribe] of Shimon. In all cases we find that [the tribe of] Shimon is greater than [that of] Levi.
D. They said leave him [Pinḥas] and let him enter [the tent to kill Zimri].
E. The Separatists [or Pharisees] permitted the matter.
F. When he entered God performed six miracles for him. The first miracle is that their [Zimri and the Midianite woman] way was to separate from each other but the angel held them fast. The second miracle was that the angel sealed their mouths and they were not able to speak. The third miracle was that his lance went through his "malehood" and her "femalehood" and all would see his "malehood" inside her vagina so that the fault-finders would not say that there was no impurity there, [or] even that he entered to engage in intercourse [himself]. The fourth miracle was that they [the bodies and genitals] were not detached from his lance, but held firm. The fifth miracle was that the angel raised the lintel so that they could be seen between his shoulders. The sixth miracle was that the angel was wounding before him and he went out.
G. When Pinḥas went out and saw that the angel was hurting the people too much, he cast them [the bodies] to earth and stood and intervened, as it is written, "Pinḥas stepped forth and intervened, and the plague ceased," [Ps. 106:30].[113]

This tradition is somewhat difficult, and is possibly corrupt. (B) is addressed to Pinḥas by those around him, supposedly members of the tribe of Levi. Pinḥas's response (C), apparently addressed to the members of his tribe, implies that he is embarking on a mission of honor. The tribe of Levi is greater than that of Shimon (Zimri's tribe), and Shimon's outrageous effrontery will be bested by Pinḥas, who will assert his tribe's superiority. The behavior of Levi, not Shimon, will serve as an example to the people.[114] (D) and (E) are crucial to the understanding of the passage, but unclear. Who says (D)? Is it the members of the tribe of Levi, or has Pinḥas arrived at the tent of Zimri and the members of the tribe of Shimon are addressing him, allowing him to enter Zimri's tent (per the Bavli)? Is (E) a continuation of the statement begun in (D), or is it a statement of fact? That is, this story can be read in one of two ways. According to the Bavli's reading, Pinḥas arrived at Zimri's tent, declared his tribe's greatness (insinuating sexual prowess, perhaps), and was allowed to enter, with the members of the tribe of Shimon thinking that the Pharisees permitted this activity. As we have it, the *Sifre Num.* text does not allow for such a reading. Pinḥas's own tribe asks him where he

---

[113]*Sifre Num.* 131 (p. 172).
[114]The Bavli's version, cited below, has a much clearer reading that contradicts this one.

is going, and (C) must respond to them. Because there is no verb expressing movement to the camp of Shimon at this point, (D) and (E) might continue to take place in his own camp. If so, it would be a tribal deliberation on the permissibility of Pinḥas's intended action.

If this reading is correct, the story departs in four main respects from the biblical account. First, Pinḥas is motivated by honor. No longer is his zeal as pure as it appears in the Bible. Second, he receives permission from who appear to be the leaders of the community, and not coincidentally, those in whose footsteps the rabbis profess to be following. Third, Pinḥas is helped by miracles, showing that his enterprise was divinely sanctioned. Finally, almost all of the miracles create easy public viewing of the spectacle. The public nature of the event is important, as it shows that Pinḥas's action was warranted and just. Pinḥas is transformed from a renegade zealot to an instrument of the communal leaders and God. Read like this, the emphasis of the story is on authority and justification of Pinḥas's action within a communal framework rather than on sex.

The Yerushalmi's version does not contain the exegetical problems of the *Sifre Num.* This version is virtually identical to the latter, except for sections (B) through (E), which the following passage replaces:

A. He supported himself on his staff [i.e., lance] until he reached the opening [of Zimri's tent].

B. When he reached his tent, he said to him [Pinḥas], from where [do you come] and to where [do you go]?

C. Pinḥas said to them, do you not agree with me that the tribes of Levi and Shimon go together everywhere?

D. They said, let him enter. Perhaps the Separatists permit the matter.[115]

Pinḥas's motivation was pure, and he acted on his own, without the authority of the Separatists.[116] The insertion of the detail in (A) that he arrived at the tent prior to the action of (B) and (C), is clearer than in *Sifre Num.*'s version.

The Bavli contains a version of the Pinḥas story very similar to the one found in the Yerushalmi, but places it in a broader context:

A. Rav Kahana [BA 1] asked Rav [BA 1] [82a], if the zealots do not injure him [who has intercourse with a Gentile woman], what is the law?

---

[115]*y. Sanh.* 10:2, 27d.
[116]Support for this reading can be found in a tradition in *y. Sanh.* 9:11, 27b, attributed to a PA 4: "they [the Sages] wanted to excommunicate him [Pinḥas], were the Holy Spirit not resting on him..."

Sex Between Jews and Gentiles

B. Rav completely forgot, and Rav Kahana read in a dream, "Judah has broken faith; abhorrent things have been done in Israel and in Jerusalem. For Judah has profaned what is holy to the Lord – what He desires – and espoused daughters of alien gods," [Mal. 2:11].

C. He [Rav Kahana] came, and said to him, this is what I read. Rav completely remembered [the answer to (A)].

D. [Rav interprets each clause of Mal. 2:11, ending with:] "and espoused daughters of alien gods" – this is one who has intercourse with a Gentile woman *(kutit)*, and it is written after it, "May the Lord leave to him who does this no descendants *('er v'onah)* dwelling in the tents of Jacob and presenting offerings to the Lord of Hosts," [Mal. 2:12][117] – if he is a scholar, he shall have no light *('er)* [=teaching] among the Sages, nor answer *('onah)* in disciples. If he is a priest, he will not have a son to offer the meal offering to the Lord of Hosts.

E. R. Ḥiyya bar Abuyah said, any man who has intercourse with a Gentile woman *(kutit)*, it is as if he wed (מתחתן) an idol, as it is written, "and espoused daughters of alien gods." What daughter does an idol have? Rather, this [refers to] one who has intercourse with a Gentile woman...[An unrelated story involving R. Ḥiyya bar Abuyah follows]

F. When Rav Dimi [BA 3-4] came he said, the Court of the Hasmoneans decreed that one who has intercourse with a Gentile[118] woman is liable because of NSGA. When Ravin [BA 3-4] came he said, because of NSGZ [the mnemonic for intercourse with] a menstruant, slavewoman, Gentile woman, and *zōnah*, but not because of marriage [i.e., adultery, designated by the A in NSGA], because they [=Gentiles] do not have it [=marriage]. And the other [R. Dimi, how would he reply]? Certainly they [=Gentiles] do not leave their wives open [to all].

G. R. Ḥisda [BA 3] said, if one comes for counsel [whether to kill a man engaged in intercourse with a Gentile woman], we do not advise him [to do so].

H. It was also stated, Rabah bar bar Ḥanah [BA 3] said in the name of R. Yoḥanan [PA 2], if one comes for counsel [whether to kill a man engaged in intercourse with a Gentile woman], we do not advise him [to do so].

I. And not only this, but also had Zimri separated [withdrawn from intercourse] and Pinḥas killed him, he [Pinḥas] would have been killed because of him [Zimri]. Had it been reversed, and Zimri killed Pinḥas, he [Zimri] would not have been killed because of

---

[117] On this biblical passage, see Beth Glazier-McDonald, "Intermarriage, divorce, and the *Bat-'Ēl Nēkār:* Insights into Mal 2:10-16," *Journal of Biblical Literature* 106 (1987): 603-11.

[118] The printed edition reads כותית. I am following MS Munich 95.

him, because he [Pinḥas] was a pursuer [and could thus legally be killed in self-defense].

J. "So Moses said to Israel's officials, 'Each of you slay those of his men who attached themselves to Baal-peor'," [Num. 25:5]. The tribe of Shimon went to Zimri ben Salu. They said to him, they are sitting in a capital court, and you sit and are silent? What did he do? He stood and gathered 24,000 men from Israel and went to Kozbi. He said to her, hearken to me. She said to him, I am the daughter of a king, and my father commanded me to hearken only to the greatest among them. He said to her, even [I am] the prince of a tribe and not only that but [I] am greater than [Moses], for [Zimri's tribe] is second in birth, and [Moses's tribe] is third in birth. He grabbed her by her plait and brought her to Moses. [Zimri] said [Moses], Son of Amram, is she forbidden or permitted? And if you say that she is forbidden, who permitted the daughter of Yitro to you? The law [concerning the ability of the zealots to harm those in intercourse with Gentile women] slipped away from him [Moses]. All the people burst out crying, that is as it is written, "[Just then one of the Israelites came and brought a Midianite woman over to his companions, in the sight of Moses and the whole Israelite community,] who were weeping at the entrance of the Tent of Meeting," [Num. 25:6].

K. "When Pinḥas, son of Eleazar son of Aaron the priest, saw this..." [Num. 25:7]. What did he see?

L. Rav said, he saw the act and remembered the law. He said to [Moses], Brother of my father's father, did you not teach me when you descended from Har Sinai, that if one has intercourse with a Gentile woman that zealots injure him. He said to him, let him who dictates the letter be its carrier.

M. Shmuel said, he saw that "No wisdom, no prudence, and no counsel can prevail against the Lord," [Prov. 21:30]. Every place God's name is being desecrated, one does not accord honor to his teacher.

N. R. Yitzḥak [PA 3] said in the name of R. Eleazar, he saw that the angel came and was slaying the people.

O. And he rose in the assembly and detached the point [of his spear]...and placed it in his garment and was leaning on his staff [i.e., the lance] and he set out. When he arrived at the tribe of Simon he said to them, where do we find that the tribe of Levi is greater than the tribe of Shimon? They said, leave him and let him enter to have intercourse. The Separatists [or Pharisees] permit the matter.[119]

The *sugya* continues with a version of the six miracles performed for Pinḥas that is nearly identical to the one cited above from *Sifre Num.* As noted above, the Bavli's version (O) of the tradition in *Sifre Num.* is much

---

[119]*b. Sanh.* 81b-82b.

clearer. Here Pinḥas uses his statement about the superiority of his tribe as a stratagem to gain access to the tent. It is clearly the tribe of Shimon that utters the statement "the Separatists permit the matter," injecting a bit of irony before the massacre that immediately follows.

Unlike the Yerushalmi's version, the Bavli's firmly puts the story into a context that disapproves of intercourse between Jewish men and Gentile women. The Bavli too reflects the tensions between Pinḥas's act and communal authority. Sections (G) and (H) say that if a zealot comes to ask a rabbi whether or not he is permitted to slay such a person he is to be told that he is not. Yet these sections, as well as the rest of the *sugya*, also display an ambivalence. Men are not prohibited from being zealots; if they do not ask, they will not necessarily be told to refrain from such an act. To be sure, zealots are warned of the danger (I) of taking the law into their hands, but ultimately the choice is left to them. Correspondingly, the danger to the men who choose to participate in such liaisons is heightened.

Even if the Jewish lover escapes punishment at the hands of the zealots, he still faces a variety of divine punishments inflicted by God (D). (F) defines intercourse with a Gentile woman as a violation of a negative precept. This is to my knowledge the only statement in the literature to this effect, although the stories of Babylonian rabbis flogging those men who have intercourse with Gentile women might assume it. As noted above, the provenance of (F) is questionable; I speculated that it might be Babylonian. In any case, the entire passage must be considered from a single place, either Palestine or Babylonia. In the Bavli's version of the Pinḥas story, Moses himself is indicted for intermarriage, and is punished by forgetting his own teaching and losing honor from Pinhas (J).

A similar but slightly different set of concerns is evinced in a *sugya* that contains many parallels to the one just cited. In this *sugya*, the law against intercourse with a Gentile woman is attributed to the Court of Shem, and that law prohibiting a Jewish man from even remaining alone with a Gentile woman is attributed to the disciples of Hillel and Shammai.[120]

---

[120]*b. 'Abod. Zar.* 36b. The relevant sections are either anonymous or attributed to Babylonian amoraim. See also Josephus, who attributes the law against marriage between Jews (probably just men) and non-Jews (probably just women) to Moses (*Ant.* 8.191).

NON-RABBINIC PARALLELS

Philo's and Josephus's opposition to intercourse and marriage between Jewish men and Gentile women has been mentioned above.[121] The *Temple Scroll* bans kings (and perhaps by extension the rest of the community it was addressing) from marrying the daughters of Gentiles.[122]

The Christian rhetoric on sex between Christians and non-Christians is largely unstudied.[123] In 388 C.E. a harsh law prohibiting marriage *("in matrimonio...accipiat")* between Christians and Jews was promulgated, but no reason for the legislation is given.[124] This is the only civil law regulating intercourse between Christians and Jews: non-marital intercourse was not even termed *stuprum*.[125] Early canon law denies communion to those who give their Christian daughters to pagans or Jews.[126]

Along with the promulgation of these civil and canon regulations, the fourth century saw the beginning of a Christian rhetoric against marriage between Christians and non-Christians.[127] Much of this rhetoric appears based on a wide interpretation of 1 Cor. 7:39: "A wife is bound to her husband as long as he lives. But if the husband dies, she is free to marry whom she will, provided the marriage is within the Lord's fellowship." The Church Fathers use this verse to justify their condemnation of all sexual liaisons, not just those involving a widow, between Christians and non-Christians. How the rhetoric is deployed remains to be studied.

It is interesting to note that in 385, St. Ambrose wrote a letter to Vigilius, a bishop, against sexual liaisons between Christians and non-Christians. In the beginning of this letter he alludes, through reference to

---

[121]See for example Philo *Moses* 1.303; *Spec. Laws* 1.56-57 (on Pinḥas, but emphasizing the fact that the couple were engaged idolatry); Josephus *Ant.* 8.191.
[122]*11QTemple* 57:15-19 (ed. Yadin 1:353-54).
[123]But see 1 Cor. 7:12-16.
[124]*CTh* 3.7.2 = *CTh* 9.7.5. See Amnon Linder, *The Jews in Roman Imperial Legislation* (rpt. Detroit: Wayne State University Press, 1987) 178-82 for commentary. Such liaisons were to be treated under the law of adultery, and any citizen was given the right to bring charges against those who violated it.
[125]*CTh* 16.8.6 (339 C.E.) has been interpreted by some to refer to Jewish intercourse with Christian slaves, but this is probably not correct. See Juster, *Les Juifs*, 47, n. 1; Linder, *The Jews* 149-50, n. 8. On civil legislation on Jewish intercourse, see Walter Pakter, *Medieval Canon Law and the Jews* (Eblesbach: Rolf Gremer, 1988) 289.
[126]*Council of Elvira* 15-17 (306 C.E.). This sentiment is echoed in a letter from Augustine, who tells a Christian man that it is proper to give his daughter only to a Christian *(Ep. 255 [CSEL 57:602-3])*.
[127]See Margaret S. Schatkin, "Marriage," in *Encyclopedia of Early Christianity*, ed. Everett Ferguson (New York and London: Garland, 1990) 574.

the story of Pinḥas more or less as interpreted also by the rabbis, to the danger of the believer being "led astray" by the non-believing partner. This theme, though, is quickly dropped in favor of a long and rambling retelling of the story of Samson. At the end of this story he asserts that sex with non-Christians should be avoided because of the danger of "treachery."[128]

Conclusions

Sexual liaisons between Jews and Gentiles are not widely discussed in the rabbinic literature. In Palestinian sources, the few passages that address this issue are skewed toward intermarriage rather than intercourse. This does not necessarily indicate such liaisons were rare. In fact, the rhetoric that does survive might suggest the opposite.

Rabbinic rhetoric on the legal status of children of Jews and Gentiles is lopsided, with far more discussion revolving around children of Jewish women and Gentile men than those of Jewish men and Gentile women. Instead of attributing this to legal necessity (the former case perceived as not being adequately addressed in the legal sources), I suggest that it reflects assumptions about the dynamics of such liaisons. The children of Jewish women and Gentile men could ultimately be left with the woman and her family. By stigmatizing such children, it creates an added incentive for a Jewish man to keep his daughter far from Gentiles, for if he marries her to a Gentile his grandchildren would be stigmatized. If the child results from a more casual liaison, he would be saddled with a potential heir who brought disgrace to the family and who legally lacked the means of procreating Jewish children. This is not to mention the difficulty that he, the father, would have finding a husband for his daughter and her child *mamzer*. By tightening these rules, the Palestinian rabbis were really threatening the maternal grandfathers of such children, forcing them to keep control over their daughters.

Lack of discussion about the children of Gentile women and Jewish men can be understood similarly. If men had relatively free sexual access to slaves and other lower class women, as in the rest of antiquity, then any children that they might beget were not truly their problem. That is, the children of such unions would remain with their mothers in any event. To stigmatize such a child would have been pointless.[129]

---

[128] Ambrose, *Ep.* 19 (*PL* 16:1024-36). In 19.34: "*hoc ergo exemplo liquet alienigenarum consortia refugienda; ne pro charitate conjugii proditionis insidiae succedant.*" Ambrose might be responding to 1 Cor. 7:14.

[129] This might be reflected in a tradition found in *b. Naz.* 23b (par. *b. Hor.* 10b) in which Tamar's act, which generated righteous children, is contrasted with Zimri's, which caused "many myriads of Israelites" to die. Communal

I do not suggest that these considerations consciously informed the rabbinic legal discourse. The rules, however, would serve to reproduce those societal assumptions that generate such sexual asymmetry. Calling the child of a Gentile man and Jewish woman a Gentile would have been onerous for the father of the mother. Labeling the child of a Jewish man and a Gentile woman a Jew would disrupt male sexual freedom, for it would obligate a man to care for and support, and his community to assume some responsibility for, this child. This is also not to say that Jewish male sexual freedom with Gentile women was condoned by the rabbis; surely it was not. But this rhetoric of children seems to acknowledge that it existed.

This sexual asymmetry might also be reflected in the rabbinic rhetoric of apologetics. Male biblical figures were not excused for their actions, and the single female figure was lightly dismissed. Perhaps in a society where these liaisons were easily accessible it was seen as too dangerous to excuse the male figures. Proper Jewish women, on the other hand, would normally have had little sexual access to Gentiles.

The real threat of the male Jew taking advantage of this freedom is reflected in the primarily Babylonian rhetoric of threat. Jewish men who have intercourse with Gentile women are threatened with instant death if caught in the act; flagellation if the act was discovered after the fact; and personal divine punishment if they escaped detection. Regardless of the ability of the Jewish community to enforce these sanctions, the threats implied in the texts themselves were most likely intended to influence the behavior of their listeners.

Palestinians focus on the communal nature of the act, its impact on the family (rhetoric of progeny) or the community at large (in the few sources on divine retribution). Babylonians threatened personal punishment. We will see in the next chapter if this is a distinction that is maintained in the rabbinic rhetoric on other non-marital forms of sexuality.

---

punishment, rather than children, is the preferred rhetoric when discussing intercourse between Jewish males and Gentile females, although in this instance this preference ruins any sense of parallelism.

4

Non-Marital Sex

The Hebrew Bible repeatedly and stridently condemns sexual contact between a man and a woman married to a different man. Prohibitions of "adultery" (לא תנאף) are found in the biblical legal codes, and the term is frequently used in prophetic writings as a metaphor for Israelite idolatry.[1] Pre-marital sexual contact, on the other hand, is hardly mentioned in the Hebrew Bible, and where it is it is always placed in a marital context, usually centering on the expectation that a woman would be a virgin at marriage.[2] The Hebrew Bible does not appear to link conceptually adultery and pre-marital sexual contact.

In the rabbinic period, however, a link between the two did exist. Although rabbinic and later Jewish (and even non-Jewish) writings devote more space to discussions of adultery than they do to pre-marital sexuality, these topics do share a fundamental characteristic: the control of female sexuality. Adultery represents more to the rabbis than a breach of God's command; it is also the "theft" of a woman's reproductive potential from her husband. Similarly pre-marital sex reflects poorly on the father, who is expected by the rabbis and his society to control his daughter's sexuality. In this chapter I explore the rhetorical strategies deployed to discuss both of these topics, and will attempt to show both

---

[1] See Ex. 20:14; Deut. 5:17; Lev. 20:10; Num. 5; Jer. 3:9, 5:7; Ezek. 23:37, 45. See further Michael Fishbane, *Biblical Interpretation in Ancient Israel* (New York: Oxford University Press, 1985) 169-70; Henry McKeating, "Sanctions Against Adultery in Ancient Israelite Society, with Some Reflections on Methodology in the Study of Old Testament Ethics," *Journal for the Study of the Old Testament* 1 (1979): 57-72.

[2] Deut. 22:13-29. Pre-marital sex might also be alluded to in some biblical uses of the term זנה, although this term often seems to refer to adultery or more general sexual promiscuity. For a discussion of this issue see below.

the great differences and the underlying similarities in their treatment by the rabbis.³

Rhetoric of Definition

Despite the heated biblical and rabbinic rhetoric that surrounds adultery, the rabbis – like the biblical authors – never explicitly define the term.⁴ Only by precisely defining marriage, thus allowing a man to identify "another man's wife," do the rabbis implicitly attempt to define what exactly adultery is.⁵ Underlying these definitions, however, is the assumption that adultery can occur only between a man (married or not) and a woman who is "married" to another man.⁶

The rabbis do attempt to define other forms of non-marital sexuality. Pre-marital sex is frequently subsumed under the rabbinic term bi'ilat znut. I conclude this section with a brief discussion of the rhetoric of the defining act of all forms of non-marital sex.

---

³Here I am indebted to, and enter into a dialogue with, Judith Romney Wegner, *Chattel or Person?* Romney Wegner argues that the mishnaic system treats women as "chattel *whenever this was necessary to establish or enforce the sexual rights of the man solely entitled to benefit from a woman's biological function,*" (171, original emphasis). Although her use of the term "chattel" has been justly criticized, this framework helps to clarify the non-mishnaic rabbinic rhetoric of adultery and pre-marital sexuality.

I do not here deal with concubinage because (1) there are very few rabbinic sources regarding intercourse with a concubine and (2) it is unclear if the rabbis would have regarded intercourse with a concubine as "non-marital." See Louis M. Epstein, "The Institution of Concubinage Among the Jews," *Proceedings of the American Academy for Jewish Research* 6 (1935): 153-88, esp. 179-82. A new study of Jewish concubinage in the context of the Jewish family and in light of Greek and Roman sources is a desideratum.

⁴On adultery generally, see Lichtschein, *Die Ehe* 54-61; L. Epstein, *Sex Laws* 194-234; Haim Cohn, "Adultery," *Encyclopedia Judaica* 2:313-16; Adolf Büchler, "Die Strafe der Ehebrecher in der nachexilischen Zeit," *MGWJ* 55 (1911): 196-219.

⁵Within the *Mishnah* and Palestinian and Babylonian Talmuds much of the tractates *Yebamot, Gittin,* and *Qiddushin* are devoted to establishing the definition of marriage. Women too are frequently held responsible for knowledge of their marital status: under *mishnaic* law she may, for example, lose her marriage settlement if she marries a man while mistakenly believing that her husband is dead *(m. Yebam.* 5. See also *y. Yebam.* 10:1, 10c).

⁶It is interesting to note that this rhetoric differs fundamentally from the idea offered by Jesus that a man can commit adultery against his own wife. See Mark 10:11-12 (the parallels to this, Luke 16:18 and Matt. 5:32, leave out the critical phrase: μοιχᾶται ἐπ' αὐτήν). See further C.G. Montefiore, ed., *The Synoptic Gospels,* 2 vols. (New York: Ktav, 1968) 1:233-34.

It has been argued that CD 4:20-5:2, which prohibits marriage to two women "in their (masc.) lifetime," also prohibits serial monogamy. More likely, however, it bans polygamy. See Geza Vermes, "Sectarian Matrimonial Halakhah in the Damascus Rule," *Journal of Jewish Studies* 25 (1974): 197-202.

Non-Marital Sex

B'ILAT ZNUT

Most other forms of non-marital sexual activity are subsumed under the rabbinic term *b'ilat znut*. The term is not used in the Bible, although the root *znh* alone does refer to the Bible to various, though usually unspecified, sexual activities and liaisons.[7] The biblical *zōnah*, always female, is a prostitute. In rabbinic usage, activities termed *b'ilat znut* usually fall into one of two categories, non-marital intercourse or non-procreative intercourse.

Non-Marital Intercourse

Various tannaitic sources attempt to define *b'ilat znut*. The sexual liaisons that comprise *b'ilat znut* are: intercourse between a levir and his levirate widow when one of them is infertile;[8] intercourse between a man and a "wife" to whom he pledged less than the minimum marriage settlement;[9] intercourse between a man and a woman whom he captured in war but did not properly follow the laws governing her treatment;[10] and intercourse not for the sake of marriage (see below).[11] While these liaisons are diverse, they all concern non-marital liaisons. That is, in the cases of sexual contact between both a man and a woman to whom he pledged a substandard marriage settlement and of a man with his captive "wife," he never fully effected the marriage, hence all acts of intercourse are termed *b'ilat znut*. A similar logic underlies application of the term to the levirate marriage. Intercourse within improperly formed levirate unions is stigmatized.

The application of the term *b'ilat znut* to pre-marital intercourse is derived from a scriptural source that addresses itself to priests:

A. "Do not degrade [or, profane[your daughter and make her a whore (*zōnah*)...," [Lev. 19:29 – is it possible that a man should not give her to a Levite and not give her to a non-priest [i.e., is this what is meant by "do not degrade your daughter"]? Scripture says, "to make her a whore."

B. I said only that "degradation" is for the sake of *znut*. And what is this? This is one who gives his unmarried daughter to his fellow not for the sake of marriage.

C. Similarly, if she gives herself not for the sake of marriage.[12]

---

[7]On *znut* in the bible, see, S. Loewenstamm, "זנות, זנונים," *Encyclopedia Biblica* 2:935-37.
[8]*m. Yebam.* 8:5.
[9]*m. Ketub.* 5:1.
[10]*Sifre Deut.* 213 (p. 247).
[11]*Sifra Qod.* 7 (90d); *Sifra Emor* 1:7 (94b).
[12]*Sifra Qod.* 7 (90d).

According to the rabbis, Lev. 19:29 defines "profanation" (a term that more typically refers to the association of priests with non-priestly things) of one's daughter with making her a "whore." (B) defines what it means to make one's daughter a whore: to allow a man non-marital sexual access to her. Similarly, (C) states that if a woman has pre-marital sex she renders herself a *zōnah*. The pericope moves from penalization of a *priest* who actively prostitutes his daughter to penalization of any man who has not adequately controlled the sexuality of his daughter. That is, (C) leaves open the possibility that if a woman, on her own initiative, has non-marital intercourse with a man, that her father might be held responsible for violation of Lev. 19:29. In any case, her status as a *zōnah*, rendering her forbidden to marry a priest, could cause both status and monetary loss to her father.

This same sentiment is echoed a few pages later: "Rabbi Eleazar says, even an unmarried man who has intercourse with an unmarried woman not for the sake of marriage [engages in *bĩilat znut*]."[13] This statement is cited three times in the Yerushalmi, and in each case is introduced as a tannaitic source and considered authoritative.[14] The Bavli cites a modified version of this tradition seven times: "Rabbi Eleazar says, even an unmarried man who has intercourse with an unmarried woman not for the sake of marriage renders her a *zōnah*."[15] Unlike the Yerushalmi's version, the Bavli's version never introduces Rabbi Eleazar's dictum as tannaitic.[16] Moreover, the dictum is almost always cited in the Bavli as counter-normative, and is frequently directly refuted. Pre-marital sex *per se* does not, in the Bavli, qualify as *bĩilat znut*.

This same difference between Palestinian and Babylonian sources can be seen in their treatment of the *mishnah* in which Rabbi Meir states that intercourse with any virgin wife who receives a marriage settlement of less than the minimum (200 zuz) is *bĩilat znut*. The Yerushalmi understands this to refer to a concubine: "What is a wife and what is a concubine? Rabbi Meir says, a wife has a *ketubah* and a concubine does not have a *ketubah*."[17] This statement is paralleled in Greek (especially) and Roman sources, which distinguish a wife from a concubine precisely

---

[13] *Sifra Emor* 1:7 (94b).
[14] *y. Yebam.* 6:5, 7c; 7:5, 8b; 13:1, 13b.
[15] *b. Yebam.* 59b, 61b (2), 76a; *b. Sanh.* 51a; *b. Tem.* 29b, 30a.
[16] The other difference, substituting "he renders her a *zōnah*" for "engages in *bĩilat znut*" is minor. Participation in *bĩilat znut* would, by definition, render her a *zōnah*. It is possible, though, that a goal behind this change is to shift the focus to the woman rather than the activity in order to integrate the dictum more smoothly into the *sugyot*, many of which are directly addressed to the status of the woman.
[17] *y. Ketub.* 5:2, 29d.

Non-Marital Sex 123

by the economic protection accorded to the wife.[18] Intercourse with a concubine, according to the Yerushalmi's interpretation of Rabbi Meir's statement, could qualify as *bĩ'ilat znut*.

The Bavli, on the other hand, cites opinions attested in no tannaitic corpus from Rabbi Yosi and Rabbi Yehudah that a marriage in which the husband has pledged less than the rabbinically determined minimum marriage settlement is permitted and, presumably, not *bĩ'ilat znut*.[19] The Bavli's *sugya* continues with a discussion of the logical consistency of these arguments, without any reference to concubinage. By first offering opinions to counter R. Meir's opinion as expressed in the *Mishnah*, and then by ignoring the assumptions that appear to underlie this opinion (at least according to the Yerushalmi), this *sugya* appears unwilling to term such a liaison as *bĩ'ilat znut*.

Non-Procreative Intercourse

There is a disagreement in the *mishnah* over the identity of the *zōnah*. According to R. Yehudah, a *zōnah* is an infertile woman, but according to the Sages she is a woman who has had, or is suspected of having engaged in, *bĩ'ilat znut*. The Bavli attempts to reconcile these opinions:

A. [*Mishnah:*] Rabbi Yehudah says, although he [a priest] has a wife and children, he cannot marry an *'ilonit* [congenitally infertile woman], because she is a *zōnah* of the type mentioned in the Torah. The Sages say, *zōnah* refers only to a proselyte woman, a freed female slave, and one who had been *bĩ'ilat znut*.

B. ...Rav Huna [BA 2] said, what is the reason of R. Yehudah? As it is written, "Truly they shall eat, but not be sated, they shall fornicate,

---

[18]See Sarah B. Pomeroy, *Goddesses, Whores, Wives, and Slaves* (New York: Schocken Books, 1975) 62-63; Susan Treggiari, "Concubinae." See also David Konstan, "Between Courtesan and Wife: Menander's *Perikeiromen*," *Phoenix* 41 (1987): 122-39. This is not to ignore potentially large differences between R. Meir's statement and these parallels. In the Greek world, it was the absence of a *dowry* that was used by orators to prove that the relationship in question was one of concubinage rather than marriage. The "marriage settlement" *(ketubah)* referred to by R. Meir might refer to a dowry, though the word is more usually employed to refer to a sum of money from her husband or his estate due to her on the termination of the marriage. See Michael Satlow, "Reconsidering the Rabbinic *ketubah* Payment," in *The Jewish Family of Antiquity*, ed. Shaye J.D. Cohen (Atlanta: Scholars Press, 1993) 142-44.

[19]*b. Ketub.* 56b. The Yerushalmi's connection between concubinage and the lack of economic protection is paralleled in a tradition in *b. Sanh.* 21a recorded in the name of Rav as told by Rav Yehudah. The context is entirely different, and the tradition is cited almost in passing. Considering Rav's strong connection with Palestine, it still appears likely that this attitude was mainly confined to Palestine.

but not increase," [Hos. 4:10][20] – every act of intercourse that is not for procreation is an act of *bĕ'ilat znut*.

C. But is it not taught: *zōnah* [stated in Scripture, what does this mean?] – this is a *zōnah*, as is her name [i.e., an adulteress],[21] these are the words of Rabbi Eliezer. Rabbi Akiba says, *zōnah* – this is a woman who makes herself "available." R. Matiah ben Harash says, even if her husband went to make her drink [for performance of the *sotah* ordeal] and had intercourse with her on the way [to Jerusalem] he renders her a *zōnah*. Rabbi Yehudah says, a *zōnah* – this is an *'ilonit*. And the Sages say, a *zōnah* is only a female proselyte, a freed female slave, and a woman engaged in *bĕ'ilat znut*. Rabbi Eleazar[22] says, an unmarried man who has intercourse with an unmarried woman not for the sake of marriage renders her a *zōnah*.[23]

D. ..."Rabbi Eleazar said a single man who has intercourse with a single woman not for the sake of marriage renders her a *zōnah*." Rav Amram[24] [BA 2 or 4] says, the law is not in accordance with R. Eleazar.[25]

This passage occurs in the midst of a discussion of a priest marrying a (pre-pubescent) girl. Rav Huna (B) interprets *bĕ'ilat znut* as referring to marital, non-procreative sex. (C) is attributed as tannaitic, and contains several competing definitions of the *zōnah*. (D) rebuts R. Eleazar's dictum.

The Babylonian contributions in (B) and (D) appear to interpret *bĕ'ilat znut* differently than do the tannaitic sources. Although R. Yehudah labels an *'ilonit* a *zōnah*, Rav Huna's statement goes beyond this, using Scripture to extend the concept of *bĕ'ilat znut* to all acts of non-procreative

---

[20]The verse reads, אכלו ולא ישבעו הזנו ולא יפרוצו. I have modified the *NJPS* translation.
[21]Following Rashi: "It means, 'straying' – straying from under the authority of her husband to other men, and according to R. Eliezer a *zōnah* is an adulteress."
[22]According to the printed edition, this is R. Eliezer, but parallels and manuscripts make it clear that the preferred reading here and in the subsequent mentions of his name is R. Eleazar.
[23]This *baraitha* has several manuscript variants. In several manuscripts, the order of the statements following R. Akiba's is different. First comes R. Yehudah's, followed by the Sages' and then R. Matiah ben Harash's. See *Tal. Bab.* 3.2:377.
[24]In a parallel in *b. Yebam.* 60a, this is the name of Rav, though "in the name of Rav" is missing in several manuscripts. See *Tal. Bab.* 3.2:354.
[25]*b. Yebam.* 61b.

Non-Marital Sex 125

intercourse. This opinion is echoed repeatedly in the Bavli.[26] Palestinian amoraim in the Yerushalmi also suggest such a labeling.[27]

Non-Rabbinic Parallels

Both Greek and Roman legal terminology are, to some extent, parallel to rabbinic use of *bi'ilat znut*. Although the Greek *moicheia* usually refers to adultery, it occasionally also refers to non-marital intercourse, such as the seduction of an unmarried woman.[28] The Roman term *stuprum* is slightly clearer. Beginning with Augustus' *lex Julia*, adultery was separated from other sexual crimes, the latter grouped together and subsumed under the term *stuprum*.[29] According to the *Digest*, "*Stuprum* is committed by someone who keeps a free woman for the sake of sexual relations not marriage, unless indeed she is a concubine...*stuprum* is committed with a widow, a virgin, or a boy."[30] *Stuprum*, then, is the term used to describe all non-sanctioned sexual behavior between a male and another person that was not adultery (*adulterium*).

The term *bi'ilat znut* is not found in any pre-rabbinic Jewish literature.[31]

Conclusions

Despite significant differences in the definitions of *stuprum* and *bi'ilat znut*, both label non-sanctioned, non-adulterous sexual liaisons. It is possible that early rabbinic sources used Roman legal terminology as a guideline for their own interpretations of *bi'ilat znut*. By forming the

---

[26]See for examples *b. Yebam.* 107a (intercourse with a minor); *b. Ketub.* 62b (reference to a man's sterile wife), 63a (reference to man's wife); *b. Sanh.* 76a (shifting a tannaitic source that discusses pimping to one condemning a man who marries off a daughter too young to procreate). See Chapter 6.
[27]*y. Yebam.* 6:5, 7c.
[28]See Aristotle *N.E.* 1134a, 19; 1138a, 25; *Rhetoric* 1375a; Demosthenes 59.65-7. See David Cohen, "The Athenian Law of Adultery," *RIDA*, 3d ser., 31 (1984): 147-65; Douglas M. MacDowell, "The Enforcement of Morals," *The Classical Review*, n.s. 42 (1992): 345-57. On μοιχεία generally, see Kurt Latte, "Μοιχεία," *P.W.* 15.2:2446-49.
[29]See Treggiari, *Roman Marriage* 278.
[30]*D.*48.5.35(34)-48.5.35(34).1 (ed. Watson, p. 814). See also *D.*48.5.6.1, which equates *stuprum* with φθορά. Cf. Philo *Spec. Laws* 3.65. On the Roman definition of *stuprum*, see now Angelika Mette-Dittmann, *Die Ehegesetze des Augustus: Eine Untersuchung im Rahmen der Gesellschaftspolitik des Princeps* (Stuttgart: Franz Steiner, 1991) 40-42. See also Pfaff, "Stuprum," *P.W.* 4A.1:423-24.
[31]The term *znut* alone is, of course, found in the Bible. Among the Dead Sea Scrolls there are four occurrences of the term *znut*; see James H. Charlesworth, *Graphic Concordance to the Dead Sea Scrolls* (Louisville: Westminster/John Knox, 1991) 249. None of these occurrences are biblical citations and none of them appear with any form of the root *b'l*. See *1QS* 1.6 and 4.10; *CD* 2.16, 19.17.

cognate *bĕ'ilat znut* from the biblical root *znh*, the Palestinian rabbis, beginning with the tannaim, succeeded in maintaining the conceptual grouping of sexual offenses that would have been known to them from Roman legal categories, while at the same time extending the appearance of biblical authority over a group of offenses that by and large have no biblical basis. So whereas the legal force of *bĕ'ilat znut* is limited to disqualifying a woman from marrying a priest, the assumptions and resonances encoded in the term, which include both the Roman *stuprum* and harlotry (to be discussed below), extend well beyond the confines of legal application. Like the Roman use of *stuprum*, the Rabbis used *bĕ'ilat znut* as a linguistic control of (especially female) sexuality.[32]

Later rabbinic sources, perhaps unfamiliar with the legal terminology, extended the scope of *bĕ'ilat znut* to include non-procreative intercourse.

Defining Act

According to almost all rabbinic sources, sexual intercourse is the act that constitutes adultery. Most rabbinic rhetoric on this issue occurs in rabbinic discussions of the *soṭah*.[33] The *soṭah* is a woman suspected by her husband of having an adulterous relationship:

> If any man's wife has gone astray and broken faith with him in that a man has had carnal relations with her unbeknown to her husband, and she keeps secret the fact that she has defiled herself without being forced, and there is no witness against her – but a fit of jealousy comes over him and he is wrought up about the wife who has defiled herself; or if a fit of jealousy comes over one and he is wrought up about his wife although she has not defiled herself – the man shall bring his wife to the priest...[34]

This passage is followed by a lengthy description of the *soṭah* ordeal, in which the suspected woman must drink a liquid that will "test" her, punishing her if guilty and rewarding her if not.

In order for a man to accuse his wife of adultery witnesses must testify that she was previously warned not to spend time with that man, and that she was secluded with him for enough time for them to "have had sex":

> A. How does he warn her regarding his jealousy? If he says to her before two [witnesses]: Don't speak with a certain man, and she

---

[32] See Fantham, "Stuprum," and on Roman sexual invective generally Richlin, *Garden of Priapus*.
[33] Throughout this chapter I return to the topic of the *soṭah*. Here I deal only with traditions relevant to defining the act necessary for "adultery."
[34] Num. 5:11-15.

speaks with him – she is still permitted to her house and to eat the *terumah* [if she is the wife of a priest].

B. If she enters with him to a clandestine place, and stays with him for enough time for defilement – she is forbidden from her house and from eating *terumah*...[35]

What does it mean by "enough time for defilement" (כדי טומאה)? For whatever this means, it defines the act of adultery. The *Tosefta* explains,

A. How much [time is necessary for] "defilement?" Enough time for intercourse.

B. How much [time is necessary for] intercourse? Enough time for the first stage of intercourse (העראה).

C. How much [time is necessary for] the first stage of intercourse? R. Leazar says, enough time for going around a palm tree. R. Yehoshua says, enough time for mixing the cup. Ben Azzai says, enough time for mixing the cup and drinking it. R. Akiba says, enough time to roast an egg. R. Yehudah ben Petirah says, enough time to swallow three eggs in a row. R. Leazar ben Yermiah says, enough time as a weaver needs to knot a fringe. Hanan ben Pinhas says, enough time for her to put her finger into her mouth. Pelimo says, enough time for her to put her hand [into] and take a loaf from the basket. Although there is no proof to this there is a hint for the matter, as it is written, "The last loaf of bread will go for a whore...," [Prov. 6:26].[36]

According to (A) and (B), a married woman who is first warned not to seclude herself with a particular man and then is witnessed secluding herself with that man for enough time for them to begin the act of sexual intercourse, even if it is not enough time for him to ejaculate, must undergo the ordeal. (C) can be read on two levels. If read literally, as it is commonly interpreted, then it is a gloss on (B), specifying almost hyper-literally the amount of time that it takes to commence intercourse. What appears more likely to me, however, is that this passage is meant euphemistically. The activities specified are hardly helpful in determining a precise amount of time. Each of the activities is sexually suggestive: the palm tree might represent a penis; the word "cup" (כוס) both as an image and by virtue of its similarity to the word for "vessel, cavity" (כיס) is evocative of a vagina; and the use of food imagery, both in rabbinic and Hellenistic and Roman sources, is often identified with sex. "Finger," "mouth," and "basket" are all sexually evocative. While it would be difficult, if not impossible, to identify precisely what activities this passage might be alluding to, it is likely that it is not meant to be

---

[35]*m. Soṭ.* 1:2.
[36]*t. Soṭ.* 1:2. See the shortened parallel to (C) at *Sifre Num.* 7 (p. 12) and on this, Lieberman, *Tos. Kip.* 8:610. See also *y. Soṭ.* 1:2, 16c, ; *b. Soṭ.* 4a.

taken literally. If this reading is correct, then (C) disagrees with (B), specifying that activities other than actual insertion of the penis would make a woman liable for the ordeal. Even if, however, this is the correct reading, it is clear that later sources prefer the first alternative: adultery is defined by intercourse.

According to both Talmudim too the defining act is sexual intercourse. The Yerushalmi, citing a tradition attributed to Rabbi Yoḥanan, reads the participants in (C) as referring to their own experiences: the images represent the amount of time necessary for each of these rabbis to begin intercourse.[37] In another passage in the Yerushalmi, a particularly harsh mishnaic rule that says that a woman seen talking with a man in the market is suspected of having intercourse with that man is reinterpreted to be referring from the beginning to intercourse: "What is 'talking?' She had intercourse. Then why does it teach 'talking?' It is a euphemism."[38] Adultery occurs only upon sexual penetration.

Similarly, in the Bavli the redactor both includes and then questions the need for the *Tosefta's* tradition on the amount of time that a woman must spend secluded with a man in order to make her liable for the *soṭah* ordeal. While the redactor of course does find reasons for the verbosity of the tradition, the definitional premise is taken for granted.[39] This underlying assumption is also displayed in statements attributed to Babylonian amoraim and on the redactorial level of the Bavli: "Does God forbid simple licentiousness?" Abaye asks. The answer, according to the redactor, is no.[40] Intercourse, not "simple licentiousness," is the crucial act.

Non-Rabbinic Parallels

The Romans also defined the adulterous act. In the *Digest*, there are repeated references to a woman and her lover being caught "in the act" – this is defined as referring to intercourse.[41] Jesus, on the other hand,

---

[37] *y. Soṭ.* 1:2, 16c.
[38] *y. Ketub.* 1:8, 25c.
[39] *b. Soṭ.* 4a-b. The way in which the Bavli reports this tradition further testifies to the literalness with which this tradition is read. After almost each clause of this tradition the redactor inserts questions of Babylonian amoraim who try to understand exactly how much time is signified by each of these activities.
[40] *b. Soṭ.* 26b; *b. Yebam.* 55b.
[41] See, for example, *D.*48.5.24 (23), attributed to Ulpian: "*Quod ait lex 'in filia adulterum deprehenderit,' non otiosum videtur: voluit enim ita demum hanc potestatem patri competere, si in ipsa turpitudine filiam de adulterio deprehendat. Labeo quoque ita probat, et Pomponius scripsit* in ipsis rebus Veneris *deprehensum occidi: et hoc est quod Solo et Draco dicunt ἐκ ἔργωι.*" Note, though, that this definition is given in the context of when a man is allowed to kill his daughter for adultery.

Non-Marital Sex

appears to see divorce as adultery and strongly implies a link between lustful thoughts and adultery.[42] Neither ever acquire in rabbinic rhetoric the appellation "adulterer."

Definitions of the act in other forms of non-marital sexual activity are not discussed,to my knowledge, in other Jewish, Christian, Hellenistic or Roman literature.

Rhetoric of Categorization

Rabbinic categorization of non-marital sexual liaisons closely follows those categories specified in the Bible. For adultery, these divisions include intercourse with a betrothed woman or a married woman; adultery (or pre-marital sex) with a priest's daughter or a non-priest's daughter; and the authority (father's or husband's) the woman is under at the time of the adulterous liaison. The scant categorical rhetoric employed in discussion of other non-marital liaisons, which centers on the seduced or raped virgin, is again biblically determined.

INTERCOURSE WITH A MARRIED OR BETROTHED WOMAN

"Do not commit adultery," the Bible declares, apparently referring to intercourse with a married woman.[43] According to biblical law, adultery warrants the death penalty for both the adulterer and the adulteress (Lev. 20:10). The Bible distinguishes "adultery" (designated by the root נאף) from intercourse with a betrothed girl:

> In the case of a virgin who is engaged to a man – if a man comes upon her in town and lies with her, you shall take the two of them out to the gate of that town and stone them to death: the girl because she did not cry for help in the town and the man because he violated another man's wife...[44]

Although the wording is different, here using the phrase "violated another man's wife" (ענה את-אשת רעהו) for the more succinct "adultery," the action is similar. This tension, between the apparent similarity of the acts and the difference of the wording, finds expression in the rabbinic sources.

The main form by which this division is expressed is the type of death penalty for which transgressors are liable. Deut. 22:24 specifies stoning for the betrothed girl and her lover; Lev. 20:10 does not specify the type of death penalty incurred through adultery. Correspondingly, the *Mishnah* specifies a penalty of stoning for the betrothed girl and her

---

[42]Matt. 5:27-30.
[43]Ex. 20:13; Deut. 5:17; Lev. 20:10.
[44]Deut. 22:23-24. On this law and its parallel, Ex. 22:15-16, see Moshe Weinfeld, *Deuteronomy and the Deuternomic School* (Oxford: Oxford University Press, 1973) 284-88.

lover and strangulation – the standard death penalty applied by the rabbis to those transgressions for which the Bible proscribes a death penalty but fails to specify which one – for the adulterers.[45] Following Lev. 18:29, the rabbinic sources also prescribe extirpation for the adulterer, but not for the man who has intercourse with a betrothed girl.[46]

On the *mishnah* dealing with the betrothed girl, the Yerushalmi focuses on the age of the girl (discussed below), and offers no commentary on the *mishnah* dealing with intercourse with a married woman.[47] The Bavli appears to accept the tannaitic categories without comment: only when dealing with more complicated conflicts (e.g., a betrothed daughter of a priest, who crosses several categories) does the Bavli offer discussion.[48]

In Roman law, intercourse with a betrothed woman is called adultery: no separate legal category exists for it.[49]

Woman, Maiden, Minor

Deut. 22:23, which deals with the betrothed girl, uses the phrase נער בתולה מארשה, literally, "a girl, virgin, betrothed." Regardless of how this phrase may have been meant, the rabbis seize upon the term *na'ara*, a girl or maiden, which in even early rabbinic law has a very precise and narrow meaning: a woman who is between 12 years and a day old and 12 years and six months old.[50] The force of this interpretation is to severely limit the applicability of the biblical law:

> A. One who has intercourse with a betrothed maiden is only liable when she is a *na'ara*, a virgin, and betrothed, and when she is in the house of her father.
>
> B. If two men have intercourse with her – the first [is sentenced to] stoning, and the second to strangulation.[51]

All three attributes are necessary for the penalty of stoning to apply. This is illustrated in (B): the first man is to be stoned because he had intercourse with a betrothed virgin between twelve and twelve and a half

---

[45] *m. Sanh.* 7:4 (betrothed woman with a partial parallel at *b. Yoma* 82a); *m. Sanh.* 11:1 (married woman). Death by strangulation for an adulterer is assumed in *Mekh. Mishpatim* 4 (pp. 261-62). One tanna, R. Shimeon, appears to dissent, prescribing burning for a betrothed woman who had intercourse with a man other than her husband (*t. Sanh.* 12:2).
[46] *m. Ker.* 1:1.
[47] *y. Sanh.* 7:114, 25c.
[48] See *b. Sanh.* 59b-51b.
[49] See *D*.5.14(13).3. The law changes under Constantine. See *CTh* 3.5.4-6.
[50] See *m. Nid.* 5:7.
[51] *m. Sanh.* 7:9. See also *Sifre Deut.* 242 (p. 272).

years old, but the second is strangled because she is no longer a virgin, hence comes under the law of adultery. Similarly, intercourse with a betrothed woman over (or under) twelve and a half would make one liable for a charge of adultery rather than one of intercourse with a betrothed maiden.

The Yerushalmi and the Bavli differ in their use of the category of age. A *sugya* in the Yerushalmi cites Palestinian sources that eliminate the qualification that the law of the betrothed maiden applies only to a *na'ara*.[52] Significantly, the Babylonian amoraim cited in this *sugya* disagree, maintaining the use of this age category. The Bavli too maintains the limitation of the law of the betrothed maiden to the *na'ara*.[53]

AUTHORITY

Rabbinic sources are also concerned about whose authority the woman is under at the time of her "adulterous" action. The *Mishnah* clearly applies the law of the betrothed maiden only when the incident occurs while she is still living in her father's house.[54] Although not cited, the scriptural basis for this limitation appears to be Deut. 22:20-21, which specifies that a woman who was found to be a non-virgin on her wedding day was to be stoned by her father's house, because the incident occurred while under her father's authority. The *Tosefta* specifies that the law of the betrothed *na'ara* does not apply if she is in the house of her husband.[55] Both the Yerushalmi and the Bavli take this categorization for granted.[56] Although the Bavli more explicitly uses this category to limit applicability of the law of the betrothed maiden (as it did with the issue of age), both Talmudim accept with little comment the tannaitic categories.

In Roman law, "authority" is not particularly relevant or discussed. Even when married, a woman had a fair degree of contact with her own family, and her father continued to hold a right even stronger than her husband to kill her and her lover if he caught them committing adultery (if she was married *sine manu*).[57]

PRIEST'S DAUGHTER

The Bible gives special attention to the priest's daughter: "When the daughter of a priest defiles herself through harlotry, it is her father

---

[52]*y. Ketub.* 3:9, 27d (par. *y. Sanh.* 7:15, 25c). See also *y. Ketub.* 3:3, 27c.
[53]*b. Sanh.* 66b. See also *b. Ketub.* 40b, 48b.
[54]*m. Sanh.* 7:9. See also *m. Sanh.* 11:6.
[55]*t. Sanh.* 10:8-9.
[56]See the discussions at *y. Sanh.* 7:15, 25c; *b. Sanh.* 66b.
[57]See *D.*48.5.21(20)-25(24); Sarah B. Pomeroy, "The Relationship of the Married Woman to Her Blood Relatives in Rome," *Ancient Society* 7 (1976): 215-27.

whom she defiles; she shall be put to the fire," (Lev. 21:9). The punishment of burning for a priest's daughter who commits "harlotry" is accepted in the tannaitic sources.[58] Another tannaitic tradition defines the "harlotry" of a priest's daughter s adultery.[59]

Both the Yerushalmi and the Bavli use this category as a didactic device. In discussions of the adulterous priest's daughter all the categories mentioned above are applied and synthesized.[60]

The non-applicability of the punishments detailed in these passages is underscored by two sources that specifically refer to the burning of a priest's daughter who commits adultery. Both of these sources condemn the application (or method of application) of this punishment.[61] For the rabbis, these are biblically determined didactic categories, not judicial guidelines.

SEDUCTION AND RAPE

As already mentioned, most of the rabbinic discussion of non-adulterous, non-marital sex falls into the undifferentiated terms *znut*, and occasionally, *'arayot*. The Bible, however, does treat as distinct two forms of non-marital intercourse, rape and seduction:[62]

> If a man seduces a virgin for whom the bride-price has not been paid, and lies with her, he must make her his wife by payment of the bride-price. If her father refuses to give her to him, he must still weigh out silver in accordance with the bride-price for virgins.[63]

> If a man comes upon a virgin who is not engaged and seizes her and lies with her, and they are discovered, the man who lay with her shall pay the girl's father fifty [shekels of] silver, and she shall be his wife. Because he has violated her, he can never have the right to divorce her.[64]

Both of these deal only with the case of a non-married woman, mandating payment of a fine or bride-price to the woman's father.[65] Rape differed in that the rapist also had to marry the woman he raped,

---

[58]*m. Sanh.* 9:1.
[59]*Sifra Emor* 1:15 (94c); *Sifre Deut.* 240 (p. 271). See also *m. Sanh.* 9:3.
[60]See *y. Ter.* 7:2, 44d; *y. Ketub.* 3:9, 27d; *b. Sanh.* 59b-51a, 66b.
[61]*m. Sanh.* 7:2; *b. Sanh.* 52b. The former, attributed to a pre-70 C.E. sage, is cited in order to refute the Sadducean method of punishment by burning. The latter records application of the punishment by Rav Hama bar Tuviya, only to condemn it.
[62]Note that some scholars maintain that these two passages refer to the same law. See Moshe Weinfeld, *Deuteronomy and the Deuternomic School* 284-88. As I will show, the rabbis read these passages as referring to two separate scenarios.
[63]Ex. 22:15-16.
[64]Deut. 22:28-29.
[65]On these passages, see L. Epstein, *Sex Customs* 181-83.

without the option of divorce. In a very literal way the rabbis maintain this distinction.

Two major themes run through the rabbinic discussion of the categories of rape and seduction, which are often treated together.[66] The first is a highly developed, and not unexpected, rhetoric of categorization. The age of the raped or seduced woman and the identity of the man who had authority over her at the time of her rape or seduction are important issues in these discussions.[67] The second major theme is that of the monetary damages for which the rapist or seducer is liable. The tannaitic sources very clearly focus on the monetary penalties for these activities.[68]

Tannaitic literature also considers two non-biblically specified issues. As noted in Chapter 2, tannaitic literature discusses the repercussions that rape, seduction, and the offspring of these unions might have on the laws dealing with incest.[69] Tannaitic sources also consider the effects of rape and seduction on a woman's eligibility to marry a priest.[70]

In all of these discussions, rape and seduction are considered in tandem and apply only to pre-marital sex. The tannaim conceptualized the "rape" of a married woman entirely differently from that of a non-married woman: a list, for example, of the three people that one is allowed to kill to "save them" from sin includes a man who is trying to kill a fellow man and a man attempting to rape a male or a betrothed woman.[71] Rape of married women, because outside of the biblical rape/seduction categories, is not considered here. Rape and seduction threaten, in the Bible, to deprive a father of the economic benefit of the *mohar*, or bride-price. Although the custom of bride-price had ceased by the rabbinic period, these biblically determined categories persisted.[72]

With a single exception, the Talmudim adhere closely to the tannaitic rhetoric on rape and seduction.[73] The Talmudim – primarily the redactor

---

[66]See ibid., 201.
[67]See *Mekh. Mishpat* 17 (pp. 307-9); *Sifre Deut.* 244 (pp. 273-75).
[68]*m. Ketub.* 3:1-4; 6; 9; 4:1; *m. Bekh.* 7:7; *m. Shebu.* 5:4; *m. Sheb.* 10:2; *m. Sanh.* 1:1; *t. Ketub.* 3:6-7; 4:1; 12:6; *t. Shebu.* 3:16; *t. Ark.* 2:10; *Mekh. Mishpatim* 17 (p. 308); *Sifre Deut.* 245 (p. 275); *Sifra Vayokra* 12:9 (28b), 12:11 (28b).
[69]*m. Yebam.* 11:1; *t. Yebam.* 3; *t. Sanh.* 10:2; 12:1; *Sifra Qod.* 9:15 (92c).
[70]*m. Yebam.* 7:5; *m. Ketub.* 1:10; *m. Ark.* 3:4; *t. Yebam.* 8:3; *Sifre Deut.* 215 (p. 248).
[71]*m. Sanh.* 8:7.
[72]See also *Sifra Emor* 11 (94a) and *Sifre Deut.* 244 (pp. 273-75) for midrashim explicitly limiting the application of these categories to unmarried women.
[73]Incest: *y. Yebam.* 1:1, 2c; 2:3, 3d; 3:2, 4d; 11:1, 1c-d; *y. Sanh.* 9:1, 26d; *y. Ketub.* 3:1, 27a (par. *y. Meg.* 1:8, 71a; *y. Ter.* 7:1, 44d); *b. Yebam.* 5a, 9b, 10a, 97a; *b. Sanh.* 58a, 76a, 87b; *b. Ker.* 3b.

Priesthood: *y. Yebam.* 6:2, 7b; 6:4, 7c; *y. Ketub.* 1:10, 25d; *y. Soṭ.* 1:2, 16c; *b. Yebam.* 56b; *b. Ketub.* 51b; *b. Ned.* 90b; *b. Soṭ.* 6a; *b. B. Batra* 145a.

of the Bavli – consider the effects of rape on a married woman. These discussions focus on whether or not she is permitted to return to her husband.[74]

Non-Rabbinic Parallels

In Greek and Roman, as well as Jewish-Hellenistic, writings rape and seduction were not viewed as having an equivalent valence. If rape was a violation of a woman and to some extent of the property of the *pater familias*, seduction was a violation of a family's honor. Seduction was seen as more insidious, threatening not only the "commodity" of a woman's virginity – which often could indirectly translate into economic gain for the family – but also the very connection of the daughter to her family.[75] Through elopement, for example, the daughter's family could lose the economic gain that could accrue through her, the possibility of political alliances of benefit to the whole family, and the honor that comes with efficient "shielding" of the family's females.[76]

In Jewish-Hellenistic sources, this attitude is reflected only in Ben Sira: "A daughter is a secret anxiety to her father, and the worry of her keeps him awake at night...when she is a virgin, for fear she may be seduced...," (Ben Sira 42:9-10). Seduction, not rape, is feared most. Other Jewish-Hellenistic sources either do not discuss this topic, or in the case of Philo, conflate both rape and seduction into a single category, "corruption."[77] This "corruption," Philo tells us, is akin to adultery but differs from it in that adultery effects many households, but that corruption effects only the woman, treating her "like servant-girls."[78] Philo here steers a middle course between the unity of the biblical categories and the difference, based in assumptions of honor and shame, perceived in Hellenistic and Roman society.

Monetary penalties: *y. Ketub.* 1:2, 25b; 3:1, 27a-b; 4:1, 28a-b; *y. Qidd.* 1:5, 60c; *b. Ketub.* 41a-42b; *b. Git.* 18a; *b. B. Qam.* 5b; *b. Qidd.* 11b (par. *b. Bekh.* 51a).
[74]*b. Yebam.* 33b; *b. Ned.* 90b-91a; *b. Ketub.* 26b-27a; 51b; *y. Soṭ.* 4:5, 19d.
[75]See for example Lysias, *On the Murder of Eratosthenes* 33-4. See Pomeroy, *Goddesses, Whores* 86.
[76]For examples from the Greek world, see Foucault, *The Use of Pleasure* 146; Kenneth J. Dover, "Classical Greek Attitudes to Sexual Behavior," reprinted in *Sexualität und Erotik in der Antike*, ed. Andreas Karsten Siems (Darmstad: Wissenschaftliche Buchgesellschaft, 1988) 267-69; David Cohen, *Law, Sexuality and Society: The Enforcement of Morals in Classical Athens* (Cambridge: Cambridge University Press, 1991) 99.

For Rome see Judith Evans-Grubb, "Abduction Marriage in Antiquity: A Law of Constantine (*CTh* 9.24.1) and Its Social Context," *Journal of Roman Studies* 79 (1989): 59-83.
[77]φθορά . See Philo *Spec. Laws* 3.65. He justifies this conflation and relates it to adultery by stating that they both derive from a single "mother," ἀκολασία.
[78]Ibid., and 3.69.

Only once, to my knowledge, in the rabbinic literature surveyed here does an equivalent distinction between rape and seduction appear, and then only in passing. One *sugya* in the Bavli cites Ben Sira 42:9-10 in a discussion on the ambivalent nature of women, especially wives.[79]

SUMMARY

The rabbinic rhetoric of categorization concerning non-marital sexual liaisons cleaves closely to the biblical categories. Hence, because, for example, Scripture uses only the categories of rape and seduction in discussions of pre-marital sexual activities, these are the only categories used in rabbinic sources to discuss these activities. All of these categories have legal import, and all are found in tannaitic sources. Neither the Bavli nor the Yerushalmi create their own categories, nor do they explicitly reject any of the tannaitic categories (although they may nullify their legal import). This rabbinic categorization has no substantial parallels to contemporary non-rabbinic rhetoric.

Rhetoric of Liability

Rabbinic rhetorics of liability focus concerning non-marital sex acts focus almost exclusively on adultery. These sources generally address one of three issues. First, they discuss which transgression(s) one is liable for when a single act can be defined as violating more than one law. The primary subject of these discussions is incest, especially with one's father's wife, which by definition is also adulterous.[80] The single area in which this kind of rhetoric is not applied to an adulterous relationship is the high priest, who can be held accountable for multiple transgressions stemming from a single act of intercourse.[81]

A second area of concern is assessing liability when more than one sex act has been committed within the same illicit relationship. To my knowledge, this rhetoric occurs only in reference to the *soṭah*, with whom each act of intercourse (by her husband) is accounted as a separate transgression.[82]

Finally, the discussions of the legal effects of age on adultery are of this type of rhetoric. According to the *Mishnah*, a woman begins her life as a sexual being, with full legal ramifications, at the age of three years and a day: "A girl three years and a day is betrothed by intercourse, and if a levir has intercourse with her, he acquires her. And others are liable

---

[79]*b. Sanh.* 100b. This passage is considered below.
[80]*m. Sanh.* 7:4; *m. Ker.* 3:5; *y. Sanh.* 7:8, 24d; *y. Yebam.* 3:12, 5a; *b. Yebam.* 32a-b; *b. Ker.* 14b; *b. Sanh.* 54a. See also Chapter 2.
[81]*t. Mak.* 4(3):9; *y. Sanh.* 9:9, 27b; *b. Qidd.* 77a.
[82]*t. Soṭ.* 2:4; *Sifra Qod.* 5:10 (89d).

on her account for [transgression of the law against] adultery..."[83] Because a woman can be legally married by intercourse at that age, those who have intercourse with a married girl who is three years and a day old or older are legally liable for adultery. This rule is assumed without further discussion throughout the rabbinic literature.

A physiological logic underlies discussion of male liability. According to tannaitic sources, neither a boy nor one who has intercourse with the wife of a boy can be held liable for adultery.[84] Because a boy is considered incapable of sexual intercourse, he is presumed to be unable to either commit adultery or to properly consummate his own marriage. This rule is justified through scriptural exegesis but it, like the *Mishnah's* rule about the three year old girl, appears to be based on physiological assumptions.

Rhetoric of Impurity

In the Hebrew Bible certain non-marital sexual liaisons were considered "impure" or defiling (טמא). An adulteress is termed "defiled," as is a woman who is divorced from her first husband, remarries, and then divorces her second husband and returns to her first husband.[85] The biblical use of this term is not entirely clear. It might, on the one hand, designate a ritual status, "defiled" as opposed to "pure." Alternatively, it might simply be another way of saying that she sinned.[86]

The term "defilement," as referring to a woman who has had non-marital intercourse, is used infrequently in rabbinic literature, and then almost only as an appropriation of the biblical terminology of the *soṭah*.[87] Even in these quotations, it is clear that "defilement" means "sin" rather

---

[83]*m. Nid.* 5:4. See also *y. Soṭ.* 1:2, 16c; 2:1, 17d.
[84]*Sifra Qod.* 9:11 (92a); *b. Qidd.* 19a; *b. Sanh.* 52b.
[85]Num. 5:13-14; Deut. 24:4. On the former, see Tikva Frymer-Kensky, "The Strange Case of the Suspected Sotah (Numbers V 11-31)," *Vetus Testamentum* 34 (1984): 11-26.
[86]For examples of this usage see Lev. 16:16, 30. See also Tikva Frymer-Kensky, "Pollution, Purification, and Purgation in Biblical Israel," in *The Word of the Lord Shall Go Forth: Essays in Honor of David Noel Freedman in Celebration of his Sixtieth Birthday*, ed. Carol L. Meyers and M. O'Connor (Winona Lake: Eisenbrauns, 1983) 399-413. Frymer-Kensky sees the force of טמא in sexual contexts as polluting the land, not simple ritual pollution or moral opprobrium (407-8).
[87]For examples see *m. Soṭ.* 1:5, 3:3; *m. Ned.* 11:12. In each of these examples, as with many of the uses of the term "defilement" in this context, the words are direct quotations attributed to women: "I am defiled," she says, meaning that she has committed adultery. I am not sure what the significance of this fact is. Perhaps "defilement" was used as a synonym in common speech for adultery, although, as I will show, it would have lost its overtones of "impurity" if, indeed, it ever had any.

than actual ritual impurity.[88] In the rabbinic period adultery did not belong to the sacred sphere of ritual purity.

"Harlotry," (*znut*) is, according to the Bible, defiling (Lev. 21:7). Never in rabbinic sources, to my knowledge, is "defilement" ever applied to those who engage in non-adulterous, non-marital sex.[89]

The absence of the application of a rhetoric of impurity applied to illicit sex would be entirely consistent with common Hellenistic and Roman rhetoric, which only rarely associates illicit sexual activity with impurity.[90] The only example of a rhetoric of purity in Jewish-Hellenistic writings is a statement in Jubilees that *fornication* defiles.[91] This intent of this passage might be similar to the rabbinic *bĕ'ilat znut*, which would prohibit the subsequent marriage of the female participant to a priest.

Rhetoric of Progeny

Because adultery can endanger certainty of paternity, hence inheritance and family continuity, one would expect a significant rhetoric to develop around the issues of children and paternity in relation to adultery. Surprisingly, this is not the case. Only a few sources directly address this issue. As with the sources of this type of rhetoric examined in Chapters 2 and 3, Palestinian and Babylonian sources use this rhetoric differently.

According to Palestinian sources, the child of an adulterous union is a *mamzer/et*. Because adultery is both a crime punishable by death and one of the *'arayot*, children of adulterous liaisons, according to two different opinions expressed in the *Mishnah*, would be *mamzerim*.[92] Other passages in the *Mishnah* more explicitly, though always in a strictly legal context, call the children of adulterous liaisons *mamzerim*.[93] There

---

[88] The absence of the element of ritual defilement from rabbinic use of the term טמא in connection to non-marital intercourse is evident in *m. Soṭ.* 3:3 states that if a woman, before being subjected to the *soṭah* ordeal in the Temple, says "I am defiled" then the ordeal ceases. *m. Soṭ.* 3:4 states that if she drinks and the potion begins to take effect she is ousted from the Temple for fear that she may defile it, presumably through her death. Death, in contrast to adultery, conveys real impurity, and the rhetoric of defilement that surrounds it is not an empty metaphor. A second example can be found in *b. Yebam.* 11a, where the relationship between defilement and prohibition is explicitly explored.

[89] For examples of sources that discuss this verse, see *b. Yebam.* 56b, 61b; *b. Soṭ.* 26a; *b. Qidd.* 77b.

[90] See Robert Parker, *Miasma;: Pollution and Purification in Early Greek Religion* (Oxford: Oxford University Press, 1983) 94. Adulteresses in Athens were barred from temples, but this appears to have been due to shame and dishonor rather than ritual impurity.

[91] *Jub.* 33:20 (ed. Charlesworth, 2:120).

[92] *m. Yebam.* 4:13; *m. Qidd.* 3:12.

[93] See *m. Yebam.* 10:1, 3; *m. Git.* 8:5.

appears to be no question in the Yerushalmi that a child of an adulterous liaison is considered a *mamzer/et*.[94] Several statements in the Bavli, on the other hand, and even one cited in the Yerushalmi in the name of a Babylonian amora, emphasize that the children of an adulterous woman are not only not considered *mamzerim*, but they are not even to be avoided or stigmatized.[95]

More striking is the difference between Palestinian and Babylonian sources on the children of a suspected adulteress. A tannaitic source declares that the children of suspected adulteress were still presumed to have been fathered by her husband.[96] The Yerushalmi attempts to give a reason: "...as Rabbi Yohanan [PA 2] said, a married woman who plays the whore, the children are credited to her husband because with him occurred the majority of acts of intercourse."[97]

The Bavli presupposes Rabbi Yohanan's opinion (but ascribed to R. Abahu [PA 3]) in the following *sugya*:

A. R. Amram asked, if she was a promiscuous woman (פרוצה), then what is the law [i.e., are her children still considered fit]?

B. According to the one who holds that a woman conceives only close to [i.e., right before] her period, it is not a good question because he does not know and cannot guard her.

C. Can you ask according to the one who holds that a woman conceives only close to [i.e., right after] her ritual immersion?

D. Because he knows he can guard her, or perhaps she is most licentious?

E. The matter remains unresolved.[98]

Can a "loose" woman, one who has intercourse more frequently with others than with her husband, be assumed to bear only the children of her husband? Underlying the redactorial commentary in (B) to (E) is an assumption that a man can watch his wife if she is suspected of adultery.[99] What matters here is the woman's fertile period. There were two opinions as to when a woman was fertile, either right before her period or immediately after his ritual immersion.[100] A husband could guard his "loose" wife more carefully during her fertile period. If, though, one thinks that a woman conceives only before her period, then

---

[94]See *y. Qidd.* 3:14, 64d. This passage was discussed in Chapter 3.
[95]See *b. Sot.* 26b-27a; *y. Sot.* 1:7, 17a.
[96]*t. Yebam.* 12:8.
[97]*y. Sot.* 1:7, 17a.
[98]*b. Sot.* 27a.
[99]This rhetoric, which deals with control of one's wife, will be considered below.
[100]See *b. Nid.* 31b.

because this time is unknowable (B), there can be no sufficient guarding. Even in the case of (C), if the woman is very licentious her husband perhaps could not guard her sufficiently (D). Hence, because ultimately one cannot totally control one's wife, the status of her children is open to question.

This passage is revealing. First, the redactor assumes that a man has more interest in his wife's extra-marital sexual interests when she is fertile. Second, in spite of this interest in the paternity of these children, the redactor fails to resolve the problem. That is, according to the logic of the position advanced by R. Abahu, children of a woman who had the majority of acts of intercourse with a man other than her husband should be legally penalized. The Bavli, however, refuses to pursue the discussion to this conclusion.

This reluctance on the part of the Bavli to penalize the children of non-marital sex is confirmed by the rhetoric concerning children of single mothers. According to the *Mishnah*, a child born of a single mother who does not now the identity of his or her father, is called a *shituki*, and is not allowed to marry a "fit" Jew.[101] The Yerushalmi does not comment on this rule, apparently accepting it. The Bavli, however, begins its discussion of this rule by citing Raba's [BA 4] opinion that in fact such a child is fit to marry any Jew, the assumption being that the father was fit for the mother. Two reasons are then offered by the redactor for the position of the *Mishnah*: (a) fear that man might accidentally marry his paternal sister, and (b) that the rabbis were particularly careful in matters of genealogy.[102] The first of these suggestions is rejected as unlikely. Although the *sugya* does not resolve the final law, there can be little doubt that the overall effect of the passage subverts the straightforward law of the *Mishnah*.

In sum, as with the incest restrictions, only the Palestinians use the status of children as a controlling device.[103] Curiously, however, it is only from the Bavli's redactor that we find a linkage between adultery and fear of paternity.

Rhetoric of Association

Rabbinic literature uses two general terms to group what the rabbis saw as sexual misdeeds, *'arayot* and *znut*. The former is primarily used to indicate sexual liaisons prohibited by Scripture, with special attention given to incest (see Chapter 2). Adultery too often gets lumped in this

---

[101] *m. Qidd.* 4:1-2.
[102] *b. Qidd.* 73a. See also *b. Qidd.* 75a.
[103] See also Ben Sira 23:22-27, which stigmatizes the children of adulterous relationships.

group, sometimes quite explicitly. *Znut*, discussed above, is a much vaguer grouping, roughly translating into "licentiousness," and usually indicates non-biblically prohibited sexual liaisons that are strongly condemned by the rabbis. It is thus important to note that when these terms occur in "vice catalogues," appearing in close proximity to other transgressions, the referent can be broader than, for example, simply adultery. The use of *znut* almost always refers to some kind of non-marital, non-adulterous sexuality, but here too there is often no specification of a single precise activity. In this section I review the deployment of these terms in their broader contexts, as well as marshaling the sources that more precisely associate non-marital sexual activities with other transgressions.

ADULTERY

While the term *'arayot* is commonly associated with idolatry and murder, occasionally, especially in the Bavli, the inclusion of adultery in the term *'arayot* is explicit.[104] These associations between adultery, murder, and especially idolatry continue in other contexts as well. In one tannaitic source murder, adultery, and idolatry are in passing grouped together as examples of capital crimes.[105] The *Mekhilta* forcefully uses the metaphor of adultery to refer to idolatry.[106] Following biblical usage, many rabbinic parables use adultery to represent idolatry.[107] The Bavli links adultery and murder in a word play.[108] This rhetoric echoes a commonplace of both Jewish-Hellenistic and early Christian writing.[109]

Association with Theft

Adultery is also associated with coveting and theft.

A. Why are faces [of men] different from each other? Because of the deceivers, so that everybody will not leap into [i.e., seize] the fields of his neighbor and have intercourse with the wife of his neighbor, as it is written, "Their light is withheld from the wicked, and the upraised arm is broken," [Job. 38:15].

---

[104]See *b. Pes.* 25a-b; *b. Yoma* 75a; *b. Sanh.* 38a, 57b; *b. Ḥul.* 23a. Statements attributed to tannaim and, in the Bavli, to Palestinian and Babylonian sources all occasionally employ the term *'arayot* to indicate adultery. Use of the term in the Yerushalmi is more indeterminate.
[105]*t. Shebu.* 3:4.
[106]*Mekh. Yitro Baḥodesh* (p. 233).
[107]See David Stern, *Parables in Midrash* (Cambridge: Harvard University Press, 1991) 171.
[108]*b. Shab.* 105a. It is attributed to a BA 3.
[109]See *Sib. Or.* 1:174-98 (ed. Geffcken, 14-15); *Test. Jacob* 7:19-20 (ed. Charlesworth, 1:379); *Test. Simon* 5:3 (ed. Charlesworth, 1:786); 1 Cor. 5:10-11; Acts 15:20. Haenchen thinks that this last passage refers only to incestuous relations, but a more general "fornication" is most likely meant (*Acts of the Apostles* 449).

Non-Marital Sex

B. R. Meir says, God changed [men's] faces, physical disposition, and voice. Face and physical disposition because of the violent men and the thieves, and voices because of the immorality (*'ervah*).[110]

This tradition carries an intriguing assumption, namely that women, like fields, are in some sense "property" of men, which can be "seized" by other men.[111] If all men had similar faces (A) or voices (B), they could deceive each other's wives and engage in adultery.[112] The connection between adultery and theft will emerge more clearly later in this chapter and in Chapter 7. This association is also common to Greek society, and is found in one Jewish-Hellenistic writer.[113]

Shame

Another association is that of adultery with shaming. In the middle of an extended passage discussing the evil of shaming another, the Bavli records this tradition:

A. ...As Rabbi Ḥanina [PA 1][114] said, all descend into Gehenna except for three.

B. Can you think "all?"

C. Rather, say, all those who descend to Gehenna rise [from there] except for three who descend and do not rise.

D. And these are: one who has intercourse with a married woman; one who shames his fellow in public; and he who calls his fellow by a nickname.[115]

Later in the same *sugya*, a tradition attributed to Rabbi Yoḥanan [PA 2] in the name of Raba bar bar Ḥanah [BA 3] states that it is better for a man to put himself into a situation where he is suspected of adultery rather than shame another in public. This is followed by a story attributed to Raba [BA 4] in which King David claims that the adulterer, although punished by death, has a share in the world-to-come, in contrast to one who shames another in public, who has no share in the world to come.[116]

---

[110]*t. Sanh.* 8:6. See also *y. Sanh.* 4:13 22b; *b. Sanh.* 38a. The Bavli's version is slightly different, but the association of theft and adultery is clear.
[111]See also *Sifra Aḥare* 13:10 (86a).
[112](B) seems to assume that intercourse takes place in the dark. See Chapter 7.
[113]See Philemon/Menander (ed. Charlesworth, 2:830). Zoroastrian sources appear to associate covert adultery with theft. See M. Shaki, "The Sassanian Matrimonial Relations," *Archiv Orientalni* 39 (1971): 343.
[114]According to MS Florence 7-8 I II, this reads "R. Yoḥanan" [PA 2].
[115]*b. B. Meṣ.* 58b. The order of the transgressions listed in (D) are different in some manuscripts. See *D.S.*9:161, n. ה. The translation of the last clause, המכנה, follows Jastrow 648, s.v., כנה, כני.
[116]*b. B. Meṣ.* 59a (par. *b. Sanh.* 107a).

Without doubt, one of the reasons for this association is to (over)emphasize the gravity of shaming another in public. Yet it is also possible that adulterer, and not for example murder or idolatry, was chosen as the foil for a reason. Modern anthropological studies have shown that a shame culture (always revolving at least in part around control of female sexuality) is a fundamental, if not the, characteristic of what they feel can be called "Mediterranean society."[117] This insight has been applied to aspects of both Greek and Roman society with success.[118] This same attitude informs these rabbinic traditions that associate adultery and public shaming. Committing adultery with another man's wife *is* a form of public shaming: her husband is shown to be unable either to satisfy or to control her sexually. The traditions themselves at once make the association and then break it, declaring that truly public humiliations, unlike adulterous liaisons which are presumably (at least in theory) kept less public, are even greater than the shame of the cuckold. If this reading is correct, then the force of these statements is further strengthened, for the message becomes that publicly humiliating a man is even worse than the shame of cuckolding him.

Support for this reading can be found in other traditions in the Bavli. One tradition, attributed to PA 1 or 2, associates pride with adultery.[119] A statement attributed to Rav Naḥman [BA 3] says that haughtiness leads to adultery.[120] This association between haughtiness and adultery is telling: it is not sexual lust, nor deep emotional attachment, nor mid-life crisis that is said to lead to adultery. Rather, adultery is seen as an

---

[117]See David D. Gilmore, "Introduction: The Shame of Dishonor," in *Honor and Shame and the Unity of the Mediterranean*, ed. David D. Gilmore (Washington, D.C.: American Anthropological Association, 1987) 10; and, "Honor, Honesty, Shame: Male Status in Contemporary Andalusia," in *Honor and Shame* 90-103; Maureen Giovannini, "Female Chastity Codes in the Circum-Mediterranean: Comparative Perspectives," in *Honor and Shame* 61-74; Stanley Brandes, "Reflections on Honor and Shame in the Mediterranean," in *Honor and Shame* 122; Bette S. Denich, "Sex and Power in the Balkans," in *Women, Culture and Society*, ed. Michelle Zimblast Rosaldo and Louise Lamphere (Stanford: Stanford University Press, 1974) 254-55.
[118]See especially D. Cohen, *Law, Sexuality, and Society;* Winkler, *Constraints;* Halperin, *Before Sexuality.* The connection between shame and adultery in Roman Egypt was noted by Sarah B. Pomeroy, *Women in Hellenistic Egypt: From Alexander to Cleopatra* (New York: Schocken, 1984) 98. For a short summary of the roles of honor and shame in the New Testament, see Joseph Plevnik, "Honor/Shame," in *Biblical Social Values and Their Meaning: A Handbook*, ed. John J. Pilch and Bruce J. Malina (Peabody, MA: Hendrickson, 1993) 95-104.
[119]*b. Soṭ.* 4b. The attributions are quite messy here, but all alternatives offered by the manuscripts appear to be Palestinian amoraim. See *Bab. Tal.* 2.1:34 and MS British Museum 406.
[120]*b. Ta'an.* 7b. The printed edition reads that he will succumb to עבירה. MS Munich 140 replaces this with אשה איש.

assertion of one's power over another man, the "theft" of the reproductive potential of his wife. Here is the expected "flip side" of the cuckolded husband. Rabbinic culture, of course, does not ascribe any honor to the adulterer – he is, in fact, said in this tradition to "fall" through his adultery – but underneath this tradition might lurk the assumption that the society revealed here maintains, like other Mediterranean societies, a zero-sum honor code.[121] When one man "takes" another's wife, the cuckold must lose honor. The rabbinic variation on this pervasive attitude is not that there is no shame, but that the adulterer does not gain in honor.[122]

The source-critical unlayering of these texts is particularly difficult. Babylonian amoraim and the redactor play active roles in these discussions. These sources then must a some level reflect a Babylonian outlook. Yet statements from Palestinian sources are cited in these *sugyot*. The problem is not so much in considering the attributed sources to be authentically Palestinian – these same views are after all also characteristic of non-Jewish antiquity – as in finding corroboration. To my knowledge, no source in any of these Palestinian rabbinic documents explicitly link shame or honor to adultery. Hence this discussion might also apply to Palestine, but more evidence would be necessary to make this case adequately.

The association between shame and adultery appears fleetingly in many other rabbinic discussions. Because the texts so rarely give us the coffee-house and bath-house gossip, the knowing glances and leers, our sight of the societies in which rabbinic cultures operated is overly corrected to legal and legislative issues. Thus, readings such as the one I offered might be difficult to accept. Yet adultery was clearly a more complex institution than the legal sources would allow. A series of stories from the Bavli demonstrates this:

> A. A certain man used to close himself and a woman in a house. The master of the house came, and the adulterer broke through the hedge [fence] and fled.[123]

---

[121]See Richlin *Garden of Priapus* 215-19.

[122]One of course must distinguish between genres of literature. In Rome, for example, legal codes do not give honor to the adulterer, although the epigrams and satires indicate that the adulterer did in fact achieve some degree of status in his society. See Amy Richlin, "Approaches to the Sources on Adultery at Rome," in *Reflections of Women in Antiquity*, ed. Helen P. Foley (1981; rpt. New York: Goren and Breach, 1984) 397.

[123]The text is garbled. I have followed the manuscript versions here. See *Bab. Tal.* 4.2:318-19, esp. n. 20.

B. Raba [BA 4, but maybe Rabah, BA 3] said, the woman is permitted [to return to her husband]. If he had committed some forbidden act, he would have hidden himself.

C. A certain adulterer came [to the house of] a certain woman. A man [her husband] came. The adulterer fled, and found himself in the guardhouse at the gate.[124] Cress was lying there, and a snake tasted it. The master of the house came to eat of this cress, without the knowledge of his wife. The adulterer said to him, do not eat from it because a snake tasted it.

D. Raba said, the woman is permitted [to her husband]. If he [this same adulterer][125] had committed some forbidden act, it would have been fine for him [the adulterer] to let him eat and die, as it is written, "For they have committed adultery, and blood is on their hands...," [Ezek. 23:37].

E. Is this not obvious?

F. You might think that he committed a forbidden act. He [the adulterer] told him [the husband] because it was fine with him [the adulterer][126] that the husband not die, so that the woman may be for him[127] "stolen waters are sweet, and bread eaten furtively is tasty," [Prov. 9:17]. Thus we are informed [otherwise].[128]

For a moment, the veil is lifted. These stories, told in Babylonian Aramaic and unparalleled in other rabbinic sources, reflect a society in which adultery did occur, in which even rabbis occasionally counseled the deliberate oversight of women's affairs, in which the concept of "forbidden love" was known. The text acknowledges that the men in (A) and (C) were adulterers, but Raba in both cases argues that the wife should remain permitted to her husband, based on an argument from human nature. "Forbidden love" is stolen love, love that properly "belongs" to the husband, an assumption that was discussed above. These texts cannot by themselves be used to assert that the Babylonian Jewish community was a promiscuous one. But they should heighten the reader's alertness to possible interpretations that go deeper than the strictly legal.

OTHER FORMS OF NON-MARITAL SEX

The Bible frequently uses harlotry, *znut*, as a metaphor for Israel's behavior vis à vis the Almighty. Unsurprisingly, this metaphor is picked

---

[124] The manuscripts give many alternatives to the place to which the adulterer fled. See *Bab. Tal.* 4.2:319-20, nn. 29-30.
[125] This phrase is found in several manuscripts. See *Bab. Tal.* 4.2:320, n. 38.
[126] Added in several manuscripts. See ibid., 321, n. 43.
[127] Some manuscripts replace this clause with the phrase: ... ותהא אנתתיה מנא עלויה 'כדכת. See ibid., 321, n. 44.
[128] *b. Ned.* 91b.

up in rabbinic writings, which often associates idolatry, the ultimate act of Israel's rejection of God, and *znut*. One of the fuller examples of this association is found in the Bavli, but incorporates ideas found in tannaitic sources. Discussing why the biblical passage on the fringes *(tzitzit)* is included among the biblical passages recited after recitation of the *Shema*, the Bavli responds:

A. Rav [sic] Yehudah bar Zivida [PA 3] said, because it [i.e., the passage] contains five things: going out from Egypt, commandment of the fringes, yoke of the commandments, sinful thought, and idolatrous thought.

B. It is understandable, the going out from Egypt and the commandment of the fringes – they are explicitly written. But the yoke of the commandments, sinful thought, and idolatrous thought, where do we learn them?

C. As. R. Yosef taught, "...look at it and recall all the commandments of the Lord and observe them..." – this is the yoke of the commandments.

D. "so that you do not follow your hearts" – this is heresy, and thus it says, "The benighted man thinks [lit. "says *in his heart*"], 'God does not care'," [Ps. 14:1].

E. "and eyes" – this is sinful thought, as it is said, "But Samson answered his father, 'Get me that one, for she is the one that pleases me [lit., "she is straight *in my eyes*"]," [Judges 14:2].

F. "you whore after them"[129] – this is idolatrous thought, and thus it says, "[The Israelites again] went astray *(zinu)* after the Baalim," [Judges 8:33].[130]

Selections (C) to (F) atomize Num. 15:39 in order to show how the passage refers also to the yoke of the commandments, the prohibition of even a sinful (i.e., sexual) thought, and the prohibition of even idolatrous thought. Looking at one's fringes is supposed to keep one from lust and idolatry.[131] The assertions are proved by recourse to other biblical verses that use similar phrases in clearer contexts. Many of the associations

---

[129]Modified from *NJPS*.

[130]*b. Ber.* 12b. This translation follows MS Paris 671, whose readings are confirmed in other manuscript versions. See *D.S.* 1:57. Note that even in this reading (D) is extraneous, and in fact indicates a *sixth* referent of the passage. The presence of (D) no doubt led to the modifications made to (A) in the printed edition.

[131]Below I survey a number of stories in which fringes are portrayed doing exactly that.

made in (C) through (F) are found in tannaitic sources.¹³² Other stories too associate *znut* with idolatry or heresy, usually in a rhetoric of the "other."¹³³

Witchcraft

Biblical and rabbinic texts associate women, witchcraft, and *znut*.¹³⁴ The connection between women, sexual license, and witchcraft is often implicit in these sources, although there are sources that explicitly link them. A parable tells of a woman afraid that her reputation will be tarnished by people thinking that she is either an adulteress or a witch.¹³⁵ "The Sages say, *znut* and witchcraft destroy the world," the *Mishnah* somewhat cryptically states.¹³⁶ This tradition is cited in the Yerushalmi, which also contains a tradition, cited below, linking discord, witchcraft, and *znut*.¹³⁷ Another well-known story in the Yerushalmi about Shimon ben Shetaḥ's slaying of seventy witches, recounts how Shimon ben Shetaḥ persuaded the witches to let into their coven a number of warriors who would kill them: he suggests that these men would give them "pleasure," which in this context has clearly sexual overtones.¹³⁸ To my knowledge, in the Bavli there is but a single tradition that links witchcraft and female sexual licentiousness.¹³⁹

Rhetoric of the Other

In all the sources, both adultery and *znut* are identified as characteristic of the "other," that is, Gentiles. These identifications are also almost always in the context of vice-catalogues. A passage in the

---

¹³²See *Sifre Num.* 115 (p. 126); *Sifra Aḥare* 9:8 (84a); *Sifra Qod.* 8:15 (91c). According to a tradition in the Yerushalmi, the entire ten commandments are contained in the passages recited after the Shema. See *y. Ber.* 10:8, 3c.
¹³³See *b. 'Abod. Zar.* 17a; *b. Sanh.* 106b.
¹³⁴See Ex. 22:17; *b. Qidd.* 49b; *b. 'Erub.* 65b; *b. Ber.* 53a; *b. Pes.* 110b; *b. Sanh.* 67a; 100b, and on this passage Jonas C. Greenfield, "Ben Sira 42.9-10 and its Talmudic Paraphrase," in *A Tribute to Geza Vermes*, ed. Philip R. Davis and Richard T. White (Sheffield: Sheffield Academic Press, 1990) 171. More generally, see Ludwig Blau, "Das altjüdische Zauberwesen," *Jahresbericht der Landes-Rabbinerschule in Budapest* (Budapest, 1898): 23-26.
The association of women and witchcraft is very common. For example see Sue Rollin, "Women and Witchcraft in Ancient Assyria (c. 900 – 600 B.C.)," in *Images of Women in Antiquity*, ed. Averil Cameron and Améile Kuhrt (Detroit: Wayne State University Press, 1985) 34-45.
¹³⁵*Sifre Deut.* 26 (p. 36-37).
¹³⁶*m. Soṭ.* 9:13.
¹³⁷*y. Soṭ.* 9:15, '4b; *y. Ta'an.* 4:5, 69a. See also *y. Ta'an.* 4:8, 69a.
¹³⁸*y. Sanh.* 6:2, 23c (par. *y. Ḥag.* 2:2, 77d-78a). The men will, according to the text, ומחדיי חדי. See Chapter 7 for a discussion of this passage.
¹³⁹*b. Git.* 45a.

Non-Marital Sex

Tosefta, for example, identifies seven areas in which the prophets rebuke the Gentiles:

- A. "...Thus said the Lord God: You eat with the blood, [you raise your eyes to the fetishes, and you shed blood...] you have relied on your sword, [you have committed abominations, you have all defiled other men's wives...,]" [Ezek. 33:25-26].
- B. "You eat with the blood" – this is [cutting a] limb from a living animal.
- C. "You raise your eyes to the fetishes" – this is idolatry.
- D. "You shed blood" – this is murder.
- E. "You rely on your sword" – this is the matters of justice and theft.
- F. "You have committed abominations" – this is homoerotic intercourse.
- G. "You have all defiled other men's wives" – this is forbidden sexual practices (*'arayot*).[140]

Another passage from the *Tosefta* links the biblical character Ishmael, who here is paradigmatic for all Gentiles, to idolatry, homoerotic intercourse, general forms of non-marital sex, and murder.[141]

The association is found also in the tannaitic midrashim. Moab and Amnon, for example, when offered the Torah by God before He offered it to Israel, refused it because it forbade adultery, and "we are all from adultery."[142] A tannaitic source explains why a captive woman must wear "captive garb" when she first enters her captive's house (Deut. 21:12-13):

- A. It teaches that he takes from her nice garments and dresses her [in] garments of widowhood,
- B. Because the daughters of these accursed nations adorn themselves in war in order to cause others to whore after them.[143]

Gentile women were given license to adorn themselves in order to attract their enemies, thus weakening their resolve. For this action, the

---

[140] *t. Sot.* 6:9.
[141] *t. Sot.* 6:6.
[142] *Mekh. Yitro Bahodesh* 5 (p. 221); *Sifre Deut.* 343 (p. 396). The midrash is somewhat strained. The reference is to their origins as children of an incestuous liaison between Lot and his daughters (Gen. 19:30-38). In this passage, the confusion of adultery and incest appears intentional. The intention, it seems to me, is to come as close as possible within the confines of biblical material and the structure of the rest of the midrash to calling Moab and Amnon a nation *of* adulterers. The association of Moav with adultery recurs in a statement attributed to Rav Nahman bar Yitzhak at *b. Shab.* 105a.
[143] *Sifre Deut.* 213 (p. 246): ...בשביל להזנות אחרים אחריהן

captive Gentile woman is punished "measure for measure": she is forced to dress in deliberately unattractive garb.[144]

The Talmudim maintain the identification of Gentile with non-marital sexual activity. Part of the *soṭah* ordeal,[145] described in the Bible for the suspected adulteress, involves binding the suspected woman with, as the *Mishnah* says, "Egyptian rope."[146] Egyptian rope is specified, according to a statement attributed to R. Yitzḥak, "because she did as the Egyptians."[147] The connection in rabbinic literature between Egyptians and forbidden sexual liaisons occurs also with incest and homoeroticism (see Chapters 2, 5). The application in all of these cases goes beyond the Egyptians to Gentiles generally. Moreover, there are several other traditions recorded in the Bavli and attributed to Babylonian sources that simply assume Gentile proclivity to promiscuity and adultery.[148] These sources primarily comment on the lack of sexual control exhibited by Gentile men.

LICENTIOUSNESS

Gentiles are associated in rabbinic sources with lack of sexual control as well as with leading Israelites astray through sex. The most prominent example of the latter is the story of Balaam. According to the Bible, Balaam was summoned by the king, Balak, to curse Israel. Although trying three times, he was not able to curse Israel (Num. 22:2 – 24:25). This story is followed by the statement that the Israelites "profaned themselves by whoring with the Moabite women," (Num. 25:1). Later Jewish sources connect these two events.[149] In the rabbinic telling of the tale, the association between Gentiles, lust, and self-control are highlighted:

---

[144]See also *Mekh. Bo*, 13 (pp. 45-56). If this interpretation is correct, this tradition parallels the attitude found in the stories involving Balaam, cited below. It is also possible to read this passage as referring to women who, in a time of war, become sexually promiscuous with troops from their own side (e.g., army prostitutes) or with other men, their own husbands being away at war. In any case, the Gentile woman is still punished for this "leading astray" of men.

[145]Although it has been argued that the *soṭah* ceremony is, in the Bible, no ordeal at all, the rabbis do appear to view it as such. See Fryer-Kensky, "The Strange Case" 24-25.

[146]*m. Soṭ.* 1:6.

[147]*y. Soṭ.* 1:6, 17a.

[148]See *b. Soṭ.* 42b; *b. Shab.* 33b (par. *b. ʿAbod. Zar.* 2b); *b. Giṭ.* 56b; *b. Qidd.* 49b; *b. Yoma* 75a; *b. B. Meṣ.* 71a; *b. Men.* 43a. See especially *b. ʿAbod. Zar.* 22b (par. *y. ʿAbod. Zar.* 2:1, 40c), in which a Gentile man who goes to his lover's home and does not find her home will even have intercourse with animals there. Nothing is safe from the Gentile male sexual urge: even Balaam, according to a Babylonian amora, had intercourse with his ass (*b. Sanh.* 105a).

[149]See Josephus *Ant.* 4.129-38.

Non-Marital Sex 149

A. What did the evil Balaam do?

B. He gave advice to Balak ben Tzipur to cause the Israelites to fall by the sword.

C. He said to him, the god of this nation hates *znut*. Set up your daughters in licentiousness and you will dominate them.

D. He [Balak] said to him, will they [i.e., the Midianites] listen to me?

E. He [Balaam] said to him, set up your daughter first, and they will see and listen to you.

F. Concerning this it is written, "'[The name of the Midianite woman who was killed was Cozbi daughter of Zur;] he was the tribal head of an ancestral house in Midian," [Num. 25:15].

G. What did they do? They built latticed screens[150] from Beit Hishimon to Har HaSheleg and they placed there women selling kinds of deserts. They placed the old woman outside and the maiden inside. The Israelites used to eat and drink and one of them would go for a walk in the market and he would take for himself something from the shop-keeper. And the old woman used to sell the thing to him for what it was worth, and the maiden said to him, come and take it for less. Thus [it happened] on the first day and the second day. On the third day she said to him,[151] from now on you are like a member of the house. Enter and chose [something] for yourself. When he entered there was there a vessel filled with Amonite wine, which is strong and unlocks the body to *znut*, and its scent was piecing.

H. Still Gentile wine for libation was not prohibited to Israelites.

I. And she would say to him, do you desire to drink a cup of wine? And he would say to her, yes. And she would give it to him, and he would drink, and after he would drink the wine would burn in him as the venom of a *kakina* [a large snake], and he would say to her, hearken to me [i.e., have intercourse with me]! And she would say to him, do you wish that I will hearken to you? And he would say, yes. Immediately she would bring forth an image of Ba'al Peor from her bosom, and she would say to him, bow to this and I will hearken to you. And he would say to her, can I worship an idol? And she would say to him, you worship merely by uncovering yourself to it.

J. ...there was there a vessel filled with Amonite wine, which is strong and unlocks[152] the body to *znut*, and its scent was piecing. Still Gentile wine for libation was not prohibited to Israelites. And she would say to him, do you desire to drink a cup of wine? And he

---

[150]Jastrow substitutes קלע, shops, for קנקל (1394). The text demands this reading, but the emendation is not supported by the manuscripts.

[151]From "...and the maiden said to him..." to here is only in the margins of MS Leiden.

[152]MS Leiden appears to read מפתה, "seduce," in place of מפתח.

would say to her, yes. And she would give it to him, and he would drink, and after he would drink the wine would burn in him as the venom of a snake, and he would say to her, hearken to me [i.e., have intercourse with me]! And she would say to him, separate yourself from the Torah of Moses and I will hearken to you. This is like it was written, "[I found Israel (as pleasing) as grapes in the wilderness; your fathers seemed to Me like the first fig to ripen on a fig tree.] But when they came to Baal-peor, they turned aside to shamefulness; then they became as detested as they had been loved," [Hos. 9:10].[153]

The Yerushalmi presents two very similar versions of the same story. (A nearly identical version of this story is reported in the Bavli).[154] The Midianites ensnare the Israelites with an elaborate scheme. First they establish their women as merchants. After these women accustom the Israelites to doing business with them, they use wine as a tool to inflame the passions of the Israelite men in order to get them to commit idolatry. The second version (J) is a bit more inclusive, equating idolatry, which may have been seen as so extreme that it was not particularly applicable to Palestinian Jews of late antiquity, to the more common, and threatening, separation from the "Torah of Moses." Considering the statement that begins this story, "the god of this nation hates *znut*" (C), the story itself seems to overkill. That is, the story would be tighter if it ended after the seduction of the Israelites. The point of continuing this tradition with the slide into idolatry is to emphasize the slippery slope of *znut*. *Znut*, like idolatry, represents a loss of control.

Wine leads to lust, and lust to idolatry, the story suggests. All share the characteristic of loss of control. Indulgence in one of these vices would have been seen as correlative with, and probably predicative of, the "other." All are signs of weakness, of a lack of discipline which should be the mark of the "good Jew" according to rabbinic standards (see below). Gentiles, in contrast to Jews, are characterized as lacking this self-control, and often they tempt Israel.[155] Promiscuity thus becomes a component in a much broader rabbinic strategy of defining Jews by emphasizing their self-control in contrast to Gentiles.

---

[153] *y. Sanh.* 10:2, 28c-d.
[154] *b. Sanh.* 106a. The differences are more of redactorial interest than relevance to this topic. The two versions presented in the Yerushalmi are conflated into one story, and the emphasis on the contemporary Jew rather than the ancient Israelite is sharpened. On this passage, see Judith R. Baskin, *Pharaoh's Counselors: Job, Jethro, and Balaam in Rabbinic and Patristic Tradition* (Chico: Scholars Press, 1983) 88-89.
[155] See also *b. Yebam.* 103a-b (par. *b. Hor.* 10b; *b. Naz.* 23b) attributed to R. Yohanan that suggests that Sisera's fall at the hands of Yael (Judges 4:18-21) was due to his weakness after having had intercourse with her seven times. In a *baraitha* at *b. Qidd.* 49b, Arabs are attributed with exceptional sexual desire.

Babylonian stories that identify Gentiles and sexual control often focus on the lack of control exhibited by Gentile men.[156] Some are reported in a decidedly Persian milieu. For example:

A. Raba brought a gift to Bar Shishakh on one of their festivals. He said [to himself], I know that he will not worship [it] in an idolatrous fashion.

B. He found him sitting up to his neck in roses and naked whores were standing around him.

C. He said to him, do you have something like this in the world-to-come? He said to him, ours is more preferable than this one. He said to him, is there something more preferable than this? He said to him, you are afraid of the government, but we are not afraid of the government. He said to him, I, at any rate, what fear do I have of the government?

D. While they were sitting a certain soldier of the government and said to him, get up, because the government needs you.

E. When he got up he said, let the eye that wants to see evil of you burst.

F. Raba said to him, Amen, and the eye of Bar Shishak burst.[157]

Bar Shishak is portrayed as a paragon of overindulgence, bathing (?) or luxuriating in flowers as naked prostitutes stood before him, pontificating to Raba on the poor fate of those who have something to fear. Of course, here Raba gets the last laugh, for Bar Shishak was not as completely insulated as he believed himself to be. This story not only effectively links Gentiles to promiscuity and overindulgence, but does so in a way that promises that they will eventually pay the price for their laxity. Other traditions in the Bavli, attributed to Babylonian amoraim, also record Gentile use of prostitutes.[158]

The Bavli also links promiscuity to heretics. One tradition records that the first transgression that Elisha ben Abuye committed after his apostasy was to go to a prostitute.[159] Another tradition interprets several dreams of a heretic *(min)* as all referring to forbidden sexual liaisons.[160]

---

[156]See, for example, the redactorial comment on *b. B. Meṣ.* 71a that a male Gentile slave, in contrast to a Jewish one, is sexually dissolute.

[157]*b. ʿAbod. Zar.* 65a.

[158]See *b. Sanh.* 39b, 95b. See below on rhetoric involving rabbis and prostitutes.

[159]*b. Ḥag.* 15b. His very name, אחר, "the other one," implies both a rhetoric of the other and a connection to promiscuous sexuality. See Henoch Yalon, *Studies in the Hebrew Language* (Jerusalem: Bialik Institute, 1971) 293-94 (Hebrew).

[160]*b. Ber.* 56b. See also *b. Sanh.* 44a, in which Ahan (Josh. 7:24) is accused of raping a betrothed woman.

One tradition is exceptionally pointed in linking the "other" to this loss of sexual restraint:

> A. Rav Yehudah [BA 2] said in the name of Rav [BA 1], the men of Jerusalem [before the destruction of the Second Temple] were obscene. A man would say to his fellow, what is at the meal today? bread of well worked dough, or bread not of well worked dough? [Inferior] white wine or [superior] red wine? A wide couch or a narrow couch? Good company or bad company?
>
> B. R. Ḥisda [BA 3] said, it was all for *znut*.[161]

Rashi interprets all the references in(A) as euphemisms for sex. Regardless of whether he is correct, there is a clear association made by these Babylonian amoraim between laxity in eating and drinking and sex. Instead of Gentiles, "the men of Jerusalem" is used as the "other."[162]

Although there are too few sources to draw any firm conclusions, it appears that Palestinian and Babylonian rabbis deploy this rhetoric differently. Palestinian sources appear to emphasize the promiscuity of Gentile women,[163] and Babylonian sources the lack of control exercised by Gentile men.[164] This would be consistent with differences in Palestinian and Babylonian rhetorics on the nature of desire (see below).

NON-RABBINIC PARALLELS

Herodotus describes the "shameful custom" of the Babylonian women, who once in their lives go to the Temple of Aphrodite and, in what appears to be a fund-raiser for the Temple, sleep with the first man who ritually acquires her.[165] Livy links the Bacchanalia to illicit sexual

---

[161] *b. Shab.* 62b-63a.
[162] It is unclear to me what this group is supposed to represent in this context. In other appearances of the term in the Bavli the overtones are positive. See *b. Sukk.* 41b.
[163] This assumption might inform Rabbi Yoḥanan's statement recorded in the Bavli, that "When the snake had intercourse with Eve, he infused lust in her. When Israel stood at Sinai, their lust ceased. But the Gentiles, who did not stand at Sinai, their lust did not cease," (*b. Yebam.* 103b; *b. Shab.* 146a; *b. 'Abod. Zar.* 22b). While the lust appears to affect both men and women, its emphasis is on women.
[164] There are a few exceptions to this trend. *t. Qidd.* 5:10 mandates that a woman cannot be alone with even 100 Gentiles, for, we are to presume, Gentile men cannot be trusted to restrain themselves. On the placement of this tradition, see Lieberman, *Tos. Kip.* 8:978-980, *b. 'Abod. Zar.* 44a records a tradition of the licentiousness of a Gentile woman, but this might be a tannaitic tradition. *y. 'Abod. Zar.* 2:1, 40c, as seen just above, records a tradition emphasizing the promiscuity of Gentile men, but this might be Babylonian: in the Bavli (*b. 'Abod. Zar.* 22b) it is attributed to Mar Ukba bar Ḥama, and in the Yerushalmi it is unattributed.
[165] Herodotus 1.199-202.

liaisons,[166] and Tacitus calls Jews "prone to lust" (*proiectissima ad libidenem gens*).[167] Although I have been able to find few other examples of Greek and Roman writers attributing non-sanctioned forms of non-marital sex to the "other," it does appear to have been a commonly accepted trope.[168]

Not surprisingly, the early Christians too used to associate heedless fornication, with its attendant loss of control, with the "other."[169] As remarked in Chapter 2, lustful practices generally (including but not limited to incest) were routinely leveled against the Christians by the pagans, and against Gnostics by more "orthodox" Christians.

Jewish-Hellenistic writers use this rhetoric frequently; indeed, sexual immorality is made a "boundary" issue, "separating Jew from Gentile. In this literature, Gentiles are constantly, and somewhat indiscriminately, accused of adultery and fornication.[170]

Rhetoric of Divine Retribution

There are few examples in rabbinic literature of the idea that God imposes either personal or communal punishment on those who are promiscuous or who commit adultery. Two tannaitic sources assume that those who commit adultery are destined for Gehenna (hell), a theme that is reiterated, as shown below, in the Bavli.[171] Other Palestinian traditions focus on communal retribution for non-marital sex. Hence, we read in the Yerushalmi:

> R. Simlai [PA 2] said, in every place that you find *znut* you find that the seizure of men (אנדרולמסיה)[172] comes into the world.[173]
>
> The census rolls of three cities were brought to Jerusalem in a cart [i.e., they were very populous]: Kabul, Sihin, and Migdal Tziviah, and the three of them were destroyed. Kabul because of

---

[166]Livy *Annals* 39.8. On the Bacchanalia, see Ross Kraemer, *Her Share of the Blessings: Women's Religions Among Pagans, Jews, and Christians in the Greco-Roman World* (New York: Oxford University Press, 1992) 43-49.
[167]Tacitus *His.* 5.1.2.
[168]See too Chapter 5 on the Roman labeling of homoeroticism, "Greek love."
[169]See for example 1 Thess. 4:3-8.
[170]For examples, see *Jub.* 20:3-5 (ed. Charlesworth, 2:93-94); 2 *Enoch* 34 (ed. Charlesworth, 1:158-59); *Sib. Or.* 3.594-600 (ed. Geffcken, 78-79); 4.33 (ed. Geffcken, 93); 5.166 (ed. Geffcken, 112). See Larry O. Yarbrough, *Not Like the Gentiles: Marriage Rules in the Letters of Paul* (Atlanta: Scholars Press, 1985).
[171]*m. 'Abot* 1:5 *t. Ḥag.* 1:7. See also *t. 'Abod. Zar.* 6(7):7, which threatens divine judgment for the "fools" (שטים) who commit adultery.
[172]This might also have a more general meaning of "punishment" of people. See Krauss, *Lehnwörter* 65.
[173]*y. Soṭ.* 1:5, 17a.

disagreements; Sihin because of witchcraft; and Migdal Tziviah because of *znut*.[174]

In both traditions, God, through the agency of humans (more specifically, Rome), brings communal suffering on the people due to their promiscuity.

The Bavli also contains a few examples of the rhetoric of divine retribution, all focusing on divine punishment of the individuals. For example:

> A. Raba [BA 4] said, anyone who has intercourse with a married woman, even if he learned Torah – as it is written about it [Torah] "[it] is more precious than rubies," [Prov. 3:15], [that is,] than a high priest who enters before [God] – she [Torah] will chase to the judgment of Gehenna.
>
> B. ...Rav [BA 1] said, anyone who has intercourse with a married woman, even if he acknowledges that possession of heaven and earth is God's, like Abraham our father, as it is written about him, "[But Abram said to the king of Sodom,] I swear to the Lord, God Most High, Creator of heaven and earth...," [Gen. 14:22], he will not be cleared[175] from the punishment of Gehenna.[176]

Two Babylonian amoraim emphasize that whatever his other merits, the adulterer awaits an unpleasant after-life. In both traditions, in fact, it is his very merit that is related to the punishment. In (A) it is the Torah that will demand judgment; and in (B) the word-play between the Hebrew words for "he gives possession" and "be cleared" denote a link between merit and judgment. Another tradition in the Bavli also includes the threat of eternal damnation for the adulterer.[177]

Surprisingly, especially in light of the divine punishment that according to the Bible is incurred by the adulteress forced to undergo the *soṭah* ordeal, the rhetoric of divine retribution and punishment is not applied to women. Below I examine in more detail the rabbinic treatment of the *soṭah* ritual, but it is worth noting here that the *Mishnah* only mentions the horrible punishments spelled out in Num. 5:21-22, and that neither tannaitic sources nor the Talmudim in their commentary on this *mishnah* expand upon the supernatural punishments.[178] The only reference to divine punishment for the adulteress that I have been able to locate is a short and somewhat ambiguous statement in the Bavli

---

[174]*y. Ta'an.* 4:8, 69a.
[175]There appears to be word play here on קנה, designating God's creation, and the word used here, ינקה.
[176]*b. Soṭ.* 4b.
[177]*b. B. Meṣ.* 58b (cited above). The relevant part of this tradition is unattributed. See also *b. Soṭ.* 37b.
[178]*m. Soṭ.* 3:4; *Sifre Num.* 15 (p. 20); 18 (p. 22); *y. Soṭ.* 3:4, 18d; *b. Soṭ.* 16b.

Non-Marital Sex

attributed to R. Akiba that if a husband and wife do not "merit," then "fire consumes them."[179] "Merit," according to Rashi, means that neither commit adultery, although the intention is probably much broader.

Jewish-Hellenistic writers and Christians, when they do employ this rhetoric (which Christians do quite frequently), focus on divine punishment of individuals.[180]

Finally, it should be noted that according to a tradition placed at the end of *Mishnah Soṭah*, the turning of the court to *znut* will precede the coming of the Messiah.[181] *Znut*, among many other events and phenomena disapproved of by the rabbis, thus becomes a symbol for the end of the world. This is not a rhetoric of divine retribution – *znut* is not a cause, but a symptom in these traditions – but it is linked to the final upheaval of the world.

Rhetoric of Temptation

Rabbinic literature attributes to women a dual threat relating to non-marital sexual activities. The first imagined threat was that which wives and daughters, through their own uncontrolled sexual activity, posed to husbands and fathers. The second was the imagined threat that women posed to men as temptresses and seductresses, tempting men into sexual promiscuity and adultery. Each of these rhetorics derive from rabbinic anthropological assumptions about the nature of human desire. Although Palestinian and Babylonian anthropological assumptions relating to human sexual desire are similar, the two societies construct different rhetorics and institutions to deal with the same perceived problems.

WOMEN AS DAUGHTERS

Babylonian rabbis appear to be concerned with the shame caused for a man when his daughter engages in unsanctioned sexual behavior.[182] In one *sugya* in the Bavli (cited below), Rav Pappa states that a promiscuous woman threatens the reputation of her family.[183] This assumption of

---

[179] *b. Soṭ.* 17a. This is a subtle exegetical tradition: דריש ר׳ איש ואשה זכו שכינה ביניהן לא זכו אש אוכלתן. The midrash plays off the *yod* in the word איש and the *heh* in the word אשה, spelling the name of God. When they no longer merit divine sanction, God withdraws, leaving the letters אש, fire. This tradition is more useful as an example of rabbinic exegesis than for anything it may reflect about sexual assumptions of its framers.

[180] See *Jub.* 39:6 (ed. Charlesworth, 2:129); *Sib. Or.* 2:258 (ed. Geffcken, p. 40); Matt. 5:27-30.

[181] *m. Soṭ.* 9:15; *b. Sanh.* 97a.

[182] This rhetoric is never applied to the mother or brother of a woman whose father may have died or otherwise left the family.

[183] *b. Sanh.* 75a.

shame is at the base of another *sugya* in the Bavli, in which Ben Sira's verses on the worry of a woman's father are cited.[184]

The Bavli's treatment of "the priest's daughter" is also telling. According to Leviticus 21:9, "When the daughter of a priest defiles herself through harlotry, it is her father whom she profanes;[185] she shall be put to the fire." Tannaitic sources do not discuss the nature of this profanation. The Bavli, on the other hand, elevates the priest's daughter's profanation of her father to a paradigmatically heinous sin. The Bavli then uses this elevation to place the death penalty of burning at the peak of the hierarchy of death penalties.[186] At the end of one of these long theoretical discussions, the Bavli cites the following tradition:

> R. Yermiah [PA 4] says, why does Scripture say, "it is her father whom she profanes?" If they treated him as holy they now treat him as profane. If they treated him with honor they now treat him with shame...[187]

Profanation, in this Palestinian source, is made equivalent to the loss of honor. In a time without a Temple, when "profanation" has little concrete meaning, the priest can still be "profaned," that is, shamed, by his daughter. This tradition would most likely have resonated in an audience beyond the priests.[188]

WOMEN AS WIVES

Fear of female infidelity is reflected in all the sources. Male suspicion of his wife's infidelity is institutionalized in the *sotah* ordeal. The *sotah* ordeal is initiated, the Bible tells us, when "... a fit of jealousy comes over him and he is wrought up about the wife who has defiled herself; or if a fit of jealousy comes over one and he is wrought up about his wife although she has not defiled herself," [Num. 5:14]. The nature of this "fit of jealousy" is turned in tannaitic sources into an announcement:

---

[184]*b. Sanh.* 100b. On the verses from Ben Sira, see Warren Trenchard, *Ben Sira's View of Women: ; A Literary Analysis* (Chico: Scholars Press, 1982) 129-65. On its restatement in the Bavli, see Greenfield, "Ben Sira 42.9-10."

[185]The *NJPS* translates מחללת as "defiles."

[186]See especially *b. Sanh.* 59b.

[187]*b. Sanh.* 52a. The attribution follows MS Munich 95 and variants; the printed edition reads "R. Meir taught..." See E.Z. Melamed, *Halachic Midrashim of the Tannaim in the Babylonian Talmud* (1943; rpt. Jerusalem: The Magnes Press, 1988) 288 (Hebrew).

[188]At least one intended audience of this tradition may have been the rabbis. Their focus on sexual shame along with their possible desire to seize the priestly mantle of authority (especially in Palestine), would have made them a group to whom this tradition particularly spoke.

> How does he accuse his wife on infidelity [מקנא לה, the same word that is used by the Bible to denote "jealousy"]? He says to her in front of two [witnesses]: Do not speak to so-and-so....[189]

The *Mishnah* here subverts the emotive "jealousy" of the Bible into a juridical act. This is the first of what we will see are several major differences between the biblical and rabbinic account of the ordeal.[190] The *mishnah* might here reflect an unease with the possibility that a man might suddenly, without warning or witnesses, initiate such a solemn and serious ordeal. The husband's right to suspect and control his wife is maintained, but now control over the ordeal is shifted to the courts. The Yerushalmi retains this technical, juridical, meaning to the term "jealousy."[191]

The Bavli, on the other hand, struggles with the emotive element implied in the Bible:

> A. It was taught in the School of Ishmael: A man only accuses his wife of infidelity when a "spirit" *(ruah)* enters him, as it is said, "but a fit *(ruah)* of jealousy comes over him and he is wrought up [about the wife]..." [Num. 5:14].
>
> B. What is a "spirit?"
>
> C. Our rabbis hold, it is an impure spirit. Rav Ashi [BA 6] says it is a pure spirit.[192]

An unparalleled *baraitha* asserts that some kind of "spirit," or emotion, must enter a man before he begins the formal accusation. If authentically tannaitic, this *baraitha* nevertheless offers what appears to be a non-normative and non-authoritative view, rejected by other Palestinian sources. (B) and (C) expand on this *baraitha*, asking if the "spirit" is impure or pure, that is, an evil emotion sent by Satan or one motivated by a "true" hatred of adultery.[193] In either case, these Babylonian amoraim restore "feeling" to the procedure. Men get jealous, they appear to be saying, and are entitled to act on that jealousy.

What appears to be a trivial legal disagreement actually implies a much broader difference between Palestinian and Babylonian assumptions about women. By retaining the possibility that a husband's *feeling* could initiate the *sotah* ordeal, this Babylonian text facilitates easier initiation of the ordeal. Since at the time of the text the ordeal no longer

---

[189]*m. Sot.* 1:2.
[190]Neusner views the tractate *Sotah* as entirely dependent on Scripture ("From Scripture to Mishnah" 150). I will argue that although it seems to be, it diverges in many important respects.
[191]*y. Sot.* 1:1, 16b.
[192]*b. Sot.* 3a.
[193]This explanation of the terms is offered by Rashi.

exists, the legal discussion is moot. Nevertheless, the text itself *threatens* women. Male jealousy in and of itself is sufficient to subject his wife to a cruel and humiliating ordeal. The message appears to be that women ought not to provoke their husband's jealousy. This text attempts to exert greater control over female sexuality.

This contrast between Babylonian and Palestinian approaches is also reflected in a well-known Palestinian story that records a husband's ire and suspicion when his wife returns home late from synagogue. He demands that she publicly shame the rabbi who gave the long sermon that detained her.[194] The point of the story is to show that the man's suspicion, although understandable, was also unreasonable. Jealousy and unfounded suspicion alone are not enough to accuse a woman of adultery.

In sum, Babylonian sources appear to show more concern than Palestinian sources with the potential that daughters and wives have to shame their fathers and husbands through sexual activity.

RHETORIC OF WOMEN AS TEMPTRESSES AND SEDUCTRESSES

Sexual attraction was perceived by both Palestinian and Babylonian rabbis to be a constant danger. Both men and women were thought to be sexually desirous. Only men, however, were thought capable of controlling this overwhelming desire. Where Palestinian and Babylonian rabbis diverge is on their assessment of the strength and effectiveness of male sexual self-control. Palestinians were far less optimistic than Babylonians in the male's ability to exercise self-control.

Female Sexual Desire

Both Palestinian and Babylonian rabbis view women as more "light-headed" than men, lacking self-control. "A woman prefers one *qav* [of material substance] and sex (תפלות) to nine *qavs* [of material substance] and abstinence," reads one *mishnah*.[195] *Baraithot* in the Bavli share this assessment: "What is the reason [that a man cannot be alone with two women]? As it is taught of the School of Eliyahu, because women are light-headed."[196] Another *baraitha* asserts that the more wine a woman consumes the more sexually solicitous she becomes, emphasizing the link between her ability to control herself and her sexual desires.[197]

---

[194]*m. Soṭ.* 1:4, 16d (partial par. *b. Ned.* 66b).
[195]*m. Soṭ.* 3:4. See A.A. Halevi, *Arkhe ha-Aggadah v'ha-Halakhah*, 4 vols. (Tel Aviv: Dvir, 1982) 3:198-207 (Hebrew); Wegner, *Chattel or Person?* 153-62.
[196]*b. Qidd.* 80b. This statement is also cited, in a very different context, in *b. Shab.* 33b. See also *b. Soṭ.* 32b.
[197]*b. Ketub.* 65a. By the time she drinks four cups, the *baraitha* asserts, she will solicit even an ass. Both Babylonian and Palestinian sources in the Bavli are

Non-Marital Sex   159

The amoraim share this view of women as not in control of themselves and prone to adultery and promiscuity. "Everyone knows why a bride enters the wedding canopy," A Babylonian amora slyly states.[198] Women are depicted not only as temptresses, but also as seductresses, actively testing male sexual control.[199] The Bavli's redactor claims that female sexual desire can "seize" them, making them unaccountable for their loss of self-control.[200] A *sugya* in the Bavli recounts stories of women who pretended that either they or their children were dead in order to gain a pretext to find the privacy needed for a liaison.[201] Only rarely are portraits of women who resist sexual temptation found in this literature.[202]

Men too were thought to have an overpowering sexual urge. Unlike women, though, they were thought capable of restraint.

Male Sexual Desire

Rabbinic sources are insistent about the strength of a man's *yeṣer ha-raʿ*, "evil desire." According to a *mishnah*, it is a strong man indeed who can conquer his desire.[203] Sources attributed to Palestinians in the Bavli comment on the strength of the male sexual urge.[204] The Bavli cites several other extended passages, of mostly Palestinian provenance, on the strength of the male *yeṣer*.[205] According to a passage in the Yerushalmi, even the priest who brings the meal offering to the suspected adulteress in the course of her ordeal must guard against touching her, lest he become aroused.[206]

---

ambivalent about the idea of wives asking their husbands for sex. See *b. ʿErub.* 100b; *b. Ned.* 20b.

[198]*b. Ketub.* 8b (par. *b. Shab.* 33a). The answer, as is clear from the continuation (although everyone knows, one should not discuss it), is that she wants sex.

[199]See *y. Soṭ.* 3:4, 19a; *b. Shab.* 62b (par. *b. Yoma* 9b. Although attributed to a Babylonian amora, the sources is most likely Palestinian. See *D.S.* 5:17, n. ח; *Lev. Rab.* 16:1 [pp. 340-43]).

[200]*b. Ketub.* 62b (women lust for sex); 51b, 54a; *b. Qidd.* 81b (on women being overcome by their sexual urge).

[201]*b. Qidd.* 80b according to the interpretation of Rashi.

[202]See, for example, *b. Soṭ.* 11b, in which the Israelite midwives are said to have resisted Pharaoh's sexual advances.

[203]*m. ʾAbot* 4:1.

[204]See *b. Qidd.* 40a (par. *b. Moʿed Qaṭ.* 17a [here given tannaitic attribution]; *b. Ḥag.* 16a); *b. Qidd.* 80b.

[205]See especially *b. Sukk.* 51b-52a (par. *b. Qidd.* 30b); *b. Ber.* 61a (par. *b. ʿErub.* 18b – tannaitic attribution); *b. Sanh.* 99b; *b. Moʿed Qaṭ.* 24a (threatens death and mutilation for those who have sex during mourning). See the sources and commentary of Urbach, *The Sages* 471-83 for a more complete discussion of the *yeṣer*.

[206]*y. Soṭ.* 3:1, 18c.

Amoraim too regard male sexual desire as a constant threat. Palestinian and Babylonian amoraim pray that they be saved from the *yeṣer ha-raʿ*.[207] One Babylonian amora says that although generally a woman can remain alone with two men, in the case when the men are "loose," or prone to promiscuity, she is not allowed to be left alone even with ten men, for fear that they will not restrain each other.[208] In heaven, according to an unattributed source in the Bavli, a man can claim to be "sensual," one who has a stronger than usual sexual urge.[209] Another tradition begins by citing a Palestinian statement that compares anyone who eats bread without first washing his hands to one who has had intercourse with a prostitute. The Babylonians reinterpret this to mean that one who has intercourse with a prostitute will eventually go begging for bread.[210] Men can become so addicted to sex, this tradition suggests, that they will squander everything they own in order to continue satisfying their urges. One Babylonian amora puts it succinctly:

> R. Ḥiyya bar Yosef said to Shmuel, what is the difference between the rebellious man and the rebellious woman [i.e., why is the man who refuses to sleep with his wife fined less than a wife who refuses to sleep with her husband]? He said to him, go and learn from the market of prostitutes. Who hires whom?[211]

A woman is fined more for refusing to sleep with her husband than is a man for refusing to sleep with his wife because, since a man's sexual desire is thought to be stronger than a woman's, he is thought less likely to be able to go for long periods of time without sex.

The Temptress

Rabbinic perceptions of the overwhelming power of male sexual desire, and of passive female acquiescence to it, gird their general wariness of women as temptresses. Through no initiative or fault of her own, a woman can tempt a man into succumbing to his own desire. The results can sometimes be deadly:

> A. Once a certain man fell in love with a woman in the time of R. Eleazar and grew ill. They came and asked him [R. Eleazar] if she may pass before him, so that he may live. He said, let him die and

---

[207]Babylonians: *b. Ber.* 17a (but see *D.S.* 1:78, n. מ), 60b; *b. Qidd.* 81b. Palestinians: *b. Ber.* 17a (see *D.S.* 1:77, n. י); *y. Ber.* 4:2, 7d. See also *Gen. Rab.* 23:5 (pp. 225-26).
[208]*b. Qidd.* 80b; *b. Soṭ.* 7a; *b. ʿAbod. Zar.* 25b. A similar statement is found attributed to a Babylonian amora at *y. Qidd.* 4:11, 66c.
[209]*b. Yoma* 35b. The term is סרוד ביצרו. This source might be tannaitic. See *D.S.* 5:90, n. מ.
[210]*b. Soṭ.* 4b.
[211]*b. Ketub.* 64b. On the "rebellious" wife, see Chapter 7.

not [do] such. May he hear her voice [they asked,] and not die? He said, let him die and not [do] such.

B. What was she?

C. R. Ya'akov bar Idi [PA 2-3] and R. Yitzhak bar Nahman [PA 3]. One said that she was married, the other said that she was unmarried.

D. According to the one who said that she was married, it is fine [i.e., we understand the severity]. And the one who said she was unmarried?

E. But Bar Koha Nagra loved a woman in the days of R. Eleazar and he permitted her [to pass before him]!

F. Here [E] she was unmarried, and here [A] she was married.

G. And even if you say that in both cases she was unmarried, solve it thus: he desired her until she was a married woman.

H. It is necessary to say that she was a great woman and he did not marry her.

I. And every thing that he [could] do was prohibited.

J. Because of this he forbade her.[212]

A woman's beauty alone is enough to physically sicken, even endanger, a man. The *sugya* is intriguing because it presents two different voices. The first, heard in (A), is the stringent one: even in the most extreme situation men and women are to be separated in order to avoid the possibility of promiscuity. Beginning with (B), however, a different voice is heard. R. Eleazar's stringency is comprehensible to the redactor only if she was married (F). Promiscuity might be dangerous, but the threat of adultery is far more so, and merits at times extreme preventive measures.

Whereas the Yerushalmi dismisses the possibility that the woman in this story is unmarried, the Bavli, in a parallel version, focuses on it. Because the situation itself (A) is slightly different, I cite in full:

A. Rav Yehudah [BA 2] said in the name of Rav [BA 1]:[213] Once a man was attracted to a woman and a vehement passion seized him. They came and asked the doctors and said that there is no cure [for him] until he has intercourse [with her]. The Sages said, let him die and not have intercourse [with her]. Let her stand before him naked [the doctors suggested]. Let him die and her not stand before him naked [the Sage replied]. Let him talk with her from behind a screen [the doctor suggested]. Let him die and not talk with her from behind a screen [the Sages replied].

---

[212]*y. Shab.* 14:4, 14d (par. *y. 'Abod. Zar.* 2:2, 40d).
[213]Rav's name is left out in some manuscripts. See *D.S.* 11:210, n. ר.

B. There was a disagreement between R. Ya'akov bar Idi [PA 2-3] and R. Shmuel bar Naḥmani [PA 3]. One said she was a married woman, the other that she was unmarried.

C. According to the one that said she was a married woman, it is fine [it is understandable], but according to the one who said she was unmarried, why to such an extent [did the rabbis forbid her to have any contact with him]?

D. Rav Papa [BA 5] said, because of discredit to her family.

E. Rav Aḥa son of Rav Ika [BA 5] said, so that the daughters of Israel will not become sexually loose.

F. So let him marry her!

G. No, that would not satisfy him, in accordance with R. Yitzḥak [PA 3] as R. Yitzḥak said, from the day that the Temple was destroyed the "taste" [i.e., enjoyment] of intercourse was taken and given to the committers of sin, as it is said, "Stolen waters are sweet, and bread eaten furtively is tasty," [Prov. 9:17].[214]

The story itself (A) is expanded. Unlike the version in the Yerushalmi, it begins with desire for intercourse and moves to cures that one expects to be progressively less problematic. These too the Sages (instead of R. Eleazar) reject. While the same question is asked at the end of the story (B), the focus of the answers are quite different. In the Yerushalmi, the working assumption was that she must be a married woman. This assumption is echoed in the Palestinian contributions to the *sugya* (B, G). Babylonian amoraim and the redactor of the *sugya*, on the other hand, explore in depth the possibility that she is unmarried. Shame for the family and setting a bad precedent for other Jewish women are proffered as reasons for forbidding sex with an unmarried woman. The *sugya* concludes with a statement attributed to R. Yitzḥak, imported from a discussion on adultery in *b. Ned.* 91b. In our *sugya* the redactor subverts this statement, applying it generally to all forbidden liaisons, not just adultery.

Many other rabbinic dicta reflect the power of women to tempt men into sexual transgression. One rabbi advises avoidance in conversation with *any* woman, even one's own wife and all the more so another man's wife, in order to avoid "inheriting Gehenna."[215] What appears to be an unexplained expiation offering recorded in the Bible (Num. 31:50) is interpreted by a tanna as necessary to atone for lusting eyes.[216] Even the

---

[214]*b. Sanh.* 75a.
[215]*m. 'Abot* 1:5.
[216]*Sifre Num.* 139 (p. 185).

Non-Marital Sex

debasement of the woman undergoing the *sotah* ordeal poses the threat of arousing the young priests.[217]

In the Yerushalmi, David's "fall" is attributed to his act of adultery with Bathsheba.[218] A *baraitha* found only in the Yerushalmi says that even a "pious man among pious men" should not be appointed as a guardian over female relatives, presumably due to the fear that he will be sexually attracted to her.[219] Women are advised to proceed behind men in a mourning procession, so the men will not be aroused by looking at them.[220] Abigail was said to be so beautiful that the sight of her would immediately arouse men.[221] The Bavli cites a prayer of an unmarried woman that no man "fall" through her.[222]

Tales of active female seduction are much rarer. The Bavli attributes to a Palestinian amora a tradition that women used to spray men with a perfume that incited their passions.[223] The Yerushalmi records a tradition that wanton women would attempt to seduce men by reciting to them suggestive biblical verses.[224] Females were dangerous simply because they were females, tempting males. No activity on their part was necessary.

Controlling Desire

As already noted, the main weapon employed by the rabbis to foil sexual desire were laws against social intercourse between, or seclusion (*yiḥud*) of, men with women. According to the *Mishnah*, for example, a man cannot be alone even with two women:

> A man should not be alone with two women, but a woman can be alone with two men. Rabbi Shimon says: even one man may be alone with two women when one of them is his wife, and sleep with them in an inn, because his wife guards him...[225]

---

[217] *m. Soṭ.* 1:5 says that if a woman's hair or breasts are attractive, they should not be exposed. According to *t. Soṭ.* 1:7 this is because of פרחי כהונה. See also *Sifre Num.* 11 (p. 17).
[218] *y. Sanh.* 2:3, 20b.
[219] *y. Ketub.* 1:8, 25d. See also *y. Ketub.* 1:9, 25a.
[220] *y. Sanh.* 2:4, 20b.
[221] *y. Sanh.* 2:3, 20b: 'ותפגוש אותם- הוקרו כולם'. According to the *Pnei Moshe* this means that upon meeting Abigail men would ejaculate. More likely, the meaning is that they would have erections. See Sokoloff 244, s.v. יקר. Although Abigail is not explicitly said to have done anything to encourage this response, the passage and its context also implies that she is not entirely innocent.
[222] *b. Soṭ.* 22a (R. Yoḥanan).
[223] *b. Shab.* 62b (par. *b. Yoma* 9b).
[224] *y. Soṭ.* 3:4, 20a. See also *Gen. Rab.* 80:1 (pp. 952-53) which states that Dinah seduced Shekhem (Gen. 34:2).
[225] *m. Qidd.* 4:12.

Because women are thought to have no sexual restraint, it was thought that one woman would not stop the (illicit) amorous activities of a couple in the same room. When two men, however, are in the same room, each would be restrained by the other. Similarly, a man would be shamed by the presence of his wife. The *Tosefta* and the Talmudim contain similar strictures.[226]

Despite these restrictions against seclusion, Palestinian and Babylonian rabbis recognized that a man's *yeṣer* could rise to dangerous levels. Palestinian rabbis advised men who felt their sexual desire overpowering them to engage in Torah study or to think of the day of their death, among other things.[227] Even so, only the truly exceptional man was thought able to restrain himself: "R. Yoḥanan said, it is similar to a man who had a son. He washed him, anointed him, fed him, gave him drink, and hung a purse around his neck and left him at the door to a brother. How could this son not sin?"[228] Sexual restraint was attributed only to biblical characters.[229] One rabbi even tells men how to fulfill their desire with a minimum amount of shame, acknowledging that a man will ultimately lose the battle with his sexual desire.[230]

Babylonian dicta are, on the other hand, much more optimistic about man's ability to resist his desire. Scattered dicta seem to limit the scope of the *yeṣer*.[231] This optimism comes out most clearly in a series of stories about rabbis who deliberately put themselves into situations in which they might be sexually tempted, and then resist temptation. While the rabbis who are said to have done this are both Palestinian and Babylonian, all the stories are found in the Bavli, and all are told in Babylonian Aramaic.[232]

Other stories about rabbis or holy men who are exposed to sexual temptation also might demonstrate this difference between Palestinian and Babylonian assessments of the ability of a man to control himself sexually:

---

[226] According to the *Tosefta*, even shopkeepers who have frequent business transactions with women may not remain alone with them (*t. Qidd.* 5:14. See also *t. Qidd.* 5:9-10). See *y. Soṭ.* 1:3, 16d; *b. Qidd.* 80b-81b.

[227] See *y. Ber.* 4:1, 7d; *y. Sukk.* 5:2, 55b; *b. Ber.* 5a; *b. Sukk.* 52a-b; *b. Qidd.* 30b; *b. San.* 107a. See further Boyarin, *Carnal Israel*, pp. 134-66.

[228] *b. Ber.* 32a.

[229] For examples see *b. Sanh.* 19b-20a and *y. Sanh.* 2:3, 20a-b.

[230] *b. Qidd.* 50b; *b. Mo'ed Qaṭ.* 17a; *b. Ḥag.* 16a.

[231] See *b. Sanh.* 45a (attributed to Rabah but in *D.S.* 11:132 *ad loc.* to Rav); *b. Qidd.* 21b: לא דברה תורה אלא כנגד יצר הרע. The attribution is tannaitic, but the parallel in *Sifre Deut.* 212 (pp. 245-46) lacks this phrase. See also *b. Sanh.* 105a (with correction of *D.S.* 11:324, n. ש).

[232] See *b. Ber.* 20a; *b. Pes.* 113b (and see *D.S.* 4:351, nn. ז ,מ); *b. 'Abod. Zar.* 17a-b. See also *b. Ketub.* 17a.

A. R. Natan says, there is no commandment in the Torah that gives its reward indirectly [i.e., that does not give an immediate award]. Go and learn from the commandment of the fringes.

B. Once there was a man who was fastidious about [keeping the] commandment of the fringes. He heard that there was a prostitute in the coastal cities and she charged for her fee 400 zuz of gold. He sent her 400 zuz of gold and she set a time for him. When his time came, he went and was seated on the threshold of her house. Her female slave came and said to her, that man with whom you made an appointment is now seated on the threshold of the house. She said to her, let him enter.

C. When he entered he saw seven beds of silver and one of gold and she was on the highest one, and between each [bed] were ladders of silver and the highest of gold. When he arrived at that place [where she was lying] his four fringes came and appeared as four witnesses and slapped him on his face. Immediately he slipped away and sat on the ground. She too slipped off and sat on the ground. She said to him, by the capital of Rome, I will not leave you until you tell me what blemish you saw in me. He said to her, by the service [of God], I did not see in you a blemish, [indeed] there is no one in the whole world as beautiful as you. But the Lord our God commanded us an easy commandment. He wrote in it [i.e., the Torah] "I am the Lord your God," "I am the Lord your God" twice. "I am the Lord your God" – I will give you reward; "I am the Lord your God" – I will punish you [for transgressions].

D. She said to him, by the service [of God], I will not leave you until your write for me your name and the name of your city and the name of the study house where you learn Torah. He wrote for her his name and the name of his city and the name of his teacher and the name of the study house where he learned. She gave away all her money: a third to the government; a third to the poor; and a third she took with her and stood at the study house of R. Ḥiyya. She said to him, Rabbi, convert me. He said to her, perhaps you are attracted to one of the students. She brought forth the writing in her hand. He [R. Ḥiyya] said to him [the student], stand, [you] merit your acquisition. Those beds [that formerly] you gazed at in prohibition, [now] look upon in permissibility. If this is the reward in this world, in the world-to-come I do not know how much![233]

When the student arrives at the prostitute's, he is confronted with extreme luxury: the beds, gold and silver, are clichéd representations of hedonism. Having climbed up the various beds and ladders, on the verge of succumbing to temptation, only the miraculous slap of his fringes "saves" him.[234] His behavior is so puzzling, and ultimately

---

[233] *Sifre Num.* 115 (p. 128-29). See also *b. Men.* 44a.
[234] I take the "slapping" of the fringes to be a miracle. The previous phrase, that "his four fringes came and appeared as four witnesses," also implies a miracle.

impressive, to the prostitute that she eventually converts and then in a storybook ending she and the pious student are able to consummate their relationship in holiness. The teacher praises the student, declaring that he will be rewarded for both his restraint and the model that he set for the Gentile prostitute.[235]

There is no rabbinic law against intercourse with a prostitute.[236] At stake in this story is not the sexual transgression (because there is none), but the loss of control and what it represents.[237] The young student is faced with temptation: to yield to it is to lose control, to begin the slide down the slippery slope that always, invariably, leads to idolatry. To the rabbis, the idea of the scholar, who is supposed to embody the virtue of control, succumbing to temptation is abhorrent.[238]

Similarly, a *baraitha* in the Bavli attributes Joseph's control when seduced by Potiphar's wife to a divinely sent vision.[239] In contrast to the Babylonian stories in which rabbis deliberately expose themselves to temptation and resist, these two Palestinian stories suggest that when one fails to avoid temptation, it is nearly impossible for an ordinary man to resist without some kind of divine help.

A Babylonian story of a rabbi exposed to temptation has a different focus:

Admittedly, it is possible to read this story as devoid of divine intervention: in the heat of passion his fringes fly up to his face.
[235]The idea that a man acquires merit by helping to transform a prostitute is found also in a series of stories in *y. Ta'an.* 1:4, 64d.
[236]But rabbinic law does, apparently, forbid Jewish women from serving as prostitutes. See *b. Sanh.* 82a (attributed to Rav).
[237]See *b. Shab.* 105b (par. *b. Nid.* 13b). This folk motif is present in other Jewish literature, as well as in much non-Jewish folk literature. See Dov Neuman (Noy), *Motif-index of Talmudic-Midrashic Literature* (Ann Arbor: University Microfilms, 1954) 730. In Thompson's index, this motif is labeled T331.5, "Anchorite saved by miracle" from sexual temptation. See Stith Thompson, *Motif-Index of Folk-Literature*, 6 vols. (Bloomington: Indiana University Press, 1955) 5:380. This motif is a significant departure from the phenomenon of the Jewish miracle worker, which has previously been investigated. See William Scott Green, "Palestinian Holy Men: Charismatic Leadership and Rabbinic Tradition," *ANRW* 2:19.2 (1979): 619-47.
[238]Another illustrative example can be found at *b. Ḥag.* 15a. Elisha ben Abuye, after apostasizing, goes to a prostitute who thinks she recognizes the famous rabbi. He proceeds to dig a radish out of the ground on the Sabbath, thus convincing her that he is "someone else." Ironically, digging a radish on the Sabbah is portrayed as more incomprehensible and sinful than going to a prostitute. See also *m. 'Abot* 4:1.
[239]*b. Soṭ.* 36b. See also *b. 'Abod. Zar.* 3a. Note that in earlier versions of this tradition human memory, not a vision, saved Joseph. See James L. Kugel, *In Potiphar's House: The Interpretive Life of Biblical Texts* (San Francisco: Harper, 1990) 98-101.

Non-Marital Sex 167

> Certain captive women who were brought to Nehardea were taken to the home of Rav Amram the Pious [BA 3]. The ladder was removed before them [i.e., they were on the second story of the house and the ladder was removed to prevent sexual access to them]. When one of them passed by [the opening to the downstairs, where the ladder usually was], light fell on the skylight. Rav Amram the Pious took the ladder, which ten men could not raise, and raised it. He went up, and when he was half way up the ladder her forced himself to stand still, and raised his voice, "A fire at Amram's," [he shouted]. The rabbis came and they said to him, you frightened us. He said to them, better that you should be ashamed at Amram's house in this world than you should be ashamed of me in the world to come...[240]

Here Amram himself clearly resists temptation. His response – to shame himself – seems to hint at an underlying assumption that men were expected to help each other resist temptation through shaming.[241] Regardless, it appears from these sources that Babylonian rabbis gave men more of a "fighting chance" against their *yeṣer* than did their Palestinian counterparts.[242]

NON-RABBINIC PARALLELS

Not only the rabbis considered women as temptresses and seductresses. Greeks and Romans too considered women as full of lust and lacking sexual self-control.[243] In the third century B.C.E., according to a Roman historian of the first century C.E., the statue of Venus Verticordia was consecrated in order to encourage women, who were thought to be naturally lustful, to remain chaste.[244] According to [Pseudo-] Lucian, the seer Teirsias – who at various times was both a man and a woman – reported that a woman's sexual pleasure was twice that of a man's.[245] The motif of woman as seductress or temptress was

---

[240]*b. Qidd.* 81a.
[241]See also *b. Ber.* 23a. Both stories presume that shame would or could be a powerful controlling mechanism. See also *b. Sukk.* 52a.
[242]But see also *b. Qidd.* 81b, in which a BA 2 succumbs to seduction.
[243]See especially Kenneth James Dover, *Greek Popular Morality in the Time of Plato and Aristotle* (Berkeley and Los Angeles: University of California Press, 1974) 101-2; Juvenal 6.352-65; Livy 34.2.13-14. See further P. Walcot, "Romantic Love and True Love: Greek Attitudes to Marriage," *Ancient Society* 18 (1987): 7; Richlin, *Garden of Priapus* 134.
The view of women as "weak" manifested itself even in Roman legal codes. See *CII* 5.37.22.5 (326); *CTh* 3.16.1 (331). See further Suzanne Dixon, "Infirmitas Sexus: Womanly Weakness in Roman Law," *Tijdschrift voor Rechtsgeschiedenis* 52 (1984): 343-71.
[244]Valerius Maximum 8.15.12. See Kraemer, *Her Share* 56-57; Mary Beard, "The Sexual Status of Vestal Virgins," *Journal of Roman Studies* 70 (1980): 12-27.
[245]Pseudo Lucian *Erotes* 26.

well-known in both the Jewish Hellenistic and contemporaneous non-Jewish world. Ben Sira, for example, contains several passages on the dangers that women present.[246] Other Jewish-Hellenistic works, particularly the *Testament of the Twelve Patriarchs*, also contain strong rhetorics of the woman as seductress, as, of course, does early Christian rhetoric.[247]

At the same time, the emphasis on male sexual desire and the necessity of sexual self-control was well-known to Greek, Roman and the Jewish-Hellenistic writers. A man, according to several Greek authors, must work continuously to fight his sexual desire.[248] Romans linked sex to other "appetites," and preached an ethic of self-control.[249] Apollonius, according to Philostratus, in his youth subdued his "maddening" sexual passion.[250] Excessive intercourse, even with prostitutes and slaves, was disapproved because it displayed weakness.[251]

Christian rhetoric tends to mirror that of the Palestinian rabbis. The Synod of Elvira, echoing rabbinic rules of *yiḥud*, ruled that clerics were

---

[246] For a survey of these passages, see Trenchard, *Ben Sira's View of Women* 95-128; Claudia V. Camp, "Understanding a Patriarchy: Women in Second Century Jerusalem Through the Eyes of Ben Sira," in *"Women Like This:" New Perspectives on Jewish Women in the Greco-Roman World*, ed. Amy-Jill Levine (Atlanta: Scholars Press, 1991) 1-39.

[247] See Brown, *Body and Society* 206-7; Salisbury, *Independent Virgins* 23-25; John Lewis Eron, *Ancient Jewish Attitudes Towards Sexuality: A Study in Ancient Jewish Attitudes Towards Sexuality as Expressed in the Testaments of the Twelve Patriarchs* (Ann Arbor: University Microfilms, 1987) 293, 297.

[248] See, for example Xenophon *Mem.* 1.2.1; 2.1.1; 2.6.1; 4.5.9; *Oec.* 12.11-14; Lysias 21.19. See further Dover, *Greek Popular Morality* 208-9.

[249] See Gail Paterson Corrington, "The Defense of the Body and the Discourse of Appetite: Continence and Control in the Greco-Roman World," *Semeia* 57 (1992): 65-74.

[250] Philostratus *Life of Apollonius* 1.13.

[251] It must be remembered that prostitutes and slaves were common and easily obtained in the Roman world. Where sex was so easy to obtain, self-restraint was praised. For examples see [Dem.] 59; Xenophon *Oec.* See further Aline Rousselle, "Personal Status and Sexual Practice in the Roman Empire," in *Fragments for a History of the Human Body*, ed. Michel Feher (New York: Zone, 1989) 3:301-333, and, *Porneia* 97. See also Treggiari, *Roman Marriage* 301.

Philo proclaims that a prostitute should be put to death. See Philo *Spec. Laws* 3.51; *Jos.* 43 and on these passages Samuel Belkin, *Philo and the Oral Law: The Philonic Interpretation of Biblical Law in Relation to the Palestinian Halakah* (Cambridge: Harvard University Press, 1940) 256-56. Josephus *Ant.* 4.244-45 forbids a man from marrying a consort or a slave, using in regard to the latter the language of self-control. Cf. 1 Cor. 6:15-18, in which Paul argues (1) in our body is Christ; (2) to have intercourse is to make one body; (3) to have intercourse with a prostitute is to make Christ one with a prostitute. Later Christian sources prefer rhetorics of self-control.

not allowed to live with unrelated women.[252] When Christian women were not being reviled, they were being spurred on to sexual abstinence. That is, women were "safe" only when masculinized, only when they exercised the same sort of self-control as expected from men.[253] The Roman Syriac church became a violent, and misogynistic, proponent of asceticism in response, partly, to the perceived threat of women.[254] These short, general statements hardly do justice to the rich rhetorics on this topic. Nevertheless, they do capture the strong, if not dominant, feeling prevailing in the milieu of the rabbis.

CONCLUSIONS

The rabbis attributed to both women and men an overwhelming desire for sex, but whereas women were subjects of this desire, men were viewed as having the ability to control it. Like some Christian writers, Palestinian rabbis took a bleak view of a man's ability to control his *yeṣer*: the best solution to the temptations it offered was enforced separation and Torah study (presumably, away from women). While theoretically having the ability to control their sexual desire, men were advised not to tempt it, and could resist the opportunity to appease it only in exceptional circumstances.

Babylonian rabbis tended toward a more "optimistic" view of male sexual desire. Men could indeed, with a little help from the community, control their own sexuality. Public shaming was expected to help men keep their sexuality under control. Shame was also employed by Babylonians to help keep control over the sexuality of their daughters and wives.

Rhetoric of Threat

The scripturally ordained death penalty for adultery was, as noted above, dealt with by the rabbis didactically. The biblical penalties were used more as a device for categorization than as a true judicial threat. There are only two reported cases, from rabbinic literature or any other source, of Jews putting adulterers or adulteresses to death in late antiquity.[255] There is, however, evidence for other institutions and rhetorical strategies that threaten to punish those engaged in non-marital sexual liaisons. Two of these institutions are legal penalties for the

---

[252]Canon 27.
[253]See Brown, *Body and Society* 140-59; Clark, "Sex, Shame, and Rhetoric;" Karen I. Torjesen, "In Praise of Noble Women: Gender and Honor in Ascetic Texts," *Semeia* 57 (1992): 41-64.
[254]See Susan Ashbrook Harvey, "Women in Early Syrian Christianity," in *Images of Women* 294-95.
[255]These two sources, *m. Sanh.* 7:2 and *b. Sanh.* 52b, deal only with the adulterous daughter of a priest.

adulteress, namely, the prohibition of her returning to her husband and the forfeiture of her marriage settlement. The other is a rhetoric of threat, directed at both men and women engaged in extra-marital sex.

Most of the rhetoric of threat concentrates on the *soṭah* ordeal. In many cases, rabbinic treatments of the *soṭah* ordeal – which had long since lapsed by rabbinic times, if indeed it had ever been in effect[256] – strays far from the biblical account, and an analysis of these wanderings, as well as of the divergences between treatments by different rabbinic circles are instructive.

LEGAL PENALTIES

Prohibition of an Adulteress

The adulteress is prohibited from returning to her husband. As shown above, there is no evidence in rabbinic literature that an adulteress was prohibited to her husband because she was considered "impure." Rather, this rule appears to be adhering to classical legal formulations that seek to punish the adulteress or suspected adulteress.

In tannaitic sources, adultery causes a woman to be prohibited from returning to her husband.[257] This applies even when a woman has accidentally married two men: she is compelled to divorce each of them, and is prohibited from remarrying either of them.[258] They have each prohibited her to the other. The same applies even when she has not accidentally married another man. "Just as she is forbidden to [her] husband, she is forbidden to [her] lover," the *Mishnah* states.[259] Never do the tannaitic sources advance a reason for this prohibition. That is, is an adulteress prohibited from remaining with her husband as a punishment; or because it would be "impure," an offense against God; or for issues of the certainty of paternity?[260] In none of these sources is

---

[256]The practical irrelevance of the laws of the *soṭah* is acknowledged in the sources themselves (*m. Soṭ.* 9:9).
[257]See for example *m. Ned.* 11:12. A woman who declares herself "defiled," that is, admits to adultery, must be divorced. See below.
[258]*m. Yebam.* 10:1.
[259]*m. Soṭ.* 5:1.
[260]There is some evidence that would support each of these hypotheses. Applicable punishments, especially economic, against the adulteress are considered below. Loss of a woman's dowry and marriage settlement must be accompanied by divorce. The idea that the "impurity" of adultery is an offense against God probably prevails in the Bible. See Moshe Greenberg, "Some Postulates of Biblical Criminal Law," in *Yehezkel Kaufmann Jubilee Volume*, ed. Menahem Haran (Jerusalem: Magnes Press, 1960) 5-28; cf. Bernard Jackson, "Reflections on Biblical Criminal Law," *Journal of Jewish Studies* 24 (1973): 8-38. Finally, one tannaitic source hints that fear of paternity might underlie these rules. According to *t. Soṭ.* 5:6, only a "man," not a boy or eunuch, can prohibit a

there an idea that an adulteress would be prohibited to her husband because she is "polluted" or ritually "defiled." The Talmudim do not add to this rhetoric.[261] Both Talmudim take for granted the fact that women who commit adultery would be forbidden to their husbands.

Non-marital sex carries special weight in reference to priests, who are biblically commanded not to marry a woman "defiled by harlotry" or a divorcee (Lev. 21:7). In all sources, any discussion around this rule revolves around a definition of "harlot" – the rule itself is assumed to be in effect, and no reason for it is offered.[262]

Economic Penalties

Economic penalties apply only to adultery, and then, only to the adulteress.[263] Tannaitic sources clearly state that a Jewish adulteress must be divorced and sacrifices her marriage settlement.[264] The connection between monetary support and faithfulness of the wife is made explicit in a *sugya* in the Yerushalmi:

> A. It is written, "If a man sins against a man, [the Lord may pardon him; but if a man offends against God, who can obtain pardon for him?]," [1 Sam. 2:25].
>
> B. R. Ḥiyya bar Ba [PA 3] and R. Yehoshua ben Levi [PA 1] [disagree as to its interpretation]. R. Ḥiyyah bar Ba interpreted this verse as referring to the lover [of the woman]; R. Yehoshua ben Levi interpreted this verse as referring to the [adulterous] wife.
>
> C. R. Ḥiyya bar Ba interprets this verse to refer to the lover. "This man supports and maintains [this woman] and you come and take her."
>
> D. R. Yehoshua ben Levi interprets this verse to refer to the [faithless] wife. "This man supports and maintains you and you desire another man?"[265]

A man is supposed to respect the "investment" made by a woman's husband, and the wife is supposed to remain faithful to the man who supports her. Thus, it is no surprise that the sacrifice of an adulteress's marriage settlement is taken for granted in other discussions in the Yerushalmi.[266]

---

woman through adultery. That is, the adulterer must have the ability to procreate.
[261]They clearly accept this rule. For examples see *b. Ned.* 90b; *y. Ned.* 11:13, 42d.
[262]See *b. Yebam.* 56b, 61b; *b. Soṭ.* 26a; *b. Qidd.* 77b.
[263]I do not include in this discussion the "fines" levied for rape and seduction, which appear intended primarily to compensate the father of the woman for potential economic loss.
[264]*m. Soṭ.* 1:5; 4:1-3; *m. Ketub.* 7:6; *t. Soṭ.* 5:1-3.
[265]*y. Soṭ.* 1:15, 17a.
[266]See *y. Soṭ.* 4:1, 19c.

Discussion in the Bavli also assume that an adulteress's marriage settlement is forfeited.[267] These discussions do question the application of this principle to women of assorted marital states (e.g., betrothed, levirate widow), but the principle itself is not challenged. There are hints that tannaitic economic penalties may have gone beyond forfeiture of the marriage settlement, but that this was modified in Babylonia.[268]

A second economic consequence of non-marital intercourse is its effect on the daughter or wife of a priest or levite. Both are normally entitled to eat the tithes and other holy food brought to their fathers or husbands. If a woman married to a priest commits adultery and confesses then she is never again allowed, according to the *Mishnah*, to eat of the heave offering.[269] Another *mishnah* states that if the daughter of a priest or levite accidentally married a man while her first husband was still alive, among other ramifications is her loss of her right to eat of the tithes or heave offerings.[270]

The Yerushalmi limits the application of the mishnaic rule. According to R. Yosi, the levite's daughter is prohibited from eating the tithes in a case of mistaken marriage only when she has conceived a child from her second, mistaken husband, who is neither a levite nor a priest.[271] "Whoring" *per se*, the Yerushalmi is saying, does not disqualify her from eating tithes. Rather, the conception of a child from a Jewish non-priest accounts for the economic penalty.

Babylonian sources, however, see this mishnaic rule as a "penalty" (קנסא).[272] That is, the Bavli explicitly sees this deprivation as a punishment. When a woman remarries, she must be absolutely certain (and objectively correct) as to her marital status, or she will suffer a penalty. Women who dare to use their own judgment as to their marital status risk, if wrong, economic penalties.

Non-Rabbinic Parallels

Greek and Roman law both, with varying degrees of vehemence, encouraged men to divorce wives who committed adultery.[273] Similarly,

---

[267]See *b. Soṭ.* 17b; *b. Ketub.* 11b (par. *b. Ketub.* 46a).
[268]See *b. Ketub.* 101a-b.
[269]*m. Yebam.* 3:10; *m. Soṭ.* 1:2-3.
[270]*m. Yebam.* 10:1. See also *t. Yebam.* 8:2.
[271]*y. Yebam.* 10:1, 10d.
[272]*b. Yebam.* 91a. Judging from the continuation this opinion is accepted by the redactor.
[273]See Demosthenes 59.87, and on this law, David Cohen, *Law, Sexuality and Society* 110-22. The *Lex Iulia* also prohibited the maintenance of an adulterous wife. See *D.* 48.5.13, and on this Mette-Dittmann, *Die Ehegesetze*, 58-61. See also *D.* 48.5.2.2, 5, 6, 7 and the discussions of Judith P. Hallett, *Fathers and Daughters in Roman Society: Women and the Elite Family* (Princeton: Princeton University Press,

Non-Marital Sex

these laws assumed that an adulteress forfeits her dowry. As in the rabbinic law, no reason for these penalties are offered.

To my knowledge, there are no Greek or Roman laws equivalent to those that deal with a priest's daughter.

RHETORIC OF THREAT

Three major themes run through rabbinic commentary on the *soṭah*: public display; humiliation and shaming; and "measure for measure." In this section, I show how the rabbinic treatment of the *soṭah* ordeal consistently deviates from the biblical account, and integrating other rabbinic sources that share these themes I investigate one complex of rabbinic rhetorical strategies that control both male and female sexual behavior.

Public Display

According to the Bible, the *soṭah* ordeal involves three actors: the suspicious husband, the suspected wife, and the priest who conducts the ordeal. The ordeal itself takes place before the priest (Num. 5:15), where he "bring[s] her forward and [has] her stand before the Lord," (Num. 5:16). There are hints that the ordeal beings inside the Tabernacle (Num. 5:17) and ends at the altar (Num. 5:25). As far as we are told, the ordeal is conducted privately among these three actors.

An essential part of the rabbinic portrayal of the *soṭah* ordeal is that it is public. According to the *Mishnah*, after the *soṭah* is abjured by the Great Court (instead of by a single priest), she is led outside where "anyone who wants to see comes and sees ... and all the women are permitted to see her, as it is said, '... and all the women shall take warning not to imitate your wantonness,' [Ezek. 23:48]."[274] The public nature of the ordeal is essential: the *soṭah* is made an example for the women. This seemingly minor shift, from a private to public ceremony, changes the entire nature of the ordeal. In the *Mishnah's* portrayal the ordeal is no longer primarily a true test before God of a woman's guilt or innocence. Rather, it becomes a didactic exercise, a rhetoric that even if not put into effect threatens public announcement of even suspected female philandering.

Another tannaitic source suggests that the public shaming of the adulteress was rooted in societal practice.

> A parable: [It is similar] to a king who decreed and said that anyone who eats figs of the seventh year [which, because the land should lay fallow in the seventh year, are forbidden by the Bible],

---

1984) 237-40, 327-28; A.H.J. Greenidge, *Infamia: Its Place in Roman Public and Private Law* (Oxford: Oxford University Press, 1894), 171-76.
[274]*m. Soṭ.* 1:4 (Court), 1:6 (all coming to see her).

that they make him go around in the campus.²⁷⁵ One woman, from a good family, came and gathered and ate figs of the seventh year, and they made her go around in the campus. She said to him, please, my lord, let the king announce my sin so that all the subjects of the kingdom will not say that she is [i.e., I am] similar to an adulteress or a witch. [Let] them see figs dangling from my neck and they will know that it is for them that I am paraded thus.²⁷⁶

Adultery and public shaming of the woman were so linked that the woman in this parable simply assumes that when people saw her being publicly shamed they would assume that it was for her adultery. To protect her reputation, she requests that spectators be informed of the true nature of her sin.

There are several other examples in tannaitic literature of the intersection between public perception and non-marital sex. Repeatedly, a man is urged to divorce a woman whose reputation is the subject of gossip.²⁷⁷ A "profligate" woman was seen as casting aspersions on all Jewish women,²⁷⁸ and a bad reputation for a wife was to be feared.²⁷⁹ Adultery and sexual reputation were seen as public affairs. All of these tannaitic sources point to the dependence placed by the rabbis on public shaming for the enforcement of their set of sexual values.

Passages in the Yerushalmi suggest that in the post-tannaitic period shaming remained an important controlling strategy. In one passage, the Yerushalmi mentions the possibility of people overhearing gossip about a woman's sexual indiscretions.²⁸⁰ Another source is more explicit:

> Once a guard of vineyards came to have intercourse with a married woman. When they were searching for a *mikvah* where they [could] immerse, passers-by came and went and the sin was averted.²⁸¹

---

²⁷⁵Reading קמפון for קנפון, as sense demands and supported by manuscripts. See the notes on this line in *Sifre Deut.* 26 (p. 36), and Krauss, *Lehnwörter* 2:510. See also Steven D. Fraade, "Sifre Deuteronomy 26 (ad Deut. 3:23): How Conscious the Composition?" *Hebrew Union College Annual* 54 (1983): 264, n. 45; Saul Lieberman, *Greek in Jewish Palestine* (New York: Jewish Theological Seminary of America, 1942) 162-64.

²⁷⁶*Sifre Deut.* 26 (pp. 36-37). See also *Sifre Num.* 137 (p. 183); *b. Yoma* 76b. According to Fraade, the "original" version of this parable is in *Sifre Num.* The differences are, however, not relevant for this discussion. See Fraade, "Sifre Deuteronomy" 271-77; Lieberman, *Greek* 162-64.

²⁷⁷*m. Soṭ.* 6:1; *m. Ketub.* 7:6.

²⁷⁸*Sifre Deut.* 240 (p. 271); *b. Sanh.* 50b.

²⁷⁹*m. Yebam.* 13:1; *m. Soṭ.* 3:5.

²⁸⁰*y. Ketub.* 2:10, 24d. On this, see Lieberman, *Greek* 163-64.

²⁸¹*y. Ber.* 3:4, 6c. It is interesting to note that a somewhat parallel story at *b. Ber.* 22a (attributed to a PA 1) omits the elements of shaming from this story (*contra* Ginzberg). On this passage, see Ginzberg *Palestinian Talmud* 2:243, who notes the importance of shame in this passage. Based on a "logical" argument about the

It is the shame of the couple that averts the sin.²⁸² It is likely that this reflects a broader societal attitude – namely, that adultery was shameful, and that shame was deployed by the society in order to prevent it.

As we might expect from the discussion above on the use of shaming in the rhetoric of Babylonian amoraim, the Bavli uses the rhetoric of public shaming of the suspected adulteress. A *baraitha* found only in the Bavli records Joseph's recoil from the temptation of Potiphar's wife because of fear that he would be shamed.²⁸³ More telling, though, is a simple comment by a Babylonian amora on *m. Soṭ.* 1:5, which permits women to see the shamed, suspected adulteress: "Raba said, 'all who want to see her see,' there is no difference between men and women but women *are obligated* to see her..."²⁸⁴ Because the suspected adulteress is made into an example, all women are obligated to see her, in order to scare them all into proper behavior. On a *mishnah* that specifies that a woman who violated "Jewish law" by going out with her head uncovered, the Yerushalmi asks what is meant by "going out" and if she may wear a wig.²⁸⁵ The Bavli, though, begins by discussing the importance of head covering for women ("the Torah commands it") and then several Babylonian amoraim articulate very stringent rules in this regard, in contrast to the lone Palestinian amora cited in the *sugya*.²⁸⁶ In each of these disparate examples there is an increased use by Babylonians in utilizing a rhetoric of shame as a controlling device.

Humiliation

Rabbinic sources go beyond public shaming of the adulteress, prescribing actual humiliation and physical abuse. According to the Bible, the priest beings the *soṭah* ordeal by baring the woman's head (Num. 5:18). The discourse of the *Mishnah* is far more violent:

---

behavior of the woman in this story, however, he proposes that the woman referred to here is actually single rather than married, and that a scribe mistakenly expanded the abbreviation 'א 'א to אשה איש when אשה אחת was meant. No manuscript support for this emendation has subsequently been found.

²⁸²The purpose of this story within its *sugya* is to illustrate one rabbi's position that immersion should be maintained because it makes intercourse less convenient and hence helps to avert sin. A story later in this same *sugya* in which a man who has had intercourse with a married woman immerses in a dangerous place despite a rabbi telling him not to might attest to a popular folk connection between immersion and purification from (especially) illicit sexual liaisons.

²⁸³*b. Soṭ.* 36b.
²⁸⁴*b. Soṭ.* 8b, my emphasis.
²⁸⁵*y. Ketub.* 7:7, 31b.
²⁸⁶*b. Ketub.* 72a-b.

> The Priest grabs her garments – if they rip, they rip; if they tear open, they tear open – until he reveals her heart and loosens her hair ...
>
> If she was covered in white garments, he covers her in black garments; if she has gold jewelry and chains, earrings and rings – they strip [them] from her, in order to disgrace her. And afterwards he brings Egyptian rope and binds her above her breasts.[287]

The *Mishnah's* description of the ordeal finds no biblical support. Not only is the woman publicly accused of her transgression, but she is first subjected to physical violence and then disfigured. She is forced to hold her offering "in order to oppress her," a phrase softened in the Bavli but linked by the Yerushalmi to the deliberate scare tactics inherent in this ritual.[288] This language resurfaces later, when in describing what happens to the meal offering and potion that she is to drink if she confesses at different stages of the ordeal, the *Mishnah* says that at a certain point even if she confesses, "they cajole her and force her to drink against her will."[289] R. Yehudah expands on this in the *Tosefta*, saying that "they force her mouth open with tongs."[290] In a passage that I will consider in more depth below, the *Tosefta* relates the illnesses that she will suffer from the ordeal in uncomfortable detail.[291] Again, whether or not these things actually occurred is in a sense irrelevant. What is relevant is the rhetoric of violence and humiliation that is applied to a suspected adulteress.

The few sources of this rhetoric in the Yerushalmi both extend and justify this humiliation. Citing a *baraitha*, the Yerushalmi specifies that a woman is to be dressed in black only if it does not look good on her.[292] Another *baraitha* cited in the Yerushalmi reads: "Shimon ben Eleazar taught, even if it is a pure woman who drinks [the ordeal], her end is that she will die with evil diseases because she caused herself to enter this great uncertainty ..."[293] The punishments and humiliation that a woman endures are here justified by her previous behavior that led to the ordeal.

---

[287] *m. Soṭ.* 1:5-6.
[288] See *m. Soṭṭ.* 2:1; *b. Soṭ.* 14a; *y. Soṭ.* 2:1, 17d. On the meal offering, see Adriana Destro, *The Law of Jealousy: Anthropology of Sotah* (Atlanta: Scholars Press, 1989) 89-106, who holds that the meal offering is constructed in the *Mishnah* as non-expiatory. Rather, her sacrifice is different because she is different, representing the antithesis of God's plan.
[289] *m. Soṭ.* 3:3.
[290] *t. Soṭ.* 2:3. The same phrase is used in *m. Sanh.* 7:2, describing how execution by burning is carried out.
[291] *t. Soṭ.* 3:4-5.
[292] *y. Soṭ.* 1:7, 17a.
[293] *y. Soṭ.* 3:5, 19a. See also *y. Soṭ.* 1:5, 17a; 4:1, 19c.

Whether or not she is guilty of adultery, she is guilty of at least giving the wrong impression, and this alone is worthy of humiliation, even death.

In the Bavli too there are few sources of this type, but they also seek to justify the humiliation. An unparalleled *baraitha* seeks to justify through citation of Scripture the harm caused to the woman's body.[294] Interestingly, although the ordeal is connected to disgrace for the woman, the Bavli's version does not invoke the reasoning of the Yerushalmi, that she deserves the punishment for behaving in a way that caused her husband to suspect her.[295] R. Yehudah's statement on forcing the suspected woman to drink against her will is also cited without comment in the Bavli.[296] Here, as in the Yerushalmi, the rhetoric of public humiliation is attributed to tannaim.[297]

"MEASURE FOR MEASURE"

Reciprocity (also called the *lex Talionis*) – the idea that those who engage in forbidden or uncountenanced sexual liaisons will be equally and justly punished – is the overriding rhetoric of threat on non-marital sexual liaisons and the only one that to any significant degree discusses men.

ADULTERESSES

The link between an adulteress or suspected adulteress and her punishment is explicit even in the *Mishnah*:

> The measure with which man measures they will measure out to him. She adorned herself for sin – God disgraces her. She revealed herself for sin – God uncovers her. With the thigh did she begin in sin first, and afterwards the belly [i.e., womb], therefore the thigh withers first, and afterwards the belly ...[298]

Each element of the ordeal, from the procedure leading up to the drinking of the potion to its effects, is based on reciprocity. Each of the adulteress's actions subjects her to a distinct punishment. As shown in

---

[294] *b. Soṭ.* 8a.
[295] *b. Soṭ.* 8b.
[296] *b. Soṭ.* 19b.
[297] Saul Lieberman states that public humiliation of the adulteress gained in popularity from the talmudic to gaonic periods. See Saul Lieberman, "Shaving of the Hair and Uncovering of the Face among Jewish Women," reprinted in *Texts and Studies* (New York: Ktav, 1974) 52-56. There is, however, no talmudic evidence for this.

It is interesting to note that the Romans too did not employ this strategy. Tacitus *Germ.* 19.1-2 comments that the Germans, unlike the Romans, did humiliate their wives if they committed adultery. See also Hallett, *Fathers and Daughters* 326-27.

[298] *m. Soṭ.* 1:7.

the paragraphs that follow this source, and in countless other rabbinic parables and traditions, the application of this principle is not limited to the adulteress. Yet it is this idea that is most seized upon by the rabbinic sources to justify the prescribed treatment of the adulteress. Thus, the *Tosefta* expands considerably on the *Mishnah* cited above:

A. Thus you find with the *sotah* that the measure with which she measured they measure out to her. She stood before him so that she would be pretty before him, therefore the priest stands her before all, to show her disgrace, as it is said, "... [and the] priest will have her stand before the Lord," [Num. 5:16].

B. She put on a head-covering for him,[299] thus the priest takes the covering from her head and places it at her feet.

C. She braided her hair for him, thus the priest loosens it.

D. She adorned her face for him, thus her face turns green [from the potion].

E. She painted her eyelids for him, thus her eyes bulge.

F. She pointed at him with a finger [thus designating him as her lover],[300] thus her nails are clipped.

G. She showed him her flesh, thus the priest rips her garment and shows her disgrace to many.

H. She girded herself in an undergarment,[301] thus the priest brings Egyptian rope and binds her above her breasts,

I. And all who want come and see.

J. She offered him her thigh, thus her thigh falls off.

K. She received him on her stomach, thus her belly withers.

L. She fed him dainties, thus her offering is the food of beasts.

M. She gave him fine wine to drink in fine cups, thus the priest causes her to drink bitter waters in a vessel of clay.[302]

This passage not only explains the strange rites of the ordeal; it systematically threatens the potential adulteress, showing how every single act leading up to actual adultery will eventually be punished.[303]

---

[299]This follows Lieberman's suggestion (*Tos. Kip.* 8:637). The force of this action – a woman putting on a head-covering for her lover – is obscure.
[300]Following Lieberman, ibid.
[301]Following Lieberman, ibid.: עישלין.
[302]*t. Sot.* 3:2-4.
[303]See also *t. Sot.* 4:10. Note that whereas the *mishnah* showed how each part of the ordeal corresponds to an action on the part of the adulteress, this *tosefta* links each act of the adultery to a part of the ordeal. Thus, although the effects of the

In fact, the *Tosefta* and other tannaitic texts go beyond articulation of "measure for measure." "Because she set her eyes upon another who is not fitting for her, what she requested is not given to her and what she has is taken from her."[304] What she has, according to the midrash, is her honor.[305] The adulterous wife is punished beyond her measure.

The Yerushalmi lacks this rhetoric in regard to the adulteress.[306] Moreover, the Yerushalmi neither comments relevantly on the *mishnah* that discusses the concept of "measure for measure" nor does it cite any of the tannaitic material discussed here on this topic. The Bavli does cite the passages from the *Tosefta* discussed above, but offers little or no commentary on them or additional statements of the rhetoric in reference to the adulteress.[307] Apparently, only the *Tosefta* uses this rhetoric to any effect.

ADULTERERS

When we move to deployment of this rhetoric in discussion of male adulterers, however, the picture is somewhat different. Both Talmudim, especially the Bavli, utilized this rhetoric against men engaged in extramarital liaisons.

Tannaitic Sources. The *Mishnah* applies the rhetoric of "measure for measure" in two different ways to adulterers. First, although it is the woman who undergoes the ordeal, the ordeal is said to also effect her lover: "just as the waters check (בודקין) her, so the water check him [the lover], as it is written, 'come,' 'come' [Num. 5:22, 27]."[308] The exegesis derives from an extra letter in the Hebrew word for "come" (ובאו), used twice to indicate the potion entering the woman's body.[309] According to this *mishnah* this extra letter indicates that her lover, too, will be affected by the waters "and even he will die the same death."[310]

The second mishnaic application of this rhetoric is to threaten male adulterers with infidelity of their own wives. Citing Hos. 4:14 ("I will not punish their daughters for fornicating nor their daughters-in-law for committing adultery; for they themselves turn aside with whores ..."), the *Mishnah* asserts that the *sotah* ordeal ceased to work when adulterers

---

potion (D, E) obviously result from her drinking the potion (M), the *tosefta* places the former first.
[304]*t. Sot.* 4:16.
[305]*Sifre Num.* 21 (p. 25).
[306]*y. Sot.* 1:7, 17a links the results of drinking the potion to the actions involved in adultery, but this is more in reference to the man.
[307]See *b. Sot.* 8b-9a (citing *t. Sot.* 3:5); *b. Sot.* 9a-b (citing *t. Sot.* 4:16).
[308]*m. Sot.* 5:1.
[309]For a discussion of the exegesis, its versions and its difficulties, see Albeck, *Mishnah* 3:384.
[310]Notes by Albeck on *m. Sot.* 5:1, 3:244.

increased.[311] The cessation of the ordeal is dated by the *Mishnah*, along with the cessation of many other indications of divine grace, to the end of the Second Temple period.

The ideas that the waters also check an adulteress's lover and that female infidelity is linked to the behavior of their husbands are also found in other tannaitic sources. But whereas the first of these themes, that the ordeal also effects her lover, is treated sparsely, the second theme is given ample expression.[312] According to one tradition, God says to the Israelites, "because you run after whores the waters will not test your wives ..."[313] Curiously, the *Tosefta* offers an alternative reason why the waters ceased: "the bitter waters work only in cases of doubt. Now already many have increased who see [them] openly."[314] Because the *soṭah* ceremony is only for the suspected adulteress, and people "now" publicly and shamelessly commit their sexual transgressions, the waters have lost their effectiveness. Although the *Tosefta* does seem to reject the ideas that an adulterer is affected by or has any effect upon the bitter waters, it still finds an application for the rhetoric of "measure for measure" to the male adulterer: Samson is blinded because he sinned with his eyes, and Absalom was pierced with a lance for each one of his father's concubines whom he violated.[315] By accepting these traditions (the former is from the *Mishnah*[316]) and rejecting the others, the *Tosefta*, it appears, is more comfortable with extending the concept of "measure for measure" in a very literal manner to men that with positing than male infidelity is rewarded with female infidelity.

Yerushalmi. In contrast to the *Tosefta*, the Yerushalmi expands on both the themes presented in the *Mishnah*. In its commentary on the mishnaic assertion that the waters "check" the lover of the suspected adulteress, the Yerushalmi considers the reasons that may account for a case in which one of the lovers becomes sick after the ordeal and the other does not.[317] The premise, that an adulterer is tested along with his lover, is not questioned. Likewise, the Yerushalmi follows the *Mishnah* in asserting that there is a causal link between male infidelity and the

---

[311]*m. Soṭ.* 9:9.
[312]See *Sifre Num.* 15 (p. 20).
[313]*Sifre Num.* 21 (p. 25).
[314]*t. Soṭ.* 14:2.
[315]*t. Soṭ.* 3:15-16.
[316]*m. Soṭ.* 1:8.
[317]*y. Soṭ.* 5:1, 20a. The *sugya* also deals with the exegetical problems posed by the *mishnah*. See also *y. Soṭ.* 1:3, 16d.

fidelity of their wives. For the waters to work, one tradition asserts, men must be free from sin.[318]

Bavli. Linking a man's sexual activities to those of this wife appears to be the Bavli's primary rhetoric of control of male sexuality. The Bavli accepts the *Mishnah's* assertion that just as the waters test the woman, they test "him," but it questions who the "him" is: husband or lover?[319] Although at the end the lover is seen as the correct referent, the bulk of the short *sugya* asserts that a *particular* man's wife can only be tested if her husband is "free from sin," an assertion that is never effectively refuted. Not only did an increase in adulterers cause the bitter waters to lose their potency, but, the redactor suggests, even other non-marital liaisons played a role.[320] The concept of a man "getting what he deserves" is expanded in the Bavli. A statement attributed to Reish Lakish [PA 2] (tradent: Shmuel bar Rav Yitzhak [PA 3]) said in regard to a *sotah* that a man gets a wife "according to his deeds."[321] If he is sexually promiscuous, his wife will be promiscuous. This sentiment is echoed in a statement cited in the Bavli attributed to R. Yohanan [PA 2] and supported by a Babylonian proverb.[322] If the attributions are correct, it would indicate that both Palestinian and Babylonian rabbis shared this assumption, but that only the Bavli employs it as a significant rhetorical strategy.[323]

Non-Rabbinic Parallels. This rhetoric would not by any means have been new. Roman philosophers had from the time of Augustus spoken out against the double standard.[324] Even Roman law codified this opinion: "A judge [in a case] of adultery ought to keep before his eyes and to inquire into whether the husband by his own chaste life was also setting his wife an example of cultivating sound morals..."[325] Jewish-Hellenistic sources are also familiar with this concept.[326]

---

[318]*y. Sot.* 9:9, 24a. This opinion is based upon the irregular wording of Num. 5:31.
[319]*b. Sot.* 27b-28a.
[320]*b. Sot.* 57b. This *sugya* cites *Sifre Num.* 21 (p. 25), which is also cited elsewhere in the Bavli: *b. Sot.* 28a; *b. Shebu.* 5a; *b. Yebam.* 58a; *b. Qidd.* 27b. See also *y. Sot.* 9:9, 24a.
[321]*b. Sot.* 2a.
[322]*b. Sot.* 10a.
[323]Another example of the Bavli's use of this rhetoric is the Babylonian tradition that Balaam, who induced Israel to fornicate, was punished by being condemned after death to seep in boiling semen (*b. Git.* 57a). In this short tradition, we also see a rhetoric of divine punishment of the individual.
[324]See Treggiari, *Roman Marriage* 312-13.
[325]D.48.5.14(13).5.
[326]See *Sent. Syr. Men.* 245-247 (ed. Charlesworth, 2:599); *Philemon/Menander* (ed. Charlesworth, 2:830); *Jub.* 20:5-6 (ed. Charlesworth, 2:94).

Summary and Conclusions

Adultery (ניאוף) was defined by all our sources (except perhaps the *Tosefta*, which might have included other forms of sexual contact in its definition) as intercourse between a man, married or not, and a married woman. Although the punishment mandated in the Bible for such a transgression is death, the capital punishment here is considered in the rabbinic sources in a strictly academic or didactic context. According to rabbinic law adultery on the part of a woman led to mandatory divorce and economic penalties.

Non-marital, non-adulterous intercourse was all subsumed under the rubric *bʿilat znut*. Among tannaitic sources, use of this term, and its occasional application even to adulterous liaisons, resembles the linguistic field of the Latin *stuprum*. The term *bʿilat znut* appears to have been first used by the rabbis, who may have created a biblical cognate in order to add authority to a category that derived from non-Jewish sources. In amoraic sources, however, the term is extended to cover non-procreative intercourse. In legal discussions on other topics as well there is close correspondence between rabbinic and Roman law.

Palestinians continue to emphasize a rhetoric of children and marital sexuality. Female sexual activity outside of marriage was heavily stigmatized. Shame and the threat of public humiliation were used as controlling strategies. Non-marital male sexual expression came under increasing attack in Palestinian sources, mirroring the tone of Roman and Christian writers.

Babylonian sources reflect a much more complex attitude toward non-marital sexuality. While also disapproving of adultery and non-marital female sexual activities, these sources also recognize that such activities took place and that they played a role in the apportionment of honor and shame.

Another difference between Palestinian and Babylonian rabbis was their response to a shared anthropological assumption that both men and women have strong sexual desires, but that only men have the capability and obligation to control these desires. Palestinian rabbis offer a bleak picture of male sexual self-control: men should stay as far away as possible from temptation, because although they theoretically can control themselves, in practice they are unlikely to be able to. Babylonian rabbis believe that men can, with a little help from the community and the fear of societal shame, control these desires.

Self-control, or its inverse, the succumbing to sexual desire, held a very important place in the thought of both Palestinians and Babylonians. Rabbis were expected to be paradigms of self-control in all matters. Following Roman attitudes, this might have been perceived as indicative of the power that they held as elite men: mastery over oneself was symbolic of the power that they held (or thought they deserved to hold) over others. Gentiles were paradigmatic of the opposite, of those who had no discipline. To surrender self-control was, to the rabbis, the beginning of a slide that ends in idolatrous in practice, like the Gentiles. Hence, this rhetoric of sexual self-control appears to be a part of a much wider discourse of power.

Similar parallels between this Jewish and non-Jewish discourse can be seen in the increasingly powerful movement away from the "double-standard." Men never are treated with the same harshness as are women, but the adulterer will pay "according to his measure." His unchastity, even with a non-married woman, could lead to his wife's unchastity. This is the rabbinic equivalent to the "new marriage morality" sweeping through Rome at this time. A man was supposed to set an example in controlled living for his wife, who was beginning to be perceived more as a partner than an instrument to create babies to augment either his lineage or the city's army. The double-standard remained "legal," but men were forcefully told what they risked if they took advantage of this opportunity.

The glimpses that these texts allow us of the scene behind them – the world of real rabbis, their society, and their constituency – are tantalizing. It must always be borne in mind that these are primarily legal texts, prescriptive texts, that do not represent the subtle and complex textures and dynamics that swirl in all societies around matters of sexuality. I have attempted to apply, where possible, an honor/shame model to these texts to show how they might reflect certain assumptions and function in a broader context. No matter how many Babylonian texts, for example emphasize that an adulterer will be paid back for his crime, it is difficult to erase that image presented at the end of Tractate *Nedarim* of an adulterer saving the life of his lover's husband, and the surprising rabbinic responses to this story. The issue that this raises, the correlation between the rhetoric and the reality, will be discussed in the Conclusion.

5

Homoeroticism[1]

Homoerotic contact stands at the nexus of two different groups of sexual rhetoric.[2] To this point, the rhetoric examined has concerned sexual partners, "who" is prohibited as a sexual partner, and why. In Chapters 6 and 7 I discuss the regulation of sexual activity, "how" sex is to be performed, and why. Homoeroticism contains both aspects. The scriptural verse prohibiting male homoeroticism, "Do not lie with a male as one lies with a woman; it is an abhorrence," (Lev. 18:22) itself contains

---

[1]Scholarship on Jewish homoeroticism has been plagued by polemical and apologetic overtones. For recent examples, see Epstein, *Sex Laws* 134-38 (grouped under the sub-title, "sex perversions"); I. Jakobovits, "Homosexuality," *Encyclopedia Judaica* 8:961-62; Samuel Dresner, "Homosexuality and the Order of Creation," *Judaism* 40 (1991): 309-21; William Orbach, "Homosexuality and Jewish Law," *Journal of Family Law* 14 (1975): 353-81; Novak, *The Image of the Non-Jew* 211; Gershom Frankfurter and Rivka Ulmer, "Eine Anfrage über Homosexualität im jüdischen Gesetz," *Zeitschrift für Religions- und Geistesgeschichte* 43 (1991): 49-56. See also the sources in Tom Horner, *Homosexuality and the Judeo-Christian Tradition: An Annotated Bibliography* (Metuchen, NJ: Scarecrow, 1981).

The many recent studies of homoeroticism in Greek, Roman, and Christian society usually only make passing reference to the "Jewish view" of homosexuality. See, for example, John Boswell, *Christianity, Social Tolerance, and Homosexuality: Gay People in Western Europe from the Beginning of the Christian Era to the Fourteenth Century* (Chicago: University of Chicago Press, 1980) 26, n. 48 and 101, nn 32, 34; Brown, *Body and Society* 34-64 (for general comments about Jewish sexuality). Robin Scroggs, *The New Testament and Homosexuality* (1985; rpt. Philadelphia: Fortress Press, 1987) 66-84, is an exception.

[2]It is unclear whether there was a conceptual category in antiquity similar to our "homosexual," applied to people based upon the gender of the object of their sexual desire. See David Halperin, "One Hundred Years of Homosexuality," in *One Hundred Years of Homosexuality*, ed. David M. Halperin, 15-40. Hence, I use the more neutral term "homoerotic" to designate only sexual activities between members of the same gender.

both a "who" and a "how" element. Rabbinic rhetoric too, I attempt to show, integrates both kinds of regulations into a complex but discernible discourse on gender and gender expectations.

Rhetoric of Definition

That Scripture prohibits male homoerotic contact is clear; exactly what form of homoerotic contact is prohibited is more ambiguous. Aside from Lev. 18:22, the only other biblical legal dictum on homoerotic contact is Lev. 20:13: "If a man lies with a male as one lies with a woman, the two of them have done an abhorrent thing; they shall be put to death – their bloodguilt is upon them." These verses leave two primary ambiguities. First, they are addressed only to men: what of women and those who are, strictly, neither men nor women, such as the hermaphrodite? Secondly, what exactly does "as one lies with a woman" (לא תשכב משכבי אשה) mean – which activities are prohibited?

PROHIBITED PARTNERS

Hermaphrodites

Before the discovery of genes gender determination was a much simpler affair: genitalia was the sole determinant. The hermaphrodite, termed in rabbinic literature an *androgunos* (a loan-word from the Greek ἀνδρόγυνος, "man-woman," a person with both male and female genitalia),[3] generated a great deal of rabbinic discussion. Which laws apply to an *androgunos*, those that normally apply to women or to men?[4] It is not surprising that this confusion spilled over to the rabbinic discussions of the hermaphrodite vis-à-vis restrictions on male homoerotic contact. The *Mishnah*, for example, states that intercourse with a hermaphrodite is equivalent to homoerotic intercourse.[5] The *Tosefta* cites and glosses this tradition:

> A. R. Eleazar (or Eliezer) said, I heard that regarding a *androgunos* that those who lie with him deserve stoning, like [lying with] a male.
>
> B. To what does this [opinion] apply? In a time when he comes upon him the way of males (דרך הזכרות), but if he does not come upon him [in] the way of males, he is not liable.[6]

---

[3]See *b. Yebam.* 83b.
[4]For an overview of regulation concerning the hermaphrodite, see *Encyc. Talm.* 2:55-60 (Hebrew), (Eng. edition: 1:386-99). Some of this rhetoric was no doubt inspired by the rabbinic, especially mishnaic, tendency to categorize. See Jacob Neusner, *Judaism: The Evidence of the Mishnah* (Chicago: University of Chicago Press, 1981) 256-70.
[5]*m. Yebam.* 8:6.
[6]*t. Yebam.* 10:2.

In the *Mishnah*, according to (A), the hermaphrodite is counted as a male for sexual purposes, so a man who penetrates a hermaphrodite either vaginally or anally would be as liable as if he penetrated another male. The *Tosefta's* gloss in (B) limits this to intercourse in "the way of males," most likely anal penetration,[7] but declares vaginal intercourse not to be a capital crime. For this tradition, the possession of male genitalia is not in itself determinative of being "male." That is, when an *androgunos* is sexually passive in vaginal intercourse, the act is not a capital crime. Only when passive in anal intercourse does the act come perilously close to male homoeroticism, and is thus prohibited.[8] The tradition is cited in slightly different versions in the Yerushalmi and Bavli.[9]

The rabbinic anxiety about male penetration is crucial. While the case of the *androgunos* is special, the attitude that is shown here pervades the Palestinian rhetoric on homoerotic intercourse.

Non-Rabbinic Parallels

The anxiety reflected in rabbinic writings over the sexuality of the hermaphrodite, whether and how to treat him/her as man or woman, is reflected in other classical sources. Hermaphrodites appear with regularity in classical and hellenistic art.[10] Classical Greek writers use the term *androgunos* to refer to effeminate men.[11] Roman writers appear

---

[7] This is one of the few places in the rabbinic corpus that the term דרך זכרות is employed. I have followed the traditional understanding of the phrase. See Lieberman, *Tos. Kip.* 6:94-96.

[8] Anal intercourse with females is normally not prohibited. See Chapter 6. This explanation might also explain use of the peculiar term דרך הזכרות instead of another more common term that signifies anal intercourse. This term emphasizes the "maleness" of the passive participant.

[9] *b. Yebam.* 82b, 83b; *y. Yebam.* 8:6, 9d. According to Lieberman, *Tos. Kip.* 6:94, the version from the *Tosefta* is "certain," or original. At *b. Yebam.* 83b there is an unparalleled *baraitha* in the name of Rabbi Simmai that repeats the opinion of R. Eleazar but in more biblical language. It is possible that the curious phrasing of the *Tosefta* confused the ancients as well. Both Talmudim attempt to justify the distinction between treating the hermaphrodite as a man or a woman through alternative interpretations of the ambiguous biblical phrase, "as one lies with a woman," (Lev. 18:22). In *b. Yebam.* 83b this is attributed to רבא בר המדורי (in MS. Munich 95 it is reported as ר' אבא בר המדורי). In *y. Yebam.* 8:6, 9d it is unattributed.

[10] See Marie Delcourt, *Hermaphrodite: Myths and Rites of the Bisexual Figure in Classical Antiquity* (1956; rpt. London: Studio Books, 1961).

[11] See Plato *Symp.* 189e; Menander *Aspis* 242. See also Saara Lilja, *Homosexuality in Republican and Augustan Rome* (Commentationes Humanarum Litterarum 74; Helsinki: Societas Scientiarum Fennica, 1983) 35.

to think of hermaphrodites as effeminate males, exactly the fear shown by the rabbis.[12]

Of the Jewish-Hellenistic authors only Philo discusses the *androgunos*. Following classical Greek writers, Philo uses the term to refer to men who act effeminately or mutilate their genitals.[13] The *androgunos* in Philo's writings always meets with condemnation. While most rabbinic rhetoric on the *androgunos* is morally neutral (for the rabbis view the *androgunos* as a biological fact rather than a mode of behavior), the rhetoric on the sexuality of the *androgunos* might well be informed by the same uneasiness that Philo so forcefully expresses.

Clement of Alexandria, like Philo, condemns the *androgunos* (by which he means both the hermaphrodite and the passive male partner in homoerotic intercourse) as effeminate.[14]

Female Homoeroticism

The biblical prohibition against homoerotic contact is addressed exclusively to men. In the rabbinic literature only a few sources discuss female homoerotic contact. The only tannaitic reference to female homoeroticism is found in the *Sifra*:

A. "You shall not copy the practices of the land of Egypt ... or the land of Canaan ..." [Lev. 18:3]

B. Is it possible that one should not build buildings or not plant vineyards like them?

C. Scripture says, "nor shall you follow their laws." I am only talking about those laws which are legislated [i.e., distinctive] for them and for their fathers and for their fathers' fathers.

D. And what would they do?

E. A man would marry a man; and a woman [would marry a] woman; and a man would marry a woman and her daughter; and a woman would marry two [men].

F. Therefore it says, "nor shall you follow their laws."[15]

---

[12]See Pliny 7.3.34; Val. Max. 8.3.1. See also James M. Saslo, *Ganymede in the Renaissance: Homosexuality in Art and Society* (New Haven: Yale University Press, 1986) 77-84; Judith P. Hallett, "Women as *Same* and *Other* in Classical Roman Elite," *Helos* 16 (1989): 59-78. Roman legal codes more explicitly link the hermaphrodite to masculinity. See *D*.22.5.15.1.

[13]See Philo *Sacr. Abel and Cain* 100; *Who is the Heir* 274; *On Dreams* 1.126; *Spec. Laws* 1.325; *Spec. Laws* 3.38, 40-41; *Virtues* 18-21; *Cont. Life* 60.

[14]Clement Alex. *Paed.* 2.10 (GCS 12:208). See also Wayne A. Meeks, "Image of the Androgyne: Some Uses of a Symbol in Earliest Christianity," *History of Religions* 13 (1973-74): 165-208.

[15]*Sifra Aḥare* 9:8 (85c-d).

The rhetorical strategy of this passage, which uses homoerotic marriages to differentiate the "other," will be considered below. (E) includes the reference to marriage between women. Of the four liaisons mentioned, only this liaison is nowhere hinted at or mentioned in Lev. 18.[16] Without explicitly justifying a prohibition against female homoerotic marriages through Scripture, this passage nevertheless suggests to a non-observant reader or listener that in fact there is a prohibition and that it is scripturally based. One can only guess at the reason for this inclusion: it is possible that the evocation of the marital relationship indicates a strong disapproval or even fear of the rejection of men and the family ideal. Alternatively, perhaps this is a response to an actual social phenomenon. In either case, it should be noted that this is a condemnation not of homoerotic sex acts, but of *marriage*. This passage does not explicitly comment upon female homoerotic sexual acts.

The Talmudim briefly discuss female homoeroticism. According to the *Tosefta*, "If a woman 'rubs' with her minor son, and he penetrates her, the School of Shammai disqualifies her [from marrying a priest], but the School of Hillel permits it."[17] The Yerushalmi records a slightly different version:

> A. If a woman 'rubs' with her son, the School of Shammai forbids her [from marrying a priest]. The School of Hillel allows [her to marry a priest].
>
> B. If two women 'rub' with each other the School of Shammai forbids her [from marrying a priest]. The School of Hillel allows [her to marry a priest.][18]

(A) omits the phrase "he penetrates her." This omission is crucial, as "rub with" now becomes so ambiguous that it can be taken to refer to sexual acts that do not involve penetration. Only from this omission can (B) follow. If (A) does not refer to penile penetration, then the question arises as to the status of women who conduct this activity with other

---

[16]The prohibition of polyandry is implied throughout Lev. 18, and is in fact a violation of the laws against adultery.

[17]*t. Soṭ.* 5:7. The term for "rub, sport with," המסללת, is found in some manuscripts as המסלסלת. The continuation of the tradition, הערה בה, appears to refer to penetration of a woman by a penis (see the parallel at *b. Sanh.* 69b), implying that המסללת is something short of actual penetration. Otherwise, the term is obscure: non-sexual uses of the root סלל include "swing," "be light," neither of which help to elucidate the sexual activity being performed in this tradition and the ones cited below. See Jastrow 995, s.v., סלל.

[18]*y. Giṭ.* 8:10, 49c.

women.¹⁹ This is the only source referring to female homoeroticism in the Yerushalmi.²⁰

A parallel in the Bavli more explicitly dismisses the import of female homoeroticism:

A. ...R. Hunah [BA 2] said, women who 'rub' with each other are ineligible to marry a priest,

B. And even according to Rabbi Eleazar who said that a single man who has sex with a single woman not for the sake of marriage makes her a *zōnah* [i.e., ineligible to marry a priest, then the same conclusion follows because]

C. These words apply to a man [who has intercourse with a woman not for the sake of marriage], but for a woman, it is only licentiousness [i.e., a woman 'rubbing' with another woman does not render her a *zōnah* and therefore unfit to marry a priest.]²¹

(A) attributes to a Babylonian amora the same law attributed in the Yerushalmi to the School of Shammai.²² In (C), Rav Huna's statement is rejected by Raba (or possibly the redactor). Female homoeroticism is deemed inconsequential.

Another Babylonian source demonstrates the same reluctance to legislate legal disabilities for female homoeroticism. *b. Shab.* 65a-b first cites Rav Huna's statement in order to reject it. The *sugya* continues with Shmuel's father's prohibition against his daughters sleeping together. The reason for this prohibition, according to the redactor, is so "they will not grow accustomed to a strange body." Rashi understands this to mean that because they would be accustomed to sleep with someone, they would be more likely to have sex with a man – his body would not be considered "strange" and frightening. If this is correct, the redactor

---

¹⁹Note that the Yerushalmi, unlike Roman authors (see below), apparently can conceive of female homoerotic contact that does not involve penetration of a woman.

²⁰The redactional issues involved in this passage are complex. Did the redactor of the Yerushalmi receive this tradition or manufacture it? Can parts (A) and (B) be from different sources? I think it probable that the passage is unified and probably post-tannaitic. The tradition presents itself as an alternate to *t. Soṭ.* 5:7. If the primacy of *t. Soṭ.* 5:7 is accepted, then it appears that at some point the phrase הערה בה was first eliminated, and then (B) was added based on a new understanding of מסלדת. Otherwise, it is necessary to postulate that two very different competing versions of the same tradition were in circulation.

²¹*b. Yebam.* 76a. פריצותא has a general meaning of laxity, though it is often used opposite צניעות. See *b. Ketub.* 96a, *b. Qidd.* 80b; *b. Sanh.* 21a for sexual meanings. For some non-sexual usages, see *b. Ketub.* 13b and *b. ʿErub.* 64b.

²²This is an additional reason to doubt the authenticity of the "tannaitic" parallel in the Yerushalmi. Had the Bavli received this version it would no doubt have been cited, in place of attributing it to R. Huna (who can also be assumed not to have known the Yerushalmi's version).

has again refused to confer any legal prohibition on female homoeroticism. Even if Rashi's interpretation is not correct, and that the fear is that the daughters would become accustomed to a "different" – i.e., a woman's body, thus being less likely to engage in heterosexual activity, the redactor still rejects Rav Huna's statement without further comment. There is only minor condemnation of female homoerotic contact. It is of course possible that Palestinian and Babylonian rabbis would have been shocked at and disgusted by these relationships, but they do not develop any rhetoric that would lead to such a conclusion.

Non-Rabbinic Parallels

Writers in the Roman period frequently discussed female homoeroticism, which they strongly condemned.[23] Roman authors generally employed two modes of condemnation: that it was "other," (usually Greek), and that it involved gender blurring.[24] Roman authors, it seems, could only perceive of female homoeroticism in terms of penetration – one partner must be active, the other passive.[25] For a woman to take the active role in intercourse blurred gender distinctions, and thus was harshly denounced by these male authors.

Pseudo-Phocylides and Paul condemn female homoeroticism through appealing to arguments from "nature" and gender expectation.[26]

---

[23]For a review of sources on female homoeroticism in the classical world, see Scroggs, *The New Testament and Homosexuality* 140-44; Bernadette J. Brooten, "Paul's View on the Nature of Women and Female Homoeroticism," in *Immaculate and Powerful: The Female in Sacred Image and Social Reality*, ed. Clarissa W. Atkinson, Constance H. Buchanan, and Margaret R. Miles (Boston: Beacon Press, 1985) 65-70. Brooten concludes that Roman authors, "*did* regard sexual relations between women as harmful, bizarre, immoral, and threatening," (79).

[24]On female homoeroticism as "Greek," see Ovid *Met.* 9.666 ff; Seneca *Mor. Ep.* 95.20.2; Martial 1.90, 7.67, 7.70. On these and other passages, see Judith P. Hallett, "Female Homoeroticism and the Denial of Roman Reality in Latin Literature," *Yale Journal of Criticism* 3 (1989/90): 209-27, esp. 213. On gender blurring, see below.

[25]The use of the term *tribiades*, which derives from the Greek word meaning "rub" (a parallel to the rabbinic use of מסוללות?), usually denotes the *active* female partner. This linguistic shift testifies to the strength of the active/passive dichotomy in Roman sexual assumptions. See Seneca *Contr.* 1.2.23; *Phaed.* 4.15-16; Lucian *Dial, merctricii* 5 (289-92); Martial 1.90, 7.67, 7.70. See also Hallett, "Female Homoeroticism" 209-10; Eva Cantarella, *Bisexuality in the Ancient World*, trans. Cormac O. Cuillemain (New Haven: Yale University Press, 1992) 164-71.

[26]Pseudo-Phocylides 1.192; Rom. 1:26. See Scroggs, ibid. 114-15; Bernadette J. Brooten, "Early Christian Women and Their Cultural Context: Issues of Method in Historical Reconstruction," in *Feminist Perspectives on Biblical Scholarship*, ed. Adela Yarbro Collins (Chico: Scholars Press, 1985) 72-75, and, "Paul and the Law: How Complete Was the Departure," in *The Church and Israel: Romans 9-11*, ed.

Female homoeroticism is wrong, according to these authors, because it involves a reversal of women's "normal," passive sexual role. Among the Church Fathers, Chrysostom and Augustine are among the few to mention it. Augustine rebukes a group for nuns for the "shameless playing with each other" that immodest women do.[27] Here, as with Chrysostom, the condemnation of female homoeroticism is based upon a perception that gender expectations have been violated.[28]

Gender blurring, as shall be shown, was very much a part of rabbinic assumptions about male homoeroticism. That the rabbis, unlike these Roman and early Christian sources, were relatively undisturbed by female homoeroticism. For the rabbis, female homoeroticism did not involve any form of penetration. Sex without penetration was not truly sex, thus not deserving of special consideration (see below). Had the rabbis conceived of a penetrating female homoeroticism, their response might have been quite different.

One should note that only in the *Sifra* are male and female homoeroticism grouped together. That is, conceptually the rabbis appear not to have had a category equivalent to our "homoeroticism" or "homosexuality," a group categorized by their preference of same-gender sexual partners. Male homoeroticism was prohibited biblically, and female homoeroticism might have been seen as lewd, but no talmudic rhetoric links these two activities.

THE DEFINING ACT

What sex act does Scripture mean to prohibit between men? What does "as one lies with a woman" mean? Tannaitic sources nowhere discuss this. According to the Yerushalmi, however, it is clear that anal penile penetration was assumed to be the act that defined homoerotic intercourse:

> A. R. Yosi [PA 3] asked, what about insertion among men [are they guilty of "homoerotic intercourse"]? What about insertion with an animal?
>
> B. Do not [the rules of the] *niddah* [i.e., menstruant] teach of the *'arayot*? A male is of her kind [i.e., insertion with an animal is like with that with a menstruant].[29]

Daniel L. Miglione, *Princeton Seminary Bulletin*; Sup. issue 1; (1990): 71-89, esp. 80-89.
[27]Augustine *Epistles* 211 (PL 33:964).
[28]On Chrysostom, see Bernadette J. Brooten, "Patristic Interpretations of Romans 1:26," *Studia Patristica* 18 (1985): 288.
[29]*y. Qidd.* 1:1, 58c (par. *y. Ketub.* 1:3, 25b).

According to tannaitic literature, penile penetration is necessary for violation of any of the ʿarayot, the sexual prohibitions of Lev. 18.[30] It is questionable whether R. Yosi (A) assumes that male homoerotic acts and bestiality are included in the ʿarayot; clearly the redactor of the Yerushalmi (B) does. The answer (B) cites the tradition from the *Sifra*, which uses the rules governing the menstruant as a paradigm that generates restrictions that also govern the remaining ʿarayot. Whether or not the *Sifra's* passage really means to include homoerotic intercourse, the Yerushalmi reads it as if it does.

This rhetorical strategy shifts somewhat in the Bavli. In a near-parallel to the Yerushalmi, a tradition in the Bavli records a discussion between Ravina and Rabah (BA 4) about the case of insertion of a penis into a male. Such an act renders one culpable, because, we are told, it is written "as one lies with a woman" (Lev. 18:22).[31] Again, the negative answer is derived from the case of the menstruant, but unlike the earlier cases, this discussion completely bypasses the equation with the ʿarayot. That is, the application of the rules of the menstruant to the case of homoerotic intercourse is not based on the fact that the verse is located in Lev. 18 among a group of verses called the ʿarayot and therefore governed by the paradigm of the menstruant. Rather, the wording of the verse itself invites an analogy to women and hence the menstruant.

Although relatively silent about male homoerotic activity, Roman law too defines male homoerotic intercourse as the act that defines its understanding of homoerotic activity. According to Paulus, the punishments for seduction, of a boy or a woman, differ according to whether intercourse took place. If intercourse did take place, the seducer is liable for capital punishment; but if the act was "incomplete," i.e., without penetration, he is liable only for deportation.[32] Other homoerotic activity might bring public ridicule, but as with at least part of the rabbinic rhetoric, it would not legally be grouped with male homoerotic intercourse.

Rhetoric of Categorization

Rabbinic sources categorize homoerotic intercourse on the basis of punishment. The Bible prescribes extirpation (Lev. 18:29) and death (Lev. 20:13) for male homoerotic intercourse. The *Mishnah* includes male homoerotic acts in its list of thirty-six transgressions punished by

---

[30]See *Sifra Qod.* 11:2 (93a); Chapter 2 above. It is unclear here, as in other passages, if homoerotic intercourse is to be understood as a member of the ʿarayot.
[31]*b. Yebam.* 54b, (par. *b. Sanh.* 55a [attributed to the redactor]).
[32]D.47.11.1.2.

extirpation and specifies stoning as the means of death.³³ A tannaitic source explains the choice of punishments:

A. He must die by stoning.

B. You say "by stoning," [but can it be] one of the other [means of] death specified in the Torah?

C. Scripture says, "their bloodguilt is upon them" [Lev. 20:13] and below it says "[A man or a woman who has a ghost or a familiar spirit shall be put to death; they shall be pelted with stones] their bloodguilt is upon them" [Lev. 20:27]. Just as "their bloodguilt is upon them" below denotes stoning, so too ["their bloodguilt is upon them"] here denote stoning.³⁴

Scriptural analogy is used here to explain the punishment. These tannaitic sources cleave closely to the bible in their categorization. This category, punishment, is then used didactically in later rabbinic sources.

Whereas the rabbinic sources prescribe the death penalty only didactically, Roman law prescribed punishments meant to be applied. In Roman law, the earlier legal sanctions against homoerotic intercourse appear to have been directed against seduction of boys.³⁵ Later, after the Empire became Christian, burning was ordained for the pathic (i.e., penetrated) partner of male homoerotic intercourse.³⁶ Only around 533 C.E. was the active (i.e., penetrating) homoerotic partner legally punished.³⁷ In light of the particular contempt in which the pathic was held in these societies (see below), the earlier application of legal penalties to him is hardly surprising.

Rhetoric of Liability

Within this type of rhetoric two issues are discussed. First is the liability of active vs. passive males engaged in homoerotic intercourse. Second is the concern with the effect of age on determining liability.

ACTIVE AND PASSIVE MALE LOVERS

The *Sifra* writes:

A. We heard the punishment, but the formal prohibition we did not hear.

---

³³*m. Ker.* 1:1; *m. Sanh.* 7:4.

³⁴*Sifra Qod.* 9:14 (92b); *y. Sanh.* 7:9, 25a (the derivation for extirpation is also given here); *b. Sanh.* 54a-b.

³⁵The *lex Scatinia* appeared to have penalized either seducers of boys or passive homoerotic partners. See Juvenal 2.36ff; Cantarella, *Bisexuality* 106-14; Derrick Sherwin Bailey, *Homosexuality and the Western Christian Tradition* (London: Longmans, Green, 1955) 68-69; Boswell, *Christianity* 70-71. Cf. Lilja, *Homosexuality* 112-21.

³⁶See *CTh.* 9.7.3, 6. See also *Coll.* 5.3 (390).

³⁷See Justinian *Nov.* 77.1; 141.1.

B. [Thus] Scripture says, "Do not lie with a male as one lies with a female," [Lev. 18:22].

C. I only have [here] a warning for the penetrator (שׁכב), where is there a warning for the one penetrated (נשׁכב)?

D. Scripture says, "[No Israelite woman shall be a cult prostitute,] nor shall any Israelite man be a cult prostitute," [Deut. 23:18], and it also says "...there were also male prostitutes in the land; (Judah) imitated all the abhorrent practices of the nations that the Lord had dispossessed before the Israelites]," [1 Kings 14:24].

E. R. Akiba says, "Do not lie with a male as one lies with a female," read it: "Do not be laid..."[38]

Sections (A) and (B) dispose of the problem of the seeming redundancy of Lev. 18:22 and Lev. 20:13 by identifying the former to refer to the prohibition and the latter to the punishment for male homoerotic acts. (C) poses a new problem. The Bible refers only to the penetrator: it does not command that a man should not lie with a man as a woman lies with a man. Working from the *a priori* assumption that to be penetrated must also be prohibited, the *Sifra*, claiming to report R. Ishmael's opinion, enlists the support of Deut. 23:18 and 1 Kings 14:24. The logic is: (1) the occurrence of the term "abhorrent practices" (תועבה) in both 1 Kings 14:24 and Lev. 18:22, allows for an association between these verses. Because Lev. 18:22 refers to homoeroticism, (2) we can understand the term "male prostitute" *(qadesh)* in 1 Kings 14:24 as referring to men engaged in some type of homoerotic activity; (3) because the term "male prostitute" appears also in Deut. 23:18, this verse can be linked to 1 Kings 14:24, and (4) because the term "female prostitute" also appears in Deut. 23:18, a logical analogy is made that associates the role of the male prostitute as analogous to that of the female, that is, passive. Rabbi Akiba, in (E), will have none of this. he derives the prohibition against a male assuming a passive role in intercourse from Lev. 18:22 itself, repunctuated into the *niphal* conjugation, thus including the passive partner.

The history of the tradition that associated the male prostitute mentioned in these two verses with a passive male partner in homoerotic intercourse is by no means clear. Originally, the term *qadesh* most likely designated a male cult prostitute, whose role, connected to fertility, was decidedly heterosexual.[39] Both the LXX and Targum Onkelos interpret this term in ways that differ from both each other and the rabbinic

---

[38]*Sifra Qod.* 9:14 (92b).
[39]See S.E. Loewenstramm, "Qadesh," *Encyclopaedia Biblica* 7:35-36 (Hebrew).

interpretation.⁴⁰ In fact, other tannaitic parallels of this tradition do not as clearly assign the passive role to the *qadesh* as does the *Sifra*:

> ["They incensed Him with alien things,] vexed Him with abominations" [Deut. 32:16] – this is homoerotic intercourse. Thus it says "Do not lie with a male as one lies with a woman; it is an abhorrence," [Lev. 18:22] and "there were also male prostitutes in the land..." [1 Kings 14:24].⁴¹

It is not clear here whether or not 1 Kings 14:24 is being used to refer to passive homoerotic activity; in a parallel source 1 Kings 14:24 is cited together with Deut. 23:18 a the sole prooftexts for the prohibition (אזהרה) of what is presumably all homoerotic activity.⁴² It is possible, then, that these sources reflect a rabbinic association of homoeroticism with cultic prostitution, active or passive. The *Sifra* is the first source to focus this association on the passive role of the male prostitute.

Later discussions that incorporate this passage from the *Sifra* focus on the liability of the penetrated male. One version of the disagreement attributed to Rabbis Akiba and Ishmael can be found in the Yerushalmi:

> A. According to R. Ishmael, whence do we derive [the punishment that the offender is] cut off [from his people]?
>
> B. Rabbi Yermiah [PA 4] in the name of R. Abbahu [PA 3]: It is said here "cult prostitute" and it is said there, "... there were also male prostitutes in the land...," [1 Kings 14:24]. You learn "prostitute" from "prostitute" [and] "prostitute" from "abhorrence." [The end of 1 Kings 14:24 mentions the word "abhorrent practices." Because Lev. 18:22 uses the same term applied to homoerotic activity, a correspondence is made between the term "cult prostitute" and homoerotic activity. This identification is then applied to the prohibition on this activity found in Deut. 23:18].
>
> C. R. Ḥiyyah bar Ada [PA 2?] in the name of R. Ḥaninah [PA 1]: [You learn] "abhorrent" from "abhorrent."
>
> D. R. Yosi ben R. Bun [PA 5] said: We learn thus, "the two of them have done an abhorrent thing." [This teaches that] both of them [are punished] by stoning; both of them [have a] warning; both of them [are subject to being] cut off [from their people.]⁴³

This *sugya* begins with a stylized version of the disagreement between Rabbis Akiba and Ishmael from the *Sifra* (cited above). (A) asks

---

⁴⁰The LXX on Deut. 23:18 reads: Οὐκ ἔσται πόρνη ἀπὸ θυγατέρων Ισραηλ, καὶ οὐκ ἔσται πορνεύων ἀπὸ υἱῶν Ισραηλ. The confusion extends to 1 (=3) Kings 14:24, as translated in the LXX: Καὶ σύνδεσμος ἐγενήθη ἐν τῇ γῇ καί ἐποίησας ἀπὸ πάντων τῶν βδελυγμάτων... Targum Onkelos on Deut. 23:18, on the other hand, reads לא תהי אתתא מבנת ישראל לגבר עבד ולא יסב גברא מבני ישראל אתתא אמה.
⁴¹*Sifre Deut.* 318 (p. 364).
⁴²*Midrash Tannaaim ad Deut.* 32:16 (pp. 194-95).
⁴³*y. Sanh.* 7:9, 25a.

the reason for R. Ishmael's exegesis, which (B) and (C) attempt to answer. (D) is the most interesting and original statement of the unit. R. Yosi ben R. Bun effectively rejects the exegeses of both R. Akiba and R. Ishmael, preferring the most obvious solution: Lev. 20:13 explicitly includes both the active and passive partners. It might be that this fifth generation Palestinian amora is somewhat mystified at the tortured reasoning used by his predecessors to derive the punishment of extirpation (as well as death penalty and warning) for both partners.

Although the discussion in this passage is ostensibly about the different exegetical styles of Rabbis Akiba and Ishmael, there are more serious legal implications. Two parallels in the Bavli cite a tradition in the name of R. Abbahu [PA 3] that, following R. Ishmael's reasoning, a man penetrated by another man is liable for two transgressions, one from Lev. 20:13 and the other from Deut. 23:18.[44] To be a passive partner of homoerotic intercourse is worse than to be an active one, even though only the active one is explicitly forbidden by Scripture.

This emphasis on the culpability of the pathic might also be reflected in R. Yosi ben Bun's statement. To the tannaim, the absence of discussion of the pathic in the Bible might have been deafening. Whichever exegetical method was used, the topic had to be dealt with. Only later, when this bipolar construction of male homoeroticism (i.e., penetrator vs. penetrated) perhaps lost some of its strength, could R. Yosi ben Bun return to the obvious solution of the legal problem. This might also explain why the discussion in the Bavli is composed solely of sources attributed to Palestine: this same concern with the penetrated male did not exist in Babylonia. I return to this point below.

AGE

Age effected the liability of those men engaged in homoerotic intercourse. Focusing on the passive partner, the *Tosefta* states that a man incurs liability for homoerotic intercourse if the passive partner is over nine years old.[45] Flatly contradicting this, the *Sifra* reports, "'[If] a man' – this excludes a minor; 'lies with a male' [Lev. 20:13] – this includes a minor."[46] The *Sifra* accounts any male who takes the active role with any passive male whatsoever liable. The Talmudim reject this position: liability is assessed differently in the case of intercourse with minors (defined as those under the age of nine or three).[47]

---

[44]*b. Sanh.* 54b; *b. Ker.* 3a.
[45]*t. Sanh.* 10:2.
[46]*Sifra Qod.* 9:14 (92b).
[47]*b. Sanh.* 54b (partially paralleled at *y. Sanh.* 7:9, 25a with different attribution; *b. Nid.* 13b; *b. Qidd.* 82a.

Non-Rabbinic Parallels

In Roman law (at least from the third century C.E.) the age of the partners of male homoerotic intercourse too had an effect on legal liability: a law attributed to Modestinus groups intercourse with a boy as with that with a widow or virgin, calling them all *stuprum*.[48]

It is interesting to note that sources other than the *Sifra* do not penalize pederasty. In ancient Greece, pederastic relationships were generally with boys between seven and fourteen.[49] Hence, boys between seven and nine might have both been considered sexually attractive and were permitted by rabbinic law as passive sexual partners, for they were not yet "men." This "loophole" again underscores that rabbinic assumptions on homoerotic intercourse were rooted in conceptions of activity and passivity shared with surrounding non-Jewish cultures rather than in more "objective" readings of Scripture.

Rhetoric of Association

Male homoeroticism is commonly discussed in association with other transgressions. Most commonly, this association occurs within vice-catalogues. A more complex association is that between homoeroticism and bestiality.

Vice-Catalogues

Because one of the two biblical verses that deal with homoerotic activity is located in Lev. 18 with the incest restrictions, male homoerotic activity is often lumped together with the other sexual prohibitions, termed the '*arayot*.[50] If '*arayot* is read to include homoerotic intercourse, then this activity is also associated with murder and idolatry.

One passage more clearly associates homoerotic intercourse with other sexual transgressions. *m. Sanh.* 8:7 groups attempted murder and

---

[48]D.48.5.35.1. Papinian saw homoerotic intercourse as coming under the rubric of "adultery:" D.48.5.6.1 is virtually identical to Modestinus's D.48.5.35.1, except Papinian leaves off intercourse with a boy *(puero)* as a form of *stuprum*. Clearer is D.48.5.9, which prohibits one fro making his or her house available for "*stuprum adulterimue...cum masculo.*"

[49]See *Anth. Graec.* 12.4, 186, 228; H.I. Marrou, *History of Education in Antiquity*, trans. George Lamb (rpt. Madison: University of Wisconsin Press, 1982) 102; Cantarella, *Bisexuality* 36-42.

[50]The '*arayot* have been discussed in Chapter 2. Note that the wording of the biblical prohibition against homoerotic intercourse does not contain the word ערוה, from which term '*arayot* derives. Hence, it would be a mistake to automatically include reference to homoerotic intercourse in every occurrence of the term '*arayot*.

For another possible example of the use of '*arayot* arayot as a euphemism for homoerotic intercourse see *t. Ḥag.* 1:1, as interpreted by Lieberman, *Tos. Kip.* 5:1286-87.

the attempted rape of a betrothed woman, as actions for which it is permissible to kill somebody rather than let him succeed.[51] Behind this law probably lies the shame of being penetrated. The abhorrence accorded the possibility of, as a male, being penetrated was so great that one could kill the aggressor.

A second term used to designate homoerotic intercourse is *to'evah*, "abomination" or "abhorrence," which Lev. 18:22 and 20:13 specifically apply to homoerotic activity. The identification to *to'evah* with homoerotic activity can be seen clearly in the *Tosefta*:

A ...It is written, "...Thus said the Lord God: You eat with the blood, you raise your eyes to your fetishes, and you shed blood – yet you expect to possess the land! You have relied on your sword, you have committed abominations, you have all defiled other men's wives – yet you expect to possess the land! [Ezek. 33:25-26].

B. "You eat with blood" – this is [the prohibition of ripping a] limb from a live animal;

C. "You raise your eyes to your fetishes" – this is idolatry;

D. "You shed blood" – this is the shedding of blood [i.e., murder];

E. "You have relied on your sword" – this concerns justice and [the prohibition against] theft;

F. "You have committed abominations" – this is male homoerotic intercourse;

G. "You have all defiled other men's wives" – [this concerns] *giluy 'arayot*.[52]

Note that homoerotic intercourse is not included in the term *giluy 'arayot* (G), which here refers to adultery. Instead, it is serious enough to warrant its own listing, rating it on a more or less equal level of immorality as ripping a limb from a living animal, idolatry, murder, theft, and adultery. Out of this list, references to idolatry, murder, and adultery are the only ones clearly inherent in the verse from Ezekiel. Ripping a limb from a living animal, the perversion of justice, and homoerotic activity are all added by exegesis to the three "baseline" transgressions, thus emphasizing their severity.[53]

Other identifications of *to'evah* with homoerotic intercourse are scattered throughout the literature. Within the tannaitic corpus there is only one other passage that identifies the term with homoerotic intercourse, and it does not contain nearly the force expressed in the

---

[51] See *t. Sanh.* 11:11, which expands the group to include the idolatry and the attempted rape of any woman whose relationship to the perpetrator is incestuous.
[52] *t. Soṭ.* 6:9. See also *Sifre Deut.* 31 (p. 50).
[53] See also *t. Soṭ.* 6:6.

Tosefta passage cited above.⁵⁴ Among the later material is a tradition very similar to that of the *Tosefta* passage, which atomizes Mal. 2:11 to refer to a series of heinous offenses: idolatry, homoerotic intercourse, prostitution, and intercourse with a non-Jewish woman.⁵⁵ Nearly all of these passages that associate the term *toʿevah* with homoerotic activities do so in the form of these exegetical vice-catalogues.

Rabbinic literature does not use the term *toʿevah* exclusively in reference to homoerotic activity. The Bible uses the term to refer to a wide range of practices including eating customs (Gen. 43:32; Deut. 14:3); other sexual transgressions (Lev. 18:26-27); idolatry (Deut. 7:26); and soothsaying (Deut. 18:9, 12). As expected, the rabbinic sources, tannaitic and amoraic, follow the biblical terminology in referring to these and other transgressions.⁵⁶ These cases far outnumber those that apply the term *toʿevah* to homoerotic acts. It appears, then, the rabbis use the identification of *toʿevah* with homoerotic acts only in exegetical contexts in which (1) the term has an ambiguous referent, and (2) it lists a number of offenses, which can then be broken down into a vice catalog.⁵⁷

Non-Rabbinic Parallels

The rabbis did not originate the inclusion of homoerotic intercourse in the vice-catalogue. Jewish-Hellenistic writers often group it with illicit heterosexual activities, adultery being the most common of these.⁵⁸ Occasionally, homoerotic behavior is grouped with idolatry or

---

⁵⁴*Sifre Deut.* 318 (p. 364).
⁵⁵*b. Sanh.* 81b-82a, cited in the name of Rav.
⁵⁶Sacrifices: *t. Shebu.* 1:3; *Sifre Deut.* 99 (p. 160); 261 (p. 283); 147 (p. 202); *b. Sanh.* 112b; *b. Tem.* 29b. Idolatry: *Mekh. Mishpatim* 20 (p. 332); *b. Pes.* 6a; 48a; *b. Soṭ.* 4b; *b. ʿAbod. Zar.* 2a. Haughtiness: *b. Soṭ.* 4b. Corruption of justice: *Sifra Qod.* 4:1 (88d-89a). Prayer (recited improperly): *b. Ber.* 23a; *b. Shab.* 10a; *b. ʿErub.* 64a. Cross-dressing: *Sifre Deut.* 226 (p. 258); *b. Naz.* 59a. Woman who returns to the man who divorced her: *b. Yebam.* 54b.
⁵⁷In *b. Ned.* 50b-51a a story is cited in which *toʿevah* is explained as, "you go astray because of it," (תועה אתה בה). This has traditionally been interpreted as referring to homoeroticism. Judging from the context however it is likely that it refers to the whole range of sexual prohibitions, the *ʿarayot*. Whatever the true referent, the explanation is clearly no more than a word-play, which reflects no assumption about or argument against homoerotic activity. The entire passage is comic, a game that ends when one of the participants, disgusted, stalks out.
⁵⁸Pseudo-Phocylides 1.3 (ed. van der Horst, 111) (specifies it with adultery as part of the decalogue); Philo *Hyp.* 7.1 (identification of pederasty with rape and prostitution); *Abraham* 135 (adultery); *Sib. Or.* 3:764 (ed. Geffcken, 87), 4:33-36 (ed. Geffcken, 93-fragmentary), 5:166 (ed. Geffcken, 112), 5:430 (ed. Geffcken, 125) (all adultery), 5:386-396 (ed. Geffcken, 123) (prostitution, incest, bestiality); *T. Jacob* 5:8, 7:19-20 (adultery); *Letter of Aristeas* 152 (incest and promiscuous unions); Josephus *Ag. Apion* 2.199 (adultery, non-reproductive sex).

bloodshed.⁵⁹ In these lists neither Scripture nor the term *to'evah* is explicitly invoked. Josephus never uses the Septuagint's translation of *to'evah* – βδέλυγμα – and Philo uses this word only when citing biblical verses that deal with things other than homoerotic intercourse.⁶⁰

Scroggs argues that the New Testament imitated the form of the Jewish Hellenists in including homoerotic intercourse in two vice-catalogues. As in the Jewish lists, homoerotic intercourse *per se* bears no special weight in these vice-catalogues.⁶¹ Later Christian writers follow this form and often include homoerotic intercourse in their vice-catalogues. Some, in the same vein as Pseudo-Phocylides, assert that the prohibition against homoerotic intercourse was part of the decalogue.⁶² If there was an association that the New Testament authors favored for homoerotic intercourse, it appears to have been idolatry.⁶³

BESTIALITY

Rabbinic sources link homoeroticism to bestiality. This may have in part been occasioned by the fact that the scriptural prohibition of bestiality – "Do not have carnal relations with any beast and defile yourself thereby; and let no woman lend herself to a beast to mate with it; it is perversion," (Lev. 18:23) – directly follows that of homoerotic intercourse. Rabbinic sources often achieve this link contextually: frequently sources discuss homoeroticism and bestiality together, or use similar language in their discussions.⁶⁴ Hence, in a passage from the *Mekhilta* the form that establishes liability for the passive male partner of

---

⁵⁹Pseudo-Phocylides ll. 3-4; 2 *Enoch* 10:4 (ver. J.?); *Sob. Or.* 2.73 (become an informer, murder); *T. Jacob* 7:19-20 (idolaters, "accursed"); Josephus, *War* 4.563 (murder); See also Romans 1:22-24 (idolatry), and on this passage, Kenneth Wayne Hugghins, *An Investigation of the Jewish Theology of Sexuality Influencing the References to Homosexuality in Romans 1:18-32* (Ann Arbor: University Microfilms, 1986).
⁶⁰See Philo *Abel and Cain* 51 (a shepherd to Egyptians); *Mig. Abr.* 64 (food); *Quis rerum* 162 (false weights); *De Fuga* 18 (sacrifices).
The Septuagint departs from translating תועבה as βδέλυγμα in only a few places, all in Proverbs. See Prov. 3:32; 6:16; 16:5; 20:10. In this places it is translated as ἀκάθαρτός or ἀκαθάσια, and it would be difficult to see how any of these references could have been understood as referring to homoerotic intercourse.
⁶¹1 Cor. 6:9-10. See Scroggs, *New Testament and Homosexuality* 101-9. The term also appears in a vice-catalogue in 1 Tim. 1:9-10.
⁶²See *Didache* 2.2 (ed. Lake, pp. 310-1); *Ep. Barn.* 19:4 (ed. Lake, pp. 402-3). For its general inclusion in these vice catalogues, see David F. Wright, "Homosexuals or Prostitutes? The Meaning of ΑΡΣΕΝΟΚΟΙΤΑΙ (1 Cor. 6:9, 1 Tim. 1:10)," *Vigiliae Christianae* 38 (1984): 135-36.
⁶³See Scroggs, *New Testament* 116; Hugghins *Jewish Attitudes* 208-23.
⁶⁴For examples, see *Mekh. Nez.* 17 (p. 310); *b. Sanh.* 54b; 58a. See also *m. Qidd.* 4:14; *b. Qidd.* 82a; *y. Qidd.* 1:1, 58c; *y. Ketub.* 1:3, 25b.

a bestial relationship mirrors – even down to the same biblical verses – that for establishing the liability for a passive homoerotic partner.[65]

This identification is also made linguistically. Lev. 18:23 and Lev. 20:16 use the root *rb'* (רבע), "mount," to designate intercourse between a human and an animal. The Bible uses the same word to designate the breeding of mixed animal species.[66] These two meanings for the root *rb'* continue in the rabbinic literature. In the later literature, however, a third meaning appears: male homoerotic intercourse.[67] To my knowledge, no source in the rabbinic corpus surveyed here uses this word to denote heterosexual intercourse.[68] The word is reserved for animal intercourse, intercourse between a human and an animal, and homoerotic intercourse.

A second, less clear but also indicative terminological distinction between hetero- and homoerotic intercourse is the use of the root *zqq*, usually in the passive *(niphal)* conjugation. In my survey of the tannaitic literature and the Talmudim, I have found only a few cases where this root is used to indicate marital, heterosexual intercourse.[69] In other cases it refers either to heterosexual intercourse involving a slave or rape,[70] or to intercourse involving animals.[71] One source in the Yerushalmi uses the term to refer to two men engaged in some type of homoerotic activity.[72]

These contextual and linguistic uses suggest a strategy of linking homoerotic activity and bestiality. A wide range of vocabulary was available to the rabbis to indicate homoerotic intercourse.[73] While they

---

[65]*Mekh. Nez.* 17 (p. 310).
[66]See Lev. 19:19.
[67]*b. Yebam.* 25a; *b. Sanh.* 9b; 70a; *b. Mak.* 6a.
[68]The evolution of this term might be based on the position of intercourse. As animals mount each other in intercourse, so too were male lovers perceived to do so. Regardless, the word choice is significant. Not once to my knowledge is *rb'* applied to heterosexual anal intercourse.
[69]In *b. Sot.* 11b and *b. B. Meṣ.* 107b the word appears in a very positive context in unparalleled *baraitot*. *b. Nid.* 31b (par. *b. Shebu.* 8a; *b. Ker.* 26a; *Gen. Rab.* 20:7 [p. 191]) records a woman swearing during childbirth not to have sex with her husband. In *y. Ketub.* 2:5, 26c it is a redactorial statement about a sage who desired his wife: כהדא שמואל בעא איזדקוקי לאיתתיה. This is the only attestation of the word in its *ithpael* form.
[70]*b. Yebam.* 99a (breeding slaves); *y. Ber.* 3:4, 6c (adultery and intercourse with a maid-servant); *b. Ketub.* 51b (attempted rape).
[71]*b. Sanh.* 106a; *b. B. Bat.* 74b; *b. 'Abod. Zar.* 20b all refer to animals copulating. *y. Sanh.* 6:6, 23b-c uses the term to refer to intercourse between a man and a dog.
[72]*y. Sanh.* 6:6, 23c; מזקקין זה לזה.
[73]For example, הבא על הזכור (*m. Sanh.* 7:4). To indicate anal intercourse, the term ביאה שלא כדרכה is commonly employed for heterosexual anal intercourse (it is never used for male homoerotic intercourse). See Chapter 6.

did occasionally use these more neutral terms, later rabbinic sources tended to choose verbs that typically designate animal copulation. These choices could reflect a deeper attitude that may view homoerotic intercourse as beneath human dignity. At the very least, there can be little doubt that the terminology indicates rabbinic disapproval.[74]

Writings of some early Church Fathers rarely use this rhetoric; for the most part their use of animals in discussions of homoerotic intercourse concentrates on arguments from nature. Whether or not animal behavior is to be imitated or avoided (argued by some early Church Fathers), never is homoerotic intercourse condemned as "animalistic."[75]

Rhetoric of the Other

Rabbinic sources actively associate homoerotic intercourse with Gentiles. According to *m. 'Abod. Zar.* 2:1, a man should not remain alone with Gentiles, "because they are suspected of murder." The *Tosefta* adds or comments: "One should not entrust a child to him [i.e., a Gentile] in order to teach him a craft and to be alone with him."[76] It is likely that underlying this passage is an assumption that Gentiles are particularly prone to homoerotic intercourse, especially with boys.[77] In another passage in the *Tosefta*, the biblical character Ishmael is identified with the three transgressions of murder, idolatry and *'arayot* – where *'arayot* is identified as referring to both general sexual promiscuity and to homoerotic intercourse.[78]

This same tune is taken up by the *Sifra*. "Just as 'the practices of the Canaanites' [Lev. 18:3], [who] are steeped in idolatry, *'arayot*, murder, homoerotic intercourse and bestiality, so too 'the practices of the Egyptians,' [Lev. 18;3]."[79] Again we see the connection of male

---

[74]This is analogous to English usage. We would rarely use the term "making love" to indicate animal behavior or "copulation" to refer to human intercourse. A similar attitude might also underlie the Greek πυγίζω. See *LSJ* 1550, *ad. loc.* Though translated as "paedico," the range of meanings for this root clearly suggests anal intercourse, and its use is in quite course contexts. Prof. Brooten informs me that later usages of this term, especially as found in magical papyri, are more neutral.

[75]See *Ep. Barn.* 10.6 and Clement of Alex. *Paed.* 2.10 (*GCS*, 12:208). Boswell, *Christianity* 152-56 summarizes the use of animals in the argument from nature.

[76]*t. 'Abod. Zar.* 3:2.

[77]For this interpretation see also Yehezkial Cohen, "The Image of the Gentile in the Tannaitic Period," *Eshel Beer-Sheva* 2 (1980): 61 (Hebrew).

[78]*t. Soṭ.* 6:6. The "authentic" description of Ishmael's activity, found in the Erfurt manuscript, is curious: נכבש על הגנות. See Lieberman, *Tos. Kip.* 8:670 for the identification of this phrase with homoerotic intercourse.

[79]*Sifra Aḥare* 13:7 (86a).

homoeroticism with other horrible offenses, but here the source highlights the proclivity toward these things as inherent characteristics of both the Canaanites and the Egyptians, i.e., Gentiles. The trigger for this interpretation is of course Lev. 18:3, which introduces the long list of prohibitions that include the incest restrictions, homoerotic intercourse, and bestiality. yet absent from the biblical list are murder and perhaps idolatry. This suggests that biblical interpretation alone does not lie behind this text. A second related passage from the *Sifra*, cited above, identifies homoerotic and incestuous marriage as characteristic of Canaanites and Egyptians, or again Gentiles.[80] As noted above, homoerotic marriages and polyandry are nowhere discussed in the biblical text. The midrash has gone out of its way to make this identification.

Among amoraim from both Palestine and Babylonia, in both Talmudim, the association between Gentiles and homoeroticism persists. A tradition in the Bavli attributed to Rav and Samuel (BA 1) suggests that Ham raped his father, Noah, when he was drunk.[81] Although not explicit, this tradition probably also probably derives from Lev. 18:3. Ham is considered the father of Egypt and Canaan (Gen. 10:6). By emphasizing the homoerotic activity of the progenitor of the Egyptians and Canaanites, this tradition suggests that this form of activity is characteristic of both of these peoples, and by extension, of the Gentiles.[82] A tradition in the Bavli attributed to a third generation Babylonian amora also associates homoerotic activity with Nebuchednezzar, the paradigm of the evil gentile monarch.[83]

A related tactic was the extension of the restriction against homoerotic activity to Gentiles. Several traditions mention the application of the 'arayot to Gentiles.[84] In later sources homoerotic activity is singled out, and its prohibition to Gentiles biblically justified. Gen. 2:24 becomes the biblical justification:

---

[80] *Sifra Ahare* 9:8 (85c-d).
[81] *b. Sanh.* 70a. A parallel, *Gen Rab.* 36:7 (p. 341) ignores this suggestion.
[82] It is important to note that Lev. 18:3 is not interpreted within rabbinic literature as referring solely to homoerotic intercourse. For other very different interpretations given to this verse see *b. Sanh.* 52a (par. *b. 'Abod. Zar.* 11a; *y. Sanh.* 7:3, 24b; *t. Sanh.* end Ch. 9); *Mekh. Yitro Bahodesh* 6 (pp. 222-23); *Sifre Deut.* 38 (pp. 73-77).

See also *b. Hul.* 92a-b, in which Ulla is attributed with a statement that out of the thirty commandments to which Gentiles can adhere, they adhere to only three, among which is the prohibition against homoerotic intercourse.
[83] *b. Shab.* 149b. Compare this to the rhetoric on incest, which associates transgressions with evil *Israelite* kings.
[84] See also Novak, *The Image of the Non-Jew* 199-222.

A. R. Leazar [=R. Eleazar, PA 3] in the name of R. Haninah [PA 1] [said]: From where do we know that Gentiles are prohibited[85] [to have intercourse with] the 'arayot as Israel?

B. Scripture says, "... and clings to his wife" – not to the wife of his neighbor.

C. "... and clings to his wife" – not a male and not to an animal.[86]

Because Gen. 2:24 takes place prior to the establishment of Israel as a separate people with unique obligations to their God, it can be used to extend the prohibition supposedly lurking within this verse to Gentiles. Although this tradition appears to be late, it is possible that this interpretation circulated earlier.[87]

Most of these sources, even when found in the Bavli, are attributed to Palestinians. Only one tradition, accusing Nebuchednezzar of homoerotic intercourse, is attributed to a "late" Babylonian, and this kind of accusation, equating active homoeroticism with haughtiness and power is a stock one.[88] While the rhetorical strategy identifying homoerotic intercourse with Gentiles might still have been in use in Palestine, it was rarely used by the Babylonians. Survival of these sources in the Bavli might only indicate the reproduction of received traditions, which also helps to explain why these Palestinian traditions receive no elaboration in the Bavli.

NON-RABBINIC PARALLELS

Jewish-Hellenistic literature preceded rabbinic literature in identifying homoerotic intercourse with Gentiles. According to the *Letter of Aristeas*:

> For most of the rest of mankind defile themselves by their promiscuous unions, working great unrighteousness, and whole countries and cities pride themselves on these vices. Not only do they have intercourse with males, but they even defile mothers and daughters. But we have been kept apart from such things.[89]

In the *Sibylline Oracles*, book 3, male homoerotic intercourse is associated with Rome (as also in a passage in the fifth book) and pederasty with Phoenicia, Egypt, Greece, Persia, Galatia, and all Asia as

---

[85]The standard edition reads מחזרין מחזרין but see Jastrow 501, s.v., חרר.
[86]y. Qidd. 1:1, 58c. See also *Gen Rab.* 18:24 (p. 167).
[87]See b. Sanh. 58a, which is given a tannaitic attribution. It is possible that the first part of the interpretation cited there is tannaitic, with the rest – part of which is the tradition I have cited here – added to make a coherent unit. The first part of the tradition cited in b. Sanh. 58a is cited independently at y. Yebam. 11:2, 12a. Note also the connection of homoerotic intercourse and bestiality.
[88]b. Shab. 149b. See below.
[89]Let. Ar. 152 (ed. Hadas, 160-61).

well.⁹⁰ Josephus, or the writer from whom he cribbed, makes an implicit argument of this kind in *Against Apion*.⁹¹

The same argument, that "they," in contrast to "us," engage in male homoerotic intercourse, is used even by the Romans in reference to particularly effeminate homoerotic courting customs and the assumption by the male of the passive role: they called it "Greek love."⁹²

The few applications of this rhetoric by the Church seem limited to the Gnostics.⁹³

Rhetoric of Divine Retribution

Rhetorics of both personal and communal divine punishment for homoerotic activities are found in rabbinic literature. Only one source, to my knowledge, personally threatens men engaged in homoerotic intercourse with divine retribution. Commenting on the name of Potiphar as it appears in Gen. 39:1 Rav says: "He [Potiphar] was jealous of him [Joseph] for himself, [so] Gabriel came and emasculated him. [That is why] at the beginning it is written "Potiphar" [Gen. 39:1] and at the end "Potiphara" [Gen. 41:45, 50]."⁹⁴ There are two word-plays in Rav's statement. The first revolves around the textual problem that Rav is attempting to resolve: why does the text record two different spellings of Potiphar's name? Rav postulates that the later addition of an *ayin* to Potiphar's name means that sometime between the first mention of Potiphar's name and the second mention (with the *ayin*), Potiphar was emasculated – a meaning of *para*⁹⁵ – the last three letters of Potiphar's "new" name.⁹⁶ Why, then, was he emasculated? Rav's second word-play is to substitute *kan'*, meaning "to be jealous or desirous of," for the word *kanah*, "Buy," which appears in the biblical text (Gen. 39:1). Hence

---

⁹⁰For homoerotic intercourse: *Sib. Or.* 3.185-87 (ed. Geffcken, 57-58). For pederasty, *Sib. Or.* 3.595-600 (3ed. Geffcken, 78-79). See also *Sib. Or.* 5.386-96 (ed. Geffcken, 123).

⁹¹Josephus *Ag. Ap.* 2.275.

⁹²See Cicero *Tusc.* 4.70. See also Ramsay MacMullen, "Roman Attitudes to Greek Love," *Historia* 31 (1982): 484-502; Lilja, *Homosexuality* 122-27.

⁹³See for example Hippolytus *Refu. Omn. Haer.* 5.26.23-23 (ed. Marcovich, 205); Tertullian *Adv. Marc.* 1.29 (GCS 47:330-33).

⁹⁴*b. Soṭ.* 13b. An expanded, and unattributed, parallel can be found in *Gen. Rab.* 86:3 (pp. 1054-55). The statement reads, שקנאו לעצמו. בא גבריאל ופירעו מעיקרא כתיב פוטיפר ולסוף פוטיפרע. Some variant readings replace פרעו with סריסו, and other use both. See *Tal. Bab.* 2.1:202-3.

⁹⁵See Jastrow 1235. The main source for this definition is from this passage, but the linguistic range can easily include it, and the context practically demands it.

⁹⁶This word-play of course depends on the reading פרעו. If the "original" text was actually סריסו, then the thrust of the midrash is different: it instead explains why Potipher is called a eunuch. In either case, he is emasculated for desiring to commit homoerotic intercourse.

the midrash successfully combines two word-plays with a commitment to the rabbinic principal of "measure for measure:" because Potiphar desired to commit a sexual offense, he was punished by loss of his sexual organ. His homoerotic desire led to his pre-emptive emasculation. This text is so dependent on Scripture and word-plays, however, that it is doubtful if it reflects any kind of real threat or assumption. That is, its force is to delight its audience because of its cleverness rather than to scare them because of its implied threat.

Two other sources assume that God punishes not just the perpetrator of homoerotic intercourse, but the entire society that produces such sinners. The sin is not personal but societal; the punishment therefore is not only personal but societal, even global. An allegedly tannaitic source groups homoerotic intercourse, inadequately mourning for the death of the second-in-command of the Sanhedrin, and slaying a man with his brother together: all are said to result in an eclipse of the sun.[97] A second source, cited below, attributes earthquakes to homoerotic intercourse.[98]

NON-RABBINIC PARALLELS

Jewish-Hellenistic writers mention both personal and communal divine retribution for homoerotic intercourse, although the former emerges more prominently. Paul, apparently basing himself on Scripture, denies entrance to the kingdom of God to those who commit homoerotic acts, a strategy followed by the Council at Elvira in their denial of communion to those engaged in homoerotic intercourse.[99]

---

[97] *b. Sukk.* 29a (partial par. *t. Sukk.* 2:5). I can discern no common feature to these offenses or any reason that would adequately explain why an eclipse would serve as a just punishment for each of them. Possibly, this *baraitha* is a concatenation of three unrelated, and no longer extant, *baraitot* that link each of these sins with an eclipse. Scholars have unwarrantedly seen in this tradition historical allusions.
[98] *y. Ber.* 9:3, 13c.
[99] 1 Cor. 6:9-10. Although he doesn't actually quote Scripture, the word he uses – ἀρσενοκοῖται – strongly suggests the LXX rendering of Lev. 18:22: μετὰ ἄρσενος οὐ κοιμηθήσηι κοίτην γυναικός. Boswell, *Christianity* argues strongly that (1) ἀρσενοκοῖται refers to prostitution rather than homosexual activities *per se* (335-83, supported mainly by its juxtaposition with πόρνοι 1 Tim. 1:10), and that (2) Christian writers, including Paul, never invoke the Levitical rules in their discussions (101-2). These arguments have been refuted by Wright, "Homosexuals or Prostitutes." Cf. William L. Petersen, "Can ΑΡΣΕΝΟΚΟΙΤΑΙ be Translated by 'Homosexuals'?" *Vigilae Christianae* 40 (1986): 187-91; D.F. Wright, "Translating ΑΡΣΕΝΟΚΟΙΤΑΙ," *Vigiliae Christianae* 41 (1987): 396-98. For other criticisms of Boswell's reading, see Richard B. Hays, "Relations Natural and Unnatural: A Response to John Boswell's Exegesis of Romans 1," *Journal of Religious Ethics* 14 (1986): 184-215.

See also Hugghins, *Jewish Attitudes* 242-44. On the Council at Elvira, see Bailey, *Homosexuality* 86.

"[S]ometimes I am a man who craves the bodies of effeminate boys and when I touch them, they suffer great pain ..." the demon says to Solomon, alluding to a particularly painful punishment awaiting habitual pathics.[100] The *locus classicus* for discussions of communal punishment for homoerotic intercourse is Sodom. Some Jewish-Hellenistic traditions and Philo identify homoerotic intercourse as the cause of Sodom's destruction.[101] A late second-century Christian source, the *Apocalypse of Peter*, mentions stoning in hell as a punishment for homoerotic contact, for both male and in one witness, female.[102]

The Church Fathers seized upon the story of the destruction of Sodom and Gemorrah as one of their principle rhetorics against homoerotic intercourse.[103] A few other references to communal punishment for homoerotic intercourse also survive in this literature.[104]

Rhetoric of Temptation

As desire between men and women (even when related) was perceived as a constant threat, so too the desire between men. Among a number of restrictions in the *Mishnah* regarding the separation of the sexes is a statement attributed to Rabbi Yehudah that prohibits two unmarried men from sleeping under a single blanket.[105] The Sages, according to this *mishnah*, disagree. Commenting upon this statement, the *Tosefta* states:

---

[100]*T. Sol.* 2:3 (ed. Charlesworth 1:963). For other examples of personal punishments, see 2 *Enoch* 10:4 (ver. J. ?); *Sib. Or.* 3:764-66; *T. Jacob* 5:8, 7:20.
[101]2 *Enoch* 10:4 (ver. J. ?); *T. Naph.* 3:4-5; Philo *Abraham* 135-136; Josephus *Ant.* 1.200-1 (sin that they wanted to rape the angels).
[102]For the dating, see Wilhelm Schneemelcher, ed., *New Testament Apocrypha*, 2 vols. (1964; Philadelphia: Westminster Press, 1965) 2:663-68. The passages that refer to the stoning are in the Akhmim fragment (reference to female homoeroticism) 32, and in the Ethiopic (probably more "original") 10. See ibid. 2:676-77.
[103]See Bailey, *New Testament* 25-27.
[104]*Sib. Or.* 3:185-87 and *Wis. of Sol.* 14:23-26 (if a reference to homoeroticism) argue that homoerotic intercourse will throw the world into a "confusion;" *T. Naph.* 3:4-5 (associates it both with Sodom and the Flood); *Sib. Or.* 5:386-96 (will lead to the destruction of Rome).
[105]*m. Qidd.* 4:14. This *mishnah* continues with rules about male and female sexual contact. According to J. N. Epstein the statements that follow Rabbi Yehudah's were added later (*Introduction* 977). If correct, this would indicate that (1) Rabbi Yehudah's statement was emphatic, by virtue of its placement at the very end of the Tractate, and conversely (2) that the addition of statements concerning proper male and female sexual behavior served to refocus the emphasis of both Rabbi Yehudah's statement and the Tractate itself.

A. "Rabbi Yehudah said: A non-married man should not pasture small cattle, and two unmarried men should not sleep under one blanket." [m. Qidd. 4:14].

B. The Sages said: Israel is not suspected of this.[106]

While in the *Mishnah*, the Sages permit what Rabbi Yehudah forbids, the *Tosefta* alleges the reason why they permit it: one should not even think that the people of Israel could engage in homoerotic intercourse (as well as bestiality). The difference is telling. Rabbi Yehudah clearly assumes a danger inherent in the close contact of men. although the Sages in the *Mishnah* disagree with him on the legal implications, there is no sign that they disagree with the assumption that a danger of temptation does exist. On the other hand, the *Tosefta* not only rejects the possibility of a danger, but implicitly advances the claim that only Gentiles are suspected.[107] The *Tosefta's* strategy is adopted by the Yerushalmi, where a citation of the *Tosefta's* gloss (B) is prefaced with the exclamation, "God forbid" (חס ושלום).[108] The Bavli too cites the *Tosefta's* statement to dismiss the idea that a Jew might be suspected of homoerotic intercourse.[109] All these sources appear to deny forcefully the existence of any danger due to the sexual temptation of a man for another man.

Their denials do not comprise the whole story.

A. We have learnt: Six things are a disgrace for a disciple: he should not go to the market when he is fragranced ...

B. "He should not go to the market when he is fragranced:"

C. Rabbi Abba son of Rabbi Ḥiyyah son of Rabbi Abba said in the name of Rabbi Yoḥanan [PA 3]: This prohibition obtains in a place where they are suspected of homoerotic intercourse (משכב זכור).

D. Rav Sheshet [BA 3] said: They only said this concerning his clothes, but concerning his body, [fragrance conceals] the sweat.

E. Rav Pappa [BA 5] said: His hair is like his clothes [i.e., should not be perfumed].

F. Some say it [a different version of (E)]: It [i.e., his hair] is like his body [hence, may be perfumed].[110]

From the other items in (A) (omitted here), it appears that the reason behind the tannaitic source is to prevent disciples from intimate contact

---

[106]*t. Qidd.* 5:2; *y. Qidd.* I4:11, 66c.
[107]*t. Bik.* 2:5 (see Lieberman, *Tos. Kip.* 2:840) might acknowledge a danger by forbidding a man to remain alone with an hermaphrodite. It is unclear, however, whether the fear is of anal or vaginal penetration.
[108]*y. Qidd.* 4:11, 66c.
[109]*b. Qidd.* 82a.
[110]*b. Ber.* 43b.

with the *opposite* sex.[111] Ironically, Rabbi Yoḥanan then limits the application of (A) to situations that involve the danger of homoerotic intercourse. A disciple should not use perfume in a place (a city and/or Gentile markets?) where people are suspected of homoerotic intercourse lest he becomes suspected of homoerotic activity. R. Yoḥanan assumes that most people, upon seeing a perfumed man in the market in a place where this activity was common would presume that he was engaged in homoerotic activity. Not in line with the other sources surveyed above, Rabbi Yoḥanan clearly suggests that Israel can indeed at times be "suspected" of homoerotic intercourse.

The Babylonian amoraim in (D) to (F) further limit R. Yoḥanan (or perhaps just the *baraitha*), but their focus is different. Their concern is identifying exactly what one can and cannot perfume. Whether the *baraitha* itself refers to the danger of heterosexual or to homoerotic liaisons becomes irrelevant for these amoraim. The redactor reports R. Yoḥanan's comment and then leaves it dangling. While the *Tosefta* and Yerushalmi might protest against the possibility of danger of homoerotic temptation, for (at least some) Palestinian rabbis this was still a live issue.

It was still apparently a live issue among the Babylonian amoraim as well. Thus we read in the Bavli:

A. ... as Rav Aḥa bar Ada [BA 3] says in the name of R. Yitzḥak [PA 3]: They forbade their [i.e., Gentile] bread because of their oil and their oil because of their wine ...

B. [Instead, read] "they forbade their bread and their oil because of their wine and their wine because of their daughters and their daughters because of *davar 'aḥer* [lit: something else, commonly used as a euphemism] and *davar 'aḥer* because of *davar 'aḥer* .

C. What is *davar 'aḥer* ?

D. Rav Naḥman bar Yitzḥak [BA 4] said: They decreed that a Gentile boy impurifies as a *zav* [i.e., one who has genital emissions other than semen and urine] so that an Israelite boy will not get used to homoerotic intercourse with him.[112]

Rav Naḥman bar Yitzḥak attempts to explain the elliptical phrase found at the end of (B) by recourse to the rule that a Gentile was to have a statutory status of a *zav*, a rule that was considered to be one of the

---

[111]There is a parallel to this tradition in the later tractate *Derekh Eretz*. See Higger, *Treatises Derek Erez* 290. In his commentary on this parallel, Sperber interprets this passage, using Greek and Roman parallels that indicate a connection between perfuming and effeminacy, to be referring to homoerotic activity (Daniel A. Sperber, *Commentary on Derech Erez Zuta* [Ramat-Gan: Bar-Ilan University Press, 1990] 53-54).

[112]*b. Shab.* 17b (par. to Rav Naḥman's statement at *b. 'Abod. Zar.* 36b).

eighteen decrees of the School of Shammai.[113] In this list of eighteen decrees all the components of this tradition (C) save *davar 'aḥer*, a euphemism for some unspecified activity, are mentioned. Rav Naḥman bar Yitzḥak trying to determine what else on that list could be referred to euphemistically, came up with the statutory impurity of Gentiles. (B) continues that this was decreed because of some other euphemistically referred to thing. This "other thing" Rav Naḥman's bar Yitzḥak identifies as fear of homoerotic intercourse. It is the unexpectedness of this interpretation that is striking. The assumption that the first *davar 'aḥer* refers to the statutory impurity of Gentile men is not far-fetched, but the obvious reason for this, especially in light of the contexts both of (B) and the original Eighteen Decrees, is to prevent Jewish women from intercourse with non-Jewish men.[114] One expects a heterosexual interpretation. The force of this twist might have been to warn those Jews who thought that a Gentile's statutory impurity does not prevent association, and maybe even intercourse, between Jewish and Gentile adolescent boys (or men) that they were mistaken. Purity is used as the weapon to keep Jewish and non-Jewish adolescent boys apart, due to the fear that a Jew who becomes acquainted with and accustomed to a non-Jew will succumb to the temptation of homoerotic intercourse. It may be that the application of this logic only to unions between Jews and Gentiles relates to an idea that the Gentile would be at least partially to blame for the Jew's transgression. Even if this was the case, Rav Naḥman bar Yitzḥak's statement is still addressed to the Jew, and does not assume that the Jew would be other than a willing partner in the liaison.[115]

NON-RABBINIC PARALLELS

The Romans did not perceive any difference between the desire by men for women and their desire for other men. One was sexually attracted to the "beautiful," whether embodied in a woman, girl, boy, or man.[116]

Early Christians, Boswell argues, also assumed that men sexually desired other men, and warned against placing oneself in situations where temptation might couch.[117] Boswell supports this argument by

---

[113] *y. Shab.* 1:7, 3c. See Chapter 3.
[114] But see Chapter 3.
[115] See also *b. B. Meṣ.* 84a, a story about R. Yoḥanan and Reish Lakish that contains homoerotic overtones.
[116] See Catallus 99; Lucretius *De rerum natura* 4.1052-5; Cantarella, *Bisexuality* 128; Brown, *Body and Society* 30.
[117] Boswell, *Christianity* 159-61.

reference to a sermon by Basil about asceticism.[118] I have been unable to find earlier material to support his claim.

Passivity/Activity, Female/Male

Much of the rhetoric surveyed thus far intimates sexual assumptions, concentrated especially in Palestinian sources, that identify male sexual passivity with effeminacy. A few scattered passages more explicitly discuss this identification, and add to it the converse: that male sexual activity, even when penetrating other males, implies power. These attitudes are tightly linked to broader gender expectations.

PASSIVITY

As noted above, for a male to allow himself to be anally penetrated was tantamount to his surrendering that which made him distinctively male. By betraying his masculinity in this way he becomes "feminized." An example of this attitude can be found in a Palestinian tradition:

> It is written, "May [the guilt] fall upon the head of Joab ... May the house of Joab never be without someone suffering from a discharge or an eruption, or a male who handles the spindle, or on slain by the sword, or one lacking bread." "A male who handles the spindle" – this is Joash, "... they inflicted punishments on Joash," [2 Chr. 24:24]. Taught R. Ishmael: This teaches that they appointed over him cruel guards who never knew a woman and they would abuse him the way one abuses a woman. Just as when it is said, "Israel's pride will be humbled before his very eyes," [Hos. 5:5]. [Read instead:] "And he will abuse Israel's pride before his very eyes."[119]

The midrash identifies the later king Joash, a descendent of Joab, as the referent of the prophecy "the male who handles the spindle," one like a woman. To be like a woman, the midrash says, means to be sexually penetrated. The physical penetration of Joash represents more than just a form of torture, it conveys complete humiliation. Although the setting of the midrash is "exceptional" – penetration is used in a prison setting as a form of abuse – rhetorically the message is clear. Penetration,

---

[118]See Basil, *De serm. ascetic.* 323 (*PG* 31:880), mistakenly referred to by Boswell, *Christianity* 160 n. 96 as volume 32.

[119]*y. Qidd.* 1:7, 6a. See also *Mekh. Beshelaḥ Amalek* 1 (p. 177), and the parallel in *Mekh. d'RASHSBI* (p. 119). The exegesis derives from a word-play on שפטים שפטים. On the meaning and derivation of this word, which clearly refers here to "sport, sodomy," see Kaurss, *Lehnwörter* 2:582-83; J. Perles, "Miscellen zur rabbinishen Sprach- und Alterthumskunde," *MGWJ* 21 (1872): 271-72; L. Ginzberg, "Review of Festscrift zu Israel Lewy's siebzigstem Geburtstag," *Revue des Études Juives* 66 (1913): 297-315; Daniel Sperber, "פויסינון," in *Studies in Hebrew and Semitic Languages Dedicated to the Memory of Prof. Eduard Yechezkel Kutscher* (Ramat-Gan: Bar-Ilan University Pres, 1980) 155-58 (Hebrew).

emphasized by the implied reference to the sexual frenzy of the guards, is equated with "feminization" and humiliation.

This sentiment, linking penetration, feminization, and power, can be seen even more clearly in a statement attributed to a third generation Palestinian amora. Referring to Esau, Israel laments to God, "is it not enough that we are subjugated to the seventy nations, but even to this one, who is penetrated like women?"[120] A man who is penetrated, the assumption is, cannot rule like a man. Here, as in other places in rabbinic literature, Esau probably represents Rome.[121] Israel, seeing that homoerotic intercourse occurs in Rome, complains that Rome, in effect, has no right to rule not because Romans are engaged in homoerotic intercourse *per se*, but specifically because they allow themselves to be penetrated.[122] By allowing themselves to be penetrated, they sacrifice their "maleness," a characteristic deemed necessary for political power.

Condemnation of effeminacy might also underlie the rabbinic discussions on the cross-dresser. Deut. 22:5 prohibits a man from wearing a woman's clothes and vice versa. Curiously, the rabbis invoke this verse in their justification of a prohibition forbidding a man to pluck out his grey hairs.[123] These discussions, although found only in the Bavli, are attributed either to tannaim or to third generation amoraim from Palestine. The prohibition, as will become clearer below from a comparison with non-rabbinic parallels, seems originally to have been aimed at the pathic. Precisely in these traditions can a difference between Palestinian and Babylonian assumptions about homoerotic intercourse and the pathic be discerned. In *b. Naz.* 59a, the redactor explains this prohibition as due to the fear that a man, by appearing like a woman, will slip disguised among women, leading to a greater chance of heterosexual immorality. If I am correct that the original discussions assumed the subject to be the male pathic, this would be further evidence of different discourses about homoerotic intercourse among rabbis from Palestine and Babylonia. That is, the redactor did not understand the sexual assumptions and anxieties that originally informed this Palestinian tradition.

To some degree, the equation of homoerotic intercourse with women is dictated by the biblical terminology: one who "lies with a male as one

---

[120]*Gen. Rab.* 63:10 (p. 693).
[121]See Gerson D. Cohen, "Esau as a Symbol in Early Medieval Thought," reprinted in *Studies in the Variety of Rabbinic Cultures* (Philadelphia: Jewish Publication Society, 1991) 243-61.
[122]See also *t. Bik.* 2:4, according to which an hermaphrodite can "marry, but not be married." Although this probably refers to vaginal intercourse, the same assumption, that a man should not be penetrated, is present.
[123]*b. Shab.* 94b; *b. Naz.* 59a; *b. Mak.* 20b.

lies with a woman" (מִשְׁכְּבֵי אִשָּׁה). One must also assume that anal penetration was not only seen to be inherent in the biblical language, but was also a description of what was actually observed.[124] Yet neither fact fully explains the force of these traditions. The particular confluence of the tropes of penetration-feminization-power is neither in the biblical text nor readily "observable." Rather, it represents a rhetorical strategy shared also by the Romans and the Jewish Hellenistic writers.

Non-Rabbinic Parallels

Interest in and condemnation of the pathic was perhaps the primary rhetorical trope about male homoeroticism among Hellenistic and Roman authors. As early as Plato the pathic was seen as betraying his nature, that is, his "manliness:"

> ... one certainly should not fail to observe that when male unites with female for procreation, the pleasure experienced is held to be due to nature, but contrary to nature when male mates with male or female with female, and that those first guilty of such enormities were impelled by their slavery to pleasure.[125]

His argument, that these activities were παρὰ φύσιν, "against nature," was widely used by Hellenistic writers in the Roman period.[126] The exact meaning of this critical phrase is a subject of continuing debate. Winkler has argued that the phrase, when employed in sexual contexts in the dream interpretation manual of Artedmidoros, signifies "culture," that is, sexual relationships outside of the social hierarchy.[127] The term "nature," according to Winkler, is articulated as "norm-enforcing" language in legislative texts.[128] Boswell, along with other scholars, argues that in this context φύσις refers to a person's own, inborn nature. That is, a man is "born" to be an active sexual partner, not a passive one. Thus, a man assuming a passive role in sexual intercourse acts against

---

[124]This is not as obvious as it might seem. According to Dover the predominant mode of male homoerotic intercourse in Greece was intercrural (*Greek Homosexuality* 100-6). Moreover, there are, of course, a wide range of possible homoerotic activities, any of which might have predominated.

[125]Plato *Laws*, 636B (trans. *LCL* 1.41).

[126]For examples see Dionysius of Halicarnassus XVI, 4; Plutarch *Whether Beasts are Rational* 990D-F; Pseudo-Lucian *Erotes* 22; Athenaeus *Deinosophist* XIII, 565C, 605D; Diogenes Laertus 6.65.

[127]Winkler, *Constraints* 43.

[128]Ibid. 69.

his "nature."[129] Note that this limits the applicability of the argument to the passive role, a limitation borne out by the texts themselves.[130]

The "unnatural" male desire to be penetrated was harshly condemned. In Rome, as in classical Athens, the pathic was despised; homoerotic intercourse was, as noted, derisively called "Greek love."[131] The fear of the pathic was so great that physiognomic works spring up whose primary goal it was to enable the reader to identify the pathic by looking at his face.[132] To be penetrated was to be turned into a woman, an anathema to the privileged men of antiquity, be they from Athens or Rome.[133] Of course, these arguments did not apply to a boy or a male slave. Those who did not socially hold "manly" power violated no norms by assuming a passive sexual role.

The background helps to explain some references made by the Jewish-Hellenistic writers, who also employ an argument based on nature. The clearest (and perhaps earliest) example can be found in Pseudo-Phocylides:

> Transgress not for unlawful sex the natural limits of sexuality.
> For even animals are not pleased by intercourse of male with male.
> And let not women imitate the sexual role of men.[134]

Nature, φύσις, limits sexual expression, and in the case of male homoeroticism, shows its law clearly among the animals. Women, for reasons not stated explicitly (though are possibly connected to the argument from nature), are told to shun the active sexual role.

Both Josephus and Philo term male homoerotic activities "against nature."[135] *T. Naph.* 3:4-5 equates the activities at Sodom with a deviation

---

[129]Boswell, *Christianity* 13, n. 22.
[130]See for example Seneca *Epistle* 122, 7-8: "*Non videntur tibi contra naturam vivere qui commutant cum feminis vestem? Non vivunt contra naturam qui specant, ut puritia spledeat tempore alieno?*"
[131]See Richlin, *Garden of Priapus* 220-26. For the term, "Greek love," see MacMullen, "Greek Love." MacMullen, in attempting to refute Boswell's assertion that Romans fully accepted homosexual activities, overcompensates. Nearly every source he cites to support his thesis that Roman attitudes were more ambivalent than portrayed by Boswell refers only to the passive role. See also Lilja, *Homosexuality* 122-27.
[132]See Maud W. Gleason, "The Semiotics of Gender: Physiognomy and Self-Fashioning in the Secondary Century C.E.," in *Before Sexuality* 389-415.
[133]See Aeschines *Ag. Timarchus* 113, 126; Musonius Rufus 12.3; Boswell, *Christianity* 70-71; Hans Ankum, "La *captiva adultera*: Problèmes concernant l'*accusatio adulterii* en droit romain classique," *RIDA*, 3d ser., 32 (1985): 154, n . 4. For a link between men who use the spindle and effeminacy, see Cicero *De Or.* 2.277; Juvenal 2.54-6.
[134]Pseudo-Phocylides II. 190-92 (trans. van der Horst, 237-40).
[135]Josephus *Ag. Apion* 2.275; Philo *Spec. Laws* 3.39; *Abraham* 135-6. See Helmut Koester, "ΝΟΜΟΣ ΦΥΣΕΩΣ: The Concept of Natural Law in Greek Thought," in

from nature and, presumably, homoerotic intercourse, and one manuscript tradition of *2 Enoch* equates Sodom, pederasty, and an argument that it was against nature.[136] Hence it is no surprise to also see in this corpus the same abhorrence of the pathic as found in the Roman literature. Philo fulminates against the pathic when speaking both about pederasty[137] and (presumably) non-pederastic male intercourse.[138] But it is Josephus who uses this rhetoric most vividly, in order to describe the abominable activities of the loathsome Galilean contingent, commanded by his arch-enemy John:

> With an insatiable lust for loot, they ransacked the houses of the wealthy; the murder of men and the violation of women were their sport; they caroused on their spoils, with blood to wash them down, and from mere satiety unscrupulously indulged in effeminate practices, plaiting their hair and attiring themselves in women's apparel, drenching themselves with perfumes and painting their eyelids to enhance their beauty. And not only did they imitate the dress, but also the passions of women, devising in their excess of lasciviousness unlawful pleasures and wallowing as in a brothel in the city, which they polluted from end to end with their foul deeds. Yet, while they wore women's faces, their hands were murderous, and approaching with mincing steps they would suddenly become warriors and whipping out their swords from under their dyed mantles transfix whomsoever they met.[139]

Josephus combines a "grotesque" and exaggerated portrayal of effeminization with visions of bloodshed and confusion of sexual roles. It is bad enough, he seems to be saying, that they imitated women. But it is much worse that they imitate women while engaging in bloodshed, a particularly masculine vice. It is the confused gender expectations that are worthy of particular opprobrium.

The Church too shared the abhorrence of the pathic. Paul mentions the *malakoi*, the effetes, in a very negative context.[140] The repulsion at

---

Religions in Antiquity: Essays in Memory of Erwin Ramsdell Goodenough, ed. Jacob Neusner (Leiden: E.J. Brill, 1968) 521-41. Philo appears to use the term "against nature" to refer even to males penetrating other males.

[136] See *2 Enoch*, 10:4 (ver. J.) (see Charlesworth, 1:119, n. 1). It is possible that *Wisdom of Solomon* argues against homoeroticism on the basis of an argument from nature, but this is not clear. See *Wis. Sol.* 14:26 and the note on it in *The Wisdom of Solomon*, ed. David Winston (*Anchor Bible* 43; rpt. Garden City: Doubleday, 1984) 280.

[137] Philo *Spec. Laws* 3.37; *De Vita* 49-52.

[138] Philo *Spec. Laws* 1.325.

[139] Josephus *War* 4.560-62 (trans. LCL 3.164-67).

[140] 1 Cor. 6:9-10. On this word, see especially Scroggs, *New Testament and Homosexuality* 62-65. See also the comments in Fee, ed., *The First Epistle to the Corinthians* 243-44.

homoerotic anal intercourse, as well as at general effeminacy, was picked up by the Church Fathers, particularly Clement of Alexandria.[141] In the East, John Chrysostom shared this abhorrence, and in the West it was appropriated by Augustine and Lactantius, among others.[142]

Islamic culture (and perhaps their Arab predecessors) too distinguished between active and passive male homoerotic acts. According to one scholar, "It is, however, abundantly clear that in classical Islamic culture in general 'active' and 'passive' homosexuality were considered essentially two different, albeit complementary, phenomena."[143] Similarly, the Hadith literature shows an abhorrence of the pathic.[144]

In sum, the anxiety caused by the idea of a man being penetrated by another man was shared in antiquity and was used rhetorically by Jew, Christian, and pagan. The rabbis never did develop an argument from nature about homoeroticism, but they did appear to share the widespread assumptions linking women, passivity, powerlessness, and the pathic. This attitude probably also informs the Palestinian rabbinic discussions of liability of the pathic partner. Pathics generally commanded attention in antiquity, and the concentration of these discussions among sources attributed to Palestine (even if occasionally quoted in the Bavli) meshes precisely with the rhetoric of Roman and Hellenistic writers.

ACTIVITY AND POWER

For the rabbis, the sexual penetration of one man by another represents haughtiness, power that has gone beyond its God-given bounds. On the one hand, sexual penetration of another male is seen as a sign of dominance, but on the other this way of expressing that dominance is seen as an affront to God. Pharaoh and Nebuchednezzar, both noted for their power and arrogance (which in rabbinic legend led to their fall), are portrayed as penetrators of other males.

> [Referring to Ex. 15:9: "The foe said, 'I will pursue, I will overtake, I will divide the spoil; My desire shall have its fill of them. I will bare my sword – my hand shall subdue them.'"] It is not written here, "shall be satisfied upon them," but "my desire shall have its fill of them" – they will satisfy their desire upon me ... In the past if you

---

[141]See *Paed.* 2.10 (GCS 12:210) and *Paed.* 3.3 (GCS 12:244-50).
[142]Chrysostom *In Epist. ad Rom.*, 4.2-3 and *Adv. oppug. vit. mon.* 3.8 (trans. Boswell, *Christianity* 131-32); Augustine *Contra mendacium* 7.10 (PL 40:496); Lactantius *Institutiones divinae*, 5.9. See Bailey, *Homosexuality* 82-83; Boswell, ibid. 156-58; H. Herter, "Effeminatus," in *Reallexikon für Antike und Christentum* 4:642-50.
[143]See Everett K. Rowson, "The Effeminates of Early Medina," *Journal of the American Oriental Society* 111 (1991): 685.
[144]Ibid. 673-74.

sought to violate their wives and their sons and their daughters, I used to hold you responsible by the laws of the kingdom. But now, "my hand shall subdue them." Some say: It is not written "I will point my sword," but "I will bare my sword," [Pharaoh] intended to have intercourse [as the active partner] with their males, like it is said "... they shall unsheathe their swords against your prized shrewdness ..." [Ezek. 28:7] – it is said "they will *unsheathe* their swords," and because he was haughty and proud of heart God brought him low and the nations abused him.[145]

This midrash gradually builds on the theme of Pharaoh's arrogance and his ultimate punishment. Each of Pharaoh's outrageous desires is punished appropriately. The midrash culminates with an exegesis that attributes to Pharaoh a desire for homoerotic intercourse. From the last line of the unit – "and because he was haughty and proud of heart ..." – it appears that of all the examples of arrogant acts perpetrated by Pharaoh, this was perceived as being the worst. Not only, though, does the desire for homoerotic intercourse serve as an example of his arrogance; it also sets up the most dramatic portrayal of his punishment. The nations "abuse him" (בזוהו), which following the pattern of the rest of the unit and in line with the general rabbinic hermeneutic of "measure for measure," probably refers to Pharaoh being repeatedly penetrated in homoerotic intercourse, an interpretation made explicit in one later version of the story.[146] Pharaoh's extreme expression of arrogance leads to his extreme punishment and humiliation at the hands of the nations.

The Bavli relates a thematically similar tradition in the name of Rabbah bar Rav Huna [BA 3] that Nebuchednezzar used to cast lots of noblemen to see whom he would penetrate that day. When, the story continues, he came to penetrate Tzidkiyah, a former king of Judah, his foreskin rolled back "300 cubits."[147] Here Nebuchednezzar's arrogant demeanor is further emphasized by relating the enormous proportions of his phallus. Like Pharaoh, Nebuchednezzar is portrayed through his active homoerotic activity as having committed hubris, exceeding his God-given power.

A Palestinian source, utilizing a rhetoric of divine retribution, captures this attitude. Earthquakes occur, R. Aha [PA 4] says, "... on account of the sin of homoerotic intercourse. God said, You cause your

---

[145]*Mekh. Beshelaḥ* (p. 140) (par. *Mekh. d'RASHBI* [p. 89]). The translation is slightly modified from Lauterbach, *Mekhilta of Rabbi Ishmael*, Shirata 7 (2:56-57). See also Judah Goldin, *The Song of the Sea* (New Haven: Yale University Press, 1971) 182-83. His view of this passage as referring specifically to pederasty, though possibly correct, misplaces the emphasis of the passage and detracts from the force of the last phrase.

[146]*Yalk. Shimoni*, 249. See the apparatus in *Mekh.*, p. 140.

[147]*b. Shab.* 149b. Attributed to Rav Yehudah [BA 2] in the name of Rav [BA 1].

limb to quiver over something that is not yours. By your life, I shall cause my world to shake on account of that very man."[148] Underneath the obvious (and not particularly successful) word play lurks the concept that homoerotic intercourse is an act of hubris, of sexually using something not belonging to one. The appropriation of this forbidden object of desire warrants divine punishment.[149]

Non-Rabbinic Parallels

Non-Jews, and Philo, had a similar rhetoric concerning males who sexually penetrate males. Active male homoeroticism was, of course, an accepted part of both Greek and Roman culture. As noted in Chapter 4, though, a man was expected to moderate his sexual desires: keeping control of one's own passions, in effect, gave a man warrant to wield power over others. Excessive, uncontrolled desire was equated with women, thus also bringing with it a charge of "softness."[150] Ironically, excessive sexual activity, irregardless of gender, was equated with loss of control and effeminacy.[151]

At the same time, penetration of another man was in Rome seen as an aggressive act in which a man asserts his dominance. Latin literature and graffiti abounds with boasts of sexual prowess and threats of sexual violence. In particularly vivid displays of their power, Roman writers occasionally threaten oral rape *(irrumatio).*[152]

---

[148]*y. Ber.* 9:3, 13c. אמר רבי אחא בעון משכב זכור.   אמר הב"ה אתה זיעזעתה איברך על דבר שאינו שלך. חייך שאני מזעזע עולמי על אותו האיש...

[149]R. Aḥa's suggestion follows another one suggesting that earthquakes arise from non-observance of the agricultural laws of *terumah* and *ma'asrot*. The word play would work if עולם is a euphemism for penis, but I have not been able to find an example of that usage.

[150]This can be seen even in Plato *Laws* 636C. See also Boswell, *Christianity* 74-77 (and the sources cited there); Polybius 31.25.5.

[151]All the Roman early emperors except Claudius are depicted by Suetonius as engaged in homoerotic activities. See Suetonius, *Aug.* 68; *Tib.* 42-4; *Calig.* 24, 36; *Nero* 29-9; *Galba* 22; *Otho* 12; *Divus Titus* 7; *Dom.* 1.

A particularly interesting passage equates Julius Caesar's adultery with his playing the pathic to males. "Every woman's man and the woman of every man," Cato is said to have stated of him (Suetonius *Jul.* 52.3).

[152]On the aggressive tone of the graffiti from Pompei, see Lilja, *Homosexuality* 97-102. On oral rape, see Richlin, *Garen of Priapus* 27, 220-26; David F. Greenberg, *The Construction of Homosexuality* (Chicago: University of Chicago, 1988) 156-58. An example of the force and comic effect of *irrumatio* can be seen in Catallus 21:

pedicare cupis meos amores...
frustra: nam insidias mihi insruentem
tangam te prior irrumatione.

In Egypt too male penetration was seen as an aggressive act. See D. Greenberg, ibid. 132.

Although the belief in a God and His commandments separates the rabbinic from non-rabbinic rhetoric, the fundamental assumptions might be similar. To penetrate is to assert power, and any man who penetrates "excessively" (however defined) is condemned.[153]

Conclusions

In this survey, one theme kept coming repeatedly to the fore, the interest in and concentration on the penetrated partner in male homoerotic intercourse. Both legal and non-legal rabbinic material display a persistent and consistent "rhetoric of the pathic." Not only was a special effort made to stigmatize the pathic legally, but also a withering discourse was developed to link the pathic to effeminacy and thus, humiliation. This discursive strategy went hand in hand with the rhetoric toward the active partner, who through homoerotic intercourse demonstrates his complete domination (sinful as it may be).

Secondly, this "rhetoric of the pathic" is fundamentally similar to that of Jewish-Hellenistic, Greek, Roman, and Christian writers. All shared the same assumptions, even anxiety, about a male who allowed himself to be penetrated. Where the rabbinic rhetoric differed was its additional application of biblical verses, strained as it sometimes was, to this basic posture. Effeminacy, according to the rabbis, was not only abhorrent because it was "unmanly," but in addition it was forbidden by the word of God. Scripture became a handmaiden. That is, it appears that the scriptural justification followed these common assumptions about the pathic.

The rabbinic "rhetoric of the pathic," with its parallels to non-rabbinic antiquity, is predominately found in Palestinian sources. Although many of these statements are cited in the Bavli, their treatment ironically only highlights the difference in attitudes of the framers of the statements and their ultimate redactors. In almost every case in which Palestinian statements of this sort are cited in the Bavli, they are either ignored or reinterpreted by Babylonian amoraim and the redactor. Thus, despite the lack of evidence from Sassanian Babylonia, it is probably safe to conclude that Palestinian and Babylonian rabbis held fundamentally different assumptions about homoeroticism, and that these differences are rooted in the different cultural milieu of the two groups of rabbis.

---

[153] It is interesting to note, in this regard, Josephus *Ant.* 16.229ff, in which Josephus phrases male penetration of eunuchs merely "unseemly." Seth Schwartz writes: "Could it be that Josephus did not believe that sex with eunuchs falls under the prohibition of male homosexuality...? Or that the law was not considered to apply to slaves?" (*Josephus and Judaen Politics* [Leiden: E.J. Brill, 1990] 157 n. 162).

There are as well other differences between the rhetoric of rabbis of Palestine and those of Babylonia. Vice-catalogues containing homoerotic intercourse, and their identification with non-Jews, are mainly confined to Palestinian sources, a rhetoric again shared with the non-Jewish writers surveyed.

The overwhelming sense of these Palestinian sources is that sex, and modes of sanctioned sex, were intricately bound with gender expectations. Sex, these sources assume, requires a penetrator, identified with the role of the male who is also assumed to hold other forms of societal power, and of a penetrated partner, identified with the role of the disenfranchised female. A sexually passive male threatens these boundaries.

Babylonian sources have a more nuanced rhetoric. To be sexually active is indeed to assert one's power, but sexual passivity in men appears not to have roused the same degree of antipathy. Indeed, as we shall see in Chapter 7, Babylonian rabbis ascribe more mutuality to sex. Male passivity was not the societal "sin" (though God was certainly perceived as disapproving) in Babylonia that it was in Palestine.

Female homoeroticism is thus relatively neglected. Not involving penetration, it hardly counted as sex for the rabbis. One Palestinian source voices strong objection to female homoerotic *marriage:* such a marriage would necessarily include an "active" partner, blurring gender boundaries. Babylonian sources show a discomfort with female homoeroticism, but do not go so far as to posit legal repercussions.

For the rabbis Scripture and the threat of the death penalty were not thought sufficient enough rhetoric to argue against homoerotic intercourse. In the Roman period there was a popularization of literary debates on the advantages and disadvantages of "boy-love" compared to heterosexual relations.[154] For the rabbis, there never was a "pro" side to homoerotic intercourse, only a "con" side. But it was not enough for them to say that homoerotic intercourse was forbidden simply because God forbade it. The scriptural prohibition of course deeply informed their opinion, but its invocation was sporadic and, as we have seen, at times forced. Although there is a death penalty and extirpation associated with the transgression, these too were not emphasized in their rhetoric. Instead, the Palestinian rabbis offered other arguments against homoerotic intercourse, arguments that one presumes would have been more persuasive to their intended audience(s): homoerotic intercourse is

---

[154]See Foucault, *Care of the Self* 189-232. These arguments shared a common organization "around the symmetrical and reciprocal relationship of a man and a woman, around the high value attributed to virginity, and around the complete union in which it finds perfection," (232).

as serious as the three "mortal sins" (an argument, incidentally, also used for theft and slander); it is a definitional activity, by which one identifies with "them;" it is animalistic; it is effeminate and humiliating; and it can lead to divine punishment. We should not conclude, though, that even among the Palestinian rabbis there was a completely shared set of assumptions. The *Sifra* and the *Tosefta* are much more strident than the other sources in associating homoerotic intercourse with Gentiles, and the idea of divine retribution is quite fuzzy, and might be somewhat late. In any case, male homoerotic intercourse was considered to be a serious threat, "requiring" several different rhetorics to be used against it.[155]

The Babylonian rabbis, on the other hand, did not employ a variety of rhetorics against homoerotic intercourse. They may have shared a perception of male homoerotic intercourse as animalistic, and they seemed to continue in the rhetoric of the vice catalogue and the association of homoerotic intercourse with non-Jews. Libido, and self-control, may have been more at the root of their own perceptions. But Babylonian rabbinic rhetoric is not as varied or spirited as among those statements attributed to Palestinian rabbis. Can this difference be explained rhetorically? Did the Palestinian rabbis simply parrot the rhetoric of their milieu? If this is not the case, then it is likely that the reason is that homoerotic intercourse, while still forbidden, simply did not arouse the same level of anxiety for Babylonian rabbis. This lack of anxiety might be due to societal factors, such as a lack of incidence in their intended audience, or as is more likely to a different set of assumptions about homoerotic intercourse. For Babylonians, male sexual passivity was not fraught with the same danger, the tight association of effeminacy with humiliation.

---

[155]Many modern scholars have assumed that "homosexuality" was in fact not common among the Jews in antiquity. Needless to say, the evidence does not support such a conclusion. Nor, however, do I mean to argue that it was common. What is clear is that it was perceived as an imminent danger and a varied rhetoric was marshalled against it. The data allows no conclusions as to actual frequency.

6

Non-Procreative Sex

Rabbinic Judaism valued procreation and promoted the procreative goal of sexuality.[1] The rabbis made procreation a religious duty for men: "A man shall not cease from procreating unless he has children. The School of Shammai said, two males. The School of Hillel said, a male and a female...'"[2] The rhetoric of procreation in early Jewish law has been fully discussed by scholars.[3] In this chapter I examine the flip side of the coin: the rabbinic attitudes toward non-procreative sexual activities. Did the rabbinic emphasis on procreation include rhetoric intended to discourage non-procreative liaisons and sexual outlets? How were their discussions of this issue informed by the great weight put on procreation? Does the rabbinic rhetoric on non-procreative sexual activities exhibit unity?

Non-procreative sex can occur within two contexts, that of liaison and that of activity. In this chapter, I first examine the rabbinic rhetoric on intercourse with an infertile partner. Subsequently I examine issues of family planning and non-procreative sexual activities. Although this material does not easily conform to the previously discussed rhetorical categories, many of these by-now familiar rhetorical strategies are present in these discussions. I conclude with a discussion of the issue of

---

[1]See especially Jeremy Cohen, *'Be Fertile and Increase, Fill the Earth and Master It:' The Ancient and Medieval Career of a Biblical Text* (Ithaca: Cornell University Press, 1989) 67-165.
[2]*m. Yebam.* 6:6. Rabbi Yoḥanan ben Beroqa extends the commandment to procreate to women. On this, see David Daube, "Johanan ben Beroqa and Women's Rights," *Zeitschrift der Savigny-Stiftung für Rechtsgeschichte-römanishische Abteilung* 99 (1982): 22-31.
[3]For examples see David M. Feldman, *Birth Control in Jewish Law: Marital Relations, Contraception and Abortion* (1968; rpt. Westport, CT: Greenwood, 1980) 46-56; David Daube, *The Duty of Procreation* (Edinburgh: Edinburgh University Press, 1977); J. Cohen, *'Be Fertile and Increase'* 76-144; Boyarin, *Carnal Israel* 134-66.

"wasted seed," which has traditionally been used (wrongly, I argue) to impose a unity on these topics.

Non-Procreative Liaisons

SEX WITH AN INFERTILE WOMAN

Any intercourse with a congenitally infertile, pre-menstrual or post-menopausal woman is non-procreative. Within tannaitic sources, discussions of intercourse with non-procreative women occur in three contexts: the obligations of the levir; the *soṭah* ordeal; and "mistaken" marriage. The Talmudim add to these categories discussions of non-procreative intercourse *per se* with infertile women, usually emphasizing the "licentiousness" of such liaisons.

Levirate Marriage

"When brothers dwell together and one of them dies and leaves no son, the wife of the deceased shall not be married to a stranger ... Her husband's brother shall unite with her: take her as his wife and perform the levir's duty. The first son that she bears shall be accounted to the dead brother, that his name not be blotted out in Israel," (Deut. 25:5-6). The goal of levirate marriage is procreation. Not surprisingly, then, the rabbinic sources prohibit levirate marriage (as it would normally be a violation of incest restrictions) if the levirate widow is infertile. According to the *Mishnah*, a congenitally infertile levirate widow (*'ilonit*) both is exempted from the obligation of the levirate marriage,[4] and releases her co-wives as well, upon whom the obligation should now descend, from this obligation.[5]

The *Mishnah* directly applies these prohibitions only to the *'ilonit*; other infertile women are not mentioned. In discussions on this topic, other tannaitic sources explicitly separate the *ilonit* from other infertile women.[6] The *Tosefta*, for example, prohibits intercourse between a levir and his pre-pubescent levirate widow not because she is infertile at that

---

[4]The *'ilonit* is defined as a woman who never physically matures and remains incapable of procreation (*m. Nid.* 5:9; *t. Yebam.* 10:7; *t. Nid.* 6:2). See *m. Yebam.* 1:1; 8:5.

[5]*m. Git.* 8:7; *t. Yebam.* 1:2; *t. Git.* 6(8):6-7; *y. Yebam.* 8:5, 9d; 13:1, 13c; *b. Yebam.* 12a-b, 91b.

[6]See *t. Yebam.* 2:5; *Sifre Deut.* 289 (pp. 307-8). The former reads the *Mishnah's* omission to signify that post-menopausal and other infertile women are, like all other women, subject to the obligations of levirate marriage. The later atomizes Deut. 25:6-7, and attributes the prohibitions on levirate acquisition of an *'ilonit* and of other infertile women to different parts of the verses. See also *b. Yebam.* 24a.

time, but for fear that when she reaches puberty she will be found to be an *'ilonit*.[7]

According to the *Mishnah*, intercourse between a levir and his *'ilonit* levirate widow is *bi'ilat znut* and thus would make the woman ineligible to marry a priest.[8] These sources are repeatedly cited in the Talmudim. All of this rhetoric concerns only the *'ilonit:* cases of post-menopausal levirate widows, for example, are not discussed.

Soṭah Ordeal

As noted in Chapter 4, according to Num. 5:11-31, a man who suspects (but cannot prove) that his wife is unfaithful is entitled to bring his wife to a priest who will put her through a trial by ordeal (through drinking a potion). If she survives the ordeal, she will be rewarded with pregnancy (Num. 5:28). The *Mishnah* asks about the infertile woman's obligation to undergo the ordeal:

- A. A woman pregnant by another [man, other than her husband] or one nursing the child of another [man, other than her husband] can neither be forced to drink [i.e., undergo the ordeal] nor does she take her marriage settlement *(ketubah)*. These are the words of R. Meir.
- B. And the Sages say, it is possible for him to separate from her, and then to take her back after a while.
- C. An *'ilonit,* an old woman, and a woman who cannot bear a child –she can neither be forced to drink [i.e., undergo the ordeal] nor does she take her marriage settlement.
- D. Rabbi Eliezer says: It is possible for him to marry another woman and to procreate from her.
- E. And all other women either drink or do not take their marriage settlement.[9]

(A) and (B) form a unit parallel to (C) and (D). The rabbinic perception that these women were infertile links (A) and (C). The women in (A), however, will again be fecund, while the women in (C) are permanently infertile. (B) and (D) appear to dissent from (A) and (C), respectively. It is not clear whether they give the man in each case a third option, or whether they offer alternative rulings. In either case,

---

[7]See *t. Yebam.* 1:5, 6:9; *y. Yebam.* 1:1, 2d; 1:2, 2d; 4:1, 5c; 12:5, 12d; 13:8, 13d; 13:12, 14a; 13:14, 14a; *b. Yebam.* 119a; *b. Nid.* 32a.
[8]*m. Yebam.* 8:5; *y. Yebam.* 8:5, 9d. See also *m. Yebam.* 6:5 and below. According to Rabbi Yehudah's opinion in *m. Yebam.* 6:5, an *'ilonit* is considered a *zōnah*. The Sages in that *mishnah*, and the uncontested opinion in this *mishnah*, clearly do not accept that opinion. See Chapter 4.
[9]*m. Soṭ.* 4:3.

there is a concern that a man be married to a fertile woman. The opinions that these women do not receive marriage settlements is explained by Albeck to be based on the fact that the marriages are to begin with illegal.[10] Albeck adduces no evidence that shows that the women enumerated in (C) are forbidden in marriage.[11] Rather, it is possible that this passage testifies to a conceptual link between adultery (and the *sotah*) and paternity. Because adultery with these women would not involve issues of mistaken paternity, the *sotah* ordeal is, in a sense, irrelevant for them.

The withholding from the suspected wife of a chance to acquit herself through the ordeal, and the loss of her rights to her marriage settlement, appear intended to make it easier for her husband to divorce her. A man who marries a barren woman and suspects her of adultery has only two legal options: to remain quiet or to divorce his wife, the option of submitting her to the ordeal being closed to him. By depriving the suspected wife of her marriage settlement, the rabbis in effect nullify the protection that her marriage settlement gives her, encouraging him to pursue divorce. The reason for this might be that once the *sotah* ordeal had already ceased, the rabbis were afraid of not penalizing these women at all. Otherwise, the fear might have been, women will have no incentives to refrain from committing adultery secretly. The objections proffered in (B) and (D) support this reading over Albeck's. The concern is not the original legality of the marriage, but issues of procreation.

The *Tosefta* contains an alternative version of this *mishnah*:

A. A single man who marries an infertile woman, or an old woman, and does not have a wife and children, she neither drinks nor receives her marriage settlement.

B. R. Eleazar says, it is possible for him to separate from her, then take her back after a while.[12]

Here the status of the infertile wife is made dependent on whether or not she is the only wife and whether or not she is married to a fertile man.[13] According to Lieberman, even the apparently contradictory statement in the *Tosefta* that an infertile woman can be forced to undergo the ordeal, is to be interpreted as referring to a case where the man has

---

[10]See the notes in Albeck, *Mishnah* 3:243 *ad loc.*
[11]His argument appears to rest on the parallelism between clause (A) and *m. Sot.* 4:1.
[12]*t. Sot.* 5:5; *y. Sot.* 4:1, 19c.
[13]See also *t. Sot.* 5:2. I take הרובה, the first word in both these texts, to refer to a fertile bachelor.

another, fertile, wife.¹⁴ In a similar tradition in the *Tosefta*, a rabbi attempts to justify the exclusion of the infertile woman from the ordeal by recourse to Num. 5:28:

> Rabbi Shimon ben Eleazar says, an infertile woman does not undergo the ordeal and does not take [her] marriage settlement, as it is written, '[But if the woman has not defiled herself and is pure,] she shall be unharmed and able to retain seed,' [Num. 5:28]. This excludes one who cannot bear children.¹⁵

The *sotah* ordeal is explicitly linked to procreation. An alternative, non-biblical justification for exclusion of the infertile woman from the ordeal is presented in several other sources.¹⁶

Mistaken Marriage

Rabbinic sources exhibit anxiety over the possibility that the *'ilonit* would conceal her condition from her prospective husband. According to the *Mishnah*, if a man did not know that the woman he was marrying was an *'ilonit*, then the woman loses her economic entitlements, including her marriage settlement. If, on the other hand, he knew that she was an *'ilonit*, then she maintains rights to her marriage settlement.¹⁷ According to the *Tosefta*, even if a man did not know that his wife was an *'ilonit*, and after discovering this fact elects to keep her as wife, he must provide a marriage settlement.¹⁸ The Bavli accepts the principle that as long as there is no deceit an infertile wife is entitled to full marital economic benefits.¹⁹

Licentiousness

A few rabbinic sources consider intercourse with an infertile woman to be licentious. The *Tosefta*, in a passage contradicting its assumption in other places that an infertile woman is permitted to marry, flatly prohibits the marriage of a Jewish man to any woman not capable of

---

¹⁴*t. Yebam.* 5:4, and Lieberman, *Tos. Kip.* 8:654-655. See also *y. Sot.* 3:4, 18d; *b. Sot.* 26a.

¹⁵*t. Sot.* 5:4. Rabbi Shimon ben Eleazar's statement, to the biblical citation, is missing in the Vienna manuscript. This appears to be a scribal error.

¹⁶*Sifre Num.* 19 (p. 23); *b. Sot.* 26a; *b. Ber.* 31b. The attributions are reversed in the two sources from the Bavli. See also *D.S.* to *b. Ber.* 31b and Melamed, *Halakhic Midrashim* 339, n. 39. In a similar tradition in the Yerushalmi (*y. Sot.* 3:4, 18d) the redactor is much more accepting of the possibility of a miracle.

¹⁷*m. Ketub.* 11:6. Presumably, she is also entitled to the other economic benefits denied to women in illicit "marriages."

¹⁸*t. Ketub.* 1:3.

¹⁹*b. Ketub.* 101b.

bearing children.[20] The *Mishnah* contains an opinion that an *'ilonit* is prohibited to a priest alone:

    A. A common priest shall not marry an *'ilonit*, unless he has [already] a wife and children.

    B. Rabbi Yehudah says, even if he has a wife and children, he shall not marry an *'ilonit*, for she is a *zōnah* as stated in the Torah [thus prohibited to marry a priest].

    C. The Sages say, the only [women to whom are applied the label] *zōnah* are a proselyte, a freed-slave, and one who had engaged in *bĕ'ilat znut*.[21]

Note again the inclusion only of an *'ilonit*, but of no other infertile woman. The ruling is also limited, even in its most extreme expression (B), to priests. The basis of Rabbi Yehudah's statement is definitional: according to the Bible, a *zōnah* is prohibited from marrying a priest; an *'ilonit* is a *zōnah*; thus a priest, regardless of circumstances, is prohibited from marrying her. Yet as shown in Chapter 4, the term *zōnah* includes in its semantic field the meaning "prostitute," and is frequently used in the literature with more than the narrow legal meaning prohibiting a woman from marrying a priest. It is impossible to say here whether Rabbi Yehudah is using this term only in its narrow meaning, or also means to cast general aspersion on marriage with such a woman. Later sources are clearer.

Both Talmudim question the reason for Rabbi Yehudah's opinion. In the Yerushalmi, we read:

    A. "A common priest shall not marry an *'ilonit*, etc." [citing the *Mishnah*].

    B. But a Jew [non-priest] who does not already have a wife and children can marry her [i.e., an *'ilonit*]?

    C. [No,] he too is prohibited to her.

    D. But because we learned there, "The only [women labeled a] *zōnah* are the female proselyte, a freed-slave, and one who engaged in *bĕ'ilat znut*," and all of these [are in reference to] a priest [marrying them]; because of this we did not learn [concerning the non-priest].

---

[20]*t. Yebam.* 8:4. Lieberman, *Tos. Kip.* 6:69 following later rabbinic laws thinks that this passage refers only to the case in which a man does not already have a wife or children, but I see no evidence that compels such an explanation. This *tosefta* is paralleled nowhere else.

[21]*m. Yebam.* 6:5; *Sifra Emor* 1:7 (94b). It is interesting to note that the opposing view of the Sages, that she is not considered a *zōnah*, is effectively bypassed in the case of the levir and his infertile levirate widow, intercourse with whom is termed *bĕ'ilat znut*, thus also rendering her unfit for a priest. See *m. Yebam.* 8:6.

E. Rabbi Yehudah ben Pazi [PA 4] said, it is written "Between rows [of olive trees] they make oil, [and, thirsty, they tread the wine presses]," [Job 24:11] [and, referring to adulterers,] "[May they be flotsam on the face of the water; may their portion in the land be cursed;] may none turn aside by way of their vineyards," [Job 24:18]. Because his act of intercourse was not for the sake of children.

F. Rabbi Simon [PA 3] said, it is written, "Truly, they shall eat, but not be sated; they shall swill, but not be satisfied, [because they have forsaken the Lord to practice lechery]," [Hosea 4:10-11], because their acts of intercourse were not for the sake of children.

G. It is written, "Lamech took to himself two wives: [the name of the one was Adah, and the name of the other was Zillah]," [Gen. 4:19]. "Adah" because he used to be refreshed through her body, and "Zillah" because he would sit in the shade of [her] children.[22]

In (A) through (D) the redactor attempts to show that the *Mishnah's* ruling also applies to all Jewish men who have not yet fulfilled the commandment to procreate. (E) and (F), attributed to third and fourth generation Palestinian amoraim, attempt to show that verses from the Prophets actually refer to non-procreative intercourse.[23] (G), which is unattributed, suggests by using word-plays on Lamech's wives' names that Lamech had one wife to satisfy him sexually, and another to produce children.[24] It appears from the context that the reader is meant to assume that this is a mark of wicked men. This condemnatory tone is echoed in another tradition, attributed to R. Zeira [PA 4], that recognizes that men keep infertile wives because they satisfy them.[25]

A parallel in the Bavli is similarly flavored:

A. The Reish Galutha asked Rav Huna [BA 2], what is the reason [for the *mishnah*]?

B. [He replied,] because of procreation.

---

[22]*y. Yebam.* 6:5, 7c.

[23]The verses from Job (E) are nowhere else in rabbinic literature explained in this sexual context. Hos. 4:10 is used in *b. Yebam.* 61b (considered below).

[24]This midrash, unattested in any earlier sources, is not particularly successful because (1) Lamech's wives' names are not similar enough to the words being used to explain them; and (2) Adah, the wife who is said to serve his physical needs in contrast to the procreative Zillah, also in fact bears children (see Gen. 4:20-21). A parallel resolves the first problem by switching the roles of the wives. See *Gen. Rab.* 23:19 (pp. 222-23). Cf. Yaakov Elman, "Babylonian Echoes in a Late Rabbinic Legend," *Journal of the Ancient Near East* 4 (1972): 12-19. Elman sees this text as a vestige of a far older tradition going back to ancient Babylonia, but I find his argument too speculative to be convincing.

[25]*y. Git.* 4:8, 46a. Presumably the satisfaction, נחת רוח, is sexual. "Satisfaction" could, however, be more generally intended, the point being that men prefer good wives, even if they are infertile, to their obligation to procreate.

C. If [because of] procreation, are only priests commanded (מפקדי) [in this regard] the Jews [non-priests] are not?

D. He said to him [Rav Huna to the Reish Galutha], because it is necessary to teach the end, "Rabbi Yehudah says, even though he has a wife and children, he is not permitted to marry an *'ilonit* because she is a *zōnah*," and concerning a *zōnah* priests are commanded [being prohibited from marrying one] and Jews [non-priests] are not. Because of this it teaches "priest" [in the first part of the *mishnah*].

E. Rav Huna said, what is the reason for Rabbi Yehudah? As it is written, "Truly, they shall eat, but not be sated; they shall swill, but not be satisfied, [because they have forsaken the Lord to practice lechery]," [Hosea 4:10-11]. Any act of intercourse that is not for increase [i.e., procreation] is *b'ilat znut*.[26]

As in the Yerushalmi, the *mishnah* is interpreted to be referring to procreation, incumbent upon all Jews, not merely the priests. (C) and (D) attempt to explain then why the *mishnah* refers specifically to priests. (E), attributed to a BA 2, is similar to the treatment of the verse found in the Yerushalmi. Rav Huna's argument appears to be that because any non-procreative intercourse is *b'ilat znut*, and any intercourse with an *'ilonit* is by definition not procreative, any intercourse with an *'ilonit* is *b'ilat znut*, rendering the *'ilonit* a *zōnah*, thus ineligible to marry a priest. This, Rav Huna holds, is Rabbi Yehudah's reasoning in declaring an *'ilonit* a *zōnah*. According to this logic, any non-procreative intercourse (e.g., with a post-menopausal woman) should disqualify a woman from marrying a priest. It is not clear from the context of this tradition whether Rav Huna would agree with that conclusion (or ascribe it to Rabbi Yehudah). Lacking in the Bavli are the two other traditions found in the Yerushalmi that emphasize the wickedness inherent in non-procreative intercourse.

SEX WITH AN INFERTILE MAN

The single context in which intercourse with an infertile man (including eunuchs, both congenital and self-made, one with crushed testicles or a severed penis) is discussed is that of levirate marriage. A man known to be congenitally incapable of procreation not surprisingly frees his levirate widow from both the obligation of levirate marriage and the formal release from this obligation. If in fact the congenitally infertile man does have intercourse with his levirate widow, the intercourse is termed *b'ilat znut*; an old man or one who could at one time procreate but is no longer able, on the other hand, is free to take or release his levirate widow.[27] The divergence between laws relating to the

---

[26] *b. Yebam.* 61a-b.
[27] *m. Yebam.* 8:5; *t. Yebam.* 2:6, 11:2, *b. Yebam.* 20b, 79b.

congenitally infertile man and other types of infertile men is similar to that found regarding an infertile woman. To my knowledge, however, only a single, unparalleled tradition in the *Tosefta* condemns marriage to an infertile man.[28]

CONCLUSIONS

All the sources surveyed here save one (*t. Yebam.* 8:4) accept the ability of a man to contract a full and binding marriage with an infertile woman, providing that he know about her condition. Even a woman who exhibits no physical abnormalities, but has proven herself barren by living with three husbands and not bearing children is allowed to marry, although only to a man who either has another fertile wife or has fulfilled his obligation to procreate.[29] Other discussions too do not disapprove of a man's marriage to an infertile woman.[30] The only objections to such intercourse in the tannaitic literature are based on procreation: as long as marriage to such a woman will not prevent a man from fulfilling his obligation to procreate, there is no objection. Non-procreative intercourse *per se* is not condemned in the tannaitic literature. The same lack of disapproval can be seen in the case of intercourse with an infertile man. This attitude is very much in line with Roman law: older, infertile, men and women are exempted from the penalties of celibacy and are allowed to marry freely.[31]

The only rhetoric that suggests that non-procreative liaisons are anything but accepted can be found in a single *sugya* in the Yerushalmi and a single tradition in the Bavli. It is possible that the redactor of the Bavli deliberately muted his source; as noted, its context appears to limit a statement with potentially wide-reaching repercussions. In any case, all of these traditions employ a rhetoric of licentiousness. That is, the only reason that non-procreative liaisons might be bad is that they radiate a certain luxuriousness and hedonism that, as noted in Chapter 4, would have been anathema to the rabbis, who advocate strict discipline as necessary for piety.

---

[28]*t. Yebam.* 8:4: ‏והאשה אינה רשאה להנשא אפי' לסריס‎... The ‏אינה‎ is missing from both MS Erfort and the first printed edition of the *Tosefta*. See Lieberman, *Tos. Kip.* 6:69.
[29]See *m. Yebam.* 6:6; *t. Yebam.* 8:5-6; *b. Yebam.* 64b-65a.
[30]On the remarriage of an infertile woman, see *t. Yebam.* 6:6; *b. Yebam.* 42b; *b. ʿErub.* 47a (with a different attribution); *y. Yebam.* 4:11, 6b. for discussions of other issues in which the ability of a man to contract a marriage with an infertile woman is taken for granted, see *m. Git.* 4:8; *t. Yebam.* 8:3; *t. Ketub.* 3:4; *t. Git.* 3:5; *y. Yebam.* 1:1, 2c; *y. Ketub.* 1:4, 25c; *b. Ketub.* 101b.
[31]See Percy Ellwood Corbett, *The Roman Law of Marriage* (Oxford: Oxford University Press, 1930) 52-53.

Family Planning

According to David Feldman, the rabbinic attitude toward contraception can only be understood in reference to their attitude toward the wasteful emission of semen.[32] In this section I review the various types of family planning mentioned in the rabbinic literature and the rhetoric surrounding them. One of the goals of this review, as well as my review of literature regarding wasted semen in the next section, is to test Feldman's assertion.

CONTRACEPTIVE SPONGE (MOK)

Most discussions of the rabbinic view of contraception begin with a discussion of the *mok*, some type of contraceptive sponge. A *baraitha* regarding its use is first found in the *Tosefta*:

A. Three women [are permitted/accustomed to] use a *mok*: a minor, a pregnant woman, and a nursing woman.

B. A minor lest she will conceive and die. Who is a minor? One who is between eleven years and a day old to twelve years and a day old. Less than that and more than that he has intercourse in his regular way (*kĕdarkō*) and does not fear.

C. A pregnant woman lest her fetus will become a *sandal* [i.e., a type of deformed fetus].

D. A nursing mother lest she will kill her son [because pregnancy would lead to her cessation of lactation],

E. As Rabbi Meir used to say, all twenty-four months he threshes inside and winnows outside.

F. The Sages say, he has intercourse in his regular way and God watches over him, as it is written, "The Lord protects the simple..." [Ps. 116:6].[33]

A voluminous halakhic literature has grown around (A): does it mean that these three women *must* use a *mok*, implying that others may, or that they *may* use one, implying that others may not?[34] In the absence of other evidence that points to a ban on the *mok*, as well as the context, it appears more probable that (A) either mandates or suggests use of the *mok*, for these women; reading a ban on other women's use of the *mok* in this passage is not warranted. This is borne out by sections (B) to (D), which describe the health risks associated with pregnancy in these three women. In (E), Rabbi Meir appears to be commenting on (D), recommending that during the two years that a woman is presumed to

---

[32] Feldman, *Birth Control* 109.
[33] *t. Nid.* 2:6.
[34] For a summary of this literature, see Feldman, *Birth Control* 194-98.

be nursing they practice *coitus interruptus* (see below). The Sages (F) disagree, suggesting instead that God will protect "him." Note that although in the case of intercourse with a girl (B) it is the woman who will suffer the effects of non-protected intercourse, "he," apparently the son being nursed, is the one who is seen as needing protection.[35]

Why is the girl, the fetus, and the baby son worth saving? Is it due to the intrinsic worth of these three beings? If this was so, then the total absence from rabbinic literature of dicta that protect the sexual health of grown women (e.g., women who consistently miscarry, have had difficult deliveries, or who are physically misdeveloped) would be curious. Rather, I suggest that what links this particular list of beings is their relationship to the man. The young wife has procreative potential, and the fetus and young son represent potential heirs. Use of a *mok* would protect these assets. If this reading is correct, then use of the *mok* is advised rather than mandated. Furthermore, there can be no condemnation here of "wasted semen." If there was knowledge or assumption of such a concept, it would be strange that (1) it is allowed to waste semen in this case (E); and (2) no mention is made of abstinence. In any case, there is no indication that use of the contraceptive sponge is otherwise prohibited.

The Bavli appears to modify this tradition:

A. Rav Bibi [BA 4] taught before Rav Naḥman [BA 3]:

B. Three women use a *mok*: a minor, a pregnant woman and a nursing woman.

C. A minor lest she will conceive and perhaps she will die;

D. A pregnant woman lest her fetus will become a *sandal*;

E. A nursing woman lest she will wean her son and he will die.

F. And who is a minor?

G. From eleven years and one day old to twelve years and one day old. Less than this or more than this she has intercourse as she usually does.[36] These are the words of Rabbi Meir.

---

[35]Pregnancy was thought by the rabbis to halt lactation, endangering any child still nursing. The idea that a nursing woman who becomes pregnant ceases lactation was well-known in antiquity: contracts for wet nurses in Roman Egypt stipulate that the women remain sexually abstinent for the duration of the contract. See Soranus *Gyn.* 2.19; Keith R. Bradley, "Sexual Regulations in Wet-Nursing Contracts From Roman Egypt," *Klio* 62 (1980): 321-25. Bradley cites this rabbinic tradition as evidence of *coitus interruptus*. A study of Jewish wet-nursing is a desideratum.

[36]There are some textual variations of this phrase. See *Tal. Bab.* 3.1:117-18, esp. n. 32. The *Tosefta's* masculine reading is found in none of these variations.

H. The Sages say, in both cases she has intercourse as she usually does and let Heaven have mercy, as it is written, "The Lord protects the simple ..." [Ps. 116:6].[37]

The primary variation in this *sugya* is the suppression of R. Meir's statement advising *coitus interruptus*. This suppression, as I argue below, dovetails with an overall condemnation of the non-procreative emission of semen found in the Bavli. The suppression of this statement causes a shift in the remaining traditions. In the *Tosefta*, Rabbi Meir and the Sages disagree over the preferred mode of intercourse with a woman who is nursing her baby. But in the Bavli, the disagreement is over whether a woman between the ages of eleven and twelve should or must use a contraceptive sponge. Every *sugya* that contains this tradition cites it as part of a discussion of the age at which a girl can safely conceive (and be called a "woman"). Not once is this tradition cited in the Bavli for its information regarding the *mok* or even contraception generally.

A second tradition on the *mok* in the Bavli hints at a difference between the Palestinian and Babylonian rabbis. While Palestinian sources do not acknowledge any link between female contraception and female sexual freedom, this source in the Bavli does:

A ...As it is taught: the female proselyte, the female captive and slave woman who have been redeemed or converted or released must wait three months [to marry]. These are the words of Rabbi Meir.

B. Rabbi Yosi permits them to be betrothed and marry immediately.

C. Raba [BA 4] said, what is the reason for Rabbi Yosi?

D. [It is] that Rabbi Yosi holds that a whoring woman (אשה מזנה) uses a *mok* so that she will not conceive.[38]

Rabbi Meir insists that women who are normally assumed to have had intercourse must wait three months in order to ascertain the paternity of any child that she may be carrying (A), while Rabbi Yosi does not require a waiting period (B) in this case.[39] Raba justifies R. Yosi's dictum by ascribing to him the idea that a woman who has non-marital sexual relations will be shrewd enough to use contraception. The Bavli's interpretation of R. Yosi is forced. The *sugya* continues with the alternative suggestion that women engaged in non-marital intercourse use "inverted" sex to prevent conception: should we assume that a captive or female slave has the opportunity and forethought to use contraception or dictate the position of intercourse? Raba's (or possibly

---

[37]*b. Yebam.* 12b. See also *b. Yebam.* 100b; *b. Ketub.* 39a; *b. Nid.* 45a; *b. Ned.* 35b.
[38]*b. Yebam.* 35a. See also *b. Ketub.* 37a.
[39]Rabbi Yosi's true reason is obscure. This tradition also appears in *t. Yebam.* 6:6 (which reads Rabbi Yehudah in place of Rabbi Meir here).

the redactor's) interpretation of R. Yosi's statement reflects a familiarity with the relationship between contraception and women's sexual freedom. As noted in Chapter 4, the acknowledgment of female sexual freedom is generally confined to Babylonian sources. To my knowledge, there is no evidence that this relationship was recognized by the rabbis in Palestine.[40] Despite the recognition of this relationship, at least by Raba, the Bavli did not attempt to forbid the use of contraceptive devices.

ORAL CONTRACEPTION

There are few passages that mention contraceptive drugs. One such drug, apparently made of some kind of roots, caused sterilization.[41] In the midst of a discussion on the duty of a male to procreate, the *Tosefta* tells us that "a man is not permitted to drink a sterilizing drug so as not to procreate."[42] It is not clear from the continuation of this passage whether a woman is permitted to drink sterilizing drugs; the manuscripts present both options.[43] In any case, the Bavli makes a clearer distinction between the use of sterilizing drugs by men and women. A story about Rabbi Ḥiyya, an early Palestinian amora, (though possibly composed by the redactor) tells of him being tricked into giving his wife permission to drink a sterilizing drug. When the truth emerges, he protests that he lost his opportunity to continue to fulfill the commandment to procreate.[44] Another passage in the Bavli debates the legal ramifications of taking a drug that has an indirect effect of causing sterilization. This mainly Babylonian composition leaves no doubt that for a man this is absolutely forbidden.[45]

I have found only a single mention of an oral contraceptive that was not perceived to have permanent, sterilizing effects. This is the abortifacient "the drug of scattering," mentioned once by the redactor of

---

[40]For examples of Palestinian discussions where one might expect to find such a recognition, see *t. 'Abod. Zar.* 6(7):7 (par. *b. 'Abod. Zar.* 54b); *y. Yebam.* 6:11, 6a.
[41]The drug is called עיקרין, which usually means "roots." It might have derived its name from the word עקרה, "infertile, barren." It is possible that the amulet known by this name was supposed to serve as a contraceptive. See *b. Shab.* 61b.
[42]*t. Yebam.* 8:4.
[43]*t. Yebam.* 8:4. According to MS Vienna she is not permitted, but according to other manuscript versions she is permitted to drink sterilizing drugs. See Lieberman, *Tos. Kip.* 6:68. Because the rabbis thought it incumbent upon men, but not women, to procreate, this passage would read "better" permitting the woman to use a sterilizing drug. On the woman's duty (or non-duty) to procreate, see J. Cohen, *'Be Fertile and Increase'* 141-44; Daube, "Johanan ben Beroqa" 23-31; Feldman, *Birth Control* 240-41.
[44]*b. Yebam.* 65b.
[45]*b. Shab.* 110b-111a.

the Bavli.⁴⁶ In this passage the redactor uses the possibility that a number of Cleopatra's female slaves took this drug in order to explain two rabbinic interpretations of the story. This suggestion, of their taking the abortifacient, meets with no other comment or disapproval.⁴⁷

COITUS INTERRUPTUS AND ANAL INTERCOURSE

In a passage in the *Tosefta* cited above, Rabbi Meir recommends *coitus interruptus* as a means of birth control for a nursing mother: "all twenty-four months he threshes inside and winnows outside."⁴⁸ This act is in other sources connected to the deeds of Er and Onan, the sons of Judah. According to the Bible,

> Judah got a wife for Er his first-born; her name was Tamar. But Er, Judah's first-born, was displeasing to the Lord, and the Lord took his life. Then Judah said to Onan, 'Join with your brother's wife and do your duty by her as a brother-in-law, and provide offspring for your brother.' But Onan, knowing that the seed would not count as his, let it go to waste [lit. "spoil on the ground"] whenever he joined with his brother's wife, so as not to provide offspring for his brother. What he did was displeasing to the Lord, and He took his life also.⁴⁹

Onan engages in what appears to be repeated acts of *coitus interruptus* in order that he not impregnate his levirate widow. "The act of Onan" becomes in one unattributed comment in the Yerushalmi the euphemism for *coitus interruptus*.⁵⁰ The Bavli's discussion of the sins of Er and Onan is more extensive:

A. No woman is impregnated by her first act of intercourse.

B. Raba [BA 4] said to Rav Naḥman [BA 3] but Tamar conceived at her first act of intercourse! [there follows a short discussion of whether Tamar, before intercourse, ruptured her hymen with her finger]...

---

⁴⁶*b. Nid.* 30b. The printed editions read סמא דנזפרא; MS Munich 95 has סמא נפע'. Regardless, the meaning is clear from context.

⁴⁷In antiquity the difference between what we call contraceptives and abortifacients was recognized only sporadically. See Soranus, *Gyn.* 1.19.60 (pp. 62-63) and Keith Hopkins, "Contraception in the Roman Empire," *Comparative Studies in Society and History: An International Quarterly* 8 (1965-66): 136-39.

⁴⁸*t. Nid.* 2:6. The euphemism "thresh" (דש) is used in a sexual context elsewhere in rabbinic literature. See *b. Nid.* 41b; *b. Pes* 87b.

⁴⁹Gen. 38:6-10.

⁵⁰*y. Ketub.* 7:5, 31b. The term is used as an explanation of the mishnaic rule (*m. Ketub.* 7:5) that a man who vows to make his wife continually draw water and dump it in a trash heap must divorce her. In the Bavli, a tradition attributed to Shmuel at *b. Ketub.* 72a interprets the same *mishnah* to refer to making a woman "scatter" the semen within her – that is, some type of abortion-causing activity.

Non-Procreative Sex 237

C. [No,] there was Er and Onan [who had intercourse with Tamar before her single sexual encounter with Judah].

D. Er and Onan had [only] anal intercourse *(shamshu shêlō' kĕdarkan)* [with her].[51]

E. An objection: All twenty-four months he threshes inside and winnows outside. These are the words of R. Eliezer. They [?] said to him, this is like the deed of Er and Onan.

F. [It is] like the deed of Er and Onan, and not like the deed of Er and Onan.

G. Like the deed of Er and Onan as it is written, "[But Onan, knowing that the seed would not count as his], let it go to waste [lit. "spoil on the ground"] whenever he joined with his brother's wife, so as not to provide offspring for his brother," [Gen. 38:9];

H. And not like the deed of Er and Onan because there it is anal intercourse and here it is vaginal intercourse.

I. It is fine [i.e., the reason for God's killing him] for Onan, but from where do we learn [the sin of] Er?

J. Rav Naḥman bar Yitzḥak [BA 4] said, it is written, "and He took his [= Onan's] life *also*," [Gen. 38:10], he too [Er] died the same death [hence was guilty of the same sin].

K. It is fine for Onan [i.e., the reason he engaged in this act], because [he did it] "so as not to provide offspring for his brother," [Gen. 38:9]. But what is the reason that Er did it? So that she would not conceive and her beauty would diminish.[52]

This passage is part of a larger discussion on the likelihood of a woman conceiving from her first act of intercourse. In the context of this discussion, the appearance of Tamar, married first to Er, then passing as a levirate widow to Onan, before finally seducing and conceiving by he father-in-law Judah (Gen. 38:18), is surprising. The Bible explicitly states that *coitus interruptus,* not anal intercourse, was committed.[53] Only in the arrangement of the *sugya* and in the unattributed material (D, H) in this passage are we presented with the possibility of anal intercourse. The question is how to reconcile Tamar's conception by a single act of intercourse with Judah with the rabbinic belief that a woman never conceives as a result of her first act of intercourse. (E), reading the Bible at its word, states that Tamar had had intercourse before her encounter

---

[51]The meaning of *lō' kĕdarkah* will be considered below. Throughout this passage I have translated it as anal intercourse.
[52]*b. Yebam.* 34a-b. On this passage, see J. Cohen, *'Be Fertile and Increase'* 136-38.
[53]The Septuagint, Onkalos, and Pseudo-Jonathan on this passage all remain faithful to the biblical text, and no tannaitic traditions that ascribe and intercourse to Er and Onan survive.

with Judah. (D) rejects that idea, attributing anal intercourse to Er and Onan. (E) cites the tradition from the *Tosefta* (*t. Nid.* 2:6) with an additional clause that specifically links *coitus interruptus* with Er and Onan. (G) and (H) resolve the objection. It is possible that this continuing defense of the possibility that Er and Onan had anal intercourse with Tamar results from a desire on the part of the rabbis to attribute virginity – thus certainty of paternity – to the mother of the ancestors of David and the Messiah.

Here there is no doubt that the *sugya* understands *bi'ah shelo' kědarkah* as "anal intercourse." (G) and (H) are only understandable as suggesting that Er and Onan had anal intercourse with Tamar, but ejaculated onto the ground. Further, only in the redactorial layer of the *sugya* is there even a hint of equivalency between wasted semen and anal intercourse ([F] - [H]). The condemnation of anal intercourse, though, is here just implicit. As (J) and (K) point out, the real sin is the avoidance of procreation (J) or selfish hubris (K).[54]

Later is this same *sugya* there is another discussion about a contraceptive sexual position. "Abaye [BA 4] said, a woman engaged in promiscuous intercourse 'turns herself over' so that she will not conceive."[55] This probably refers to some other sexual position, perhaps with the woman on top (see below). In any case, this contraceptive mode of sex, like a *mok*, is seen by the Babylonians as a contraceptive that can serve to sexually "liberate" women.

Bi'ah Shelo' kědarkah

The phrase *lo' kědarkah* translates literally something like "not customary," and is found throughout rabbinic literature in a variety of legal applications. *Bi'ah Shelo' kědarkah*, these sources tell us, has virtually identical legal effect as does vaginal intercourse. Hence, this mode of sex can be used to acquire a wife, for example, or its commission with the wrong partner can make one liable for a charge incest or adultery.[56]

---

[54]The difference between non-procreative emission of semen and anal intercourse is already noted by the Tosafot, *b. Yebam.* 34b, s.v., ואונן ער כמעשה ולא.

[55]*b. Yebam.* 35a; *b. Ketub.* 37a. The phrase is מתהפכת. Immediately after this opinion the redactor says that according to a disagreeing amora, the woman לא מתהפכת יפה יפה. Whatever it is that she is doing, she is not doing it correctly.

[56]For examples see *m. Yebam.* 6:1; *t. Ker.* 1:16; *Sifre Num.* 13 (p. 19); *Sifre Deut.* 239 (p. 270); *y. Yebam.* 6:1, 7b; *y. Ketub.* 3:6, 27d; *b. Qidd.* 22b; *b. Yebam.* 59a-b; *b. Ketub.* 40b, 97b-98a; *b. Hor.* 4a; *b. Ker.* 11a-b. A particularly interesting discussion attributed to an early Palestinian amora forbids *Gentiles* from *bi'ah shelo' kědarkah*. The reply (from either Raba or, in MS Munich 95, the redactor) is swift: "Can there be any [transgression] for which a Jew is not liable while a Gentile is liable?" See *b. Sanh.* 58b (par. *Gen. Rab.* 18:24 [p. 167]).

Non-Procreative Sex

Because, as we saw above (Chapters 2, 4) liability for incest and adultery depend upon penetration (it is the defining act), it is most likely that this phrase refers to anal intercourse. Note, though, that although *bi'ah shelo' kĕdarkah* is often translated "unnatural sex/intercourse" neither the phrase itself nor any other rabbinic rhetoric implies the attachment of an argument from nature to anal intercourse.[57] Both anal and vaginal intercourse were seen as part of the same legal category, as intercourse.[58]

"Overturning the Table"

Another phrase that has often been seen as referring to anal intercourse is the euphemistic phrase "overturning," either oneself or "the table." This terminology is found only in the Bavli. The phrase is vague enough, however, that it might instead refer to rear-entry intercourse or "inverted" intercourse, with the woman on top. In the *sugya* cited above, "overturning" was only seen as non-procreative if done "well." This might refer to a woman moving or gyrating in order to "scatter" the seed, a technique known from non-Jewish sources in antiquity.[59] Other uses of the term are equally indecisive: one even suggests that this sexual position is procreative, with children conceived therefrom being "cripples."[60] In this same *sugya*, two stores are related:

> A. ... anything that a man wants to do with his wife, he does. A parable: [The matter is similar to] meat that comes from the slaughterhouse. If he wants to eat it salted, he eats it [that way]; [if he wants to eat it] roasted, he eats it [roasted]; [if he wants to eat it]

If *bi'ah shelo' kĕdarkah* signifies a sex act in which ejaculation occurs outside or on the woman, then we should expect that mention of that sex act should have the same legal consequences associated with *bi'ah shelo' kĕdarkah*. This appears not to be the case. See *y. Ned.* 11:13, 42d, in which a woman upon whom a Roman soldier ejaculates is still permitted to eat the tithes.

[57]The phrase לא כדרכה, as well as with other possessional suffixes, is applied to a large variety of activities, none of which have anything "natural" about them. It is applied to methods of pruning (*m. Sheb.* 4:5); the way an animal is slaughtered (*m. Ḥul.* 2:3); the way impurity is transferred between vessels (*t. Kel. B. Kama* 7:12); the language of the Torah (*y. Yebam.* 19:1, 17a); types of transference between courtyards (*y. 'Erub.* 8:3, 25a); women's custom of buying "halves" of things (*y. Qidd.* 2:1, 62c); and modes of idol worship (*b. Sanh.* 55a, 56b, 60b; *b. Zeb.* 106a).

[58]Another less common phrase used to denote anal intercourse is דרך זכרות. See Chapter 5 and *y. Ketub.* 3:9, 27d (par. *y. Sanh.* 7:14, 25c, in the name of R. Avin [PA 5]).

Once in the Bavli (*b. Soṭ.* 42b) the word ערם is also used to denote anal intercourse.

[59]See Lucretius *De rerum natura* 4.1263-77.

[60]*b. Ned.* 20a, cited in the name of a late tanna, Rabbi Yoḥanan ben Dahavei. This threat occurs within a list of frowned-upon sexual activities that will have eugenic effects. See Chapter 7.

> boiled, he eats it [boiled]; [if he wants to eat it] seethed, he eats it [seethed]. Thus [too] a fish that comes from the nets ...
>
> B. A certain woman came before Rabbi [Yehudah ha-Nasi]. She said to him, Rabbi, I set my table for him[61] and he overturned it! He said to her, my daughter, the Torah has permitted you [to him in this way], what can I do for you?
>
> C. A certain woman came before Rav [BA 1]. She said to him, Rabbi, I set my table for him and he overturned it! He said, is this different from a fish? [i.e., just as a man can eat a fish in any way he desires, so too can he "overturn the table" if he desires].[62]

In both (B) and (C), a woman complains to a rabbi regarding her husband forcing her into "inverted/overturned" intercourse. From this passage, it is again not clear what activity is being performed.[63] Clearly, though, these women do not like it.

There is, to my knowledge, only a single Babylonian tradition that expresses clear disapproval of anal intercourse.

> A. R. Yosef [BA 3] said, it is also forbidden to read the Book of Ben Sira.
>
> B. Abaye [BA 4] said to him, what is the reason? I could say that it is because it is written in it, "Do not strip the skin of a fish even from its ear, lest you spoil it, but roast it [all] in the fire, and eat two loaves with it."
>
> C. If [you wish to explain it] literally, [the same thing] is written in the Torah. "[When in your war against a city you have to besiege it a long time in order to capture it,] you must not destroy its trees ..." [Deut. 20:19].
>
> D. If [you wish to explain it] allegorically [i.e., as a *drash*], it teaches what is customary (ארעא אורח), [as] we learn that one should not have *bi'ah shelo' kĕdarkah*.[64]

In (A), the question is raised, in the midst of a discussion on the permissibility of reading "foreign" books (ספרים החיצונים), whether one is allowed to read the book of Ben Sira. Abaye, seeking to explain Rav Yosef's reasoning, cites a verse which he thinks Rav Yosef might find offensive.[65] A prohibition against waste informs (C). Because the Torah,

---

[61]See *Tal. Babl.* 4.1:174, esp. n. 56.
[62]*b. Ned.* 20b.
[63]The dictionaries and commentators take this to mean anal intercourse. See *Wörterbuch* 1:485, s.v., הפך and the remarks of Kohut in the *Arukh* 3:232, s.v., הפך and vol. 8:81, s.v., שלחן.
[64]*b. Sanh.* 100b.
[65]This verse is not attested in any edition of Ben Sira. See S. Schechter, "The Quotations From Ecclesiasticus in Rabbinic Literature," *Jewish Quarterly Review*, o.s., 3 (1891): 682-706; Moshe Segal *Sefer Ben Sirah ha-Shalem* (Jerusalem: Bialik

through its injunction against chopping down trees wantonly, teaches the same thing as the verse in Ben Sira, this particular verse from Ben Sira cannot be used to ban reading the book. The exegesis at (D) is not as clear. It is possible that the same argument of waste is applied to sex.[66] *Bi'ah shelo' kĕdarkah* is associated with this waste. This waste might, more specifically, refer to semen. Whether it refers to anal intercourse (which I think it does) or not, this sex act would have been non-procreative and thus involved a "waste" of semen.[67]

Alternatively, if interpreted to refer specifically to anal intercourse, the "waste" might be the preference of anal intercourse when vaginal intercourse is available. This explanation better parallels the sense of the citation from Ben Sira: as one should consume one's fish, wasting none of it, so too should one "consume" one's wife, taking advantage of the sexual satisfaction that she, in contrast to a man, has to give.[68] If correct, this explanation suggests that Abaye says that what is wrong with anal intercourse is that it is not vaginal intercourse, and thus, wastes the woman's unique attributes.[69]

Institute, 1953) (Hebrew). Schechter argues that the verse is not part of the *"real"* (his emphasis) Ben Sira (683), while Segal maintains that the verse came from an edition of Ben Sira that was simply "גרועה מאד," full of common Aramaic sayings (41).

A number of other verses are cited in the continuation of the *sugya*, all examples of possible reasons why Rav Yosef would prohibit the book. The others share a concern with sexuality. It is unclear to me what the perceived problem with this verse is.

[66]אורח ארצא is the Aramaic equivalent of דרך ארץ, which means both "normal, customary" and "sex."

[67]Several later commentators explain the *sugya* in this manner. See for example *Yad Ramah*, ad loc.

[68]For the idea of a man sexually "consuming" his wife as he might a fish see b. Ned. 20b; b. Soṭ. 11b.

For a possible parallel, see Pseudo-Lucian *Amor.* 87. The identification of women to fish, for male sexual consumption, might have been a cliché. See, for example, Athenaeus 10, 457d. Women as "consumable," which will be further discussed below, was a concept known in non-Jewish antiquity. See Madeline M. Henry, "The Edible Woman: Athenaeus's Concept of the Pornographic," in *Pornography and Representation in Greece and Rome*, ed. Amy Richlin (New York: Oxford University Press, 1992) 250-68.

[69]Rashi understands this exegesis differently: דאין הגון לאדם לשנות את דרכו והיינו דקאמר מאודניה. He arrives at his conclusion through the word used for "ears" from the verse in Ben Sira. It is unclear to me how this exegesis functioned.

It is also unclear whether (D) should be attributed to the redactor or to Abaye. Condemnation of "wasted semen," as we shall see below, is characteristic of the redactor. Formally, there is no necessary reason to assign this clause to Abaye.

OTHER NON-PROCREATIVE SEXUAL ACTIVITIES

Only a few other apparently non-procreative sexual activities are mentioned in the rabbinic sources, and none are rhetorically linked to contraception. There is a single reference to cunnilingus, "kissing that very place."[70] It is possible that there is a reference to fellatio: if so, it was seen by Babylonian amoraim as something that women wanted to do, probably in order to avoid pregnancy.[71] Other scholars have argued that women manipulated the laws of menstrual purity as a contraceptive ruse.[72]

An enigmatic practice that appears to have involved male ejaculation on, rather than within, a woman, *derek 'averim*, literally "way of the limbs," is mentioned only in the Bavli:

A. ...As it is taught, why is [it specifically written] "had carnal relations with (שכבת זרע)" [concerning the *sotah*, in Num. 5:13]? It is to exclude [when her husband warned her concerning] "something else."

B. What is "something else?"

C. Rav Sheshet [BA 3] said, it excludes when he warned her concerning *bi'ah shelo' kĕdarkah*.

D. Raba [BA 4] said, but it says "[Do not lie with a male] as one lies with a woman," [Lev. 18:22].

E. Rather, Raba said, it excludes when he warned her concerning *derek 'averim*.

F. Said Abaye [BA 4] to him, did God prohibit promiscuity (פריצותא)?

G. Rather, said, Abaye, it excludes when he warned her concerning a "kiss."[73]

---

[70] *b. Ned.* 20a.
[71] *b. Yebam.* 63b: אמר אביי מקשטא ליה תכא ומקשטא ליה פומא. רבא אמר מקשטא ליה תכא ומדרא ליה גבא. According to Rashi, this refers to women who prepare meals for their husbands and then vex them, either through cursing or ignoring them. Compare the interpretation of Romney Wegner: "On the one hand, Abaye defines an 'evil woman' as one who , having aroused her husband by 'preparing the dish,' offers him her mouth instead and Raba reviles the wife who 'prepares the dish, then turns her back.' Of course, these objections may stem less from prudery than from disapproval of clumsy attempts at birth control by wives overburdened with children," (Judith Romney Wegner, "The Image and Status of Women in Classical Rabbinic Judaism," in *Jewish Women in Historical Perspective*, ed. Judith R. Baskin [Detroit: Wayne State University Press, 1991] 80).
[72] See R. Kraemer, *Her Share of the Blessings* 103-4. Kraemer appears to be following the suggestion made by Shaye J.D. Cohen, "Menstruants and the Sacred in Judaism and Christianity," in *Women's History and Ancient History*, ed. Sarah B. Pomeroy (Chapel Hill: University of North Carolina Press, 1991) 299 n. 63.
[73] *b. Yebam.* 55b. See also *b. Sot.* 26b; *b. Nid.* 13b.

The problem is why is the term used for the effusion of semen used specifically in the verse which is about a man warning his wife to avoid seclusion with a certain man. It is to teach us, according to Rav Sheshet, to exclude the case of *bi'ah shelo' kĕdarkah*. Raba's objection (D) is based on the use of a plural word in Lev. 18:22 to designate the manner of lying with a woman: anal intercourse (how he understands *bi'ah shel'o kĕdarkah*) is included as one of the two "lyings" of women (the other being vaginal sex), and thus cannot be singled out and excluded on the basis of the term "carnally." That is, anal and vaginal intercourse are both considered intercourse, period. Hence, he says, the real lesson concerns *derek 'averim* (E). Abaye in turn dismisses this activity as inconsequential (F), and suggests that it really teaches concerning a "kiss" (G), which the *sugya* continues to define as only partial penile penetration of a woman by a man. It is not clear from this passage what exactly is meant by *derek 'averim*, nor is it clear even if this activity was generally discouraged. Below I will consider the single statement that does disapprove of this activity.

A second obscure activity is *ma'aseh ḥidudim*, mentioned once in the Bavli only to be dismissed lightly by Babylonian amoraim.[74] The Bavli also cites a *baraitha* that might mention ejaculation on a woman's breasts, which is again dismissed as having no legal ramifications.[75] Discussion of the "rhythm method" in the rabbinic sources is confined to those times that a woman was thought *most* fertile: there is no discussion about when she is least fertile or hint that this was considered a contraceptive technique.[76]

ABSTINENCE AND CHILD ABANDONMENT

According to David Biale, "... the norm of procreation did not go unchallenged and ... and ideal of sexual abstinence had penetrated rabbinic culture to the point that it became a bone of contention."[77] He supports this assertion with two midrashim that link both Moses and Noah to sexual abstinence and a special degree of holiness.[78] A more famous source on rabbinic abstinence is a tradition that a tanna, Ben

---

[74]*b. Sanh.* 66b. According to Rash, this is similar to *derek 'averim*: מחדר ומקשה אברו בבשרה מבחוץ דהוא נהנה והיא אינה נהנית...

[75]*b. Ketub.* 36b; *b. Git.* 81a.

[76]*b. Nid.* 31a; *b. Soṭ.* 27a. Intercourse during menses is of course forbidden to Jews biblically, but it is never discussed as having contraceptive results. In fact, although a woman is considered in Hellenistic medical writings to be infertile during menstruation, there is evidence that some rabbinic circles thought that a woman was fertile at that time. See *b. Me'il.* 17a.

[77]Biale, *Eros and the Jews* 34-35.

[78]Moses: *Sifre Num* 99-100 (p. 98-99); *b. Shab.* 87a. Noah: *Gen. Rab.* 35:1 (p. 328).

Zoma, abstained from sex due to his love for study of the Torah.[79] The ideas reflected in these sources might also inform a series of rabbinic stories that contrast male study of Torah with marital obligations.[80] These sources, however, are only peripherally about abstinence: more to the point, they are about the relationship between desire, self-control and rabbinic piety. That is, the dialectic that Biale sees in rabbinic culture between sexual asceticism and procreation and sexual pleasure – one that had great currency in Christian circles at that time – is far from certain. It is likely, in fact, that the issue of sexual asceticism *per se* was of little interest to the rabbis.

There is no evidence that sexual abstinence was used for family planning (although it is likely that it was), and scant evidence survives on Jewish female abstinence in late antiquity.[81]

Tacitus comments that Jews do not abandon or expose their infants, a practice common in antiquity.[82] There is, however, evidence in the rabbinic sources that children may have been either abandoned or given to others to be raised. Most of these sources are Babylonian.[83]

Non-Rabbinic Parallels

Greeks and Romans approached contraception pragmatically. While on the one hand, both Greek and Roman men generally desired heirs, a large family could lead to economic ruin. For women, every pregnancy was a serious health risk. Hence, a wide range of family planning techniques were developed, from the rhythm method to "the application before coitus of cedar gum, vinegar, brine or olive oil to the vagina or male genitals and a gamut of vaginal plugs and occlusive pessaries...."[84] Plato was a vigorous supporter of family planning.[85] Almost never in pagan religious texts is there any condemnation of family planning

---

[79] *t. Yebam.* 8:7; *b. Yebam.* 63b. Ben Zoma reportedly says in response to those who accused him of abstaining from procreation, מה אעשה? השקה נקשי בתורה, יתקיים עולם באחרים. On this passage, see Steven D. Fraade, "Ascetical Aspects of Ancient Judaism," in *Jewish Spirituality From the Bible Through the Middle Ages*, ed. Arthur Green (New York: Crossroad, 1986) 274-75; Boyarin, *Carnal Israel* 134.

[80] *b. Ketub.* 61b-63a. On this passage see Chapter 7.

[81] Aphrahat, in fact, testifies that Jews used to attack Christians for their abandonment of God's blessing, procreation. See Aphrahat *Dem.* 8.

[82] Tacitus *Hist.* 5.3. See the commentary of Stern, *Greek and Latin Authors* 2:41.

[83] The אסופי is defined in the *Mishnah:* "anyone taken in from the market who does not know his parents," (*m. Qidd.* 4:1) and mentioned in the *Tosefta* (*t. Qidd.* 5:1). The Yerushalmi discusses the *'asufi* only briefly (*y. Qidd.* 4:2, 65d). Comments of Babylonian amoraim in the Bavli (*b. Qidd.* 73a-b) on the *'asufi* acknowledge child abandonment among Jews in their communities. Unsurprisingly, these sources seek to allow abandoned children to marry any Jew. See also *b. Sanh.* 19b.

[84] Hopkins, "Contraception" 134.

[85] Plato *Leg.* 5, 740b-e; *Rep.* 5 459d-461c.

techniques.⁸⁶ Abortion and child abandonment were relatively free of legal or social opprobrium.⁸⁷

Yet at the same time, there is a weak but discernible unease with certain modes of family planning. Musonius Rufus alludes to "forbidden" contraceptive techniques.⁸⁸ Later, Soranus speaks warily of both abortifacients and contraceptives.⁸⁹ Soranus, as well as roughly contemporaneous Christian writers, begin to advocate sexual abstinence.⁹⁰ For Christian women, abstinence often translated into freedom from male sexual control and avenues for increased power and prestige.⁹¹ Christians vigorously condemned abortion.⁹²

In Jewish-Hellenistic authors also there is a "religious" flavor to contraception. If one could speak of a single view of Jewish-Hellenistic writers to non-procreative sexual activity, it would be that intercourse should be for children. Josephus tells us that "the only sexual liaison that the law recognizes is the natural union of man and wife, and that only for the procreation of children."⁹³ In the *Testament of the Twelve Patriachs* there are also two condemnations of non-procreative intercourse, and the

---

⁸⁶See Emiel Eyben, "Family Planning in Graeco-Roman Antiquity," *Ancient Society* 11-12 (1980-81): 56-58.

⁸⁷For abortion, see below. On child abandonment in late antiquity generally, see Sarah B. Pomeroy, "Infanticide in Hellenistic Greece," in *Images of Women in Antiquity* ed. Averil Cameron and Amélie Kuhrt, 207-22; John Boswell, *The Kindness of Strangers: The Abandonment of Children in Western Europe From Late Antiquity to the Renaissance* (New York: Panteon, 1988).

⁸⁸Musonius Rufus fr. 15a (ed. Hense, 77-8, with emendation proposed by Keith Hopkins, "A Textual Emendation in a Fragment of Musonius Rufus: A Note on Contraception," *Classical Quarterly* 15 [1965]: 72-74).

⁸⁹Soranus *Gyn.* 1.19.60.

⁹⁰Ibid. 1.8.30. The literature on Christian abstinence is vast. See Robin Lane Fox, *Pagans and Christians* (New York: Alfred A. Knopf, 1987) 351-74; Brown, *Body and Society.*

⁹¹See Brooten, "Early Christian Women;" Pagels, *Adam, Eve* 20; Brown, *Body and Society* 263-64; Jan Willem Drijvers, "Virginity and Asceticism in Late Roman Western Elites," in *Sexual Asymmetry: Studies in Ancient Society,* ed. Josine Blok (Amsterdam: J.C. Gieben, 1987) 241-73; Brown "Bodies and Minds." Not all Christians promoted abstinence: as late as the fourth century Ambrosiaster was defending marriage (Question 127, *CSEL* 50:399-416). See David G. Hunter, "On the Sin of Adam and Eve: A Little-known Defense of Marriage and Childbearing by Ambrosiaster," *Harvard Theological Review* 82 (1989): 283-99.

⁹²See *Diadache* 2.2; Franz Joseph Dölger, *Kulter-und religiounsgeschichtliche Studien, Antike und Christentum* (Münster, Westfalen: Aschendorff Münster) 4:23-27.

⁹³Josephus *Ag. Apion* 2.199.

second book of the *Sibylline Oracles* forcefully condemns abortion and child exposure.[94]

Wasted Seed

As we have seen, the rabbis did not formulate a rhetoric of "wasted seed" around non-procreative sexual liaisons and acts. Yet Babylonian rabbis did develop a very complex rhetoric around the non-procreative emission of semen in other contexts. The lengthiest and most stylized of these discussions is from the Bavli, *b. Nid.* 13a-b. Below is a translation, with sources indicated: sources attributed as tannaitic are italicized; those attributed to amoraim are in boldface; and the redactorial strata is in regular type:[95]

m. Nid. 2:1: Every hand that frequently checks [for genital fluxes]: in women, it is praiseworthy but in men you should cut [it] off.

    A. What's the difference between men and women?

- With women, who are not *běnot hargashah* [Rashi: men, unlike women, feel their genital flux], it is praiseworthy, but for men, who are *bnei hargashah*, you should cut [the hand off].
- If so, why does [the Mishnah] teach "frequently" – is it not frequently as well?
- The "frequently" is for men.

    B. *It is taught: To what does this apply to? To the case of the emission of semen but for a man emitting a genital flux, even he is as praiseworthy as women; and even in the case of an emission of semen if he checks with a sack or potshard, he checks.*

- but with a strip [of cloth], he does not.

    C. *But we learnt: One checks himself with a strip [of cloth] and with anything else that he wants,*

- as **Abaye** [BA 4] **said, with a thick strip** [it is meant in F], so here too [in E] a thick strip [is meant].

    D. Referring to what was Abaye's statement made? *As we learnt: A man was eating terumah [i.e., sacred food] and he felt his limbs shaking he holds his penis and swallows the terumah.*

- "Holds?" But we learnt: *Rabbi Eliezer says, anyone who holds [his] penis and urinates, it is as if he brings a flood into the world.*
- **Abaye said, with a thick strip. Raba (רבא)** [BA 4] **said, you can even say with a soft strip because since it was uprooted, it**

---

[94] See *T. Jud.* 10 and *T. Iss.* 2. On these passages, see Eron, *Ancient Jewish Attitudes* 179-80; 210-16. See also *Sib. Or.* 2:281ff (ed. Geffcken, 42); Stephen D. Ricks, "Abortion in Antiquity," *Anchor Bible Dictionary* 1:32-34.

[95] On using type-face to differentiate strata in the Babylonian Talmud, see S. Friedman, "A Critical Study of *Yebamot* X" 37-38.

Non-Procreative Sex 247

  was uprooted [i.e., in the case of I the emission was unavoidable, so there is no fear of causing an emission].
- Abaye fears lest he brings an additional [seminal emission], but Raba does not fear lest he brings an additional [seminal emission].
- *Have we not learnt: To what is this thing similar? To one who puts his finger in his eye, that every time that a finger is in an eye, the eye tears. And if he returns [the finger to the eye], the eye tears [again].*
- [What is the response of] Raba? It is not common to "get heated" [i.e., have an orgasm] and then "get heated" again in a short time.

E. [Reverting to] the text: *Rabbi Eliezer says, anyone who holds [his] penis while urinating, it is as if he brings a flood into the world.*

F. They said to Rabbi Eliezer, will the spray not splash on his legs, and he will appear as one with a maimed penis and [this will cause] slander about his children that they are *mamzerim* [because he will be thought incapable of procreation, the children will be assumed to have another father by his own wife]?

G. He said to them, it is better that there be slander about his children that they are *mamzerim* than that he make himself a wicked man before God for even a moment.

H. Another *baraitha* taught: *Rabbi Eliezer said to the Sages, it is possible that a man stands in a high place and urinates, or urinates in loose earth, and does not make himself a wicked man before God for even a moment...*

I. And what is all this [about]? Because he had a non-procreative emission of semen.

J. As R. Yoḥanan [PA 3] said, anyone who emits seed wastefully is liable for the death penalty, as it is said, "What he [Onan] did was displeasing to the Lord, and He took his life also," [Gen. 38:10].

K. Rabbi Yitzḥak [PA 3] of the School of Rabbi Ami [PA 3] said, it is as if he spilt blood, as it is written, "You who inflame yourselves among the terebinths, under every verdant tree; who slaughter children in the wadis, among the clefts of the rocks," [Is. 57:5]. Don't read "slaughter" (שחטי), but "cause to flow" (סחטי).

L. Rav Ashi said, it is as if he committed idolatry: it is written here "under every verdant tree," and it is written there "[You must destroy all the sites at which the nations you are to dispossess worshipped their gods,] whether on lofty mountains and on hills or under every verdant tree," [Deut. 12:2].

M. Rav Yehudah [BA 2] and Shmuel [BA 1] once stood on the roof of a synagogue of *Shef v'yativ* in Nehardaeah. Rav Yehudah said to Shmuel, I have to urinate. He said to him, Moron, take hold of your penis and urinate outside [i.e., over the roof].

N. How could he do this?

- Is it not taught: Rabbi Eliezer says, anyone who holds his penis and urinates it is as if he brings a flood to the world?

O. **Abaye said, he made it like [the case of a] reconnoitering troop,** as we learnt: if a reconnoitering troop enters the city when there is peace, then open jars are forbidden and closed jars are permitted. But if in a time of war, both are permitted because they [i.e., the soldiers] are not free [i.e., do not have time] to make a libation.

- Thus, because they are frightened they do not come to pour a libation. So too here, because he was frightened, he did not come to lustful thoughts.
- But here what is the fear? If you like, I could say fear of the night and of the roof. Or, if you like I could say fear of his master, and he will not come to lustful thoughts.
- And what is fear of his master?

1. Some say, fear of the Lord, but here it is different, for fear of the Lord was upon R. Yehudah, **about whom Shmuel said that this one was not born of a woman.**
2. Or, if you like I could say that he was married, **and Rav Naḥman used to say, if he was married it is permitted.**
3. Or, if you like I could say that it was this that he taught him, that which *Abba the son of Rabbi Mineyomi bar Ḥiyya taught, he can help his testicles from below.*
4. Or, if you like I could say that it was this that he taught him, **that Rabbi Abahu [PA 3] said that Rabbi Yoḥanan [PA 3] said, there is a limit to it, from the corona and below it is permitted, from the corona and above is forbidden.**

P. **Rav said, anyone who willingly causes himself to have an erection will be banned.**
- Say [that it is] "forbidden" [instead of 'banned"] because he incites his evil inclination against himself,

Q. **Rabbi Ami [PA 3] said, he is called a renegade because this is the craft of the evil inclination. Today it says to him, do this, and the next day it says to him, do this, and the day after it says to him, worship an idol, and he goes and worships.**

R. Some say, **Rabbi Yosi said, anyone who incites himself lustfully is not brought in to the precinct of the Holy One, blessed be He.** It is written here, "What he did was displeasing to the Lord, [and He took his life also]," [Gen. 38:10], and it is written there, "For You are not a God who desires wickedness; evil cannot abide with You," [Ps. 5:5].

S. **R. Eliezer said, why is it written, "Your hands are full of blood," [Is. 1:15]? These are those who commit adultery with their hand.**

T. *It was taught from the School of R. Ishmael, "You shall not commit adultery," [Ex. 20:13] – there will be no adultery in you, whether by hand or by foot.*

U. *Our rabbis taught: Converts and those who play [or sport] with children delay the Messiah.*

V. It is fine with converts, as according to R. Helbo [PA 3], **as R. Helbo said, converts are as difficult for Israel as a thorn.** But what is "one who plays with children?"
    - I could say that [this refers to] male homoerotic intercourse, but these are liable for stoning [hence they do not delay the Messiah].
    - Rather, [I could say those who practice] *derek 'averim*, but they are accounted with bringing the flood.
    - Rather, it is those who marry young girls not of child-bearing age, as R. Yosi said, the Messiah ben David will only come after all the souls in the treasury are exhausted...

W. "But in men you should cut [it] off" – The question was raised, is the *Mishnah* teaching a law or a curse?

X. "Is the *Mishnah* teaching a law," as in the case of Rav Huna [BA 2] who cut off a hand [see *b. Sanh.* 58b]. Or perhaps it is teaching a curse?

Y. Come and hear what was taught: *Rabbi Tarfon says, one who puts his hand on his penis, you should cut off the hand on his belly. They said to him, but would his belly not split? He said to them, it is better that his belly split and he does not descend into the pit of destruction.*
    - It is fine [if] the *Mishnah* is teaching a law [that is, those who say "would his belly not split" makes sense]. But if you say that "the *Mishnah* teaches a curse," what does "his belly split" [mean]?
    - Rather, is "the *Mishnah* teaches a law" not sufficient that [the cutting of the hand] is not on the belly? Rather, Rabbi Tarfon meant: anyone whose hand goes below his belly, his hand should be cut off. They said to Rabbi Tarfon, if a thorn lodges in his belly should he not remove it? He said to them, no.
    - [They said to him], will his belly not split? He said to them, it is better that his belly splits and he does not descend into the pit of destruction.[96]

The *sugya* can be outlined roughly as follows:

(A):	Why the *Mishnah* differentiates men from women
(B) - (D):	On touching one's penis generally
(E) - (H):	On touching one's penis while urinating
(I) - (L):	On the non-procreative emission of semen
(M) - (O):	On touching one's penis while urinating
(P) - (T):	On male self-arousal

---

[96] *b. Nid.* 13a-b, according to MS Munich 95.

(U) - (V):   Marrying girls who cannot bear children

(W) - (Y):   Punishment for touching one's penis

As a whole, this *sugya* argues strongly against men arousing themselves (whether intentionally or, as in the case of touching one's penis while urinating, unintentionally) because this will lead to the non-procreative emission of semen. When, however, the individual pericopes that compose this *sugya* are examined, it appears that this idea is found only in the redactorial strata of the *sugya* and in the contextualization of earlier source material. In fact, as will become clear from a detailed examination of the components of this *sugya* arranged by attribution, such a notion is foreign to these earlier sources.

Tannaitic Sources. According to *m. Nid.* 2:1, a woman should frequently check to see if she has begun menstruating, whereas a man who frequently checks (presumably for a seminal emission) deserve to have it (presumably his hand, the subject of the clause) amputated. The *mishnah* does not explain why a man should not check frequently with his hand for genital emissions, although a *baraitha* offers an intriguing parallel:

> It was also taught ... [R. Muna or R. Matyah][97] used to say, Let the hand to the eye be cut off; let the hand to the nose be cut off; let the hand to the mouth be cut off; let the hand to the ear be cut off; let the hand to the vein be cut off; let the hand to the penis be cut off;[98] let the hand to the anus be cut off; let the hand to the casket be cut off; [because[the hand [leads to] blindness, [because] the hand [leads to] deafness, [because] the hand causes polyps[99] to rise.[100]

Even if the reference to "the hand to the penis" is a corruption based on our *mishnah*, the argument is here made explicit: one should avoid touching certain parts of one's body because it can lead to ill-health. Medical reasons underlie the stricture. Hence it is possible that *m. Nid.* 2:1 too proscribes men from touching their genitals too frequently for fear that such an activity will lead to health problems.[101]

---

[97] See *D.S.* 2:238.

[98] This phrase is missing in some manuscripts. See *D.S.* 2:238. It may have found its way into our text due to influence from *m. Nid.* 2:1.

[99] These might be specific to the nose. See Preuss, *Biblical and Talmudic Medicine* 296.

[100] The prospect of a disease that would render a man infertile would have not seemed trivial to the tannaim. *t. Yebam* 8:4, for example, condemns men who endanger their ability to procreate. On this passage, see Lieberman, *Tos. Kip.* 6:68.

[101] The prospect of a disease that would render a man infertile would have not seemed trivial to the tannaim. *t. Yebam* 8:4, for example, condemns men who endanger their ability to procreate. On this passage, see Lieberman, *Tos. Kip.* 6:68.

Alternatively, and perhaps more likely, the *mishnah* can be read as condemning a man for sexually arousing himself. Other tannaitic dicta within this *sugya* support this interpretation. For example, according to (D) (paralleled at [E] and [N]): "But isn't it taught: R. Eliezer says, that anyone who holds his penis when he urinates, it is as if he brings a flood unto the world." This *baraitha*, found also in two shorter but similar *sugyot*,[102] suggests that (1) some kind of male sexual transgressions brought about the flood in the time of Noah; and (2) those who continue to do such things threaten the world with another divinely caused flood. Both claims are singular. The idea that the flood was brought about by sexual sins of the people of that generation is foreign to tannaitic sources.[103] Moreover, no other tannaitic source, to my knowledge, threatens sexual transgressions with the communal punishment of flooding. The peculiarity of this source, when compared to other tannaitic material, as well as its lack of attestation in tannaitic documents, thus throws the attribution into question. Regardless of the veracity of the attribution, however, the same tannaitic condemnation of a man touching his penis while urinating is found in (F) - (H) (if tannaitic and not a later addition) and (0.3) in our *sugya*, as well as elsewhere in tannaitic literature.[104] This condemnation is apparently based on the idea of self-arousal: there is no mention in this source of the emission of semen.

Several of the other relevant tannaitic sources are paralleled by a toseftan *baraitha* that explicitly comments on *m. Nid.* 2:1:

1. ... Rabbi Tarfon says, it [his hand] should be cut off on the belly. He [?] said to him, but his belly will split!

2. He said to them, I only intended this: To what is the matter similar? To one who presses his finger hard upon his eye. All the time that he presses tears come out.

---

[102]*b. Shab.* 41a; *b. Nid.* 43a (D) is imported from the latter.

[103]Connection of sexual sins to the generation of the flood seems to first appear in rabbinic writings attributed to R. Yoḥanan. See *b. Sanh.* 108a, which however, also goes onto impute a wide variety of non-sexual transgressions to the generation of the flood. It is interesting to note that another statement attributed to R. Yoḥanan in *y. Sanh.* 10:3, 29b describes the flood waters as being very hot: only in the Babylonian Talmud is the heat of the water linked to the sexual sinfulness of the people. See *b. Rosh. Hash.* 12a; *b. Zeb.* 113b. The redactor also connects the non-procreative emission of semen to the generation of the flood at *b. Ned.* 20b.

[104]See the parallels at *b. Shab.* 41a, 118b; *b. Nid.* 16b, 43a. Note that in *b. Nid.* 16b this dicta is assigned originally to Ben Sira. While part of the passage attributed to Ben Sira parallels Ben Sira 21:22-3, the clause about touching one's penis while urinating has no parallel in the book. I have been unable to locate parallels to the condemnation of touching one's penis while urinating in tannaitic documents.

3. To what does this apply? To the emission of semen, but for a genital flux every hand that frequently checks is praiseworthy.[105]

This *tosefta* is found in a quite different form in our *sugya*. (1) forms the basis for the latter part of our *sugya* (Y); (2) is equivalent to (E); and (3) is the basis for (B). (2) is the only tannaitic source, as I argue below, that might plausibly be read as expressing disapproval of the non-procreative emission of semen. Yet even this source is not as clear as might be hoped. First, (2) might simply suggest natural consequence: if one touches his penis, some natural consequence that is negatively charged (erection or the emission of semen) will inevitably follow. Second, (2) is somewhat obscure: what does "I only intended" (אף אני לא נתכוונתי אלא) mean, and how does it fit with the rest of the pericope?[106] It seems to imply that (1) is an exaggeration, intended to emphasize the condemnation of a man who checks his genitals frequently. If this is so, then by splitting up this tradition (if indeed it was before them) the editor/redactor of our *sugya* caused (1) to be read out of context. That is, while in its original context (1) is softened by (2), its citation in (Y) allows it to be read more literally. To R. Tarfon's statement in the *Tosefta* is added the threat of divine retribution, of descent into the "pit of destruction." Responding to his students, who complain that cutting a man's hand off on his belly will result in rupturing his stomach, R. Tarfon responds that even that is better than descent into "the pit of destruction." Rabbi Tarfon's threat of descent into the pit of destruction is not found in parallel traditions in either the *Tosefta* or the Yerushalmi.[107] Thus, if the redactor was using the same version of the tradition as is currently found in the *Tosefta*, he apparently

---

[105]*t. Nid.* 2:8.

[106]Elsewhere in the *Tosefta* the phrase only occurs at *t. Naz.* 3:10 and here too the sense is somewhat obscure. The *Tosefta* concerns a woman who makes a vow: if another woman heard her and replied, "Me too," the vow is considered binding on her also, even if the husband of the first woman releases his wife from the vow. If, however, the second woman says that she only meant that she should "be like her [the first woman]," then she too would be released when the first woman is released. The ambiguity is whether the second woman makes her stipulation (1) instead of, or (2) later than and in addition to, her declaration, "Me too." If, as is more likely, (2) is meant, then the phrase serves to explain and modify the first statement, as I am interpreting the phrase in its present context.

[107]In *t. Nid.* 2:8, cited above, there is no additional threat. In the version in *y. Nid.* 2:1, 49d, when his students asked if cutting off his hand on his belly will lead to bursting of the stomach, R. Tarfon replies, "death is better than life for him." Both lack any element of divine retribution. The phrase and concept of the pit of destruction, however, are found in tannaitic and Palestinian sources. See *t. Soṭ.* 3:19, 8:6; *y. Ber.* 4:2, 7d (par. *b. Ber.* 28b, with tannaitic attribution). See also *b. ʿErub.* 19a and *b. Soṭ.* 35b.

reworked it, adding a stronger form of rhetoric in order to emphasize the heinousness of the activity.

A clearer case of editorial tinkering with tannaitic sources is found at (T). In its original context, this *baraita* almost certainly referred to different kinds of heterosexual activities: "foot" probably refers to sexual intercourse, and "hand" to some other kind of physical contact.[108] Only the placement of the *baraitha*, immediately after (S), suggests that the "hand" is to be taken as a reference to male masturbation.[109]

The other tannaitic sources in this *sugya* also show no concern with the issue of the non-procreative emission of semen. (C), an unparalleled *baraitha*, is not even concerned that a man who checks himself with a soft cloth will become aroused. Both (D) and (O) cite *mishnayot* that do not deal with this issue.[110] (U), a strange tradition that those who "sport" with children delay the coming of the Messiah, will be discussed below.

In sum, no passage attributed as tannaitic in this *sugya*, with the possible but by no means certain exception of the parallel to the *Tosefta* in (D), show disapproval of the non-procreative emission of semen. They do, however, condemn a man who touches his own penis, and self-arousal generally. Why they condemn such a man is not clear from these sources. It also appears that the editor and/or redactor both positioned

---

[108]If foot, רגל here is a euphemism for "penis," the exegesis might be that any sexual intimacy with a married woman, even if it does not involve intercourse, can be termed "adultery." The dictionaries do not give this meaning for רגל in rabbinic literature, but it is clearly attested in the Bible and rabbinic sources (see for example Judges 3:24; Ezek. 6:25; b. Yebam. 103a). See also Elliot R. Wolfson, "Images of God's Feet: Some Observations on the Divine Body in Judaism," in *People of the Body: Jews and Judaism from an Embodied Perspective*, ed. Howard Eilberg-Schwartz (Albany, NY: State University of New York Press, 1992) 164; Siegman Schultze-Galléra, *Fuss- und Schusymbolik und-Erotik* (Leipzig; 1909). "Hand" is used to mean penis in 1QS 7 (ed. Vermes, 71). On sexual euphemisms in rabbinic literature, see Ezra Z. Melamed, "Euphemisms and Textual Alterations of Expressions in Talmud," in *Benjamin deVries Memorial Volume*, ed. Ezra Z. Melamed (Jerusalem: Tel-Aviv University Research Authority, 1968) 137-43 (Hebrew). The opinion of the Tosafist that it means that he rubs his penis with a hand or foot is far-fetched (b. Nid. 13b, s.v., בין ביד).

[109]On this *baraitha*, see Melamed, *Halachic Midrashim* 123.

[110](G): *m. Nid*. 5:2, on a priest grabbing his penis to hold back ejaculation for fear of pollution while eating heave-offerings; (W): This is a citation of *m. 'Abod. Zar.* 5:6, which discusses under what circumstances wine left within reach of pagan soldiers is permissible for Jews to drink. It is cited in order to draw an analogy between the fear of the troops engaged in battle and therefore their neglect of the Jewish wine and the fear of a man urinating off a roof or at night, and therefore he will not come to arouse himself. This *mishnah* is also cited at *b. Shab.* 41a; *b. Ketub.* 27a. The latter citation uses this mishnah to draw an analogy between wine and sex: Rav Mari argues that if the troops are too busy to make libations, they are also too busy to have intercourse with the women in the town.

these traditions in contexts which distort their original meanings, and perhaps even modified traditions in order to reinforce the message of the *sugya*.

Amoraic Dicta. Because Palestinian and Babylonian amoraim appear to share the assumptions about self-arousal, dicta attributed to both will be considered together.

Like the tannaim, the amoraim condemn those acts that lead to self-arousal. This can be seen most clearly in (P) through (T).[111] These passages condemn the man who brings himself to erection. In (P), Rav (BA 1) threatens excommunication for such a man; in (Q) R. Ami (PA 3) calls him an "apostate,"[112] and justifies this appellation by suggesting that if one yields to the "evil desire" in a relatively small matter, it will lead one into progressively more serious transgressions, presumably ending with idolatry and apostasy.[113] In (R), R. Yosi (PA 3)[114] states that one who excites himself with fantasies (perhaps merely synonymous with one who causes himself to have an erection) removes himself from God's presence. The source of this exegesis is a scriptural analogy based on the appearance of the word for "evil" (רע) in both Gen 38:10 and Psalms 5:5. The former verse discusses the death of Onan, the latter states that "evil" cannot dwell in God's presence.[115] According to the Bible, Onan was killed by God when he did not properly discharge his duty as a levirate husband, because, knowing that the child would not be his, he spilled his seed on the ground (Gen 38:9). What Onan did is termed "evil," but his exact transgression is not specified. R. Yosi connects Onana's "evilness" to lustful thoughts, but not necessarily to his non-procreative emission of semen.

Condemnation of self-arousal is also indicated in (S). R. Eleazar (PA 3) applies Isaiah 1:15, "your hands are full of blood," to "those who commit adultery with the hand." This serves as an introduction to the tannaitic statement (T), which as shown above probably had nothing at all to do with masturbation. Similarly, there is no compelling reason to interpret R. Eleazar's statement as referring to men who masturbate.

---

[111]It is interesting to note that the redactorial comment in (P) adds nothing substantive to the statements of the amoraim. Its phrasing suggests that it is responding to an objection (now lost) made to (O), which (P) is not. Moreover, its meaning is close to (Q), but its language suggests some kind of play on (R).

[112]Note that according to the printed version he is called a "transgressor," עבריין.

[113]Curiously, this reason – in exactly the same language – is found in another place attributed to a different Palestinian amora, in a discussion of an entirely different matter. See *b. Shab.* 105b.

[114]R. Ami in the printed version.

[115]Or, following Rashi and the emendation proposed by *Masoret ha-Shas*, evil cannot dwell "in Your dwelling (מגורך)," thus more closely paralleling R. Yosi's statement that such a man removes himself from God's מחצה.

Rather, it was most likely a comment on (T), condemning this "adultery by hand," whatever activity that may have been. Only the editorial placement might lead a reader to interpret the unit as referring to male masturbation.

Like the tannaitic source, amoraic sources consider the case of a man touching his penis while urinating. These sources, like their tannaitic parallels, appear to be concerned with self-arousal, rather than non-procreative emission of semen. (M) relates the story of Shmuel and Rav Yehudah, who are said to be in a synagogue when the latter has to urinate. Because, presumably, it would be awkward for him to do so in this place without using his hands, he asks Shmuel for his opinion. Shmuel disparagingly tells him simply to use his hand and urinate outside. Amoraic and tannaitic dicta are cited in a redactorial attempt to explain, in (O), Shmuel's ruling in (M). None of the reasons given imply a condemnation of non-procreative emission of semen. Note that one of the reasons offered, Rav Naḥman's ruling that a married man is allowed to touch his penis when he urinates, does not appear to be based on the idea of non-procreative emission of semen (unless we assume that married men were thought less arousable by touch), but on inciting oneself to sexual transgression. That is, Rav Naḥman suggests that a married man, when aroused, will approach his wife rather than looking for another, non-sanctioned sexual partner.

The punishment for male masturbation is discussed in the last part of the *sugya*. In (X), Rav Huna (BA 2) asks, should a man really lose his hand for such an activity, or is it merely a "curse" (לטותא). As mentioned above, the question is odd: *t. Nid.* 2:8, which parallels this section, suggests that R. Tarfon did not intend that this comment be taken literally. Hence, R. Huna (or better, the redactor's use of R. Huna's statement) either distorted the tannaitic tradition, or was unfamiliar with the order in our present *Tosefta*.

None of the amoraic dicta surveyed above suggest any concern with the non-procreative emission of semen. The only amoraic dicta, in fact, that do suggest such a connection are (J), (K), and (L). Sections (J), (K), and (L) form a highly stylized unit that associates the wasteful emission of seed with the death penalty, bloodshed, and idolatry, echoing the three rabbinic "mortal sins" of murder, idolatry, and sexual transgressions.[116] In (J), Rabbi Yoḥanan asserts that Onan's sin was the wasteful emission of semen, and that those who waste semen deserve,

---

[116]On the grouping of three amoraic statements generally, see S. Friedman, "A Critical Study of *Yebamot X*" 38-43.

like Onan, to die.[117] This is the single instance in rabbinic literature (known to me) that the phrase, "wasteful emission of semen" (שכבת זרע לבטלה) is attributed to a Palestinian rabbi. Rabbi Yitzḥak's exegesis in (K) is quite rich. The exegesis is based on the transposition of a letter of a word in Is. 57:5, with the result that the verse is made to apply to those who "cause children to flow in the wadis." Not only is the sin of murder suggested in the transposition alone (the word for "murder" is changed, through the transposition, into "cause to flow"), but it is also suggested in the verse. Semen is seen as bearing potential children, and masturbation thus becomes murder in a very real sense. This exegesis evokes the tannaitic traditions that equate the restraint from procreation with bloodshed (see below). Note, however, both that the statement is qualified with the words "as if," acknowledging that the parallel is not to be taken too literally.[118] In (L), Rav Ashi (BA 6) utilizes scriptural analogy to "fill out" the trilogy. Dependent on (K)'s association of masturbation with Isaiah 57:5, Rav Ashi compares similar phrases in Isaiah 57:5 and Deut. 12:2. As the latter verse discusses idolatry, masturbation is associated with idolatry.

In sum, *only two or three amoraic statements, (J), (K), and (L), discuss the non-procreative emission of semen*. The remainder of the relevant amoraic statements discuss *self-arousal*. The import of this distinction, as well as the exceptional (J) – (L), are discussed below. Despite the fact that most of these amoraic statements (like the tannaitic traditions) on their own say nothing about the non-procreative emission of semen, their placement in the *sugya* suggests that they in fact do. This further suggests that the editor molded the available materials to form this polemic against masturbation.

Redactorial. As we have seen, the editorial placement of, and perhaps tinkering with, earlier materials distorted the original meanings of those sources. The redactorial molding of and contribution to this *sugya* is even clearer.

The redactorial contribution to the *sugya* begins at the very beginning, with (A). Attempting to explain why the *mishnah* treats males and females differently, (A) asserts that men feel when they have a

---

[117] MS Munich 95 reads שם רע in place of שכבת זרע. Although this reading would further support my thesis (see below), it is, judging from the continuation of the dicta, almost certainly a scribal mistake.

[118] For examples of the phrase "as if he spilled blood" used in different and unrelated contexts, see *b. B. Meṣ.* 58b; *b. Sanh.* 35a. The phrase can be used as a threatening association, not fraught with the other implications that our tradition (K) might suggest. The idea that sperm in some way was already the "child" is unparalleled in late antiquity. Note that no other contemporary exegesis of Isaiah 57:5 remotely suggests this interpretation.

genital flux, whereas women do not (e.g., menstrual bleeding). Hence, a male need not touch himself to ascertain if he has had a flux.[119] The focus on genital emissions, primarily male orgasm, is not found explicitly in the *mishnah* itself, and this interpretation helps to introduce, and direct, the ensuing *sugya:* the discussion will be about male genital emissions.

(B) – (D) is an example of redactorial use and shaping of other sources. Within this unit, transferred from *b. Nid.* 43a, the redactorial contribution to (B), as well as the shaping of the argument in (D), imply redactorial concern with the non-procreative emission of semen. Moreover, although the unit as a whole apparently concludes with permission for men to check themselves for genital fluxes with any type of cloth, the *sugya* uses it in order to develop R. Eliezer's statement in (D).

The thrust of the redactorial contribution is clearer in the second half of the *sugya.* (I) is the fulcrum of the *sugya.* According to (H), a man should urinate in certain ways so "he will not make himself wicked for even a moment before God" (presumably referring to self-arousal). This is followed by (I): "What is the point of all this? Because of the non-procreative emission of semen." The *sugya* turns on this short statement. Not only does it interpret (H) (which says nothing about this issue), but it also (1) puts the entire first half of the *sugya* into this context; and (2) introduces the strong traditions of (J), (K), and (L), which in turn begin the second half of the *sugya,* which is more direct and forceful than the first half. According to (I), this *sugya,* and the traditions contained therein, *are all about the non-procreative emission of semen.* Were we not told this in (I) through (L), we might well miss this point.

Redactorial misreading of earlier sources continues in (V). In this intriguing comment, the redactor attempts to understand a clause in (U), that those who "sport" with children delay the coming of the Messiah. The redactor offers and rejects two suggestions: that this refers to male homoeroticism or *derek 'averim*. Both are rejected because they already have punishments associated with them, stoning for male homoeroticm and "flooding" for the latter. Why were these two sexual activities suggested? Perhaps because they share, in the eyes of the redactor, the characteristic on non-procreative emission of emission. Yet nowhere else in rabbinic literature is homoeroticism associated with this concept, and elsewhere in the Babylonian Talmud, *derek 'averim,* as seen above, is neither associated with the non-procreative emission of semen nor is it even really condemned. Its association with flooding apparently derives from within this *sugya:* identified by the redactor here as an activity that

---

[119]This interpretation follows Rashi, *ad loc.;* Jastrow 1:365 s.v., הרגשה. See also *b. Nid.* 43a.

involves the non-procreative emission of semen, the activity is compared to (D), similarly interpreted by the redactor. Thus, activities that are regarded as conceptually distinct in the rest of the rabbinic literature are here brought under the common rubric of "activities that involve the non-procreative emission of semen." Even having rejected these alternatives, (V) settles on a third intriguing activity, marriage to (or sex with) a female not old enough to bear children. While this activity is prohibited elsewhere in rabbinic literature, it is never linked to the non-procreative emission of semen. Hence, this tradition groups three activities, not otherwise thought of as linked, thus including them in its general polemic.

Finally, as mentioned above, (W) allows for a reshading of the *Tosefta's* interpretation of the last clause in the *mishnah*. The *sugya* ends with advocating the physical loss of the hand of the male who masturbates.

Comparing this *sugya* to its parallel in the Yerushalmi puts the contribution of the redactor into even greater relief. The passage is short enough to cite in full:

A. The *mishnah* means that [it is like] anyone who frequently puts his hand in his eye tears much.

B. Rabbi Tarfon says, let it be cut off on his belly.

C. They said to him, but his stomach will split!

D. He said to them, Thus I said, because death is better than life for him.

E. The *haverim* said, R. Tarfon curses him with a curse that touches his body.

F. Rabbi Yosi [PA 3] said, it [section B] derives [from] the *Mishnah* [that] it is forbidden to touch from the belly down.

G. This [teaching] that you said applies to the emission of seed, but in the matter of [checking for] genital flux anyone who frequently checks is praiseworthy.[120]

The *sugya* continues with an extensive discussion of the first part of the *mishnah*, dealing with women checking themselves. Although the Yerushalmi's parallel *sugyot* are often much more concise than the Bavli's, the striking difference in the tenor of the two *sugyot* further highlights the work of the redactor of the Bavli's *sugya*. (G) condemns those men who check to see if they have had an orgasm, assuming that because one will know there is no need to check. Such checking is

---

[120] *y. Nid.* 2:1, 49d.

condemned, but it is not clear why. There is not even a hint of a polemic against the non-procreative emission of semen.

Summary. A source-critical analysis of the *sugya* has shown that the editor and redactor of *b. Nid.* 13a-b actively shaped their materials into a polemic against the non-procreative emission of semen. Most of the tannaitic and amoraic material used in this *sugya* condemns self-arousal rather than non-procreative emission of semen, a difference that will be discussed below. The *sugya* uses material from *t. Nid.* 2:8, but in a way that suggests that the editor either did not know the tradition as it now survives, or distorted it. In almost no source outside of the redactorial strata is there evidence of condemnation of the non-procreative emission of semen *per se*.

The Bavli's redactor's concern with the male waste of seed can also be seen in a tradition that revolves around Joseph's relationship to Potiphar's wife. According to the version in the Yerushalmi:

A. It is written, ["Archers bitterly assailed him (Joseph); they shot at him and harried him.] Yet his bow remained taut, [and his arms were made firm]," [Gen. 49:23-24].

B. R. Shmuel bar Naḥman [PA 3] said, the bow was relaxed and returned [to its natural state].

C. R. Abun [PA 5] said, his seed was scattered and went forth from his fingernails.[121]

D. "His arms were made firm," [Gen. 49:24].[122]

E. Rav Huna [BA 2] said in the name of Rav Manah [BA 2], he closes his eyes and saw a likeness of our father and immediately he relaxed [i.e., his erection].[123]

Like the Yerushalmi, the Bavli also sees Joseph as tempted by Potiphar's wife nearly to the point of succumbing. But in recounting the same exegesis offered in the Yerushalmi, the Bavli adds a strong moral flavoring of its own.

A. ... Immediately, "his bow remained taut," [Gen. 49:24].

B. Rabbi Yoḥanan said in the name of R. Meir, his "bow" subsided.

C. "and his limbs were made firm," [Gen. 49:24] – he stuck his hands in the ground and his seed come forth from between his fingernails ...

---

[121] Although it appears from the order of the *sugya* that this exegesis derives from the first half of the verse, it only makes sense when connected to the second half: (C) and (D) should be transposed.
[122] Hebrew: ויפזו זרעי ידיו.
[123] *y. Hor.* 2:5, 46d.

D. It is taught: Joseph was worthy to have twelve tribes issue from him like they issued from Jacob, as it is said, "This, then, is the line of Jacob: [at seventeen years of age,] Joseph ..." [Gen. 37:2],

E. Except that his seed came forth from between his fingernails.[124]

Both *sugyot* contain a tradition that Joseph scattered his seed from his fingernails rather than have sexual relations with Potiphar's wife. Yet only in the Bavli does this become the reason that he did not issue twelve tribes. Whether (E) is authentically tannaitic or not is unclear. The entire tradition is unparalleled in tannaitic corpora, and in some manuscripts of this *sugya* "it is taught" (D) is replaced by "they said," a phrase that does not usually introduce tannaitic material.[125] Assuming that (D) and (E) are a unit, a later date would show further evidence of the Bavli's redactor's concern with the waste of male seed. In any case, the difference between the Palestinian and Babylonian treatment of this topic is telling.[126]

The different approaches of the Bavli and the Yerushalmi can also be seen in the complete absence from the Yerushalmi of the phrase used in the Bavli for the wasteful emission of semen.[127] To my knowledge, the phrase in the Yerushalmi that most closely approximates the phrase is the "waste [of an opportunity] for procreation," a very different idea.[128] Further evidence for a difference between Babylonian and Palestinian assumptions about wasted seed might be found in *Genesis Rabbah*. This work, compiled in Palestine close to the time of the redaction of the Yerushalmi, also shows no knowledge of the concept of wasted seed.[129]

NON-RABBINIC PARALLELS

Although Roman epigrammists have a distinct disdain for semen, they never develop an idea that there can be a "wasteful" emission of it.[130] Some Roman medical writers counsel against too frequent ejaculation, especially as a result of masturbation, due to the

---

[124]*b. Sot.* 36b.
[125]See *Tal. Babl.* 2.2:136, n. 137.
[126]See also *b. 'Erub.* 18b, in which the redactor suggests that male masturbation results in the begetting of demons.
[127]Hebrew: שכבת זרע לבטלה.
[128]*y. Mo'ed Qat.* 1:7, 80d; *y. Git.* 4:4, 46a: ביטול פרייה ורבייה.
[129]For examples from *Gen. Rab.* that virtually mirror the issues expressed in the Palestinian sources cited in this chapter, see 26:4 (pp. 246-47), 36:4 (pp. 338-39), 45:3 (p. 449), 80:2 (p. 956), 87:11 (pp. 1071-73), 98:20 (p. 1270). Even the midrashim about Er and Onan (85:5, pp. 1038-39) do not focus on the waste of semen as their sin.
[130]See for example Juvenal 6.365 (Boudleian MS Canonicianus 41). The rhetoric here and elsewhere seems to link semen to pollution.

dangerousness of the "seizure" that accompanies male orgasm.[131] At the same time, the Stoics linked masturbation with a lack of self-control. Self-arousal incites the "evil desire," potentially leading one into an actual sexual sin. Thus it is not the vain emission of semen that is feared as much as the potential for other transgressions.

Philo is the earliest source known to me that articulates an idea of the wasteful emission of semen:

> Whenever the menstrual issue occurs, a man must not touch a woman, but must during that period refrain from intercourse and respect the law of nature. He must also remember the lesson that the generative seeds should not be wasted fruitlessly for the sake of a gross and untimely pleasure. For it is just as if a husbandman should in intoxication or lunacy sow wheat and barley in ponds or mountain streams instead of in the plains, since the fields should become dry before the seed is laid in them. (33) Now nature also each month purges the womb as if it were a cornfield ... (34) They too must be branded with reproach, who plough the hard and stony land. And who should they be but those who mate with barren women? For in the quest of mere licentious pleasure like the most lecherous of men they destroy the procreative germs with deliberate purpose ... (36) [T]hose who sue for marriage with women whose sterility has already been proved with other husbands, do but copulate like pigs or goats, and their names should be inscribed in the lists of the impious as adversaries of God ...[132]

Men who have intercourse for reasons other than procreation sin because they waste their semen, scattering their seed on "hard and stony land." The connection of non-procreative sexual activity and the waste of semen is one that is later adopted by the Church, being most famously expressed in the "Alexandrian rule," in which Clement of Alexandria forbids all intercourse not for the sake of procreation.[133] In spite of this, the Church Fathers never develop a rhetoric against (non-abortive) contraceptives.[134]

---

[131] See especially Thomas Laqueur, "Orgasm, Generation, and the Politics of Reproductive Biology," *Representations* 14 (1986): 5-7.

[132] Philo *Spec. Laws* 3.32-36 (trans. LCL 495-97). On this passage, and Philo's view in general, see Heinemann, *Philons* 262-63.

[133] The history of the Church on non-procreative sexual practices is well summed up in John T. Noonan, Jr., *Contraception: A History of Its Treatment by the Catholic Theologians and Canonists* (1965; rpt. Cambridge: Harvard University Pres, 1986) 786-81. See also Jean-Louis Flandrin, "La vie sexuelle des gens mariés dans l'ancienne société: de la doctrine de l'Église à la réalité des comportements," in *Sexualités ocidentales*, ed. Phillippe Ariès (Paris: Le Centre d'Études Transdisciplinaires, 1982) 102-15; Eyben, "Family Planning" 62-74; Brown, *Body and Society* 132-36; Brundage, *Law, Sex* 51-123.

[134] See A.M. Dubarle, "La Bible et les péres ont-ils parlé de la contraception?" *La vie spirituelle, Supplement* 15 (1962): 608-10. He notes that this does not imply that

Another parallel to the concept of wasted semen can be found in Sassanian Babylonia. "Rendering one's sperm ineffective, no matter in what manner, is itself a sin, *DkM*. 490, 6-7 ... 'Who sleeps with a barren woman shall be condemned for annihilating sperm.' And according to the *Phil. Riv. Dd*. 34, 14-15 he who renders semen ineffective ... is guilty ..."[135] The relationship between Zoroastrian and rabbinic (especially of the redactor of the Bavli) beliefs that impinge upon sexuality requires further study, but it might inform the redactorial statements against wasted semen.

Conclusions

All rabbinic circles appear to share the idea that the primary goal of sexual intercourse is procreation, and they condemn non-procreative sexual liaisons and acts *when they interfere with procreation*. In this, they held views no different from those of contemporary Christians and pagans.[136] Yet there is no single idea linking rabbinic views of non-procreative sexual liaisons, contraceptives, and wasted semen, and the points of intersection between shared concepts on these issues are sometimes enlightening, but as frequently coincidental. That is, parallels between Jewish, pagan, and Christian discussions in this matter are occasionally deceiving. Comparisons, as we will see, can be helpful but must be used with caution.

The tannaim (1) counseled against marrying an infertile woman when it would interfere with procreation; (2) advised women to use contraceptives when not doing so would endanger them or their children; and (3) condemned the man who arouses himself. We have already seen how (1) is shared with Jewish-Hellenistic, pagan, and Christian writers. (2), I have argued, is based in the view of a woman as an economic asset to her husband, an investment to be protected. What (2) is not is a condemnation of contraception, a theme entirely absent from any attributed tannaitic source. (3) is more enigmatic (medical? licentiousness?). If these explanations are correct, then comparisons of tannaitic views on self-arousal (not to mention the more problematic area of procreation in general) to those of the Church Fathers can only be misleading. Following Philo, the Church did fear the waste of semen.[137]

---

the Church Fathers would have approved of contraception. Whether or not they would have, they clearly did not discuss contraceptives.

[135]Shaki, "Sassanian Matrimonial Relations" 344.

[136]See especially, Daube, *Duty of Procreation* 3-39; Rousselle, *Porneia* 40; Paul Veyne, "The Roman Empire," in *A History of Private Life: From Pagan Rome to Byzantium* 36-40; Brown, *Body and Society* 21; Eyben, "Family Planning" 32.

[137]It is interesting to note that the Church Fathers never use the biblical story of Er and Onan to justify their sexual restrictions, perhaps again pointing to extra-

Although the rules themselves might be similar, underlying them might be very different sets of assumptions.

The Roman sources, on the other hand, help to explain the views expressed by the Palestinian amoraim. The problem with a liaison with an infertile woman is no longer rooted only in her interference with procreation. Now it is also a sign of dissoluteness, of lack of control. For the Palestinian amoraim keeping a woman only for sexual pleasure was a sign of luxuriant "softness," a condition ridiculed and condemned (see Chapter 4). This idea might also resonate behind those statements on the waste of seed attributed to the Palestinian amoraim.

Comments attributed to Babylonian amoraim on this topic show both similarities and differences with those of their Palestinian counterparts. Like the Palestinian amoraim, the Babylonian amoraim seem to share the idea that the sexuality of women is controlled by men. On the other hand, there is a recognition that this control is not absolute, and that women might engage in non-controlled sexual activity, and are smart enough to use contraception when they do. One should not conclude from this that Palestinian women were faithful or did not think to use contraception when committing adultery. Rather, again we see in the Palestinian sources an overriding concern with issues of marriage and marital sexuality.

Like the Palestinian rabbis, the Babylonian amoraim also inveighed against male self-arousal. Yet in the statements attributed to them there is a much more "relaxed" attitude. Abaye is credited with the dismissal of the sexual practice of *derek 'averim* as inconsequential. Rav, an early Babylonian amora with much contact with Palestine says that one who arouses himself should come under a ban, yet the redactor of the same *sugya* struggles with a tradition attributed to later Babylonian amoraim that does not question a man touching his own penis while urinating. Because these statements are few and scattered, and without the availability of more comparative material, it would be rash to try to construct a single "attitude" that informs these opinions.

When we reach the level of the redactor of the Bavli, however, we see a shift. For the first time a rhetoric around the non-procreative emission of semen develops. The waste of semen, for selfish reasons, is connected to the sin of Er. An artful *sugya* is crafted which expresses the redactor's condemnation of the waste of male semen. Male self-arousal will lead not only to sexual sin encouraged by lust, but will in fact set off a kind of chain reaction that will lead straight-away into idolatry. "[He] incites the evil desire against himself," the redactor says, introducing a tradition co-

---

biblical origins of Church attitudes. See Noonan, *Contraception* 101-2; Dubarle "La Bible" 608-10.

opted from another context. *b. Nid.* 13a-b is a polemic – it is tantalizing to speculate about its intended audience and goal.[138] There are hints in this *sugya* and others (such as the Bavli's version of the Joseph story) that it is the actual emission of semen in vain that is problematic. If we are to judge from the rhetoric, this view does not rest on a condemnation of self-pollution.[139] Rather, it is possible that the rhetoric against the wasteful emission of semen was connected to contemporary Zoroastrian beliefs.

Glaringly absent from this discussion has been women. Because the rabbis, as the world around them, appeared to adhere to the medical opinion that women as well as men emit "semen" that is necessary for conception, it is at first surprising that rabbinic discussions of "waste of semen" never include women's "seed."[140] If, however, current Greek and Roman thought on male self-control actually was at the root of these rabbinic dicta, then the absence of discussion of the waste of female semen follows. This would help explain the off-handed dismissal of both female homoeroticism and the only source (known to me) on female masturbation in this literature (*b. Yebam.* 34a-b).

As controlling and degrading as these texts can be in discussing female sexuality that does not involve procreation, they can also, as we shall see in the next chapter, be warm and protective in discussions of marital intercourse for procreation.

---

[138] As with any discussion of "intended audiences" of this literature, any guesses must remain speculative. Nevertheless, it is tempting to see this as a polemic against masturbation, perhaps directed against the young husbands who leave their wives to study for long periods in the Academies.

[139] The lack of rhetoric about self-pollution regarding masturbation is surprising, but might relate to increasing de-emphasis placed on the ritual effect of male emissions. See S. Cohen, "Menstruants and the Sacred" 283-84.

[140] See Preuss, *Biblical and Talmudic Medicine* 387-88; Rousselle, "Observation féminine" 1100-1; Jan Blayney, "Theories of Conception in the Ancient Roman World," in *The Family in Ancient Rome,* ed. Beryl Rawson, 230-36.

7

Marital Sexuality

As by now (hopefully) shown, Palestinian rabbis, and the Jewish-Hellenistic writers who preceded them, consistently related their rhetoric on the expression of sexuality to marriage.[1] While Palestinian rabbis do not absolutely prohibit non-marital sexual liaisons, they do, as we have seen, deploy a number of rhetorical strategies to control them. Babylonians, too, develop rhetorics to control non-marital sexuality, but are at the same time more willing to acknowledge the occurrence of sexual activities outside of marriage.

That the rabbis attempt to control who one can have sex with or marry is unsurprising: many of the prohibited and condemned liaisons are prohibited in the Bible. Rhetoric on the *mode* of sex, however, how one is to have sex, is unprecedented in Scripture. Yet the rabbinic corpus contains an extensive discourse on sexual activities, even those that take place within marriage. In Chapter 6 I explored some of this rhetoric. In this chapter I will examine the other rabbinic rhetorics that focus on marital sexuality. These rhetorics fall broadly into two groups, those that discuss the rights and obligations for sexual intercourse, and those that discuss sexual activities.

Sexual Obligations Between Husband and Wife

FEMALE SEXUAL RIGHTS

The 'Onah

The biblical text that anchors most rabbinic discussion of the sexual obligations of a husband to his wife is Ex. 21:7-11:

---

[1] See, for example, Philo *Jos.* 42-44, in which Joseph tells Potiphar's wife that Jewish men never frequent prostitutes; marry as virgins; and have intercourse only for procreation.

(7) When a man sells his daughter as a slave, she shall not be freed as male slaves are. (8) If she proves to be displeasing to her master, who designated her for himself, he must let her be redeemed; he shall not have the right to sell her to outsiders, since he broke faith with her. (9) And if he designated her for his son, he shall deal with her as is the practice with free maidens. (10) If he marries another, he must not withhold from this one her food *(shi'erah)*, her clothing *(kîsutah)*, or her *'onah*. (11) If he fails her in these three ways, she shall go free, without payment.[2]

Verse 10 enumerates three things to which a female Hebrew slave is entitled from her husband/master. Even if her husband/master marries another woman, she maintains these three rights. It is not entirely clear, however, exactly what these three rights are, and the last, *'onah* is the most obscure of these. The *NJPS* translates the word as "conjugal rights," following, among other sources, the Septuagint.[3] This would be the only such biblical use of the word, which normally is used to denote "season, period."[4]

Rabbinic discussion on *'onah* with some dissent, accepts this as referring to female sexual rights. Palestinian and Babylonian sources, however, differ in the rhetoric that they use to discuss this right.

Tannaitic Traditions

The problem of translating verse 10 is addressed early in rabbinic literature:

A. *Shi'erah* – this is her food, and thus it says, "You have devoured My people's flesh *(shi'er)*," [Mic. 3:3], and it is written, "He rained meat *(shi'er)* on them like dust," [Ps. 78:27]. *kîsutah* – as its meaning [i.e., clothes].

vi'onatah – this is sex *(derek 'ereṣ)*, as it is written, "[Shechem son of Hamor the Hivite, chief of the country, saw her, and took her] and lay with her by force (ויענה)," [Gen. 34:2]. These are the words of Rabbi Yoshiah.

B. Rabbi Yonathan says, *shi'erah kîsutah* – clothes that are fitting for her.[5] If she is young, he should not give to her [clothes] of an old woman; if she is old, he should not give to her clothes of a young woman. *vi'onatah* – that he should not give to her summer [clothes] in the winter, or winter [clothes] in the summer, but he should give each [set] in its season *(bi'onatah)*.

---

[2]See Adrian Schenker, "Affranchissement d'une esclave selon Ex 21, 7-11," *Biblica* 69 (1988): 547-56, for a text-critical analysis of this passage.
[3]The Septuagint translates *'onah* as ὁμιλίαν.
[4]But see *BDB, ad loc.*, which derives the noun *'onah* from the verb meaning "answer, respond." S. Paul defines *'onah* as "oil." See Shalom Paul, "Exod. 21:10: A Threefold Maintenance Clause," *Journal of Near Eastern Studies* 28 (1969): 52-53.
[5]This follows the manuscripts. See apparatus *ad loc.*

C. Where do we learn [that a husband cannot withhold] food [from his wife]? Say it is an argument a fortiori. If he is not permitted to withhold from her things not essential to her life, all the more so that he is not permitted to withhold things that are essential to her life.

D. Where do you learn that [a man cannot withhold] sex [from his wife]? Say it is an argument a fortiori. If one is not permitted to withhold things on account of which [a woman] did not marry at first, for things on account of which she did marry at first, a fortiori he is not permitted to withhold them from her.

E. Rabbi [Yehudah] says, *shî'erah* – this is sex, as it is written, "None of you shall come near anyone of his own flesh *(shî'er bîsaro)*," [Lev. 18:6], and it is written, "Your father's nakedness *(shî'er)* ... the nakedness *(shî'er)* of your mother [you shall not uncover ...]," [Lev. 18:7].

kîsutah – as its meaning.

'onatah – this is food, as it is written, "He subjected you to the hardship of hunger, *(vayî'ankah vayar'ibekah),*" [Deut. 8:3].[6]

Four opinions are expressed in this passage. In (A) and (E), the verse is interpreted as referring to three obligations, clothes, food, and sex. Rabbis Yoshiah and Yehudah differ only in assigning the three biblical words to their proper referent. According to (B), neither food nor sex is referred to in this verse, only clothes. (D) asserts that the obligation for sex, like food (C), can be derived logically. The Targumim too appear to translate *'onah* as referring to sex.[7]

Like the biblical text itself, the rabbinic traditions that translate Ex. 21:10 as referring to sex do not go beyond the limited scope of the application of the verse. That is, Ex. 21:7-11 refers to a specific case that presupposes both the involvement of a Hebrew slave woman and polygamy. In tannaitic sources, the verse is not specifically applied to the sexual obligations of a husband toward his wife. Aside from a single clause, this passage from the *Mekhilta* is exegetical rather than explicitly prescriptive. The possible exception is clause (D), which assumes that women marry expecting sex. Unlike the other clauses, (D) uses logic rather than Scripture, in order to imply that because all women marry expecting sex, their husbands may not decrease their sexual "allotment."[8]

---

[6]*Mekh. Mishpatim* 3 (pp. 258-59) (par. *Mekh. d'RASHBI* [pp. 167-68] with different attributions).

[7]Targum Onkelos: ועתנה. Targum Jonathan: ומעייל לה. Targum Yerushalmi: מעילה ומפקה לווחה.

[8]Although speculative, it is possible that the "original" core of this tradition lacked (C) and (D). One version of this tradition, preserved in the *Mekh. d'Rashbi*,

The *Mishnah* explicitly obligates a man to have intercourse with his wife. This obligation is made dependent on a man's profession:

- A. If one vows not to have intercourse with his wife, the School of Shammai says, [he is allowed to maintain it for only] two weeks. The School of Hillel says, one week.[9]
- B. Students who leave for study of Torah without permission [of their wives, can do so] for thirty days. Workers, one week.
- C. The 'onah [obligation] which is stated in the Torah: *Tayalin*,[10] every day. Workers, twice a week. Donkey drivers, once a week. Camel drivers, once every thirty days. Sailors, once every six months. These are the words of R. Eliezer.[11]

The passage progresses from general to specific application. (A), attributed to the Schools, commands a man to divorce his wife if he vows to abstain sexually from his wife for any substantial length of time.[12] (B), stated anonymously, legislates that even without a vow, a man is allowed to refrain from sexual intercourse with his wife for only a limited period without her permission. Section (C) expands on (B), by both linking a husband's sexual obligation to Ex. 21:10 ("the 'onah which is stated in the Torah"), and by detailing further occupations and their sexual obligations. The generating principle for (C) appears to be simple economic need. A man's occupation, measured by the amount of time that it requires him to be away from his wife, is the sole determinant of his sexual obligation.

Thus, the tannaitic sources declare that a wife has a right to sex, the amount of which depends on the husband's occupation. A married man may not, without permission of his wife, take a vow of celibacy. No reason is given for this sexual right.

---

lacks both (C) and (D), remaining entirely exegetical. Would the reader of this exegetical tradition have applied the interpretations to contemporary society?
[9]There is a parallel to this statement at *m*. '*Ed*. 4:10.
[10]הטיילין. The Talmudim discuss the meaning of this word. Because the dictionaries derive their meanings from the discussions in the Talmudim, they offer conflicting interpretations. According to *Wörterbuch*, it is a "Müssiggänger," an unemployed person, while the *Arukh* (4.28) interprets it to refer to a day student.
[11]*m. Ketub.* 5:6.
[12]Jacob Neusner regards this tradition as "verified" at Yavneh by (C) (Neusner, *Rabbinic Traditions About the Pharisees* 3:200). (C), however, does not depend on (A). This interpretation of the *mishnah* follows *t. Ketub.* 5:1.

Yerushalmi

The Yerushalmi integrates the passage from the *Mekhilta* into the mishnaic sexual obligations of the husband, in the process significantly expanding the field of discourse:

A. Students who leave for study of Torah without permission of their houses,[13] [can do so] for thirty days. [If they leave w]ith permission of their houses, for any amount [of time they can be away from their wives].

B. Rabbi Shmuel bar Naḥman [PA 3] said [i.e., cited in this matter a verse] in the name of R. Yoḥanan [PA 3], "He sent them to the Lebanon in shifts of 10,000 a month: [they (i.e., those chopping lumber in Lebanon for the building of the Temple under King Solomon) would spend one month in the Lebanon and two months at home]," [1 Kings 5:28].

C. R. Avin [PA 5] said, the Holy One loves procreation more than the Temple.

D. What is the reason? "... they would spend one month in the Lebanon and two months at home," [1 Kings 5:28].

E. Rav said, "[The number of Israelites ...] who worked in monthly shifts all the months of the year ...," [1 Chr. 27:1].

F. Here [concerning workers] you say once a week [they are obligated to have sex with their wives], and there [concerning workers also in *m. Ketub.* 5:6] you say twice a week!

G. Bar Kapra taught: Workers go away to work without permission of their houses for one week.

H. "'Onah' which is stated in the Torah" – It is taught, *shî'er*, this is sex *(derek 'ereṣ); 'onah*, this is food. It is taught, *'onah*, this is sex; *shî'er*, this is food.

I. The one who says "*shî'er*, this is sex," [justifies himself with the verse] "None of you shall come near anyone of his own flesh *(shî'er bîsaro)*," [Lev. 18:6], *'Onatah* – this is food, as it is written, "He subjected you to the hardship of hunger, *(vayî'ankah vayar'ibekah),*" [Deut. 8:3].

J. The one who says, "*shî'er*, this is food," [justifies himself with the verse,] "He rained meat *(shî'er)* on them like dust," [Ps. 78:27]. "'*Onah*, this is sex," [he justifies with the verse] "if you ill-treat

---

[13]Hebrew: ברשות בתיזן. This phrase is also found in MS Leiden, apparently means "with permission of their household" (Sokoloff 92). The *Pnei Moshe* interprets this phrase as "permission of their wives." This is possible, but the phrase, which occurs in the Yerushalmi only in this *sugya*, is more general. Note, however, that the word for "house" *(oikos)* in Greek sometimes can refer to "wife." See Lysias 1.6-7.

(tî'anêh) my daughters," [Gen. 31:50, Laban is speaking to Jacob in reference to his daughters Leah and Rachel], this is sex.

K. R. Eliezer ben Yaakov interpreted the verse shî'erah kîsutah, that her clothes be fitting for her, that he should not give the clothes of a young woman to an old woman, nor [clothes] of an old woman to a young woman. kîsutah vî'onatah, that the clothes should be according to the season, that he should not give summer [clothes] in the winter, nor winter [clothes] in the summer.

L. Where do we learn [that a man is obligated to give his wife] food [since it is omitted in K]? If he is not permitted to withhold from her things not essential to her life, all the more so that he is not permitted to withhold things that are essential to her life.

M. Where do we learn about 'onah? If he is not permitted to withhold from her things for which she did not marry [permitted to her only] at that moment, all the more so things for which she did marry [permitted to her only] at that moment, all the more so things for which she did marry [permitted to her] at that moment.[14]

N. From the gift that Jacob our father sent to Esau his brother R. Eliezer learned, because he sent [it] to him in the correct fashion (kĕderek 'êreṣ). "200 she-goats and 20 he-goats," [Gen. 32:15] one to ten. "200 ewes and 20 rams," [Gen. 32:15], one to ten.[15] "30 milch camels with their colts," [Gen. 32:16]. R. Berakhiah [PA 4] said, this is because [the camel] is modest in sex, so Scripture did not publicize [the ratio of males to females]. "40 cows and 10 bulls," [Gen. 32:16] one to four because they work. "20 she-asses and 10 he-asses," [Gen. 32:16], one to two because they work.

O. R. Yermiah [PA 4] asked, does it not follow to make students like tayyalin [for purposes of their sexual obligation, i.e., every day]?

P. R. Mana [PA 5] said, does it not follow that they should be treated as harvesters, because they toil more.

Q. Rav said, "she eats with him every Friday night," this is euphemistic.[16]

Sections (A) to (E) comment on the mishnaic rule limiting scholars to thirty days at a time away from their wives. (A) expands the *mishnah's* enigmatic comment "with permission" to include the agent (the household, or perhaps wife), and adds that if the student did receive permission then he is released from his obligation. (B) justifies the time limit, thirty days, with a scriptural verse, effectively linking study of Torah and building of the Temple. (C) and (D) comment on the ratio of time spent at home vs. the time spent working. (C) uses this ratio to

---

[14]In MS Leiden, the question of (L) is posed, and then answered with the answer of (M). Everything in the middle is supplied in the margin.
[15]This clause is missing in the Vienna edition, but is found in MS Leiden.
[16]y. Ketub. 5:8, 30a-b.

Marital Sexuality 271

prove that God loves "procreation" more than the Temple (and by extension, Torah study). The use of the term "procreation" may be significant: it might assume that the rule of the ʿonah is predicated on procreation, a question to which I will return below. In (E), Rav appears to disagree, for the verse suggests that the ratio is one to one rather than two to one, that is, that they used to work for one month and then go home for a month. He concludes from this that a scholar too should go away for one month and then return to his wife for no less than one, instead of two, months. This contradicts R. Avin's reasoning in (C). The placement of Rav's statement after the chronologically later R. Avin might suggest that the redactor wanted to emphasize Rav's opinion at R. Avin's expense.

(F) and (G) deal with a seeming contradiction in the *mishnah*: are workers obligated to have sex with their wives once or twice a week? According to (G), the mishnaic reference to "once a week" indicates only the maximum amount of time that a worker can be away from his wife without her permission. That is, because this rule refers only to workers who have to leave their homes for economic reasons, it does not contradict the rule that a worker is obligated to have intercourse with is wife twice a week. (H) through (M) restate the tradition from the *Mekhilta* cited above. (N) attempts to justify the obligations enumerated in the *Mishnah* by R. Eliezer. They derive, according to this anonymous tradition, from the ratios of male and female animals delivered by Jacob to Esau. Because both goats and rams were thought not to work, the males would be less tired and have sex more frequently, and thus the ratio of females to males can be higher. On the other hand, because both bulls and asses work, the ratio of females to males is lower. Only the ratio of camels, due to their sexual modesty, is not mentioned. While clever, the explanation is inexact and incomplete. It accounts only for the principle that the difficulty of a man's work results in decreased sexual obligations. Neither the frequencies recommended by R. Eliezer, nor the principle that sexual obligations are also dependent on the amount of time that a job requires a man to travel, are explained. This passage explains only the difference between the sexual obligations of the *tayyalim*, who are presumed not to work, and the workers.

(O) and (P) continue in the same vein as (N). They question the nature of a student's work: is it more like a *tayyal* or a laborer?[17] The

---

[17] It is possible, though unlikely, that (O) assumes that students remain in their house, and are thus obligated to have intercourse with their wives every day. The beginning of this *sugya*, which assumes with other statements in the Yerushalmi that men leave their homes to study, mitigates against this interpretation.

premise accepted by (N), (O), and (P) contradicts the *mishnah*. Whereas the *mishnah* bases many of its rules on sexual obligations on a man's economic or spiritual need to be away from home, the Yerushalmi prefers a principle predicated on the physical difficulty of work. Rather than accepting and codifying the frequencies enumerated in the *mishnah*, the Yerushalmi treats the *mishnah* as advisory, and develops a general principle meant to govern a husband's sexual obligations toward his wife: the harder the job, the less frequently he is obligated to have sex with is wife. From the *mishnah's* view, a "harvester" is treated no differently from any other worker who remains at home or who engages in week-long temporary work outside of town. In the Yerushalmi, context indicates that a harvester, because his work is hard, is obligated to have sex with his wife less frequently, although exactly how much less is left unstated.

In (Q), Rav comments on *m. Ketub.* 5:9: "He [=a man who has gone away] gives her [his wife] 1/6 dinar for her needs, and she eats with him every Friday night." This clause appears to be misplaced, and will be considered below.

Hence, the Yerushalmi appears in principle to accept the tannaitically determined sexual rights of a wife. Instead of being determined by the amount of time that a man is home though, the frequency of a wife's conjugal rights is linked to the difficulty of her husband's work. The Yerushalmi thus transforms the more objective, legal obligations of the *mishnah* into a subjective principle (i.e., difficulty of work) that can be used to determine the sexual obligation.[18]

Bavli

The Bavli's discussion of *m. Ketub.* 5:6 is more detailed than the Yerushalmi's. Because, despite substantial overlap with the Yerushalmi's *sugya*, it also contains differences of both detail and focus, I cite a substantial part of the *sugya*:

A. "Students may go away [for 30 days] ..." With permission, how long [can they go away]? As long as they want.

B. And how much is the usual time [a student is allowed away from his wife]?

C. Rav said, a month here [in the study-house] and a month in the house, as it is written, "[The number of Israelites ...] who worked in monthly shifts all the months of the year ...," [1 Chr. 27:1].

---

[18]For this "dietetic" strategy in non-Jewish antiquity, see Ludwig Edelstein, "The Dietetics of Antiquity," in *Ancient Medicine: Selected Papers of Ludwig Edelstein*, ed. Oswei Temkin (rpt. Baltimore: The Johns Hopkins Press, 1987) 303-16.

Marital Sexuality

D. And R. Yoḥanan [PA 3] said, a month here and two in his house, as it is written, "[He sent them to the Lebanon in shifts of 10,000 a month:] they would spend one month in the Lebanon and two months at home," [1 Kings 5:28].

E. What is the reason that Rav did not use this [i.e., 1 Kings 5:28] text? Because building the Temple is different [from Torah study] because it [= the Temple] can be built by others.

F. What is the reason that R. Yoḥanan did not use that text [1 Chr. 27:1]? It is different there because each man had provision.

[There follows an exegetical disagreement between Rav and R. Yoḥanan on the effects of grief on a person, culminating in a redactorial application to the destruction of the Temple].

G. "*Tayyalim* [are obligated to have intercourse] every day." What is a "*tayyal*"? Raba [BA 4][19] said, students at circuit sessions (בני פירקי).[20]

H. Abaye [BA 4] said, they are those about whom it is written, "In vain do you rise early and stay up late, you who toil for the bread you eat; He provides as much for His loved ones while they sleep," [Ps. 127:2].[21]

I. Rav Yitzḥak [PA 3?] said, these [referred to in the last clause of Ps. 127:2] are the wives of students who chase away sleep from their eyes and watch for their husbands in this world and come to the world-to-come.[22]

J. And you say they [i.e., the "*tayyalim*"] are students at circuit sessions? [i.e., if Ps. 127:2 as interpreted by R. Yitzḥak refer to students who toil at night, how can they be expected to have sex with their wives every night?]. Rather, Abaye said, it is as Rav's [explanation], as Rav said, for example Rav Shmuel bar Shilat [BA 1] who ate from his own means, drank from his own means, and sleeps in the shade of his palace and there does not pass an official courier (פריסחקא דמלכה)[23] by his gate.

---

[19]In some versions, Rabah. See *Tal. Bab.* 1.2:70, n. 29.
[20]So Jastrow 1240. These students do not leave home in order to study.
[21]The rendering of this last clause is uncertain: בן יתן לידידו שנא
[22]"and watch for their husbands" is found only in MS Munich 95. This statement offers numerous exegetical problems. The phrase used, מנדדות שינה מעיניהם seems to indicate that the women chased sleep from the eyes *of their husbands*, although it is used elsewhere as an expression for a person staying awake and watching over something. Although there is no manuscript support for changing the suffix, "their (m) eyes" – especially in light of the addition in MS Munich 95 – appears to refer to the eyes of the women. Moreover, there are two parallels to this tradition. In *b. B. Bata* 10a, R. Naḥman bar Yitzḥak interprets Ps. 17:15 to refer to the students themselves who "chase away sleep from their eyes." A closer parallel, *b. Yoma* 77a, omits "from their eyes."
[23]Some manuscripts have דרוקא, a troop of soldiers. See *Tal. Bab.* 1.2:71.

K. When Rav in [BA 3-4]²⁴ came [from Palestine] he said, they [the *"tayyalim"*] are, for example, the delicate men (מפנקי) of the West.

[There follows a digression of two stories on the physical, non-sexual strength enjoyed by two Palestinian rabbis].

L. "Workers [are obligated to have intercourse with their wives] twice a week." But we learnt [in the same *mishnah*], "workers [are obligated] once a week!"

M. R. Yosi [PA 3?] said in the name of R. Haninah [PA 3?], this is no problem. Here [in reference to the obligation of twice a week] it is when they work in their own city; there [in reference to the obligation of once a week] it is when they work in another city.

N. Similarly, we learnt, to what do these words apply? To those who do their work in their cities, but if they work in another city, once a week.

O. "Ass drivers [are obligated] once a week."

P. Rabah bar Rav Hanan²⁵ said to Abaye [BA 4], was it necessary for the Tanna to take pains to be so explicit about the *"tayyalim"* and the worker [when one would think that only these cases would be covered in the first, more general part of the *mishnah*]?

Q. He said to him, no regarding all [classes the first part of the *mishnah*, dealing with vows, speaks].

R. But it says "[once in] six months," [for a sailor, for whom the first part of the *mishnah* regarding vows of one to two weeks would be irrelevant].

S. One who has bread in his basket is not similar to one who does not have bread in his basket.

T. Rabah bar Rav Hanan²⁶ said to Abaye, what is the law about an ass driver who became a camel driver?

U. He said to him, a woman prefers one *qav* [of provisions] and licentiousness (תיפלוח) to ten²⁷ *qavs* [of provisions] and abstinence.²⁸

V. "Sailors [are obligated] once every six months, these are the words of R. Eliezer."²⁹

---

²⁴Some versions have Rav Dimi [BA 3-4]. See *Tal. Bab.* 1.2:71.
²⁵According to MS Munich 95, Rav Hanin bar Papa. Other manuscripts offer alternatives, all Babylonian amoraim. See *Tal. Bab.* 1.2:72.
²⁶According to MS Munich 95, Raba bar Hanin.
²⁷Most manuscripts read "nine." See *Tal. Bab.* 1.2:73.
²⁸This is a citation of *m. Sot.* 3:4. See also *b. Sot.* 21b.
²⁹This clause is missing in MS Munich 95 and other manuscripts. See *Tal. Bab.* 1.2:73, n. 12.

W. Rav Berona [BA 2] said in the name of Rav, the law is like R. Eliezer.[30]

X. Rav Ada bar Ahavah [BA 2] said in the name of Rav,[31] this is R. Eliezer, but the Sages say that students leave [their homes] for study for two or three years without permission.

Y. The rabbis relied on Rav Ada bar Ahavah and acted thus in exchange for their souls [i.e., they died prematurely as a result].

[There follows a story of a Babylonian rabbi who, neglecting to make his *yearly* visit home, is killed in an accident.]

Z. When [= how much] is the *'onah* [obligation] of students? Rav Yehudah [BA 2] said in the name of Shmuel,[32] once a week.

AA. "[He is like a tree planted beside streams of water,] which yields its fruit in season," [Ps. 1:3]. Rav Yehudah, and some say Rav Huna, and some say Rav Naḥman, said this is one who has intercourse with his wife once a week [lit., "from Friday to Friday"].[33]

The *sugya* continues with several stories of rabbis who attempt to balance their study time away from home with their marital obligations. These rabbis spend anywhere from a week to twelve years away from their wives at a time. Boyarin has shown that these stories reflect a Babylonian ambivalence to what was most likely a "common" practice of men traveling far from their homes to study.[34] On the one hand, the Babylonian rabbis supported the right of the husband to travel to an academy and spend a long period of time there. On the other hand, they recognized the tension that this caused in marriages, and the stories implicitly caution a man not to neglect his marital duties.

The Bavli contains other important differences from its parallel in the Yerushalmi. Sections (A) to (D) are very similar to the beginning of the parallel *sugya* in the Yerushalmi: two biblical verses are adduced in order to support opinions that scholars should spend one or two months every three months at home. In (E) and (F), however, the redactor of the Bavli diverges significantly from this line of argumentation. Torah study is unlike the building of the Temple because (1) no one can learn Torah in another's place; and (2) students of Torah, unlike those building the Temple, are not receiving wages, so their wives cannot as easily tolerate their husbands being away for half the year. Although both (E) and (F)

---

[30] This statement is missing in some manuscripts, and attributed to Rav Kahana in others. See *Tal. Bab.* 1.2:73, nn. 13-15.
[31] "in the name of Rav" is missing in many mss.
[32] The attribution is completely missing in MS Munich 95, and only Rav Yehudah's name is indicated in several other manuscripts.
[33] *b. Ketub.* 61b-62b.
[34] See Boyarin, "Internal Opposition."

represent what the redactor thinks that one amora might say in answer to the other, the overall effect of these statements is to undermine the relevance of Scripture in this discussion. Because Torah study is different from work on the Temple, both (E) and (F) imply, scriptural verses that discuss the Temple are not germane to derivations of law on female conjugal rights. The questioning of biblical support for this law foreshadows statements made later in the *sugya* that expand the amount of time that a man is allowed to remain away from home studying.

Sections (G) to (K) attempt to define what is meant by a *"tayyal."* (G) to (I) interpret this phrase as referring to day students, who live at home with their wives. (J) begins to move the focus from students to wealthy individuals. By including the example of a wealthy scholar, (J) serves as a transition to (K) which finally defines the term as referring to those like the "delicate men of the West," rich and spoiled men of Palestine.[35] Whereas the Yerushalmi directly addresses the question of whether a student is to be considered like a *"tayyal,"* (J) in the Bavli deftly dismisses this possibility by redefining the term *"tayyal."*

In its discussion of the sexual obligation of workers and the seeming contradiction between two views in the *mishnah*, the Bavli comments briefly that it depends on where the worker finds employment. This answer, (L) to (N), of uncertain attribution and supported by a *baraitha* paralleled nowhere else, stands in contrast to the *sugya* in the Yerushalmi, which ignores the entire issue of men traveling for employment. Correspondingly, the Bavli ignores both the context of the vow and the issue of permission of his wife as possible explanations of the internal contradiction in the *mishnah*.

Section (O) is superfluous, a section from the *mishnah* with no commentary. (P) through (S) discuss the application of the first clause of the *mishnah*. Why does the *mishnah*, (R) asks, discuss vows of abstention for one or two weeks when dealing with the case of the sailor (and donkey-driver, etc.), who is obligated to have intercourse with his wife only once every six months. The answer, (S), is elliptical. Apparently, it compares a woman whose husband has taken a vow of abstinence to one who has no "bread," and the sailor's wife to one who has "bread" (i.e., a husband).[36]

---

[35]It is unclear to me what this term would have meant to its audience. The term "delicate men of the West" appears nowhere else in the Bavli, nor to my knowledge are Palestinians considered by the Bavli to be more delicate. *b. Shab.* 109a, in fact, records a tradition attributing particular fastidiousness to residents of Mahoza, a Babylonian town.

[36]According to Rashi, it means that a woman whose husband vows not to have intercourse with her despairs, while a woman whose husband is away is always comforted knowing that he could return at any moment. In other places in the

In (T), a Babylonian amora questions whether a man is permitted to switch his profession to one which lessens his sexual obligation to his wife. The answer (U) is that his wife would not like this, because she, like all women, prefer sex to any possible material gain that might result from the change of professions. The legal issue – whether a man's change of professions resulting in decrease of a woman's sexual rights violates the original implied agreement regulating frequency of sexual relations – is avoided. (V), like (O), cites the *mishnah* but does not comment on the clause.

(W) and (X) offer conflicting opinions on the legal application of the *mishnah*. (W) accepts it as law, but (X) disagrees, and instead almost nullifies a man's sexual obligation to his wife. (Y) is a remarkable statement of ambivalence: although rabbis accepted the opinion expressed in (X), they did so at risk to their lives. (Z) and (AA), which is based on two word-plays between the words in Ps. 1:3 and the Hebrew words for reproduction and *'onah*,[37] attempt to define the sexual obligation of students to once a week, but the stories punctuating this section, and those that follow, clearly portray rabbis doing so much less frequently.

There are three main differences between this *sugya* and its parallel in the Yerushalmi: (1) the Yerushalmi links difficulty of work to the husband's sexual obligation and the Bavli does not; (2) the Bavli focuses the vast majority of its discussion on the sexual obligation of students; (3) the Bavli omits the tannaitic tradition, cited in the Yerushalmi, which justifies the husband's marital obligations to his wife with biblical support. Overall, it appears that the redactorial thrust of this *sugya* is to mitigate the strict legal obligations enumerated in the *mishnah*, and to express the tensions between marital sexual life and Torah study.[38] Perhaps tellingly, at the very end of the *sugya* a story is related of a rabbi who returned earlier than expected – after only three years – from his house of study in order to see his wife, only to have his father meet him

---

Bavli, the phrase ("one who has bread in his basket is not similar tone who does not have bread in his basket") is used to indicate that one who has something, usually food, is concerned about or desires that thing less than one who does not. See *b. Yoma* 18b (par. *b. Yebam.* 37b), 67a, 74b. Women do not serve as the subject (the one who has or lacks bread) in any of these sources.

[37]The word פריו, "his fruit," is meant in the exegesis to evoke the phrase פרייה ורבייה, "reproduction." בעתו is in one sense (i.e., its meaning as "time, season") a synonym of *'onah*, which in the exegesis is then employed in its second sense of "sexual obligation."

[38]Even though many of these stories end with disasters or near disasters, legally the obligation has been lessened. A husband can legally abstain from conjugal relations but court disaster at the same time.

with a weapon and say, "You remembered your whore!"[39] That he returned after "only" three years causes his father to accuse him of lack of sexual control. By terming his wife a whore, the father implies that his son (her husband) cannot control himself, coming home in order to have sex. That is, by terming the man's wife a whore the father is really directing his attack at his son, who by not exercising self-control turns his wife into a "whore." This story too reflects ambivalence, but it is still a long way from the beginning of the *sugya*. The *sugya* begins with concern over the wife's right to sex, but ends with concern over the husband's right to study. What begins as a woman's right ends as a man's burdensome – even if only occasional – obligation.[40]

Elsewhere too in the Bavli we find a redactorial drift to lessening female conjugal rights. Tannaitic traditions that provide biblical support for female conjugal rights are cited in the Bavli only to demonstrate a man's obligation to provide *food* for his wife.[41] Other tannaitic traditions on female sexual rights are cited in the Bavli only in entirely different contexts.[42] The Yerushalmi, by contrast, more directly accepts the biblical support given to female conjugal rights.[43]

Sex on Friday Night

Tannaitic sources never directly link the conjugal obligation to Friday night. both the Yerushalmi and the Bavli suggest that Friday night is a particularly auspicious time for marital intercourse, though they proffer no reason.

As noted above, *m. Ketub.* 5:9 obligates a man to "eat" with his wife each Friday night. This is taken by Rav, in the Yerushalmi, to be euphemistic for sex.[44] On this *mishnah*, the Yerushalmi says:

A. This thing is stated euphemistically.

B. Shimon bar Ba [PA 3] said in the name of R. Yoḥanan, it really means "eat."

---

[39]*b. Ketub.* 63a.
[40]See also *b. Sanh.* 107a, in which Babylonian amoraim say that David, even when sick, fulfilled all of his conjugal obligations. While when isolated this tradition appears to praise David, in context it is clear that it was used to emphasize David's extreme lust, which is connected to his downfall.
[41]*b. Ketub.* 47b-48a.
[42]See *t. Kid.* 3:7; *b. Kid.* 19b; *b. Ketub.* 56a; *b. B. Meṣ.* 51a, 94a; *b. B. Batra* 126b.
[43]*y. Ketub.* 1:2, 59c.
[44]Melamed accepts Rav's assertion that the *mishnah* is using euphemistic language. See E. Z. Melamed, "Lashon nikiyya v'kinuyim bîmishnah," *Leshonenu* 47 (1982-83): 8 (Hebrew). Melamed bases himself on the Gen. 39:6 and the Talmudim. See *y. Ketub.* 5:9, 30b; 5:13, 30b.

C. According to the opinion of Rav, she eats from his; according to the opinion of R. Yoḥanan, she eats from hers.⁴⁵

When the *mishnah* states that a man is obligated to eat with is wife every Friday night, does it literally mean "eat" or is it a euphemism for sex? This short *sugya* relates the dispute but does not resolve it. The reasoning for Rav's opinion, that it means sex, (C), is obscure.⁴⁶ Another tradition in the Yerushalmi states that Ezra instituted that one eat garlic on Friday night because "it causes love to enter and desire to go forth," presumably a reference to sex.⁴⁷

The Bavli too suggests that Friday night was appropriate for intercourse. According to one *sugya*:

A. What is the *'onah* of students?

B. Rav Yehudah said [in the name of Shmuel], from Friday night to Friday night.

C. "[He is like a tree planted beside streams of water,] which yields its fruit in season," [Ps. 1:3]. Rav Yehudah, and some say Rav Huna, and some say Rav Naḥman, said this is one who has intercourse (והמשמש ממטה) from Friday night to Friday night.⁴⁸

"From Friday night to Friday night" might refer specifically to those times, or it might refer more generally to a weekly obligation: other usages of this phrase in the Bavli suggest that it might just mean "weekly."⁴⁹ A parallel *sugya* in the Bavli links the *'onah* to Friday night and to garlic, which as in the Yerushalmi is said to increase semen.⁵⁰

The Bavli too discusses *m. Ketub.* 5:9, which prescribes that a man eat with his wife every Friday night:

---

⁴⁵*y. Ketub.* 5:13, 30b. Part of this last clause (C) is found in the margins in MS Leiden, whose main body lists only the opinion of R. Yoḥanan recorded here.

⁴⁶The words משלו, משלה typically indicate possession. Rav, then, should mean that the woman's husband supports her, while R. Yoḥanan that she supports herself. This is not the same as saying that she eats with him or alone, as the *Pnei Moshe* attempts to explain it. Moreover, the explanation of the *Pnei Moshe* requires the assumption that these opinions refer to the behavior of husband and wife during the week, an assumption that is not at all explicit. To further confuse the issue, the *Korban HaEdah* records a variant reading that reverses the opinions (although MS Leiden corresponds to the printed version).

⁴⁷*y. Meg.* 4:1, 75a.

⁴⁸*b. Ketub.* 62b (par. *b. B. Kama* 82a with different attributions).

⁴⁹See *b. Ber.* 17b, 44a; *b. Pes.* 57a; *b. Ketub.* 65a; *b. Men.* 103b; *b. Ḥul.* 84a.

⁵⁰See *b. Yoma* 18a. On the medical, and aphrodisiac effects of garlic generally, see Immanuel Löw, *Die Flora der Juden*, 2 vols. (1924; rpt. Hildesheim: Georg Olms, 1967) 2:138-49.

A. Rav Naḥman [BA 3] said, it is really "eating." Rav Asi[51] [PA 3] said, it is sex.

B. We learnt, "she eats with him Friday night." It is fine according to the one who says she [really] eats, because it is taught, "she eats." But according to the one who says "sex," why [does the *mishnah* say] "eats?"

C. It is euphemistic, as it is written, "[Such is the way of an adulteress;] she eats, wipes her mouth, and says, 'I have done no wrong'," [Prov. 30:20].

D. An objection: R. Shimon ben Gamliel said, she eats [with him][52] Friday night and Shabbat.

E. It is fine according to the one who says "eating," because it is taught [in (D)] "and Shabbat." But according to the one who says ["eating' really means] "sex," is there sex on Shabbat [during the day]?

F. But Rav Huna [BA 2] said, Israel is holy and they do not have intercourse by day.

G. But Raba said, in a darkened house [during the day] it is permitted[53]

The same disagreement over the interpretation of *m. Ketub.* 5:9 recorded in the Yerushalmi occurs in (A), but here the opinions are attributed to Babylonian amoraim. (B) and (C) are a redactorial attack and defense of R. Asi's opinion. (D) begins another assault of R. Asi's interpretation with the citation of an unparalleled *baraitha* that is apparently taken out of context. If "eat" really means "sex," the continuation of the *sugya* argues, then in (D) too "eat" should mean "sex," and this would create a contradiction with those (E, F) who maintain that it is forbidden to have intercourse in the day. (G) saves the opinion (D), leaving the question open as to what is really meant by the word "eat" in these passages.

In summary, there is a predominantly Babylonian suggestion that Friday night is the best time for a husband, especially if a student, to fulfill his conjugal obligation. No reason for this opinion is given, nor is it suggested that intercourse on Friday night is additional to other conjugal obligations.

Other Discussions of Female Conjugal Rights

One other passage in the Bavli discusses the husband's sexual obligations:

---

[51]This might refer to a BA 6. I follow here several manuscripts, including Munich 95. The printed text reads "R. Ashi."
[52]Following MS Munich 95 and other manuscripts.
[53]*b. Ketub.* 65b (partial par. *b. Ketub.* 64b).

A. R. Yehoshua ben Levi [PA 1]⁵⁴ said, any man who knows that his wife is a fearer of heaven and does not "visit her" (פוקדה) is called a sinner, as it is written, "You will know that all is well in your tent, [when you visit your wife you will never fail]," [Job. 5:24].

B. And R. Yehoshua ben Levi said, a man is obligated "to visit" his wife when he [is about] to go on a journey, as it is written ... [Job 5:24 is cited again]

C. Does it [really] come from here [i.e., this biblical text]? [Rather,] derive it from here: "... your urge shall be for your husband," [Gen. 3:16, God is telling Eve]. It teaches that a woman has an urge for [= sexually desires] her husband when he goes on a journey.

D. Rav Yosef [BA 3] said, it is only necessary when it is near her period [even though our rabbis said that a man must separate from his wife close to her period].⁵⁵

E. How much is that?

F. Raba said, an 'onah.

G. These words apply to a voluntary [or optional journey], but one for the sake of a commandment, he is anxious.⁵⁶

This *sugya* begins with two exegeses, the second (B) more forceful ("a man is obligated ...") than the first (A), of the same biblical verse. They are (allegedly) made by a Palestinian amora, and emphasize, in stronger terms than the obligations enumerated in *m. Ketub.* 5:6, a husband's sexual obligations to his wife.⁵⁷ The first exegesis is a fairly straightforward word — play on Job 5:24. The second exegesis (B) is puzzling: nothing in the verse suggests anything about a man going out on a journey. In (C), the redactor recognizes this and proffers an alternative proof-text. Gen. 3:16, oddly, also does not prove that a man should visit, or have sex, with his wife before going on a journey.⁵⁸ Instead, it shows

---

⁵⁴MS Oxford 248 omits "ben Levi."
⁵⁵This phrase is added in many versions. Other versions substitute לאשתו נדה. See *Tal. Bab.* 3.2:403 n. 123.
⁵⁶*b. Yebam.* 62b.
⁵⁷These statements attributed to R. Yehoshua ben Levi are not paralleled in the Yerushalmi. His citation of the same verse, without commentary, can be found in the Bavli in reference to a man checking his home before Shabbat (*b. Shab.* 34a). It is possible that the tradition in *b. Shab.* 34a was imported and revised in this *sugya*. Revised or not, the use of the biblical term פקד as a euphemism for sex is not attested elsewhere in the Bavli (although possibly hinted at in Gen. 21:1). Some commentators have maintained that פקד here literally means visit, rather than intercourse, but context makes that highly unlikely. See *Tosafot, b. Yebam.* 62b. s.v., חייב אדם.
⁵⁸Unless the journey from the Garden of Eden is intended, but I think that this is unlikely. This statement is paralleled in a statement attributed to R. Yitzḥak b.

only that a woman has a general sexual desire for her husband. Citation of the verse is followed by a rather remarkable implicit claim, that a man should have intercourse with is wife because his wife's desire is strong. (D), (E), and (F) all deal with the case when one's wife, at the start of the journey, is either a menstruant or close to menstruation. It is interesting to note that Raba (F) uses the word 'onah with its meaning of "a specific period of time," rather than the contextually expected "sexual obligation."[59] (G) closes this section of the sugya, further limiting the application of (B).

A HUSBAND'S RIGHT TO SEX

Economic Penalties for Refusal of Sex

Although the Yerushalmi and the Bavli differ in their interpretation and emphasis on a husband's marital sexual obligation, both Talmudim assume that a husband is obligated to have sex with his wife. Wives have sexual rights. But what if the women decide not to exercise that right? Is there a female sexual obligation to their husbands, and how is this matter discussed in the sources?

Nowhere in rabbinic literature is a man explicitly given sexual rights. Yet these "rights" are implicitly imposed in the Talmudim. The source of this imposition is the mishnaic discussion of the "rebellious" spouses:

A. If a woman "rebels" (*moredet*) against her husband, they subtract from her marriage settlement seven dinars a week.

B. Rabbi Yehudah says, seven *tropics* [= 3 1/2 dinars]

C. To what point do they subtract? To the entire sum of the marriage settlement.

D. Rabbi Yosi says, really he continues to subtract [beyond the sum of the marriage settlement], for perhaps she will receive an inheritance from elsewhere and he [will then be able to] collect from her.

E. And similarly a man who "rebels" against his wife, they add to her marriage settlement three dinars a week.

Abdimi [PA 1] or R. Yitzhak [PA 3] (see *D.S.* 3:197, n. 7) at *b. 'Erub.* 100b. See also the parallel at *ADRN* ver. A (p. 4).

The euphemism "visit" for marital intercourse appears to be based upon its use in Gen. 21:1 and 1 Sam. 2:21. Its use in this fashion in rabbinic literature is rare, attributed only to Palestinians, and almost always has the connotation of impregnation. See, for examples, *y. Soṭ.* 3:4, 18d; *Gen. Rab.* 39:2 (p. 376, but some manuscripts replace the term with ילדות); 53:8 (pp. 562-63).

[59](F) was apparently imported from *b. Nid.* 63b. See also *b. 'Abod. Zar.* 75a for a discussion of the length of time that is meant by 'onah in an entirely different context.

Marital Sexuality

F. Rabbi Yehudah says, three *tropics* [1 1/2 dinars].[60]

"Rebellious" spouses suffer economic fines. What, however, does "rebel" mean? The *Tosefta* comments on the imposition of the fines on the rebellious wife without defining what it means to rebel, and makes no comment at all on the rebellious husband.[61]

The Talmudim link this *mishnah* with, among other things, withholding sex. Again, a comparison between the Yerushalmi and Bavli is informative. Beginning with the Yerushalmi:

A. Here [in the case of the rebellious wife] you say [that you lessen her marriage settlement] seven [dinars a week].[62] Here [in the case of a rebellious husband] you say [that you add to her marriage settlement] three [dinars each week].

B. Rabbi Yosi bar Haninah [PA 2] said, she: because she is obligated for seven [kinds of work. See *m. Ketub.* 5:5], he subtracts [seven dinars each week from her marriage settlement]. He: because he is obligated for three [things, namely, food, clothes and sex], he adds three [dinars a week to her marriage contract].

C. But bear in mind: if she brought slaves to him [as pat of her dowry] she would not be obligated to him at all [i.e., she should be exempt from personally doing the work, so could not be fined for being rebellious].

D. And bear in mind: if he stipulated with her [that he was not obligated for her] food, nor clothes, nor sex, then he would not be obligated to her at all [and if rebellious, could not be fined].

E. Why is this [i.e., the difference noted in (A)] so?

F. It is as R. Yohanan [PA 3] said, the grief of a man is greater than that of a woman.

G. This is as it is written, "Finally, after she [Delilah] had nagged him [Samson] and pressed him constantly, he was wearied to death," [Jud. 16:16].

H. What does "pressed him" mean?

I. R. Yitzhak ben Eleazar [PA 4][63] said, she would pull away from under him.

J. "He was wearied to death" – he was wearied to death, she was not wearied to death.

---

[60]*m. Ketub.* 5:7.
[61]*t. Ketub.* 5:7. Melamed, following the Talmudim, thinks that the *mishnah* here does refer to denial of sex ("Lashon Nikiyyah" 12).
[62]This clause, missing in the printed edition, is found in MS Leiden.
[63]In *b. Sot.* 9b this statement is attributed to "Rabbi Yitzhak in the name of Rabbi Ami [PA 3 or 4]."

K. And some say, she had sex [lit., would do her need] with other men.

L. All the more so that she desired, as R. Naḥman [PA 5?] said in the name of R. Naḥman, that organ – if she starves it, she satisfies it. If she satisfies it, she starves it.[64]

(A) asks why the penalties for rebellious husbands and wives differ. (B) offers both an answer and, in the process, a definition of "rebellious." A "rebellious" spouse is one who refuses to perform his or her obligation to the other spouse. For the wife, these obligations are the seven kinds of work enumerated in *m. Ketub.* 5:5 (and which do not include sex); for the husband they are the three obligations derived from Ex. 21:14. Rabbi Yosi bar Ḥaninah perhaps assumes that a "rebellious" spouse is one who reneges on *all* of his or her obligations, and who is thus penalized a dinar a week for each one. (C) and (D), cited anonymously, refute the logic of (B). If "rebelliousness" was linked to these obligations, cases could be imagined in which the obligations were eliminated, thus making moot the category of the "rebellious spouse." The *sugya* then offers an alternative answer, beginning with (F): "rebelliousness," at least of the wife, is the denial of sex to her husband. Because this denial is more painful to the husband than the wife, the wife receives a heavier fine.

If in (F) R. Yoḥanan is really referring to the denial of intercourse rather than refusal of a wife to perform her seven kinds of obligated work, then it assumes that men have no sexual outlet other than their wives. This assumption, possibly in idyllic vision by R. Yoḥanan, was apparently not shared by the redactor of the *sugya*. The redactor (G) cites a verse from the story of Samson and Delilah that seemingly has nothing to do with sex and gives three alternative interpretations to it. (I) goes beyond R. Yoḥanan's statement, declaring not that she would simply deny him sex, but that she would sexually arouse him and leave him frustrated.[65] As a result (J), he (Samson), but not she (Delilah), "was wearied to death," thus accounting for the larger fine given to the "rebellious" wife.

Women, on the other hand, need not be specially aroused in order to become frustrated: (K) suggests that Delilah herself may have suffered more that Samson from sexual abstinence. She, unlike Samson, is attributed with a sexual outlet.[66] (L) attempts to refute (K), proposing that because the more sex one has the more one wants (an assumption made by Rabbi Naḥman), if she was having sex with others she would

---

[64] *y. Ketub.* 5:10, 30b.
[65] The reason for this exegesis is unclear to me.
[66] The phrase, "she did her need," is curious. although commonly employed as a euphemism for male sexuality ("he did his need"), its use in the feminine usually designates "urination." See *m. Nid.* 9:1 and Melamed, ibid. 6-7.

demand it also from Samson. Curiously, the statement attributed here to R. Naḥman, which appears twice in the Bavli attributed to other amoraim, apparently refers there only to the *male* organ.[67] Here, the tradition is applied to female sexual desire. Female sexual desire becomes the focus of the *sugya*, even as it justifies the harsher economic penalties levied on women for the denial of sex to their husbands. The issue, or even definition, of a "rebellious" husband is almost completely ignored.

The parallel *sugya* in the Bavli even more forcefully assumes that a rebellious wife is one who denies her husband sex.[68] The Bavli, however, adds a consideration of motive:

A. What is meant by a "rebellious woman?"

B. Amimar [BA 5-6] said, that she says, I desire my husband[69] and I will torment him, but if she says, he is repulsive to me, we do not compel her.

C. Mar Zutra [BA 5-6] says, we compel her.

D. Such a case occurred, and Mar Zutra compelled [her], and R. Ḥaninah[70] came out from it [i.e., was conceived as a result].

E. It is not this – there, it was the help of heaven.[71]

Amimar suggests that *motive* of a woman is important in assessing whether or not she is to be called rebellious. Now assuming that "to rebel" means to deny sex, a wife is permitted to use the excuse that her husband is repulsive to her to avoid sex with him without suffering the penalties of a "rebel." Mar Zutra (C) disagrees with this, suggesting that motive is not a factor and that the action of refusal alone is sufficient to label her a rebel. (D) records how "compelling" through application of this fine can have happy consequences, if not for the wife, at least for the Jewish people, for it led to the birth of a great scholar. The redactor (E) qualifies this example by stating that it was a special case; Heaven intervened and brought about the birth of R. Ḥaninah. Not in all cases could such happy results be assured.

---

[67]See *b. Sanh.* 107a (Rav Yehudah); *b. Sukk.* 52b (R. Yoḥanan). In the latter source this opinion is said to derive from Hos. 13:6: "When they grazed, they were sated; when they were sated they grew haughty ..." In both places, the maxim is clearly applied to the penis.

[68]*b. Ketub.* 63a-64b.

[69]MS Munich 95 add: רעיא ליה, "I take delight in him."

[70]Following MS Munich 95 and other manuscripts.

[71]*b. Ketub.* 63b. Some manuscripts attribute the conception of R. Ḥaninah not to heaven, but to the special merit of Mar Zutra. The better manuscripts, however, preserve the reading here. See *Tal. Bab.* 1.2:88.

As we saw, the Yerushalmi focuses its passage on female sexual desire. The Bavli shifts to male desire:

A. R. Ḥiyya bar Yosef said to Shmuel, what is the difference between a rebellious husband and a rebellious wife?

B. He [Shmuel] said to him, go learn from the market of prostitutes, who hires whom.

C. Another explanation: His urge is external, her urge internal.[72]

(B) assumes that the male sexual drive is stronger than the female sexual drive, a view common in the Bavli.[73] (C) seems to have a similar implication.[74]

The husband, not the wife, has a sexual obligation. But in the Talmudim, it is the wife, not the husband, who suffers the more severe economic punishment for refusal of sex. While both Talmudim subsume the wife's denial of sex under the term "rebellious wife," the Bavli and Yerushalmi, as we have seen, differ in the focus of their commentary. Perhaps it was thought by the redactor of the Yerushalmi that a woman's voracious sexual appetite would mitigate against her use of sex as a weapon against her husband. For the redactor of the Bavli, however, a woman who refused to have sex with her husband was potentially a more serious problem. Because male sexual desire was thought by these Babylonians to be more problematic for men than women, "rebelliousness" was seized upon as a way to insure that a woman would exercise her right to sex.

Marital Rape

The sexual rights and obligations between spouses were seen as contractual. Thus, refusal to fulfill the terms of the "contract" were punished economically. When Mar Zutra, in *b. Ketub.* 63b, says that "we may compel" a woman who denies sex to her husband, he means that one fines her until she yields. Only one source in this literature, found in the Bavli, might be construed to indicate that a man may compel his wife to have sex.[75] Several commentators, ancient and modern, are correct in asserting that this passage in fact does not give any justification to rape of a wife.[76] Additionally, it is likely that in Jewish society women were almost certainly protected by their relatives against sexual abuse by their

---

[72]*b. Ketub.* 64b.
[73]See Chapter 4.
[74]Its exact force is unclear to me. Rashi writes, קשויו ניכר ומתגנה. ויצרו מבחוץ.
[75]*b. Ned.* 20b. See citation and discussion of this *sugya* in Chapter 6.
[76]See Maimonides, *Hilkhot Ishut*, 14:8; Naḥum Rackover, "Coercive Marital Relations Between a Man and His Wife," *Shenaton ha-Mishpat ha-Ivri: Annual of the Institute for Research in Jewish Law* 6-7 (1979-80): 295-317 (Hebrew).

husbands.[77] There are also several talmudic sources that explicitly denounce marital rape. Most of them do so using identical rhetoric, that of children.

The clearest expression of this prohibition, and rhetoric, is in a short passage in the Bavli:

A. Rami bar Ḥama [BA 4][78] said in the name of Rav Asi [BA 1?], it is forbidden for a man to force his wife for a *davar miṣvah* [= sex], as it is written, "[A person without knowledge is surely not good;] he who moves hurriedly blunders," Prov. 19:2].[79]

B. R. Yehoshua ben Levi said, any man who forces his wife for a *davar miṣvah* will have children who are not fit (מהוגנין).

C. Rav Ika bar Ḥaninah [n.a.][80] said, what is the meaning of "A person without knowledge is surely not good?"

D. As we have similarly learnt, "A person without knowledge is surely not good" – this one forces his wife for a *davar miṣvah*. "He who moves hurriedly blunders" – this is one who has intercourse and then repeats [it].

E. But Raba said, if one wants his children to be males, he should have intercourse and repeat!

F. This is not a problem. Here [E] it is with her consent, there [D] it is without her consent.[81]

In (A), a Babylonian amora, apparently playing off Prov. 19:2, forbids marital rape.[82] (B), attributed to a Palestinian amora, introduces the rhetoric of children: sex committed by compulsion will result in children who are somehow deformed.[83] The continuation, in (C) through (F), also employs a eugenic rhetoric dealing with sexual compulsion.[84] The *sugya* continues with discussions of how to conceive worthy children (see

---

[77]It is possible that Jewish, like Roman, women found protectors in their brothers and fathers. See Pomeroy, "The Relationship of the Married Woman" 215-27.
[78]In some versions Rami bar Abba [BA 3]. See *D.S.* 3:392.
[79]The citation of this verse is missing – probably mistakenly – in some versions. See *D.S.* 3:392, n. פ.
[80]Some versions have the equally unknown Raba bar Ḥaninah. See *D.S.* 3:392-392, n. ש.
[81]*b. 'Erub.* 100b.
[82]The verse reads, ואץ ברגלים חוטא. Apparently, רגלים is being taken in the sense of "sex," and חוטא is read more literally than in the *NJPS* translation.
[83]This "deformity" is probably moral, but might also be physical. See the section on "Eugenic Rhetoric" below.
[84]The term "eugenics" acquired negative connotations during the Nazi period. Here I use the term as defined by the *OED*: "Pertaining or adapted to the production of fine offspring." No connotations, positive or negative, are intended.

below) and female solicitude of sex from their husbands. To my knowledge, there is no discussion of marital rape in the Yerushalmi.

Palestinian sources cited in the Bavli, then, employ eugenic rhetoric in their rejection of marital rape. A man should not rape his wife because unworthy children will result. Babylonian amoraim, and the redactor, do not utilize this rhetoric for sexual compulsion.

NON-RABBINIC PARALLELS

The obligation of sexual intercourse is rarely discussed in Greek and Roman sources. Plutarch reports that Soon required the husband of the *epikleros*, a woman who with her father's property is "claimed" by a relative of her deceased father, to have intercourse with her at least three times each month.[85] The objective of this law was to produce a son who would be considered his grandfather's heir. Whether or not this report is accurate, it is clear that Plutarch, whose attitude toward marital intercourse is further considered below, admired this rule. In fact, in another report of this rule Plutarch neglects to mention that Solon's rule applied only to the *epikleros*, thus implying that Solon mandated marital sexual intercourse for everyone.[86] Considering Plutarch's generally positive evaluation of marital intercourse, his admiration of Solon's law is not surprising. He never suggests, however, that such a law should be established in his own day. Nor do any other writers from this period.

The reason that Greek and Roman writers and legislators do not dwell on obligations of marital intercourse appear clear. Because in Roman law divorce could be unilateral and upon demand, there was less of a need to legislate particular rights of the spouses.[87] If a man was not satisfied sexually he could turn, with only the scorn of the philosophers to reckon, to slaves, boys, and prostitutes; a woman could divorce her husband. In rabbinic law, a woman could not initiate divorce, and thus needed more protection within marriage.[88] Moreover, Roman women

---

[85]Plutarch *Solon* 20.2-3. On this, see W.K. Lacey, *The Family in Classical Greece: Aspects of Greek and Roman Life* (Ithaca: Cornell University Press, 1968) 89; David M. Schaps, *Economic Rights of Women in Ancient Greece* (Edinburgh: Edinburgh University Press, 1979) 36 and esp. 126, n. 80.

[86]Plutarch *Moralia* 769A.

[87]Roman marriage was dependent on continuous mutual consent. On this, see for example Buckland, *A Manual of Roman Private Law* 66-69.

[88]Recently there has been some controversy on this issue. See Bernadette Brooten, "Donnten Frauen im alten Judentum die Scheidung betreiben?" *Evangelische Theologie*, 42 (1982): 65-80; Hans Weder, "Perspektive der Frauen?" *Evangelische Theologie* 43 (1983): 175-78; Bernadette J. Brooten, "Zur Debatte über das Scheidungsrecht der jüdischen Frau," *Evangelische theologie* 43 (1983): 466-78. Although Brooten has discovered traces of laws that allow for the initiation of

were afraid of pregnancy, and were often grateful when their husbands turned to other outlets. "An amorous husband was a catastrophe," as one scholar writes.[89]

For Christians, the issue is far more complicated. Paul writes:

> It is a good thing for a man to have nothing to do with women, but because there is so much immorality, let each man have his own wife and each woman her own husband. The husband must give the wife what is due to her, and the wife equally must give the husband his due. The wife cannot claim her body as her own; it is her husband's. Equally, the husband cannot claim his body as his own; it is his wife's. Do not deny yourselves to one another, except when you agree upon a temporary abstinence in order to devote yourselves to prayer; afterwards you may come together again; otherwise, for lack of self-control, you may be tempted by Satan.[90]

Paul develops a theory of mutual sexual obligations as a guard against temptation. Women and their husbands have sexual obligations, or debts, toward each other.[91] These obligations are never precisely specified.

The conception of marital sex as a mutual obligation continued in later Church theologians.[92] As the Church's stance toward sexuality changed, however, this idea of mutual obligation weakened in some circles. Origen's lionizing of virginity and his degradation of sex contributed to a growing unease within the Church with the idea that one's body belongs to anyone except oneself.[93] John Chrysostom preached that the only purpose of marital sex was to avoid fornication, a passable but hardly positive interpretation of Paul's dictum.[94] Augustine, among other Western Church Fathers, accepted the permissibility of marital intercourse but nevertheless recommended that

---

divorce by the wife, there can be little doubt that the assumption throughout the *Mishnah* and later rabbinic writings is that a wife did not have this legal capacity.
[89] Aline Rousselle, "Body Politics in Ancient Rome," in *A History of Women in the West: From Ancient Goddesses to Christian Saints*, ed. Pauline Schmitt Pantel, trans. Arthur Goldhammer (Cambridge: Harvard University Press, 1992) 322. This claim is probably exaggerated, as Roman women appeared to utilize contraception. See Hopkins, "Contraception," Eyben, "Family Planning." Moreover, there was general encouragement of fertility.
[90] 1 Cor. 7:1-5.
[91] See William F. Orr, ed., *1 Corinthians* (The Anchor Bible 32; Garden City: Doubleday, 1976) 208; Hermann L. Strack and Paul Billerbeck, *Kommentar zum Neuen Testament aus Talmud und Midrasch*, 6 vols. (1922; rpt. München: Beck, 1963-1965) 3:368-69, n. 8; Jean-Louis Flandrin, "La vie" 104-5.
[92] See Flandrin, "La vie" 104.
[93] See Brown, *Body and Society* 170-74.
[94] See Brown, "Bodies and Minds" 488.

couples avoid it.[95] As in the Yerushalmi and the Bavli, the idea of conjugal obligations was de-emphasized in favor of service to God.

REASONS FOR SEXUAL RIGHTS AND OBLIGATIONS

According to Plutarch, intercourse between husbands and wives gives rise to "honor, grace, love (ἀγάπη), and trust."[96] He adds that regular intercourse removes strife from marriage. Plutarch reflects a general sense of a "new marital morality": the conjugal couple became an increasingly important focus of discourse.[97] Harmony between the spouses was seen as mirroring the idealized civic harmony. Sex, like the political treaty, according to Plutarch, was intended to renew ties of affection and obligation.

This "new marital morality" does not find direct expression in rabbinic literature. Although tannaitic sources oblige men to have sex with their wives, and even give this obligation a biblical foundation, they never attempt to explain why they are doing so. The Talmudim offer, in a few scattered statements, some hints as to how they may have conceptualized the purpose of marital sex.

"Happiness"

Babylonian and Palestinian rabbis differ over whether sexual pleasure is an approved or valid reason for marital intercourse. Babylonian rabbis appear to accept female sexual pleasure as a rationale for intercourse, whereas Palestinian rabbis do not.

According to Deut. 24:5: "When a man has taken a bride, he shall not go out with the army or be assigned to it for any purpose; he shall be exempt one year for the sake of his household, to give happiness to the woman he has married." While it is not clear from this passage what kind of "happiness" is meant (most likely sexual), the Bavli, echoing this language, links the idea of "happiness" and the marital sexual obligations:

> A. ... R. Yoḥanan [PA 2] said, if a man had intercourse with his wife, a menstruant, he is liable [for having intercourse with a menstruant].

---

[95]See Augustine *De bono conjugali*, ch. 3; Henry Chadwick, *Augustine* (Oxford: Oxford University Press, 1986) 89, 114-15.

[96]Plutarch *Moralia* 769A. See also Plutarch *Solon* 20.3.

[97]On this, see Paul Veyne, "La famille et l'amour sous le haut-empire romain," *Annales: économies, sociétés, civilisations* 33 (1978): 48; Veyne, "The Roman Empire" 24-25; Brown, "Late Antiquity" 297-311; Suzanne Dixon, "The Sentimental Ideal of the Roman Family," in *Marriage, Divorce, and Children in Ancient Rome*, ed. Beryl Rawson, 99-113; Walcot, "Romantic Love" 5-33; Gordon Williams, "Some Aspects of Roman Marriage Ceremonies and Ideals," *Journal of Roman Studies* 48 (1958): 24-28.

Marital Sexuality 291

> If he had intercourse with his levirate widow, a menstruant, he is not liable ...
>
> B. How does "his levirate widow" differ [from his wife in this case]?
> C. He performed a commandment [of taking his levirate widow].
> D. But with his wife too he performed a commandment!
> E. With his pregnant wife [we are dealing, for whom there is no commandment].
> F. But there is the happiness of her *'onah*.
> G. It was not at the time of her *'onah*.
> H. But Raba [BA 4] said, a man is obligated to cause his wife to be happy with a *davar miṣvah* [= sex].
> I. It was close to the time of her period.[98]

The original context of R. Yoḥanan's comment (A) is not clear; it is hard to imagine that he really meant that intercourse with one's levirate widow while she was a menstruant did not make one liable for a sin offering. The redactor (I) ultimately understands this statement to apply to the time when a woman is about to get her period. (B) through (H) explore R. Yoḥanan's differentiation between the commandments of "acquiring" one's levirate widow and of his *'onah* obligation.

The redactor argues first that one is also commanded to have intercourse with one's wife, presumably for procreation (D). (E) answers by saying that if that were the case, intercourse with one's pregnant wife would not be a commandment. The redactor replies (F) that the issue is not procreation, but the "happiness (*śmḥ*) of her *'onah*," that is, marital, even perhaps non-procreative, intercourse, per a husband's sexual obligation to his wife. (G) objects that then when a husband has already fulfilled his sexual obligation, then there would be no commandment. (H), attributed to Raba, objects to (G) by asserting that a husband has a continual obligation to make his wife happy through intercourse. (I) continues with another objection, that then when a woman is near her period, and her husband is warned to stay away from her, there is no commandment for him to have intercourse with her.

Of interest in this passage is the use of the term *śmḥ*, happiness. In this *sugya* it is used, at least in (F), with an almost technical sense, as a synonym for intercourse. Raba's use of the term (H) is more ambiguous, and might reflect an actual linkage between female happiness and marital sex. His use of the causative verb and the proximity to another euphemism for intercourse, *davar miṣvah*, seems to assume that

---

[98] *b. Pes.* 72b.

intercourse makes women happy, and that this happiness might justify extending a husband's sexual obligations. "Happiness," or joy, thus becomes a reason for fulfillment of sexual obligations. This assumption appears elsewhere, also attributed to Babylonian amoraim, in the Bavli.[99]

That Babylonians employed a rhetoric of pleasure in dealing with marital intercourse might find confirmation in a terminological switch that occurs in discussion on vows. According to the *Mishnah*, a man can vow that a woman not "be enjoyed to me forever."[100] The phrase means that a man vows not to have intercourse with his wife. This simple meaning is changed in the Bavli. According to the redactor of the Bavli and a Babylonian amora, men or women can vow that they will abstain from the *hana'ah* of sex, a different idea.[101] The mishnaic euphemism is assumed by the redactor of the Bavli to refer to real "pleasure" in sex. Only a single tradition in the Yerushalmi appears to employ this language, and it might be attributed to a Babylonian amora.[102]

Another example of this emphasis on the "pleasure" of sex can be found in the redactorial response to a tradition in the Bavli, attributed to the Palestinian amora R. Yoḥanan, which accuses Sisera of having repeatedly had intercourse with Yael (Judges 4:18-23). To this tradition, the redactor objets, "did she [Yael] not enjoy it?" The assumption is that women derive pleasure from intercourse.[103]

---

[99]*b. Ketub.* 8a (the marriage blessings); *b. Mo'ed Qaṭ.* 8b. The link with sex, rather than the "happiness" of marriage and its celebration generally, is not as clear in this *sugya*. Anderson sees *śmḥ* used with this same nuance in other passages in the Bavli also (Gary A. Anderson, *A Time to Mourn, a Time to Dance: The Expression of Grief and Joy in Israelite Religion* (University Park, PA: Pennsylvania State University Press, 1991) 27-37. I find his explanations of *b. B. Batra* 144b-145a and *b. Sukk.* 25b unconvincing. In both of these passages, as with *t. Ketub.* 1:1 which he cites for support, *śmḥ* is closely associated with and can directly refer to the marriage-feast. The Bible and other Ancient Near Eastern languages do use the cognate *śmḥ* and associated words to refer to intercourse, and its association in rabbinic literature with the marriage-feast intimates a further connection with marital sexuality. This, however, is not identical to positing that the idea that underlies this nuance – sex makes a woman "rejoice" – is present. See also Gary Anderson, "Celibacy or Consummation in the Garden? Reflections on Early Jewish and Christian Interpretations of the Garden of Eden," *Harvard Theological Review* 82 (1989): 121-48.

[100]*m. Ned.* 8:7.

[101]*b. Ned.* 15b (par. *b. Ned.* 81b). Note that in *b. Ned.* 15b, the word *hana'ah* is missing in MS Munich 95 from Rav Kahana's dictum that a woman can vow to abstain from תשמיש המטה. See also *b. Ketub.* 71b.

[102]*y. Ned.* 11:1, 42c (par. *y. Naz.* 9:1, 57c). Attribution is to Rav Huna.

[103]*b. Yebam.* 103a-b (par. *b. Hor.* 10b; *b. Naz.* 23b). For another example of Babylonian rhetoric on the "fun" and pleasure of sex see *b. Ber.* 62a.

Palestinian sources, on the other hand, almost never use female sexual pleasure as a rationale for marital sex. Tannaitic sources seem totally unaware of this concept.[104] The only source attributed to a Palestinian rabbi known to me that links marital intercourse and female sexual pleasure is a *baraitha* found in the Bavli:

A. An objection: What should a man do to have male children?

B. R. Eliezer says, he should disperse his money to the poor.

C. R. Yehoshua ben Karḥa says, he should make his wife happy in *davar miṣvah*.[105]

Even if this unparalleled *baraitha* is authentically tannaitic, (C) only indicates that female sexual pleasure might be useful for the conception of male children. Female sexual pleasure in itself is not considered by any Palestinian source known to me an "approved" reason for intercourse.

Procreation

If Babylonian sources employ the idea of female sexual pleasure as a legitimate reason for marital intercourse, Palestinian sources legitimate sexual intercourse through a rhetoric of procreation. An example of how the two rabbinic groups differ in this respect can be found in a tradition cited in the Bavli:

A. ... as it is written, "On the eighth day he let the people go. They bade the king good-bye and went to their homes, joyful (*śmeḥim*) and glad of heart over all the goodness that the Lord had shown to His servant David and His people Israel," [1 Kings 8:66].

B. "and [they] went to their homes" – where they found their wives pure [i.e., not menstruating].

C. "joyful" – that the wife of each one conceived and bore a male child.[106]

This source is most likely Palestinian.[107] In it we can see a use of the term "happy" almost converse to the way that the Babylonians employed it. The wives are not made happy by sex. Rather, the husbands are made happy by the conception of male children.

The Palestinian use of this rhetoric of children in discussions of marital sexuality is confirmed in other sources. The point of ʿonah

---

[104]See for example *Sifre Deut.* 271 (p. 292).
[105]*b. B. Batra* 10b. (C) follows the reading indicated in D.S. 10:44, n. ס.
[106]*b. Shab.* 30a. This tradition is in the margins of MS Munich 95. Modified versions are found at *b. Moʿed Qaṭ.* 9a; *Gen. Rab.* 35:15 (p. 332).
[107]It is attributed as tannaitic at *b. Moʿed Qaṭ.* 9a and is paralleled in *Genesis Rabbah* with a Palestinian attribution.

obligation is that it leads to procreation, which is thought at least by the rabbis (and probably by the women themselves) to be highly desired by women. To deny a woman sex was to deny her children and the status that they confer. R. Avin, cited above, in a discussion of 'onah, says that God loves "procreation more than the Temple."[108] The obligation of 'onah is made synonymous with that of procreation. Another example of this assumption is found in the Bavli:

A. ... As Rav Daniel bar Katina [BA 3] said in the name of Rav, what is the scriptural authority [for the statement in the Mishnah that] one does not marry women during a festival? As it is written, "You shall rejoice in your festival," [Deut. 16:14] – "in your festival" and not "in/with your wife."[109]

B. Ulla [PA 3] said, [it is forbidden] because of the labor.

C. Rabbi Yitzhak Napha [PA 3] said, because of the abrogation of procreation.[110]

(A) and (B) connect marriage to "rejoicing" (śmḥ) (A) and the trouble of making the party (B). According to Rashi, (C), attributed to a Palestinian amora, argues that if marriage was allowed during the festival then all would wait until the festival to marry, presumably leading to fewer marriages with the result being less procreation. The parallel passage in the Yerushalmi – attributed to a different Palestinian amora – discusses this reason at length.[111] The opinion ascribed to Ulla in the Bavli (B) is attributed in the Yerushalmi, without comment, to R. Abbahu in the name of R. Eleazar. Halivni argues that the difference between the sugyot result from use of different versions of the mishnah.[112] While this partially explains some of the finer differences, the more fundamental difference is caused by the Palestinian assumptions that tightly link marriage, sex, and procreation. For the Palestinians, procreation, not female sexual desire, is a good reason for granting a woman sexual rights.[113]

---

[108] y. Ketub. 5:8, 30a-b.
[109] This section is paralleled at b. Ḥag. 8b.
[110] b. Mo'ed Qaṭ. 8b.
[111] y. Mo'ed Qaṭ. 1:7, 80d. The sugya does not, however, explain why avoidance of marriage on the festival leads to a lessening of procreation.
[112] Halivni, Sources and Traditions 2.3:532-34.
[113] There is a possible exception to this dichotomy at y. Ḥag. 2:2, 78a (par. y. Sanh. 6:9, 23c. This story is cited and discussed in Chapter 4). Shimon ben Shetaḥ, after gaining entrance to a witches coven, fools them into letting his warriors into slaughter them by asking them if they would like to receive men who will "make them rejoice" (ḥda). This is the only use of this word as meaning "sex" in either Talmudim, and its use is clearly derogatory. On this passage see Anderson, A Time to Mourn 34-35.

Non-Rabbinic Parallels

Palestinian emphasis on procreation as the goal of sex is very similar to contemporary Greek, Roman, and Christian rhetoric on sex. This concept can be seen as early as Plato, and seemed ascendant among the Pythagoreans and later, the Stoics.[114] The *Corpus Hippocratium* advises sex for women for their health, but does not appear to connect female sexual desire to "pleasure."[115] Some Roman philosophers also preached that sex should be only for procreation.[116] Musonius Rufus, flourishing shortly after Augustus and his promulgation of a number of laws aimed at increasing procreation and the number of Roman citizens, states succinctly:

> Men who are not wantons or immoral are bound to consider sexual intercourse justified only when it occurs in marriage and is indulged in for the purpose of begetting children, since that is lawful, but unjust and unlawful when it is mere pleasure seeking, even in marriage.[117]

Paul, as we have seen above, does not advance the argument that intercourse is for procreation. Rather, Paul, immersed as he was in the belief that the eschaton was imminent, advocated sex only as remedy for temptation. According to one scholar, "Paul, in effect, defined marriage as a context for the mutual satisfying of erotic desires."[118] Among the Church Fathers, the Stoic goal of procreation was so completely accepted that Paul's reasoning is virtually ignored. Clement of Alexandria bluntly declared the only virtue of sex to be procreation.[119] The "Alexandrian Rule" became normative in later Christian writings.[120]

Among modern Arabs, too, procreation is greatly valued. According to Patai, female desire for children, and the status that accrued to them

---

[114]See Plato *Laws* 841D-E and the discussion in Brundage, *Law, Sex* 16-21.

[115]See Lesley Dean-Jones, "The Politics of Pleasure: Female Sexual Appetite in the Hippocratic Corpus," *Helios* 19 (1992): 72-91, esp. 82.

[116]See David Herlihy, *Medieval Households* (Cambridge: Harvard University Press, 1985) 6; Dabue, *Duty of Procreation* 29.

[117]Musonius Rufus 12 (trans. Lutz, 87).

[118]Roy Bowen Ward, "Musonius and Paulon Marriage," *New Testament Studies* 36 (1990): 286-87. See also Herbert Preisker, *Christentum und Ehe in den ersten drei Jahrhunderten* (Berlin: Trowitsch & Sohn, 1927) 126-27, 137-41; Willy Rordorf, "Marriage in the New Testament and Early Church," *Journal of Ecclesiastical History* 20 (1969): 193-210.

[119]Clement Alex. *Paed.* 2.10.91; *Str.* 3.7.58. See Brown, *Body and Society* 130-33. On the transition of the idea from the Stoics to the Church Fathers, see Nonan, *Contraception* 47-48.

[120]See Elizabeth A. Clark, "Sexuality," in *Encyclopedia of Early Christianity*, ed. Everett Ferguson (London and New York: Garland, 1990) 843.

through procreation, is very strong.[121] It is possible that this attitude reflects a more ancient tradition.

Marital sexuality among these groups was conceived of as being for procreation, not pleasure.[122]

Marital Sexual Behavior

To my knowledge, no tannaitic source comments upon or attempts to control marital sexual behavior. Within the Talmudim, however, there is a substantial discourse on "sanctioned" sexual behavior. These discussions center on three issues: restraint during menstruation ("*niddah*"); "modesty" in marital sexual behavior; and "eugenics," the assumption that sexual behavior effects the nature of the thereby conceived child.

Niddah

Within the two major law codes on sexuality in the Hebrew Bible are two verses that command a man not to "draw near" to a woman while she is menstruating (Lev. 18:19; Lev. 20:18). Considering the massive quantity of discussion of the laws of menstrual purity in rabbinic literature, the minuscule amount devoted to the encouragement of keeping these laws is surprising.[123] Most of the talmudic tractate *Niddah* concerns itself with laws of menstrual purity, yet the vast majority of it focuses on specific questions of application: when, precisely, does *niddah* begin and end? How does it transmit ritual impurity? How long after the end of menstruation must a woman wait before ritual immersion? The fundamental question – why should anyone follow the laws of menstrual purity – is left virtually unattended. This focus on issues of purity over other issues is no doubt what led this tractate to be included in most orderings of the Talmudim in the Order of Purities rather than that of Women.[124]

According to the *Mishnah*, "for three transgressions do women die in childbirth: not being scrupulous with regard to [the laws of] *niddah*;

---

[121] See Raphael Patai, *Sex and Family in the Bible and the Middle East* (New York: Doubleday, 1959) 79.

[122] I have not been able to find support for Mopsik's statement that "Thus, by reproducing, religious man [sic] imitates the divine work of the original organization of the cosmos and his procreative act is perhaps considered as the ritual reenactment of cosmogony." Charles Mopsik, "The Body of Engenderment in the Hebrew Bible, the Rabbinic Tradition and the Kabbalah," in *Fragments for a History of the Human Body*, ed. Michel Feher (New York: Zone, 1989) 53.

[123] For a survey of laws concerning the menstruant, see Israel Ta-Shema, "Niddah," in *Encyclopedia Judaica* 12:1141-48. See also S. Cohen, "Menstruants and the Sacred."

[124] MS Munich 95 is an exception to this ordering.

ḥallah; and the lighting of candles [on Friday night]."[125] This cryptic statement is explained in later rabbinic sources as a form of punishment: because the first woman caused mortality to descend on the first man, she is punished with menstruation.[126] Although driven by a "measure for measure" hermeneutic, this explanation seems to shy away from the force of the *mishnah*. Whereas the *mishnah* seems to threaten women to keep an eye on their menstrual cycle (and keep their husbands informed), the later rabbinic explanations focus only on the "curse" of menstruation, totally ignoring the implications for the sexual violations that would be incurred thereby. Other tannaitic sources are hardly more enlightening, usually defining the meaning "drawing near" (i.e., the defining act) or categorizing according to punishment (extirpation).[127]

Only a handful of sources actually encourage adherence to the laws of *niddah*. These sources offer both positive and negative reasons. Adherence in the laws of *niddah*, according to one source, will make a wife "more beloved" by her husband (who would, presumably, desire her more).[128] A second source attributes eugenic benefits to adherence to these laws.[129] Another source, on the other hand, attributes the death of a man to the less than strict adherence by a woman to the laws of *niddah*.[130]

What might account for the lack of rhetoric on this topic? Unlike other sexual transgressions, there is richness of neither quantity nor quality. It is possible that the rabbis felt that acceptance of the idea of this law (if not all the particulars) was commonly accepted and therefore there was no need to encourage people to observe it. Although speculative, this explanation would help to explain one source that attributes to the Romans a decree ordering Jews to restrain from observance of Shabbat and circumcision, and to have intercourse while the wives were menstruating.[131] The first two restrictions would certainly have been seen as fundamental affronts. Perhaps the last one was too.[132]

---

[125] *m. Shab.* 2:6. "*Ḥallah*" refers to the laws governing the separation and burning of a piece of dough before any baking of bread.
[126] *y. Shab.* 2:5, 5b; *b. Shab.* 31b-32a.
[127] These themes of course continue in later literature too. See *b. Ketub.* 61a on defining what contact is appropriate between a menstruant and her husband.
[128] *b. Nid.* 31b. The printed version prefaces this tradition with תניא, which is missing from MS Munich 95.
[129] *b. Shebu.* 18b. See below for a discussion of this source and eugenic rhetoric.
[130] *b. Shab.* 13a-b. This is attributed as tannaitic.
[131] *b. Me'il.* 17a-b.
[132] Alternatively, of course, the inclusion of the order to violate the laws of *niddah* in this list might have been included here precisely to give it more authority.

MODESTY

Sexual intercourse should occur, according to all the sources, in private. According to one *baraitha* in the Bavli, a man should not marry his daughter to a boor (*'am ha'areṣ*) because he will have sex with her "shamelessly."[133] The Yerushalmi contains a tradition that one rabbi had sex "by way of the sheets," a puzzling but assuredly chaste mode of intercourse.[134] Another story explains that the flogging of a man who had intercourse with his wife in a semi-public place was administered "because of the disgrace."[135] In one story in the Bavli, a disciple hides under the bed of his master to observe how he has intercourse. When discovered, his master rebukes him.[136] A second tradition associated with Rav assumes that if a man sleeps in a room with a husband and wife that they will not have intercourse.[137] Most of the remaining rhetoric that promotes sexual modesty centers on condemnation of sex in the light.

Sex in the Light

Sex in the light is frowned upon in non-tannaitic documents. According to the *Mishnah*, "The School of Shammai said, two testing strips are necessary for each act of intercourse, or intercourse [should take place] by light of candle. The School of Hillel said, two testing strips are sufficient for the whole night."[138] These "testing strips," pieces of cloth, were to be used by women before and after intercourse to check for blood, which would render her a menstruant with its concomitant restrictions. Alternatively, the School of Shammai suggests, sex can take

---

There is, however, nothing in this story or its context that would suggest this motivation.
[133]*b. Pes.* 49b (partial par. *b. Sanh.* 90b). The tradition is placed in a series of *baraithot* which condemn *'amey ha'areṣ*.
[134]*y. Yebam.* 1:1, 2b: דרך סדין. The context of the passage, discussing the right motives for intercourse with one's levirate widow, indicate the chaste nature of this sexual contact.
[135]*y. Ḥag.* 3:2, 78a. Curiously, the parallel in the Bavli explicitly interprets the flogging as necessary only due to the "exigency of the hour," i.e., the rabbis were stricter when the nation was under persecution (*b. Sanh.* 46a; *b. Yebam.* 90b).
[136]*b. Ber.* 62a. The disciple is Rav Kahana [BA 2], his master Rav [BA 1]. Rav tells him that his behavior is דלאו אורח ארעא, not polite. It is a fairly mild rebuke.
[137]*b. 'Erub.* 63b. Although not explicitly stated, the application of Micah 2:9 implies that the deprival of intercourse affects the woman. This is further support for the Babylonian view that a woman's desire is a reason to have intercourse with her. Another possible example of modesty during intercourse might be found at *b. Nid.* 70b-71a, which states that a man should "sanctify" himself during intercourse. Rashi understands this to mean that he should conduct himself modestly. See Adolph Büchler, *Types of Jewish-Palestinian Piety from 70 B.C.E. to 70 C.E.* (1922; rpt. New York: Ktav, 1968) 43 n. 3.
[138]*m. Nid.* 2:3.

place in the light. A source attributed to the tannaitic period, which appears in both the Yerushalmi and the Bavli, takes issue with this pronouncement:

> Our rabbis taught, even though they said one who has intercourse by light of candle is indecent (מגונה), the School of Shammai said, two testing strips are necessary for each act of intercourse, or intercourse [should take place] by light of candle. The School of Hillel said, two testing strips are sufficient for the whole night.[139]

This *baraitha* is not paralleled in any tannaitic document. The School of Shammai labels intercourse by light "indecent," a word that in rabbinic sources is also applied to such acts as reciting the *Shema* twice successively or talking obscenely.[140] The Talmudim, especially the Bavli, use other rhetoric too in its discussions on sex in the light. The most extensive deployment of these rhetorics occurs later in the same *sugya* cited above:

A. R. Yohanan [PA 3] said, it is forbidden for a man to have intercourse in the day.

B. Rav Huna[141] [BA 2] said, what scriptural basis is there [for this statement]? "Perish the day on which I was born, and the night it was announced, 'A male child has been conceived'," [Job 3:3]. The night was set given for conception, the day was not given for conception.

C. Reish Lakish [PA 3] said, it [A] is derived from this verse: "... he who is heedless of his ways will die," [Prov. 19:16].

D. How does Reish Lakish then interpret the verse used by R. Yohanan [as explained by R. Huna in (B)]?

E. He needs it according to the interpretation of Rabbi Haninah bar Pappa [PA 3] as Rabbi Haninah bar Pappa interpreted, that angel appointed over conception, his name is "Night," and he takes a drop [of semen] and brings it before the Holy One and says before Him, Master of the World, what will this drop be, strong or weak; wise or stupid; rich or poor? ... [here follows a digression on free-will].

F. And [how would] R. Yohanan [respond]? If it was so [E], Scripture would have written "she conceived a male child," so what is the meaning of "A male child is conceived?" That night [which in Job 3:3 is closer to "male child"] is given to conception, and day is not given to conception.

G. And how would R. Yohanan interpret the verse [used by] Reish Lakish? [He applies it] as is written in Ben Sira: Three things I hate

---
[139]*b. Nid.* 16b; *y. Nid.* 2:3, 50a.
[140]*Shema: b. Ber.* 33b (par. *b. Meg.* 25a); Talking obscenely: *b. Pes.* 3a.
[141]Attribution is missing in the printed text. This is following MS Munich 95.

and four I do not love. A prince who frequents the banquet-houses, and some say a prince who gossips; one who sets up a place in the heights of the town; one who holds his penis while urinating; and one who enters the house of his neighbor suddenly, and R. Yohanan said, even his own house.[142]

H. R. Shimon b. Yohai[143] said, four things the Holy One hates and I do not love. One who enters his house suddenly, and it is not necessary to say the house of his neighbor; one who holds his penis while urinating; one [who stands] naked before his bed; and one who has intercourse in front of anything living.

I. Rav Yehudah [BA 2] said to Shmuel, even in front of mice?

J. He said to him, moron [?] (שוטא), no, rather, for example, the house of so-and-so who had intercourse in front of their male and female slaves.

K. What biblical support is there? "[Then Abraham said to his servants,] You stay here with the ass...," [Gen. 22:5]. People similar to the ass.

L. Rabbah bar Rav Huna [BA 3] knocked bells on his curtained bed [during intercourse].

M. Abaye chased flies away [during intercourse].

N. Raba chased mosquitoes away [during intercourse] ...

[There follows a number of traditions that advise proper conduct in non-sexual matters].

O. Rav Hisda [BA 3] said, it is forbidden for a man to have intercourse in the day, as it is written, "Love your fellow as yourself," [Lev. 19:18]. How do you infer it? Abaye said, perhaps he will see in her some repulsive thing and she will become repulsive to him.

P. Rav Huna said, Israel is holy, and they do not have intercourse in the day.

Q. Raba said, in a darkened house it is permitted, and a scholar [can] darken with his cloak and have intercourse.

R. We learnt, "... or he has intercourse by light of candle."

S. I could say, she checks [for menstrual blood] by light of candle.

T. Come and hear: Although they say that one who has intercourse by light of candle is indecent,

U. I could say that one who checks his bed [for blood] by light of candle is indecent.

---

[142]Part of this tradition is found at Ben Sira 21:22-23. The rest is not found the extant version of Ben Sira.
[143]"b. Yohai" is missing in MS Munich 95.

V. Come and hear: Those of the house of Monbaz the king did three things that caused them to be remembered well. They had intercourse during the day; they checked their beds with clean wool; and they observed [rules of] purity and pollution with snow. It is taught, at any rate, "they had intercourse during the day!"

W. I could say, they checked their beds in the day. It also follows [logically]: if one thought "they had intercourse," [would it say,] "caused them to be remembered well?"

X. Yes, because sleep overwhelms [him] she is made repulsive before him.[144]

(A) is the only section in the *sugya* in which a Palestinian amora explicitly condemns intercourse by light. The reason (B), supplied by a Babylonian, is entirely exegetical: the night is for sex because the Bible says that the night is for sex. Reish Lakish's exegesis (C) might not necessarily have been connected to this issue. He apparently is interpreting the word "ways" in a sexual context, but in this verse there is no hint of a reference to "night." (D) through (H) explore how Reish Lakish and R. Yoḥanan would differ over their interpretation of relevant verses. (E) recounts a Babylonian tradition that links intercourse at night to divine intervention and conception. (G) interprets Prov. 19:16 much more literally than Reish Lakish, extending it to allude to the variety of ill-chosen paths mentioned by Ben Sira. (H) through (N) ([H] serves as a pivot for two sections) form a unit that condemns intercourse in front of any living creature as immodest. (J) and (K) attempt to limit this sweeping statement to slaves, allusion to whom is perceived in the word "asses" found in Gen. 22:5. Because "asses" are counted as the "anything living" referred to in (H), the prohibition is taken to apply to them rather than animals. (L) through (M) show the extreme modesty exhibited by three Babylonian rabbis, with Rabah bar Rav Huna even clanging bells before intercourse in order to scare away any living creatures (L).

With (O), the *sugya* returns to intercourse in the light. Both (O) and (P) are obscure. In spite of Abaye's interpretation in (O), the verse is never shown to refer to Rav Ḥisda's dictum. (P) fails to show explicitly why the claim of "holiness" preempts intercourse in the light. (Q) suggests that the issue is not that one cannot have intercourse in the "day," but rather, by light.[145] (R) responds to this objection. (R) through (W) twice propose and reject the proposition (accepted in the Yerushalmi)[146] that the *mishnah* refers to checking the bed for blood during the day. (X) (reverting to Abaye's answer given in [O]) responds

---

[144]b. Nid. 16b-17a.
[145]There are parallels to this part of the *sugya* at b. Shab. 86a and b. Ketub. 65b.
[146]y. Nid. 2:3, 50a.

to (W): sex during the day might be better than at night, because at night he is sleepy and does not want sex. Sex by light is thought to be dangerous to a man's sexual attraction of his wife. This argument seems to assume that a man normally does not see his wife naked, and that intercourse in the light would reveal "blemishes" normally hidden. An echo of this attitude might be found in another *sugya* that praises a Babylonian reported to have uncovered just "a handbreadth" of flesh during intercourse.[147] On the other hand, intercourse while fully clothed is condemned elsewhere in the Bavli as a Persian practice.[148]

Outside of the short comment cited above, the only other relevant statement in the Yerushalmi is attributed to Rabbi Ba and Rabbi Simon: a "modest" (צנוע) man does not have intercourse by candlelight.[149] Modesty is the only motive in the Yerushalmi for avoidance of intercourse in the light. It is interesting to note that although modesty plays an important role in the *sugya* cited above, it is never made directly into an argument for the disapproval of intercourse in the light.

There is a single eugenic argument in the Bavli for avoidance of intercourse by light:

A. "Do not stand in front of a candle naked" – as we have learnt, one who stands in front of a candle naked will become epileptic.

B. And one who has intercourse by candlelight[150] will have epileptic children.[151]

This is the only example of the Bavli attributing deformed children to intercourse by light.[152] As we shall see, however, discourse on most other areas of marital sexual activities does use the rhetoric of eugenics.

NON-RABBINIC PARALLELS

Contemporaneous pagan authors also discussed modestly during sex, often using similar rhetorics. Xenophon comments on the shameful barbarians who have no regard for privacy during sex.[153] Plutarch

---

[147] *b. Ned.* 20b.
[148] *b. Ketub.* 48a, attributed as תני רב יוסף, with a similar statement attributed to Rav Huna. See also *b. Ber.* 8b.
[149] *y. Pes.* 4:3, 31a. See also *t. Pes.* 3:17; *y. Pes.* 4:5, 31a; *b. Shab.* 53b; *b. Yoma* 8a. These passages express a fear that a man might see his wife in the light, become aroused, and have sex with her on the Day of Atonement.
[150] Some variants read "naked" in place of "by candlelight," but this is probably mistaken. See *D.S.* 4:348 n. ג.
[151] *b. Pes.* 112b.
[152] A *baraitha* on *b. Ned.* 20a, that asserts that looking at the female genitals will lead to blind children, might also be using a eugenic argument to advise, implicitly, intercourse in the dark. See below for a citation of this passage.
[153] Xenophon *Anab.* 5.4.34. See further Dover, *Greek Popular Morality* 206.

disagrees with Herodotus that a woman's shame leaves her with her underwear: the wise woman, he says, always keeps her sense of shame.[154] Even when the lights are out, Plutarch says, a woman should maintain her virtue and chastity.[155]

A more striking parallel can be found in Ovid. Advising men and women in the "Art of Love," Ovid suggests to women that they choose their sexual positions based on which pat of their body they want their man to see. That is, a woman who thinks that she has a blemish will choose a sexual position that will conceal it.[156] He follows this with advice not to let light in, for it will expose "too much" of the body, again risking discovery of blemishes.[157] Testimony to this same trope by both Ovid and Abaye probably testifies to its strength in antiquity.

RHETORICS OF EUGENICS

Passages such as *b. Pes.* 112b (cited above) are not common in the Bavli. More typically, passages that use eugenic rhetoric discuss several different activities, not all necessarily sexual.[158] Many of these passages present somewhat coherent and self-contained discourses on behavior leading to the conception and bearing of healthy, beautiful, righteous, and often male children.

At its most simple, the rabbinic rhetoric of eugenics relates sexual conduct, nature of the conceived child, and biology.

A. Rabbi Yitzḥak [PA 3] said in the name of R. Ami [PA 3], if the woman emits her seed first [climaxes?] she will bear a male. If the man emits his seed first she will bear a female, as it is written, "... When a woman who brings forth seed bears a male [she shall be unclean seven days] ...," [Lev. 12:2, modified].

B. Our rabbis taught: at first they would say that if the woman emits her seed first she would bear a male. If the man emits his seed first she would bear a female. And the Sages did not explain the matter until Rabbi Zadok came and explained, "Those were the sons whom Leah bore to Jacob in Paddan-aram, in addition to his daughter Dinah," [Gen. 46:15]. The males depend on the females, and the females on the males.

---

[154]Plutarch *Moralia* 139C. See also 140C.
[155]Ibid. 144E-F.
[156]Ovid *Ars* 3.769-92.
[157]Ibid. 807-8: "*Nec lucem in thalamos totis admitte fenestris/Aptius in vestro corpore multa latent.*"
[158]The eugenic character of many of these texts was noted by Reichler (Max Reichler, "Jewish Eugenics," in *Jewish Eugenics and Other Essays* [New York: Bloch, 1916]). Despite the apologetic nature of this essay (Reichler argues that Jews have "good blood" due to their knowledge of eugenics), it collects and categorizes most of the relevant passages.

C. "The descendants of Ulam – men of substance, who drew the bow, had many sons and grandsons," [1 Chr. 8:40]. Is man able to increase sons and grandsons? Rather, it is because they restrained themselves on the stomach so that their wives would emit seed first, so that their children would be male. And Scripture attributes to them as if they increased sons and the sons of sons.

D. And this is what Rav Katina [BA 2] said, I am able to make all my children male.

E. Raba said, all who want all his children to be male should have intercourse and then repeat.

F. Rabbi Yitzhak said in the name of R. Ami, a woman conceives only close to her period, as it is written, "Indeed I was born with iniquity, [with sin my mother conceived me]," [Ps. 51:3].

G. But R. Yohanan said, [she only conceives] close to her ritual immersion [after her period] ...[159]

(A) and (B) offer alternative verses whence to derive the same conclusion, that the timing of female "emission of seed" – presumably thought to be orgasm – determines the child's gender. According to R. Ami (A), this is derived from the identification of female emission of seed with male children in Lev. 12:2, while R. Zadok (B) derives it from the attribution of Jacob's sons to Leah and Leah's daughter to Jacob in Gen. 46:15. In (C), an anonymous exegesis of 1 Chr. 8:40 is used to demonstrate the effectiveness of the maxims presented in (A) and (B). (D), attributed to a Babylonian amora, has the same purpose, and (E), also attributed to a Babylonian amora, suggests a different technique for bearing male children. (F) and (G), attributed to Palestinians, then discuss the time a woman is most fertile.

Many of the themes struck in this *sugya* are found throughout the Bavli. The view that if a woman climaxes first she will bear a male child (A) is found elsewhere in the Bavli attributed only to Palestinian amoraim.[160] As (D) and (E) show, Babylonian amoraim also subscribed to the belief that one's sexual behavior could influence the gender of the child.[161] The concern over the influence of mode of intercourse and time of month on female and male fertility is also found throughout the Bavli.[162]

---

[159]*b. Nid.* 31a-b.
[160]*b. Ber.* 60a (R. Yitzhak b. Ami); *b. Nid.* 25b (R. Yitzhak b. Ami), 28a (R. Yitzhak), 71a (R. Hama b. R. Haninah [PA 3]).
[161]See also *b. 'Erub.* 100b.
[162]See *b. Ber.* 5a; *b. Sanh.* 38a; *b. Nid.* 38a-b; *b. Sot.* 27a; *b. Shebu.* 18b; *b. Nid.* 43a (par. *b. Hag.* 14b-15a). For a summary of medical knowledge about fertility recorded in talmudic literature, see S. Itzchaky, M. Yitzchaki, and S. Kotteck,

Two other passages in the Bavli go well beyond the physiological links evidenced in the passages cited above.

A. Our rabbis taught, "You shall put the Israelites on guard against their uncleanness ...," [Lev. 15:31]. Rabbi Yiashiah [PA 3] said, whence the prohibition to Jews that they should separate from their wives close to their periods.

B. How long? Raba said, an 'onah.

C. R. Yoḥanan [PA 2] said in the name of R. Shimon bar Yoḥai, anyone who does not separate from his wife close to her period, even if he has sons [virtuous] as the sons of Aaron, they will die, as it is written, "You shall put the Israelites on guard against their uncleanness ... and concerning her who is in menstrual infirmity ...," [Lev. 15:31, 33] and next to it, "[The Lord spoke to Moses] after the death [of the two sons of Aaron]," [Lev. 16:1].

D. R. Ḥiyya bar Abba [PA 3] said in the name of R. Yoḥanan, he who separates from his wife near her period will have male children, as it is written, "... for distinguishing between the clean and the unclean ...," [Lev. 11:47] and near it, "When a woman at childbirth bears a male ...," [Lev. 12:2].

E. R. Yehoshua ben Levi said, he will have sons fitting to teach, as it is written, "[You] must distinguish [between the sacred and the profane, and between the unclean and the clean] and you must teach [the Israelites all the laws] ...," [Lev. 10:10-11].

F. Rabbi Ḥiyya bar Abba said in the name of R. Yoḥanan, anyone who says [the prayer] havdalah ["separation"] over wine at the end of Shabbat will have male children, as it is written [Lev. 10:10, 11:47]. This is followed by a repetition of (E)].

G. Rabbi Benyamin bar Yapat [PA 3] said in the name of R. Eleazar, all who sanctify themselves at intercourse will have male children, as it is written, "[For I the Lord am your God:] you shall sanctify yourselves and be holy, [for I am holy]," [Lev. 11:44], and near it, "When a woman at childbirth bears a male ...," [Lev. 12:2].[163]

The *sugya* is composed almost entirely (with the exception of the digression at [B]) of statements attributed to Palestinian amoraim. Each statement is an exegesis that employs the hermeneutical technique of *śmikut*, using two Scriptural verses juxtaposed to each other to derive a rule. An assumption of fertile periods might underlie (A) through (E), though certainly part of the impetus behind this recommendation is the avoidance of the possibility of intercourse when the woman gets her period. (F) connects the birth of male children to a completely non-

---

"Fertility in Jewish Tradition (Ethno-Medical and Folkloric Aspects)," *Koroth* 9:1-2 (1985): 126-27.
[163] *b. Shebu.* 18b.

sexual activity. (G) derives a link between "sanctification" and male children, but nowhere is it made clear what exactly that means.[164]

A second extended eugenics passage in the Bavli marshals several of the rhetorics and assumptions discussed above. I have discussed this *sugya* in another context in Chapter 6, but present here a translation of the relevant sections.

> A. Rabbi Aḥa bîRabbi Yishayah says, anyone who gazes at women will eventually come to sin, and anyone who gazes at the heel of a woman will have unfit (מהוגנין) children.
>
> B. Rav Yosef [BA 3] said, and [even when] his wife is a menstruant.
>
> C. Rabbi Shimon ben Lakish [PA 3] said, when he teaches "heel," it is the defiled place opposite the heel.
>
> [There follows a *baraitha* about why a man should be modest].
>
> D. Rabbi Yoḥanan ben Dahavei said, the ministering angels taught me four things: Why are there lame [children]? Because they [= the parents] "overturned their table."[165] Why are there dumb [children]? Because they [= the parents] kissed that very place [i.e., oral sex]. Why are there deaf [children]? Because they [= the parents] talked during intercourse. Why are there blind [children]? Because they looked at that very place [i.e., the female genitals].
>
> E. An objection: They asked Ima Shalom, why are your children most beautiful? She said to them, he does not "talk" to be either in the beginning of the night or at the end, but in the middle of the night, and when he "talks" he reveals a handbreadth and covers a handbreadth, and he is similar to one whom a demon[166] forces. And I asked him, what is the reason? And he said to me, so that I will not think of another woman and his sons are found to come into *mamzerut*.
>
> F. This is not a problem. here (E) the words concern intercourse, and there (D) the words refer to other things.

---

[164]Rashi explains that it means "modesty." Visotzky, "Three Syriac Cruxes," *Journal of Jewish Studies* 42 (1991): 173-75 links the term "holy" and modesty in other rabbinic contexts. This nuanced use of the term "holy" also appears in Syriac sources. See Arthur Vööbus, *History of Asceticism in the Syrian Orient*, 2 vols (Louvain: Secrétariat du Corpus SCO, 1958) 1:104-6; Sebastian Brock, "Jewish Traditions in Syriac Sources," *Journal of Jewish Studies* 30 (1979): 215-18. None of these parallels, however, provide an exact meaning for the term in this context. There is a less complete parallel at *b. Nid.* 70b-71b. See also *b. Yebam.* 20a.
[165]"Inverted" intercourse of some type. See Chapter 6.
[166]MS Munich 95 reads, "prince."

G. Rabbi Yohanan [PA 3][167] says, that Sages say that the law is not as Rabbi Yohanan ben Dahavei, but that whatever a man desires to do with his wife, he can do ...

[There follows traditions that support (G)].

H. "[That shall be your fringe; look at it and recall all the commandments of the Lord and observe them,] so that you do not follow your heart [and eyes in your lustful urge]," [Num. 15:39]. From this R. Natan [PA 4][168] said, a man shall not drink out of one cup and think of another. Rabina [BA 3] said, this is only necessary when both are his wives.

I. "I will remove from you those who rebel and transgress against Me ...," [Ezek. 20:38]. Rabbi Levi [PA 3] said,[169] these [i.e., those who rebel and transgress], are of nine types, ASNT MShGAH[170] [the mnemonic for:] children of a female slave;[171] children of a raped woman;[172] children of a hated wife;[173] children of a man under a ban; children of an "exchange" [i.e., a man thought he was having intercourse with another woman]; children of strife; children of drunkenness; children of a woman whom one intends to divorce; children of confusion; children of an impudent woman.[174]

This *sugya* provides a virtual catalogue of things to avoid in order to bear "fit" children. According to a Palestinian amora (A), licentious thoughts of a woman, caused even by gazing at a woman's heel, can lead to "unfit" children.[175] (B) fortifies this stricture. According to Rav Yosef, "unfit" children will result even from gazing upon the heel of one's wife

---

[167]Following most manuscripts. See *Tal. Bab.* 4.1:172.
[168]Following most manuscripts.
[169]The attribution is missing in MS Munich 95.
[170]The mnemonic is missing in many manuscripts.
[171]This might also mean "fear," as the printed text reads. Manuscripts are more ambiguous. See *Tal. Bab.* 4.1:176, n. 87.
[172]As noted in Chapter 4, this refers to an unmarried woman who is raped, not to a wife.
[173]H.A. Szubin has suggested to me that this is not an emotive term, but is instead a technical term that in earlier times designated a woman who was repudiated and demoted in status, but not yet divorced. The institution would have fallen into disuse by the rabbinic period, but the nuance remains. If this explanation is correct, then this tradition refers to one who repudiated his wife – a practice frowned upon within the Bible itself – and then had a child by this woman. There is, however, little direct evidence for survival of this nuance into the rabbinic period.
[174]*b. Ned.* 20a-b.
[175]Compare *b. Ber.* 24a, in which a Palestinian, and several Babylonian, amoraim discuss female temptation without using eugenic rhetoric.

when she is a menstruant, and thus sexually prohibited to him.[176] The case evinced in (B) signifies the "safest" one for licentious thoughts, the one in which a man is least likely to act on his desires. On the other hand, the Palestinian amora in (C) limits (A) by saying that "heel" really refers to the female genitalia. By implication, he would allow gazing on a woman's heel.[177]

(D) articulates a eugenic approach that goes beyond the four specific cases cited there: the mode of intercourse directly influences the nature of the child conceived through that act. This principle of "measure for measure" is in fact explicitly stated in some later versions of this tradition.[178] (E) objects to a clause in (D), that those who talk during intercourse bear deaf children, by stating a tradition that beautiful children resulted from a union that did involve "talking." (F) reads (E) as using "talk" literally, though here also connoting intercourse.[179] According to (D) and (E), the content of the conversation differed, thus resolving the contradiction. Although (E) is ostensibly cited only for this clause, the eugenic assumptions embedded within it are evident. It advocates an extremely modest approach to marital intercourse. The suggestion that a man should have intercourse as if compelled has traditionally been read to refer to hurried intercourse. This reading, when combined with the recommendations for the exposure of only a small amount of flesh as well as intercourse in the middle of the night, seems correct. Sex was to take place quickly, with a minimal amount of lust, totally in the dark.[180] All of these strictures, the text says, are to avoid bringing his children into *mamzerut*, making them *mamzerim*. According to the halakhic texts we have surveyed in previous chapters, it

---

[176]This is apparently how the redactor understands this statement, although it probably was not originally connected to (A). See Halivni, *Sources and Traditions* 3:289.

[177]It is also possible that the "heel," עקב, (A) really does mean vulva. This use is attested in the redactorial layer of *b. Naz.* 51a. Then (C) would simply be clarifying (A).

[178]See *Tal. Bab.* 4.1:170, n. 146. See also *b. Ber.* 10a, another Babylonian tradition that condemns looking at "that place," i.e., the vagina.

[179](F) reads: לא קשיא. הא במילי דתשמיש הא במילי אחרנייתא. R. Nissim takes this to refer to the content of the conversation. It is also possible that (E) originally used the word "talk" only euphemistically for intercourse. In that case, (F) might have misunderstood the passage. MS Munich 95, however, reads בתשמיש in place of במילי דתשמיש, which better supports this alternative reading.

[180]R. Nissim reads the advice to have intercourse in the middle of the night as based in the assumption that "women go into the market and he will think of them."

is of course impossible for thoughts alone to create a *mamzer*.[181] Yet this text suggests that if a man were to consider another, presumably married, woman at time of intercourse with his wife, his children would be affected.

Another Palestinian amora in (H) again implies the assumptions made in (E). Although it never says why a man should not "drink out of one cup and think of another," the assumption appears to be again that it will influence the child. Interestingly, Ravina appears not to share this assumption. His limitation of this rule to a case of one man thinking of one wife while having intercourse with another appears based on interfamilial relations. That is, there is no *eugenic* reason that could stand behind his limitation.

(I) is another eugenic catalogue, but this time listing children of "semi-married" liaisons. All of the liaisons listed in (I) are either not between fully married partners or in some way involve incomplete consent, knowledge, or intention. Only children conceived with good intention and full knowledge in sanctioned unions are "fit." The strength of the eugenic assumption helps to explain the lack of connection to the verse cited, Ezek. 20:38. Those "who rebel and transgress" are simply identified as those who were conceived in less than ideal conditions. The manner of conception itself can turn children into "rebellers" and "transgressors."[182]

Most of the passages on eugenics, although found in the Bavli, are of Palestinian provenance. Only rarely do Babylonians contribute to this rhetoric, and when they do, the contribution is more exegetical. For example:

> A. Rabbah b. Rav Huna [BA 3][183] said, if a man marries a woman not fit for him, Scripture considers him as if he plowed the earth and strewed salt, as it is written, "The following are those who came up from Tel-melah, Telpharsha...," [Neh. 7:61].
>
> B. Raba said in the name of Rav, if a man marries a woman for the sake of money he will have children who are not fit, as it is written, "They have broken faith with the Lord, because they have begotten alien children," [Hos. 5:7] ... [there follows an attempt to explain how this verse applies]

---

[181]Note *t. Yebam.* 6:9, cited in Chapter 2. here the child of a levirate husband and his brother's ex-wife, if he makes love to her for the sake of her beauty or money, is "almost a *mamzer*."

[182]See also *b. Git.* 70a. An unparalleled *baraitha* asserts that intercourse performed standing, sitting, or with the woman in a superior position results in physically deformed children.

[183]Following MS Oxford Opp. 248.

C. Rabah said in the name of Rav Huna [BA 2],[184] if one marries a woman who is not fit for him, Elijah binds him and the Holy One whips him ...[185]

(A) is an extremely clever word-play, that depends on similarities between three words.[186] The same scriptural verse is used in the Yerushalmi in a far more conventional exegesis.[187] (B) is the only clause to use a eugenic argument, although it too is based on clever exegesis. Finally, in (C) the *sugya* reverts to a rhetoric of personal divine retribution, which is common in the Bavli's discussion of the violation of sexual laws and mores. In this *sugya*, whose focus was marriage rather than the generation of children, only Rav employs a eugenic rhetoric, and even then this rhetoric is primarily informed by exegesis.[188]

Palestinians and Babylonians

It is striking that these passages that discuss eugenics are composed almost solely from material attributed to Palestine. But it is even more striking that neither these statements, nor the eugenic ideas upon which they are based, are paralleled in rabbinic documents redacted in Palestine. These eugenic passages are unique to the Bavli. Several statements attributed to Babylonians show an interest in eugenics, especially in the conception of male children. Yet repeatedly we have seen Babylonians using eugenic rhetoric out of its "medical" context. These phenomena require some comment.

The idea that mode of intercourse influences the character of the conceived child squares firmly with contemporary currents in the Roman empire. Gynecological manuals in Roman times were virtually fertility manuals, written for men in order for them to produce fit heirs.[189] "The gynecological writings of Soranus and Rufus of Ephesus were manuals on fertilization written for husbands," Rousselle writes.[190] These

---

[184]Following MS Oxford Opp. 248.
[185]*b. Kid.* 70a.
[186]The verse reads: ‎וכל העולים מתל מלח תל חרש... "World," "salt," and "plot" all are derived from this simple statement.
[187]See *y. Kid.* 4:1,65b. In this exegesis, those who ascended from the various places enumerated in this scriptural passage are identified as representing the various groups said to have returned with Nehemiah to Palestine.
[188]See also *b. B. Meṣ.* 84b (*b. Ber.* 20a), and on this passage, Boyarin, *Carnal Israel* 197-225. Here, R. Yoḥanan is said to sit at the *mikvaot* so that when women look upon him after purifying themselves after their menstrual period, they will conceive children as beautiful as him. Although the story is about a Palestinian amora, it is told about him (rather than being attributed to him) and is in Babylonian Aramaic.
[189]See Rousselle, "Observations" 1092.
[190]Rousselle, *Porneia* 40.

manuals, of which Soranus's *Gynecology* is among the most complete, are handbooks for husbands, meant to help them to choose wives fit to bear their heirs, and then control and protect their fertility. These manuals advise not only when one should have intercourse, but in what state of mind:

> What is one to say concerning the fact that various states of the soul also produce certain changes in the mold of the fetus? For instance, some women, seeing monkeys during intercourse, have borne children resembling monkeys. The tyrant of the Cyprians who was misshapen, compelled his wife to look at beautiful statues during intercourse and became the father of well-shaped children ... Thus in order that the offspring may not be rendered misshapen, women must be sober during coitus because in drunkenness the soul becomes the victim of strange fantasies ...[191]

This passage, itself based on a common and ancient medical assumption, bears striking parallels to some of the talmudic passages cited above.[192] Concern over the states of mind of the spouses during sex has potentially serious consequences.[193] This assumption was so widespread that it can be found even in the *Gospel of Philip*. "Frequently, if a woman sleeps with her husband out of necessity, while her heart is with the adulterer with whom she usually has intercourse, the child she will bear is born resembling the adulterer."[194] Distinctions between adultery and thoughts of adultery are blurred.

These views, expressed by Roman doctors and apparently part of common folk-wisdom, are so similar to the Palestinian rabbinic attitudes found in the Babylonian Talmud that it is hard to avoid the conclusion that these rabbinic dicta were influenced by the Roman medical sources (or the assumptions that underlie them). Without question, this is to some degree true. Both Roman and Palestinian societies were concerned about procreation, especially in producing male heirs. As doctors and philosophers in Rome created manuals to aid in this goal, and the knowledge spread to the populace (or, perhaps, vice-versa), Palestinian rabbis most likely appropriated some of these ideas.[195] The timing of sexual intercourse, ideas about when a woman was most fertile, and the

---

[191] Soranus *Gyn.* 1.10.39 (trans. Temkin, 37-38).

[192] For other parallels see the sources cited by Temkin, ibid. 37-38, n. 71.

[193] On this, see also Hanson, "The Medical Writers' Woman" 315-16. Note that these passages refer to thoughts of the *wife*. See also Eduard Zeller, *Die Philosophie der Griechen in ihrer geschichtlichen Entwicklung* (Leipzig: Fues's Verlag, 1869-81) 1:399.

[194] *Gospel of Philip* 2.3.78 (trans. Isenberg in *Nag Hammadi Library* 156).

[195] Philosophy and medicine were closely related in antiquity. See Ludwig Edelstein, "The Relation of Ancient Philosophy to Medicine," in *Ancient Medicine* 349-66.

link between which partner climaxes first and the gender of the child conceived as a result, probably derive from these non-Jewish influences.

Yet closer scrutiny also reveals a very striking difference. According to the Roman and folk wisdom surveyed, the thoughts and actions of the *woman* impact on the character of the child.[196] In the rabbinic sources, however, it is the *man's* thoughts and actions that are determinative.

It is difficult to know what the primary goal of this shift was. On the one hand, men are given more responsibility for proper sexual behavior. Physically deformed children are proof of improper male sexual conduct. On the other hand, men are credited with greater control over reproduction. This schema lessens the perceived female contribution to the fetus. This dialectic, I believe, underscores the androcentric nature of these texts. Men choose their sex partners, and men determine the sexual activities and when they would occur. Men have intercourse modestly and with a sense of purpose, of *gravitas*, in order to conceive worthy heirs. Women thus become accessories to sex.

To summarize: Palestinian rabbis appropriated common "medical" assumptions. The assumptions that easily meshed with their values and concerns were assimilated virtually unchanged. Other assumptions, though, are modified to fit into a more pervasive rabbinic sexual rhetoric. Men control both the choice of sexual partners and the mode of intercourse, both the "who" and the "how." The consequences of bad judgment are stigmatized or deformed heirs.

It is more difficult to explain the absence of these ideas in Palestinian documents. Very few sources in Palestinian documents contain this eugenic trope.[197] Selective, and eclectic, source preservation is, as always, a possible explanation. A second, and what I think is the most likely possibility, is that the Bavli preserves this material because of its applicability. It is possible that the eugenic knowledge of Palestinians was a major source of Babylonian eugenic knowledge.[198] Contributions

---

[196]Aristoxenus, as expanded upon by Iamblichus, might provide an exception to this generalization. Even his advice that a man should eat right and not be drunk while impregnating his wife, however, appears rooted in assumptions of seriousness and *gravitas* rather than eugenics. See the fragment preserved in Johnnes Stobaeus 4.37.4 (*Anthologium*, ed. Johnnes Stobaeus, 5 vols. [Berlin: Weidmann, 1884] 4:878-79); Iamblichus, *De Vita Pythagorica* 210-211 (ed. Ludovicus Deubner [Teubneir, 1937], 114-15).
[197]See for example *Gen. Rab.* 26:4 (p. 254), which links the nature of children to a *woman's* thoughts during sex.
[198]There is no evidence that Babylonians connected practical eugenic knowledge to the story of Jacob and his husbandry with sheep (Gen. 30:37-39). In fact, the only citation of this story in rabbinic literature of this period occurs in *Gen. Rab.* 73:10 (p. 854). Even here the story is not used to learn anything about human eugenics.

to these discussions by Babylonian amoraim demonstrate a shallow understanding of the assumptions underlying the eugenic statements of Palestinian amoraim. The Bavli's redactor might have preserved these traditions due to a practical interest in the conception of fit, male children.[199]

The Yerushalmi's redactor, on the other hand, in contrast to both the redactor of the Bavli and the Palestinian amoraim, demonstrates no interest in eugenic statements. Apparently, despite the Yerushalmi's demonstrated preference in discussions on sexuality for rhetoric that deals with children and procreation, the conception of fit, male heirs, was not a concern. Possibly, but speculatively, the idea of influencing the nature of the child through eugenic practices was theologically offensive to the redactor of the Yerushalmi: God, not people, determine the character of the child. Alternatively, there may simply have been less concern with production of a heir at the time of the redaction of the Yerushalmi. Reproduction of the Jews, not production of individual heirs, was the goal of procreation. This explanation also, however, is highly speculative.[200]

Conclusions

There is never any question of disagreement in rabbinic literature that marital sex is the preferred sexual outlet. Yet this did not stop the rabbis from legislating and controlling marital sex, to an extent that went far beyond Augustus's comparatively mild inducements to procreate. Combining the roles of legislator, philosopher, and doctor, the rabbis articulated a series of regulations and opinions on marital sexuality. These opinions occasionally changed in the course of time, and certainly differed according to locale.

One aspect of this rhetoric in which Palestinians and Babylonians were somewhat similar was that of the sexual rights and obligations of spouses. Neither group accepted the well-defined tannaitic mandates for marital sex. For Palestinians, a set frequency for intercourse became a

---

[199] According to Edelstein: "For Egypt and Babylon were unfamiliar with medical dietetics. To be sure, even their rules of living, of avoiding taboos ... have been, although they formed part of divine worship. Nevertheless, there can be no doubt that to the people themselves they were religious rather than medical prescriptions," (Ludwig Edelstein, "The Distinctive Hellenism of Greek Medicine," in *Ancient Medicine* 380). If the source of these Palestinian dicta were "medical," their incorporation into the Bavli might have been based on either practical or "religious" criteria.

[200] It is also possible that this absence in the Yerushalmi is related to a global redactorial phenomenon. Richard Kalmin informs me that in several instances concepts attributed only to Palestinians in the Bavli are completely lacking from the Yerushalmi.

strategy, similar to the general Greek and Roman rhetoric of dietetics. That is, sexual conduct was linked with one's health and way of life. Hence, according to Palestinian amoraim, if one worked hard, one's sexual obligation was decreased. Both Palestinians and Babylonians "eroticized" the study of Torah, although the Babylonians were far more engaged in this rhetoric: study of Torah was in constant tension with, and occasionally superseded, marital duties. This too is much in line the changing role of philosophy and its relation to passion in the contemporary pagan world.[201] Palestinians, like their pagan and Christian neighbors, saw procreation as the value of sex. Babylonians were more accepting of the idea that happiness, or pleasure, was a legitimate and good reason to have sex. This is also based to some degree on differing conceptions of the nature of male and female desire.

The rabbinic discussion of sexual frequency indicates the two forces that are at work in other rhetoric on marital sexuality: conceptions of the nature of desire and outside influence. In some areas, such as modesty, Palestinians and Babylonians were in accord. Greek, Roman, and Persian societies also appear to put an emphasis on this. Yet in other areas, especially eugenics, the two communities diverge. Palestinians adopted select Greek and Roman "medical" explanations but by the time of the redactor of the Yerushalmi apparently had little interest in applying them. The redactor of the Bavli, however, thought these traditions – probably received as units – worth preserving.

Although the rabbinic discourse on "how" one is to have sanctioned sex differs in many ways from the discussion of with whom one is permitted to have sex, there are many points of contact between them. Differences between Palestinian and Babylonian rabbis; common sexual assumptions that underlie seemingly disparate discussions; and rhetorical strategies that seek to persuade people to follow a certain set of sexual practices, are all common to the subjects surveyed thus far. These topics are discussed in the final chapter.

---

[201] For the Jewish eroticization of Torah, see Boyarin, "Internal Oppositions": Gary Anderson, "The Expression of Joy as a Halakhic Problem in Rabbinic Sources," *Jewish Quarterly Review*, n.s., 80 (1990): 248-52. For non-Jewish parallels, see Musonius Rufus 14 ("Is Marriage a Handicap for the Pursuit of Philosophy?"); Rousselle, "Body Politics" 330.

8

Conclusions

In the beginning of this study I posed two primary clusters of problems: (1) identification of the kind of rhetorics employed by the rabbis in their discussion of sexuality; and (2) the assumptions that might underlie these rhetorics, and their relationship to real social institutions. Although I have primarily examined the rhetorics, these modes of persuasion are intrinsically linked to the assumptions of the societies in which they were employed. That is, to be effective a mode of persuasion must "speak" to its audience. After sketching what I perceive to be some of the sexual assumptions of the rabbis in late antiquity, I will summarize the rhetorical strategies themselves and offer some suggestions as to how they might have been intended to function. I conclude with brief discussions of some implications of this study outside the area of sexuality.

Assumptions: Toward a History of Rabbinic Sexuality

This study is not a history of the rabbinic constructions of sexuality. Rather, it is a preliminary step toward the investigation of these constructions. Throughout this study I have gathered, rhetorically classified, and analyzed the data upon which any such sexual history will be based. Out of the many issues that this study raises, I believe that the most obvious and crucial ones are (1) what sexual assumptions are reflected in these rhetorics, and (2) what is the relationship between these rabbinic assumptions and actual social practice. Here, in anticipation of a more complete study of these questions, I offer some preliminary thoughts.

Palestinian and Babylonian rabbis appear to have held differing assumptions about sexuality. Despite contact between these rabbinic communities, they were separated geographically, were dominated by different super-powers, and were part of vastly different cultural milieus.

Palestinian assumptions and attitudes are closely paralleled in contemporary, Western, non-Jewish sources. We know far less about Babylonia, and the non-Jewish milieu in which the Jewish (and especially rabbinic) community lived, and the interaction between this milieu and the Babylonian rabbis.

What, then, were these differing sexual assumptions? I believe that three broad primary areas of disagreement can be discerned in these sources: (1) gender expectations; (2) focus on the family and procreation; and (3) sexual desire.

THE NATURE OF SEX AND GENDER EXPECTATIONS

For Palestinians and Babylonians, "sex," that is, the act within a physical relationship that had legal consequences, was defined as the penetration of the penis into a woman's vagina or anus. For the majority of liaisons, this penetration need not result in male or female orgasm. To my knowledge, only a single source – Palestinian – might suggest that other forms of non-penetrating sexual contact could result in legal repercussions.

This seemingly trivial legal fact points toward a far more reaching assumption. Sex was about penetration. An active male penetrates a passive female. Remember that we are not here dealing with mere "biological" fact: it is as easy to conceptualize intercourse in terms of mutual pleasure, or even other dichotomies, such as "engulfer" and "engulfed," as it is to conceptualize sex as penetration.

The language of sex reinforces the impression generated by this legal observation.[1] The most common rabbinic expression for intercourse is בא עליה, a term which is not found in the Bible and implies this active/passive dichotomy. Other terms that linguistically should imply a more mutual sexual relationship, such as מזדקק or נתעלל, are almost always employed in rabbinic literature in negative contexts.

The "acting out" of this sexual assumption, and the different emphases put on it by Palestinian and Babylonian rabbis, can best be seen in rabbinic discussion of homoerotic intercourse.[2] I use the term "homoerotic" rather than "homosexual" intentionally: I have not found any evidence that rabbis in late antiquity, Palestinian or Babylonian, knew of such a creature as the "homosexual," a person defined on the basis of the gender of the primary object of sexual desire. Rabbinic

---

[1] This topic was briefly addressed by E.Z. Melamed, "Euphemisms." A fuller study is a desideratum.
[2] For a fuller discussion of this topic, see Michael L. Satlow, "'They Abused Him Like a Woman': Homoeroticism, Gender Blurring, and the Rabbis in Late Antiquity," *Journal of the History of Sexuality* 5 (1994): 1-25.

discussion of homoeroticism reveals the depth in which this sexual dichotomy of activity and passivity operated.

Female homoeroticism, as has been frequently noted, is relatively neglected in rabbinic sources. The reason for this can be traced to this active/passive conceptualization of sexuality. Because the rabbis, both Palestinian and Babylonian, did not think that female homoerotic activity involved any form of penetration, it was, in a sense, inconsequential. It was not truly "sex."

The rabbinic discourse on male homoeroticism was more complex. The Bible clearly prohibits homoerotic contact between males. Yet Palestinian sources develop an extensive rhetoric against the passive partner of male homoerotic intercourse. For a male to allow himself to be anally penetrated was tantamount to him surrendering that which made him distinctively male. By betraying his masculinity in this way he becomes "feminized." This complex, discursive web of masculinity/activity/penetration/power, vs. femininity/passivity/being penetrated/weakness, permeates the Palestinian sources. Palestinian rabbinic rhetoric both reflects the assumptions and speaks to the community in which the Palestinian rabbis worked. Babylonian rabbis, working in a different community, never develop this rhetoric: in a different community with different assumptions about gender roles and expectations, such a discourse would not have made sense.

Constructions of gender and gender expectations have wide implications for the future study of rabbinic sexuality. Ultimately, what, for Palestinian and Babylonian rabbis, does it mean to be "male" or "female?" What are the relationships between gender expectations and sexual activity? This study can only raise these questions.

MARITAL AND NON-MARITAL SEXUALITY

The second area of disagreement is focus on family and procreation. Palestinians nearly always frame their discussions about sex around marriage and procreation. Babylonians are much more sensitive to issues of non-marital and non-procreative sexuality. I will examine the assumptions of each group separately.

The Bible prohibits incest, that is, intercourse between certain kin. Palestinians rabbis consistently read these incest restrictions as prohibitions against *marriage* with prohibited kin. The danger, for Palestinian rabbis, is not that men and women who are related to each other will engage in occasional sexual liaisons, but that they will marry. The result of this reading is the creation of a rule of endogamous restrictions. Incest restrictions are important only insofar as they circumscribe a rule of exogamy.

Discussions of sex between non-Jews and Jews exhibit an identical focus. Palestinian sources focus the danger of intermarriage, almost to the exclusion of discussions on sex between Jews and non-Jews. For Palestinian rabbis, the marriage of a Jewish man to a Gentile woman was a fairly serious offense. The focus of the Palestinian rabbis on intermarriage is also reflected in their discussions of Samson and Solomon. It is Samson's marriage to a Philistine woman, not his whoring, that is worthy of particular opprobrium. Some rabbis even suggest, in an effort to exculpate Solomon's marriage to many foreign women, that he did not actually marry them, but just had intercourse with them. Even the Palestinian reading of the story of Pinḥas, who in the Bible is credited with murdering Zimri as he was having intercourse with a Midianite woman, does not emphasize that evil of intercourse between Jewish men and Gentile women.

Palestinian concern with marital and procreative intercourse founds the well-developed rhetoric that deals with the children of forbidden liaisons. Palestinian rabbis were more prone than Babylonian rabbis to label children of forbidden liaisons *mamzerim*, and more actively promoted the social stigma attached to such a status.

For Palestinians, the ideal expression of sex was in marriage. Female sexuality before marriage was strictly condemned; it was termed *bĕʿilat znut* by many Palestinian rabbis, a position apparently accepted by the redactor of the Yerushalmi. Female adultery too was condemned in the strongest of terms. Male non-marital sexuality was also condemned, although the rhetoric used, "measure for measure," was different.

For Palestinian rabbis, procreation was the primary goal of sex within marriage. Palestinian sources do not acknowledge that a woman gets pleasure from sex: her "right" to sex is best understood as a "right" to procreate. That is, although men are given the halakic obligation to procreate, women are given the right to bear children, which no doubt would have added to their own protection and status within their communities. Where Palestinians condemn non-procreative sex, though, the condemnation is based only upon the abhorrence of excess. Certain non-procreative liaisons represented the loss of self-restraint. It is important to note that Palestinians probably had no concept that "wasted semen" was worthy of condemnation. Anal intercourse, then, is never condemned in Palestinian sources, nor is contraception.

Palestinians also employed a rhetoric of eugenics to control *how* sex was to be conducted. Sanctioned sexual intercourse done modestly in a proper state of mind, produces beautiful children.

The Palestinian emphasis on marriage and procreation, like Palestinian anxiety about the pathic, is paralleled in contemporary non-Jewish sources. Both the residents of Hellenistic cities, *poleis*, and the

Romans, considered the production of worthy heirs and citizens to be a civic duty. Around the turn of the millennium, Augustus instituted special incentives for couples to have children, and special penalties for those sexual liaisons that interfered with the procreation of citizens. As in Palestinian rabbinic sources, female sexuality was tightly controlled. Philosophers, and Christians, too began to subject male sexuality to increasing control. The second and third centuries of this era saw a profusion of Greek so-called gynecological manuals, which were actually little more than fertility handbooks. In these manuals, men could discover how to identify a fertile spouse; how to keep her fertile; and how to have intercourse in order to produce the best male heirs. Together, these elements of pagan sexuality, which are also closely paralleled in Jewish-Hellenistic writings, the Dead Sea Scrolls, and contemporary and later Christian sources, form a striking backdrop by which we can illuminate the scattered and often cryptic rabbinic statements on sexuality.

Babylonian sources reflect a much more complex, and conflicted, set of sexual assumptions than do Palestinian sources.

Marriage was not the only focus of Babylonian commentary on forbidden sexual liaisons. Truer to the biblical text than the Palestinians, Babylonian rabbis, and I include in this term the redactor of the Bavli, forcefully condemned incestuous non-marital liaisons. In discussions on sex between Jews and Gentiles, Babylonians focus on the danger of sex between Jewish men and Gentile women. Interestingly, very few sources address the issue of sexual liaisons between Jewish women and Gentile men.

When, following a well-worn apologetic, modern scholars argue that Judaism had a "positive" view of sex, the majority of sources to which they invariably refer are Babylonian. Whether or not it is useful to ask if Babylonian rabbis charged sex as "positive" or "negative," it does appear that they were more accepting of non-marital and non-procreative expressions of sexuality than were Palestinians. Pre-marital sex, for example, was not condoned, but neither were women who engaged in it termed *zōnōt* or those who engaged in *bi'lat znut*. Adultery, of course, was also not condoned by Babylonians, but there are hints in Babylonian sources that adultery was a more complex institution than the legal sources allow. In Babylonian discourse on sexual activity we might be observing a clash between Jewish law and its interpretation and the credos of the honor-shame culture that most likely prevailed in Babylonia at that time. That is, the ideal coexists uneasily with the realities of a society in which honor is achieved by acquiring the love of another man's woman. Unfortunately, in this as in many other areas we know so little about Sassanian Babylonia that it is impossible to test this thesis against the prevailing milieu, as is possible in our discussion of Palestinian sexuality.

Not surprisingly, then, it is the Babylonians who posit a link between a woman's sexual desire and her conjugal rights. Men are obligated to attend sexually to their wives because it gives their wives pleasure. Procreation remains important in Babylonian discourse, but it does not occupy the place that it does in Palestinian discourse. Contraception, and non-procreative sexual positions, remain permitted by the Babylonian rabbis, but this is brought into conflict with the growing unease among later amoraim and the redactor of the Bavli with the ejaculation of semen in no-procreative activities. The Bavli itself never resolves this tension.

SEXUAL DESIRE

For the rabbis, both Palestinian and Babylonian, Jewish piety was linked to self-control. At its (relatively rare) extreme, piety could manifest itself as asceticism. More commonly, however, self-control was exercised through adherence to the law, and above all, through moderation even in legally permitted activities. Self-control was seen as a defining issue: Gentiles are not Jews because, above all, they do not have self-control, do not set limits for their own behavior. Other Gentile activities, such as idolatry, are seen as manifestations of this state.

Thus, sexuality and sexual desire is part of a much broader discourse. For Palestinians especially, sexual excess was linked to decadence, femininity, and Gentiles. Desire was to be kept under control at all costs, but never did sexual continence become a viable option, or even an issue of apparent importance to the rabbis. Palestinians were also not very optimistic about a man's ability to control his sexual urge: women were often to blame for male surrender to his sexual desires. On the other hand, we see an assumption that women could exercise some degree of sexual control. This assumption is parallel to those present in Rome and among Christians.

Rabbinic Rhetorics of Sexuality

Although I have organized this study around topics, the rhetorics themselves can be discussed. The "rhetorics" that I have labelled throughout this study can roughly be divided into two types, legal and non-legal. The legal rhetorics function, I believe, within the legal community, presenting the modes in which legal texts *qua* legal texts are to be discussed and analyzed. They reflect prevailing assumptions, but the audience(s) to which they are addressed and that they are intended to persuade is (are) narrow. Non-legal rhetorics appear to be intended for a wider audience.

LEGAL RHETORICS

The three legal rhetorics are "definition," "categorization," and "liability." Sexual transgressions are defined (exactly *who* is sexually prohibited and *what* sexual activity is prohibited between them) and discussed by means of various categories, which are themselves used either as principles for organization or as paradigms for derivation. "Liability" is concerned with detailing the factors that influence the decision of whether or not one is to be considered "liable" (חייב) for a transgression.

The vast bulk of discussion on identification of the sexually prohibited partners centers on the *'arayot*, those sexual partners prohibited to a man and enumerated in Lev. 18. Lev. 18 and Lev. 20 prohibit incest, adultery, and male homoeroticism. These form the major topics that attract rhetorics of definition: which kinswomen are prohibited; what constitutes a valid marriage, thus defining "your neighbor's wife;" who exactly is a man (e.g., the *'androgynos*). Rhetorics of definition on two topics that have no scriptural antecedents, female homoeroticism and pre-marital sex, ironically underscore the importance of Scripture in defining prohibited sexual liaisons and activities. Female homoeroticism is mentioned by Palestinian sources in a context that suggests that it is prohibited by Scripture. Pre-marital intercourse for women is given the term (by Palestinian rabbis) *bi'ilat znut*, a legal category parallel to, and perhaps derived from, the Roman category of *stuprum*. The conceptual framework might derive from Hellenistic and Roman models, but the language suggests a (non-existent) scriptural basis.

The ways in which justification for these definitions were extended does vary by locale.[3] Palestinian documents (especially the *Sifra*) and dicta (even those found in the Bavli attributed to Palestinians) all prefer to employ arguments from Scripture. Babylonian amoraim and the redactor of the Bavli nearly always attempt to justify their definitions logically. Palestinians also use an argument from appearances to extend prohibitions: an otherwise permitted liaison can be forbidden because it might appear to others as forbidden. Babylonians use sociological factors in order to define prohibited sexual partners: what people actually do, especially in patterns of family visitation, can lead to additional prohibitions.

---

[3] I do not deal here with the entire question of what legal arguments are considered "good" and why, which is just beginning to receive scholarly attention. The question of why rabbis employ the legal justifications and hermeneutics that they do is an intriguing one.

The rhetoric of categorization also demonstrates a strong reliance upon Scripture. Although it is the Talmudim that realize the argumentative potential of these categories, synthesizing, comparing, and contrasting them in sometimes seemingly endless permutations, the actual categories that they use are almost always tannaitically determined. That is, the Talmudim, when they use a rhetoric of categorization, use only those categories that are attested in tannaitic sources. These, in turn, are usually scripturally derived. For example, rabbinic discussions that categorize non-marital sex use the categories of the status of the woman at the time of the offense (i.e., married or betrothed); age of the woman at time of the offense; under whose authority the woman was under at the time of the offense; the priest's daughter; and rape and seduction. Each one of these "categories" is mentioned in Scripture. In tannaitic literature, they are used as organizational principles. The Talmudim use these – and only these – categories as part of their argumentative discussions on this topic. As these categories are biblically determined, it should come as no surprise that this rhetoric is used only for biblically prohibited liaisons. Because intercourse between Jews and Gentiles, for example, is not biblically prohibited, a rhetoric of categorization is not employed in its discussion.

The most common "category" used in these sources is that of punishment. Scripture usually declares a punishment (sometimes a general one, such as death, sometimes more specific, such as death by burning) for violation of its sexual regulations. These punishments, mentioned by Scripture in an almost *ad hoc* way, become in the tannaitic literature ways by which these liaisons can be organized, compared, and occasionally derived. By the tannaitic period, and all the more so during later times, the Jews had lost their authority to administer the death penalty.[4] Biblically mandated death penalties thus became academic categories, to be used for organization and exegesis rather than application.

Like "categorization," the rabbinic rhetorics of liability are tannaitically determined; any differences between tannaitic and later discussions are quantitative rather than qualitative. Similarly, I could discern no significant differences between the way Palestinian and Babylonian rabbis employed this rhetoric. The factors discussed in this rhetoric are: determination of the transgression when a single sex act

---

[4]This is not to say that occasionally permission was not given to Jewish leaders to put someone to death, but these cases appear to be exceptional. See Origin *Ep. ad Africanus* 14 (*PG* 11:41); *b. Git.* 67b; *b. B. Qam.* 59a-b. See further Isaiah M. Gafni, *The Jews of Babylonia in the Talmudic Era* (Jerusalem: Zalman Shazar Center for Jewish History, 1990) 99-100 (Hebrew).

violates more than one law (e.g., intercourse with one's mother is both incest and adultery); intention of the participants; and mitigating factors such as age and wakefulness (another type of intention).

These issues are not biblically determined (rabbinic efforts to derive biblical support for them notwithstanding). But they do find close parallels in Roman legal writings. The determination of liability was a relevant issue to the Jews of this period, despite their inability to bring expiatory sacrifices. These issues of liability could only serve to lessen guilt. In the Bible, factors such as age and intention have no bearing on one's liability. According to the rabbis, these factors can erase one's liability.[5] It may be that in seeking to exculpate those whom the rabbis felt should not be held liable for such transgressions, the tannaim turned to Roman legal reasoning (whether directly or indirectly). Later rabbis accepted these issue without further elaborating on them.

Rhetorics of definition, categorization, and liability comprise the rabbinic legal discourse. The rhetorics of definition and liability comprise the practical, applied side of legal discussions on sexual transgression. The rhetoric of categorization is more academic and theoretical, especially as employed n the Talmudim. Scholars have often used the categories legal/non-legal (*halakic/aggadic*) in study of rabbinic literature. This dichotomy is imprecise, and in many cases misleading. Legal ramifications in areas of sexuality are generated from three distinct forms of rhetoric. Further study in other topics is necessary to confirm whether what is now known as "legal," or *halakic*, writings can really be classified more precisely as the rhetorics of definition, categorization, and liability.

NON-LEGAL RHETORICS

When promoting their sexual mores, what arguments did different rabbinic groups think would be persuasive? I have identified seven kinds of non-legal rhetorical strategies that, I believe, were thought (by some) to be persuasive: progeny; association; other; threat of divine retribution; pollution; apologetics; and punishment. The assumptions reflected in one other non-legal rhetoric, "temptation," were discussed above.

Progeny: This rhetoric concerns the children of forbidden (or disapproved) liaisons. The bulk of this rhetoric concerns the legal status of these children: are they *mamzerim;* forbidden (if a woman) to marry a priest; or fully fit to marry any other fit Jew? As was demonstrated repeatedly throughout the course of this study, this rhetoric was most

---

[5]See Howard Eilberg-Schwartz, *The Human Willin Judaism: The Mishnah's Philosophy of Intention* (Atlanta: Scholars Press, 1986).

often employed by Palestinians. Palestinians were also quicker than Babylonians to legally penalize the children of such forbidden liaisons. This rhetoric has close parallels to both Greek and Roman legal rhetorics that deal with legally disqualified children of non-sanctioned sexual liaisons.

Palestinian preoccupation with the rhetoric of children also manifests itself in other, non-legal arenas. Children of intercourse between Jewish men and Gentile women are called in a tannaitic source and in the Targumim enemies of God. The social stigma borne by the *mamzer* is emphasized in Palestinian sources. Palestinian sources, for the most part in the Bavli, assume a link between proper sexual conduct and the physical stature of the children produced thereby.

The Palestinian partiality to this rhetoric is probably related to the concentration by Palestinian rabbis on marriage and procreation. To a society in which procreation was the goal of sex, arguments about the status of the progeny produced thereby are bound to carry some weight. In Babylonia, on the other hand, where the understanding of the goals of sexuality were more nuanced, this rhetorical strategy was less frequently used.

The rhetorics of *association* and the *other* are frequently linked. The most common forms that "association" take are linguistic grouping and the vice-catalogue. The point of such associations is to "smear" the sexual activity by associating it with a complex of other forbidden activities. Association creates a multi-layered intertextual web, by which the understanding of transgressions is informed by other, seemingly unrelated transgressions. Single terms, such as ʿ*arayot* and *znut*, cover a wide range of forbidden or non-sanctioned sexual behavior, effectively associating all the members of the group. These groupings are tannaitically determined.

The most common vice-catalogue in rabbinic literature is the group of three "mortal sins," idolatry, murder and ʿ*arayot*. The formation of this group was probably quite early, as traces of it can be seen in Jewish Hellenistic and early Christian writings. By the rabbinic period the force of the association was not to devalue any of these individual acts by linking them to other "heinous" acts. Rather, the catalogue was utilized as a whole, a trope, whose force was to designate absolute evil. Thus, vice-catalogues other than this group of "mortal sins" that include a sexual reference can be more informative. Associations between sex, theft, and shame for example might reveal underlying sexual assumptions.

One of the primary applications of vice-catalogues and other associations that involve sexual references is identification of the activity to the sectarian or non-Jew. The attribution of these activities to the "proximate other" helps to define the group itself by implicitly stating what it is not.

The identification of Gentiles with prohibited sexual liaisons is mainly confined to Palestinian sources, and among these sources, the *Tosefta* and tannaitic midrashim (especially the *Sifra*) are most vocal. These sources ascribe incest, adultery, and male (and to a lesser degree female) homoeroticism to Gentiles. By contrast, Babylonian sources associate incest with *Jewish sectarians*, and make no identification of male homoerotic intercourse with Gentiles.

Another more complex association that appears in Palestinian and Babylonian sources is a linkage between Gentiles, promiscuity, loss of self-control, and idolatry. Palestinian and Babylonian rabbis in all documents appear concerned with maintenance of male self-control and discipline. By ascribing laxity to Gentiles, the rabbis are warning their audience: loss of self-control will begin a slide that will lead to promiscuity and idolatry, just like the Gentiles! I suggested that the focus of this rhetoric might be slightly different in Palestinian and Babylonian sources, with the former emphasizing the promiscuity of Gentile women, and the latter the promiscuity of Gentile men.

Evaluation of this data depends on what exactly was being "othered" with this rhetoric, the activity or the group to whom it was ascribed. Did, for example, the tannaitic midrashim seek to condemn certain sexual practices and liaisons by identifying them with the "other"? Or, as was more likely, were these sources attempting to distance Jews from Gentiles using a variety of identifying characteristics? If the latter is true, then the data presented here can only be evaluated along with "othering" statements concerning a range of different prohibited activities. In either case, however, it is noteworthy that it is the Palestinians who make prohibited sex a definitional issue. Whether this is due to simple rhetorical borrowing from Roman, Hellenistic, and Christian writers, all of whom commonly slandered carefully targeted groups with sexual misbehavior, or whether it reflects a heightened perception of danger of social proximity to Gentiles, remains an open question.[6]

---

[6]See Jonathan Z. Smith, "What a Difference a Name Makes," in *"To See Ourselves as Others See Us:" Christians, Jews, "Others" in Late Antiquity*, ed. Jacob Neusner and Ernest S. Frerichs (Chico: Scholars Press, 1985) 3-48; François Hartog, *The Mirror of Herodotus: The Representation of the Other in the Writing of History*, trans. Janet Lloyd (Berkeley and Los Angeles: University of California Press, 1988) 226; S.C. Humphreys, *The Family, Women and Death: Comparative Studies*, 2d ed. (Ann Arbor: University of Michigan Press, 1993) 51-54; Arnaldo Momigliano, *Alien Wisdom: The Limits of Hellenization* (Cambridge and New York: Cambridge University Press, 1975).

The rhetoric of *divine punishment*, in which the offender of a sexual prohibition is threatened with divine retribution, is used only infrequently. It occurs in discussions of incest, sex between Jews and Gentiles, non-marital sex, and male homoeroticism, but the number of sources for each is small. One curious consistency among these sources is that Palestinian sources most often employ a rhetoric of *communal* retribution, while Babylonian rabbis more often employ a rhetoric of *personal* retribution. Sexual transgressions, for the Palestinians, seem to endanger the entire community. Babylonian rabbis use this rhetoric to threaten the offender himself (it is always directed at men) with divine punishment. It is possible that this again is related to the Palestinian emphasis on family and procreation, institutions that were commonly seen in antiquity as inextricably linked to the society at large. Communal punishment followed not from the defilement of the Land of Israel, as Scripture says, but from what may have been seen as an offense against the Jewish people. The effect of this Palestinian rhetoric might have been to encourage neighbors to keep close watch on each other, in order to prevent communal harm. Babylonian rhetoric, on the other hand, would merely have frightened the individual.

The rhetoric of *pollution* is rarely used by the rabbis to discourage certain sexual liaisons or practices. Despite, for example, a certain vehemence in the Bavli's opposition to wasted semen not once does it employ an argument that refers to "self-pollution." The only references to pollution occur in discussions of intercourse between Gentiles and Jews and of non-marital sexual activity, and in both these cases the rhetoric plays only a very minor role.

The rhetoric of *apologetics*, used to exculpate biblical characters who appear to have violated rabbinic sexual restrictions, is used only in the discussions on incest and sex between Jews and Gentiles. In the former, Babylonians go to further extremes than Palestinians in their attempt to forgive biblical characters of "seeming" violations of the incest restrictions. In the case of sex between Jewish men and Gentile women the relevant sources, the vast majority of them Palestinian, exaggerate the seriousness of the transgression rather than apologize for it. In the case of sex between Jewish women and Gentile men, only Esther is discussed, and her relationship with the Gentile king is not seen as a threat by the rabbis.

In contrast to the rhetoric of categorization, which uses the biblically mandated punishments for academic exercises, the rhetoric that I have called *punishment* threatens concrete retribution for sexual transgression. In some cases, especially when dealing with the refusal of one spouse to fulfill their sexual obligations to the other, this punishment is economic, presumably enforceable by the court. Occasionally flogging is threatened. More common, however, is a non-enforceable, rhetorical threat. That is, a rhetoric whose function appears to be to threaten, although it sometimes leaves open what exactly is being threatened. Hence a text might objectify and treat with harsh language a woman who violates rabbinically sanctioned sexual mores; or another text will threaten men with ostracism or imply that they leave themselves open to vigilante action.

The rhetorics surveyed here account for the rabbinic discussions on "who" sexual prohibitions. The "how" prohibitions, discussed in Chapters 6 and 7, are not as neatly classified. These discussions are diverse; it would do violence to these discussions to attempt to dissect and classify their rhetoric as was possible in Chapters 2 to 5. There is little or no precision in these discussions, with many key terms, such as descriptions of non-procreative sexual activities, left obscure. While traces of many of the rhetorics surveyed above are integrated into these discussions (association, "other," divine retribution, punishment), they are better suited to topical study. This in itself is significant. There appears to be a rhetorical integrity in discussions of "who" prohibitions, most of which derive from Scripture.[7] The "how" discussions, which do not derive from Scripture, are most focused on topics, less rhetorically stereotyped. In discussing "how" restrictions the rabbis were to some degree extending their authority into the bedroom, totally obfuscating the barriers between public and private (there are no pre-rabbinic antecedents for Jewish legislation on how sexual activities were to be performed).[8] Perhaps there is a relationship between this rabbinic venture and the rhetoric they employ. Not secure with their new, self-conferred (we assume) authority, they use different rhetorical structures, distinct from those used to discuss sexual liaisons which are discussed in Scripture.

Implications for Future Research

This study has implications beyond the history of rabbinic sexuality. It also raises several issues that require future study.

---

[7] There are also sociological reasons behind such strictures: by prohibiting sex between those who are maritally prohibited to each other, there is less of a chance that love between them will destabilize highly instituted and regulated marital strategies. See William J. Goode, "The Theoretical Importance of Love," *American Sociological Review* 24 (195): 38-47.
[8] The closest that one finds to such restrictions in pre-rabbinic sources are the restrictions dealing with sex during menstruation.

IMPLICATIONS FOR THE STUDY OF RABBINIC LITERATURE

As mentioned in the Introduction, Jacob Neusner has argued extensively that rabbinic documents must be considered as data only in their final forms. That is, the Bavli, for example, speaks with a single "voice." The implication of this position is that statements within these documents that are attributed to earlier sources cannot be used as historical evidence for the period or place to which they are ascribed. While Neusner acknowledges that rabbinic documents are comprised of sources, and even offers (for the Bavli) one criterion by which these sources can be differentiated from the "homogeneous" whole of the document, his approach precludes historical investigation that relies upon attributions. That is, he holds that the method employed here, of assembling rabbinic dicta on a given topic and depending on the attributions attached to those dicta, is, a priori, not valid.[9]

Although Neusner and others have demonstrated the heavy hand of the editor of these rabbinic documents, no test has yet been derived by which the veracity, or lack of veracity, of attributed sources in the Talmudim can be verified.[10] If the "redactors" of each of these documents comprised a single, like-minded group which consistently changed those sources that did not agree with their own "agenda," then we should expect that these documents would exhibit evidence of consistency and uniformity about issues of importance to the redactors. Each document might preserve disagreements (in line, even, with its overall redactorial "strategy") but all statements within a document should share the same "language." If they do not, this constitutes

---

[9]For summary of his ongoing work on the Bavli, see Jacob Neusner, *The Principal Parts of the Bavli's Discourse: A Preliminary Taxonomy* (Atlanta: Scholars Press, 1992).
[10]See William Scott Green, "What's in a Name? – The Problematic of Rabbinic 'Biography'," in *Approaches to Ancient Judaism: Theory and Practice*, ed. William Scott Green (Missoula: Scholars Press, 1978) 77-96; Louis Jacobs, "How Much of the Babylonian Talmud is Pseudepigraphic?" *Journal of Jewish Studies* 28 (1977): 45-59; David Kraemer, "On the Reliability of Attributions in the Babylonian Talmud," *Hebrew Union College Annual* 60 (1989): 175-90; Sacha Stern, "Attribution and Authorship in the Babylonian Talmud" *Journal of Jewish Studies* 45 (1994): 28-51.

The same can be said, of course, for the tannaitic documents, which are even more heavily stylized. Throughout this study I have treated the tannaitic sources as a unity. I have done this partly for methodological reasons, and partly because, due to the scarcity of the data, even if the attributed statements in the tannaitic documents were "true," it would add little to a study of the rabbinic rhetorics of sexuality.

evidence that despite extensive and stylized editing, the sources that comprise the documents were left more or less intact.[11]

Throughout this study I have tried to present my data as it emerges from each document, thus giving organizational primacy to the claims that (1) each tannaitic document maintains its own "program," or agenda, and (2) that attributions within the Talmudim that cannot be otherwise verified cannot be trusted. This study, limited only to those dicta that directly discuss sexuality, offers no significant contribution to the first claim: there is too little data, and those relevant dicta that do exist all appear to share assumptions about sexuality. The surprise came when dealing with the second claim. The statements on sexuality in the Bavli, as well as the Yerushalmi, do not all appear to share the same assumptions, that is, they do not all "speak the same language." Rather, the line of division is geographical rather than documentary. Statements attributed to Palestinians often display similar assumptions about sexuality, as do those statements attributed to Babylonians. Similarly, and expectedly, the contributions of the redactors are fairly uniform. Often, for example, the Bavli will cite sources attributed to tannaim or to Palestinian amoraim, the assumptions of which the redactor appears not to understand. Far less frequently, although occasionally, the Yerushalmi cites a statement attributed to a Babylonian amora, which again often stands out both for its incongruity with the statements attributed to Palestinian amoraim and for its similarity to statements attributed to Babylonians cited in the Bavli.

Although the redactors of both the Yerushalmi and the Bavli are heavily involved in shaping and stylizing the form of their products, they do not, for the most part, appear to have modified the substantive content of the sources reviewed here. Attributed statements dealing with sexuality apparently genuinely originate in the locale to which they are attributed. This data does not, however, support (or contradict) claims for *chronological* veracity of attributions.[12]

---

[11]Why this might have been is beyond the scope of this discussion. Perhaps the redactors did not notice these discrepancies; the redactors noticed but did not care, because the discrepancies were in an area that was not central to their concerns; or the redactors did not, in fact, constitute a single homogeneous group.

[12]For attempts to verify that attributed statements in the Bavli are chronologically trustworthy, see, David C. Kraemer, *Stylistic Characteristics of Amoraic Literature* (Ann Arbor: University Microfilms, 1984).

Note that the manuscript evidence too supports this geographical distinction. Rarely do manuscript variants attribute statements that display Palestinian assumptions to Babylonians or vice-versa. My conclusion here coincides with those of other scholars. See my brief review of this issue in Chapter 1.

Two caveats to this conclusion are necessary. First, the methodology by which this conclusion was reached is not an entirely objective one. It involves first collecting all statements within a rabbinic corpus that deal with a particular topic, and then determining whether these statements share more in common with (1) other statements on this topic attributed to chronologically or geographically similar personages or with (2) statements on this same topic found in the same document. This determination is far from certain or objective. Throughout this study I have sought to apply this method and to demonstrate in each case its merit. Ultimately, however, the usefulness of this methodology must be confirmed through its application to other topics. Can similar results be obtained through systematic study of the rabbinic dicta, for example, on topics such as "power" or "knowledge?" Again, it is important to emphasize that it is unity of underlying assumptions, not general agreement or disagreement within the same "language," that should be the guide for such a study. That is, sources working within the same set of assumptions can agree or disagree on specific propositions. In this study I have tried to unearth cases where similar sets of assumptions were not shared.

Second, I do not mean to obscure the often very real differences between rabbinic documents. The *Sifra* for example seems to use a rhetoric of the "other" more frequently than other documents; the Bavli has a unique polemic against wasted semen. Both of these polemics occur in the redactorial layer, and the Bavli's polemic even results in the (verifiable) modification of at least one tannaitic source. The documents *are* edited extensively, and the redactors do often have points to make. Yet despite these differing agendas, and the often violent twisting of sources in order to fit those agendas, the Talmudim (at least) do for the most part maintain the integrity of the attribution of sources. Fraade has argued that tannaitic documents were neither "compilations" nor "scrapbooks," but instead formed a hybrid genre.[13] I would make a similar argument for the Talmudim.

HELLENISM AND THE RABBIS

According to Fergus Millar, no part of the Near East was free from Hellenistic and Roman influence, and the extent of that influence was vast:

> The social and cultural history of the Near East in this period is no simple matter of a conflict between 'Classical' and "Oriental' ... Whatever metaphor we use for the interplay of cultures in this

---

[13]Steven D. Fraade, "Interpreting Midrash 1: Midrash and the History of Judaism," *Prooftexts* 7 (1987): 179-94.

region, every aspect of society and culture was influenced both by Greek civilisation and by the progressive extension of Roman rule.[14]

A lively literature has developed around the extent to which "the rabbis" were influenced by Hellenistic and Roman practices.[15] This study has shown that the influence of Hellenism and the Romans on Palestinian rabbis went far beyond the occasional practice, linguistic oddity, or legal institution: many of the assumptions that generated Palestinian rabbinic rhetoric on sexuality almost certainly derived from those of the Greeks and Romans. Although Palestinian rabbinic rulings on sexuality occasionally differ from their Greek and Roman equivalents, all are based upon a common language, shared thought-categories and assumptions. Greeks, Romans, and Palestinian Jews, for example, all shared many of the same assumptions about homoeroticism, although each culture enacted different forms of legislation dealing with it. To talk of particular points of "Hellenistic influence" thus largely skirts around the issue. Whether or not particular customs or practices are consciously adopted or rejected by the Palestinian rabbis, their fundamental way of thinking at least about sexuality is virtually identical to those whom they label the "other."

Conversely, the Babylonian rabbis are at times so alienated from these sets of assumptions that they appear not to grasp fully the import of the dicta transmitted to them from Palestine. Babylonian rabbis were apparently working with quite different assumptions about sexuality. This study suggests that the difference in sexual assumptions between Babylonian and Palestinian rabbis can in large measure be traced to their broader milieus.

RHETORIC AND REALITY

Whence arose these differences between Palestinians and Babylonians? Were these assumptions shared by the Jewish community

---

[14]Fergus Millar, *The Roman Near East 31 B.C. – A.D. 337* (Cambridge: Harvard University Press, 1993) 235. See also G.W. Bowersock, *Hellenism in Late Antiquity* (Ann Arbor: University of Michigan Press, 1990).
[15]For examples see S. Lieberman, *Greek in Jewish Palestine*, and, *Hellenism in Jewish Palestine* (New York: Jewish Theological Seminary of America, 1950); David Daube, "Rabbinic Methods of Interpretation and Hellenistic Rhetoric," *Hebrew Union College Annual* 22 (1949): 249-64; Henry A. Fischel, ed., *Essays in Greco-Roman and Related Talmudic Literature* (New York: Ktav, 1977); B. Cohen, *Jewish and Roman Law*. The state of the field is summarized in Sandra R. Shimoff, "Hellenization Among the Rabbis: Some Evidence from Early Aggadot Concerning David and Solomon," *Journal for the Study of Judaism* 18 (1987): 168-73. See also, Adam Kamesar, "The Narrative Aggada as Seen from the Graeco-Latin Perspective," *Journal of Jewish Studies* 45 (1994): 52-70.

that the rabbis purported to serve? Did the social conditions advocated in these sources ever exist? How were institutions such as honor and shame deployed in the different Jewish communities in late antiquity? These issues, which depend on a much broader study of the relationship between rabbinic rhetoric and reality, await further study. The data surveyed here, however, suggest confluences and motifs that are too strong and consistent to be assigned to mere rhetorical "borrowing" or active rabbinic imagination. In fact, these texts most likely reflect more common societal assumptions, while at the same time seeking to maintain and reproduce those assumptions and the institutions that rest upon them. At the same time, it must be recognized that words such as "common" must be considered cautiously. "Common societal assumptions" might ultimately represent only the assumptions of two relatively small, elite groups of Jewish scholars. This issue impinges on that of the intended audience of these texts, a question to which I believe this data gives no answer.

Regardless of the assumptions informing these rhetorics, how were these texts intended to be read? Several of the sources examined here are polemical: did the authors of *b. Nid.* 13a-b, for example, expect their text to scare male masturbators into more "sanctioned" behavior? I have interpreted several of these texts as preserving older material but subverting it. Did such reading strategies really exist among Jews in antiquity?

Finally, there is the all-important questions of actual practices and gender relations (see below). Can we learn from these texts what Jews, or at least rabbis, actually did sexually? To this question, too, I think that these sources cannot give an answer.

GENDER RELATIONS

Rabbinic texts are androcentric. The relationship between rabbinic rhetoric, even rabbinic constructions of sexuality and actual Jewish female life and practice is far from clear. One thing that seems to emerge from these texts is that sexuality is rarely, if ever, discussed by the rabbis with the good of the woman in mind. Even the Palestinian sources on a woman's sexual rights from her husband are concerned with procreation, not female sexual pleasure. Moreover, until we know more about the relationship between the rhetoric and reality, between rabbinic legislation and its acceptance, application, and enforcement, we can derive very little from this literature as to actual female sexual lives and thoughts. Did women view themselves as the rabbis viewed them? Was female asceticism, frowned upon by Palestinian rabbis but lionized in early Christian sources, an option for Jewish women in Roman Palestine or in Babylonia? How did these assumptions affect relationships between and among Jewish families in late antiquity? What strategies did women use to conform with and rebel against androcentric societal expectations and institutions? Even female contraceptive strategies are masked by the androcentrism of these texts.

However one answers these questions, there can be little doubt that they impact upon broader issues of gender relations. Many of these texts very clearly objectify women. One scholar has explained similar kinds of Greek texts as "coffeehouse talk," inconsequential male boasting. Even if we accept this view, the impact of these texts could hardly be called inconsequential.[16] Societal assumptions about gender roles are reproduced within these kinds of texts. How do assumptions about sexual desire relate to social controls imposed upon women? Did Palestinian and Babylonian differences in assumptions about sexual desire result in different legal responses to women's roles in private and public spheres?

Rabbinic writings are our primary source for the study of Jews and Judaism in late antiquity. Yet if this study has been successful, it has shown that rabbinic culture was not monolithic. Rabbinic assumptions about sexuality were as historically as textually determined, to the point where rabbinic texts created under one set of assumptions were misunderstood when read in societies that held different assumptions. Only in academic writing is it possible to separate sex; the constructions of sexuality; strategies (especially rhetorical) of sexual (and other types of) control; gender assumptions and expectations; social relationships between dominant and minority cultures as well as different classes within the society; and the relationship between texts and real lives and social institutions. In reality, all of these threads are finely interwoven. The study of rabbinic sexuality, although only a small part of the complex fabric of which it is a part, offers a glimpse of some of these complex relationships.

---

[16]See Winkler, *Constraints* 70; Richlin, "Zeus, Metis" 172.

Bibliography

PRIMARY SOURCES

The Acts of the Apostles: The Greek Text with Introduction and Commentary. Edited by F.F. Bruce. Grand Rapids: William Eerdmans, 1990.

The Apostolic Fathers. LCL. 2 vols. Translated by Krisopp Lake. London: Heinemann, 1977.

The Aramaic Bible. Translated and edited by Bernard Grossfeld. Edinburgh: T. & T. Clark, 1988.

Aristeas to Philocrates (Letter of Aristeas). Translated and edited by Moses Hadas. New York: Harper & Brothers, 1951.

Avot D'Rabbi Nathan. Edited by S. Schechter. Frankfurt: J. Kauffmann, 1888.

The Babylonian Talmud. Codex Munich 95. 3 vols. Jerusalem, 1971.

The Babylonian Talmud. Seder Nezikin: Codex Hambourg. A Facsimile of the Original Manuscript. Jerusalem, 1969.

The Babylonian Talmud with Variant Readings. Tractates Yebamot, Ketubot, Nedarim, Sotah. Institute for the Complete Israeli Talmud. 4 vols. Jerusalem: Yad HaRav Herzog, 1977 – 1991.

Biblia Hebraica. Edited by R. Kittel. 12th ed. Stuttgart: Deutsche Bibelgesellschaft, 1984.

Catullus. *Works.* LCL. Translated by F.W. Cornish. London: Heinemann, 1976.

Cicero. *Works.* LCL. 28 vols. Translated by E.W. Sutton, H. Rackham, et al. London: Heinemann, 1979.

Clement of Alexandria. *Protrepticus and Paedagogus*. Edited by Otto Stählin. GCS, vol. 12. Leipzig: J.C. Hinrichs'sche, 1905.

―――――. *Stromata*. Edited by Otto Stählin and Ludwig Früchtel. 2 vols. GCS. Berlin: Akademie, 1985.

Codex Theodosianus. Edited by P. Krueger. Berlin: Weidmannos, 1923.

The Dead Sea Scrolls in English. Edited by G. Vermes. 3d edition. London and New York: Penguin, 1987.

The Digest of Justinian. Edited by Theodor Mommsen and Paul Krueger. Translated by Alan Watson. 4 vols. Philadelphia: University of Pennsylvania Press, 1985.

Dikduke Soferim. Edited by Rabbinovicz. 14 vols. 1867-1897. Reprint Brooklyn and Jerusalem: Me'ain Hahohmah, 1959/60.

Epiphanius of Salamis. *The Panarion of Epiphanius of Salamis*. Translated by Frank Williams. Nag Hammadi Studies. Leiden: E.J. Brill, 1987.

―――――. *Ancoratus and the Panarion*. Edited by Karl Holl. GCS, vol. 25. Leipzig: J.C. Hinrichs'sche, 1915.

The First Epistle to the Corinthians. Translated and edited by Gordon D. Fee. Grand Rapids: William B. Eerdmans, 1987.

Galen. *On the Usefulness of the Parts of the Body*. Translated and edited by Margaret Tallmadge May. Cornell Publications in the History of Science. Ithaca: Cornell University Press, 1968.

Greek and Latin Authors on Jews and Judaism. Edited by Menahem Stern. 3 vols. Jerusalem: The Israel Academy of Sciences and Humanities, 1980.

Herodotus. *History*. LCL. 4 vols. Translated by A.D. Godley. London: Heinemann, 1981.

Hippolytus. Edited by Miroslav Marcovich. Patristische texte und studien. Berlin: Walter de Gruyter, 1986.

The Jews in Roman Imperial Legislation. Edited by Amnon Linder. Detroit: Wayne State University Press and Jerusalem: The Israel Academy of Sciences and Humanities, 1987.

Josephus Flavius. *Jewish Antiquities. Jewish War. The Life. Contra Apionem.* LCL. 9 vols. Translated by H. St.J. Thakeray, R. Marcus, and L.H. Feldman. London: Heinemann, 1925-1965.

Juvenal. *Satire*. LCL. Translated b9 G.G. Ramsay. London: Heinemann, 1979.

Lucretius on Love and Sex: A Commentary on De Rerum Natura IV, 1030-1287 with Prolegomena, Text, and Translation. Edited by Robert D. Brown. Columbia Studies in the Classical Tradition. Leiden: E.J. Brill, 1987.

The Manual of Discipline. Edited by P. Wernberg-Møller. Leiden: E. J. Brill, 1957.

Martial. *Epigrams*. LCL. 2 vols. Translated by Walter C.A. Ker. London: Heinemann, 1979.

Mekhilta D'Rabbi Ishmael. Edited by H.S. Horovitz and I.A. Rabin. 1930; Reprint Jerusalem: Wahrmann, 1970.

Mekhilta of Rabbi Ishmael. Edited by Jacob Lauterbach. 3 vols. Philadelphia: Jewish Publication Society, 1933 – 1935.

Mekhilta D'Rabbi Shimon B. Yohai. Edited by J.N. Epstein and E.Z. Melamed. Jerusalem, Hillel Press, n.d.

Midrash Bereshit Rabba. Edited by J. Theodor and Ch. Albeck. 3 vols. 2d ed. Jerusalem: Wahrmann, 1965.

Midrash Debarim Rabbah. Edited by Saul Lieberman. Jerusalem: Wehrman, 1964.

Midrash Tanaim on Sefer Devarim. Edited by David Tzvi Hoffman. n.d.

Minucius Felix. *Octavius*. Edited by C. Halm. Corpus Scriptorum Ecclesiasticorum Latinorum, vol. 2, 1-56. Vindobonae: C. Geroldi 1868.

_____. *The Octavius of Marcus Minucius Felix*. ACW. Translated by G.W. Clark. New York: Newman, 1974.

The Mishnah. Edited by Ch. Albeck. 6 vols. Tel Aviv and Jerusalem: Dvir; The Bialik Institute, 1988.

Musonius Rufus. *Reliquiae*. Edited by O. Hense. Bibliotheca Scriptorum Graecorum et Romanorum. Lipsiae: B.G. Teubneri, 1905.

_____. "Musonius Rufus: The Roman Socrates." Edited by Cora B. Lutz. *Yale Classical Studies* 10 (1947): 3-147.

The Nag Hammadi Library in English. Edited by James M. Robinson. Leiden: E.J. Brill and New York: Harper and Row, 1977.

The New Oxford Annotated Bible with the Apocrypha. Revised Standard Version. New York: Oxford University Press, 1973.

New Testament Apocrypha. Edited by E. Hennecke and Wilhelm Schneemelcher. Translated by R. McL. Wilson. Philadelphia: Westminster Press, 1965.

Novem Testamentum Graece. Edited by E. Nestle and K. Aland. Stuttgart: Deutsche Bibelstiftung, 1979.

The Old Testament Pseudopigrapha. Edited by James H. Charlesworth. 2 vols. Garden City: Doubleday, 1983.

Die Oracula Sibyllina. Edited by John Geffcken. Leipzig: J. C. Hirrichs'sche Buchhandlung, 1902.

Ovid. *Works* LCL. 6 vols. Translated by Frank Justus Miller, et al. London: Heinemann, 1977.

Patrologia Graeca. Edited by Migne.

Patrologia Latina. Edited by Migne.

The Palestinian Talmud. Leiden Ms. Cod. Scal. 3. A Facsimile of the Original Manuscript. 4 vols. Jerusalem, 1970.

Philo. *Works.* LCL. 10 vols and 2 suppl. vols. Translated by F.H. Colson et al. London: Heinemann, 1929-1961.

Philostratus. *The Life of Apollonius of Tyana.* LCL. 2 vols. Translated by F.C. Conybeare. London: Heinemann, 1969.

Plato. *The Laws.* LCL. 2 vols. Translated by R.G. Bury. London: Heinemann, 1926.

The Elder Seneca. *Controversiae.* LCL. 2 vols. Translated by M. Winterbottom. London: Heinemann, 1974.

Seneca. LCL. 10 vols. Translated by John W. Basore, et al. London: Heinemann, 1970.

The Sentences of Pseudo-Phocylides. Edited by P.W. van der Horst. Leiden: E.J. Brill, 1978.

Septuaginta. Edited by A. Rahlfs. 2 vols. 4th ed. Stuttgart: Privilegierte Wurttembergische Bibelanstalt, 1935.

Sifra. Edited by J.H. Weiss. Wien: Jacob Schlossberg, 1862.

Sifre Numbers. Edited by H.S. Horovitz. 1966; Reprint Jerusalem: Shalem, 1992.

Sifre on Deuteronomy. Edited by Louis Finkelstein. 1939; Reprint New York: Jewish Theological Seminary of America, 1969.

Soranus. *Gynecology*. Edited and translated by Owsei Temkin. Baltimore: The Johns Hopkins Press, 1956.

Talmud Babli. Nehardea ed. 20 vols. Jerusalem, 1988.

Talmud Yerushalmi. Venice Edition. Leipzig, 1925 (=Venice 1523).

Tanakh: The Holy Scriptures. The New JPS Translation according to the Traditional Hebrew Text. Philadelphia: The Jewish Publication Society, 1988.

The Temple Scroll. Edited by Yigal Yadin. 3 vols. Jerusalem: The Israel Exploration Society and The Institute of Archaeology of the Hebrew University of Jerusalem, 1983.

Tertullian. *De pudicitia*. Edited by Augusti Reifferscheid and G. Wissowa. Corpus Scriptorum Ecclesiasticorum Latinorum, vol. 20, 219-73. Prague: F. Tempsky, 1890.

_____. *Adv. Marc.*. Edited by A. Kroymann. Corpus Scriptorum Ecclesiasticorum Latinorum, vol. 47, 290-650. Vidobonae: F. Tempsky, 1906.

Theodosian Code. Translated and edited by Clyde Pharr. Princeton: Princeton University Press, 1952.

The Tosefta: The Orders of Zeraim, Moed, Nashim, Nezikin. Edited by S. Lieberman. 4 vols. New York: Jewish Theological Seminary of America, 1955-1988.

Tosephta. Edited by M.S. Zuckermandel. Jerusalem: Wahrmann, 1970.

The Treatises Derek Erez. Edited by Michael Higger. New York: Manchester, 1935.

The Ways of the Sages and the Way of the World. Translated and edited by Marcus van Loopik. Texte und Studien zum Antiken Judentum. Tübingen: J.C.B. Mohr (Paul Siebeck), 1991.

The Wisdom of Solomon. Edited and translated by David Winston. Anchor Bible. 1979; Reprint Garden City: Doubleday, 1984.

The Zadokite Documents. Edited by Ch. Rabin. 1954; Reprint Oxford: Oxford University Press, Clarendon Press, 1958.

SECONDARY SOURCES

Adams, J.N. *The Latin Sexual Vocabulary*. London: Duckworth, 1982.

Albeck, Ch. *Mavo L'Talmudim*. Tel Aviv: Dvir, 1987.

———. *Das Buch der Jubiläen und die Halacha*. Berlin: Hochschule fur die Wissenschaft des Judentums 47, 1930.

Alexander, P.S. "The Rabbinic Lists of Forbidden Targumim." *Journal of Jewish Studies* 27 (1976): 177-91.

Alon, G. "Studies in Philonic Halacha (C)." *Tarbiz* 6 (1934): 30-37 (Hebrew).

———. *Jews, Judaism and the Classical World*. Translated by Israel Abrahams. Jerusalem: Magnes Press, 1977.

Anderson, Gary. "Celibacy or Consummation in the Garden? Reflections on Early Jewish and Christian Interpretations of the Garden of Eden." *Harvard Theological Review* 82 (1989): 121-48.

———. "The Expression of Joy as a Halakhic Problem in Rabbinic Sources." *Jewish Quarterly Review*, n.s., 80 (1990): 221-52.

———. *A Time to Mourn, a Time to Dance: The Expression of Grief and Joy in Israelite Religion*. University Park, PA: Pennsylvania State University Press, 1991.

Ankum, Hans. "La *captiva Adultera*: Problèmes concernant l'*accusatio adulterii* en droit romain classique." *Revue internationale des droits de l'antiquite*, 3d series, 32 (1985): 153-205.

Aptowitzer, V. "Spuren des Matriarchats im jüdischen Schriftum." *Hebrew Union College Annual* 4 (1927): 207-40.

———. "Spuren des Matriarchats im jüdischen Schriftum (Schluss)." *Hebrew Union College Annual* 5 (1928): 261-97.

Archer, Léonie J. *Her Price is Beyond Rubies: The Jewish Woman in Graeco-Roman Palestine*. Journal for the Study of the Old Testament Supplement Series. Sheffield: Sheffield Academic Press, JSOT Press, 1990.

Bailey, Derrick Sherwin. *Homosexuality and the Western Christian Tradition*. London: Longmans, Green, 1955.

Baskin, Judith. "The Separation of Women in Rabbinic Judaism." In *Women, Religion, and Social Change*, edited by Yvonne Yazbeck Haddad, 3-18. Albany: State University of New York Press, 1985.

———. *Pharaoh's Counselors: Job, Jethro and Balaam in Rabbinic and Patristic Tradition*. Chico: Scholars Press, 1983.

Beard, Mary. "The Sexual Status of Vestan Virgins." *Journal of Roman Studies* 70 (1980): 12-27.

Belkin, S. "Levirate and Agnate Marriage in Rabbinic and Cognate Literature." *Jewish Quarterly Review*, n.s., 60 (1969-70): 275-329.

———. *Philo and the Oral Law: The Philonic Interpretation of Biblical Law in Relation to the Palestinian Halakah*. Cambridge: Harvard University Press, 1940.

Bernstein, Richard J. *Beyond Objectivism and Relativism: Science, Hermeneutics, and Praxis*. Philadelphia: University of Pennsylvania Press, 1983.

Biale, David. *Eros and the Jews*. New York: Basic Books, 1992.

Bigger, Stephen F. "The Family Laws of Leviticus 1 in Their Setting." *Journal of Biblical Literature* 98 (1979): 187-203.

Blau, Ludwig. "Das Altjüdische Zauberwesen." *Jahresbericht der Landes-Rabbinerschule in Budapest* Budapest, 1898.

Blayney, Jan. "Theories of Conception in the Ancient Roman World." In *The Family in Ancient Rome: New Perspectives*, edited by Beryl Rawson, 230-36.

Bleich, J. David. "The Prohibition Against Intermarriage." *Journal of Halacha and Contemporary Society* 1:1 (1981): 5-27.

Bokser, Baruch M. "An Annotated Bibliographical Guide to the Study of the Palestinian Talmud." *ANRW* 2.19.2 (1979): 139-256.

———. *Post Mishnaic Judaism in Transition: Samuel on Berakhot and the Beginnings of Gemara*. Brown Judaic Studies. Chico: Scholars Press, 1980.

Boswell, John. *Christianity, Social Tolerance, and Homosexuality: Gay People in Western Europe from the Beginning of the Christian Era to the Fourteenth Century*. Chicago: University of Chicago Press, 1980.

———. *The Kindness of Strangers: The Abandonment of Children in Western Europe from Late Antiquity to the Renaissance*. New York: Pantheon, 1988.

Bourdieu, Pierre. *Outline of a Theory of Practice*. Translated by Richard Nice. Cambridge Studies in Social Anthropology, vol. 16. 1972; Cambridge: Cambridge University Press, 1991.

Bowersock, G. W. *Hellenism in Late Antiquity*. Ann Arbor: University of Michigan Press, 1990.

Boyarin, Daniel. *Carnal Israel: Reading Sex in Talmudic Culture.* The New Historicism: Studies in Cultural Poetics. Berkeley and Los Angeles: University of California Press, 1993.

———. "'This We Know to Be the Carnal Israel': Circumcision and the Erotic Life of God and Israel." *Critical Inquiry* 18 (1992): 474-505.

———. "'Behold Israel According to the Flesh': On Anthropology and Sexuality in Late Antique *Judaisms.*" *Yale Journal of Criticism* 5 (1992): 27-57.

———. "The Great Fat Massacre: Sex, Death, and the Grotesque Body in the Talmud." In *People of the Body,* edited by Howard Eilberg-Schwartz, 69-100.

———. "Internal Opposition in Talmudic Literature: The Case of the Married Monk. " *Representations* 36 (1991): 87-113.

———. "Literary Fat Rabbis: On the Historical Origins of the Grotesque Body." *Journal of the History of Sexuality* 1 (1991): 551-84.

———. "Reading Androcentrism Against the Grain: Women, Sex, and Torah-Study." *Poetics Today* 12 (1991): 29-53.

Bradley, K.R. "Sexual Regulations in Wet-nursing Contracts from Roman Egypt." *Klio* 62 (1980): 321-25.

Brandes, Stanley. "Reflections on Honor and Shame in the Mediterranean. " In *Honor and Shame and the Unity of the Mediterranean,* edited by David D. Gilmore, 121-34.

Brendel, Otto J. "The Scope and Temperament of Erotic Art in the Greco-Roman World." In *Studies in Erotic Art,* edited by Theodore Bowie and Cornelia V. Christenson, 3-108. New York: Basic, 1970.

Brener, Atalia. "Nashim zarim b'Mikra *"Beit Mikrah* 30 (1984-5): 179-85.

Brock, Sebastian. "Jewish Traditions in Syriac Sources." *Journal of Jewish Studies* 30 (1979): 212-32.

Brooke-Rose, Christine. "Woman as a Semiotic Object." *Poetics Today* 6 (1985): 9-20.

Brooten, Bernadette J. "Konnten Frauen im alten Judentum die Scheidung Betreiben?" *Evangelische Theologie* 42 (1982): 65-80.

———. "Early Christian Women and Their Cultural Context: Issues of Method in Historical Reconstruction." In *Feminist Perspectives on Biblical Scholarship,* edited by Adela Yarboro Collins, 65-91. Society of

Biblical Literature Centennial Publications. Chico: Scholars Press, 1985.

⎯⎯⎯⎯. "Patristic Interpretations of Romans 1:26. " *Studia Patristica* 18 (1985): 287-91.

⎯⎯⎯⎯. "Paul and the Law: How Complete Was the Departure." In *The Church and Israel: Romans 9-11*, edited by Daniel L. Miglione (*The Princeton Seminary Bulletin*, Suppl. 1, 1990), 71-89.

⎯⎯⎯⎯. "Paul's View on the Nature of Women and Female Homoeroticism." In *Immaculate & Powerful: The Female in Sacred Image and Social Reality*, edited by Clarissa W. Atkinson, Constance H. Buchanan, and Margaret R. Miles, 61-87. Boston: Beacon Press, 1985.

⎯⎯⎯⎯. "Zur Debatte über das Scheidungsrecht der jüdischen Frau." *Evangelische Theologie* 43 (1983): 466-78.

Brown, Francis, S.R. Driver, and Charles A. Briggs. *The New Brown – Driver – Briggs- Gesenius Hebrew and English Lexicon*. 1907; rpt. Peabody, MA: Hendrickson, 1979.

Brown, Peter. "Bodies and Minds: Sexuality and Renunciation in Early Christianity." In *Before Sexuality: The Construction of Erotic Experience in the Ancient Greek World*, edited by David M. Halperin, et al., 479-93.

⎯⎯⎯⎯. *The Body and Society: Men, Women and Sexual Renunciation in Early Christianity*. Lectures on the History of Religions, vol. 13. New York: Columbia University Press, 1988.

⎯⎯⎯⎯. "Late Antiquity." In *From Pagan Rome to Byzantium*, edited by Paul Veyne and translated by Arthur Goldhammer, 235-311. Vol. 1 of A *History of Private Life*, edited by Georges Duby, Cambridge: Harvard University Press, Belknap, 1987.

⎯⎯⎯⎯. *Power and Persuasion in Late Antiquity: Towards a Christian Empire*. Madison: University of Wisconsin Press, 1990.

Brundage, James A. *Law, Sex, and Christian Society in Medieval Europe*. Chicago: University of Chicago Press, 1987.

Buchholz, P. *Die Familie in rechtlicher und moralischer Beziehung nach mosaich-talmudischer Lehre*. Breslau: Schetter, 1867.

Buckland, W.W. *A Manual of Roman Private Law*. Cambridge: Cambridge University Press, 1939.

⎯⎯⎯⎯. *A Text-book of Roman Law from Augustus to Justinian*. 3d ed. Cambridge: Cambridge University Press, 1963.

Büchler, A. *Types of Jewish-Palestinian Piety from 70 B.C.E. to 70 C.E.* 1922; rpt. New York: Ktav 1968.

⸻. "The Levitical Impurity of the Gentile in Palestine Before the Year 70." *Jewish Quarterly Review*, n.s., 17 (1926-27): 1-81.

⸻. "Die Strafe der Ehebrecher in der nachexilischen Zeit." *Monatsschrift für Geschichte und Wissenschaft des Judentums* 55 (1911): 196-219.

Cameron, Averil. *Christianity and the Rhetoric of the Empire: The Development of Christian Discourse.* Berkeley and Los Angeles: University of California Press, 1991.

Cameron, Averil and Amelie Kuhrt, ed. *Images of Women in Antiquity.* London: Croom Helm, 1983.

Camp, Claudia V. "Understanding a Patriarchy: Women in Second Century Jerusalem Through the Eyes of Ben Sira." In *"Women Like This": New Perspectives on Jewish Women in the Greco-Roman World,* edited by Amy-Jill Levine, 1-39. Society of Biblical Literature: Early Judaism and its Literature. Atlanta: Scholars Press, 1991.

Cantarella, Eva. *Bisexuality in the Ancient World.* Translated by Cormac O. Cuillenain. New Haven: Yale University Press, 1992.

Chadwick, Henry. *Augustine.* Past Masters. Oxford: Oxford University Press, 1986.

⸻. "The Relativity of Moral Codes: Rome and Persia in Late Antiquity." In *Early Christian Literature and the Classical Intellectual Tradition in Honorem Robert M. Grant,* edited by William R. Schoedel and Robert L. Wilken, 135-53. Paris: Éditions Beauchesne, 1979.

Charlesworth, James H. *Graphic Concordance to the Dead Sea Scrolls.* Louisville: Westminster/John Knox, 1991.

Clark, Elizabeth A. "Sex, Shame, and Rhetoric: En-gendering Early Christian Ethics." *Journal of the American Academy of Religion* 59 (1991): 221-45.

⸻. "Sexuality." In *Encyclopedia of Early Christianity,* edited by Everett Ferguson, 843-45. London and New York: Garland, 1990.

Cohen, Boaz. *Jewish and Roman Law.* 2 vols. New York: Jewish Theological Seminary of America, 1966.

⸻. "Laws of Persons." *Proceedings of the American Academy of Jewish Research* 16 (1947): 1-37.

Cohen, David. "The Athenian Law of Adultery." *Revue internationale des droits de l'antiquite'*, 3d ser., 31 (1984): 147-65.

———. *Law, Sexuality, and Society: The Enforcement of Morals in Classical Athens.* Cambridge: Cambridge University Press, 1991.

———. "Sex, Gender, and Sexuality in Ancient Greece." *Classical Philology* 87 (1992): 145-60.

Cohen, Gerson D. "Esau as a Symbol in Early Medieval Thought." Reprinted in *Studies in the Variety of Rabbinic Cultures*, 243-69. Philadelphia: Jewish Publication Society, 1991.

Cohen, Jeremy. *"Be Fertile and Increase, Fill the Earth and Master It": The Ancient and Medieval Career of a Biblical Text.* Ithaca: Cornell University Press, 1989.

———. "Rationales for Conjugal Sex in RaABaD's *Ba'alei ha-nefesh*." *Jewish History* 6 (1992): 65-78.

Cohen, Shaye J.D. "Conversion to Judaism in Historical Perspective: From Biblical Israel to Post-biblical Judaism." *Conservative Judaism* 36:4 (1983): 31-45.

———. "Crossing the Boundary and Becoming a Jew." *Harvard Theological Review* 82 (1989): 13-33.

———. "The Origins of the Matrilineal Principle in Rabbinic Law." *AJS Review* 10 (1985): 19-53.

———. "Solomon and the Daughter of Pharaoh: Intermarriage, Conversion, and the Impurity of Women." *Journal of the Ancient Near East Society* 16-17 (1984-85): 23-37.

———. "From the Bible to the Talmud: The Prohibition of Intermarriage." *Hebrew Annual Review* 7 (1983): 27-39.

———. "Menstruants and the Sacred in Judaism and Christianity." In *Women's History & Ancient History,* edited by Sarah B. Pomeroy, 273-99. Chapel Hill: University of North Carolina Press, 1991.

———. "'Those Who Say They Are Jews and Are Not': How Do You Know a Jew in Antiquity When You See One?" In *Diasporas in Antiquity*, edited by Shaye J.D. Cohen and Ernest S. Frerichs, 1-45. Brown Judaic Studies. Atlanta: Scholars Press, 1993.

———. "Women in the Synagogues of Antiquity." *Conservative Judaism* 34:2 (1980-81): 23-29.

———, ed. *The Jewish Family in Antiquity*. Brown Judaic Studies. Atlanta: Scholars Press, 1993.

Cohen, Yechezkial. "The Image of the Gentile in the Tannaitic Period." *Eshel Beer-Sheva* 2 (1980): 3962 (Hebrew).

Cohn, Haim. "Adultery." In *Encyclopedia Judaica*, vol. 2, 313-16.

———. "Incest." In *Encyclopedia Judaica*, vol. 8, 1316-8.

———. "Sexual Offenses." In *Encyclopedia Judaica*, vol. 14, 1207-08.

Collins, Adela Yarbro. "The Function of 'Excommunication' in Paul." *Harvard Theological Review* 73 (1980): 251-63.

Corbett, Percy Ellwood. *The Roman Law of Marriage*. Oxford: Clarendon Press, 1930.

Corrington, Gail Paterson. "The Defense of the Body and the Discourse of Appetite: Continence and Control in the Greco-Roman World." *Semeia* 57 (1992): 65-74.

Crook, J.A. *Law and Life of Rome, 90 B. C.-A.D. 212*. 1967; Reprinted Ithaca: Cornell University Press, 1984.

Daly, Mary. *Gyn/Ecology: The Metaethics of Radical Feminism*. Boston: Beacon Press, 1979.

Daube, David. *The Duty of Procreation*. Edinburgh: Edinburgh University Press, 1977.

———. "Johanan Ben Beroqa and Women's Rights." *Zeitschrift der Savigny-Stiftung für Rechtsgeschichte- römanislische Abteilung* 99 (1982): 22-31.

———. "Rabbinic Methods of Interpretation and Hellenistic Rhetoric." *Hebrew Union College Annual* 22 (1949): 239-64.

Davidson, Arnold I. "Sex and the Emergence of Sexuality." *Critical Inquiry* 14 (1987): 16-48.

de Heusch, Luc. "Les vicissitudes de la notion d'interdit." In *Religion et tabou sexuel*, edited by Jacques Marx, 9-16.

Dean-Jones, Lesley. "The Politics of Pleasure: Female Sexual Appetite in the Hippocratic Oath." *Helios* 19 (1992): 72-91.

Delcourt, Marie. *Hermaphrodite: Myths and Rites of the Bisexual Figure in Classical Antiquity*. Translated by Jennifer Nicholson. 1956; Reprint London: Studio, 1961.

Deming, Will. "Mark 9.42-10.12, Matthew 5.27-32, and B. *Nid.* 13b: A First Century Discussion of Male Sexuality." *New Testament Studies* 36 (1990): 130-41.

Denich, Bette S. "Sex and Power in the Balkans." In *Women, Culture, and Society*, edited by Michelle Zimbalist Rosaldo and Louise Lamphere, 243-62.

Destro, Adriana. *The Law of Jealousy: Anthropology of Sotah.* Translated by Wayne Harper. Brown Judaic Studies. Atlanta: Scholars Press, 1989.

Dinaburg, B. "B. Frizzi and His Book 'Petah Enayim', on the Character of the Italian Haskalah." *Tarbiz* 20 (1949): 241-64 (Hebrew).

Dixon, Suzanne. "*Infirmitas Sexus:* Womanly Weakness in Roman Law." *Tijdschrift Voor Rechtsgeschiedenis* 52 (1984): 343-71.

———. "The Sentimental Ideal of the Roman Family." In *Marriage, Divorce, and Children in Ancient Rome*, edited by Beryl Rawson, 99-113.

Dölger, Franz Joseph. *Antike und Christentum.* Vol. 4. *Kultur- und Religiounsgeschichtliche Studien.* Münster, Westfalen: Verlag Aschendorff Munster.

Dover, Kenneth J. "Classical Greek Attitudes to Sexual Behaviour." Reprinted in *Sexualität und Erotik in der Antike*, edited by Andreas Karsten Siems, 264-81. Darmstadt: Wissenschaftliche Buchgesellschaft, 1988.

———. *Greek Homosexuality.* London: Gerald Duckworth, 1978.

———. *Greek Popular Morality in the Time of Plato and Aristotle.* Berkeley and Los Angeles: University of California Press, 1974.

Dresner, Samuel H. "Homosexuality and the Order of Creation." *Judaism* 40 (1991): 309-21.

Drijvers, Jan Willem. "Virginity and Asceticism in Late Roman Western Elites." In *Sexual Asymmetry: Studies in Ancient Society*, edited by Josine Blok and Peter Mason, 241-73. Amsterdam: J.C. Gieben, 1987.

Dubarle, A.M., o.p. "La Bible et les pères ont-ils parlé de la Contraception?" *La Vie Spirituelle* Supplement 15 (1962): 573-610.

Duncan, J., and M. Derrett. "'Handing Over to Satan': An Explanation of 1 Cor. 5:1-7." *Revue internationale des droits de l'antiquite* 3d series 26 (1979): 11-30.

Edelstein, Ludwig. "The Dietetics of Antiquity." In *Ancient Medicine: Selected Papers of Ludwig Edelstein*, edited by Owsei Temkin, edited and translated by C. Lilian Temkin, 303-16. 1967; Reprint Baltimore: The Johns Hopkins Press, 1987.

———. "The Distinctive Hellenism of Greek Medicine. " In *Ancient Medicine: Selected Papers of Ludwig Edelstein*, edited by Owsei Temkin, edited and translated by C. Lilian Temkin, 367-97.

———. "The Relation of Ancient Philosophy to Medicine. " In *Ancient Medicine: Selected Papers of Ludwig Edelstein*, edited by Owsei Temkin, edited and translated by C. Lilian Temkin, 349-66.

Eilberg-Schwartz, Howard. *The Human Will in Judaism: The Mishnah's Philosophy of Intention*. Atlanta: Scholars Press, 1986.

———. *The Savage in Judaism: An Anthropology of Israelite Religion and Ancient Judaism*. Bloomington: Indiana University Press, 1990.

———, ed. *People of the Body: Jews and Judaism from an Embodied Perspective*. The Body in Culture, History, and Religion. Albany: State University of New York Press, 1992.

Eisenstein, J.D. "Incest." In *Jewish Encyclopedia*, vol. 6, 572-74.

Elliger, Karl. "Das Gesetz Leviticus 18." *Zeitschrift für die alttestamentliche Wissenschaft* 67 (1955): 1-25.

Elman, Yaakov. "Babylonian Echoes in a Late Rabbinic Legend." *Journal of the Ancient Near East* 4 (1972): 12-19.

Elshtain, Jean Bethke. "Feminist Discourse and Its Discontents: Language, Power, and Meaning." *Signs* 7 (1982): 603-21.

Encyclopaedia Biblica. Edited by Benjamin Mazar. 9 vols. Jerusalem: Bialik Institute, 1964 – 1988.

Encyclopedia Judaica. Edited by Cecil Roth, et al. 16 vols. Jerusalem: MacMillen, 1971.

Epstein, J. N. *Introduction to the Text of the Mishnah*. Jerusalem: Magnes Press, 1964 (Hebrew).

Epstein, Louis M. "The Institution of Concubinage Among the Jews." *Proceedings of the American Academy for Jewish Research* 6 (1935): 153-88.

———. *Marriage Laws in the Bible and the Talmud*. Harvard Semitic Series. Cambridge: Harvard University Press, 1942.

_____. *Sex Laws and Customs in Judaism.* Cambridge: Harvard University Press, 1948.

Eron, John Lewis. *Ancient Jewish Attitudes Towards Sexuality: A Study in Ancient Jewish Attitudes Towards Sexuality as Expressed in the Testaments of the Twelve Patriarchs.* Ann Arbor: UMI, 1987.

Eschelbacher, Max. "Zur Geschichte des biblisch-talmudischen Eherects." Review. *MGWJ* 65 (1921): 299-322.

Evans-Grubb, Judith. "Abduction Marriage in Antiquity: A Law of Constantine (*CTh* 9.24.1) and Its Social Context." *Journal of Roman Studies* 79 (1989): 59-83.

Evans-Pritchard, E.E. *Kinship and Marriage Among the Nuer.* 1951; Reprint Oxford: Oxford University Press, Clarendon Press, 1990.

Eyben, Emiel. "Family Planning in Graeco-Roman Antiquity." *Ancient Society* 11-12 (1980-1): 5-81.

Falk, Ze'ev. "On the Historical Background of the Talmudic Laws Regarding Gentiles." *Immanuel* 14 (Fall 1982): 102-13.

Fantham, Elaine. "*Stuprum:* Public Attitudes and Penalties for Sexual Offences in Republican Rome." *Echos du monde classique/Classical Views,* n.s., 35 (1991): 267-91.

_____. "Nihil Iam Ivra Natvrae Valent: Incest and Fratricide in Seneca's *Phoenissae.*" In *Seneca Tragicus: Ramus Essays on Senecan Drama,* edited by A.J. Boyle, 61-76. Victoria: Aureal, 1983.

Feldman, David M. *Birth Control in Jewish Law: Marital Relations, Contraception, and Abortion.* 1968; Reprint Westport, CT: Greenwood, 1980.

Feldman, Louis H. "Josephus' *Jewish Antiquities* and Pseudo-Philo's *Biblical Antiquities.*" In *Josephus, the Bible, and History,* edited by Louis H. Feldman and Gohei Hata, 59-80. Detroit: Wayne State University Press, 1989.

Fischel, Henry, ed. *Essays in Greco-Roman and Related Talmudic Literature.* New York: Ktav, 1977.

Fish, Stanley. "*Fish v. Fiss.*" Reprinted in *Interpreting Law and Literature: A Hermeneutic Reader,* edited by Sanford Levinson and Steven Mailloux, 251-68. Evanston, IL: Northwestern University Press, 1988.

Fishbane, Michael. *Biblical Interpretation in Ancient Israel.* New York: Oxford University Press, 1985.

Fiss, Owen M. "Objectivity and Interpretation." Reprinted in *Interpreting Law and Literature: A Hermeneutic Reader*, edited by Sanford Levinson and Steven Mailloux, 229-49. Evanston, IL: Northwestern University Press, 1988.

Fitzmyer, Joseph A. "Divorce Among First-Century Palestinian Jews." *Eretz-Israel: Archaeological, Historical and Geographical Studies* 14 (1978): 103*-110*.

Flandrin, Jean-Louis. "La vie sexuelle des gens mariés dans l'ancienne société: De la doctrine de l'église a la réalité des comportements." In *Sexualités Occidentales*, edited by Phillippe Aries, and André Béjin, 102-15. Communications. Paris: Le Centre D'Études Transdisciplinaires, 1982.

Foley, Helene, ed. *Reflections of Women in Antiquity*. New York: Gordon and Breach Science Publishers, 1981.

Foucault, Michel. *Introduction*. Vol. 1 of *The History of Sexuality*. Translated by Robert Hurley. New York: Random House, 1980.

———. *The Use of Pleasure*. Vol. 2 of *The History of Sexuality*. Translated by Robert Hurley. New York: Viking, 1985.

———. *The Care of the Self*. Vol. 3 of *The History of Sexuality*. Translated by Robert Hurley. New York: Random House, 1984.

Fox, Robin. *Kinship and Marriage: An Anthropological Perspective*. 1967; Reprint Cambridge Studies in Social Anthropology, vol. 50. Cambridge: Cambridge University Press, 1989.

———. *The Red Lamp of Incest*. New York: E.P. Dutton, 1980.

Fox, Robin Lane. *Pagans and Christians*. New York: Alfred A. Knopf, 1987.

Fraade, Steven D. "Ascetical Aspects of Ancient Judaism. " In *Jewish Spirituality from the Bible Through the Middle Ages*, edited by Arthur Green, 253-88. World Spirituality. New York: Crossroad, 1986.

———. *From Tradition to Commentary: Torah and Its Interpretation in the Midrash Sifre to Deuteronomy*. Albany: State University of New York Press, 1991.

———. "Interpreting Midrash 1: Midrash and the History of Judaism." *Prooftexts* 7 (1987): 179194.

———. "Sifre Deuteronomy 26 (ad Deut. 3:23): How Conscious the Composition?" *Hebrew Union College Annual 54 (1983)*: 245-301.

Francus, Israel. "The Halakhic Status of Children Born from Mixed Marriages in Talmudic Literature." *Sidra: A Journal for the Study of Rabbinic Literature* 4 (1988): 89-110 (Hebrew).

Frankel, Z. "Gründlinien des mösaich-talmudischen Eherechts. " In *Jahresbericht Des Jüdisch-theologischen Seminars "Frenkelscher Stiftung."* Leipzig, 1860.

————. *Mavo HaYerushalmi.* 1870; Reprint Berlin: Louis Lamm, 1923.

Frankfurter, Gershom, and Rivka Ulmer. "Eine Anfrage über Homosexualität im judischen Gesetz." *Zeitschrift für Religions- und Geistesgeschichte* 43 (1991): 49-68.

Fraser, P. M. *Ptolemaic Alexandria.* 3 vols. 1972; Reprint Oxford: Oxford University Press, Clarendon Press, 1986.

Friedman, Shamma. "A Critical Study of *Yevamot* X with a Methodological Introduction." In *Texts and Studies: Anlecta Judaica*, edited by H.Z. Dimitrovsky, 275-441. New York: Jewish Theological Seminary of America, 1977 (Hebrew).

Frizzi, Benedetto. *Dissertazione Di Polizia Medica Sul Pentateuco in Riguardo Alle Leggi, e Stato del Matrimonio.* Pavia: P. Galeazzi, 1788.

Frymer-Kensky, Tikvah. "Pollution, Purification, and Purgation in Biblical Israel." In *The Word of the Lord Shall Go Forth: Essays in Honor of David Noel Freedman in Celebration of His Sixtieth Birthday*, edited by Carol L. Meyers and M. O'Connor, 399-413. Winona Lake: Eisenbrauns, 1983.

————. "The Strange Case of the Suspected Sotah (Numbers V 11-31)." *Vetus Testamentum* 34 (1984): 11-26.

Gadamer, Hans-Georg. *Truth and Method.* Translated by Garrett Barden and John Cumming. New York: Seabury, 1975.

Gafni, Isaiah M. *The Jews of Babylonia in the Talmudic Era.* Jerusalem: Zalman Shazar Center for Jewish History, 1990 (Hebrew).

Gardner, Jane F. *Women in Roman Law & Society.* London: Croom Helm, 1986.

Geertz, Clifford. *The Interpretation of Cultures: Selected Essays.* New York: Basic, 1973.

Geiger, Abraham. *Urschrift und Vebersetzungen der Bibel in ihrer Abhängigkeit.* Breslau: Julius Hainauer, 1857.

Gergely, Thomas. "'Vous ne suivrez pas les desirs de votre coeur et de vos yeux...' Judaisme et comportement sexuel." In *Religion et tabou Sexuel*, edited by Jacques Marx, 117-27.

Gilmore, David D., ed. *Honor and Shame and the Unity of the Mediterranean*. A special publication of the American Anthropological Association. Washington, D.C.: American Anthropological Association, 1987.

———. "Honor, Honesty, Shame: Male Status in Contemporary Andalusia." In *Honor and Shame and the Unity of the Mediterranean*, 90-103.

———. "Introduction: The Shame of Dishonor." In *Honor and Shame and the Unity of the Mediterranean*, 2-21.

Ginzberg, Louis. *A Commentary on the Palestinian Talmud*. 3 vols. New York: Jewish Theological Seminary of America, 1941 (Hebrew).

———. *The Legends of the Jews*. 6 vols. 1925; Reprint Philadelphia: The Jewish Publication Society of America, 1947.

———. "Review of *Festscrift zu Israel Lewy's siebzigstem Geburtstag*." *Revue des Études Juives* 66 (1913): 297-315.

Giovannini, Maureen. "Female Chastity Codes in the Circum-Mediterranean: Comparative Perspectives." In *Honor and Shame and the Unity of the Mediterranean*, edited by David D. Gilmore, 61-74.

Glazier-McDonald, Beth. "Intermarriage, Divorce, and the *Bat-'Él Nēkār*: Insights into Mal 2:10-16." *Journal of Biblical Literature* 106 (1987): 603-11.

Gleason, Maud W. "The Semiotics of Gender: Physiognomy and Self-fashioning in the Second Century C.E." In *Before Sexuality*, edited by David M. Halperin, et al., 389-415.

Goldberg, Abraham. "The Babylonian Talmud." In *The Literature of the Sages*, edited by S. Safrai, vol. 1, 323-45.

———. "The Mishnah – A Study Book of Halakhah." In *The Literature of the Sages*, edited by S. Safrai, vol. 1, 211-51.

———. "The Tosefta – Companion to the Mishnah." In *The Literature of the Sages*, edited by S. Safrai, vol. 1, 283-301.

Goldin, Judah. *The Song at the Sea*. New Haven: Yale University Press, 1971.

Goodblatt, David. "The Babylonian Talmud." *ANRW* 2.19.2 (1979): 257-336.

Goode, William J. "The Theoretical Importance of Love." *American Sociological Review* 24 (1959): 38-47.

Grant, Michael. *Eros in Pompeii: The Secret Rooms of the National Museum of Naples.* Antonia Mulas photographer. New York: William Mowwor, 1975.

Green, William Scott. "Palestinian Holy Men: Charismatic Leadership and Rabbinic Tradition." *ANRW* 2.19.2 (1979): 619-47.

_____. "What's in a Name? – The Problematic of Rabbinic 'Biography'." In *Approaches to Ancient Judaism: Theory and Practice*, 211-51. Brown Judaic Studies. Missoula: Scholars Press, 1978.

Greenberg, David F. *The Construction of Homosexuality.* Chicago: University of Chicago, 1988.

Greenberg, Moshe. "Some Postulates of Biblical Criminal Law." In *Yehezkel Kaufmann Jubilee Volume*, edited by Menahem Haran, 5-28. Jerusalem: Magnes Press, 1960.

Greenfield, Jonas C. "Ben Sira 42.9-10 and Its Talmudic Paraphrase." In *A Tribute to Geza Vermes*, edited by Philip R. Davis and Richard T. White, 167-73. Journal for the Study of the Old Testament Supplement Series. Sheffield: Sheffield Academic Press, 1990.

Greenidge, A.H.J. *Infamia: Its Place in Roman Public and Private Law.* Oxford: Oxford University Press, 1894.

Guarino, Antonio. "Studi Sull' 'incestum." *Zeitschrift der Savigny-Stiftung für Rechtsgeschichte (Röm. Abt.)* 63 (1943): 175-267.

Habermas, Jürgen. *Communication and the Evolution of Society.* Translated by Thomas McCarthy. Boston: Beacon, 1979.

Haenchen, Ernst. *The Acts of the Apostles: A Commentary.* 1965; Reprint Philadelphia: The Westminster Press, 1971.

Halevi, A.A. *Arkhe Ha-aggadah V'ha-halacah.* 4 vols. Tel Aviv: Dvir 1981.

Halivni, David. "Contemporary Methods of the Study of Talmud." *Journal of Jewish Studies* 30 (1979): 192-201.

_____. *Sources and Traditions.* Vol. 3 of *A Source Critical Commentary on Seder Nashim.* Tel Aviv: Dvir, 1968 (Hebrew).

Hallett, Judith P. *Fathers and Daughters in Roman Society: Women and the Elite Family.* Princeton: Princeton University Press, 1984.

———. "Female Homoeroticism and the Denial of Roman Reality in Latin Literature." *Yale Journal of Criticism* 3 (1989/90): 209-27.

———. "Women *as Same* and *Other* in Classical Roman Elite." *Helios* 16 (1989): 59-78.

Halperin, David M. "One Hundred Years of Homosexuality. " In *One Hundred Years of Homosexuality*, 15-40. New York: Routledge, 1990.

Halperin, David M., John J. Winkler, and Froma I. Zeitlin, ed. *Before Sexuality: The Construction of Erotic Experience in the Ancient Greek World*. Princeton: Princeton University Press, 1990.

Hannick, Jean-Marie. "Droit de cite et mariages mixtes dans la Grèce classique." *L'antiquité Classique* 45 (1976): 13348.

Hanson, Ann Ellis. "The Medical Writers' Woman." In *Before Sexuality*, edited by David M. Halperin, et al., 309-37.

Harrison, A.R.W. *The Law of Athens*. Oxford: Oxford University Press, 1968.

Hartog, François. *The Mirror of Herodotus: The Representation of the Other in the Writing of History*. Translated by Janet Lloyd. Berkeley and Los Angeles: University of California Press, 1988.

Harvey, Susan Ashbook."Women in Early Syrian Christianity." In *Images of Women in Antiquity*, edited by Averil Cameron and Améile Kuhrt, 288-98.

Hauptman, Judith. "Images of Women in the Talmud." In *Religion and Sexism: Images of Woman in the Jewish and Christian Traditions*, edited by Rosemary Radford Ruether, 184-212. New York: Simon and Schuster, 1974.

Hays, Richard B. "Relations Natural and Unnatural: A Response to John Boswell's Exegesis of Romans 1." *Journal of Religious Ethics* 14 (1986): 184-215.

Heinemann, Isaak. *Philons griechische und jüdische Bildung*. Breslau, M. & H. Marcus, 1932.

Henderson, Jeffrey. *The Maculate Muse: Obscene Language in Attic Comedy*. 2d ed. New Haven: Yale University Press, 1991.

Hengel, Martin. *The Zealots: Investigations Into the Jewish Freedom Movement from the Period of Herod I Until 70 A.D.* Translated by David Smith. Edinburgh: T. & T. Clark, 1989.

Henry, Madeleine M. "The Edible Woman: Athenaeus's Concept of the Pornographic." In *Pornography and Representation in Greece and Rome*, edited by Amy Richlin, 250-68.

Herlihy, David. *Medieval Households*. Cambridge: Harvard University Press, 1985.

Herter, H. "Effeminatus." In *Reallexikon für Antike und Christentum*, edited by Theodor Hauser, vol. 4, 642-650. 1959.

Hertier, Françoise. "The Symbolics of Incest and Its Prohibitions." In *Between Belief and Transgression: Structuralist Essays in Religion, History, and Myth*, edited by Michel Izard and Pierre Smith, translated by John Leavitt, 152-79. 1979; Reprint Chicago: University of Chicago Press, 1982.

Higger, Michael. "Sex Laws and Customs in Judaism." *Jewish Quarterly Review* 39 (1948-9): 425-28.

Hopkins, Keith. "Brother-sister Marriage in Roman Egypt." *Comparative Studies in Society and History: An International Quarterly* 22 (1980): 303-54.

———. "Contraception in the Roman Empire." *Comparative Studies in Society and History: An International Quarterly* 8 (1965-6): 124-51.

———. "A Textual Emendation in a Fragment of Musonius Rufus: A Note on Contraception." *Classical Quarterly* 15 (1965): 72-74.

Horner, Tom. *Homosexuality and the Judeo-Christian Tradition: An Annotated Bibliography*. Metuchen, NJ: Scarecrow, 1981.

Hugghins, Kenneth Wayne. *An Investigation of the Jewish Theology of Sexuality Influencing the References to Homosexuality in Romans 1:18-32*. Ann Arbor: University Microfilms International, 1986.

Humphreys, S.C. *The Family, Women and Death: Comparative Studies*. 2d edition. Ann Arbor: University of Michigan Press, 1993.

Hunter, David G. "*On the Sin of Adam and Eve*: A Little-known Defense of Marriage and Childbearing by Ambrosiaster." *Harvard Theological Review* 82 (1989): 283-99.

Irsai, O. "Ya'akov of Kefar Niburaia – A Sage Turned Apostate." *Jerusalem Studies in Jewish Thought* 2:2 (1982/83): 153-68 (Hebrew).

Itzchaky, Samson, Moshe Yitzhaki, and Samuel S. Kottek. "Fertility in Jewish Tradition (Ethnomedical and Folkloric Aspects)." *Koroth* 9:1-2 (1985): 122-35.

Jackson, Bernard. "Reflections on Biblical Criminal Law." *Journal of Jewish Studies* 24 (1973): 8-38.

Jacobs, Louis. "How Much of the Babylonian Talmud is Pseudepigraphic?" *Journal of Jewish Studies* 28 (1977): 45-59.

Jakabovits, Immanuel. "Homosexuality." In *Encyclopaedia Judaica*, vol. 8, 961-62.

―――. "Sex." In *Encyclopedia Judaica*, vol. 14, 1206-07.

Jastrow, M. *A Dictionary of the Targumim, the Talmud Babli and Yerushalmi, and the Midrashic Literature*. 2 vols. London, 1886 – 1903.

Juster, Jean. *Les Juifs dans l 'empire romain: Leur condition juridique, économique et sociale*. 2 vols. Paris: Paul Geuthner, 1914.

Kalmin, Richard. "Quotation Forms in the Babylonian Talmud: Authentically Amoraic, or a Later Editorial Construct?" *Hebrew Union College Annual* 59 (1988): 167-87.

―――. *The Redaction of the Babylonian Talmud: Amoraic or Saboraic*. Cincinnati: Hebrew Union College Press, 1989.

―――. "Saints or Sinners, Scholars or Ignoramuses? Stories About the Rabbis as Evidence for the Composite Nature of the Babylonian Talmud. " *AJS Review* 15 (1990): 179-205.

Kamesar, Adam. "The Narrative Aggada as Seen from the Greco-Latin Perspective." *Journal of Jewish Studies* 45 (1994): 52-70.

Kamlah, Ehrhard. *Die Form der katalogischen Paränese im Neuen Testament*. Tübingen: J. C. B. Mohr, 1964.

Kennedy, George A. *Classical Rhetoric and Its Christian and Secular Tradition from Ancient to Modern Times*. Chapel Hill: University of North Carolina Press, 1980.

―――. *Greek Rhetoric Under Christian Emperors*. Princeton: Princeton University Press, 1983.

Kittel, Gerhard. "Das Konnubium mit Nicht-Juden im antiken Judentum." *Forschungen zur Judenfrage* 2 (1937): 30-62. Hamburg: Hanseatische.

Klein, Michael L. "Not to Be Translated in Public - לא מתרגם בציבורא." *Journal of Jewish Studies* 39 (1988): 80-91.

Koester, Helmut. "ΝΟΜΟΣ ΦΥΣΕΩΣ: The Concept of Natural Law in Greek Thought." In *Religions in Antiquity: Essays in Memory of Erwin*

Ramsdell Goodenough, edited by J. Neusner, 521-41. Leiden: E.J. Brill, 1968.

Kohut, A. *Aruch Completum.* 8 vols. Vienna, 1878 – 1892 (Hebrew).

———. *Additamenta ad Aruch Completum.* Vienna, 1937 (Hebrew).

Konstan, David. "Between Courtesan and Wife: Menander's *Perikeiromen.*" *Phoenix* 41 (1987): 12239.

Kraemer, David. "The Intended Reader and the Bavli." *Prooftexts* 13 (1993): 125-40.

———. *The Mind of the Talmud.* New York: Oxford University Press, 1990.

———. "On the Reliability of Attributions in the Babylonian Talmud." *Hebrew Union College Annual* 60 (1989): 175-90.

———. *Stylistic Characteristics of Amoraic Literature.* Ann Arbor: University Microfilms, 1984.

Kraemer, Ross Shepard. *Her Share of the Blessings: Women's Religions Among Pagans, Jews, and Christians in the Greco-Roman World.* New York: Oxford University Press, 1992.

Krauss, S. *Griesche und lateinische Lehnworter im Talmud, Midrasch und Targum.* Revised by Immanuel Löw. Hildesheim: Geror Olms, 1964 (1899).

———. *Persia and Rome in the Talmud and Midrashim.* Jerusalem: Mosad HaRav Kook, 1948 (Hebrew).

Kugel, James L. *In Potiphar's House: The Interpretive Life of Biblical Texts.* San Francisco: Harper, 1990.

Kuhn, Thomas. *The Structure of Scientific Revolutions.* 2d edition. Chicago: University of Chicago Press, 1970.

Lacey, W. K. *The Family in Classical Greece.* Aspects of Greek and Roman Life. Ithaca: Cornell University Press, 1968.

Lachs, Samuel Tobias. "Sexual Imagery in Three Rabbinic Passages." *Journal for the Study of Judaism* 23 (1992): 244-48.

Laqueur, Thomas. "Orgasm, Generation, and the Politics of Reproductive Biology." *Representations* 14 (1986): 1-41.

Lassner, Jacob. *Demonizing the Queen of Sheba.* Chicago: Chicago University Press, 1993.

Latte, Kurt. "Μοιχεία." In *Real-Encyclopädie der classischen Altertumswissenschaft*, edited by Pauly and Wissowa, vol. 15.2, 2446-49.

Lee, A.D. "Close-Kin Marriage in Late-Antique Mesopotamia." *Greek, Roman, and Byzantine Studies* 29 (1988): 403-13.

Levi-Strauss, Claude. *The Elementary Structures of Kinship*. Translated by James Harle Bell and Richard von Sturmer. Boston: Beacon Press, 1969.

Levine, Baruch. *The JPS Torah Commentary: Leviticus*. Philadelphia: Jewish Publication Society, 1989.

Levine, Lee I. *The Rabbinic Class of Roman Palestine in Late Antiquity*. Jerusalem: Yad Izhak BenZvi; New York: Jewish Theological Seminary of America, 1989.

Levy, Jacob. *Wörterbuch über die Talmudim und Midraschim*. 4 vols. 1876-1889; Reprint Berlin and Wien: B. Harz, 1924.

Lichtschein, Ludwig. *Die Ehe nach mösaisch-talmudische Auffassung und das mösaische-talmudische Eherecht*. Leipzig: Otto Wigand, 1879.

Lieberman, Saul. *Greek in Jewish Palestine*. New York: Jewish Theological Seminary of America, 1942.

_____. *Hellenism in Jewish Palestine*. New York: Jewish Theological Seminary of America, 1950.

_____. *HaYerushalmi Kiphshuto*. Jerusalem: "Darom", 1934.

_____. "Shaving of the Hair and Uncovering of the Face Among Jewish Women." In *Texts and Studies*, 52-56. New York: Ktav, 1974.

_____. *Tosefta Ki-fshutah: A Comprehensive Commentary on the Tosefta*. 10 vols. New York: Jewish Theological Seminary of America, 1955 – 1988 (Hebrew).

Lilja, Saara. *Homosexuality in Republican and Augustan Rome*. Commentationes Humanarum Litterarum. Helsinki: Soceitas Scientiarum Fennica, 1983.

Loewenstamm, S. "Z'nunim, z'nut." In *Encyclopaedia Biblica*, vol. 2, 935-37 (Hebrew).

_____. "'Arayot." In *Encyclopedia Biblica*, vol. 6, 388-90 (Hebrew).

_____. "Qadesh" In *Encyclopaedia Biblica*, vol. 7, 35-36 (Hebrew)

Löw, Leopold. "Eherechtliche Studien." In *Gesammelte Schriften*, edited by Leopold Löw. 3 vols. 3:13-334. 1889; Reprint Hildesheim: Georg Olms, 1979.

———. *Die Flora der Juden*. 1924; Reprint Hildesheim: Georg Olms, 1967.

MacDowell, D.M. "Bastards as Athenian citizens." *Classical Quarterly*, n.s., 26 (1976): 88-91.

———. "The Enforcement of Morals." *The Classical Review* 42 (1992): 345-47.

Mace, David. *Hebrew Marriage: A Sociological Study*. London: Epworth, 1953.

MacKinnon, Catharine. *Feminism Unmodified: Discourses on Life and Law*. Cambridge: Harvard University Press, 1987.

MacMullen, Ramsay. "Roman Attitudes to Greek Love." *Historia* 31 (1982): 484-502.

Malina, Bruce. "Does Porneia Mean Fornication?" *Novum Testamentum* 14 (1972): 10-17.

Malinowski, Bronislaw. *The Sexual Life of Savages*. 1929; Reprint Boston: Beacon Press, 1987.

Marrou, H.I. *A History of Education in Antiquity*. Translated by George Lamb. Wisconsin Studies in Classics. Madison: University of Wisconsin Press, 1982.

Marx, Jacques, ed. *Religion et tabou sexuel*. Problèmes d'histoire des religions. Brusselles: Editions de l'Université de Bruxelles, 1990.

McKeating, Henry. "Sanctions Against Adultery in Ancient Israelite Society, with Some Reflections on Methodology in the Study of Old Testament Ethics" *Journal for the Study of the Old Testament* 11 (1979): 57-72.

Meeks, Wayne A. "Image of the Androgyne: Some Uses of a Symbol in Earliest Christianity" *History of Religions* 13 (1973-74): 165-208.

Melamed, E.Z. *Halachic Midrashim of the Tannaim in the Babylonian Talmud*. 1943; Reprint Jerusalem: The Magnes Press, 1988 (Hebrew).

———. "Lashon Nikiyyah v'Kinuyim b'Mishnah." *Leshonenu* 47 (1982-3): 3-17.

———. "Euphemisms and Textual Alterations of Expressions in Talmudic Literature." In *Benjamin deVries Memorial Volume*, edited by E.Z. Melamed, 112-48. Jerusalem: Tel Aviv University Research Authority, 1968 (Hebrew).

Mélèze-Modrzejewski, Joseph. "Un aspect du 'couple interdit' dans l'antiquité: Les mariages mixtes dans l'égypte hellénistique." In *Le couple interdit: Entretiens sur le racisme*, edited by Leon Poliakov, 53-73. Paris: Mouton, 1977.

Mette-Dittmann, Angelika. *Die Ehegesetze des Augustus: Eine Untersuchung im Rahmen der Gesellschaftspolitik des Princeps*. Historia Einzelschriften. Stuttgart: Franz Steiner, 1991.

Mielziner, M. *The Jewish Law of Marriage and Divorce in Ancient and Modern Times and Its Relation to the Law of the State*. Cincinnati: Bloch, 1884.

Milgrom, Jacob. "To'vah"' In *Encyclopaedia Biblica*, vol. 8, 466-68 (Hebrew).

Millar, Fergus. *The Roman Near East 31 BC – AD 337*. Cambridge: Harvard University Press, 1993.

Momigliano, Arnaldo. *Alien Wisdom: The Limits of Hellenization*. Cambridge and New York: Cambridge University Press, 1975.

Mommsen, Theodor. *Römisches Strafrecht*. 1899; Reprint Darmstadt: Wissenschaftliche Buchgesellschaft, 1961.

Montefiore, C.G., ed. *The Synoptic Gospels*. 2 vols. New York: Ktav, 1968.

Moore, George Foot. *Judaism in the First Centuries of the Christian Era*. 3 vols. Cambridge: Harvard University Press, 1927-1930.

Mopsik, Charles. "The Body of Engenderment in the Hebrew Bible, the Rabbinic Tradition and the Kabbalah. " In *Fragments for a History of the Human Body*, edited by Michel Feher, 49-73. Zone. New York: Zone, 1989.

Murphy, Robert F., and Leonard Kasdan. "Agnation and Endogamy: Some Further Considerations." *Southwestern Journal of Anthropology* 23 (1967): 1-14.

———. "The Structure of Parallel Cousin Marriages." *American Anthropologist* 61 (1959): 17-29.

Neubauer, Jakob. *Beiträge zur Geschichte des biblisch-talmudischen Eheschließungsrechts. Eine Rechtsvergleichend-historische Studie.*

Mitteilungen der Vorderasiatischen Gesellschaft (E.V.) 1919. Leipzig: J.C. Hinrichs'sche Buchhandlung, 1920.

Neuman (Noy), Dov. *Motif-index of Talmudic-Midrashic Literature*. Ann Arbor: University Microfilms, 1954.

Neusner, Jacob. *The Bavli's Massive Miscellanies: The Problem of Agglutinative Discourse in the Talmud of Babylonian*. South Florida Studies in the History of Judaism. Atlanta: Scholars Press, 1992.

_____. *The Formation of the Babylonian Talmud*. Leiden: E.J. Brill, 1970.

_____. "From Scripture to Mishnah: The Origins of Mishnah's Division of Women." *Journal of Jewish Studies* 30 (1979): 138-53.

_____. *A History of Jews in Babylonia*. 5 vols. Leiden: E.J. Brill, 1969-1970.

_____. *The Mishnaic System of Women*. Vol. 5 of *A History of the Mishnaic Law of Women*. Studies in Judaism in Late Antiquity. Leiden: E.J. Brill, 1980.

_____. *How the Talmud Shaped Rabbinic Discourse*. Atlanta: Scholars Press, 1991.

_____. *Judaism: The Evidence of the Mishnah*. Chicago: University of Chicago Press, 1981.

_____. *The Principle Parts of the Bavli's Discourse: A Preliminary Taxonomy*. South Florida Studies in the History of Judaism. Atlanta: Scholars Press, 1992.

_____. *Rabbinic Traditions About the Pharisees Before 70*. 3 vols. Leiden: E.J. Brill, 1971.

_____, ed. and trans. *Sifra: An Analytical Translation*. Atlanta: Scholars Press, 1988.

_____. *Sources and Traditions: Types of Composition in the Talmud of Babylonia*. South Florida Studies in the History of Judaism. Atlanta: Scholars Press, 1992.

_____. *Talmudic Thinking: Language, Logic, Law*. Columbia, S.C.: University of South Carolina Press, 1992.

Noonan, John T., Jr. *Contraception: A History of Its Treatment by the Catholic Theologians and Canonists*. 1965; Reprint Cambridge: Harvard University Press, Belknap Press, 1986.

Novak, David. *The Image of the Non-Jew in Judaism.* Toronto Studies in Theology. New York: The Edwin Mellen Press, 1983.

Orbach, William. "Homosexuality and Jewish Law." *Journal of Family Law* 14 (1975): 353-81.

Ortner, Sherry B., and Harriet Whitehead, ed. *Sexual Meanings, the Cultural Construction of Gender and Sexuality.* Cambridge and New York: Cambridge University Press, 1981.

Oxford English Dictionary. 12 vols. 1933; Reprint Oxford: Oxford University Press, 1978.

Pagels, Elaine. *Adam, Eve, and the Serpent.* New York: Random House, 1988.

Paglia, Camille. "Junk Bonds and Corporate Raiders: Academe in the Hour of the Wolf." *Arion*, 3d series, 1 (1991): 139-212.

Pakter, Walter. *Medieval Cannon Law and the Jews.* Abhandlungen zur Rechtwissenschafflichen Grundlagenforschung. Eblesbach: Rolf Gremer, 1988.

Parker, Robert. *Miasma: Pollution and Purification in Early Greek Religion.* Oxford: Oxford University Press, Clarendon Press, 1983.

Patai, Raphael. *Sex and Family in the Bible and the Middle East.* New York: Doubleday, 1959.

Patterson, Cynthia B. "Those Athenian Bastards." *Classical Antiquity* 9 (1990): 40-73.

Paul, Shalom. "Exod. 21:10 A Threefold Maintenance Clause." *Journal of Near Eastern Studies* 28 (1969): 48-53.

Perles, J. "Miscellen Zur Rabbinishen Sprach- und Alterthumskunde." *MGWJ* 21 (1872).

Peskowitz, Miriam. "Family/ies in Antiquity: Evidence from Tannaitic Literature and Roman Galilean Architecture." In *The Jewish Family*, edited by Shaye J. D. Cohen, 9-36.

Petersen, William. "Can ΑΡΣΕΝΟΚΟΙΤΑΙ Be Translated by 'Homosexuals' (1 Cor. 6:9; 1 Tim. 1 :10). " *Vigiliae Christianae* 40 (1986): 187-91.

Pfaff. "Stuprum." In *Real-Encyclopadie der classischen Altertumswissenschaft*, edited by Pauly and Wissowa, vol. 4A.1, 423-24.

Pierrugues, P. -E. *Glossarium Eroticum Linguae Latinae Sive Theologiae.* 1826; Reprint Berlin, 1908.

Plevnik, Joseph. "Honor/Shame. " In *Biblical Social Values and Their Meaning: A Handbook,* edited by John J. Pilch and Bruce J. Malina, 95-104. Peabody, MA: Hendrickson, 1993.

Pomeroy, Sarah B. *Goddesses, Whores, Wives, and Slaves.* New York: Schocken Books, 1975.

――――――. "The Relationship of the Married Woman to Her Blood Relatives in Rome." *Ancient Society* 7 (1976): 215-27.

――――――. *Women in Hellenistic Egypt: From Alexander to Cleopatra.* New York: Schocken, 1984.

Porton, Gary G. *The Traditions of Rabbi Ishmael.* 3 vols. Studies in Judaism in Late Antiquity. Leiden: E.J. Brill, 1977.

Preisker, Herbert. *Christentum und Ehe in den ersten drei Jahrhunderten.* Berlin: Trowitsch & Sohn, 1927.

Preuss, Julius. *Biblisch-talmudische Medizin: Beiträge zur Geschichte der Heilkunde und der Kultur überhaupt.* Berlin: S. Karger, 1921.

――――――. *Biblical and Talmudic Medicine.* Translated by Fred Rosner. New York: Sanhedrin, 1978.

Rabello, Alfredo Mordechai. "De Collatio Legum Mosaicarum et Romanarum." *Shenaton Ha Mishpat Ha-Ivri: Annual of the Institute for Research in Jewish Law* 1 (1974): 231-62 (Hebrew).

Rabin, Chaim. *Qumran Studies.* London: Oxford University Press, 1957.

Rackover, Nahum. "Coercive Marital Relations Between a Man and His Wife." *Shenaton Ha-Mishpat Ha-Ivri: Annual of the Institute for Research in Jewish Law* 6-7 (1979-80): 295-317 (Hebrew).

Ranke-Heinemann, Uta. *Eunuchs for the Kingdom of Heaven.* New York: Doubleday, 1990.

Rawson, Beryl, ed. *The Family in Ancient Rome: New Perspectives.* Ithaca: Cornell University Press, 1986.

――――――. *Marriage, Divorce, and Children in Ancient Rome.* Oxford: Oxford University Press, Clarendon Press, 1991.

Real-Encyclopädie der classischen Altertumswissenschaft. Edited by Pauly and Wissowa. Stuttgart: J. B. Metzherscher, 1894-.

Reichler, Max. "Jewish Eugenics." In *Jewish Eugenics and Other Essays*. New York: Bloch, 1916.

Rhodes, P.J. "Bastards as Athenian Citizens." *Classical Quarterly*, n.s., 28 (1978): 89-92.

Riccobono, Salvatore, et al., ed. *Fontes Iuris Romani Antejustiniani*. Vol. 2. *Leges*. Florence: S.A.G. Barbèra, 1941.

Richlin, Amy. "Approaches to the Sources on Adultery at Rome." In *Reflections of Women in Antiquity*, edited by H. Foley, 379-404.

————. *Garden of Priapus: Sexuality and Aggression in Roman Humor*. Rev. Ed. New Haven: Yale University Press, 1992.

————. "Zeus and Metis: Foucault, Feminism, Classics." Review. *Helios* 18 (1991): 160-80.

————, ed. *Pornography and Representation in Greece and Rome*. New York: Oxford University Press, 1992.

Ricks, Stephen D. "Abortion in Antiquity." In *Anchor Bible Dictionary*, vol. 1, 32-34.

————. "Kinship Bars to Marriage in Jewish and Islamic Law." In *Studies in Islamic and Judaic Traditions*, edited by William M. Brinner and Stephen D. Ricks. 2 vols., vol. 1, 123-41. Atlanta: Scholars Press, 1986.

Rieger, Paul. "The Foundation of Rome in the Talmud: A Contribution to the Folklore of Antiquity." *Jewish Quarterly Review*, n.s., 16 (1926): 227-35.

Rollin, Sue. "Women and Witchcraft in Ancient Assyria (900 – 600 BC)." In *Images of Women in Antiquity*, edited by Averil Cameron and Améile Kuhrt, 34-45.

Rordorf, Willy. "Marriage in the New Testament and Early Church." *Journal of Ecclesiastical History* 20 (1969): 193-210.

Rosaldo, Michelle Zimbalist and Louise Lamphere, ed. *Women, Culture, and Society*. Stanford: Stanford University Press, 1974.

Rousselle, Aline. "Body Politics in Ancient Rome." In *From Ancient Goddesses to Christian Saints*, edited by Pauline Schmitt Pantel, translated by Arthur Goldhammer, 296-336. A History of Women in the West. Cambridge: Harvard University Press, Belknap Press, 1992.

———. *Porneia: On Desire and the Body in Antiquity.* Translated by Felicia Pheasant. 1983; Reprint Family, Sexuality and Social Relations in Past Times. New York: Basil Blackwell, 1988.

———. "Observation feminine et idéologie masculine: Le corps de la femme d'après les médecins Grecs." *Annales: Economies, Sociétés, Civilisations* 35 (1980): 1089-115.

———. "Personal Status and Sexual Practice in the Roman Empire. " In *Fragments for a History of the Human Body,* edited by Michel Feher, vol. 3, 301-33. Zone. New York: Zone, 1989.

———. "Vivre sous deux droits: La pratique familiale poly-juridique des citoyens romains Juifs." *Annales: Economies, Sociétés, Civilisations* 45 (1990): 839-59.

Rowbatham, Sheila. *Woman's Consciousness, Man's World.* Baltimore: Penguin, 1973.

Rowson, Everett K. "The Effeminates of Early Medina." *Journal of the American Oriental Society* 111 (1991): 671-93.

Safrai, S. "Home and Family." In *The Jewish People in the First Century: Historical Geography, Political History, Social, Cultural and Religious Life and Institutions,* edited by S. Safrai and M. Stern, et al., vol 2, 728-792. 2 vols. Compendia Rerum Iudaicarum ad Novum Testamentum. Philadelphia: Fortress Press, 1976.

Safrai, S., ed., *The Literature of the Sages,* 2 vols. Compendia Rerum Iudaicarum ad Novum Testamentum. Philadelphia: Fortress Press, 1987.

Salisbury, Joyce E. *Church Fathers, Independent Virgins.* New York: Verso, 1991.

Sanders, Jack T. *The Jews in Luke-Acts.* Philadelphia: Fortress, 1987.

Satlow, Michael L. "*Eros and the Jews.*" Review. *Shofar* 12 (1994): 114-16.

———. "Reconsidering the Rabbinic *ketubah* Payment." In *The Jewish Family in Antiquity,* edited by S. Cohen, 133-51.

———. "'They Abused Him Like a Woman': Homoeroticism, Gender Blurring, and the Rabbis in Late Antiquity." *Journal of the History of Sexuality* 5 (1994): 1-25.

Schaps, David M. *Economic Rights of Women in Ancient Greece.* Edinburgh: Edinburgh University Press, 1979.

Schatkin, Margaret S. "Marriage." In *Encyclopedia of Early Christianity*, edited by Everett Ferguson, 572-74. London and New York: Garland, 1990.

Schechter, S. "The Quotations from Ecclesiasticus in Rabbinic Literature." *Jewish Quarterly Review*, o.s., 3 (1891): 682-706.

Schenker, Adrian. "Affranchissement d'une esclave selon Ex 21,7-11." *Biblica* 69 (1988): 547-56.

Schiffman, Lawrence H. "The Samaritans in Tannaitic Halakhah." *Jewish Quarterly Review*, n.s., 75 (1975): 332-33.

Schutz-Galléra, Siegman. *Fuss- und Schusymbolik und- Erotik*. Leipzig, 1909.

Schwartz, Seth. *Josephus and Judaean Politics*. Leiden: E.J. Brill, 1990.

Scroggs, Robin. *The New Testament and Homosexuality*. 1983; Reprint Philadelphia: Fortress, 1987.

Sealy, R. "On Lawful Concubinage in Athens." *Classical Antiquity* 3 (1984): 111-33.

Segal, Moshe. *Sefer Ben Sirah Ha-shalem*. Jerusalem: Bialik Institute, 1953 (Hebrew).

Shaki, Mansour. "The Sassanian Matrimonial Relations." *Archiv Orientalni* 39 (1971): 322-45.

Shaw, Brent D., and Richard P. Saller. "Close-Kin Marriage in Roman Society." *Man*, n.s., 19 (1984): 432-44.

Shimoff, Sandra R. "Hellenization among the Rabbis: Some Evidence from Early Aggadot Concerning David and Solomon." *Journal for the Study of Judaism* 18 (1987): 168-87.

Smith, Jonathan Z. "What a Difference a Difference Makes." In *"To See Ourselves as Others See Us": Christians, Jews, "Others" in Late Antiquity*, edited by Jacob Neusner and Ernest S. Frerichs, 3-48. Chico: Scholars Press, 1985.

Sokoloff, Michael. *A Dictionary of Jewish Palestinian Aramaic*. Ramat-Gan: Bar Ilan University Press, 1990.

Sperber, Daniel. A *Commentary on Derech Erez Zuta*. Ramat-Gan: Bar-Ilan University Press, 1990.

_____. "Phoytinun." In *Studies in Hebrew and Semitic Languages Dedicated to the Memory of Prof. Eduard Yechezkel Kutscher*, edited by

Gad B. Sarfatti et al., 155-58. Ramat-Gan: Bar-Ilan University Press, 1980 (Hebrew).

Stager, Lawrence E. "Eroticism and Infanticide at Ashkelon." *Biblical Archaeology Review* 17:4 (July/August 1991): 34-53, 72.

Stern, David. *Parables in Midrash*. Cambridge: Harvard University Press, 1991.

Stern, Sacha. "Attribution and Authorship in the Babylonian Talmud." *Journal of Jewish Studies* 45 (1994): 28-51.

Strack, Hermann L., and Paul Billerbeck. *Kommentar zum Neuen Testament aus Talmud und Midrasch*. 6 vols. 1922; Reprint München: Beck, 1963 – 1965.

Strack, Hermann L., and G. Stemberger. *Introduction to the Talmud and Midrash*. Introduction by Jacob Neusner. Translated by Markus Bockmuehl. Minneapolis: Fortress, 1992.

Ta-Shema, Israel. "Niddah." In *Encyclopedia Judaica*, vol. 12, 114-48.

Taubenschlag, Raphael. *The Law of Greco-Roman Egypt in the Light of the Papyri 332 B. C.-640 A.D.* New York: Herald, 1944.

Thompson, Stith. *Motif-index of Folk-literature*. Bloomington: Indiana University Press, 1955.

Thornton, Bruce. "Constructionism and Ancient Greek Sex." *Helios* 18 (1991): 181-93.

Torjesen, Karen I. "In Praise of Noble Women: Gender and Honor in Ascetic Texts." *Semeia* 57 (1992): 41-64.

Treggiari, Susan. "Concubinae." *Papers of the British School at Rome* 49 (1981): 59-81.

———. *Roman Marriage: Iusti Coniuges from the Time of Cicero to the Time of Ulpian*. Oxford: Oxford University Press, 1991

Trenchard, Warren C. *Ben Sira's View of Women: A Literary Analysis*. Brown Judaic Studies. Chico: Scholars Press, 1982.

Urbach, Ephraim E. *The Sages: Their Concepts and Beliefs*. Translated by Israel Abrahams. 1975; Reprinted Cambridge: Harvard University Press, 1987.

Vermes, G. "Leviticus 18:21 in Ancient Jewish Bible Exegesis." In *Studies in Aggadah, Targum and Jewish Liturgy in Memory of Joseph Heinemann,* edited by Ezra Fleischer and Jakob J. Petuchowski, 108-24. Jerusalem: Magnes Press and Hebrew Union College Press, 1981.

———. *Scripture and Tradition in Judaism*. Studia Post-Biblica. Leiden: E.J. Brill, 1961.

———. "Sectarian Matrimonial Halakhah in the Damascus Rule." *Journal of Jewish Studies* 25 (1974): 197-202.

Veyne, Paul. "La famille et l'amour sous le Haut-empire romain." *Annales: Économies, Sociétés, Civilisations* 33 (1978): 35-63.

———. "The Roman Empire." In *From Pagan Rome to Byzantium*, edited by Paul Veyne and translated by Arthur Goldhammer, 5-233. Vol. 1 of *A History of Private Life*, edited by Georges Duby, Cambridge: Harvard University Press, Belknap, 1987.

Visotzky, Burton L. "Mortal Sins." *Union Seminary Quarterly Review* 44 (1990): 31-53.

———. "Overturning the Lamp." *Journal of Jewish Studies* 38 (1987).

———. "Prolegomenon to the Study of Jewish-Christianities in Rabbinic Literature." *AJS Review* 14 (1989): 47-70.

———. "Three Syriac Cruxes." *Journal of Jewish Studies* 42 (1991): 167-75.

Vögtle, Anton. *Die Tugend- und Lasterkataloge im Neuen Testament*. Münster: Verlag der Aschendorffschen Verlagsbuchhandlung, 1936.

Vööbus, Arthur. *History of Asceticism in the Syrian Orient: A Contribution to the History of Culture in the Near East*. 2 vols. Louvain: Secretariat Du Corpus SCO, 1958.

Vorberg, G. *Glossarium Eroticum*. Stutgart, 1932.

Walcot, P. "Romantic Love and True Love: Greek Attitudes to Marriage." *Ancient Society* 18 (1987): 5-33.

Ward, Roy Bowen. "Musonius and Paul on Marriage." *New Testament Studies* 36 (1990): 281-89.

Weaver, P.R.C. "The Status of Children in Mixed Marriages." In *The Family in Ancient Rome: New Perspectives*, edited by Beryl Rawson, 145-69.

———. "Children of Freedmen (and Freedwomen)." In *Marriage, Divorce, and Children in Ancient Rome*, edited by Beryl Rawson, 166-90.

Weder, Hans. "Perspektive der Frauen?" *Evangeslische Theologie* 43 (1983): 175-78.

Weeks, Jeffrey. *Sexuality*. Key Ideas. Sussex: Ellis Horwood Limited, 1986.

Wegner, Judith Romney. *Chattel or Person ? The Status of Women in the Mishnah*. New York: Oxford University Press, 1988.

⸺. "The Image and Status of Women in Classical Rabbinic Judaism." In *Jewish Women in Historical Perspective*, edited by Judith R. Baskin, 68-93. Detroit: Wayne State University Press, 1991.

Weinfeld, Moshe. *Deuteronomy and the Deuteronomic School*. Oxford: Oxford University Press, 1972

Weisberg, Richard. *Poethics and Other Strategies of Law and Literature*. New York: Columbia University Press, 1992.

Weiss, Avraham. *Studies in the Literature of the Amoraim*. New York: Horeb, 1961/62 (Hebrew).

Weiss, Egon. "Endogamie und Exogamie im römischen Kaiserreich." *Zeitschrift der Savigny-Stiftung für Rechtsgeschichte* 29 (1908): 340-69.

Williams, Gordon. "Some Aspects of Roman Marriage Ceremonies and Ideals." *Journal of Roman Studies* 48 (1958): 16-29.

Winkler, John J. *The Constraints of Desire*. New York: Routledge, 1990.

Wolfson, Elliot. "Images of God's Feet: Some Observations on the Divine Body in Judaism." In *People of the Body*, edited by Howard Eilberg-Schwartz, 143-81.

Wright, D.F. "Translating ΑΡΣΕΝΟΚΟΙΤΑΙ." *Vigiliae Christianae* 41 (1987): 396-98.

⸺. "Homosexuals or Prostitutes? The Meaning of ΑΡΣΕΝΟΚΟΙΤΑΙ (1 Cor. 6:9, 1 Tim. 1:10)." *Vigiliae Christianae* 38 (1984): 125-54.

Yalon, Henoch. *Studies in the Hebrew Language*. Jerusalem: Bialik Institute, 1971 (Hebrew).

Yarbrough, O. Larry. *Not Like the Gentiles: Marriage Rules in the Letters of Paul*. Dissertation Series. Atlanta: Scholars Press, 1985.

Zaas, Peter. "Catalogues and Context: 1 Corinthians 5 and 6." *New Testament Studies* 34 (1988): 622-29.

Zeller, Eduard. *Die Philosophie der Griechen in ihrer geschichtlichen Entwicklung*. Leipzig: Fues's Verlag, 1869-81.

Ziskind, Jonathan. "Legal Rules on Incest in the Ancient Near East."
Revue internationale des droits de l'antiquité, 3d ser., 35 (1988): 79-109.